David C. Cook
Bible Lesson
Commentary

The Essential Study Companion *for* Every Disciple

David C. Cook
Bible Lesson
Commentary

NIV

David © Cook®

transforming lives together

DAVID C. COOK NIV BIBLE LESSON COMMENTARY 2011–2012
Published by David C Cook
4050 Lee Vance View
Colorado Springs, CO 80918 U.S.A.

David C Cook Distribution Canada
55 Woodslee Avenue, Paris, Ontario, Canada N3L 3E5

David C Cook U.K., Kingsway Communications
Eastbourne, East Sussex BN23 6NT, England

David C Cook and the graphic circle C logo
are registered trademarks of Cook Communications Ministries.

Lessons based on *International Sunday School Lessons: The International Bible Lessons for
Christian Teaching*, © 2008 by the Committee on the Uniform Series.

ISBN 978-1-4347-0068-1

© 2011 David C Cook

Written and edited by Dan Lioy, PhD
The Team: John Blase, Doug Schmidt, Amy Kiechlin, Caitlyn York, and Karen Athen
Cover Design: Amy Kiechlin
Cover Photo: iStockphoto

Printed in the United States of America
First Edition 2011

1 2 3 4 5 6 7 8 9 10

012811

Tradition and Wisdom

Unit I: Teaching and Learning

Unit II: Jesus Teaches Wisdom

God Establishes a Faithful People

Unit I: God's Covenant

Unit II: God's Protection

Unit III: God's Redemption

God's Creative Word

God Calls for Justice

A Word to the Teacher

The youngest of my nieces and nephews is now a first grader. When I asked Emily what her favorite subject was at school, I was expecting her to tell me it was gym or art, as her older brothers had always replied. Instead, she promptly answered, "Computers!" Computers? For a 7-year-old? For a child in first grade?

I find it amazing that the computer has become so much a part of our children's daily lives. Some people, in fact, insist that the computer age will mean the end of the traditional Sunday school class and teacher. After all, they point out that Bible software now exists and maintain that electronic study can be done at any time and anywhere by anyone without the need of a class or teacher.

These gadgetry wizards insist computer-based tools offer programs that eliminate traditional forms of Christian education. For instance, they tell us tiny devices exist that can store every bit of Bible information, that thousands of religious discussion groups can be found on the Internet, and that just as many websites deal with spiritual matters.

There are now too many companies to count with electronic concordance products on the market. And a number of leading theological seminaries conduct graduate courses solely on the Internet. In fact, one professor told me that he never will see any of his students, but will communicate with them only through the computer.

Does all this glitzy technology mean that Sunday schools will soon die out? Does the prevalence of the gadgetry mean that the teacher has become as obsolete as lamplighters and cave dwellers? Absolutely not! Your role as a Sunday school teacher is more important than ever!

No electronic device can replace the presence of a live human guiding a group of people on the quest for a Christ-filled existence. No microchip can fill the role of a person exemplifying the power and presence of Jesus in a local setting. No computer-based tool can know the hurts and needs of persons struggling to serve as the Savior's community. Only you as a teacher can!

When suitable, feel free to use modern technology as an implement to assist you in learning. But don't be intimidated by the claims of those who insist that you as a Sunday school teacher are redundant and unnecessary. Instead, recognize the unique calling you have from the Lord.

Be sure to carry out the task of weekly classroom leadership, which is never outdated. Most of all, rely on the promise of Jesus' goodness and nearness as you present each lesson in the upcoming year.

Your fellow learner at the feet of the Master Teacher,
Dan Lioy

Using the *David C. Cook NIV Bible Lesson Commentary* with Materials from Other Publishers

Sunday school materials from the following denominations and publishers follow International Sunday School Lesson outlines (sometimes known as Uniform Series). Because the *David C. Cook NIV Bible Lesson Commentary* (formerly *Peloubet's)* follows the same outlines, you can use the *Commentary* as an excellent teacher resource to supplement the materials from these publishing houses.

NONDENOMINATIONAL:

Standard Publishing: *Adult*
Urban Ministries
Echoes Teacher's Commentary (Cook Communications Ministries): *Adult*

DENOMINATIONAL:

Advent Christian General Conference: *Adult*
American Baptist (Judson Press): *Adult*
United Holy Church of America: *Adult*
Church of God in Christ (Church of God in Christ Publishing House): *Adult*
Church of Christ Holiness: *Adult*
Church of God (Warner Press): *Adult*
Church of God by Faith: *Adult*
National Baptist Convention of America *(Boyd): All ages*
National Primitive Baptist Convention: *Adult*
Progressive National Baptist Convention: *Adult*
Presbyterian Church (U.S.A.) (Bible Discovery Series—Presbyterian Publishing House or P.R.E.M.): *Adult*
Union Gospel Press: *All ages*
United Holy Church of America: *Adult*
United Methodist (Cokesbury): *All ages*

Righteousness and Wisdom

DEVOTIONAL READING

Psalm 115:3-11

DAILY BIBLE READINGS

Monday August 29
Malachi 4:1-6 The Sun of Righteousness

Tuesday August 30
Numbers 15:37-41 Remember All the Commands

Wednesday August 31
Psalm 115:3-11 God Is Our Help and Shield

Thursday September 1
2 Corinthians 9:6-12 God's Abundant Blessings

Friday September 2
Proverbs 3:27-35 Wisdom in Relationships

Saturday September 3
Proverbs 3:13-26 The Profit from Wisdom

Sunday September 4
Proverbs 3:1-12 Trust in the Lord

Scripture

Background Scripture: *Proverbs 3:1-35*
Scripture Lesson: *Proverbs 3:1-12*
Key Verse: *Trust in the LORD with all your heart.*
Proverbs 3:5.
Scripture Lesson for Children: *Proverbs 3:1-12*
Key Verse for Children: *Trust in the LORD with all your heart and lean not on your own understanding.*
Proverbs 3:5.

Lesson Aim

To learn how to choose God's wisdom instead of our own.

Lesson Setting

Time: During the reign of Solomon (about 970–930 B.C.)
Place: Jerusalem

Lesson Outline

Righteousness and Wisdom

I. Trusting in the Lord: Proverbs 3:1-10
   A. *Gain Peace and Prosperity: vss. 1-2*
   B. *Find Favor with God and People: vss. 3-4*
   C. *Encounter Obstacle-Free Paths: vss. 5-6*
   D. *Experience Good Health: vss. 7-8*
   E. *Enjoy Material Prosperity: vss. 9-10*

II. Valuing the Lord's Discipline: Proverbs 3:11-12
   A. *Accept the Lord's Instruction: vs. 11*
   B. *Acknowledge the Lord's Correction: vs. 12*

Introduction for Adults

Topic: *Wisdom for Living*

"Trust me. Your check is in the mail." That line is sure to produce a laugh, because trust has become a cheap commodity these days. Trust in God is also hard to find, because people know so little about His character. Sadly, many people are biblically illiterate. They live with caricatures of God in their heads.

Proverbs tells us that God is trustworthy and that keeping His commands is the basis for living in a wise manner. We listen to people we trust. We believe them and do what they say. We trust our surgeons because we believe their skills can save our lives.

So how do we build trust in God? The key is to study His commands and promises recorded in His Word. Will it really be better for us if we trust God and do what He says? Absolutely! This week's lesson gives us ample reasons for building our lives on the wise foundation of God's character and commands. After all, He alone is trustworthy. And what He promises will come true.

Introduction for Youth

Topic: *Living Right*

What values and goals are really worth striving for? Our culture offers teenagers many alluring prospects—some worthwhile and others terribly ruinous. For example, that's one reason drugs exact such a heavy toll among adolescents. The promised high turns into deadly addiction.

God's wisdom teaches teens that there's nothing more valuable than to strive for spiritual stature and success. We must consistently present them with the goal of upright living, not just by our lectures but also by our examples. When teens see their parents and other adults trusting God and heeding His Word, they will be more likely to seek spiritual values for themselves.

Adolescents need to hear and see the kinds of rewards promised in Proverbs 3: long life, prosperity, a good name, healthy bodies, and sound minds. They see more than enough violence and destruction. They need to see hope of a better way.

Concepts for Children

Topic: *Pleasing God*

1. We have to make choices between doing things our own way and God's way.
2. God promises to enrich our lives when we obey Him.
3. Finding and doing God's will is more than worth all the effort we put into it.
4. God has given us the Bible to direct our paths.
5. Trusting God helps us make important decisions.

Lesson Commentary

I. TRUSTING IN THE LORD: PROVERBS 3:1-10

A. Gain Peace and Prosperity: vss. 1-2

My son, do not forget my teaching, but keep my commands in your heart, for they will prolong your life many years and bring you prosperity.

The Book of Proverbs is a collection of moral truths on a wide range of subjects presented in poetic form. It sets forth the philosophy of practical life from a godly perspective. Its main purpose is to teach people how to apply divine wisdom to daily life and to do what is right, just, and fair. According to 1 Kings 4:32, Solomon composed about 3,000 maxims. What we have in Proverbs may be a selection from these. There were also other writers of Proverbs, such as Agur (chap. 30) and Lemuel (31:1-9). According to 25:1, a group of assistants to King Hezekiah compiled and added the proverbs of Solomon contained in chapters 25–29. This information suggests that while many of the wise sayings recorded in Proverbs came during Solomon's reign in the 10th century B.C., others may not have been completed until the time of Hezekiah, whose reign ended in 686 B.C. This varied background to the book might suggest why Proverbs reflects a threefold setting: general wisdom literature, insights from the royal courts, and instruction offered in the tender relationship between parents and their children.

An examination of Proverbs 3 indicates that Solomon listed five admonitions in the first 10 verses. Each of these exhortations is followed by a promised reward for those who obey it. Like all the Hebrew teachers of wisdom, the king was careful to emphasize that every action has a natural and logical consequence. Prudent actions will be rewarded, whereas foolish ones will be punished. One of the most typical mistakes made in the study of Proverbs is to view the wisdom sayings as a series of ironclad promises. Individual proverbs do make strong statements in regard to the benefits of wisdom. Thus many people make the assumption that these benefits are divinely guaranteed, but they're not. The maxims in Proverbs should be seen as general statements that express a basic truth or a practical concept. A good way to analyze these adages in the back of one's mind is to reason, "For the most part, if I do this, then that is more likely to happen," rather than making the more confident but faulty assumption, "If I do this, then that will happen."

In verse 1, the Hebrew word rendered "my son" was the customary way to address a student or a disciple. The term occurs 23 times in Proverbs. It was unlikely that Solomon was addressing his own biological offspring in this passage. The king began by reminding his student about the importance of keeping Solomon's teaching in focus and memory. The Hebrew noun rendered "teaching" is a term also used for the first five books of the Old Testament. The same word is used to refer to divine law. In this instance, the king used the term to communicate a standard or direction. Put differently, Solomon wanted his student to use his teachings as a guide to navigate along the path of wisdom. The king also emphasized the importance of his disciple retaining these "commands" in his "heart." "Commands" renders a noun that denotes both injunctions and precepts. "Heart" carries with it the idea of embracing and actively putting into practice what the student had learned from the teacher. This truth is echoed in James 2:26, which says that faith without deeds is dead.

Proverbs 3:2 explains the reason for heeding Solomon's injunctions. The king said they would lead to a long and full life. Moreover, those adhering to his teachings would enjoy "prosperity" (vs. 2). The latter renders a Hebrew noun that denotes the presence of contentment and peace, whether in one's relationship with God or one's fellow human beings. Generally speaking (though not in every case), the wise live longer than the foolish. In addition to a longer life, the obediently prudent person would have a fuller and more meaningful existence. While "prosperity" could refer to actual wealth, in a broader sense, the emphasis is focused on an increased sense of purpose and significance. Here the student had to make a choice. Saying *yes* to God's way meant saying *no* to the world's way (see 9:10-11; 10:27).

B. Find Favor with God and People: vss. 3-4

Let love and faithfulness never leave you; bind them around your neck, write them on the tablet of your heart. Then you will win favor and a good name in the sight of God and man.

Solomon's second admonition encouraged his student to hold on to "love" (Prov. 3:3) and "faithfulness." The Hebrew term rendered "love" refers to the presence of kindness and mercy, whereas "faithfulness" translates a word that denotes what is reliable and trustworthy. Throughout the Old Testament, these two terms consistently showed up in God's covenants with His people (see Exod. 34:6; Pss. 25:10; 26:3; 40:10; 86:15; 100:5; 108:4; 115:1; 117:2; 138:2). To be specific, "love" (Prov. 3:3) and "faithfulness" complement and reinforce one another, to the extent that they add up to integrity in the upright. Metaphorically speaking, the best way to remain characterized by covenant-keeping compassion and honesty was to bind these virtues around one's neck and inscribe them on the tablet of one's heart. Put differently, Solomon wanted his student to wear these precepts like a necklace so that they would always (figuratively) be in front of the disciple as a reminder. Moreover, having kindness and loyalty chiseled on one's heart ensured that they would be practiced so frequently that they would become second nature (see Deut. 6:6-9; Prov. 7:3; Jer. 31:33).

What is the result of being a person of fidelity? Solomon noted that the rewards included enjoying the favor of God and a reputation for trustworthiness among one's fellow human beings (see Luke 2:52). "Favor" (Prov. 3:4) renders a Hebrew noun that refers to the grace and approval of the Lord. Instead of the term rendered "name," some manuscripts use a word translated "understanding," in which the emphasis is on having insight, discernment, and prudence. In this case, the admonition is on how intensely the upright are to concentrate in obtaining and heeding wisdom from God. Collectively, these terms speak of the total integration of the Lord's commands within every facet of one's life. In brief, divine wisdom clarifies for us what our priorities should be (see Matt. 6:33).

C. Encounter Obstacle-Free Paths: vss. 5-6

Trust in the LORD with all your heart and lean not on your own understanding; in all your ways acknowledge him, and he will make your paths straight.

Solomon's third admonition is to wholly trust God (see Deut. 6:5; Ps. 37:5). In the Old Testament, the Hebrew verb rendered "trust" (Prov. 3:5) is used in a literal sense to physically lean on something for support. The term is also used in a figurative sense to rely on someone (or something) for help or protection. "Heart" metaphorically refers to one's core personality, that is, the center of one's thoughts, emotions, and will. The focus in this verse is on acknowledging the Lord and seeking His counsel when making plans. The king told his student to avoid putting all his confidence into his own limited insight and discernment. This did not mean the disciple was to completely set aside his own knowledge and experience. After all, it would be absurd to think that Solomon, after spending years teaching a student wisdom, would then direct him to forsake everything he had learned. Instead, the king was reminding his pupil to recognize the source of his awareness and prudence, and to humbly admit there was more that God could teach him.

Those who depend on God in this manner also intentionally choose to "acknowledge" (vs. 6) Him in all their attitudes and endeavors. The underlying Hebrew verb is more literally rendered "to know" (in other words, "to take into consideration"). Here the emphasis is on maintaining a clear mental awareness of who God is, with the result that the believer submits to His will in every area of life (see 1 Chron. 28:9; Hos. 4:1; 6:3, 6). When the upright are totally committed to the Lord, He in turn makes the way smooth for them. Proverbs 3:6 depicts the path of life as being even and free from obstacles, which ensures the believer's success (see 11:5). A person seeing the hilly countryside around Jerusalem would have appreciated this metaphor of a straight path. Though the actual distance between some of the towns around the capital city was relatively short, traveling on foot was often arduous. The hills of Israel had to be traveled around or climbed over. In a similar way, the Lord will clear a spiritual path for those who trust in Him for direction.

D. Experience Good Health: vss. 7-8

Do not be wise in your own eyes; fear the LORD and shun evil. This will bring health to your body and nourishment to your bones.

Solomon's fourth admonition is a call to jettison pride and self-sufficiency and embrace humility. It began with his student refusing to envision himself as being so shrewd and prudent that he could ignore the Lord's injunctions and live for himself (see Rom. 12:16). A modest disposition included fearing the Lord and turning away from evil. What does it mean to "fear the LORD" (Prov. 3:7; see Job 28:28; Ps. 111:10; Prov. 1:7; 9:10; 31:30; Eccl. 12:13)? On the one hand, it is not an irrational feeling of dread and impending doom. On the other hand, it is more than courteous reverence. Fearing the Lord involves a deep awareness of His sovereignty and power. It also includes holding God in awe and unconditionally obeying Him. This is demonstrated by doing what is right and refusing to involve oneself in wickedness. Solomon may have intended to parallel these thoughts with those in verses 5 and 6. For instance, to be wise in one's own eyes is similar to leaning on one's own understanding. Similarly, to fear God implies completely trusting in Him.

Physical and spiritual wellness is the reward for being humble and avoiding evil (Prov. 3:8). Imagine how a cool drink of water refreshes one's body on a hot summer day. Likewise, revering God and living uprightly bring vitality to one's soul. Once again, Solomon was not making an ironclad promise, but spelling out a general principle (see Ps. 73:3, 12). Indeed, some of the most humble servants in God's kingdom have struggled with chronic pain all their lives. The absence of physical health, however, stands in stark contrast to the fitness of their souls. Many physicians today unknowingly repeat Solomon's wise advice. They understand that many physical ailments can be blamed on stress. In turn, stress often comes from trusting in one's own limited wisdom instead of turning to God for insight and discernment.

E. Enjoy Material Prosperity: vss. 9-10

Honor the LORD with your wealth, with the firstfruits of all your crops; then your barns will be filled to overflowing, and your vats will brim over with new wine.

Proverbs 3:6 instructed believers to acknowledge God in all their undertakings. Solomon's fifth admonition mentioned one specific way in which this can be done, namely, by honoring the Lord with one's wealth. In this verse, the Hebrew verb rendered "honor" implies affirming God's rightful place of authority in one's life by giving Him the best part of everything one produces. This exhortation follows the offering principles recorded elsewhere in the Old Testament (see Exod. 22:29; 23:19; Lev. 23:10; Num. 18:12-13; 28:26-27; Deut. 18:4; 26:1-2). Rendering gifts of tribute to the Lord was not to be done grudgingly, but as an expression of adoration to Him. This attitude recognizes that everything we have belongs to and comes from God. Accordingly, offering Him the firstfruits is a way of constantly reminding ourselves of these truths.

The reward for following this instruction is a material one. Solomon said the pupil would be blessed with wealth in return for his faithfulness in giving. The full barns and overflowing wine vats symbolized that the student would have more resources than he could possibly imagine or ever use (vs. 10). In Bible times, barns did not resemble the red structures we often see in the countryside today. Instead, barns in the ancient Near East were often just pits in the ground, usually covered with a thick layer of earth for protection. Grain could be stored for years under such conditions. Solomon's teaching would certainly have impacted any pupil who saw his wealth. Be that as it may, we must be careful not to give to God simply in order to get back from Him. Israel's king made it clear that the only proper motive for giving is to honor the Lord. Regardless of whether we see an increase in our resources after years of faithful giving, we can be assured that there will be many treasures stored up for us in heaven (see Matt. 6:19-23).

II. VALUING THE LORD'S DISCIPLINE: PROVERBS 3:11-12

A. Accept the Lord's Instruction: vs. 11

My son, do not despise the LORD's discipline and do not resent his rebuke.

What happens to children who are not disciplined by their parents? Experience tells us that they often become rebellious and rude. Pampered children lose respect for their parents because the latter refused to set any reasonable boundaries for them, or to enforce the consequences for misbehavior. Solomon understood this phenomena, and that's why he directed his student not to abhor God's "discipline" (Prov. 3:11). The latter renders a noun that can also be translated "chastening," "correction," or "instruction." The second half of the verse carries the thought further. Those who recoil from the Lord's character-shaping discipline grow to "resent his rebuke," in which the Hebrew verb translated "resent" points to the feeling of sickening dread. It's not long before those who react in this way decide to reject God's reproof altogether.

B. Acknowledge the Lord's Correction: vs. 12

Because the LORD disciplines those he loves, as a father the son he delights in.

Proverbs 3:12 records Solomon's explanation for his exhortation in verse 11. "Disciplines" (vs. 12) renders a different Hebrew verb than the one appearing in verse 11 that is rendered "discipline." In verse 12, the verb means to "reprove" or "rebuke." The Lord deals with His spiritual children in this way, not to signal His hatred, but as an outgrowth of His covenantal compassion, in which the verb translated "loves" denotes the affection existing between members of a close-knit family.

The king illustrated his point by drawing a parallel between godly parents and their children. Because the former take delight in their children, the parents recognize that part of their responsibility includes disciplining their children from time to time. To Solomon, hardship was a small price to pay for something as valuable as wisdom. Many Israelites believed that God sent a person difficulties as a way of correcting poor behavior or as a test of that person's loyalty to Him. The king warned his pupil not to spurn God when He allowed hardship to come his way. Instead, the student was to gain a sense of security, for he knew that the Lord loved him enough to train him to become more upright and virtuous (see Deut. 8:2-5; 2 Sam. 7:14).

Discussion Questions

1. What are some practical ways believers can store God's commands in their hearts?
2. What did Solomon admonish us to do to enjoy God's favor and maintain a good reputation among others?
3. Why is it important to completely trust in the Lord?
4. When we are struggling financially, how is it possible to honor God with the best part of our wealth?
5. How can we avoid loathing those times when God chastens us?

Contemporary Application

Though many Christians love to quote from Proverbs, it is not an easy book to study. Investigating this portion of Scripture is much like searching through a used-book store. If you are in too much of a hurry, you will walk away empty-handed and frustrated. In contrast, if you take your time and browse carefully, you will discover a variety of treasures that could change your life forever. Though the 500+ wise sayings recorded in this book were written almost 3,000 years ago, they still apply to modern-life situations. And while the cultural details of the adages have changed, the truths they express are timeless.

In short, Proverbs is a practical, down-to-earth collection of wise sayings. The maxims offer sound advice for living a successful life. They also cover such timeless topics as drunkenness, gossip, laziness, stubbornness, friendship, and childbearing. The book is not particularly about theological ideas, but about practical, personal ethics. The writers did not attempt to prove the existence of God or explain the mysteries of His ways. God's existence and sovereignty are assumed throughout. The axioms are not much concerned with the age to come and heavenly wonders. Instead, they focus on the here and now on planet Earth.

Though the topics covered are varied and complex, their basic approach is straightforward. The fear of God is the beginning of wisdom. To maintain a high moral standard is to demonstrate wisdom. Success is the natural by-product of integrity. Few will choose the path of wisdom. We are prudent when we associate with those who do and become one of them.

From Generation to Generation

Scripture

Background Scripture: *Proverbs 4:1-27*
Scripture Lesson: *Proverbs 4:10-15, 20-27*
Key Verse: *Hold on to instruction, do not let it go; guard it well, for it is your life.* Proverbs 4:13.
Scripture Lesson for Children: *Proverbs 4:10-15, 20-25*
Key Verse for Children: *Do not set foot on the path of the wicked or walk in the way of evil men.* Proverbs 4:14.

Lesson Aim

To recognize the supreme value of embracing the way of wisdom.

Lesson Setting

Time: During the reign of Solomon (about 970–930 B.C.)
Place: Jerusalem

Lesson Outline

From Generation to Generation

 I. Staying on the Right Path: Proverbs 4:10-15
  A. *Listening to Wisdom: vss. 10-11*
  B. *Holding on to Instruction: vss. 12-13*
  C. *Turning Away from Evil: vss. 14-15*
 II. Guarding the Heart: Proverbs 4:20-27
  A. *Experiencing Wellness and Wholeness in Wisdom: vss. 20-22*
  B. *Carefully Safeguarding One's Integrity: vs. 23*
  C. *Always Telling the Truth: vs. 24*
  D. *Shunning Wickedness: vss. 25-27*

Introduction for Adults
Topic: *The Wise Path*

Academic excellence is a worthy goal, and in the long run it's better to study hard than to coast. However, if we get straight A's in school but flunk the lessons that God wants us to learn about the way of wisdom, we haven't really accomplished anything of eternal importance. God's course in how to live is expertly taught in the Book of Proverbs.

The Hebrew people knew all too well the perils of breaking God's laws and the blessings of keeping them. The concise sayings recorded in Proverbs reflect this ancient wisdom. In this book, we find godly counsel on how to deal with a wide variety of situations. If we neglect the wise path taught in Scripture, we are planting the seeds of our own destruction. But if we seek the book's divine counsel above everything else, we will reap rich eternal dividends.

Introduction for Youth
Topic: *Learn to Listen*

"Instruction" (Prov. 4:13) is more literally rendered "discipline." This suggests that to take hold of wise counsel is similar to committing oneself to the regimen followed by world-class athletes. Because they know they face stiff competition, they devote themselves to eating sensibly, exercising regularly, and never missing an opportunity to train. By disciplining themselves in this way, athletes recognize they are better prepared to vie with their rivals and win their sporting events.

Saved adolescents can benefit from learning about the personal benefits connected with the regimen of wisdom. Because they realize their faith will be challenged by people they encounter and situations they experience throughout life, they are prudent to give themselves fully to the regular study and deliberate application of what they learn from God's Word. This week's lesson reminds them to recognize the supreme value of embracing the way of wisdom and listening to its sensible counsel.

Concepts for Children
Topic: *Knowing Right from Wrong*

1. God wants us to gain wisdom by reading the Bible every day.
2. God also gives us loving parents to help us gain wisdom.
3. We are wise when we do what is right.
4. We please God when we say no to what is evil.
5. God wants us to encourage others to be good and kind to others.

Lesson Commentary

I. STAYING ON THE RIGHT PATH: PROVERBS 4:10-15

A. Listening to Wisdom: vss. 10-11

Listen, my son, accept what I say, and the years of your life will be many. I guide you in the way of wisdom and lead you along straight paths.

In Proverbs 4:1-9, Solomon recalled when he first received teaching from his father and mother. In much of the ancient Near East, instruction in wisdom was primarily a matter of training for service in the royal court. The elders were regarded as "fathers" to the students. In Israel, however, training in wisdom extended to the home. And so we find Solomon, as a seasoned parental figure, desiring to pass on the wealth of the wisdom he possessed to the next generation. The opening words of verse 1 convey warmth and affection, as well as Solomon's concern for the welfare of his readers. He urged the recipients of his teaching—instruction that he had obtained from his father, King David, and his mother, Bathsheba—to pay attention and in this way grow wise. The guidance being provided was "sound" (vs. 2), for its source and the effects it had upon the lives of its adherents were wholesome, virtuous, and beneficial.

There is a sense of urgency surrounding Solomon's admonition recorded in verse 10. This is seen in the Hebrew verb rendered "listen," which is more literally translated "hear" and implies carefully heeding what has been enjoined. It is the same term rendered "hear" in Deuteronomy 6:3 and 4. Moses' emphasis in these verses was not so much that he was telling the Israelites to continue to listen to his sermon, but that he was stressing his call for them to obey the Lord. Also, if they did abide by the Lord, God would fulfill His promise to bless them in a land of their own—a land flowing with milk and honey where they could become a mighty people. In verse 4, Moses did not just make a statement about God; the lawgiver was also giving a command to the people. They were always to worship only the Lord their God and never divide their devotion between the one true God and false gods. Also, they were to teach their children to be exclusively devoted to the Lord.

Against this theological backdrop, Solomon urged his pupils to willingly "accept" (Prov. 4:10) his instruction. The king assured his students that heeding his teaching would result in a long, good life. As in 3:2, the emphasis here goes beyond the concept of merely surviving to old age. Solomon envisioned an existence characterized by purposefulness and tranquility in which a love for God and one's fellow human beings was paramount. The king was like a sage who used godly instruction to point his disciples in the "way of wisdom" (4:11). The Hebrew verb rendered "guide" comes from the same root word for the noun that is frequently translated "law." This observation serves as a reminder that God's Word is the basis for living in a prudent, virtuous manner. Solomon literally referred to the latter as being "led in the tracks of uprightness." This idiomatic expression denotes paths that are straight and obstacle-free, ensuring that one's journey is safe. In an ethical sense, those who obtained understanding from what the king taught would avoid the moral pitfalls that overtake the wicked. Tragically, the course of their lives tends to be perverse and ultimately ends in ruin—both temporally and eternally.

B. Holding on to Instruction: vss. 12-13

When you walk, your steps will not be hampered; when you run, you will not stumble. Hold on to instruction, do not let it go; guard it well, for it is your life.

Proverbs 4:12 builds on verse 11 by clarifying for the upright the practical benefits associated with embracing wisdom's ways. Solomon depicted the course of life by referring to the common activity of walking on a road that was unobstructed. The Hebrew verb rendered "hampered" (vs. 12) means "to be narrow" or "to be constricted" and denotes the presence of adversity and distress. The king's point is that those who heed the prudent counsel of God's Word avoid trouble that the deviant bring on themselves. Nothing stands in the way of the upright as they operate in a discerning manner. Indeed, regardless of whether they "walk" or "run"—that is, whether their progress is steady or swift—nothing really impedes their endeavors.

This emphasis on unimpeded progression can also be found in Isaiah 40:28-31. The prophet noted that God, who is powerful enough to create all things, does not tire or grow weary (vs. 28). Then Isaiah presented the paradox that while the strongest people—the young—weaken (vs. 30), the weak become strong through trusting in God (vss. 29, 31). Eagles can soar for a long time on thermals (rising currents of warm air), and so they are a symbol of strength and endurance. The weary would gain strength to soar above their circumstances, like eagles. Furthermore, they would run and walk without tiring, unlike the young who stumble and fall. The Hebrew word translated "renew" (vs. 31) involves the idea of exchange. The term is used elsewhere of a change of clothes (Gen. 35:2). The point is that those who trust in the Lord exchange their weakness for His strength.

In Proverbs 4:13, Solomon urged his students to maintain a tight grip on "instruction." The underlying Hebrew noun is the same one used in 3:11, where it is rendered "discipline" and refers to the presence of God's "chastening" and "correction" in the lives of His spiritual children. Rather than loathe such godly instruction, Solomon admonished his pupils to firmly take hold of the same and never let go of it. The underlying idea is to always remember the lessons taught by wisdom. This emphasis is reinforced in the latter part of 4:13, where the king urged his disciples to "guard" or protect what they had learned. The reason is that the instruction they received in godliness was the basis for enjoying a successful and prosperous life.

C. Turning Away from Evil: vss. 14-15

Do not set foot on the path of the wicked or walk in the way of evil men. Avoid it, do not travel on it; turn from it and go on your way.

When the righteous see the wicked prosper, it can test their faith and tempt their souls (see Ps. 73:2-3, 13-14). Perhaps this truth explains why Solomon admonished his pupils to never enter the path of criminals or proceed in the way of evildoers (Prov. 4:14). Put another way, the king warned against following the bad example of those who are cruel and corrupt. No matter how enticing their nefarious activities seemed at times, the upright were to completely avoid the ways of evil. Even when the opportunity arose to travel on such a villainous path, the prudent were to turn away from it and keep moving in a virtuous direction (vs. 15).

Similar emphases can be found in Psalm 1:1. The writer used a dramatic three-fold parallelism to note what divinely blessed people avoid doing. They shun the thinking, practices, and fellowship of ungodly people. Notice that the progression—walk, stand, and sit—denotes successive downward steps in evil activities. There is also a threefold collection of wicked contemplations: counsel, way, and seat. Finally, three words describe the character of the ungodly: wicked, sinners, and mockers. The three clauses emphasize that godly people completely avoid all association with wickedness and evildoers. They do not adopt the principles of the wicked as a rule of life. They do not persist in the practices of notorious offenders. Additionally, they do not associate with those who openly mock God, His Word, or His people.

The psalmist next focused attention on the "law of the Lord" (vs. 2), and said it is to be the believer's rule of conduct. God's law is not an irksome restriction, but rather the object of the upright's love and constant study. Virtuous people find true happiness in the revealed will of God as recorded in His Word. The phrase "the law of the Lord" can refer to either teaching or instruction. It is also used of a body of laws, especially the laws of Moses recorded in the first five books of the Old Testament. In Psalm 1:2, the writer made the phrase synonymous with the Word of the Lord and stressed that it served as the believers' guide for life. The virtuous relate to God's Word in two ways. First, they delight in it. "Delight" does not refer to a mere external formalism, but rather to an obedient heart (37:31). Second, believers meditate on Scripture constantly. The psalmist was referring to thoughtful reflection and study in an attitude of prayer and worship.

II. GUARDING THE HEART: PROVERBS 4:20-27

A. Experiencing Wellness and Wholeness in Wisdom: vss. 20-22

My son, pay attention to what I say; listen closely to my words. Do not let them out of your sight, keep them within your heart; for they are life to those who find them and health to a man's whole body.

Proverbs 4:16-19 contrasts the priorities and fate of the wicked and the righteous. The wayward experience insomnia until they are able to harm some innocent victim. Figuratively speaking, wickedness and violence are the food and drink of reprobates. Indeed, their existence is defined by their evil deeds. While it appears as if they will continue to prosper indefinitely from the crimes they commit, the gloomy darkness of calamity and despair await them. In contrast, the destiny of the upright is like sunlight at dawn, which beams brighter and brighter until the time of high noon.

It is against this backdrop that Solomon urged his pupils to "pay attention" (vs. 20) to his words. Put another way, the king's students were to attentively "listen" to his instruction. Furthermore, they were to resist the temptation to forget or ignore the lessons they had learned. Solomon enjoined his disciples to never lose sight of a single word he uttered. The idea is that one's response to wisdom was to go beyond a merely superficial compliance. The righteous were to let the truths of Scripture penetrate deeply into their "heart" (vs. 21). As was noted in last week's lesson, the heart symbolizes one's core personality. Those who allowed God's wisdom to permeate their innermost being enjoyed a truly godly life. In point of fact, understanding the way of wisdom brought wellness and wholeness to their spiritual, psychological, and physical existence (vs. 22).

B. Carefully Safeguarding One's Integrity: vs. 23

Above all else, guard your heart, for it is the wellspring of life.

Based on what Solomon had already said, he reminded his students of the importance of carefully safeguarding their integrity. He realized that throughout their earthly sojourn, they faced the risk of morally compromising themselves. For this reason, he implored his pupils to guard their hearts with all diligence, knowing that it was the fountainhead of their spiritual existence (Prov. 4:23). An examination of Scripture reminds God's children that they are in a spiritual battle and that their foe is powerful. That is why Peter urged his readers to be self-controlled and alert to the attacks of the enemy (1 Pet. 5:8).

We often think of self-control in negative terms, as the avoidance of sin. But Peter had in mind self-control's positive virtues. Believers who are self-controlled maintain a sober disposition. This attitude is complemented by a vigilant state of mind. By remaining careful and alert, believers can do a better job of resisting the attacks of Satan. The Lord wants the godly to be aware of the challenges facing them and to do all they can to resist the enemy of their faith. Peter described the devil as a ravenous lion that prowls around looking for a victim to devour. Once the animal has found its prey, it wastes no time in launching its attack. By remaining alert, believers are better able to recognize and ward off the devil's assaults.

The apostle directed his readers to resist the devil by standing firm in the faith (vs. 9). By "faith," Peter could have been referring to one's trust in the Lord. In this case, believers could deflect the enemy's strikes by continuing to trust in God. Eventually, the devil would flee from those who resisted him (see Jas. 4:7). Another possibility is that Peter was referring to the orthodox truths of the faith. In this case, God's people were to hold fast to what they had learned about the Redeemer. They were never to surrender their beliefs just to avoid the possibility of suffering.

C. Always Telling the Truth: vs. 24

Put away perversity from your mouth; keep corrupt talk far from your lips.

Solomon directed his pupils to keep their mouths free from "perversity" (Prov. 4:24). The latter renders a Hebrew noun that literally means "crookedness" and denotes what is twisted or distorted. The noun rendered "corrupt" refers to what is deviant. Together, these terms point to speech, whether concealed or conspicuous, that is misleading and deceptive. In addition to never saying anything that isn't true, those who guard their heart refuse to have anything to do with the lies spoken by others. Ephesians 4:29 contains a similar admonition. This passage's first subject is "unwholesome talk" (vs. 29). This can include cursing, gossip, lies, or any kind of damaging speech. Little by little, this sort of speaking tears down both the speaker and the hearer. Christians, therefore, should use speech that builds up others, such as words of comfort, encouragement, and affirmation. This kind of speech conveys a "benefit," or blessing, to the hearer.

From God's standpoint, there are two kinds of speech: wise and foolish (Prov. 15:2). The wisdom people claim to have will be revealed in their choice of words. Much clever rhetoric is not necessarily wise. Rather than tearing people down, wise speech will contribute to their overall well-being. In this regard, the Bible is the standard by which all our speaking is measured. What is consistent with Scripture is wise, and what violates Scripture is foolishness. From the divine perspective, there are two kinds of words, life giving and death dealing (vs. 4). The Bible leaves us in no doubt about the tongue's potential, both for us and for others. God's Word depicts the tongue as both the bearer of life and the destroyer of the spirit. A healing tongue speaks wholesome, uplifting words, and brings life and encouragement to others. So then, the goal of our speech is both to avoid trouble and to bring healing.

D. Shunning Wickedness: vss. 25-27

Let your eyes look straight ahead, fix your gaze directly before you. Make level paths for your feet and take only ways that are firm. Do not swerve to the right or the left; keep your foot from evil.

Guarding one's heart includes doing what is appropriate and shunning what is inappropriate. This truth is symbolized by the analogy of traveling along a road. As the upright journeyed along the path of wisdom, there were many potential distractions to pull them off in a debilitating direction. That is why Solomon urged his pupils to keep looking "straight ahead" (Prov. 4:25) and resist the temptation to turn aside to follow a wicked course. Because the way of evildoers was harrowing and onerous, the king instructed his students to make the path for their feet as "level" (vs. 26) as possible. As a result, the moral direction of their lives would remain steadfast and safe. Vigilance was required to avoid getting sidetracked in either one "evil" (vs. 27) direction or another.

Discussion Questions

1. Why do you think Solomon thought it was necessary to urge his pupils to accept what he had to say?
2. How does following the way of wisdom benefit one's life?
3. What are some things believers can do to retain and apply the wise counsel of Scripture?
4. What does it mean to guard one's heart, and why is this important?
5. How can believers avoid becoming distracted by the world's temptations and remain on the path of righteousness?

Contemporary Application

During a church missionary conference, someone asked one of the missionaries why they thought their children turned out so well. The mother explained that every day she read to them from the Book of Proverbs. "We simply wanted them to understand the difference between wise and foolish behavior," she said.

Many adults have yet to learn this lesson. Their lives show the bitter consequences of having failed to heed the teachings of Proverbs. Tragically, many people think they can escape the damages caused by foolish behavior. That's why society needs to see the difference it makes when we live according to God's rules. The testimonies of Christians are valuable assets in helping others to find happiness through God's wisdom.

Thanks to modern computer technology, we can benefit from what are called search engines on the Internet. These powerful services can answer just about any questions we might have. We now have greater access to more facts than we've ever had in history. But the search engines cannot lead us to God, the fountain of life and the source of all true wisdom.

This week's Scripture passages remind us that the wisest people have not necessarily accumulated the most facts. We all know there's a difference between gaining more and more knowledge and finding redemption in Christ. We can have our heads filled with facts and still miss out on the eternal life that the Father offers through trusting in the Son.

We have noted that modern life is filled with choices. The Book of Proverbs tells us to choose the best way, namely, God's wisdom. If we fail in this regard, we will lose everything. All our intellectual achievements and academic credentials will count for nothing if we reject the truth of Scripture. What a wonderful opportunity we have as believers to show what we value most in life!

Teaching Values

Scripture

Background Scripture: *Proverbs 10:1–15:33*
Scripture Lesson: *Proverbs 15:21-33*
Key Verse: *He who ignores discipline despises himself, but
whoever heeds correction gains understanding.*
Proverbs 15:32.
Scripture Lesson for Children: *Proverbs 15:13-22*
Key Verse for Children: *A happy heart makes the face
cheerful.* Proverbs 15:13.

Lesson Aim

To let the lessons taught by wisdom influence every
area of our lives.

Lesson Setting

Time: During the reign of Solomon (about 970–930 B.C.)
Place: Jerusalem

Lesson Outline

Teaching Values

I.   Choosing Wisdom: Proverbs 15:21-24
    A. *Following the Straight Path: vs. 21*
    B. *Giving and Receiving Good Advice: vss. 22-23*
    C. *Benefiting from Appropriate Conduct: vs. 24*
II. Valuing Piety: Proverbs 15:25-29
    A. *Divine Justice against the Proud and the Wicked:
        vss. 25-26*
    B. *Greed Leading to Ruin: vs. 27*
    C. *Wisdom in Speech and Prayer: vss. 28-29*
III. Heeding Correction: Proverbs 15:30-33
    A. *Encouragement over Good News: vs. 30*
    B. *Prudence in Listening to Constructive Criticism:
        vss. 31-32*
    C. *Wisdom in Fearing God: vs. 33*

Introduction for Adults

Topic: *Good Advice*

An examination of Proverbs indicates that Solomon wrote many of the axioms recorded in the book. After his inauguration as Israel's king, his reign got off to a good start. He received great advice from his father. Solomon had sense enough to accept his inadequacies. And he knew he needed wisdom from the Lord, especially to succeed as the next monarch of Israel.

There are times in our lives when we face awesome responsibilities for which we feel unqualified. In those trying moments, we can either avoid them or seek God's help. We likely will not need to ask Him how to be the wise ruler of a whole nation, but we still need wisdom to lead our families, churches, and communities. Setting our sights on riches will only leave us dissatisfied, for even if we get the material possessions we crave, we will still want something more. But if we seek wisdom from God, He will provide it in abundance (see Jas. 1:5).

Introduction for Youth

Topic: *What's Wrong with Your Thinking?*

There are occasions when saved adolescents think what they need to survive differs from what God thinks. Society says they should have lots of money, power, and popularity. But they learn from Proverbs that this mind-set is incorrect. The book's key admonition is for them to fear the Lord. Indeed, revering Him is the basis for all godly instruction (see 15:33).

At times, when life feels uncertain, it might feel absurd to the students to make the Lord the central focus of their lives. Nonetheless, they can do so, for He has promised to supply all their needs from His glorious riches, which have been given to them (and all believers) in Christ (Phil. 4:19).

Therefore, the main goal of the class members should be on spiritually maturing as believers. This involves growing wiser, becoming more patient, demonstrating unconditional love to others, and obeying God in whatever they do (1 Cor. 13:4-7). It also means manifesting the fruit of the Spirit, rather than the acts of the sinful nature (Gal. 5:19-23).

Concepts for Children

Topic: *Words for Living*

1. We show we are wise when we read the Bible.
2. By reading the Bible, we feed ourselves spiritually.
3. The Bible teaches us to love and praise God.
4. From the Bible we learn about the importance of being patient and kind to others.
5. God is pleased when we ask wise adults we trust for advice.

Lesson Commentary

I. CHOOSING WISDOM: PROVERBS 15:21-24

A. Following the Straight Path: vs. 21

Folly delights a man who lacks judgment, but a man of understanding keeps a straight course.

Proverbs 15:21 contrasts folly and understanding. The first half of the verse is literally translated "to one who lacks heart." This is a reference to individuals who have no sense or ability to exercise sound "judgment." Indeed, their core personality is characterized by nonsensical decision-making. Because they lack the ability to make prudent choices, foolishness brings them joy. The opposite is true of people known for their discerning, judicious ways. Because they are characterized by "understanding," they consistently follow an upright path. In turn, God shines the light of His favor on all their undertakings.

Throughout Proverbs, references to fools denote individuals who are morally senseless and spiritually deficient. Even though they might be intelligent by the world's standards, they are dullards by God's standards. They reject the way of wisdom and godly instruction. Additionally, they depend upon their own immature ways of thinking. Various Old Testament passages shed light on the nature of fools. They have nothing but contempt for the name and ways of God (Ps. 74:18). Their minds, being filled with nonsense, are inclined toward wickedness (Isa. 32:5-6). Though they might prosper for a season from their ill-gotten gains, they will lose it in the end (Jer. 17:11). While fools might portray themselves as being enlightened, they really have a closed mind when it comes to the existence of God (Ps. 14:1). In their ignorance, they scoff at the Lord continually (74:22).

B. Giving and Receiving Good Advice: vss. 22-23

Plans fail for lack of counsel, but with many advisers they succeed. A man finds joy in giving an apt reply—and how good is a timely word!

Proverbs 15:22 notes that in absence of good advice, programs "fail." The latter renders a Hebrew verb that means "to break," "to frustrate," or "to go wrong." Success occurs as a result of consulting with numerous knowledgeable and seasoned "advisers."

If these mentors are conscientious and honest, they will be eager to offer appropriate and timely advice. They realize that a fitting reply given at the right time and in a winsome manner can make all the difference in the execution of a plan. Moreover, their collective input can help in the formulation of a clear, specific, and achievable goal, along with a reasonable strategy to achieve what is envisioned. The process of planning involves well-established procedures and a bit of imagination. It also entails anticipating potential pitfalls and opting for alternate approaches to reach the goal when obstacles are encountered. In short, giving and receiving good advice requires the sorts of skills and aptitudes found in godly wisdom.

There are other adages recorded in Proverbs concerning the value of sage counsel. For instance, in 1:5, the discerning are instructed to acquire guidance. According to 11:14, when a nation lacks wise leadership, it is bound to fail. Solomon noted in 12:5 that the deliberations of the upright are just, whereas the counsels offered by the wicked are treacherous. Moreover, as stated in verse 20, those plotting calamity have hearts filled with deceit. In contrast, joy is the companion of those planning peace. While individuals who devise evil go astray, those who plan to do good exhibit unfailing love and commitment (14:22).

Though people make their own plans, God directs the results—even the very words that are used to communicate those proposals (16:1). The Lord is not only aware of what people intend to do, but He also knows the motives behind their ideas. Rationalization may cover a multitude of sins, but nothing can be hidden from God (vs. 2). The Hebrew adjective rendered "innocent" was often used to describe mixed oils. The reference to God weighing motives might have a slight allusion to the Egyptian practice of weighing a person's heart after death to determine the depth of that person's integrity. In light of God's sovereignty and knowledge, the only prudent course of action is to commit one's plans to God. This type of devotion to the Lord requires an attitude of humility and a willingness to change our plans if necessary. If we demonstrate an unswerving earnestness to accomplish the will of God, then our proposals are far less likely to fail (vs. 3).

C. Benefiting from Appropriate Conduct: vs. 24

The path of life leads upward for the wise to keep him from going down to the grave.

Solomon depicted our earthly sojourn as a journey that follows a discernible "path" (Prov. 15:24). For those who are prudent, their life course tends to be "upward." In one sense, the latter is a reference to the enjoyment of temporal wellness and wholeness. In another sense, the underlying Hebrew term introduces the notion of immortality, which is developed more fully in the New Testament doctrine of the resurrection from the dead (see John 5:28-29; 1 Cor. 15:20-23). By choosing the way of wisdom, the discerning avoid a premature, untimely demise. "Grave" translates a noun that refers to the realm of the dead. It was understood to be the abode of both the righteous and the unrighteous. The ancient Israelites thought of it as being a shadowy and gloomy underground region inhabited by disembodied souls (see Gen. 37:35; Num. 16:30; Deut. 32:22; 2 Sam. 22:6; Job 30:23; Pss. 9:17; 16:10; 88:6; 139:8; Prov. 15:11; Eccl. 9:10; Isa. 38:10; Amos 9:2).

II. VALUING PIETY: PROVERBS 15:25-29

A. Divine Justice against the Proud and the Wicked: vss. 25-26

The LORD tears down the proud man's house but he keeps the widow's boundaries intact. The LORD detests the thoughts of the wicked, but those of the pure are pleasing to him.

Proverbs 15:25 reveals that the Lord is sovereign over everyone, including the "proud." The latter renders a Hebrew adjective that also can be translated "haughty" or "arrogant." It refers to individuals who put themselves first before God and their fellow human beings. For example, the proud, in an effort to amass more wealth, exploit the poor and disadvantaged. Throughout ancient Hebrew society, this would have included widows.

In Bible times, the death of a woman's husband could leave her in an abandoned and helpless state. A widow without legal protection was often vulnerable to neglect or exploitation. If a woman's husband died when her children were adolescents, they were considered orphans. There were three primary ways a widow could provide for the financial needs of herself and her children. First, she could return to her parents' house; second, she could remarry, especially if she was young or wealthy; or third, she could remain unmarried and obtain some kind of employment.

The last prospect was rather bleak, for it was difficult in ancient times for a widow to find suitable work that would meet the economic needs of herself and her family. Unfortunately, it was far too common for greedy and unscrupulous agents to defraud a destitute widow and her children of whatever property they owned. Solomon was alluding to this tragic circumstance when he noted that the Lord, in response to the efforts of the wicked, not only brought about their financial ruin, but also kept the "widow's boundaries intact." In that era, a person's property was marked by boundary stones. Furthermore, it was a crime to move these in an attempt to increase the size of one's own estate (see Deut. 19:14; 27:17; Job 24:2; Prov. 22:28; 23:10; Hos. 5:10).

Proverbs 15:26 reveals what the Lord thinks of the plans devised by the wicked. The Hebrew noun rendered "detests" is more literally translated "abomination" and denotes what is abhorrent, loathsome, and disgusting in character. This verse reflects the biblical truth that God is the moral governor of the universe and that everyone is accountable to Him for his or her actions. There is no doubt that He will one day judge all forms of deceit, hypocrisy, perversity, and abuse. In contrast, the Lord looks with favor on the thoughts of those whose motives are ethically "pure." Likewise, He is pleased with the wholesome plans of the upright.

B. Greed Leading to Ruin: vs. 27

A greedy man brings trouble to his family, but he who hates bribes will live.

Proverbs 15:27 targets those who are greedy for financial gain. They are willing to cut ethical corners (so to speak) in order to make a profit. But despite possible short-term monetary advantage, their dishonesty can make circumstances difficult for their family and ultimately bring about its ruin. This is a fitting end, particularly since Ephesians 5:5 and Colossians 3:5 equate greed with idolatry. The second half of Proverbs 15:27 mentions one form of avarice, namely, bribery. The latter refers to the giving of illegitimate gifts (for example, money or a favor) to unduly persuade the recipient to act in a certain way or influence the outcome of a decision in a specific direction. Those who deplore such behavior and refuse to participate in it will enjoy a less morally compromised life.

Tragically, some people think a bribe works like a magic charm. They are convinced that it can bring about their prosperity (Prov. 17:8). Others are willing to use bribes to pervert the judicial process (vs. 23). Admittedly, there are times in our fallen world when doling out political favors and monetary gifts can purchase access to those in positions of influence and power (18:16). Indeed, throughout history, innumerable people have claimed the friendship of those who give such gifts (19:6). In some cases, a person can be bribed for a very small price to transgress the law (28:21). According to 1:19, a disastrous end awaits all who are greedy for money. Ironically, their penchant for violence and extortion have a way of robbing them of life itself.

C. Wisdom in Speech and Prayer: vss. 28-29

The heart of the righteous weighs its answers, but the mouth of the wicked gushes evil. The LORD is far from the wicked but he hears the prayer of the righteous.

Proverbs 15:28 and 29 contrast the tendencies and destinies of the righteous and wicked. "Weighs" (vs. 28) renders a Hebrew verb that means "to muse," "to meditate," "to consider," or "to study." The core truth is that the heart of the upright reflects on God's will, as conveyed through His Word, before giving an answer. Meanwhile, the wicked blurt out evil things, sometimes even before thinking; and such haste can lead to unanticipated negative consequences (see 19:2; 20:25; 29:20). For instance, while the careful planning and hard work of the diligent result in prosperity, the haste of the greedy to get rich quick leads to poverty (21:5). Moreover, according to 10:32, the speech of evildoers is perverse, while that of the righteous is pleasing. It's no wonder that the Lord ignores the prayers of the wicked, but responds to the petitions of those who heed His commands (15:29; see 15:8; 28:9).

III. HEEDING CORRECTION: PROVERBS 15:30-33

A. Encouragement over Good News: vs. 30

A cheerful look brings joy to the heart, and good news gives health to the bones.

"Cheerful look" (Prov. 15:30) is more literally rendered "light of the eyes" and possibly refers to the gleam in the countenance of a messenger who brings an encouraging report. The latter, in turn, produces a feeling of inward vitality and jubilation in the recipients. The second part of the verse reinforces this observation by noting that the conveyance of "good news" literally "makes fat the bones." In Solomon's day, fat or greasy bones were identified with prosperity and happiness. "Bones" is used to represent the health of a person's entire body. In this instance, the communique leaves people feeling good both physically and spiritually (see Gen. 45:27-28; Prov. 25:25; Isa. 52:7-8).

B. Prudence in Listening to Constructive Criticism: vss. 31-32

He who listens to a life-giving rebuke will be at home among the wise. He who ignores discipline despises himself, but whoever heeds correction gains understanding.

The Hebrew noun translated "rebuke" (Prov. 15:31) can also be rendered "correction" or "reproof" and denotes the presence of constructive criticism. Those who are godly are not put off by such admonitions. Instead, they hear and heed the "life-giving" instruction, and thereby demonstrate to others that they are wise. While the prudent listen to reproof and improve the character of their innermost being, fools disregard correction and in the process abhor what could be beneficial for them. Even more tragic is that they remain indifferent to the harm this dismissive attitude brings them throughout their lives (vs. 32).

C. Wisdom in Fearing God: vs. 33

The fear of the LORD teaches a man wisdom, and humility comes before honor.

Ultimately, the way in which people heed godly correction reflects the extent to which they genuinely reverence the Lord. Proverbs 15:33 notes that the "fear of the LORD" provides wise instruction. A similar truth is recorded in 1:7, which reveals that the reverent fear of God is the starting point of all Hebrew wisdom. This respect for Yahweh is what sets biblical wisdom apart from all its worldly counterparts. This foundational truth is repeated throughout the Bible's wisdom literature (see Job 28:28; Ps. 111:10; Prov. 9:10; Eccl. 12:13).

Reverence for God and a commitment to His Word signal the presence of "humility" (Prov. 15:33), in which the latter renders a Hebrew noun that denotes the presence of a meek and gentle disposition. Contrary to what the world thinks, a deferential and respectful demeanor are the basis for enjoying social "honor" from others.

Discussion Questions

1. Why do you think some people find joy, rather than sorrow, in acting foolishly?
2. How is it possible to know when enough advisers have been consulted when making plans?
3. In what ways might the Lord use you to prevent injustices being done to the poor and disadvantaged?
4. How can believers encourage their peers to be more thoughtful and considerate in the responses they give to others?
5. As you seek to live uprightly, what petitions might you bring before God this week to help you achieve your goal?

Contemporary Application

When the new church softball team was formed, Ted volunteered to be the captain. In previous years, he had been on other teams and had always thought he would make a fine captain. He was a good player, he knew the game, and he was assertive with people.

There were many men who signed up for the team, enough to field a 10-play squad with several reserves. After the first few practices, they thought they would do well, even though the players on the other teams in the church league had been playing together for years. By three games into the season, however, most of their enthusiasm had evaporated. In fact, none of those games went past the fourth inning because of the "slaughter rule." That rule automatically ends a game whenever one team is more than 15 runs ahead.

A lot of the problem was Ted. He rarely played those members who were the most dedicated to the team. They had shown up for all the practices despite adverse weather conditions, but Ted did not think they were as good as those who came to practices only when they felt like it. Those he did play, he played out of position, which led to many errors. They became discouraged, which hurt their batting.

At first, Ted received friendly advice from the more seasoned captains of the other teams. But he dismissed their counsel as being inferior to his own personally held views. He even ignored the input of his own more experienced team members, convincing himself that he knew what was best for the group. But things continued to get pretty demoralizing as one game after another was lost. Even before the end of the regular season, Ted quit the team. By the end of the season, they did not have a captain or even enough players to field a full team.

None of us knows everything. In fact, in the absence of good advice, our best intentions can go wrong (see Prov. 15:22). For that reason, we are prudent to seek out the godly counsel of others and heed constructive criticism, especially as we seek to live for the Lord (see vs. 31). When we do, we operate according to biblical principles and show our reverence for the Lord (see vs. 33).

Wisdom and Discernment

Scripture

Background Scripture: *Proverbs 25:1-28*
Scripture Lesson: *Proverbs 25:1-10*
Key Verse: *If you argue your case with a neighbor, do not betray another man's confidence.* Proverbs 25:9.
Scripture Lesson for Children: *Proverbs 25:1-10*
Key Verse for Children: *A word aptly spoken is like apples of gold in settings of silver.* Proverbs 25:11.

Lesson Aim

To cultivate harmony in relationships by following the way of wisdom.

Lesson Setting

Time: During the reign of Solomon (about 970–930 B.C.)
Place: Jerusalem

Lesson Outline

Wisdom and Discernment

    I. Respecting Authority: Proverbs 25:1-3
        A. *The Proverbs from Solomon: vs. 1*
        B. *The Enigma of Earthly Rulers: vss. 2-3*
   II. Finding Harmony in Relationships:
       Proverbs 25:4-10
        A. *The Basis for a Just Government: vss. 4-5*
        B. *The Prudence of Being Deferential: vss. 6-7a*
        C. *The Value of Resolving Conflicts Tactfully: vss. 7b-8*
        D. *The Benefit of Settling Disputes Privately: vss. 9-10*

Introduction for Adults

Topic: *Neighborly Advice*

Scan your daily newspaper to see how many stories substantiate the truth found in Proverbs. How many of the reported conflicts occurred because someone, or a group of people, chose foolishness instead of wisdom? "Those who fail to find me," we can hear the wisdom of Proverbs declaring, "harm themselves." In some cases, the harm comes to others as well. Despite this, many people refuse to listen to God's Word. Tragically, some individuals listen only after they have been hurt.

In contrast, biblical wisdom is like a concerned neighbor advising, "Turn to me and find life." The deepest satisfaction comes from knowing God's Word and obeying His injunctions recorded in it. Our obligation as responsible, prudent Christians is to offer life and to warn of destruction. We must be faithful watchers on the wall, crying out with wisdom for people to be careful and to choose God's path of uprightness over the wicked, destructive ways of the world.

Introduction for Youth

Topic: *So You're Always Right*

Who among saved teens would not want to be thought of as wise and knowledgeable? Of course, they don't flaunt the fact that they strive to be discerning and prudent. It's not necessary to call attention to one's wisdom, for wisdom shows itself naturally in one's lifestyle.

What about adolescents who realize they aren't always right in what they think, say, and do? In a metaphorical sense, God has sent them an invitation marked RSVP (*Répondez s'il vous plaît*)—French for "Please reply." The offer is made through such biblical books as Proverbs. All the teens have to do is humbly accept wisdom's generous offer to navigate through life in the best way possible.

Concepts for Children

Topic: *Treasures in God's Word*

1. God is greater than we can ever imagine.
2. God wants us to work together to make the world a better place to live.
3. We are humble when we put God first in our lives.
4. God wants us to obey the laws created by our nation's leaders.
5. God wants us to be kind and caring to others.

Lesson Commentary

I. RESPECTING AUTHORITY: PROVERBS 25:1-3

A. The Proverbs from Solomon: vs. 1

These are more proverbs of Solomon, copied by the men of Hezekiah king of Judah.

The sayings recorded in Proverbs 25–29 are attributed to King Solomon. Apparently, they were from the collection of 3,000 ethical maxims he composed (1 Kings 4:32). These adages were selected, compiled, and organized by a committee of scholars appointed by King Hezekiah for the purpose of reforming Israel. The names of the collectors and the criteria they used in selecting and arranging these specific axioms remain a mystery. Apparently, this compilation of Solomon's wisdom was organized at the same time as the revival of the psalms authored by David and Asaph for use in corporate worship (see 2 Chron. 29:30). If it were not for the spiritual renewal during Hezekiah's reign, many of these biblical hymns and proverbs might have been lost forever.

Hezekiah succeeded his father, King Ahaz, at the age of 25. Hezekiah reigned in Jerusalem for 29 years (715–686 B.C.). He was one of the few monarchs who led Judah closer to God instead of further away from Him. Hezekiah cleansed the Jerusalem temple and rededicated it solely to the worship of the Lord. Then the king celebrated his famous 14-day Passover in the shrine for the first time in decades. Hezekiah was also responsible for a water tunnel that he cut through rock to connect Jerusalem to a spring outside the city. God rewarded Hezekiah's faithfulness by delivering Jerusalem from King Sennacherib of Assyria. Even though Hezekiah was a godly monarch, his pride sowed seeds of destruction for Judah.

Sometime before Sennacherib's threat, Hezekiah nearly died. In response to his prayers, the Lord extended Hezekiah's life by 15 years. When a Babylonian delegation came to congratulate the king, he boastfully showed them the great wealth of Jerusalem. Isaiah warned Hezekiah that Babylon would one day carry it all away. Hezekiah's son Manasseh succeeded his father for the longest and most wicked reign of any king of Judah. The fate of Judah was sealed during Manasseh's reign as he set up idols, first in the temple courtyards and finally in the temple itself. He worshiped the stars and consulted mediums. The Chronicler reported that Manasseh repented near the end of his life, but his son Amon ignored Manasseh's brief example of repentance and followed his lifelong pattern of wickedness. King Hezekiah's account can be found in 2 Kings 18–20; 2 Chronicles 29–32; and Isaiah 36–39.

B. The Enigma of Earthly Rulers: vss. 2-3

It is the glory of God to conceal a matter; to search out a matter is the glory of kings. As the heavens are high and the earth is deep, so the hearts of kings are unsearchable.

The first of Solomon's maxims recorded by Hezekiah's scribes deals with the importance of earthly rulers to society. Proverbs 25:2 notes that God, as the supreme Ruler of the universe, maintains the prerogative to keep His administration of the temporal and eternal realms a divine secret (see Deut. 29:29). Earthly rulers are aware of this mystery in God's ordering of existence, and their curiosity about the unknown spurs them on to investigate what they do not understand and find an explanation for their unanswered questions.

In Ecclesiastes 3:11, Solomon noted that God has "set eternity" in the human heart. Expressed differently, the Creator has made people with a deep-seated, inborn awareness of His ways in the world. This impels them to comprehend how the past, present, and future all fit together. But despite each generation's stellar intellectual abilities and attainments, people remain largely ignorant of what God has planned. They are unable even to fathom the nature and timing of events during the course of their individual lives.

Proverbs 25:3 builds on the truth implicit in verse 2 that God has given human governments awesome and sobering responsibilities. If earthly rulers are prudent, they will inquire after the Lord to discern His will, despite its unknowns. Interestingly, subordinates within the echelons of human government often find themselves uncertain about what their superiors are thinking. To them, the motivations and plans of those at the highest levels of executive power seem to be incomprehensible, like the heights of the heavens and the depths of the earth.

Jewish writings dating from the first century A.D. subdivided the heavens into three or more layers. It is unclear how much of this thinking Solomon accepted, though his wording suggests he embraced the Jewish belief in the plurality of the heavens. If we assume that the first heaven is the sky and the second heaven the more distant stars and planets, the third heaven refers to the place where God dwells. Paradise is the abode of blessedness for the righteous dead. For believers, it also signifies dwelling in fellowship with the exalted Redeemer in unending glory.

The Bible mentions three primary human institutions—the family, government, and the church. When one or more of these entities is weakened or fails, all of society is affected. God established the family first. He created Adam (Gen. 2:7), and then He created Eve to be a companion for Adam (vss. 21-23). The Lord then commanded them to be fruitful and multiply (1:28). God established human government to maintain law and order in society (1 Pet. 2:13-14). God established the church to bring Him glory and proclaim His saving message (Matt. 16:18; 28:18-20; Eph. 1:22-23).

In Romans 13:1-8, Paul talked about the importance of properly obeying the governing authorities, which God had established. The apostle's teaching expanded upon Jesus' teaching recorded in Mark 12:17. Even though believers were citizens of heaven (see Phil. 3:20; Col. 1:13), they were also members of the state. God's people were obligated to be appropriately submissive to the rulers in authority over them (Rom. 13:1). The apostle noted that all human rulers have been established in their positions of authority by God (see John 19:10-11). Therefore, obeying the government, in a way, was equivalent to heeding God. Even if the state rulers were wicked, the institution itself was not evil, and so believers were to submit appropriately to the governing authorities.

II. FINDING HARMONY IN RELATIONSHIPS: PROVERBS 25:4-10

A. The Basis for a Just Government: vss. 4-5

Remove the dross from the silver, and out comes material for the silversmith; remove the wicked from the king's presence, and his throne will be established through righteousness.

Generally speaking, the Lord has gifted some, especially godly rulers, to uncover mysteries and, presumably, to explain those mysteries to others. This would be especially important in judicial matters. Moreover, the Lord gifts devout leaders with the ability and determination to understand more than the average person. Though Solomon did not elevate earthly monarchs to divine status, he taught that the rulers' experience, wisdom, and knowledge were so great that common people would struggle to make sense of their ways. Implicit in that truth is perhaps a cautionary awareness not to question the decisions of the monarch.

Next, in Proverbs 25:4-5, Solomon compared the purification of silver to the refinement of the royal court. The process involved smelting lead ore to separate the dross (lead oxide) from the silver. Just as impurities were removed from precious metal to purge it, so deceitful advisers were to be removed from the monarch's presence (see Isa. 1:21-26; Jer. 6:27-30). The ouster of unscrupulous courtiers would ensure that the counsel being received was untainted and that justice was the foundation on which the government was established (see Prov. 16:12).

These observations balanced Solomon's earlier claims to the king's near infallibility. No matter how wise and gifted a monarch might be, the ruler was still dependent upon a cadre of advisers for accurate information and objective viewpoints to ensure wise decision-making. A discerning monarch who had trusted court officials would be richly blessed with success by God.

Today, some people consider Solomon's elevated opinion of the monarchy to be flagrant self-promotion. However, it is helpful to remember that in his day, monarchs were the undisputed leaders of nations. There was no other form of government available to the people of Israel. It is also beneficial to keep in mind that no matter how much power the monarch possessed, in the early years of Solomon's reign he was dependent upon God for his wisdom and authority. The ruler was also expected to follow God's laws just like the common people. Most importantly, the Lord held the monarch accountable for his actions.

B. The Prudence of Being Deferential: vss. 6-7a

Do not exalt yourself in the king's presence, and do not claim a place among great men; it is better for him to say to you, "Come up here," than for him to humiliate you before a nobleman.

Solomon commented on the prudence of remaining deferential, rather than arrogant and self-aggrandizing, in the royal court. He cautioned his readers never to take a place of honor at a royal feast (Prov. 25:6). Instead, they were to take a place of less honor and allow the monarch to promote them, if he wished. Verse 7 rehearses a scene in which the king, at one of his banquets, invited a subordinate to sit in a coveted spot nearer to him. In contrast is the humiliation of being demoted in public before the other nobles who served the monarch. Perhaps Jesus had these verses in mind when He spoke about a foolish person who claimed a place of honor at a wedding feast, only to be humiliated when asked to move to a lesser position (see Luke 14:7-11).

Ecclesiastes 8:2-8 contains additional observations Solomon made about the wisdom of conducting oneself with modesty before earthly leaders. For the discerning courtier, this included obeying the decrees of ruling authorities. The king appealed to the oath his subjects made before God to remain loyal to His chosen monarch (vs. 2; see 1 Chron. 29:24). Solomon urged the readers of his day not to be hasty to rush out of the ruler's presence. Otherwise, they might inadvertently signal an intent to avoid executing their assigned responsibilities. Even when the task felt unpleasant, they were to do their duty promptly. Moreover, the king's subordinates were wise when they refused to associate with a "bad cause" (Eccl. 8:3), especially a course of action that involved plotting evil against him. The prudent recognized that the monarch had the power to do whatever he wanted. Furthermore, the wise understood that the king's authority, as evidenced by the edicts he issued, was "supreme" (vs. 4) or absolute. Thus, only foolhardy individuals would dare to oppose or argue with him after he had made up his mind.

Furthermore, Solomon observed that, generally speaking, those who heeded the ruler's command would not be punished for insubordination. Also, those who were wise perceived when the time was right to initiate an endeavor and the best way to go about it (vs. 5). Solomon explained that regardless of the issue, there was a proper time and course of action. Thus, when the moment was right, the king's directive had to be carried out. This remained the case even when his subjects were going through hard times. If they refused or delayed in expediting his will, he could make their lives feel even more miserable (vs. 6).

It was foolhardy for the king's subjects to procrastinate in doing what he ordered based on the tenuous hope that the situation might somehow improve. After all, no one could predict the future or foretell specifically what would happen next (vs. 7). Not even the time of one's death—perhaps the most consequential event in a person's earthly existence (along with being born)—could be forecast with any precision. It was as impossible to do this as it was to restrain and control the "wind" (v. 8). "Wind" renders a Hebrew noun that also can be translated "spirit." If the latter rendering is adopted, the verse would be saying that no one can hold back the lifebreath (or animating force) when the time comes for it to leave one's body (see Pss. 104:29; 146:4; Eccl. 12:7).

In either case, it was reckless to attempt to thwart or undermine the monarch's authority, whether intentionally or unintentionally. Those who were guilty of such wickedness could not escape the detrimental consequences of their actions. It was as difficult to do so as a soldier trying to be discharged from the military during a "time of war" (Eccl. 8:8). Another interpretation of this verse is that Solomon compared the inevitability of death to a foreboding personal battle that everyone was obligated to experience and from which they could not escape. Not even the attempt to hide behind one's evil ways could forestall or rescue a person from eventually dying, which was the lot of every human being. In truth, people cannot cheat their way out of death.

C. The Value of Resolving Conflicts Tactfully: vss. 7b-8

What you have seen with your eyes do not bring hastily to court, for what will you do in the end if your neighbor puts you to shame?

Solomon's final teachings in this section deal with personal conflicts, especially the type that can eventually end up in court. The king mentioned a situation in which a person has witnessed something that seems ethically questionable (Prov. 25:7). In verse 8, he literally advised, "Do not go out hastily to strive," in which the Hebrew verb rendered "strive" means to engage in a legal dispute. Expressed differently, Solomon admonished his readers to slow down, speak privately with the party involved, and try to resolve conflicts tactfully before appealing to the judicial system. The king realized that most disputes result from misunderstandings and not from evil intentions. Clear communication could remedy many of these problems before they become serious. However, if Solomon's advice is ignored, those bringing the case against their "neighbor" might end up humiliated—and left with a stack of legal bills.

D. The Benefit of Settling Disputes Privately: vss. 9-10

If you argue your case with a neighbor, do not betray another man's confidence, or he who hears it may shame you and you will never lose your bad reputation.

Proverbs 25:9 deals with a situation in which two neighbors have a dispute with one another. Solomon advised that the two exercise caution when arguing their case in a legal court. In particular, the king warned against disclosing any secrets (for example, a criticism one has against a neighbor), perhaps in a desperate attempt to clear oneself of wrongdoing. If a plaintiff uses confidential information without necessity or warrant to strengthen his or her own case, then the plaintiff might lose more than the argument. The indictment might be incorrect or unable to be proved. Also, a long-standing friendship could be irreparably damaged. Moreover, the violation of a confidence could prompt the victim to claim that the gossiper defamed his or her character. In turn, the accusation could permanently damage the "reputation" (vs. 10) of the one betraying a secret. The resulting infamy would destroy whatever integrity the plaintiff had before the litigation was enacted.

Discussion Questions

1. What do you think motivated Hezekiah's scribes to compile proverbs authored by Solomon?
2. In what sense do earthly rulers bring honor to themselves by trying to discern God's will?
3. How can the presence of evil advisers in government undermine a nation's efforts to establish a more just society?
4. How can government officials resist the temptation to be self-promoting?
5. How might the decision to hastily bring a lawsuit against a neighbor backfire for the plaintiff?

Contemporary Application

I have listened to college students who were studying to be pastors fervently debate the finer points of theology. Then I have seen those same students worship together later in a spirit of unity and love.

I have also been part of a church congregational meeting called to vote on the starting time of the morning worship service. I saw a ballot on which one voter wrote that if his or her preferred time was not selected, he or she would no longer be attending the church! Other such sentiments circulated. A few people even insisted that one of the times on the ballot was more spiritual than the others, because it was more conducive to families with small children. Tempers flared. Relationships became strained. It was ugly!

What's the difference between these two examples? Was there more at stake in one situation than the other? Perhaps. But the real difference lies in the focus and attitudes of the "combatants." The college students recognized that while a group of believers will not always agree on every issue, they can work together harmoniously because of their common faith in the lordship of Christ. From this we see that inconsequential differences should never divide believers.

God has made us all with varying temperaments and backgrounds that result in our unique viewpoints. The many denominations and church bodies within Christianity today testify to believers' differing perspectives and convictions about everything from the finer points of theology to differing styles of worship.

How can we ever hope to get along with each other? It's by remembering that the most essential thing—our unity in Christ—takes precedence over every other thing. In church meetings, we need to hear the words "The Lord Jesus would want us to . . ." rather than "I think I should . . ." The two statements are not the same. From this week's study we learn that for believers to cultivate harmony in their relationships, they are prudent to follow the way of wisdom.

An Ordered Life

Scripture

Background Scripture: *Proverbs 28:1–29:27*
Scripture Lesson: *Proverbs 29:16-27*
Key Verse: *Whoever trusts in the LORD is kept safe.*
Proverbs 29:25.
Scripture Lesson for Children: *Proverbs 29:16-27*
Key Verse for Children: *Many seek an audience with a
ruler, but it is from the LORD that man gets justice.*
Proverbs 29:26.

Lesson Aim

To discern that a wise person obeys God's laws.

Lesson Setting

Time: During the reign of Solomon (about 970–930 B.C.)
Place: Jerusalem

Lesson Outline

An Ordered Life
   I. Maintaining a Future-Oriented Stance:
      Proverbs 29:16-17
      A. *The Downfall of the Wicked: vs. 16*
      B. *The Discipline of Children: vs. 17*
  II. Looking to the Lord for Significance and
      Security: Proverbs 29:18-27
      A. *The Value of Heeding God's Word: vs. 18*
      B. *The Waywardness of Fools: vss. 19-20*
      C. *The Contentious Nature of the Insolent: vss. 21-22*
      D. *The Demise of the Arrogant and the Criminal:
         vss. 23-24*
      E. *The Preservation of the Upright: vs. 25*
      F. *The Source of True Justice: vss. 26-27*

Introduction for Adults

Topic: *Law and Order*

On a warm day in early spring, lingering piles of winter snow begin to thaw and recede. Likewise, spiritual happiness tends to melt away when we sin. Also, the more we transgress God's Word, the more disorder it produces in our lives.

Proverbs 29:16-27, the passage to be studied in this week's lesson, reminds us that it is not enough to be hearers of Scripture. We must also be obedient to its commands (see Jas. 1:22). The obedience that the Lord desires comes first from within. It cannot be merely outward and superficial. We as believers seek God wholeheartedly and then proceed to hide God's Word in our hearts (see Ps. 119:11).

In short, obedience begins when we store up the Scriptures like treasures within ourselves. And once we have taken them to heart, we reflect on them and discover a genuine source of delight and cause for rejoicing (see Prov. 29:18).

Introduction for Youth

Topic: *Discipline Me?*

There's an old saying that refers to obstinate people being as stubborn as an ox. Sadly, many parents and teachers have encountered teenagers who seem like that at times. These adolescents have convinced themselves that they know more about life than others around them. Sadly, they end up making poor decisions that result in terrible consequences.

David, while serving as Israel's king, became well aware of this tendency. Perhaps that is why he encouraged God's people to learn a lesson from life. Some animals, like the horse or the mule, are so senseless that they must be bridled to be useful (see Ps. 32:9). Similarly, the Lord must hold in check those who reject wisdom's instruction and stubbornly pursue a path of ungodliness (see Prov. 29:18-19).

In contrast are those who find true and lasting freedom on the expressway of godliness. Perhaps from the time of their youth, they have a strong personal desire for holiness. Indeed, this is the basis for them drawing near to God and enjoying the eternal blessings of living in humble submission to Him.

Concepts for Children

Topic: *Follow the Right Path*

1. When we obey God, we enjoy peace and happiness.
2. We are responsible when we do what the Bible says.
3. What we do is just as important to God as what we say.
4. God will watch over us as we seek to obey Him.
5. God wants us to be a good example to help others obey Him.

Lesson Commentary

I. Maintaining a Future-Oriented Stance: Proverbs 29:16-17

A. The Downfall of the Wicked: vs. 16

When the wicked thrive, so does sin, but the righteous will see their downfall.

In Proverbs 29:16, Solomon noted a circumstance in which evil people controlled the reins of power. "Thrive" renders a Hebrew verb that means "to increase." Metaphorically speaking, the soil in which the corrupt are planted causes their "sin" to flourish. "Sin" renders a noun that denotes the presence of rebellious acts and flagrant transgressions of the law. While insurrectionists might appear to prosper for a season, those heeding God's commands will triumphantly look on the demise of the wicked. A similar mind-set is found in Psalm 37. David urged the righteous not to envy the wicked, for one day they will disappear like sun-parched grass (vss. 1-2). The king also exhorted the upright to patiently trust in the Lord and not fret over the wicked schemes of evildoers, for eventually He will wipe them out (vss. 8-9).

B. The Discipline of Children: vs. 17

Discipline your son, and he will give you peace; he will bring delight to your soul.

The Hebrew verb translated "discipline" (Prov. 29:17) implies dispensing admonishment and correction with the goal of providing instruction and training in righteousness. When godly parents, out of concern for the proper rearing of their children, use appropriate techniques to guide them along the path of wisdom, the latter will bring them inner "peace," in which the latter renders a verb that means "to rest" or "to repose." The second part of the verse carries the thought further by noting that the feeling of tranquility results in the experience of "delight." The latter renders a noun that denotes the presence of joy, pleasure, and happiness.

Solomon believed that wisdom was to be primarily taught by the parents of his students. Though the king acknowledged that other instructors might have a profound influence on a young person, he insisted that the fundamental responsibility for a child's education rested upon the parents. God has placed parents in a strategic position to mold the character of their children and develop their ability to think biblically. The process of character development starts with the establishment of godly values. Parents do this by actively modeling the ways of righteousness. Solomon viewed both parents as being vital in this teaching and modeling mission ordained by God. Indeed, Israel's king urged young people to guard the directives of their fathers and remain faithful to the instruction of their mothers (Prov. 6:20). It's no wonder that children who come from homes where one parent is gone, often suffer a lack of wisdom. When a parent is missing, mature Christians should do what they can to fill that void.

Solomon reminded his readers that no person is an island, especially when it comes to his or her family of origin. All of a person's actions will have some sort of impact on his or her family, especially the parents. This was especially true in ancient times, when the care of older family members was the responsibility of their adult sons and daughters. Depending on the wisdom or foolishness of the latter group, the family estate could be either built up or squandered. The king declared in 10:1 that wise children make a father rejoice. In contrast, foolish children bring grief to their mother. Growing up, Solomon may have seen the joy in David's face when he acted prudently. And Solomon undoubtedly witnessed his father's grief when Absalom attempted to usurp the throne.

The importance of young people choosing the path of righteousness is emphasized in 22:6. "Child" can refer to a wide range of ages, including infants, weaned children, and adolescents. Moreover, the Hebrew verb rendered "train" can also be translated "to dedicate." In fact, the verb is elsewhere used in reference to the consecration of the Jerusalem temple (1 Kings 8:63; 2 Chron. 7:5). Proverbs 22:6 is talking about children whom godly parents set apart for the Lord and morally train to follow Him. Others, however, contend that the emphasis in this verse is on figuring out a child's idiosyncrasies. It's claimed that parents should learn what captures the interest of their children, motivate them to pursue it, and thereby empower them to excel in life. An Arabic root of much later origin—nearly a millennium after the proverb was written—is the basis for this supposition. Reference is made to the practice of rubbing the palate of a newborn child with date juice or olive oil to encourage the infant to suck. But it is unlikely that this meaning was behind the Hebrew verb Solomon used.

Moreover, the verse is not talking about customizing the training of children according to their preferred style of learning (the benefit of the latter notwithstanding). The phrase translated "the way he should go" refers to the path of righteousness, as opposed to the way of fools and the wicked. Solomon believed there was only one moral standard by which people should live. Parents who trained their children to pursue godliness increased the likelihood that they would remain on this path even into old age.

Life these days seems overflowing with different things to experience. But when all is said and done, there are only two distinct options—the path of wisdom or the road of folly. The first choice leads to life, while the second option leads to death. This perspective is evident in Jesus' teaching recorded in Matthew 7:13-14. He declared that the highway to hell is broad. Also, its gate is wide for the many who choose to walk down its easy, gliding path. In contrast, the gateway to life is small. Also, the road is narrow with only a few ever finding it. By this Jesus did not mean that it is difficult to become a Christian. Rather, He was teaching that there is only one way to eternal life with God. The way of wisdom is to trust in Christ. Living His way may not be popular, but it is nevertheless true and right.

II. LOOKING TO THE LORD FOR SIGNIFICANCE AND SECURITY: PROVERBS 29:18-27

A. The Value of Heeding God's Word: vs. 18

Where there is no revelation, the people cast off restraint; but blessed is he who keeps the law.

"Revelation" (Prov. 29:18) translates a Hebrew noun that means "vision" and refers to divine oracles spoken through prophets of the Lord (see 1 Sam. 3:1; Ps. 89:19; Isa. 1:1; Dan. 1:17; 8:1). What they declared was intended to summon God's people back to Him. In the absence of moral and spiritual guidance, a society would career even faster toward lawlessness and ruin. The Mosaic "law"—and more generally, the Word of God—was the basis for these prophetic utterances. In a sense, Scripture provided the ethical framework for what the Lord's spokespersons declared. When the upright heeded the sage instruction conveyed by His ordinances, their lives were filled with blessing or an abiding inner joy.

B. The Waywardness of Fools: vss. 19-20

A servant cannot be corrected by mere words; though he understands, he will not respond. Do you see a man who speaks in haste? There is more hope for a fool than for him.

Proverbs 29:19 targets the issue of servants who are stubborn and insolent. Words alone are insufficient to induce subordinates to respond favorably to the admonishment and chastisement given to bring about reform in their attitudes, words, and actions. While the corrective instruction may be understood, wayward servants refuse to heed what they hear. In this case, more drastic measures are required. Verse 20 notes the imprudence associated with failing to think before speaking. Conducting oneself in such an impetuous manner often results in ill-advised and rash comments that the hasty individual later regrets. Because it can be very difficult to repair the relational damage done, the prospects for a brighter future are far better for fools (vs. 20).

Sadly, the imprudent often use their tongues as weapons. With a word or two, they can injure a person's feelings and even his or her reputation. Proverbs 12:18 highlights the specific kind of damage that can be done when cutting remarks are made. Speech that is rash, thoughtless, or reckless is like the lacerating thrusts of a "sword." The underlying Hebrew noun can refer to either the long-bladed sword used in war or the short-bladed dagger. Both weapons were stunningly effective in finishing off one's opponent. Those who are wise intentionally say things that bring healing, not harm. For instance, their words are wholesome and true, encouraging and uplifting, kind and gentle.

Moreover, the prudent guard their words (13:3). This means they control what they say and thus avoid getting themselves into trouble for inflammatory or insulting speech. Because they minimize the possibility of others seeking to retaliate against them for unguarded remarks, they have a greater likelihood of living a longer life. While the prudent have open ears (vs. 1) and closed mouths, the foolish have closed ears and open mouths. They recklessly blurt whatever comes to mind without considering the possible negative consequences of their rash speech (vs. 3). The quick retort might seem witty when uttered, but it will bring ruin on the speaker. There's an old Arab proverb that is apt: "Take heed that your tongue does not cut your throat."

C. The Contentious Nature of the Insolent: vss. 21-22

If a man pampers his servant from youth, he will bring grief in the end. An angry man stirs up dissension, and a hot-tempered one commits many sins.

A contentious nature can be created by overindulging the whims of others. Proverbs 29:21 mentions a circumstance in which servants are pampered from childhood. The result is sorrow, not joy. The meaning of the Hebrew noun rendered "grief" remains debated. Other suggestions include "trouble," "weakling," and "thankless one." In any case, the coddled young person grows up to be a self-centered rebel who challenges authority and thwarts the law at every turn.

Insolence can also be found in people given to anger. The noun that is rendered "angry" (vs. 22) literally refers to the nose or nostrils of the face. The image is that of a snorting sound that is produced by intense annoyance or dissatisfaction over some circumstance. This connotation is reinforced by the noun translated "hot-tempered," which refers to individuals characterized by heated emotional flare ups. When their anger rages, they become indignant in their attitude and toxic in their words. Quarrels and strife erupt, and this dissension incites acts of insurrection and other forms of wrongdoing.

Solomon, as Israel's king (see Eccl. 1:1, 12), could recount many other similar deplorable circumstances. One situation involved honoring fools with positions of high authority, while their wiser, more seasoned peers (referred to as "the rich" in 10:6) were dishonored with low-ranking appointments. The longer the wicked remained in power, the more physical and emotional distress it created for the general populace (Prov. 29:2). Another anomaly involved slaves (or servants) riding on horseback like princes, while nobles walked on the ground like slaves (Eccl. 10:7). Proverbs 19:10 notes a similar circumstance in which fools lived in luxury and slaves ruled over princes. To honor fools in these ways was as incongruous as snow appearing in summer (26:1). The situation was even more unbearable when servants became monarchs and godless fools were satiated with food (30:21-22). Presumably, these individuals prospered despite their own lack of diligence and wisdom.

D. The Demise of the Arrogant and the Criminal: vss. 23-24

A man's pride brings him low, but a man of lowly spirit gains honor. The accomplice of a thief is his own enemy; he is put under oath and dare not testify.

The Hebrew noun rendered "pride" (Prov. 29:23) is used in ancient literature to refer to the rising up or swelling of the sea. In this verse, it denotes individuals who have allowed their egos to become bloated with arrogance. Solomon observed that at the moment the haughty imagine themselves to be at the height of their power and prowess, they are most vulnerable to be overtaken by unforeseen events and unscrupulous people. In short, those filled with conceit eventually experience a disgraceful and humiliating downfall. In contrast, those who are characterized by an attitude of humility enjoy respect and prestige from others. Indeed, such honor is a reflection of their lifelong goal to revere and glorify the Lord.

Solomon desired that his readers travel on the "highway of the upright" (16:17). The king warned them that they will have to live wisely and honestly to remain on this route. If they stray from it, their physical and spiritual life will be in danger. One of the tempting side paths that will lead people astray is the detour of pride. Solomon warned his readers that taking this course will lead to their demise (vs. 18). An arrogant spirit is a sure sign that trouble is just around the corner. According to Solomon, it is better to be in poverty—even slavery—with a humble spirit than to be rich with a proud spirit (vs. 19). The implication is that the wealth of the haughty was illegally seized. Those who assisted the plunderers in their crime did so to their own peril. After all, the legal authorities could mandate that the accomplices testify under oath, which placed them in an ethical dilemma (29:24). If they spoke up, they implicated themselves; but if they refused to bear witness, society held them responsible for the transgression (see Lev. 5:1).

E. The Preservation of the Upright: vs. 25

Fear of man will prove to be a snare, but whoever trusts in the LORD is kept safe.

In a world filled with injustice and violence, it is easy for the meek and merciful to feel alarmed. Solomon cautioned, though, against being cowered into fear by the wicked and unscrupulous. Those who are petrified by the ungodly have no sense of security. As a result, they also have no courage to take a stand for what is right. In contrast, are those who anchor their trust to the Lord. By depending on Him, they find safety. The Hebrew verb rendered "kept safe" (Prov. 29:25) literally means "to be set on high." The image is that of soldiers finding security in a walled, mountaintop fortress. The impenetrable position gives them a distinct military advantage over their foes. In a similar way, the upright remain safe and sound because they are wholeheartedly committed to the Lord (see Ps. 56:11; Prov. 3:5-6).

F. The Source of True Justice: vss. 26-27

Many seek an audience with a ruler, but it is from the LORD that man gets justice. The righteous detest the dishonest; the wicked detest the upright.

Proverbs 29:26 is literally rendered "many are seeking the face of the ruler." This idiomatic expression associates "seeking the face" of national leaders with enjoying their goodwill. The underlying assumption is that by obtaining the favor of an earthly ruler, subordinates can freely make their requests and find "justice" in the decisions that are made. "Justice" translates a Hebrew noun that refers to the rendering of a verdict (whether favorable or unfavorable) in a court of law. Solomon noted that true and lasting justice only comes from the Lord. For this reason, those who are upright in conduct and disposition put their faith in God, who is characterized by truth and justice (see Deut. 32:4; Pss. 19:9; 33:4; 57:10; John 17:3). Because the righteous are His spiritual children, they abhor those who are "dishonest" (Prov. 29:27), in which the latter renders a noun that denotes those who are given to iniquity and injustice. "Wicked" translates an adjective that refers to those who are evil and villainous in their predisposition. Characteristically, they despise others who strive to be godly and virtuous.

Discussion Questions

1. What sorts of conditions do you think allow the wicked to thrive?
2. What challenges do godly parents face in rearing their children?
3. Why are some believers reluctant to heed wisdom's instruction?
4. What can people in positions of leadership do to encourage subordinates to respond favorably to constructive criticism?
5. How can believers maintain a humble attitude when society lauds the arrogant?

Contemporary Application

Right above the head of the chief justice of the U.S. Supreme Court, carved in marble, is a tablet representing the Ten Commandments. This reminds us that laws are something that bring peace and stability to a society. Solomon, being aware of this truth, noted that whoever obeys the law is "blessed" (Prov. 29:18).

On the one hand, we know that without laws, chaos results. Yet, on the other hand, from the time we become adults, we resist the restrictions that come with law. What is perceived as constrictive is actually what brings us justice, security, and tranquility (see vss. 17, 25-26). Clearly, good laws are beneficial to us. Why then do our hearts race when the police car pulls out and follows us? Most likely we fear that we have broken some law that was designed for our good.

Shame should result when we knowingly violate the law. When the law is disregarded or changes too often, the sense of shame and security is lost. Shame was the topic of a survey taken by *Newsweek* some time ago. It was noted that "ninety percent of Americans say they believe in God. Yet the urgent sense of personal sin has all but disappeared in the current upbeat style in American religion."

The loss of any definition of sin is a critical issue in this week's lesson. We learn that God's definition of sin is made against the backdrop of His law. We also discover that God's law offers clear parameters that result in fulfillment and joy for believers. They realize that even though the wicked despise the godly (see vs. 27), the Lord dearly loves His own and eternally blesses them.

Wisdom's Superiority

Scripture

Background Scripture: *Ecclesiastes 9:13–10:20*
Scripture Lesson: *Ecclesiastes 9:13-18*
Key Verse: *So I said, "Wisdom is better than strength." But the poor man's wisdom is despised, and his words are no longer heeded.* Ecclesiastes 9:16.
Scripture Lesson for Children: *Ecclesiastes 9:13-18*
Key Verse for Children: *"Wisdom is better than strength."* Ecclesiastes 9:16.

Lesson Aim

To recognize the relative value and limitations of wisdom.

Lesson Setting

Time: During the reign of Solomon (about 970–930 B.C.)
Place: Jerusalem

Lesson Outline

Wisdom's Superiority

I. The Tragedy of Rejecting Wisdom: Ecclesiastes 9:13-16
   A. *How Wisdom Fares: vs. 13*
   B. *A Besieged City: vss. 14-15*
   C. *Wisdom's Value and Limitations: vs. 16*

II. The Relative Benefit of Wisdom: Ecclesiastes 9:17-18
   A. *Wisdom vs. Fools: vs. 17*
   B. *Wisdom vs. Sin: vs. 18*

Introduction for Adults

Topic: *Subversive Wisdom*

Teachers can be quite sure that few—if any—of their students have recently studied Ecclesiastes. But teachers can also be assured that nearly everyone has asked questions about the meaning of life. Depending on how much class members trust, love, and respect each other, it may be difficult for them to admit their struggles with these big questions.

Christians are not immune to asking, "What's the point? I've tried believing God, but nothing works for me. I guess my faith is not strong enough." Some Christians are afraid to admit such questions to each other for fear of being considered subversive by their peers. They're also afraid to ask God about their doubts.

Rather than trying to solve everyone's philosophical problems, we need to concentrate on honest questions and candid answers. God was honest enough to include Solomon's soul-searching questions in the Bible. We also have to face them, and ask for God's help in finding the right answers.

Introduction for Youth

Topic: *Wisdom vs. Foolishness*

"Get off that treadmill and do some real walking," Joe yelled to his friend in the health club. Treadmills are handy devices for exercise. But to many people life itself seems like a treadmill. It's just like putting one foot down after the other.

The Book of Ecclesiastes reminds us that there are rhythms to life. The only way we can navigate safely through these times and changes—over which we have no control—is to trust in God's control of events. At times, this might feel hard for us to do, but it can be done.

When teens feel as if life has become a treadmill for them, they need to refocus their faith on the Lord. He can enable them to live wisely and avoid the pitfalls of foolish behavior. He is their source of joy, satisfaction, and peace in the midst of troubling circumstances. Ultimately, their spiritual and mental health comes from loving and obeying the Lord.

Concepts for Children

Topic: *An Example of Wisdom*

1. God wants us to see the value of being wise.
2. It's sad that some people don't think they need to be wise.
3. Being wise is better than being powerful like a superhero.
4. One wise person can help many others.
5. When we are wise, others will know that we are God's children.

Lesson Commentary

I. THE TRAGEDY OF REJECTING WISDOM: ECCLESIASTES 9:13-16

A. How Wisdom Fares: vs. 13

I also saw under the sun this example of wisdom that greatly impressed me.

Ecclesiastes deals with the stark realities of human existence. On the surface, the frank, unvarnished perspective presented in the book can leave readers wondering why it has been included in the canon of Scripture. Moreover, some struggle to accept Solomon's verdict that apart from God everything in life is absolutely futile and absurd, a declaration that appears throughout the author's treatise (see 1:2, 14; 2:11, 17, 26; 12:8). As a result, they conjecture that the sentiments of the author represent an inferior perspective, one that allegedly is supplanted by more inspired views, such as those found in the New Testament. This orientation is a grossly inaccurate misrepresentation of Ecclesiastes. Indeed, the book's lessons can be found emphasized elsewhere in Scripture.

In Solomon's discourse, he considered how people can best spend their fleeting days of life on earth (see Eccl. 6:12). He also attempted to provide an explanation for the way things are in life (see 8:1). As the author contemplated these issues, he considered the matter of death's reality and certainty. This fate awaited all people regardless of their ability, conduct, wealth, or power. Solomon made a point of commenting on those who blamelessly observed all the Lord's commands and decrees (namely, the righteous) and lived in a prudent and discerning manner (namely, the wise). Like everyone else, what the upright endeavored and experienced remained under God's complete control. From the limited perspective of human beings, no one could really know in advance what awaited the faithful. Anything could happen to them, including whether they were loved or hated by others (that is, experienced good or bad; 9:1).

The king was especially sobered by the realization that everyone shared the same "destiny" (vs. 2), namely, death. Four pairs of contrasting individuals are listed to cover the entire spectrum of humanity. In terms of their common fate, it did not matter whether people were righteous or wicked; good or bad; ceremonially clean or unclean (that is, heeding or disregarding the laws of ritual purity); or religiously observant in offering sacrifices or irreligious concerning the same. In an attempt to round out the representative list covering all humanity, two more pairs of opposites are mentioned. As a rule, the physical termination of life was the end of both good people and sinners (namely, those who pleased and those who displeased God); and those who pledged an oath to God's covenant and those who were afraid to do so (for example, a guilty person; see 2:14; 3:20).

Solomon lamented that, regardless of whatever took place on earth, death was the inescapable end for everyone. He called it "evil" (9:3), that is, an unfortunate tragedy. The deplorable reality of death spawned sinful desires and actions throughout the human race. Apparently, some individuals reasoned that since there was nothing but death ahead for everyone, why not give one's heart over to inane ideas and foolhardy behavior (see Isa. 22:13; 1 Cor. 15:32). Certainly pride and selfishness often determined what individuals chose to do in various situations. In some respects, their sinful nature dominated the trajectory of their entire life. From the horizon of temporal human existence, only those who remained alive had any hope of finding pleasure. This enjoyment of the good life that God granted to people was one of the themes the author returned to again and again (see 2:24-25; 3:22; 5:18-20; 8:15; 9:7-9).

In Ecclesiastes 9:11-12, Solomon confronted another of the harsh realities of life, specifically, that existence is filled with unpredictability. Sometimes the randomness of circumstances and events undermines the potential benefit of being wise. For instance, an untimely misfortune or even death can eliminate the gains achieved through diligent planning and hard work. To illustrate his point, the author noted that the fastest athletes do not always win footraces. Likewise, the strongest military powers sometimes do not prevail in a battle involving weaker foes. Similarly, there are occasions when the prudent go hungry, the discerning experience poverty, and those who are the most knowledgeable come up against failure. The truth is that hard work, strength, intelligence, and wealth (among other traits) do not necessarily ensure temporal success or earthly prosperity (vs. 11). In short, regardless of what talents, aptitudes, and resources people have, disaster can overtake anyone at any time for no apparent reason.

The perilous character of life neutralizing all moral distinctions is illustrated by the analogy of fish suddenly getting caught in a deadly net, or birds being abruptly ensnared in a trap. Similarly, people unexpectedly fall victim to tragic circumstances beyond their control (vs. 12). That said, the upright are admonished to wake up each morning and place the day in God's hands, trusting in His plan for them (see Matt. 5:45). In light of the reality and certainty of death, the challenge facing the prudent was to decide the best way to live (see Eccl. 6:12; 8:1). The counsel Solomon offered was based on his personal experience and his observations of how the world generally works. What he noticed about wisdom showcased its potential and limitations. It was also an irresolvable tension that profoundly affected the king (9:13).

B. A Besieged City: vss. 14-15

There was once a small city with only a few people in it. And a powerful king came against it, surrounded it and built huge siegeworks against it. Now there lived in that city a man poor but wise, and he saved the city by his wisdom. But nobody remembered that poor man.

Solomon recalled a small town that had only a modest number of inhabitants. It happened that the army of a mighty ruler surrounded and besieged the city (Eccl. 9:14). In ancient times, the purpose of this military tactic was to eliminate whatever ability a city had to defend itself. For instance, food and water supplies were cut off and outside contact was terminated. Though a siege could last for several months, the dying residents within its walls would eventually be forced to surrender.

On occasion, the invaders would accelerate the process by constructing earthen ramps and erecting ladders in an effort to scale the city's walls. Then, from this elevated position, flaming arrows and other burning objects could be launched into the city. Other strategies included breaching the gates with battering rams and tunneling underneath the walls. According to verse 15, an impoverished but prudent man lived within the besieged town under consideration. According to the NIV rendering of the verse, he used his discernment and understanding to rescue the city from its predicament; yet soon afterward, everyone forgot him. According to an alternative translation, the poor wise person could have saved the town, but no one listened to his advice, due in part to his commoner status in society.

C. Wisdom's Value and Limitations: vs. 16

So I said, "Wisdom is better than strength." But the poor man's wisdom is despised, and his words are no longer heeded.

Regardless of which rendering is preferred for Ecclesiastes 9:15, Solomon's conclusion (recorded in verse 16) remains true. On the one hand, wisdom is superior to the raw power of human might. This observation is echoed in the modern-day adage that brains are better than brawn. On the other hand, if those blessed with such prudence were poor, others scorned them and disregarded the sound counsel they offered.

Earlier, in 1:12-18, Solomon discussed the limitations of wisdom. Unlike his predecessors, he had the aptitude, determination, and resources to investigate the riddles of life. This included conducting a meticulous and methodical examination of all that is done "under heaven" (vs. 13). The latter phrase is synonymous with "under the sun" (vss. 3, 14). Thus, the world, with its all activities and enigmas, was the data that fueled Solomon's investigation. Biblical wisdom provided the king with the theological foundation and philosophical framework through which he used his mind to make sense of the material and immaterial aspects of existence.

It is difficult to imagine the enormity of Solomon's undertaking, which included fathoming God's eternal purposes. As the king looked back on what he attempted, he concluded that God had placed on people a lifetime of toil that seemed arduous and irksome. Indeed, as Solomon pondered the gamut of secular human activity on earth, all that was accomplished proved to be senseless and useless. In fact, it was as absurd and futile as "chasing after the wind" (vs. 14).

The king's search for understanding reflects the mental acuity God gave all human beings—intelligence that distinguishes them from animals. Because God created people in His image (see Gen. 1:26-27), they realize that there must be more to life than simple physical survival and existence. People also sense that there must be meaning for their lives, and this awareness prompts them to strive for ideals that eclipse themselves. For some, this involves deciphering life's mysteries, while for others it entails combatting injustice and eradicating suffering. As laudable as these and other goals might be, God has not permitted them to be attained by secular human efforts. In truth, the imperfections of life cannot be remedied. Likewise, the deficiencies encountered in this world are impossible to quantify and overcome (Eccl. 1:15; see 3:11, 14-15; 7:13; 8:16-17).

To his chagrin, Solomon admitted that even his God-given wisdom had its limitations in making sense of life. The king realized that his discernment and prudence exceeded that of any of his predecessors who reigned over Jerusalem. Indeed, he could claim to have greater insight and understanding than anyone else he knew (1:16). Moreover, the king made full use of these aptitudes and abilities. For instance, he was determined to ascertain the benefit of godly wisdom over inane ideas and foolhardy behavior. The result of his endeavor was no better than any other human pursuit. In short, the attempt to apprehend meaning and truth by reason alone was as ineffectual as "chasing after the wind" (vs. 17). Even more sobering is that those who grew in wisdom and learning experienced a corresponding increase in vexation and anguish (vs. 18).

II. THE RELATIVE BENEFIT OF WISDOM: ECCLESIASTES 9:17-18

A. Wisdom vs. Fools: vs. 17

The quiet words of the wise are more to be heeded than the shouts of a ruler of fools.

Despite the regrettable circumstance of wisdom's limitations, Solomon still believed that it was better to heed the advice of the prudent spoken in a quiet manner than the howl of a ruler made in response to the clamor of fools (Eccl. 9:17). In 2:12-14, the king commented on the long-term value of wisdom, especially in contrast to a life preoccupied with mirth and merriment. As in 1:17, "madness and folly" in 2:12 refer to inane ideas and foolhardy behavior. Solomon was convinced that he remained the best person to undertake this evaluation. After all, it was hard for him to imagine his successors having appreciably more aptitude, determination, and resources to achieve what he had already done.

The king discovered that in terms of short-term benefit, wisdom was to be preferred over folly, just as there was more profit to light than to darkness (vs. 13). From the standpoint of earning an income, people in that era tended to be more productive during the day than at night. Moreover, in terms of mental acuity and spiritual perception, the wise were like people who had two good eyes enabling them to see where they were going. In contrast, fools (that is, the morally senseless and spiritually deficient) were like individuals who were unable to see what lay ahead and consequently stumbled about aimlessly in darkness. Be that as it may, Solomon admitted that the same fate—death—overtook all people, regardless of whether they were prudent or reckless in life (vs. 14).

In 7:11, the king compared the benefit of wisdom to that of an inheritance, noting that those having both were amply provided for in times of want and protected in times of calamity. Moreover, both provided a certain measure of temporal security, especially in life's chaotic, tumultuous moments. Nonetheless, there was an unmistakable advantage for those who possessed knowledge (a counterpart of wisdom). They could use their understanding and discernment to operate in an informed, intelligent manner and thereby avoid the pitfalls that often snagged the foolhardy (vs. 12; see Prov. 3:13-18; 13:14). The preceding observations notwithstanding, it would be incorrect to conclude that the benefits of wisdom were limitless and absolute. Ultimately, only God is all-knowing and perfectly wise, and no one has ever been able to fathom His providential undertakings or change His sovereign plans (see Dan. 2:20-23; 4:34-35; Isa. 40:13-14; Rom. 11:33-36).

B. Wisdom vs. Sin: vs. 18

Wisdom is better than weapons of war, but one sinner destroys much good.

The parable recorded in Ecclesiastes 9:13-16 reinforced the truth that a small amount of wisdom offered at the right moment could do more good than a stockpile of weapons used to maim and kill in a time of war. And yet the transgression of a deviant person could wipe out all the gains made by the judicious counsel put forward by a monarch's courtiers (vs. 18). The latter observation is illustrated by the maxim appearing in 10:1. Solomon noted that an entire bottle of perfumer's ointment is made rancid by just a few dead, decaying flies. In turn, the foul odor that is produced renders the product useless and worthless. In a corresponding way, a small amount of folly can sour the benefit arising from a massive amount of wisdom and honor.

A miscellaneous collection of proverbs appears in verses 2-20, in which wisdom and folly are contrasted. Themes previously discussed in Solomon's treatise are mentioned again, and in some cases with added emphases. As before, the king maintained that while wisdom was superior to folly, the presence of the latter could neutralize the benefit offered by the former. A case in point would be the havoc and devastation brought on by a ruler's fickle decisions (the focus of verses 2-7).

For instance, the Hebrew idiom translated "right hand" (see vs. 2) denoted a circumstance or result that was characterized by goodness, protection, and blessing (see Pss. 16:8; 110:5; 121:5; Isa. 41:13). In contrast, "left hand" referred to a situation or outcome that was known to be detrimental, impotent, and wretched (see 1 Sam. 8:3; 2 Kings 21:21; Matt. 25:33, 41). Not surprisingly, the mind of the wise was inclined toward the right, while that of a fool lurched to the left. Ecclesiastes 10:3 advances the thought regarding the circumstance of fools. Even in such a straightforward activity as walking down a road, the imprudent lacked good sense. Indeed, strangers they encountered along the way could see how inept and dull witted they were in performing the most basic tasks (see Prov. 13:16).

Discussion Questions

1. What are some examples of biblical wisdom you have seen in your walk with the Lord?
2. When tragic circumstances occur in life, how can insights from God's Word help believers to cope?
3. What might you say to unbelievers to help them have a greater appreciation for biblical wisdom?
4. In heated exchanges, what can believers do to remain calm and prudent in what they say?
5. How is it possible for one foolish mistake to destroy much that is good?

Contemporary Application

Ecclesiastes presents the reflections of a person who boldly faced the complex questions of life, only to conclude in the end that true meaning and joy come from God. Solomon prefaced his treatise with the statement "Meaningless! Meaningless!" (Eccl. 1:2). Indeed, he carried this sentiment throughout the book.

The answer to this cry of despair does not become clear until the book's conclusion, in which the king declared that, to discover meaning and wisdom, people must "fear God and keep his commandments" (12:13). In fact, everything in Ecclesiastes must be seen within the framework of these opening and closing statements. From this perspective, the book proves to be a brilliant, inspired discourse that should encourage believers to work diligently toward a God-centered view of life.

Solomon examined the things that human beings live for, including wisdom, pleasure, work, progress, and wealth. And yet, no matter what they attempt to attain in life, they all meet the same destiny—they die and are forgotten by others. In this way, the king did not try to hide the futility that people face. Indeed, he emphasized that all the goals of human beings have limitations—even wisdom. Thus it is useless for them to seek to master their own destiny.

There is, however, an underlying hope in the book. Although every human striving will eventually fail, God's purposes will never fail. Through the experience of one who seemed to have tried everything, the author concluded, based on his faith in the Lord, that God had ordered life according to His own purposes. Therefore, the best thing a person can do is to accept and enjoy life as God has given it.

Wisdom for Aging

DEVOTIONAL READING

Psalm 71:1-12

DAILY BIBLE READINGS

Monday October 10
Psalm 71:1-12 Do Not Forsake Me

Tuesday October 11
Ecclesiastes 1:1-11 Nothing New under the Sun?

Wednesday October 12
Ecclesiastes 2:1-11 Nothing to Be Gained?

Thursday October 13
Ecclesiastes 5:10-20 Toiling for the Wind?

Friday October 14
Ecclesiastes 3:1-8 Everything Has Its Time

Saturday October 15
Ecclesiastes 11:1-8 Ignorance of God's Work

Sunday October 16
Ecclesiastes 11:9–12:7, 13 Remember Your Creator

Scripture

Background Scripture: *Ecclesiastes 11:7–12:14*
Scripture Lesson: *Ecclesiastes 11:9–12:7, 13*
Key Verse: *Fear God and keep his commandments, for this is the whole duty of man.* Ecclesiastes 12:13.
Scripture Lesson for Children: *Ecclesiastes 11:9–12:7, 13*
Key Verse for Children: *Remember your Creator in the days of your youth.* Ecclesiastes 12:1.

Lesson Aim

To find the answer to life's changes through our faith in God.

Lesson Setting

Time: During the reign of Solomon (about 970–930 B.C.)
Place: Jerusalem

Lesson Outline

Wisdom for Aging

  I. Living Life to the Fullest: Ecclesiastes 11:9-10
     A. Enjoying One's Youth: vs. 9
     B. Maximizing One's Life: vs. 10
  II. Revering the Creator: Ecclesiastes 12:1-7, 13
     A. The Importance of Honoring God: vs. 1
     B. The Onslaught of Old Age: vss. 2-5
     C. The Finality of Death: vss. 6-7
     D. The Purpose of Life: vs. 13

Introduction for Adults

Topic: *Life Worth Living*

Solomon was not bashful about old age and death. He evidently enjoyed the days of his youth, but he made no efforts to minimize the signs of failing mental and physical health. We cannot read his description recorded in Ecclesiastes 12:1-7 without a twinge of sadness and even fear, for we know we cannot escape this same end.

More importantly, sometimes we try to ignore the warning signs of spiritual decline and death. Jesus told us quite plainly that our souls are priceless. We cannot give anything in exchange for them. Therefore, the best way to prepare for the inevitability of death is to make sure we have trusted in the Messiah for salvation. Without His forgiveness, we are eternally lost. But through faith in Him, we have a life that is truly worth living.

Introduction for Youth

Topic: *Enjoy Life While You Are Young*

As Christians, we want our lives to count for something. If we buy into worldly values, however, we will be led to think that everything in life is relative and fleeting. Supposedly, we should live it up now, if there is no life after death.

Such notions stand opposed to the teachings of God's Word, and are to be rejected. It is true that God wants us to enjoy life while we are young. Nonetheless, there is life after death, and the decisions we make now will have eternal ramifications.

If we want our lives to have everlasting significance, we must commit ourselves wholeheartedly to the cause of Christ. This includes not only trusting in Him for salvation but also willingly serving Him regardless of the circumstances. As Scripture reveals, faithful service to the Lord brings rich and heavenly blessings.

Concepts for Children

Topic: *Remember Your Creator*

1. God made us, and we belong to Him.
2. God wants us to live for Him right now.
3. God helps us to make good choices.
4. God helps us be kind to others.
5. Throughout our lives, God wants us to love Him.

Lesson Commentary

I. LIVING LIFE TO THE FULLEST: ECCLESIASTES 11:9-10

A. Enjoying One's Youth: vs. 9

Be happy, young man, while you are young, and let your heart give you joy in the days of your youth. Follow the ways of your heart and whatever your eyes see, but know that for all these things God will bring you to judgment.

In Ecclesiastes 11:8, Solomon pointed to the sobering realization that for every person the "days of darkness" (that is, death) were not far off. It is a time when every opportunity available in this temporal, fallen world would be lost. Whatever lay ahead beyond the grave remained enigmatic and obscure to earthbound creatures (see 3:11). For unbelievers, these truths made their lives seem absurd and pointless. But for those whose existence was centered on God, the sobering awareness of death's inevitability prompted them to be more conscientious and virtuous in how they lived.

The king encouraged young people to delight in their early years, for this was an integral part of God's gift of life to them. Ultimately for believers, only in the Messiah is the abundant, deeply satisfying life made available (see John 10:10). Solomon also directed his readers to take part in whatever enterprise God allowed and to find joy in doing so. At first glance, these admonitions might seem to be advocating hedonism, or at least giving youth a license for immorality, but clearly that was not the king's intent. He reminded the upright to operate within the moral guidelines of God's Word. They were especially to keep in mind that one day the Almighty would assess everything they thought, said, and did (Eccl. 11:9; see 3:17; 12:14).

Paul likewise noted that all believers would one day be examined in the presence of the Lord Jesus. Such a prospect was not intended to take away their joy, but to spur them on to higher moral ground in their Christian walk. Put differently, they sought to please the Redeemer by how they lived (2 Cor. 5:9). The apostle noted that it was a divine necessity for believers to appear before the Son to give an account of their time on earth. This judgment would not determine whether they went to heaven or hell. That had been already determined by their decision to trust in the Messiah. The future evaluation would be an assessment of the believers' faithfulness as disciples of the Savior. All believers would be summoned before the Lord to have their works examined—and indirectly their characters (vs. 10; see Rom. 14:12).

B. Maximizing One's Life: vs. 10

So then, banish anxiety from your heart and cast off the troubles of your body, for youth and vigor are meaningless.

For the time being, Solomon advised young and old alike to rid themselves of unnecessary "anxiety" (Eccl. 11:10). Similarly, he encouraged them to discard whatever physical suffering and pain they could (for example, by remaining as healthy as possible spiritually, mentally, emotionally, psychologically, and physically). They were to pursue their God-given freedom with delight, as long as their behavior was within the context of ethical responsibility. Eventually, though, the joyous gift of youth (including one's childhood and the prime of life) would quickly fade away like a puff of air dissipating in the wind. And once it was gone, it was irretrievable.

II. REVERING THE CREATOR: ECCLESIASTES 12:1-7, 13

A. The Importance of Honoring God: vs. 1

Remember your Creator in the days of your youth, before the days of trouble come and the years approach when you will say, "I find no pleasure in them."

In Ecclesiastes 3:1, Solomon declared that God sovereignly ordered and controlled all the activities and events of life. This included Him establishing the time of birth and the moment of death (vs. 2). The existence of people and dynasties could be compared to a house. When the latter is first built, its structure is solid and strong, but over time, the wear and tear of life causes the edifice to weaken, sag, and eventually collapse (see 10:18). Even the most diligent of persons and rulers could not indefinitely forestall the inevitability of their physical demise, and once it happened, it was irreversible (see 11:10). These observations form the conceptual backdrop for Solomon's poem recorded in 12:1-8.

The king affirmed the biblical truth that God is the Creator (see Gen. 1:1; Ps. 102:25; Isa. 41:4; John 1:1-2) and that from the earliest days of one's earthly existence, the Lord of life should be remembered (Eccl. 12:1; see Deut. 8:18; Judg. 8:34; Pss. 63:6; 119:55). The latter included revering Him and obeying His commands. According to Solomon, now was the time to worship and serve God, before the vexations and burdens associated with old age came. Young people needed to understand that the further they moved away from God, the further away they departed from the real solutions to life's problems. By choosing to live for God earlier, rather than later, they would have more opportunities to give Him their best and enjoy all the wonders connected with doing His will.

B. The Onslaught of Old Age: vss. 2-5

Before the sun and the light and the moon and the stars grow dark, and the clouds return after the rain; when the keepers of the house tremble, and the strong men stoop, when the grinders cease because they are few, and those looking through the windows grow dim; when the doors to the street are closed and the sound of grinding fades; when men rise up at the sound of birds, but all their songs grow faint; when men are afraid of heights and of dangers in the streets; when the almond tree blossoms and the grasshopper drags himself along and desire no longer is stirred. Then man goes to his eternal home and mourners go about the streets.

Solomon's preceding admonitions needed to be kept in mind before experiencing the ill effects of becoming physically infirm. After all, once the suffering, pain, and deprivation associated with the final years of life set in, the pleasures of youth would be nothing more than a distant memory. Ecclesiastes 12:2-8 use some of the most beautiful and yet sorrowful poetry in literature to describe the feebleness and frailty of aging. To be sure, not everyone in our era of modern medicine will experience the drastic loss of faculties vividly portrayed by the king. Nonetheless, in old age, people are not as vigorous and agile as they were in their youth.

First, Solomon characterized old age as being like the clouds that returned to darken the sky after it had rained. This darkness was in contrast to the light given off by the sun, moon, and stars (vs. 2). The next series of images depicted in verses 3-4 can be understood in two ways. In a literal sense, when old age came, those who worked as house servants were not as strong. Indeed, they become shaky and bent. Longtime grinders of grain had to stop their work because their eyesight had grown dim (vs. 3). Even the sleep of the elderly was not always peaceful. Though they closed up their houses at night, their sleep did not last long because they were awakened by the early morning song of the birds. This remained the case even though their hearing had faded (vs. 4). In an allegorical sense, Solomon was presenting images referring to the deterioration brought on by old age. Thus, the housekeepers refer to an elderly person's arms and hands. The grinders represent decaying molar teeth, and "those looking through the windows" (vs. 3) symbolize failing eyes. The "doors to the street" refer to the loss of hearing, and the birds chirping in the morning denote the faint voice of the aged.

Verse 5 presents two literal examples of old age, followed by three metaphors from nature. Solomon apparently considered the dread of heights and the trepidation of busy streets as natural fears of the elderly. "When the almond tree blossoms" most likely refers to when the hair of an old person turns white. Though the base of the petals on a blossoming bitter almond tree turn pink, the outer tips turn white, making the entire tree appear that color. The Hebrew noun that is translated "grasshopper" can also be rendered "locust." Both are nimble when the day is warm, but slow down markedly when the temperature is cold (see Nah. 3:17). The comparison of old age to these plant-eating insects as they dragged themselves along the frigid ground probably symbolizes the immobility of old age, when one is too stiff to move as quickly as before.

The Hebrew noun that is translated "desire" (Eccl. 12:5) literally refers to the caperberry, an obscure fruit thought in ancient times to stimulate physical passion. The same word, however, was used elsewhere in ancient literature to refer to an appetizer, perhaps suggesting that the desire mentioned in verse 5 was for food. In either case, the image reflects an elderly person's declining appetite. When people reach this point in life, they are close to dying and going to the grave, which Solomon referred to as their "eternal home." He reminded his readers of how mourners wander through the streets, wailing in grief for the person who has passed away. Thus, before people reached this point, the king urged them to remember their Creator.

C. The Finality of Death: vss. 6-7

Remember him—before the silver cord is severed, or the golden bowl is broken; before the pitcher is shattered at the spring, or the wheel broken at the well, and the dust returns to the ground it came from, and the spirit returns to God who gave it.

In Ecclesiastes 12:6-7, Solomon used a series of poetic images to describe the swift termination of life. He mentioned the severing of the silver cord from which a golden lamp hung, which in turn caused the lamp (representing life) to be broken. In a parallel analogy, the sage referred to a clay pitcher being smashed so that it could no longer carry the water of life. Even the wooden waterwheel that drew the water had been broken. Another possibility is that the silver cord is the human spine, while the lamp is the head. The pitcher is the heart, which will no longer carry life-giving blood, and the wheel represents the lungs (carrying air), the heart (carrying blood), or the organs of digestion.

Solomon, after using imagery to describe the inevitable demise of people, next showed the ultimate results of the breakdown of the body. In death, the original components, or "the dust" (vs. 7), will return "to the ground" from which it came. At the same time, the breath of life, which originated from God, returns to Him (see Gen. 2:7; 6:17; 7:22; Job 34:14-15; Pss. 104:29-30; 146:4; Eccl. 3:19; Isa. 42:5; Ezek. 37:5). Understandably, all the king's talk of decline and death must have left him feeling depressed. Just as he had done at the beginning of his monologue (see Eccl. 1:2), he lamented that life seemed absolutely futile and absurd, especially when divorced from God (12:8). Indeed, Solomon discerned that none of the conjectures, possessions, or joys of life could provide the answer to his search for meaning and significance. And yet there was more for him to say. He brought his discourse to a close by revealing the ultimate purpose of humanity.

D. The Purpose of Life: vs. 13

Now all has been heard; here is the conclusion of the matter: Fear God and keep his commandments, for this is the whole duty of man.

In Ecclesiastes 12:13-14, the king summarized the conclusion to his observations and ponderings about the meaning of life. He declared that the whole duty of every person was to revere God and heed His commandments (vs. 13; see Job 28:28; Prov. 1:7; 9:10; Eccl. 5:7). The reason to abide by this all-encompassing injunction is that, despite the seemingly endless cycle of history, despite evil and greed, despite even death, what people do in life does matter. Solomon's admonition reflects what the Lord commanded Joshua and his generation of Israelites as they were about to enter the land of promise (see Josh. 1:7-8). As far as Joshua's and Israel's obedience to God's law was concerned, there was to be no deviation.

The phrase "to the right or to the left" (vs. 7) implied that the Israelites were to strictly obey the law. Expressed differently, they were to walk the fine line of obedience.

Both a promise and a condition for the fulfillment of that promise are included in verse 8. Not allowing the book of the law to "depart from [his] mouth" meant that Joshua should remember, rehearse, and obey the teaching Moses had passed on to him. God instructed Joshua to repeat aloud the words of the law while studying them or reflecting upon them. Such a practice ensured that Joshua would be thinking about the words as he spoke them. And yet God would not consider knowledge of the law to be enough. The Lord also demanded obedience. So the practice of repeating aloud the law as Joshua meditated upon it also served to remind him to "be careful to do everything written in it."

To meditate on God's Word day and night does not mean one has to live the life of a hermit. Certainly this was not true of Joshua. God intended him to fulfill this command even as he was in the process of conquering Canaan. Thus, Joshua was to keep God's law in mind as he entered into each battle. After all, God was fulfilling through Joshua what He had promised to Abraham. If Joshua kept the law and the history of his ancestors in mind as he led the people, he would be more likely to obey God's will and less likely to repeat the mistakes of previous generations. Since God had denied Moses entrance into the promised land because of his disobedience, Joshua could be sure that the Lord would not be partial to him.

Not surprisingly, during Jesus' final hours with His disciples, He urged them to continue in His love by keeping His commands. In the same way, the Son had stayed in the Father's love by remaining obedient to His will (John 15:10). Obeying the Savior was not a burden. In fact, heeding His teaching was the only way to experience lasting joy (vs. 11). Jesus summed up His teachings with one commandment: His followers were to love one another as He has loved them (vs. 12). This kind of love was demonstrated by a willingness to lay down one's life for a friend (v. 13). Indeed, the Redeemer did this very thing for humankind when He willingly subjected Himself to death, even death on the cross. Jesus set the example of the type of sacrificial love believers should demonstrate toward one another.

The basis for Solomon's concluding assertion in Ecclesiastes 12:13 is that God cares enough to evaluate every thought and action—whether obvious or hidden, and whether resulting in good or evil (vs. 14; see Matt. 12:36; Rom. 2:16; Heb. 4:12-13). Thus, God will judge all the foolish, vain, and wicked acts committed by the unrighteous. Likewise, He will take into account all the kind, good, and gentle acts performed by the righteous (see Eccl. 3:17). In this way, the king brought to an end his treatise concerning what life is really all about. He maintained that while human efforts (including rational inquiry) seem to lack eternal value (see 1:2; 12:8), people of faith should enjoy life in the fear of the Lord, whose first gift to them is life itself.

Discussion Questions

1. How is it possible to find joy at a young age and still remain faithful to God?
2. What can saved young people do to maximize the opportunities God has given them to serve Him?
3. Why do many people prefer to ignore the reality of aging rather than face up to its sobering prospects?
4. In what ways can a congregation help its elderly members deal with the physical limitations that come with aging?
5. Why do you think Solomon said that revering God is the foremost duty of every person?

Contemporary Application

Many have decided that life is meaningless. They do not arrive at their conclusion as a result of Solomon's long deliberations. Their lives have been shattered by so many disappointments that they see no purpose in existing. They have also deeply imbibed from the view of life that says human beings are just like animals and that God is dead.

Christians should directly address these issues. We must show how a God-centered worldview helps us deal with our troubles in constructive ways. We must also boldly teach that there is more to life than a cluster of experiences, some good and some bad. Indeed, we must explain how Jesus Christ makes the difference, especially the resurrection of believers from the dead.

The promise of being raised to new life is not wishful thinking. As Paul declared in 1 Corinthians 15, it is the truth we can count on. The historical fact of Jesus' resurrection guarantees it. The Gospel spread and the church was established because Jesus is alive. Of all the world's religions, Christianity alone claims that its founder was raised from the dead. This claim has been disputed, but never successfully refuted.

I once talked to a scientist about the Christian faith. He was not impressed by my arguments. Then I asked him, "What do you make of Jesus' resurrection?" He paused for a moment and then said, "I don't know. I've never thought about it." Our assignment is to help our unbelieving friends think about the meaning of Jesus' resurrection, especially in light of eternity.

The popular image of heaven—angels with harps and wings, fluffy clouds, holier-than-thou people clothed in white—is as different from the real heaven as a firefly is different from a lightning bolt. That popular image of heaven is not an eternity many people would enjoy. It's certainly not an eternity worth dying for.

And yet dying for the lost is exactly what Jesus did on the cross. He then rose from the dead so that believers can live with Him in heaven. Because of His victory over death, our lives have real meaning, both for time and for eternity.

Tradition and Love

Scripture

Background Scripture: *Song of Songs 4:8–5:1*
Scripture Lesson: *Song of Songs 4:8–5:1*
Key Verse: *Let my lover come into his garden and taste its choice fruits.* Song of Songs 4:16.
Scripture Lesson for Children: *Ecclesiastes 3:9-15*
Key Verse for Children: *There is nothing better for men than to be happy and do good while they live. . . . This is the gift of God.* Ecclesiastes 3:12-13.

Lesson Aim

To recognize that God-given love is the joy of life.

Lesson Setting

Time: During the reign of Solomon (about 970–930 B.C.)
Place: Jerusalem

Lesson Outline

Tradition and Love
  I. The Affection between the Bride and Groom:
    Song of Songs 4:8-15
    A. *The Groom's Longing for His Bride: vs. 8*
    B. *The Bride's Stunning Beauty: vs. 9*
    C. *The Bride's Incomparable Love: vss. 10-11*
    D. *The Metaphor of a Locked Garden: vss. 12-15*
  II. The Consummation of Marital Love:
    Song of Songs 4:16–5:1
    A. *The Bride's Invitation: 4:16*
    B. *The Groom's Response: 5:1*

Introduction for Adults

Topic: *A Kiss Is Still a Kiss*

"As Time Goes By" is the name of a popular song from 1931. The lyrics speak of the "simple facts of life" connected with romantic love. Even "as time goes by," a "kiss" remains "just a kiss" and a "sigh" is said to be "just a sigh."

The biblical view of love is much more profound. It is best seen in long-term marriage relationships in which husbands and wives remain committed to each other, regardless of life's ups and downs. Even such experiences as illness and financial loss can't break the bond of love that is found in these couples. They are sterling examples of the devotion that the Lord wants to see in saved men and women who get married.

Introduction for Youth

Topic: *Love in a Committed Relationship*

In 1985, American singer, dancer, and entertainer Tina Turner was awarded a Grammy for the hit song "What's Love Got to Do with It." The lyrics talk about the feelings of attraction associated with romantic love. Turner sang of love being nothing more than a "second-hand emotion" and a "sweet old-fashioned notion."

This dismissive view of love contrasts sharply with that of the Song of Songs. The bride and groom have not only strong feelings for each other, but also a committed relationship. Saved teens can appreciate the way the ballad portrays love's subtlety and mystery, its beauty and pleasures, and its captivation and enchantment.

Concepts for Children

Topic: *God Gives Good Gifts*

1. God gives purpose to everything in the world.
2. God is in control of everything that happens in our lives.
3. What God does lasts forever.
4. We are most happy when we do good to others.
5. We can trust God for the plan He has for our lives.

Lesson Commentary

I. THE AFFECTION BETWEEN THE BRIDE AND GROOM: SONG OF SONGS 4:8-15

A. The Groom's Longing for His Bride: vs. 8

Come with me from Lebanon, my bride, come with me from Lebanon. Descend from the crest of Amana, from the top of Senir, the summit of Hermon, from the lions' dens and the mountain haunts of the leopards.

The Song of Songs (sometimes called the Song of Solomon) is love poetry filled with similes and metaphors. The singers are the bride and bridegroom, the beloved and her lover. Their songs are interspersed with songs of their friends. Since God is not mentioned in the Song of Songs, we must think carefully about His place in courtship and marriage based on New Testament principles and practices.

According to 1 Kings 4:32, King Solomon composed 1,005 songs. Many Bible scholars assume that the Song of Songs is one of these. Whereas the songs of Solomon probably covered a broad range of themes, this song is specifically about love. It portrays love's subtlety and mystery, its beauty and pleasures, its captivation and enchantment. It reveals the romantic feelings of a woman and a man. The Song of Songs also portrays the power of love. In fact, in this book the power of love is shown to rival the strength of death itself. Thus, one of the main lessons to be learned from a study of the Song of Songs is that God intends for powerful love to be a hallmark of a marital relationship.

There is no clear plot in the Song of Songs as there would be in a play or a story. Interpreters have therefore suggested several different story lines. This commentary takes the view that the poem shows the love between King Solomon and one of his wives. The ballad contains a cluster of five meetings in which the lovers pass through courtship, their wedding, the consummation of their love in marriage, and later occasions in which they renew their love. According to this analysis of the action, there are three sources of the speeches in the poem: the bride, her attendants, and the groom.

The lines of the Song of Songs are short and rhythmical, and the language is rich in imagery and highly sensual. This narrative poem reflects the words and feelings between two people who are experiencing human, sexual love with all its pleasures and sorrows. The vivid, expressive language of this ballad exalts the purity of marital affection and romance. It also strongly condemns unchaste relations outside of marriage (for example, sexual experimentation before marriage). Furthermore, the Song of Songs reminds the reader about the beauty and sanctity of sexual intimacy between a husband and wife. The book reveals that such love is characterized by sacrifice, commitment, and faithfulness.

The bride was identified as a Shulammite (6:13), a dark-skinned country girl

(1:6). She was brought to the palace to become the bride of King Solomon (vs. 4). We have no details about their courtship. Their songs began with her introduction to the court from which she celebrated his love and name. Their songs fit the character and customs of an ancient Middle Eastern wedding. Brides commonly were in their teens. It will help if we try to catch the spirit of the occasion and contemplate the intimate dialogue between the bride and bridegroom. They described their love in the colorful imagery of King Solomon's time. In anticipation of their union, it was important for her to recall their young love. She celebrated her lover's physical and moral qualities. The bride used many word pictures to describe their relationship (vss. 12-14). As the two sang to each other, they rejoiced in the beauty that had attracted them to one another (vss. 15-17).

Chapters 1 and 2 reveal that it was the desire of the Shulammite to be pure in love and to consummate it only at the right time and in the proper relationship. After she and Solomon had spent some talking, they parted. Chapter 3 continues the young woman's portion of the song. Apparently, she lay down for sleeping. Thus, verses 1-5 is probably an account of her troubled dream of being away from the king. Sometime after waking up, the Shulammite described Solomon's wedding procession. The noble entourage included the monarch's carriage and a royal escort of 60 armed soldiers. The daughters of Jerusalem were called out to see Solomon wearing the wedding crown given to him by his mother (vss. 6-11).

The king responded by repeatedly extolling his bride for her ravishing beauty. Behind her veil, her eyes shone with love. They were as soft, gentle, and sparkling as those belonging to doves. As her long, dark, and unbound hair hung over her shoulders, it was comparable to the flowing movement of a flock of female Palestinian goats winding down from the grassy slopes of Mount Gilead after grazing (4:1). Gilead was located southeast of the Sea of Galilee and known for its agricultural and livestock activities. Black goat's hair was smooth and shiny and typically used in weaving tents (see 1:5).

The bride had a distinctively beautiful smile. Her white, clean teeth were perfectly formed, matched, and intact. They glistened with moisture. They were comparable to a flock of newly shorn sheep that had come up from being washed. Each sheep had its twin (that is, it was paired) and not one of them was missing (vs. 2). The Shulammite's painted lips were as red and appealing as a ribbon of scarlet, and her mouth was lovely. No doubt the words that she spoke were as delightful as her appearance. Behind the bride's veil, her temples were comparable to a slice of pomegranate (vs. 3). The latter was an orange-shaped fruit that varied in color from yellow to bright red. Like this ripe, globular fruit, the Shulammite's rosy cheeks were full in form and gleamed with youthful beauty and vigor.

The bride's neck was distinctive in its beauty and elegant in its form. It was slender and straight, giving it a graceful, regal appearance. It was comparable to a defensive tower of David built along the city wall of Jerusalem. Such a structure may have been constructed with rows of stones and intended for warfare. This armory had thousands of bucklers hanging on it, that is, all the small round shields used by officers and other infantry (vs. 4). A chain of dazzling jewels around the young woman's long neck with its stately poise might resemble the glistening shields that had been placed on the tower.

The Shulammite's exquisitely shaped torso evoked grace and youthfulness. It was comparable to the twin fawns that a gazelle might bear while gently grazing among the lilies (vs. 5; see 8:8). Solomon anticipated being physically intimate with his bride once they were married. It would not be until the early morning hours—the time when the day was coolest and the shadows of the morning began to flee away with the beaming of the first rays of light—that the king and his beloved consummated their marriage. The groom would enjoy the tender beauty of his bride, which was comparable to a mountain of myrrh and a hill of frankincense (4:6). Perhaps there was a pouch containing such aromatic spices attached to a cord hanging around the Shulammite's neck.

Solomon further remarked that his bride's appearance was not lacking in any way. Indeed, she was physically devoid of any blemish or flaw (vs. 7). The king invited his darling to hurriedly journey from her home in Lebanon. Perhaps to the king the Shulammite seemed distant and her thoughts far from him. Maybe she was preoccupied with concerns about their relationship. If so, this explains why Solomon wanted her to descend from the peak of Amana, from the heights of Senir and Hermon, from the lairs inhabited by lions, and from the mountains frequented by the leopards (vs. 8). The mountains mentioned in this verse all were located in Lebanon. The king not only wanted his bride physically close to his side, but also desired to be a haven of rest and security for her from any anxieties she might have.

B. The Bride's Stunning Beauty: vs. 9

You have stolen my heart, my sister, my bride; you have stolen my heart with one glance of your eyes, with one jewel of your necklace.

Solomon admitted that he was truly excited to be with the Shulammite. Evidently, the thought of his bride made his heart beat wildly with anticipation. One can imagine the king's emotions racing faster and faster as he caught a momentary glimpse of her soft, delicate eyes. The groom's feelings leaped with joy as he obtained a single glance at one precious gem of his darling's sparkling necklace (S. of S. 4:9). His bride had succeeded in arousing his desire to passionately love her. In ballads written during that era, it was common for couples pledged in marriage to use such terms of endearment as "sister" and "brother." The Mosaic covenant formed the backdrop of this mind-set, with the bride and groom conveying their mutual love and commitment in the most uplifting manner.

C. The Bride's Incomparable Love: vss. 10-11

How delightful is your love, my sister, my bride! How much more pleasing is your love than wine, and the fragrance of your perfume than any spice! Your lips drop sweetness as the honeycomb, my bride; milk and honey are under your tongue. The fragrance of your garments is like that of Lebanon.

The king declared that the intimate expressions of love he received from his sweetheart were incomparably beautiful and pleasing. It was more delightful and exhilarating than the choicest wine. The scent or fragrance of the Shulammite's perfumes was far more appealing than the most exotic spices (S. of S. 4:10). The bride's lips were as delectable and pleasant as nectar to her beloved. To him, her tongue was rich and full with milk and honey. The aroma of the Shulammite's clothing was as clean, fresh, and inviting as that of Lebanon's cedar forests (vs. 11).

D. The Metaphor of a Locked Garden: vss. 12-15

You are a garden locked up, my sister, my bride; you are a spring enclosed, a sealed fountain. Your plants are an orchard of pomegranates with choice fruits, with henna and nard, nard and saffron, calamus and cinnamon, with every kind of incense tree, with myrrh and aloes and all the finest spices. You are a garden fountain, a well of flowing water streaming down from Lebanon.

The woman with whom Solomon had fallen in love was a virgin. She had never known any other man and would remain exclusive in her affection and devotion to her betrothed. The sensual pleasures associated with physical intimacy are compared to a royal garden with exotic plants. Such delights were as secure as a hidden plot that had been barred, a spring that had been locked up, or a fountain that had been closed off. Only within the context of marriage would the sensual pleasures offered by the Shulammite be available to her betrothed (S. of S. 4:12).

The various distinctive physical features belonging to the king's beloved were comparable to a grove of pomegranates with the finest of luscious fruits, henna (a beautiful, aromatic blossom), and nard (an aromatic oil; vs. 13). This means she would bring her darling tremendous delight and pleasure. The sensual satisfaction and charm of the Shulammite were comparable to an array of poignant spices, oils, perfumes, and incenses (in particular, nard, saffron, calamus, cinnamon, all sorts of incense trees, myrrh, aloes, and the best spices available; vs. 14). The king's bride was as pure, refreshing, and invigorating as the headwaters of many spring-watered gardens, a well of fresh, flowing waters, and cool, scintillating brooks of melting snow cascading down the mountains of Lebanon (vs. 15).

II. THE CONSUMMATION OF MARITAL LOVE: SONG OF SONGS 4:16–5:1

A. The Bride's Invitation: 4:16

Awake, north wind, and come, south wind! Blow on my garden, that its fragrance may spread abroad. Let my lover come into his garden and taste its choice fruits.

The Shulammite had been compared to a locked garden whose delights remained to be opened. The king anticipated being enraptured in the love of his sweetheart. Now that they were officially married, she invited Solomon to come into her previously secluded orchard to fully delight in her sensual pleasures. Only within the context of matrimony is such physical intimacy sanctioned by God. The Shulammite summoned the cool north wind and directed the warm south wind to come and blow through her garden. She wanted her many fragrant scents and aromas to be gently carried along toward her friend, companion, and lover. She desired the garden of her body to exhale and send out its spices and fragrances. She longed for her darling to enter her garden and sample its most pleasant and delightful fruits (S. of S. 4:16). In a manner of speaking, the Shulammite wanted the king to become intoxicated with her love and to find full enjoyment and satisfaction in her pleasures.

B. The Groom's Response: 5:1

I have come into my garden, my sister, my bride; I have gathered my myrrh with my spice. I have eaten my honeycomb and my honey; I have drunk my wine and my milk.

The physical intimacy of marriage is very private and personal. Spouses pledge to give themselves fully and exclusively to their partners. Such an arrangement requires tremendous mutual trust and commitment. It implies that both individuals are desirous to yield the control of their bodies to each other in an encounter that is wholesome and proper (see 1 Cor. 7:1-7). In this case, Solomon did not spurn the invitation of his sweetheart to luxuriate in her beauty. He eagerly entered the garden of her body to enjoy the sensual delights she offered. The fragrances of her myrrh and balsam spices had been gathered by him and fully savored. The delectable pleasures she had to offer, her honeycomb and honey, were partaken by the king. By drinking heavily from her wine and milk, he experienced love that was rich and full, refreshing and exhilarating (S. of S. 5:1).

An unidentified voice (possibly God or a chorus of wedding guests) invited the bride and groom to eat and drink deeply. Clearly, this was an opportunity for the newlyweds to feast fully from the abundant physical delights they had to offer each other. The couple was to drink heavily from the refreshing fountain and invigorating well of sensual pleasures that marriage afforded. Here we see that physical intimacy in the context of matrimony is a great gift and creation of God to people. Both partners can become enraptured with each other's affection. The two can receive expressions of kindness and appreciation in a unique manner. Each individual can show affection to the other in tangible, meaningful ways. The couple can feel secure and wanted, especially as they partake of their mutual, sensual delights.

While the Song of Songs is likely not an allegory of God's love for His people, the metaphor of marriage is used throughout Scripture to describe the Lord's special relationship with the faith community. In the covenant of Sinai, idolatry was equated with adultery (Exod. 34:10-17). The prophets (for example, Isaiah, Amos, and Hosea) used the same comparison to describe the people's straying from God. Also, it is no accident that Jesus began His earthly ministry by blessing a wedding at Cana in Galilee (John 2:1-11). Moreover, human history began with a wedding (Gen. 2:18-25) and will end with the marriage supper of the Lamb (Rev. 19:6-9).

Discussion Questions

1. How did Solomon describe the Shulammite woman in Song of Songs 4:8-15?
2. How strong was the desire of the bride and groom for one another?
3. What was the extent of the love the couple had for each other?
4. What are some truths about marriage one can glean from the Song of Songs?
5. How can married couples keep the ardor of their affection vibrant throughout the years of marriage?

Contemporary Application

The worldly tendency is to make too much of romantic love. To listen to many popular songs, we would think that love is all that matters. As the Beatles sang, "Love is all you need." Meanwhile, the electronic and print media often present romantic love as entirely redemptive. For instance, we see this in the film titled, *What Dreams May Come*, when the husband uses love to rescue his wife from hell.

Admittedly, many unbelievers are convinced that love is mainly about sex and that sex is just as good, if not better, when experienced outside of marriage. The late actress Audrey Hepburn expressed a common opinion when she explained her decision not to marry her longtime companion by saying love was more romantic that way. A more severe sort of Christian might recoil and assert that we should care only about "spiritual" things and ignore romantic expressions of love altogether. One wonders whether that person even knows what love is!

Romantic love is by no means as important to our eternal well being as is salvation. Yet "every good and perfect gift is from above, coming down from the Father of the heavenly lights" (Jas. 1:17). And love is certainly one of those God-given gifts. As long as we obey the Lord's basic guidelines—for example, no sexual relations outside of marriage, no adultery, and so on—there's no biblical reason we can't enjoy love as much as we want. In fact, God's love for us—which is self-sacrificial, faithful, and forgiving—provides a model that should make Christians the best at showing love in the context of marriage. Regardless of what people look like, what their station in life may be, or how old they are, God is pleased to bless them with the gift of love.

Living as God's People

Scripture

Background Scripture: *Matthew 5:1-12*

Scripture Lesson: *Matthew 5:1-12*

Key Verse: *"Blessed are those who hunger and thirst for righteousness, for they will be filled."* Matthew 5:6.

Scripture Lesson for Children: *Matthew 5:1-12*

Key Verse for Children: *"Rejoice and be glad, because great is your reward in heaven."* Matthew 5:12.

Lesson Aim

To encourage believers to find true happiness by living for God and serving others.

Lesson Setting

Time: A.D. *28*

Place: Galilee

Lesson Outline

Living as God's People

   I. The Sermon's Setting: Matthew 5:1-2

  II. The Sermon's Blessings: Matthew 5:3-12

     A. *For the Poor in Spirit: vs. 3*

     B. *For the Mournful: vs. 4*

     C. *For the Meek: vs. 5*

     D. *For the Spiritually Hungry: vs. 6*

     E. *For the Merciful: vs. 7*

     F. *For the Pure in Heart: vs. 8*

     G. *For the Peacemakers: vs. 9*

     H. *For the Persecuted: vss. 10-12*

Introduction for Adults

Topic: *Seeking True Happiness*

Mother Teresa was a humanitarian who ministered for over 45 years to the poor, sick, orphaned, and dying in India. She taught those who joined her in her mission that "being happy with God means loving as He loves, helping as He helps, giving as He gives, serving as He serves, rescuing as He rescues, being with Him 24 hours, touching Him in His distressing disguise."

Mother Teresa embodies the sacrificial disposition that Jesus commended in the Sermon on the Mount. We learn that true happiness is found in living for God and serving others. The Lord blesses the poor in spirit by bestowing on them the kingdom of heaven. Because they are genuinely unpretentious and recognize their need for God, He lavishes them with eternal spiritual riches. Unlike earthly possessions, these heavenly treasures cannot be taken away. God guarantees them to His humble people.

Introduction for Youth

Topic: *What's with This Sermon?*

Undoubtedly, the Sermon on the Mount will seem alien and counterintuitive to some of the class members. Even so, as they begin to seriously consider each of the Beatitudes declared by Jesus, the Spirit can transform their thinking and give them increased self-awareness and understanding.

Teens will come to see that their lives reflect the character of individuals they admire but have never met. Adolescents also exemplify the behavior, dress, and habits of family members, friends, neighbors, and coworkers. Imitating others can be a good thing if those who serve as role models are upright people.

This week's lesson will challenge Christian teens to consider that following the Lord is the best path to take in life. They will also be encouraged to become godly examples for others to follow. The more class members focus their attention on the Savior and His Word and behave in ways that are characteristic of Him, the more they will set a godly example in their words and deeds.

Concepts for Children

Topic: *What a Blessing!*

1. Jesus took His followers away from the crowds.
2. Jesus used a hillside as a classroom as He taught His followers how to find true happiness.
3. Jesus wants His followers to help others in their community.
4. Jesus wants His followers to bring joy and hope wherever they go.
5. Jesus teaches His followers that obeying God will bring them true joy.

Lesson Commentary

I. THE SERMON'S SETTING: MATTHEW 5:1-2

Now when he saw the crowds, he went up on a mountainside and sat down. His disciples came to him, and he began to teach them, saying.

Matthew began his Gospel with a record of Jesus' descent from Abraham to Joseph and Mary (1:1-16). Not every ancestor of the Savior appears in the list. Yet as the descendant of Abraham and David—two of Israel's most esteemed ancestors—Jesus unquestionably qualifies as the nation's Messiah. Verse 17 explains that Jesus' genealogy, as Matthew presented it, comprises three sections of 14 generations each. Matthew wanted to show that the progress of biblical history had reached its fulfillment with the coming of the Messiah. In verses 18-25, Matthew recounted the Savior's birth. And in 2:1-12, we learn about the visit of the magi to the newborn king. Verses 13-18 explain the reason for Jesus' family fleeing to Egypt, while verses 19-23 detail their eventual return to Nazareth.

Chapters 3 and 4 detail the start of Jesus' earthly ministry. This included the following episodes: the work of John the Baptizer in preparing the way for the inauguration of the Messiah's redemptive work (3:1-12); John's baptism of Jesus in the Jordan River (vss. 13-17); Satan's temptation of Jesus (4:1-11); the beginning of the Savior's Galilean ministry (vss. 12-17); and His calling of four disciples (vss. 18-22). Verses 23-25 narrate how Jesus continued to travel throughout Galilee and proclaimed the Good News of the kingdom. He taught in synagogues and healed large numbers of people. His popularity grew considerably in a relatively short period of time. Consequently, many people began following Him from all over Palestine and its surrounding regions.

Part of Jesus' message included the announcement that God's kingdom was drawing near (vs. 17). What attitudes and actions were appropriate for a citizen of God's kingdom? The Messiah answered this question in what is known as the Sermon on the Mount (chaps. 5–7). Although Jesus' primary audience would have been His disciples, there was a larger crowd of people who listened to Him teach (7:28). The ethics Jesus taught in His sermon contrasted sharply with the legalism of His religious critics. Because the Pharisees and scribes coveted external forms of righteousness, Jesus launched His sermon by decrying such an approach to life.

There are two views regarding when and where the Sermon on the Mount was preached. One group asserts that it is a compilation of various teachings that were given on different occasions in several places. A second group believes the sermon was delivered early in Jesus' ministry at one time and place (for example, on the side of a mountain near Capernaum). Portions of the Sermon on the Mount are similar to Jesus' Sermon on the Plain (Luke 6:20-49). Some experts think these passages represent two different messages given on separate occasions, while others think the two passages represent the same message. According to the second view, Luke presented an abbreviated version of the longer sermon recorded in Matthew.

The "crowds" of Matthew 5:1 that came to hear Jesus' sermon are presumably the same as the "large crowds" of 4:25 that followed Jesus. They came from at least a 100-mile radius of the territory to listen to Jesus teach (5:2). As the Master Teacher, Jesus employed the normal sitting posture of a Jewish rabbi. God's supreme Old Testament revelation—the law—was given by Moses, accompanied by thunder and lightning, from Mount Sinai. One greater than Moses gave this sermon also from a mountain region probably near the Sea of Galilee. We do not know exactly where Jesus preached the Sermon on the Mount. A traditional site, however, is on a hillside near Capernaum, on the northwest shore of the Sea of Galilee. Part of the "crowds" (4:25; 5:1) Jesus drew came from the thousands of people who lived in the cities and smaller settlements that dotted the Sea of Galilee's coastline during the first century A.D.

II. THE SERMON'S BLESSINGS: MATTHEW 5:3-12

A. For the Poor in Spirit: vs. 3

"Blessed are the poor in spirit, for theirs is the kingdom of heaven."

At various times in history, there have been common misconceptions made about the Sermon on the Mount. Some have said it is nothing more than a call to social action, while others regard it simply as a list of things to do to be happy. Still others say the sermon is not applicable for this age, but rather only for the kingdom age to come. As we read the sermon, we should be careful to put it in its first-century context and let the lessons appearing in it speak for themselves. For instance, consider Matthew 5:3. In this verse, we are immediately struck by the presence of the word "blessed."

This refers to the spiritual wellness of believers. The term conveys the idea of being the privileged recipient of God's favor, and thus enjoying a happier end than the wicked. Jesus' various declarations of blessedness are commonly called the Beatitudes. This term comes from the word "beati," which is used in the Vulgate, an important Latin translation of the Bible. In short, the word refers to a state of bliss. The Messiah pronounced His first blessing on the "poor in spirit," which is a reference to humility. These are believers who have been stripped of their own securities and deeply feel their need for God. The Savior's redemption, not their own goodness, is the basis for their citizenship in heaven.

The attitude and lifestyle Jesus encouraged are foundational to all the other virtues the Savior commended. For instance, we cannot mourn without recognizing how unable we are to handle life in our own strength (vs. 4). We cannot be meek unless we humbly acknowledge our need for gentleness (vs. 5). We cannot long for righteousness if we proudly view ourselves as already righteous (vs. 6). We cannot be merciful without recognizing our need for God's mercy (vs. 7).

We cannot be pure in heart if our heart is filled with pride (vs. 8). We cannot be peacemakers if we arrogantly assert that our way is always right (vs. 9). Finally, we cannot stand up under persecution without Christlike humility (vss. 10-12).

B. For the Mournful: vs. 4

"Blessed are those who mourn, for they will be comforted."

Jesus pronounced His second blessing on the mournful, who will receive God's comfort. "Those who mourn" (Matt. 5:4) weep because they know they have transgressed against the Lord. Also, they cry in confession and repentance, which are a reflection of their humble spirit. These believers do not look to the world for satisfaction, joy, or comfort; rather, they find these things in the Savior alone. They come to Jesus in humility and faith, confessing their sins, and He enters their lives and stays there with the sweet assurance of His forgiveness.

C. For the Meek: vs. 5

"Blessed are the meek, for they will inherit the earth."

Jesus gave His third blessing to the meek and promised them the earth as an inheritance (Matt. 5:5). Meekness has two aspects. On the one hand, the meek bear up under provocations, control their feelings, and refuse to get even. On the other hand, they are courageous, generous, and courteous. They put others, not themselves, first. Here we find Jesus explaining the values of the kingdom. Relationships, possessions, information, prayer, money, and power are a few of the categories He redefined from God's perspective. Jesus showed that following Him involves radical change. For most of us this means undoing the way we have always acted and reconsidering traditional sources of wisdom from our family, friends, and culture. To become like Jesus requires us to thoroughly review our moral values and lifelong goals and dreams.

D. For the Spiritually Hungry: vs. 6

"Blessed are those who hunger and thirst for righteousness, for they will be filled."

Jesus next blessed those who longed for righteousness, and He promised to fulfill their desires (Matt. 5:6). The attitude is one of desiring God above all things and seeking to be in a right relationship with Him and others. While greed, injustice, and violence consume the unsaved, believers yearn for justice and goodness to be established. In these first four beatitudes there is a logical progression. First, we admit our spiritual bankruptcy (vs. 3). Seeing ourselves as "poor in spirit" causes us to "mourn" (vs. 4) our condition. Because we grieve over our sorrowful state, we come to a correct notion of ourselves, which is to be humble and meek (vs. 5). Thus, by accepting the appraisal arrived at in verses 3 through 5, we are ready to "hunger and thirst for righteousness" (vs. 6).

E. For the Merciful: vs. 7

"Blessed are the merciful, for they will be shown mercy."

Jesus then blessed the merciful and said they will be treated with mercy (Matt. 5:7). This verse is talking about having a gracious disposition toward others. The merciful are kind, charitable, and ready to sympathize with the sufferings of the afflicted. They long for justice, but are not harsh and cruel. Also, they seek to be generous to all by showing the love of God without partiality or preconditions. The merciful receive God's favor, for they are the beneficiaries of His mercy.

Cultivating a merciful disposition is a key virtue for those who choose to follow Jesus. They recognize the seriousness of their decision and the demands it places upon them. Jesus' disciples agree not only to obey Him in all He has said, but also to order their priorities for His sake. They seek to serve Him as a slave would serve a master. The followers of Jesus want to be like Him in their thoughts and actions. Furthermore, their desire is to abide in His words and heed His commands. The disciples of the Messiah do not merely perpetuate His teachings, transmit His sayings, or imitate His life. They bear witness in their own words and actions that their Lord dwells within them. Thus, Jesus is much more than a mere teacher or guru to His followers. In point of fact, they affirm Him to be the indwelling presence of God.

F. For the Pure in Heart: vs. 8

"Blessed are the pure in heart, for they will see God."

Jesus gave His sixth blessing on the pure in heart and promised that they would see God (Matt. 5:8). The focus here is on being genuine and honest in all one's dealings. Such purity requires spiritual discipline and self-control. It renounces self-love for the love of God. Sin is the enemy of moral purity, and popular ideas and activities conspire to undo it. Furthermore, the world ridicules and taunts the virtuous for not having fun; but instead of fun, the pure receive the greatest gift of all, namely, a personal encounter with the living God. When we come to know the Father through faith in the Son, we are truly fulfilled.

G. For the Peacemakers: vs. 9

"Blessed are the peacemakers, for they will be called sons of God."

In the seventh beatitude, Jesus pronounced a blessing on "the peacemakers" (Matt. 5:9). In saying they "will be called sons of God," Jesus meant they will become spiritual children in God's heavenly family (John 1:12; Eph. 1:5). Peacemakers do not merely stay cool, calm, and collected, but also work for peace in their families, schools, churches, businesses, and communities. Jesus is the ultimate peacemaker (Isa. 9:6), for He destroyed the enmity between sinners and God (2 Cor. 5:18-19; Eph. 2:13-18). Jesus not only brings us peace with God, but also heals our broken relationships (Rom. 5:1).

H. For the Persecuted: vss. 10-12

"Blessed are those who are persecuted because of righteousness, for theirs is the kingdom of heaven. Blessed are you when people insult you, persecute you and falsely say all kinds of evil against you because of me. Rejoice and be glad, because great is your reward in heaven, for in the same way they persecuted the prophets who were before you."

In the final beatitudes, Jesus blessed the persecuted and promised them the kingdom of heaven (Matt. 5:10). He taught that when believers stand up for truth, righteousness, and goodness, they will be slandered and insulted (vs. 11). Such persecution arises because of taking a stand for righteousness and being known as a follower of the Messiah. Jesus gave two reasons His harassed followers could accept their circumstances with an attitude of joy (vs. 12). First, they ought to realize that their eternal reward will exceed their wildest expectations. Second, they can remember that God's enemies also mistreated His prophets.

As followers of the Redeemer, we should not be shocked when we are slandered, physically harmed, or targeted for malicious rumors. Even though we feel the intense pain of such injustices, we can persevere by holding onto the promise of God's richest blessings. For instance, Jesus said that heaven belongs to the persecuted. By this He meant they would have a place of distinction in the kingdom of God. In this present world, many believers are harassed and abused by others for the cause of the Son. The world might regard them as nobodies, but God considers them as people of honor who should be given nothing less than unending joy in His presence.

Jesus encouraged His followers to influence their world with the kingdom values He previously described. In verse 13, he compared believers to salt. In ancient times, the Jews obtained their salt from the shores of the Dead Sea and the Hill of Salt (Jebel Usdum). The salinity of the chemical could be lost due to overexposure to the sun and excessively damp conditions. People used salt to season and preserve their food and to bring out its flavor. Ingesting salt also helped people to maintain their electrolytes and prevent dehydration from occurring.

Jesus noted that when salt becomes contaminated with foreign substances, it can lose its distinctive flavor and preservative qualities. When this happened, people would discard such a worthless chemical. Jesus was figuratively referring to the spiritual qualities that should be present in His disciples. In other words, they needed to have a wholesomeness about them that enabled them to be a blessing and a moral preservative in the world.

Jesus explained that a city located at the top of a hill cannot escape detection (Matt. 5:14). In Bible times, cities on hills were often built out of white limestone. These towns gleamed in the sun and could not easily be hidden. Furthermore, at night the oil lamps used by the inhabitants could be seen glowing over the surrounding area. Similarly, believers who are fully devoted to the Savior could not remain hidden, for the spiritual light of their lives will be visible to everyone. They are to radiate the knowledge and presence of God to people living in spiritual darkness or ignorance.

Jesus next made a reference to a "lamp" (vs. 15), which refers to a small clay bowl that burned olive oil drawn from a flax or linen wick. The Redeemer noted that people in His day did not light a lamp and place it under a wooden basket or clay bowl, which was used to measure ground meal or flour. Instead, they placed the lamp on a stand so that it might radiate its light to every person in the house (vs. 15). The lamp symbolized the believers' works of righteousness, the light of which shone far into the darkness of the world and gave glory to God. When the unsaved saw the good that believers performed, they were more inclined to praise the "Father in heaven" (vs. 16).

Discussion Questions

1. What do you think it means to be "poor in spirit" (Matt. 5:3)? How does this contrast with the way the world thinks?
2. What erroneous ideas might people have about meekness (vs. 5)?
3. What would you say it means to be "pure in heart" (vs. 8)? How is this possible in our age of materialism and vice?
4. What challenges do believers face as they strive to be "peacemakers" (vs. 9) in a world filled with violence?
5. Why is it possible to rejoice when we are persecuted?

Contemporary Application

Jesus began the Sermon on the Mount with the Beatitudes. These blessings list the rewards of poverty of spirit (humility), mournfulness (grieving over sin), meekness (keeping power under control), hunger and thirst after righteousness (spiritual seeking), mercy (being gracious), purity of heart (being forgiven), peacemaking (reconciliation), and persecution (suffering for taking a stand for Christ).

Contentment is at the heart of such character qualities. Satisfaction and joy are difficult in our society because so many things tell us we're lacking this or that—a bigger house, a more luxurious car, another television, a thinner figure, a better job, a gorgeous boyfriend or girlfriend, and so on. Yet we know from the teachings of Scripture that God can fill us with contentment despite our lack of these things (Phil. 4:11-13).

A godly character is the foundation upon which contentment rests. We know that as Christians our character should be godly because that's who we are. For instance, if someone asks why we are being peacemakers, our answer should be "It's just my character in Christ." At the same time, we need to cultivate a godly character each day by committing ourselves to being all Christ taught. When we do, we will grow in godly character.

Forgiving as God's People

Scripture

Background Scripture: *Matthew 5:17-26*

Scripture Lesson: *Matthew 5:17-26*

Key Verse: *"Therefore, if you are offering your gift at the altar and there remember that your brother has something against you, leave your gift there in front of the altar. First go and be reconciled to your brother; then come and offer your gift."* Matthew 5:23-24.

Scripture Lesson for Children: *Matthew 5:17-26*

Key Verse for Children: *"First go and be reconciled to your brother; then come and offer your gift."* Matthew 5:24.

Lesson Aim

To experience the joy of forgiving and being forgiven.

Lesson Setting

Time: A.D. *28*

Place: Galilee

Lesson Outline

Forgiving as God's People

I. The Fulfillment of the Law: Matthew 5:17-20
   A. *The Reason for Jesus' Advent: vs. 17*
   B. *The Permanency of the Law: vs. 18*
   C. *The Relevancy of the Law: vss. 19-20*

II. The Commandment against Murder: Matthew 5:21-26
   A. *The Intent behind the Injunction: vss. 21-22*
   B. *The Importance of Being Reconciled: vss. 23-24*
   C. *The Need for Expediency: vss. 25-26*

Introduction for Adults

Topic: *Living in Harmony with Others*

Being willing to forgive others is foundational to living in harmony with them. Tragically, though, adults often have difficulty forgiving others because they find it extremely hard to forget how they were wronged.

Because we've heard "forgive and forget" so often, we think that to fail at one part of that equation means we fail at both. Forgiveness, however, is not forgetting. As Neil Anderson suggests in his conference on resolving personal conflicts, "Forgetting may be the result of forgiveness, but it is never the means of forgiveness."

Some of your students may still be struggling with the issue of forgiveness. They may still remember being wounded. And because they remember, they feel they can't forgive. You will want to be sensitive to them and assure them that with God's help they can forgive even though the memory of the wound is still with them.

Introduction for Youth

Topic: *Should I Forgive?*

In "An Essay on Criticism," Alexander Pope wrote that "to err is human, to forgive divine." Even adolescents experience times when forgiveness truly does seem to be the privilege of the divine and to be impossible for mere mortals. Can teens learn to forgive?

It's true that forgiveness begins with God, for all of humankind has sinned and rebelled against Him (Rom. 3:23). Even so, God has chosen to forgive us (Eph. 1:7). Once saved adolescents experience God's forgiveness, He wants them to forgive others who have wronged them. This is in keeping with Paul's statement in 4:32: "forgiving each other, just as in Christ God forgave you."

Concepts for Children

Topic: *Can I Really Forgive?*

1. Jesus keeps all the promises He made to us in the Bible.
2. Jesus wants us to obey what is taught in the Bible.
3. Jesus does not want us to say mean things to others, even if they are mean to us.
4. Jesus has forgiven all our sins.
5. Because Jesus forgave us, we can forgive others, too.

Lesson Commentary

I. THE FULFILLMENT OF THE LAW: MATTHEW 5:17-20

A. The Reason for Jesus' Advent: vs. 17

"Do not think that I have come to abolish the Law or the Prophets; I have not come to abolish them but to fulfill them."

The biblical concept of the law is central to Jesus' comments in Matthew 5:17. In the Old Testament, the Hebrew noun rendered "law" can mean "direction," "instruction," or "injunction." The word appears not only in legal texts, but also in narratives, speeches, poems, and genealogies. The noun denotes ethical imperatives that are divine in origin and concern the way of life characterized by righteousness and blessing. An examination of Scripture indicates that for the ancient Hebrews, morality was not an abstract concept disconnected from the present. Rather, it signified moral edicts concerning how people of faith should live.

A similar mind-set is found in the New Testament, especially in connection with the Greek noun rendered "law." The focus of this term is on ethical standards and rules of conduct, as established by tradition. Such synonyms as "custom," "principle," and "norm" help to convey the range of meanings found in the word. The noun also is used to denote what people should do, with such terms as "ordinance," "rule," and "command" helping to capture this sense of the word. Depending on the context, the noun is used to refer to the Pentateuch (the first five books of the Old Testament), guidelines for ethical behavior, or the promises of God.

In Matthew 5:17, Jesus' collectively referred to the Hebrew sacred writings as "the Law" and "the Prophets," which mirrors how religious experts of the day would have talked about the entire Old Testament. He declared that He did not "come to abolish the Law or the Prophets." "Abolish" renders a Greek verb that means "to put an end to the effect or validity of something." The idea is that during the Savior's first advent, He did not seek to annul, repeal, do away with, or make invalid the Mosaic legal code. Instead, His primary concern was to dismantle incorrect views about the law, especially faulty interpretations put forward by the religious specialists of the day. This included a works-based form of righteousness in which it was assumed that strict adherence to the law would gain people their salvation (see Rom. 9:30-33).

Rather than tear down all that the law stood for and represented, Jesus came to "fulfill" (Matt. 5:17) the same. The underlying Greek verb has three interrelated meanings, each of which applies to what Jesus said about Himself. The Messiah fulfilled the law by carrying out its ethical injunctions, showing its true spiritual meaning, and bringing to completion all that it stood for prophetically. The idea is that Jesus obeyed the law perfectly, thoroughly, and absolutely. He is the realization of its types and prophecies and the exclusive inspired interpreter of its teachings. Furthermore, He alone fully satisfied the payment for sin required by the law. Thus, He is more than an ideal example of how God's people should act. The Son is the object of the believers' faith, enabling them to be declared righteous in the Father's sight. Jesus also leads them beyond a surface-level compliance with the law to an inward adherence to its moral expectations.

B. The Permanency of the Law: vs. 18

"I tell you the truth, until heaven and earth disappear, not the smallest letter, not the least stroke of a pen, will by any means disappear from the Law until everything is accomplished."

Throughout His time on earth, Jesus remained subject to the law (Gal. 4:4) and, as a righteous Jew, acted in accordance with its stipulations (Luke 2:21-23; 4:16). Jesus also upheld the truth that the moral teachings of the law continued to be relevant (Matt. 5:17-18). Furthermore, as Israel's greatest teacher (cf. Matt. 7:28-29; John 13:13-14), He expounded on the meaning of the law and clarified its significance for God's people (see Matt. 5:21-48). In particular, Jesus stated that love for God and all people were the foremost commandments of Scripture (Matt. 22:37-40; see Deut. 6:5; Lev. 19:18).

When Adam and Eve violated God's command (Gen. 3:1-7), sin entered the world and brought death along with it (Rom. 5:12). The law of God was within its rightful authority to condemn all people, for all Adam's descendants had violated what the Lord decreed (3:23). Through Jesus' atoning sacrifice at Calvary, the fundamental relationship between regenerate sinners and the law was radically altered. To be specific, the Messiah, through His death on the cross, rendered powerless the law's ability to condemn those trusting in Him. As a result of their spiritual union with Christ (6:1-7), they are pardoned (or acquitted) of sin and delivered from eternal damnation (8:1).

Jesus frees and empowers them to live in accordance with the law's timeless moral precepts and injunctions. After all, the "law is holy" (Rom. 7:12). Likewise, its commandments are "holy, righteous and good." The implication is that God's universal moral absolutes are eternal in nature, unchanging, and perfect. As such, they have applicability for Christians down through the centuries. The preceding observations help clarify why there is an inherent permanency to the law. This is made clear when Jesus solemnly assured His listeners that "the smallest letter" (Matt 5:18) and "the least stroke of a pen" found in the law would never "disappear" from it until everything recorded in it was achieved. Not even "heaven and earth" would vanish before God had "accomplished" all that He declared would come to pass. The Greek verb rendered "accomplished" refers to attaining to or arriving at something. As was noted earlier, Jesus satisfied all the demands of the law, fulfilled their prophetic announcements, and flawlessly explained their divinely inspired teaching.

C. The Relevancy of the Law: vss. 19-20

"Anyone who breaks one of the least of these commandments and teaches others to do the same will be

called least in the kingdom of heaven, but whoever practices and teaches these commands will be called great in the kingdom of heaven. For I tell you that unless your righteousness surpasses that of the Pharisees and the teachers of the law, you will certainly not enter the kingdom of heaven."

There are also several interrelated purposes to the law, the first of which is to increase the awareness people have of their sin (see Rom. 3:20; 4:15; 5:13; 7:7-11). They recognize that they have violated God's will and fall short of His glorious moral standard (3:23). Second, the law spotlights the transgressors' need for a Redeemer, that is, salvation through faith in the Son (Gal. 3:19-24). Third, the law helps to restrain evil by specifying the kinds of acts that are wicked. In this way, it assists governing authorities to maintain civil order, protect the innocent, and penalize the unjust. Fourth, the law helps God's people to recognize and live uprightly by giving them an ethical frame of reference. They are able to do so, for they are indwelt by the Spirit and energized by the Father's love.

The preceding observations help clarify why there is an inherent relevancy of the law. This point also explains why, in Matthew 5:19, Jesus rejected any misinterpretations and misapplications of the law. The religious leaders of the day ignored the least commandment by using the Mosaic legal code to win acceptance with God. And they encouraged others to disregard the law by perpetuating the incorrect notion that a mere outward compliance with rules and regulations ensured the intactness of one's relationship with God. In the end, the meticulous observance of human traditions and opinions is an inadequate substitute for God's law. Those who so depreciated the ordinances of Scripture would be considered least in the "kingdom of heaven." Oppositely, those who affirmed the truths of the law—from the least to the greatest of its injunctions—would correspondingly be "called great in the kingdom of heaven."

The ethical demands of the kingdom exceed what anyone can humanly achieve on his or her own. Indeed, no matter how closely people might try to abide by the technicalities of the law, their sinful nature undermines their best efforts (see Rom. 7:7-25). Even the smallest infraction makes one guilty of breaking all of God's commands (see Jas. 2:10). This was just as true for such pious leaders as "the Pharisees and the teachers of the law" (Matt. 5:20). Because they remained entrenched in their legalism and hypocrisy, they would fail to secure redemption for themselves. Only those who rely on God—completely and exclusively—will be admitted to the divine kingdom.

II. THE COMMANDMENT AGAINST MURDER: MATTHEW 5:21-26

A. The Intent behind the Injunction: vss. 21-22

"You have heard that it was said to the people long ago, 'Do not murder, and anyone who murders will be subject to judgment.' But I tell you that anyone who is angry with his brother will be subject to judgment. Again, anyone who says to his brother, 'Raca,' is answerable to the Sanhedrin. But anyone who says, 'You fool!' will be in danger of the fire of hell."

A key question concerns whether Jesus was taking issue with the Mosaic law recorded in the Old Testament or the Pharisaic interpretation of the same. This commentary understands the Messiah to be challenging the collective body of Jewish religious law, including rabbinic ordinances, customs, and traditions. There is no conflict, then, between Jesus and the Mosaic legal code. What He taught and did stood in continuity with the Old Testament, while at the same time made a break with the prevalent legalistic traditions of the day. Jesus endeavored to clarify what God originally revealed in the law, truths that had been obscured by some religious experts in the centuries that followed. The Savior made it clear that erroneous views about the law were separate from it and worthy of being rejected.

Accordingly, Jesus' goal was to replace unscriptural notions with the truth. For example, in Matthew 5:21-22, He cited the teachings of some experts concerning Exodus 20:13 (see Deut. 5:17), in which they said it was illegal to murder. The Savior also mentioned a common teaching that all murderers must be brought to judgment (Matt. 5:21). A superficial examination of these teachings might suggest that their advocates had properly understood the sixth of the Ten Commandments. Jesus revealed, however, that these interpretations were inadequate, for they failed to give a full summary of the law concerning murder. As a result, people were left with a distorted understanding of the truth.

In their writings and oral teachings, some experts had focused on the external application of the law's injunctions. While they may have faithfully read the letter of the law, they frequently missed or obscured the spirit of it. Because the majority of people in Galilee during the time of Christ could not read, they learned the Scriptures by hearing what these scholars read and explained in the synagogues. Consequently, the people adopted interpretations of the law that were distorted. Jesus went to the heart of the moral teachings of the law when He declared that any person who harbored malice against "his brother" (vs. 22) was subject to the punishment imposed by the court. Unlike the legalists, who voided the law by their misinterpretations, Jesus affirmed the sixth commandment by explaining its true meaning and significance.

Next, Jesus mentioned a Jewish decree that prohibited insulting someone using the contemptuous word "Raca." This term was reserved for those who were presumed to be totally lacking in understanding. Such words as "idiot" and "fool" might be modern-day equivalents. Whoever was guilty of this sort of insult was liable to pay the penalty imposed by the Sanhedrin (the Jewish supreme court). That injunction notwithstanding, Jesus revealed the essence of God's will by declaring that any verbal abuse made one liable to eternal damnation. The Greek noun rendered "hell" originally referred to the Valley of Hinnom, a deep ravine south of Jerusalem. The nearby residents used the Valley of Hinnom as a trash dump, and the fires in it burned constantly. The spot served as a horrifying reminder of the eternal destiny that awaits all who perish without trusting in the Messiah.

B. The Importance of Being Reconciled: vss. 23-24

"Therefore, if you are offering your gift at the altar and there remember that your brother has something against you, leave your gift there in front of the altar. First go and be reconciled to your brother; then come and offer your gift."

The Savior's remarks indicate that He wanted His followers to be thoroughly upright in their attitudes and actions. Accordingly, in Matthew 5:23-26, He provided two examples of dealing with anger by means of reconciliation. While verses 23 and 24 deal with the reconciliation of an offended "brother," verses 25 and 26 concern the issue of resolving legal conflict. The point in both illustrations is that believers are to work for reconciliation in all areas of life, whether private or public.

Jesus first had His listeners imagine that a worshiper brought some type of offering to the Jerusalem temple to be sacrificed on the altar. This would be intended as an expression of reverence and devotion to God, along with a desire to be reconciled to Him. However, if this same person remembered that his "brother" (vs. 23) had a grievance against him, the Lord considered the religious devotion of the offender to be empty of meaning. Jesus said it would be better for the devotee to leave his offering at the altar, exit from the shrine, and become reconciled to the person who had been affronted. Once the relationship was restored, the worshiper then could present an offering with a clean conscience (vs. 24; see Ps. 66:18).

C. The Need for Expediency: vss. 25-26

"Settle matters quickly with your adversary who is taking you to court. Do it while you are still with him on the way, or he may hand you over to the judge, and the judge may hand you over to the officer, and you may be thrown into prison. I tell you the truth, you will not get out until you have paid the last penny."

Jesus next had His listeners imagine a lawsuit that existed between two individuals. Since the person was summoned into court by his opponent, the case most likely concerned the owing of debts. The Savior recommended that the person being sued quickly come to peaceful terms with his accuser while they were on their way to the law "court" (Matt. 5:25). This was especially pertinent advice if the person being sued was guilty of the crime. Jesus then noted that if the two did not quickly settle their dispute, the authorities would hand the accused over to the judge, who in turn would place him in the custody of the prison ward so that the accused could be incarcerated. The Messiah solemnly assured His listeners that the authorities would not release the accused from prison until he had paid the last fraction of a cent (vs. 26). Jesus made it clear that there was no room for malicious anger. Even the presence of enmity against someone else was a violation of the sixth commandment. In fact, animosity was so evil that God would certainly judge it.

Discussion Questions

1. In what ways might the law of God be relevant for believers today?
2. How did Jesus accomplish all that is written in the Mosaic law?
3. What sort of righteousness was necessary to enter God's kingdom?
4. When believers are feeling upset with one another, how can they avoid being derogatory in their comments?
5. Why did Jesus emphasize the importance of believers reconciling with one another?

Contemporary Application

When Jesus, "through his blood" (Col. 1:20), reconciles a person with God, "peace" is the result. Where once the terrible prospect of God's wrath remained (John 3:36; Rom. 9:22; Eph. 2:3), through Jesus' reconciliation peace is made and remains (Rom. 5:1; 8:1). Hostility is canceled out. The fact that Paul started every one of his 13 letters with a greeting of grace and peace shows how important this truth is to believers.

Our peace with God is not a truce. The latter is passive. It's cease and desist. Peace, however, is active. God wants us to be mindful of the activity of His peace in our lives whenever we're anxious (Phil. 4:6-7), afraid, or discouraged (John 14:27). Our peace with God impacts our peace with each other, and peace becomes one of the guiding rules of our conduct in our relationships (Rom. 12:18; 1 Thess. 5:13). Indeed, because the Father has forgiven and reconciled us in His Son, we have ample reason to be forgiving, kind, and compassionate to one another (Eph. 4:32).

Christian author Philip Yancey writes, "Forgiveness is no sweet platonic ideal to be dispensed to the world like perfume sprayed from a bottle. It is achingly difficult." An unfaithful spouse, a rebellious child, an abusive parent, a traitorous friend—no doubt any one of these can cause inexpressible pain. When these kinds of people devastate our hopes and expectations, we wrestle with deep anger and sorrow that threaten to become bitterness.

In such onerous circumstances, how can we possibly forgive? The Bible gives the only answer that can motivate us to do so. We are able to forgive, because the Son has reconciled us to the Father. In light of this truth, the question becomes, "How can we possibly not forgive?" As our gratefulness for God's forgiveness grows, we will be better able to experience the joy of forgiving and being forgiven.

Loving as God's People

Scripture

Background Scripture: *Matthew 5:43-48*

Scripture Lesson: *Matthew 5:43-48*

Key Verse: *"I tell you: Love your enemies and pray for those who persecute you, that you may be sons of your Father in heaven. He causes his sun to rise on the evil and the good, and sends rain on the righteous and the unrighteous."* Matthew 5:44-45.

Scripture Lesson for Children: *Matthew 5:43-48*

Key Verse for Children: *"Love your enemies and pray for those who persecute you."* Matthew 5:44.

Lesson Aim

To look for ways to be more loving toward the difficult people in our lives.

Lesson Setting

Time: A.D. *28*

Place: Galilee

Lesson Outline

Loving as God's People

  I. Love Given Freely: Matthew 5:43-45

      A. *Conditional Love: vs. 43*

      B. *Unconditional Love: vss. 44-45*

  II. Love Offered without Limits: Matthew 5:46-48

      A. *Self-Serving Love: vss. 46-47*

      B. *Striving to Be Unreservedly Compassionate: vs. 48*

Introduction for Adults

Topic: *Adopting an Attitude of Love*

The story is told of an elderly pilgrim who was making his way to the Himalayan Mountains in the bitter cold of winter when a blizzard struck. An innkeeper said to him, "My good man, how will you ever get there in this kind of weather?" The aged traveler cheerfully answered, "My heart got there first, so it's easy for the rest of me to follow."

The Good News of Christ teaches that there is only one way for us to meet all the demands of love expressed in God's law. We can do so when our hearts go there first. Expressed differently, when we determine in the core of our being to love others without precondition or limit, God honors our commitment by enabling us to unreservedly show compassion.

Introduction for Youth

Topic: *Love My Enemies?*

Every small group has certain individuals who can be identified as "extra-grace people." They invariably demand extra grace on our part to accommodate their personality. Even in a Christian setting, they require a soft answer and patience. Maybe some people have come to mind as you read this. They are not enemies, just frustrating people who do not return the grace you extend toward them.

Part of the reason we have difficulty responding in love to those who have irritated us is that we don't want to appear like a doormat to others. So we become defensive instead of exhibiting the fruit of the Spirit. It's liberating to know that we don't have to respond in kind to extra-grace people. With the Lord's help and the encouragement of His people, we can look for ways to be more loving toward the difficult individuals in our lives.

Concepts for Children

Topic: *Love Your Enemies*

1. Jesus told His followers that the rules in the Bible are important to follow.
2. Jesus said that God is pleased when His children do what He commands.
3. Jesus wants His followers to be kind to unfriendly people.
4. God's children should choose to love, rather than hate, those who are not nice.
5. Prayer is one way Jesus' followers can show concern for their enemies.

Lesson Commentary

I. LOVE GIVEN FREELY: MATTHEW 5:43-45

A. Conditional Love: vs. 43

"You have heard that it was said, 'Love your neighbor and hate your enemy.'"

Last week's lesson emphasized the relevancy and permanency of God's law, especially in terms of its enduring moral precepts (see Matt. 5:17-20). We considered the example Jesus gave concerning murder and learned that He wants us to forgive those who have wronged us and seek to be reconciled with those we have offended (see vss. 21-26). In verses 27-30, Jesus discussed the sin of adultery. The religious leaders would have approved His citation of Exodus 20:14 (see Deut. 5:18). The Savior, however, went far beyond the common understanding of this commandment.

The spiritual experts had applied the seventh commandment only to the mere physical act of adultery (Matt. 5:27). But Jesus declared that if a man gazed at a woman with lustful intentions, he had already committed adultery with her in his heart (vs. 28). Here the heart represents the center of one's feelings and desires. The Savior was talking about a prolonged and deliberate stare in which the viewer harbored lustful desires for the woman. Doing this aroused forbidden passions, and the illicit yearnings would lead to sinful acts. Christ's teaching reflected the original biblical prohibition against premarital and extramarital relations.

In verses 31-32, Jesus commented on divorce. He began by mentioning Deuteronomy 24:1-4, which authorized a husband to issue a certificate of divorce to his wife (Matt. 5:31). Undoubtedly, Israel's religious leaders would have affirmed the teaching of this passage. The Jewish scholars of Christ's day debated the issue of divorce and remarriage, because in first-century Palestine, divorce was rampant and was permitted for the slightest matter. Once a divorce had occurred, the estranged wife would usually remarry, for being in a husband-wife relationship was her only means of support.

Israel's religious leaders had failed to consider fully the divine perspective regarding marriage and divorce. Rather than deal with the spirit of the law, they tried to avoid and circumvent it with a host of clever interpretations and traditions, which they added to the law. As a result, the true intent of the Mosaic legislation was concealed and nullified. Jesus brought corrective and needed balance to the topic by stating that divorce for any reason other than sexual immorality caused the rejected spouse to commit adultery. Likewise, marriage to an improperly divorced person was an act of adultery (vs. 32).

Next, Jesus discussed the issue of oaths (vss. 33-37). He mentioned the ancient teaching that it was important to heed, rather than violate, one's sworn pledge to the Lord (vs. 33). Tragically, the religious leaders had brought hypocrisy and abuse to oath taking. To eliminate these wrongs, Jesus declared that no oath should be made whatsoever (vs. 34). His preference was to abolish oaths, especially if these became occasions for lying and deceiving, rather than encouraging truthfulness. Jesus declared that heaven (the throne room of God), that earth (the footstool of His feet; see Isa. 66:1), and that Jerusalem (the city of the great King; see Ps. 48:2) were not to be cited as witnesses to any type of pledge, especially false ones.

When a person appealed to any of these places while making an oath, these became as binding as if the individual had invoked the name of the Lord. Even oaths made against a person's head were to be avoided, for no person but God could control the color of one's hair (Matt. 5:36). Christ declared that it was far better to make simple yes or no declarations of what one intended to do (see Jas. 5:12). Anything said beyond this was not only evil in character but also had its origins in Satan, the evil one (Matt. 5:37; see John 8:44). The Savior's point was that unambiguous human language must suffice for human communication.

In Matthew 5:38-42, Jesus commented on the sin of revenge. He noted the ancient teaching that the punishment the authorities gave had to be equitable and match the crime, not exceed it. The original intent of Exodus 21:24 (see Lev. 24:20; Deut. 19:21) was to limit the occurrence of vengeance, to help the court mete out correction that was neither too strict nor too lenient, and to prevent having different penalties for different social classes. Sadly, many used this law as a guideline for what they should do in all their relationships. Jesus wanted to correct this problem and go even further by urging His followers not to seek revenge, but instead to put others first and be generous beyond expectations. For instance, believers who were slapped on the right cheek were told to also offer the other cheek (Matt. 5:39).

Beginning with verse 43, Jesus addressed the issue of showing love. The experts taught others to love their neighbors and hate their enemies (see Lev. 19:18; Pss. 139:19-22; 140:9-11). In Jesus' day, the widespread opinion among scribes and Pharisees was that one's neighbors included only the upright. Supposedly, the wicked were to be hated because they were enemies of God. The religious leaders defined the wicked as sinners (such as tax collectors and prostitutes), Gentiles, and especially Samaritans. It's true that a love for righteousness will lead to a hatred of evil. However, this does not make it right to be hostile and malicious toward sinners. The upright should abhor the corrupt lifestyle of the lost but never harbor a vindictive loathing of them as human beings. Instead, the godly should display a brokenhearted grieving over the sinful condition of the lost. The foundation for this is a genuine concern for their eternal salvation (Matt. 5:44-48; Luke 6:27-36).

Tragically, the scribes and Pharisees had made a virtue out of being antagonistic toward the sinful. The result was a renunciation of Leviticus 19:18, the command to love one's neighbor. Jesus carried on His ministry in the midst of this intensely prejudiced, exclusivist, and intolerant environment. One of His goals was to tear down the walls that existed between sinners and God. Doing this would enable God's love to flow freely and not be hindered by such potential barriers as nationality, race, party, age, and gender.

B. Unconditional Love: vss. 44-45

"But I tell you: Love your enemies and pray for those who persecute you, that you may be sons of your Father in heaven. He causes his sun to rise on the evil and the good, and sends rain on the righteous and the unrighteous."

Jesus commanded His followers not only to love their enemies, but also to bless those who cursed them, do good to those who hated them, and pray for those who abused and persecuted them (Matt. 5:44). Such compassionate behavior would demonstrate that the Savior's disciples were true children of their heavenly Father (vs. 45). Jesus was stressing that goodwill must not allow itself to be limited by ill will. In fact, those who were genuine members of the Father's spiritual family demonstrated their parentage by their moral resemblance to Him who is love. For example, those who regarded showing forgiveness as a sign of weakness were hypocritical in asking God to forgive them. Likewise, those who felt enmity toward others could hardly be an effective peacemaker for the Lord.

The Father demonstrated His love for sinners by allowing His Son to die for them, even though they were His enemies (Rom. 5:8). The mercy, generosity, and fairness of God are also evident when one realizes that He provides sunshine for all people, regardless of whether they are evil or good. He likewise supplies rain for the upright and the wicked (Matt. 5:45). These truths spotlight the universal goodness of the Creator, which is to be the model for the believers' conduct. Specialists have used the phrase "common grace" to refer to the merciful favor that God bestows without discrimination on all people.

The latter notwithstanding, it would be incorrect to conclude from verse 45 that God's love is amoral. It would also be mistaken to deduce that He shows love without any distinction toward people and that therefore all people are automatically destined to be saved. Jesus taught otherwise (see 25:31-46), and the rest of the New Testament reveals that some aspects of God's love are linked to His moral character and the prerequisite of obedience (see John 15:9-11; Jude 1:21).

II. Love Offered without Limits: Matthew 5:46-48

A. Self-Serving Love: vss. 46-47

"If you love those who love you, what reward will you get? Are not even the tax collectors doing that? And if you greet only your brothers, what are you doing more than others? Do not even pagans do that?"

Since God was so gracious to His enemies, believers were also to be compassionate toward those who hated them. The Son reasoned that if the Father's spiritual children only loved those who loved them in return, there was nothing commendable or distinctive about that. Society might regard the display of mutual love to be normal, customary, and sufficient to fulfill moral expectations. Jesus, however, stated that it was ethically inadequate. Merely responding in love to those who have first shown love is indistinguishable from an exchange of favors.

Jesus urged His followers to show the love of God without precondition or self-imposed limitations.

Jesus' followers should not expect to receive any heavenly reward for displays of love that were narrowly focused and conditional in nature. After all, the most despised people of society at that time—namely, those who made a sizable profit by collecting taxes from their fellow citizens on behalf of the Roman government—showed love to the same extent (Matt. 5:46). Jesus also said there was nothing uniquely Christlike in greeting only one's "brothers" (vs. 47), for even unsaved people did that. It was unusual to display kindness not only to one's closest associates but also to one's enemies. Moreover, if believers lent their money or goods only to people from whom they expected to receive an interest payment, there was nothing commendable about that, for sinners did the same thing (Luke 6:34). It was distinctively more godly not only to lend one's possessions to other people but also to expect to receive nothing in return for one's kindness.

B. Striving to Be Unreservedly Compassionate: vs. 48

"Be perfect, therefore, as your heavenly Father is perfect."

When the Savior's disciples operated in the manner previously described, their spiritual reward in the kingdom of God would be great. They would demonstrate that they were His true children, for He extended His kindness even to people who were ungrateful and wicked. Therefore, just as God was merciful, likewise His people were to be merciful (Luke 6:35-36). The implication is that in every area of life, the members of God's spiritual family were to adhere to the perfect moral standard revealed in the Ten Commandments. They were to obey all the pertinent directives of Scripture, not just those they felt were most convenient. For instance, they were to love other people—including their enemies—with the sacrificial love of Christ. In fact, there was to be no limit to the compassion and kindness that God's people displayed, for He placed no limits on these virtues.

The consequence is that the high ethical ideals revealed in Scripture were to be the goal that believers strove to achieve. The Son went so far as to say that His followers were to be as "perfect" (Matt. 5:48) as His heavenly Father (see Lev. 19:2). The Greek adjective rendered "perfect" (Matt. 5:48) is used in the context of the Son making a comparison with the Father. Thus in this verse, the adjective means "to be fully developed in a moral sense." The word could also refer to maturity of behavior. In both cases, the Son's emphasis was on believers being completely devoted to the Father, especially as seen in being unreservedly compassionate. Just as God was unbounded in His goodness, in the same way, Jesus' disciples were to be unmitigated in their love.

Jesus' concern was for God's Word to be written (in a manner of speaking) on the hearts and minds of His followers (see Jer. 31:33). As a result, they would renounce vengeance and choose to love their enemies. With respect to the legalists of Jesus' day, they were satisfied with partial obedience to the moral imperative of love. Christ, however, wanted something profoundly different for His disciples. They were to allow their lives to be reshaped and transformed by the perfect example of their heavenly Father. If they acted in this way, they would fulfill every aspect of the ethical injunctions appearing in Scripture (see Rom. 12:8-10).

In essence, Jesus was focusing on moral purity and spiritual maturity, which were demonstrated by the willingness of believers to heed God's commands. This aspect of God's perfection is evident in His gracious provision of food and clothing to both the righteous and the unrighteous. He is not generous because He expects the wicked to respond with gratitude and reverence. In fact, He knows that apart from His saving grace the unrighteous will never appreciate His benefits. Furthermore, God's generosity to His enemies is neither a sign of weakness nor an indication of moral indifference to the good and evil practiced by humans. Scripture teaches that the Lord will one day judge the righteous and the unrighteous (see Dan. 12:2; John 3:18). In the meantime, God's gracious provisions are given freely and unconditionally, thus removing any justification the wicked might claim in wanting to hate Him.

A similar emphasis can be found in 1 John 4 on the importance of showing love. In fact, three times in these verses the apostle repeated the phrase "love one another." After the exhortation in verse 7 ("let us love one another"), it is presented as a fact of Christian responsibility in verse 11 ("we also ought to love one another") and as a conditional promise in verse 12 ("if we love one another"). Immediately following the exhortation, John explained why showing love was so important. Just as believing in Jesus' incarnation identifies one as being from God, so too does genuine love, because "love comes from God" (vs. 7).

Admittedly, love is not a natural trait or a learned behavior, for its origin is from God. So all who practice Christian love show that they have been born of God and that they have an intimate relationship with Him. John's point is that love is the natural expression of a Spirit-filled life. The ability to truly love grows out of fellowship with God. For John, the new birth, fellowship with God, and the practice of unconditional love are all intimately woven together to form the core of genuine Christian character.

John next turned to the flip side of the equation. If Christlike compassion is not present in an individual, then that person cannot possibly have an intimate knowledge of God. Though the phrase "born of God" is not present in verse 8 as it is in its counterpart in verse 7, John was likely talking about someone who has not trusted in the Savior, and is thus incapable of demonstrating genuine agape—that is, divine, unconditional love. Believers should love one another because God is the source of love and because He is in fact the essence of love. In verse 8, John was referring to an aspect of God's character. It would be theologically incorrect, however, to declare "love is God," for love is not the sole quality that absolutely defines the nature of the Lord.

John consistently taught that love must be demonstrated by one's actions if it is going to be proved genuine. The Father met this qualification by sending His Son into the world to make salvation available to all. "One and only" (vs. 9) translates a Greek word that means not only "unique," but also "especially treasured." While the truth that "God is love" may be an abstract concept, the Father sending His Son is concrete. The Father abundantly demonstrated the reality of His love by sending His cherished Son to die on behalf of sinful humanity.

The Father's sending the Son has nothing to do with humanity's love for God. The initiative was all on God's side. In fact, the Son's atoning sacrifice for sin is the supreme demonstration of the Father's love (vs. 10). The writer to the Hebrews pictured the death of Christ in terms of this festival (Heb. 2:17). In His crucifixion, Jesus was the real sacrifice, while those offered on the day of Atonement were only shadows. By offering Himself on the cross, the Son presented Himself before the Father as the final, all-sufficient atonement for the sins of the world.

Discussion Questions

1. Why is it wrong to hate our enemies while at the same time showing love to our neighbors?
2. Why did Jesus say that loving our enemies shows others we are God's spiritual children?
3. How does God's love encourage us to be compassionate, sensitive, and kind to other people?
4. How much do you depend on the Spirit to show the love of God to others?
5. In what sense are we, as believers, to be "perfect" (Matt. 5:48), in the way that our Father in heaven is "perfect"?

Contemporary Application

It's natural for us to feel angry, hurt, and sometimes bitter when others sin against us. The choice to forgive will not automatically cancel out these emotions. What, then, should we do?

First, we can begin by showing love to those who have hurt us, regardless of our feelings. It is possible to act lovingly toward an enemy even while we are struggling with the bitterness or anger we feel. Second, we should acknowledge such emotions to God and ask for His help. There is no need to hide such feelings from God, for He knows the thoughts and intents of our hearts even better than we do.

Third, we should entrust ourselves to the care of God. Jesus' words remind us that God is the only one who can ensure that true justice will be done. As long as our eyes are on the offense of the one who has hurt us, we will be drawn into the vortex of bitterness. But when our focus is on Jesus, we find both an example of forgiveness and the motivation to follow His example.

Praying as God's People

Scripture

Background Scripture: *Matthew 6:5-15*
Scripture Lesson: *Matthew 6:5-15*
Key Verse: *"When you pray, go into your room, close the door and pray to your Father, who is unseen. Then your Father, who sees what is done in secret, will reward you."* Matthew 6:6.
Scripture Lesson for Children: *Matthew 6:5-15*
Key Verse for Children: *"Pray to your Father, who is unseen. Then your Father, who sees what is done in secret, will reward you."* Matthew 6:6.

Lesson Aim

To consider ways to renew and improve our prayer lives.

Lesson Setting

Time: A.D. 28
Place: Galilee

Lesson Outline

Praying as God's People

   I. Maintaining Acceptable Motives in Prayer: Matthew 6:5-8
      A. *Genuine vs. Insincere Praying: vss. 5-6*
      B. *Mindless vs. Mindful Praying: vss. 7-8*
  II. Maintaining Correct Priorities in Prayer: Matthew 6:9-15
      A. *Prayer and Worship: vss. 9-10*
      B. *Prayer and Dependence: vss. 11-13*
      C. *Prayer and Forgiveness: vss. 14-15*

Introduction for Adults

Topic: *Valuing the Inner and Outer Actions*

People learn new skills all the time. People like to talk about how they learned to use a computer. We laugh about the mistakes we made and how we inadvertently erased some important material. We keep taking refresher courses to upgrade our computer skills.

Learning to pray is like that, because praying is a new skill. It's not something you fall into. Prayer is a developed discipline that expresses our sincere piety. Prayer takes training and discipline. While we pray, we learn more about it and find new pleasure in it, but it requires time and concentration.

Prayer is not like technology, however, because anyone can pray. That's because prayer is having a talk with God about the state of the inner and outer aspects of our lives. But for the conversation to be satisfying, we have to think about what we say and how we say it. We have to use our best thoughts and skills, conditioned by a proper attitude.

Introduction for Youth

Topic: *Talking to Our Father*

The concept of prayer as conversation with our heavenly Father has tremendous appeal. We have to take prayer out of the realm of stuffy, pious jargon. We have to show teenagers that prayer is not limited to the people who do the praying in public services. Rather, prayer pleases God because it shows that we love Him and His fellowship.

Many times, Christian teens pray for the first time on retreats, or in small campus and church groups. They touch levels of intimacy in prayer because they are vulnerable to each other, more so than many adults. Therefore, our concern is not with the right words and tone of voice, but in practicing our faith with honesty and integrity. That's what Jesus talked about.

Our goals for youth are to develop strong daily prayer habits, as well as quality prayer in fellowship groups. Then as they pray, they can develop the needed spiritual muscles for standing up in spiritual battles.

Concepts for Children

Topic: *Pray This Way*

1. Jesus said that make-believe prayers are useless because we can't fool God.
2. God loves to hear His children talk to Him in prayer.
3. God wants us to talk to Him about all of our fears and needs.
4. It is helpful to pray with our parents and friends.
5. By setting aside a special time to pray every day, we grow stronger in our faith.

Lesson Commentary

I. MAINTAINING ACCEPTABLE MOTIVES IN PRAYER: MATTHEW 6:5-8

A. Genuine vs. Insincere Praying: vss. 5-6

"And when you pray, do not be like the hypocrites, for they love to pray standing in the synagogues and on the street corners to be seen by men. I tell you the truth, they have received their reward in full. But when you pray, go into your room, close the door and pray to your Father, who is unseen. Then your Father, who sees what is done in secret, will reward you."

In Matthew 6:1-4, Jesus instructed His listeners not to perform righteous acts so as to gain attention from other people. He also warned that if they did their good deeds just to show off, they should expect no reward from the Father (vs. 1). To explain His meaning, Jesus presented three examples of righteous acts: charitable giving (vss. 2-4), prayer (vss. 5-15), and fasting (vss. 16-18). In each case, He explained how these acts should not be performed and how they should be performed. He also explained the rewards that flow from each approach to doing acts of righteousness.

Thus, after clarifying the issue of giving (vss. 2-4), Jesus commented on praying appropriately. Regrettably, some people in His day used this pious activity to obtain recognition. They loved to stand in prominent spots in the synagogues and on the corners of busy streets so the public could see what they were doing (vs. 5). In that culture, one normally prayed while in a standing position. One might lead the congregation in prayer during the synagogue service or while standing before the ark where the Torah scrolls were stored. Also, one might be standing on a street corner or in a public place during the prescribed times for prayer. No doubt many onlookers admired what appeared to be a display of godly devotion. However, God knew these practices were a charade. Jesus said that the recognition these attention-seekers received from the public was the only reward they could expect.

It is ironic that an activity that was intended to bring honor and praise to God would be used to bolster the reputation of the worshipers. This violated the first of the Ten Commandments, for the individuals made themselves, rather than the Lord, their god (see Exod. 20:1-3; Deut. 5:6-7). These persons also violated the second commandment, for they were so preoccupied with serving themselves that they had no real desire to serve God (see Exod. 20:4-6; Deut. 5:8-10).

Jesus taught that to foster a humble attitude, it would be better for His followers to pray in a private, secluded spot. By taking this approach, they would ensure that they were not drawing attention to themselves. Jesus promised His listeners that God, who is unseen, was well aware of their prayers and would reward them accordingly (vs. 6). Despite what has been said, it would be a mistake to assume that the Savior condemned praying in public, for even He prayed in open settings (see John 11:41-42). His point was that the true citizens of God's kingdom were to pray with pure motives, rather than self-serving attitudes.

B. Mindless vs. Mindful Praying: vss. 7-8

"And when you pray, do not keep on babbling like pagans, for they think they will be heard because of their many words. Do not be like them, for your Father knows what you need before you ask him."

Another problem involving prayer was that some of the unsaved engaged in meaningless repetition. The pagans believed that their gods thrived on incantation and repetition. They thought that by saying the same words over and over in prayer, they would influence the deity to hear their requests (Matt. 6:7). Jesus stated that such beliefs about prayer were based on superstition, not on trust in God. That is why the Messiah's followers were not to repeat themselves endlessly in prayer, for the Father already knew what they needed before they asked (vs. 8). Therefore, meaningless repetition was unnecessary and insulting to God. The more believers engaged in this practice, the more they violated the spirit of the third of the Ten Commandments, for they were treating the person and character of God in an empty or meaningless way (see Exod. 20:7; Deut. 5:11).

It would be incorrect, however, to infer that Jesus was condemning everyone who prayed long prayers or repeated their requests, for even He prayed all night (see Luke 6:12) and repeated His petitions (see Matt. 26:44). Rather, Jesus was censuring the notion that prayers are like incantations that can compel God to do what He otherwise is unwilling to do. Jesus was also denouncing the idea that through prayer people can overcome God's unwillingness by tiring Him with their words.

II. MAINTAINING CORRECT PRIORITIES IN PRAYER: MATTHEW 6:9-15

A. Prayer and Worship: vss. 9-10

"This, then, is how you should pray: 'Our Father in heaven, hallowed be your name, your kingdom come, your will be done on earth as it is in heaven.'"

After commenting on the detestable practices of the hypocrites, Jesus then instructed His disciples to pray in a certain manner. What He said is not a rigid magical formula that He wanted them to mechanically repeat over and over, for this would contradict what He had said earlier in this passage. Rather, Jesus intended the prayer to be a model after which to pattern other petitions.

The prayer briefly sums up the great themes of Jesus' teaching and expresses the desire of His disciples for the Father to establish His kingdom. Through this petition, they acknowledge their dependence upon the Father to supply their daily needs. They also confess that He has reconciled them to Himself and that it is only through His power that they can resist temptation. Jesus' model prayer contains various elements that should be included in all types of prayer to God. Some aspects of what Jesus said concern the believers' relationship with God, while others deal with their relationship with people. Thus, the thematic emphases of the Lord's Prayer parallel those of the Ten Commandments.

With respect to Matthew 6:9-13 and Luke 11:2-4, specialists have debated how they are related. The version in Matthew is longer than the one in Luke, and it is also more rhythmical and liturgical in its composition. In addition, all of information in the prayer recorded in Luke is contained in the one appearing in Matthew. Some think that Matthew's version of the Lord's Prayer was the original, and that Luke borrowed and condensed it. Others say that Luke's version of the model prayer is the original and that Matthew expanded on it to reflect his theological and linguistic perspective. Still others maintain that the versions in Matthew and Luke originated from different, independent sources. Each of the theories has a considerable degree of subjectivity to it, which makes it difficult to determine which one is the most accurate. Of fundamental importance to the debate is the fact that the historical contexts are quite different for the two versions of the Lord's Prayer. This suggests that Jesus taught this form of prayer on more than one occasion during His earthly ministry.

In His model prayer, Jesus first mentioned praise or adoration. The idea is that, before believers ever mention their needs and concerns, they should first acknowledge the holiness of their heavenly Father (Matt. 6:9). The Greek noun rendered "Father" is a term of intimacy that exists in a close, family relationship. Moreover, the verb translated "hallowed" means "to treat as holy" and implies the ideas of reverence, honor, and obedience. Also, in Bible times, the names of people often denoted their nature or character. Accordingly, God's name is a self-revelation of His nature, especially in terms of His saving acts in history. Thus, to say that God's name is holy is to confess that He alone is morally pure and absolutely transcendent above His creation.

This truth helps to explain the rationale behind the second of the Ten Commandments, namely, that since God is infinitely distinct and set apart from all He has made, it is an offense to make an idol to represent Him (see Exod. 20:4-6; Deut. 5:8-10). For that reason, to acknowledge the holiness of God is a corrective against any self-seeking motives in prayer. This assists us in understanding why Jesus wanted His followers to focus their attention first on God, not themselves or others. Jesus' directive reflects the concern of the first of the Ten Commandments that as we pray, we should worship only God (see Exod. 20:2-3; Deut. 5:6-7).

When believers commune with God in prayer, they are asking not only that His creatures keep His name holy, but also that He Himself would sanctify His name by being the holy Judge and Savior. These truths serve as a reminder that the Father is in heaven, that He cares for His people on earth, and that He can be approached on a personal basis. They learn that in Him they can find eternal spiritual rest, a truth made evident by the fourth of the Ten Commandments (see Exod. 20:8-11; Deut. 5:12-15).

As believers pray to God, they should focus on His continuing rule in their lives and the successful accomplishment of His will. The believer should long for God to manifest His kingdom and His will completely on earth, even as He fully implements His rule in heaven (Matt. 6:10). Believers understand that in one sense

God's kingdom already exists in the hearts and lives of those who obey the Lord and yield to His will. They also know that the kingdom will not come until God's will is perfectly done throughout the world, and it is for this that they pray.

B. Prayer and Dependence: vss. 11-13

"'Give us today our daily bread. Forgive us our debts, as we also have forgiven our debtors. And lead us not into temptation, but deliver us from the evil one.'"

The implication of the preceding truths is that believers should regularly ask God to help them and their fellow Christians remain submissive to His guidance and directives. When Jesus' followers obey God, they demonstrate that they are subject to His rule and that they want His will to be accomplished in their lives. Moreover, Matthew 6:9 and 10 indicate that when believers pray, they should first focus their attention on God and His glory. Then, as verse 11 makes clear, they should concentrate on their personal needs. From this we see that it is perfectly acceptable for believers to petition God concerning their ongoing needs, for He is the one who provides them with their daily sustenance.

With respect to the Greek adjective rendered "daily," a variety of meanings has been suggested including the following: "necessary for existence," "for the current day," and "for the following day." When the various options are considered, Jesus probably meant either "bread for tomorrow" or "the bread that is necessary." The differing views regarding the derivation and meaning of the adjective have led to a variety of interpretations concerning what Jesus meant in verse 11. Three of these explanations are worth mentioning.

One interpretation is that Jesus was referring to the bread received in the Lord's Supper. A second view is that Jesus' reference to bread symbolizes life in the coming kingdom. This would make the petition equivalent to the appeal in verse 10 for the heavenly kingdom to come. The problem with these two explanations is that they present us with an unusual figure of speech that conflicts with the simple phrasing of Jesus' prayer. A third interpretation understands verse 11 as a straightforward petition for God to supply the daily needs of His people. This explanation seems best, for it is a theme that is developed in other portions of Jesus' Sermon (see vss. 19-24).

It would be incorrect to infer from Jesus' statement that God will give believers everything they desire. Jesus wanted His disciples not only to depend on God, but also to moderate their longings. Furthermore, when believers pray to God to supply their daily needs, they are indicating their desire to be content with what He gives them. Additionally, by depending on God to meet their needs, they are less likely to worry about their continued well-being. This, in turn, will minimize their inclination to violate the eighth and tenth of the Ten Commandments, which concern stealing and coveting respectively (see Exod. 20:15, 17; Deut. 5:19, 21).

Matthew 6:12 stresses the importance of believers confessing their sins, or moral and spiritual debts, to God (see Luke 11:4). Evidently, Jesus was speaking in Matthew 6:12 about daily forgiveness, because the moment people are saved, God forgives their sins (see Eph. 1:7). Daily forgiveness is necessary to restore the believers' broken fellowship with the Lord (see 1 John 1:3, 9).

As Jesus spoke to His disciples, He instructed them to consider their relationships with others. This truth reflects what is taught in the Ten Commandments, the last six of which deal with obligations to one's fellow human beings (see Exod. 20:12-17; Deut. 5:16-21). Clearly, both the Ten Commandments and the Sermon on the Mount emphasize that one's relationships with others must not be ignored or dishonored. With respect to the sermon, Jesus stressed that God's forgiveness of His spiritual children should be reflected in their willingness to forgive people who wronged them. The idea is that the more aware and appreciative Christians are of God's forgiveness, the more inclined they will be to forgive others.

Next, Jesus encouraged His disciples to talk to God about their spiritual well-being. This emphasis is reflected in Matthew 6:13, which says, "Lead us not into temptation." On the surface, the verse seems to suggest that God is the one who leads His people into temptation. Such a conclusion, however, is theologically unsustainable (see Jas. 1:13-15). Most likely, Jesus was stressing the importance of asking God to protect believers from situations that would entice them to sin. Though God would never tempt His people to do evil, He does allow them to be tested in their faithfulness. It is also possible to translate Matthew 6:13 as "do not bring us to the time of trial." This rendering serves as a reminder that believers should regularly ask God to deliver them from all evil influences, including the father of wickedness, the devil (see John 8:44).

Some ancient Greek manuscripts add the following ending to Matthew 6:13: "For yours is the kingdom and the power and the glory forever. Amen." The doxology provides an appropriate ending to verses 9-13. It encourages believers to recognize that God is deserving of all power, authority, and honor throughout eternity. The disputed ending also fittingly balances the emphasis of Jesus' model prayer. The invocation begins by focusing on God, then proceeds to focus on human needs, and ends by once again focusing God.

C. Prayer and Forgiveness: vss. 14-15

"For if you forgive men when they sin against you, your heavenly Father will also forgive you. But if you do not forgive men their sins, your Father will not forgive your sins."

Jesus had been stressing the importance of avoiding temptation and being delivered from the evil one (Matt. 6:13). His words served as a reminder that believers daily transgress against God and others (see 1 John 2:10). The Greek noun rendered "sin" (Matt. 6:14) conveys the imagery of people taking a misstep and losing their footing. From a moral perspective, the noun denotes the violation of God's will and commands. Such terms as "offenses," "failures," "wrongdoing," and "trespass" help to convey this notion. While the noun could refer to inadvertent misdeeds, the emphasis in Matthew 6:14 is on deliberate acts against God and humankind.

In this verse, Jesus taught that His followers would enjoy God's forgiveness to the same extent that they forgave other people for transgressing against them. Also, Jesus said that His disciples would not enjoy God's forgiveness to the same extent that they refused to forgive others for transgressing against them (vs. 15). Based on this verse, some have concluded that forgiving others is a precondition to receiving God's pardon. But this supposition would contradict the truth that God's forgiveness of sin is entirely dependent on Jesus' sacrifice of atonement. Jesus was not teaching that believers had to forgive others to merit God's pardon. Rather, Jesus was stating that the outworking of believers' having been forgiven in their daily lives was linked to their willingness to forgive others who had wronged them (see Eph. 4:32).

Discussion Questions

1. What methods of praying did Jesus criticize in the Sermon on the Mount?
2. What is the connection between our forgiveness of others and God forgiving us?
3. What do you like most about praying to God?
4. What are some of your recent prayers that God has answered?
5. Who is someone you could pray for today?

Contemporary Application

Jesus taught His disciples to pray that they might do the will of God. That shouldn't be surprising, especially since the whole purpose of Jesus' life was to do His Father's will. Have you ever wondered how you can expect your prayers to be in accordance with the will of God? Matthew 6:5-15 can help us answer that concern.

First, Jesus taught that we should strip away all concerns about what anyone else thinks about our praying. We should also not be concerned with whether we are praying the way the so-called pros do. Second, we are to praise God for His character and rule among His people. How have we seen His kingdom prospering on the mission field, in our church, and in our lives? We should praise Him for those things. When we do, we align ourselves with who God is and what He is doing.

Third, we are to commit ourselves to carrying out God's will on earth just as it is carried out in heaven. We should humbly and sincerely present every concern and need we have to the Lord. We should not try to sound pious by concealing our true concerns behind religious jargon. Finally, we are to approach life with the attitudes the Lord has. The more we become like the Savior, the more we will think, act, and pray according to God's will. By doing these things, we will renew our prayer lives and our love for God.

Refusing to Worry

Scripture

Background Scripture: *Matthew 6:25-34*
Scripture Lesson: *Matthew 6:25-34*
Key Verse: *"Seek first his kingdom and his righteousness, and all these things will be given to you as well. Therefore do not worry about tomorrow. . . . Each day has enough trouble of its own."* Matthew 6:33-34.
Scripture Lesson for Children: *Matthew 6:25-34*
Key Verse for Children: *"Do not worry about your life."* Matthew 6:25.

Lesson Aim

To recognize that only God provides true security and freedom from worry.

Lesson Setting

Time: A.D. 28
Place: Galilee

Lesson Outline

Refusing to Worry

   I. Jesus' Exhortation against Worrying: Matthew 6:25-30

      A. Anxiety about Life: vs. 25

      B. Our Value to God: vs. 26

      C. Uselessness of Worry: vs. 27

      D. Lessons from Nature: vss. 28-30

  II. Jesus' Prescription for Anxiety: Matthew 6:31-34

      A. God's Awareness of Our Needs: vss. 31-32

      *B. Kingdom Priorities vs. Future Concerns:
         vss. 33-34*

Introduction for Adults

Topic: *Putting Worry in Its Place*

It's common knowledge that excessive and prolonged worrying is not good for our health. We also know that worrying can rob us of peace and contentment. It should come as no surprise, then, that Jesus told us not to worry. He saw it as an exercise in futility. How then can we stop worrying?

Many books and sermons on tape give us good practical advice. The simplest answer, of course, is to focus our attention on the Lord. When we start the day with praise and thanks to God as well as meditation on His Word, we are in good shape to deal with the problem of worrying.

It also helps to have some good friends. These would not be people who dream up more stuff for us to worry about, but rather those who are good listeners and who can draw us back to our resources in Christ. Occasionally, we all need encouragement to let go of our worries and give them to the Lord.

Introduction for Youth

Topic: *Why Worry?*

A Little League baseball game was being played one Saturday when a visitor stopped to watch. Walking up along the first baseline, he asked the boy playing nearby whether he knew the score.

"We're behind 13 to nothing," the boy replied. "Thirteen to nothing!" the visitor bellowed with a jolt. "Hey, you don't seem very worried about it." "Naw," answered the youngster. "Why should I? We haven't been up to bat yet!"

That kind of attitude is the outlook Jesus wants saved teens to have as they follow Him and serve one another every day. Just because they may be hurting and angry, or just because they might have doubts and questions, they don't need to avoid turning to Him for consolation. He is always present to help them through their struggles.

Concepts for Children

Topic: *Do Not Worry*

1. Jesus urged us not to worry about food, drink, or clothing, because life is much more than these things.
2. Jesus said that God will provide for us, especially because we are more valuable than birds or flowers.
3. Trusting God to meet our needs shows to others that our faith is in Him.
4. Jesus urged us to put God's desire and work first in our lives.
5. God is like a loving parent who will provide for us at all times.

Lesson Commentary

I. JESUS' EXHORTATION AGAINST WORRYING: MATTHEW 6:25-30

A. Anxiety about Life: vs. 25

"Therefore I tell you, do not worry about your life, what you will eat or drink; or about your body, what you will wear. Is not life more important than food, and the body more important than clothes?"

The wealthy religious professionals of Jesus' day apparently endorsed the notion that material abundance was a sign of God's blessing. Consequently, Jesus' listeners who were impoverished might have asked, "Since we are poor, where do we stand with God?" Jesus, however, did not directly address this question, for His teaching about riches was quite different from that of the scribes and Pharisees. Instead, Jesus told His followers not to spend their time hoarding increasingly greater amounts of earthly treasures. After all, He indicated, fine clothes can be eaten by moths, metal jewelry and utensils can rust, and money and valuables can be stolen (Matt. 6:19). Expressed differently, worldly wealth is never entirely secure.

Jesus was not saying that money is bad, or even that being rich is necessarily evil. He was concerned about greed, that is, the desire to acquire greater wealth no matter what. Instead of stockpiling possessions, Jesus' followers were to invest their lives in accumulating heavenly riches. Perhaps Jesus was referring to rewards from God for such things as serving others in love and forgiving those who have inflicted harm. In heaven there is no depreciation and no theft; the treasures accumulated there are safe (vs. 20). With penetrating insight, Jesus declared that one's heart will always be where one's riches are found (vs. 21). People who spend their time accumulating earthly possessions have their interests anchored in temporal concerns. People who spend their time storing up spiritual treasures are focused on eternal matters.

Jesus transitioned from talking about the heart to talking about the eye. Nonetheless, He was still focused on the problems associated with greed for worldly wealth. In first-century A.D. Palestine, the setting sun meant that it was time to light the lamps. Jesus said that just as a lamp glows in a room at night, so the eye brings light into the body. As long as the eyes work, the body has light. But if they don't work, the body is in darkness (vss. 22-23). Jesus was, of course, using physical vision metaphorically to represent spiritual vision. His point is that people who are intent on amassing worldly wealth are spiritually blind, while those who are most concerned with deserving heavenly rewards have acute spiritual vision. The Lord had a strong word for the spiritually blind. Using a paradox, He said that the "light" (vs. 23) of these people is actually "darkness," and He noted how terribly dark it was for them.

Jesus changed His metaphor again, this time to slavery. He pointed out that it wouldn't work for a slave to have two owners, for the slave would inevitably favor one over the other (vs. 24). That means that one owner would be disappointed in the service given by the slave. Jesus was still talking about financial matters when He plainly stated that it was impossible to serve both God and money. Here we learn that if our primary aim in life is to accumulate wealth, God won't receive the worship and obedience He deserves from us. Consequently, we are wise choose to serve God, for no other master is worthy.

In our age of consumerism, both poor and rich fear being out of control or overwhelmed by circumstances that will threaten their material well-being. Jesus taught that the believers' outlook was to be radically different from that of the unsaved. Christians were not to worry, for it was counterproductive and prevented them from fully trusting God. Jesus was not condemning proper stewardship and forethought. Rather, He was censuring anxiety over the future. In view of that, the Savior urged believers not to be fearful about their lives. For instance, the provision of food, drink, and clothes—matters over which the unsaved constantly fretted—were not to preoccupy the thoughts of Jesus' followers. This is because there was more to life than these things (vs. 25).

B. Our Value to God: vs. 26

"Look at the birds of the air; they do not sow or reap or store away in barns, and yet your heavenly Father feeds them. Are you not much more valuable than they?"

Jesus explained that the lives of believers were of more significance than what they wore and ate. He pointed to the wild birds that flew in the sky and stated that these creatures were not involved in planting and harvesting crops. Yet the Father in heaven abundantly supplied their material needs. The point of Jesus' illustration was not idleness, but rather freedom from anxiety. The birds could find everywhere around them the insects they needed to eat—all provided by God. It stood to reason that the person of faith was of more value to God than a bird (Matt. 6:26). This being the case, God would not fail to provide graciously for His people's needs, just as He never failed to provide for the needs of creatures such as birds.

C. Uselessness of Worry: vs. 27

"Who of you by worrying can add a single hour to his life?"

Sadly, the tendency of believers was to be consumed with worry over the most insignificant details of life. Jesus declared that being anxious is pointless and useless, and a waste of time (Matt. 6:27). Some Bible scholars think this verse should be translated as it appears in the NIV, with its emphasis on trying to "add a single hour to [one's] life." Others think the verse should be rendered as it appears in the NIV margin, with its emphasis on attempting to increase one's "height" by a "single cubit." In ancient times, a cubit varied in length from 18 to 21 inches. It was the measure taken from the length of a person's arm from the elbow to the tip of the finger. Jesus' point comes through clearly in either rendering, namely, that worry does not change things. Not only was it futile to worry about small matters one could not control, but also the larger matters of life are even further from one's control.

D. Lessons from Nature: vss. 28-30

"And why do you worry about clothes? See how the lilies of the field grow. They do not labor or spin. Yet I tell you that not even Solomon in all his splendor was dressed like one of these. If that is how God clothes the grass of the field, which is here today and tomorrow is thrown into the fire, will he not much more clothe you, O you of little faith?"

Those who were excessively concerned about clothing, food, and shelter never had any inner peace and rest. This condition is far different from the one Jesus offers to believers. He is their source of eternal rest. Jesus pointed to the lilies of the field and asked His audience to consider how such delicate flowers grew. These plants did not labor to provide covering for themselves (Matt. 6:28). Yet the great King Solomon in his entire splendor had not been clothed as magnificently as these flowers (vs. 29). To the Savior's Jewish audience, Solomon would have been the foremost example of human glory.

It stood to reason that people of faith were more valuable to God than the lilies of the field. Consequently, God would not fail to provide for the needs of His spiritual children, just as He never failed to clothe the grass of the field. Through faith in the Son, they could enter their eternal Sabbath rest (see Heb. 4:1-11). Jesus then stated that the life span of grass was very brief. One day it was alive, and the next day people removed it to burn as fuel in the clay ovens of Palestine. If God was willing to do so much to ensure the growth and development of something as seemingly insignificant as field grass, would He not do unbelievably more for His people? Jesus assured His listeners that the Lord would provide for the basic needs of His children, individuals who tended to have such "little faith" (Matt. 6:30).

II. JESUS' PRESCRIPTION FOR ANXIETY: MATTHEW 6:31-34

A. God's Awareness of Our Needs: vss. 31-32

"So do not worry, saying, 'What shall we eat?' or 'What shall we drink?' or 'What shall we wear?' For the pagans run after all these things, and your heavenly Father knows that you need them."

Since God abundantly cared for His lesser creatures, He would care even more for His highest creatures—human beings. That is why it was irrational to worry even in the face of life's brevity and death. The Savior's comments were intended to enhance the confidence of His followers' trust in God. Since the Lord would always meet the needs of His spiritual children, they were not to worry about obtaining essential items such as food, drink, and clothing (Matt. 6:31). The more they fretted about these things, the less able they would be to serve the Lord effectively. Likewise, as long as they lived in worry, they would miss what true life in the Son was all about. Jesus next stated that the basic necessities of life were constantly pre-occupying the thoughts of the unsaved. Believers, however, were not to be like them, for the Son promised that the Father would supply His people's needs (vs. 32).

B. Kingdom Priorities vs. Future Concerns: vss. 33-34

"But seek first his kingdom and his righteousness, and all these things will be given to you as well. Therefore do not worry about tomorrow, for tomorrow will worry about itself. Each day has enough trouble of its own."

While the unsaved spent their lives seeking after the things of the world, which were destined to pass away, Jesus urged His followers to make seeking God's kingdom and righteousness their foremost priority. Some think the focus in Matthew 6:33 is mainly on the end times and thus understand Jesus to be referring to the future expansion of God's active reign on earth, the vindication of the upright, and the punishment of the wicked. More likely, the connotation is ethical in nature. This means that the principal goal of believers is the establishment of God's rule in their lives and in the lives of the unconverted. Also, the highest aim of any disciple is the manifestation of Jesus' righteousness in the lives of His people and imputed to repentant sinners.

Christians need not fear making heavenly concerns their greatest priority, for the Lord would not neglect their needs. When they truly honored God by their faith, He would honor their dependence on Him by supplying their needs. His spiritual children might not become wealthy in earthly treasures, but He would ensure that they did not lack anything to serve Him effectively. When God had the foremost place in the lives of His children, they would turn to Him first for help, fill their thoughts with His desires, make His character the pattern for their behavior, and obey the ethical injunctions of His Word.

Since God would meet the needs of His people, they were not to be concerned about tomorrow. In fact, the upcoming days would have sufficient anxiety-producing moments and circumstances of their own. Moreover, worrying about the future was pointless, for people could not control it. In fact, worrying about the future could never give anyone the ability to manipulate it. Because people could not hold sway over the present with its innumerable problems, it was futile to become preoccupied with concerns of the future. The troubles believers encountered each day were too many to count and beyond their control. This being the case, they were to entrust the present and the future to God (vs. 34). The grace He gave His spiritual children was sufficient only for the day. It could not be stored for use at a future time. If Jesus' disciples encountered troubles in the future, God would give them the grace they needed to handle their difficulties.

Like Jesus' exhortations against worrying recorded in Matthew 6:25-34, Psalm 42 encourages the faithful to turn to God when they feel anxious or troubled. The author was in touch with his emotions. Though he admitted feeling sad, he did not wallow in self-pity. Instead, the writer redirected his attention to the Lord (vs. 5). The poet realized that by putting his hope in God, he would be able to once again offer up praises to Him. The psalmist could do so for he knew that one day he would experience again the presence of his Savior and God (vs. 6). None of us is immune to feelings of discouragement from time to time. One remedy is to think about how God has been good to us. When we reflect on the many ways the Lord has been kind to His people, it will shift our focus off the present situation and onto God's ability to do what seems impossible.

In verse 7, the author talked about hearing the tumult of the raging seas, as if God's vicious waves had swept over him like an angry ocean or a roaring waterfall. Some think the psalmist was referring to the mighty waters of the upper Jordan River surging down from Mount Hermon. Another possibility is that the writer was talking about a deluge from the sky dumping large quantities of water, which then filled the rivers and streams that eventually flowed into the seas. In either case, the poet's intent behind the imagery is much the same. He sensed that God was ultimately responsible for the oceans of trial in which he seemed to be drowning. It was as if God was sending one trouble after another upon him, like the relentless pounding of the surf, and causing him great distress. We should not fault the psalmist for taking such a candid look at his situation. When we are troubled, it is appropriate for us to think honestly about our circumstances. This helps us to be realistic and to anchor our hope in God, rather than in people or possessions.

Verse 8 forms the thematic center for the entire song and interrupts the laments coming before and after it. Though the psalmist's situation seemed bleak, he could still say that through each day the Lord poured out His unfailing love upon him. This helped the author sing songs of praise to God "at night." This was the writer's way of praying to God, whom he knew was the ultimate source of life. We are reminded of a similar refrain appearing in Lamentations 3:22-24. Jeremiah believed that an understanding of God's faithfulness in dealing with His people was reason for hope rather than despair. Even in his afflictions, the prophet remembered God's unfailing love and kindness, and he found reason for hope and godly self-discipline.

In Philippians 4:6, Paul told his friends not to worry about any self-centered concerns. Such anxiety can become all-consuming. It takes our minds off what is important to God and focuses attention on ourselves. We can become self-absorbed, unable to rejoice during hard times and to be gentle with friends and foes alike. So what is the best remedy for anxiousness? Paul's prescription is prayer. When we turn to God and surrender our anxieties to Him, God's peace can reach our innermost parts. The apostle did not imply that our burdens will vanish, nor was he talking about a state of mind. In fact, it is an inner peace that can come only from God and is beyond our comprehension. In addition, the Father's peace will guard our hearts and minds in the Son (vs. 7).

Discussion Questions

1. What is it about the uncertainties of life that drives many believers to be consumed with worry?
2. In the eyes of God, how much more valuable to Him are His spiritual children than birds?
3. How can increasing our faith in God result in a decrease in worrying?
4. What is the difference between worry and maintaining a proper concern for the future?
5. What does it mean to seek God's kingdom, and why is this important?

Contemporary Application

Recently, I was in a group that was asked, "What makes you worry?" I thought about myself while I listened to the various answers. Money seemed to come up often.

In a recent demographic study of the United States by the National Decision Systems and the United States Census Bureau, the response most often cited by those questioned about their greatest concern was "achieving financial security." Money is more often the source of worry in the lives of adults than anything else. This remains especially so in tough economic times. Other sources of anxiety identified in the poll included appearance, career, mate, and security.

In short, preoccupation with material things is a prime reason why adults tend to worry excessively. Moreover, an anxiety-laden desire for money can be as much of a trap as possessing it. In addition, we can become so busy that gradually our spiritual vision is blurred. As we neglect Bible study, prayer, and Christian fellowship, we move away from our first love—the Savior.

Pastor and author Warren Wiersbe says that "the average person who worries crucifies himself or herself between two thieves: the regrets of yesterday and the worries about tomorrow." Fretting strikes when what we value most is threatened. Furthermore, worrying can draw us away from trusting completely in the Lord. Since everything we have belongs to God, we are stewards, obligated to use our possessions, time, and energy as investments for our Lord. It's amazing that when we choose to live in this way, our anxieties begin to dissolve and our worrying gradually diminishes.

In light of this week's lesson, we are wise to consider where our heart is focused. Are we using our God-given resources to invest in His kingdom? Are we daily seeking His righteousness? In the final analysis, the contents of our character matter more to God than the size of our bank account.

A Blessing for All Nations

Scripture

Background Scripture: *Genesis 12:1-9*

Scripture Lesson: *Genesis 12:1-9*

Key Verse: *"I will make you into a great nation and I will bless you; I will make your name great, and you will be a blessing."* Genesis 12:2.

Scripture Lesson for Children: *Genesis 12:1-9*

Key Verse for Children: *"I will make you into a great nation and I will bless you; I will make your name great, and you will be a blessing."* Genesis 12:2.

Lesson Aim

To emphasize that faith is a journey with God.

Lesson Setting

Time: 2091 B.C.

Place: Ur of the Chaldeans and the land of Canaan

Lesson Outline

A Blessing for All Nations

I. God Summons Abram: Genesis 12:1-3
 A. *The Lord's Command: vs. 1*
 B. *The Lord's Blessing: vss. 2-3*

II. Abram Responds in Faith: Genesis 12:4-9
 A. *Abram's Obedience: vss. 4-5*
 B. *Abram's Worship of God: vss. 6-9*

Introduction for Adults

Topic: *Sharing Good Fortune*

"Not many months after my conversion . . . I poured out my soul before God . . . who had done everything for me—who had saved me when I had given up all hope and even desire for salvation—I besought Him to give me some work to do for Him . . . some self-denying service . . . however trying or however trivial."

As a young man in the 1840s, Hudson Taylor felt the call of ministry to China, a land then largely unknown to Christianity. Taylor went on in 1865 to begin the China Inland Mission, which sent over 300 missionaries to China in the next 25 years. Clearly, God's spiritual blessing and good fortune were on His servant!

But how did Taylor move from a skeptical adult who believed he was beyond salvation to a person of conviction whom God would use? The full story is worth reading in Taylor's autobiography. There you will be encouraged in your own faith journey to follow the call of God on your life.

Introduction for Youth

Topic: *A Blessing to All Nations*

Bob remembers traveling as a child with his father, a regional salesman, to visit accounts throughout southern Illinois. "On those trips, my dad relied as much on his date book as he did his map," Bob says. The book was filled with the names and addresses of his customers, directions to their businesses, their purchasing history, and of course, the date of their next appointment. "Without that book," Bob says, "my dad would have been out of business in less than a week."

The biblical account of Abram's life reveals that sometimes God has other plans for our lives than the ones we so carefully map out. For the patriarch, this included being a blessing to all nations. For us there might be a lesson we need to learn, a person we need to meet, or a task only we can do. When God calls, the date books must be set aside. We are travelers with God on a lifelong journey of faith, so His planner always takes precedence.

Concepts for Children

Topic: *A Promise to Abram*

1. When God made promises to Abram (Abraham), he believed those promises.
2. Abram obeyed God by moving his whole family.
3. God chooses people who are different from one another to be His leaders.
4. God calls people to be leaders even when they do not understand His plan.
5. God is pleased when we follow His directions for us.

Lesson Commentary

I. GOD SUMMONS ABRAM: GENESIS 12:1-3

A. The Lord's Command: vs. 1

The LORD had said to Abram, "Leave your country, your people and your father's household and go to the land I will show you."

Genesis is the book of beginnings. In this historical narrative, we find the beginnings of the material universe, human life, human sin, divine judgment on human sin, covenant promises, and the Israelite tribes—to name just a few. Genesis provides a foundation for a great deal of what we can know about life and our Lord. Genesis is also the first of five books forming a group of their own at the beginning of the Old Testament. Together, Genesis through Deuteronomy are usually called the "Torah" (meaning "law" or "teaching") or the "Pentateuch" (literally, "five-volumed [book]"). Moreover, Genesis provides the background for the Exodus and wilderness settings of the other four books.

We learn in Genesis 4–6 that some of Adam's early descendants, such as Cain and Lamech, were ungodly people, while other descendants of Adam's, such as his son Seth, were godly. Nonetheless, it appears that by the time of Noah, who lived many generations after Adam, wickedness had almost wholly eclipsed righteousness in the human race. Consequently, the Lord decided to bring judgment on the world. He did so by sending a worldwide flood to wipe out all life—all that is except for one godly man (Noah), his family, and the animals they would gather. God gave Noah instructions for building and stocking an ark that could rise up on the floodwaters. When these preparations were complete, the waters began to cover the earth and do their destructive work.

Noah was 600 years old when the Flood began (7:6), and the rains lasted 40 days and 40 nights (vs. 12), covering the earth for a total of 150 days (vs. 24). Noah, his family, and the animals were on the ark for about another six months before the Lord commanded them to come out (8:13-15)—over a year after they went into the ark. Indeed, it was only after the waters receded that all the occupants of the ark disembarked from the vessel (vs. 18). As Noah and his family exited from the ark, a new era in history began. From here on out, the small band of people would repopulate areas devastated by the Flood. It was appropriate, therefore, that God and the remnant mark the occasion by reaffirming their relationship (8:19–9:17).

From a thematic standpoint, Genesis can be looked at as having two main parts: chapters 1–11 and 12–50. The first 11 chapters cover the time from the Creation to the birth of Abram. Though in these chapters we meet certain key individuals, such as Adam and Noah, the scope takes in all humanity. Then, in the book's final 38 chapters, the time span covered is much shorter, namely, about three centuries. Also, the focus has narrowed to one family called by God to receive and transmit His blessings. From start to finish, Genesis is a book of history, and its historical account is trustworthy, for it was inspired by God. That said, we should not expect the book to provide a complete or systematic history of time from its origin until the Hebrews' Egyptian sojourn. The author's concern was not history as an end in itself. Instead, the writer used real historical people and events to teach eternal truths about God and humankind.

A case in point would be the situation on earth many years after the Flood and the Tower of Babel. In 2091 B.C., God began a new approach in His dealings with humanity. He started to devote special attention to one family (later to become a nation) that would bear His name before all the world's peoples. Then, from out of this nation, He would raise up the Messiah, who would achieve salvation for all who would believe in Him. The narrative begins with the phrase "This is the account of" (11:27). Here we find one of several places in Genesis where such wording appears. The phrase, however, introduces more than genealogies. It is a signal to the reader that the narrative is about to detail what became of the individual mentioned in the heading (in this case, Terah and his family).

We learn, in particular, that Terah was the father of Abram, Nahor, and Haran, and that Haran had a son named Lot. Verse 28 notes that, while Haran was still relatively young, he died in Ur of the Chaldeans, which was the place where he was born. In the time of Abram, the city of Ur, in the southern part of what is now Iraq, was an important commercial center with a population of at least 300,000 people. Over 100,000 clay business documents have been found at the site, as well as the remains of an extensive library. Musical instruments and statuettes found in the royal tombs indicate a high level of craftsmanship and cultural standards.

The well-educated people of Ur were proficient in mathematics, astronomy, weaving, and engraving. Walls averaging 30 feet in height protected Ur from intruders. At the heart of the city was the three-tiered ziggurat (a kind of step pyramid) dedicated to the moon god, Nanna, the protector of the city. Some two-story homes contained the best comforts available in the ancient world, including a kind of primitive air conditioning. The town's harbor on the Euphrates River brought travelers from all over the world to conduct trade.

Verse 29 supplies other details about Terah's family. While Abram married Sarai, Nahor married Milcah. The background information provided in these verses helps to prepare the reader for upcoming events discussed in Genesis. For instance, notice the brief statement in verse 30 that Sarai was barren. God would use this circumstance to mature the faith of Abram and Sarai. To set in motion His grand plan, God needed one man to become the progenitor of a holy nation (Israel), and He chose Abram of Ur for that role. We cannot be sure why God called this person and not someone else. But from later events in the patriarch's life, we know he had many fine qualities.

The preceding statement does not mean that Abram was perfect. In fact, Joshua 24:2 reveals that at the time the patriarch was living in Ur, his family was worshiping false gods. Moreover, it might appear at first glance from Genesis 11:31 that

God originally called Terah from Ur to go to Canaan. But other passages make it clear that God called Abram to leave his homeland (see Gen. 15:7; Neh. 9:7; Acts 7:2-3). The patriarch began his journey to Canaan with his father, wife, and Lot, his nephew. After traveling north along the Fertile Crescent trade route, the group arrived in Haran, where they stayed for a time, accumulating possessions and servants (see Gen. 12:5).

Why did Abram stop in Haran? Perhaps Terah, his father, was too weak to travel farther, or perhaps Terah felt at home there, since the people of Haran also worshiped the moon god. While some attribute the stay in Haran to disobedience, others suggest that the stop was just a delay necessitated by family reasons. Once Terah died (11:32), Abram continued his journey, obeying the message God had given while Abram was in Ur. God summoned Abram to leave everything that was significant to him—his culture, his relatives, and his family (Gen. 12:1). God also directed an elderly man to leave the security of his homeland and set out for an unknown destination. This must have seemed painful and risky to the patriarch. Nevertheless, along with Abram's call came a blessing that surely acted as a powerful incentive for him to obey God.

B. The Lord's Blessing: vss. 2-3

"I will make you into a great nation and I will bless you; I will make your name great, and you will be a blessing. I will bless those who bless you, and whoever curses you I will curse; and all peoples on earth will be blessed through you."

The blessing of God came in the form of a series of seven promises. (In Scripture, seven was often viewed as the symbolic number of perfection.) First, God promised to make Abram's descendants into a great nation (Gen. 12:2). Second, God would personally "bless" the patriarch. The underlying Hebrew verb means that God would give Abram and his descendants the ability to flourish and be successful in serving as the Creator's servants wherever they sojourned. Third, God would make Abram famous. Fourth, God would make the patriarch a blessing to others. Fifth, God would bless anyone who blessed Abram (vs. 3). Sixth, God would curse those who cursed Abram. Seventh, all the families of the earth would be blessed through (and because of) the patriarch.

Here we find God's blessing of creation now being carried forward to Abram in the form of a covenant. In the garden, God had blessed Adam and Eve, giving them a fruitful place, endowing them with the ability to multiply, and making them rulers over creation. That was all ruined at the Fall. Then, as God began to build His covenant people, He promised to give Abram's descendants a fruitful land, a great nation, and kingship. From our perspective in time, we can see some of the ways these covenant promises were fulfilled. Abram became the progenitor of the Hebrew nation. In his own day, he was rich, and ever since, he has been famous. His greatest descendant, Jesus Christ, has spread God's blessings to people from all nations. Of course, Abram did not know about these fulfillments. He had to accept the blessing and obey the call by faith (see Heb. 11:8-10).

In Abram's day, several types of covenants existed in the ancient Near East. One type, the royal grant covenant, consisted of a king's giving land or some other type of benefit to a servant. Normally, the terms were unconditional for the one benefiting from the gift. Another type of ancient covenant was the suzerain-vassal treaty. In this covenant, a powerful ruler (or suzerain) pledged to protect a weak king's (or vassal's) realm as long as the latter remained loyal to the stronger monarch. This covenant's continuance depended on the behavior of the weaker king. Covenants between God and people resembled either the royal grant or the suzerain-vassal type of compact. The Abrahamic covenant was of the royal grant type. In it, God promised to give the descendants of the patriarch the land of Canaan.

II. ABRAM RESPONDS IN FAITH: GENESIS 12:4-9

A. Abram's Obedience: vss. 4-5

So Abram left, as the LORD had told him; and Lot went with him. Abram was seventy-five years old when he set out from Haran. He took his wife Sarai, his nephew Lot, all the possessions they had accumulated and the people they had acquired in Haran, and they set out for the land of Canaan, and they arrived there.

In response to God's summons, Abram left Haran with his wife Sarai and his nephew Lot to travel hundreds of miles to Canaan (Gen. 12:4). The entourage took with them considerable possessions, slaves, and hired servants (vs. 5). Besides being old, Abram was also childless, so his response to God was truly a step of faith. We know, of course, that apart from God's revelation, the patriarch would not have abandoned the safety and wealth of his homeland. Perhaps from a human perspective residing in a comfortable house among friends and relatives outweighed the prospect of living in a tent as an alien in a far-off place. But when God called, Abram responded in trust, believing that God was able to do what He had promised (see Rom. 4:21).

B. Abram's Worship of God: vss. 6-9

Abram traveled through the land as far as the site of the great tree of Moreh at Shechem. At that time the Canaanites were in the land. The LORD appeared to Abram and said, "To your offspring I will give this land." So he built an altar there to the LORD, who had appeared to him. From there he went on toward the hills east of Bethel and pitched his tent, with Bethel on the west and Ai on the east. There he built an altar to the LORD and called on the name of the LORD. Then Abram set out and continued toward the Negev.

Abram journeyed by stages through the land of Canaan from north to south, stopping at Shechem, Bethel, and the Negev area (Gen. 12:6). The "great tree of Moreh" possibly refers to a well-known holy place (such as a sacred grove) for the veneration of local deities. Abram, however, worshiped the Lord there. In the patriarch's time,

Canaan was thinly populated. Some urbanization had begun to take place at several fortified cities. But the area was far behind the standard of civilization Abram had left in Ur. The Canaanites worshiped their gods with detestable practices, the worst of which was offering children as burnt sacrifices to idols.

When the patriarch arrived, the Canaanites and Amorites occupied the land. The former were descended from Canaan, the grandson of Noah. The Amorites, whose origin is disputed, moved into Canaan in the years preceding Abram, causing considerable destruction and upheaval. This made it easier for the patriarch and his group to move freely through the promised land. At this time, the Canaanites were divided into city-states in which the monarchs had wide powers to raise an army, control lands, impose taxes, and compel subjects to take part in public projects.

It was against this cultural backdrop that Abram demonstrated faith and obedience, and God honored his commitment. Specifically, when the patriarch arrived at Shechem, the Lord appeared to him and promised to give the land of Canaan to his descendants (vs. 7). This is the first time, according to the text, that God had appeared to Abram since he left Ur, and the first time we know that God explicitly promised Canaan to Abram. In response to the Lord's appearance, the patriarch built an altar and offered sacrifices. This act of devotion showed that he believed the Lord and was thankful for what He would do for him. At Bethel, Abram built another altar and again worshiped God (vs. 8). Then he continued south, where he settled for a while (vs. 9).

The name "Negev" apparently means "dry country" and is used throughout the Old Testament to denote the southernmost area of the land of Canaan. The region generally referred to as the Negev is south of Judea and west and southwest of the Dead Sea. The area has very little rainfall and few sources of underground water. Though today the area is quite dry and barren, archaeological surveys suggest the region once contained many villages. Research, in fact, indicates that Abram and his family could have sojourned through this area for long periods. They would have found both foliage and water. Furthermore, when the patriarch traveled through the Negev, he found permanent settlements there and people who were generally at peace with each other.

The biblical record outlines Abram's life in Canaan as tent pitching and altar building. Thus the patriarch did not establish a permanent settlement in the land, but lived as a nomad, moving his considerable flocks from place to place to find food and water. While he was wealthy in possessions, he did not leave behind signs of his riches or prestige, only altars left as symbols of his faith in the Lord for a witness to his new pagan neighbors. Scripture gives us few details of where Abram went in Canaan, but what we are told about his stops in the land is significant.

For instance, Shechem, Bethel, and the Negev are all important places in the life of Jacob (chaps. 33–35), who inherited Abram's covenant with God. That covenant was renewed with Moses and the Israelites. When the Israelites conquered Canaan, the battle plan after Jericho was to capture Ai. Before taking the city, the Israelites camped in the hills where Abram camped, between Bethel and Ai (see Josh. 8:9, 12). It is as if Abram and Jacob first took Canaan peacefully, by building altars and buying land. And then the Israelites in the conquest came to reclaim what God had promised them long ago. From this summary we see that the God of the patriarchs showed His faithfulness through many generations.

Discussion Questions

1. Why did God direct Abram to leave his native land to begin the journey to Canaan?
2. If you were Abram, how do you think you would have felt upon receiving the divine summons?
3. Which of the seven promises God made to Abram intrigues you the most? Why?
4. What did the Lord promise to Abram when He appeared to the patriarch at Shechem?
5. What responses from the Canaanites do you think Abram experienced as he built altars to the Lord?

Contemporary Application

God is calling each of us. Some of us He is calling to take the first step of a life-long journey with Him. Such involves admitting our sinfulness and accepting His Son, Jesus Christ, as our Lord and Savior. It is the most important step we can take.

For those who have already taken the first step, the journey has only begun. God continues to call, but often we have already scripted our life's journey ourselves. We are involved with many activities, and we do not want to listen.

What does God ask us to do? Students and athletes have been surprised when God called them to enter the ministry or become missionaries. But God may ask us to do simpler things that are also challenging—for instance, sharing the Gospel with someone seated next to us on a bus, or inviting a next-door neighbor to go to church with us.

As we live by faith, we have the privilege of serving the King of kings, Jesus, who has promised to share His inheritance with us. He invites us to share in all He has accomplished by His life, death, and resurrection. We realize that Jesus is the one who has done all the work that makes the promise of eternal life possible. That is one reason why we should point others to Him, and not to ourselves. We, in ourselves, have nothing to offer, but the Messiah has everything we need.

Living in faith means continually taking risks, stepping out of the familiar into the unfamiliar. Abram no doubt thought about the implications of obeying God and all the negatives of leaving, but he left anyway. We can learn from Abram's response what we should do when God calls. We need to recognize His call and willingly step out, no matter what the consequences.

A Promise to Abraham

Scripture

Background Scripture: *Genesis 15:1-21*

Scripture Lesson: *Genesis 15:1-6, 12-18*

Key Verse: *Abram believed the LORD, and he credited it to him as righteousness.* Genesis 15:6.

Scripture Lesson for Children: *Genesis 15:1-7*

Key Verse for Children: *After this, the word of the LORD came to Abram in a vision: "Do not be afraid, Abram. I am your shield, your very great reward."* Genesis 15:1.

Lesson Aim

To learn that God can do what we consider impossible.

Lesson Setting

Time: Between 2081–2080 B.C.

Place: Canaan

Lesson Outline

A Promise to Abraham

  I. Abram's Acceptance of God's Pledge: Genesis 15:1-6

      A. *God's Declaration: vs. 1*

      B. *Abram's Dilemma: vss. 2-3*

      C. *God's Promise of Many Descendants: vss. 4-5*

      D. *Abram's Belief in God's Promise: vs. 6*

  II. God's Reassurance to Abram: Genesis 15:12-18

      A. *Abram's Sleep: vs. 12*

      B. *God's Explanation: vss. 13-16*

      C. *God's Pledge Concerning Canaan: vss. 17-18*

Introduction for Adults

Topic: *Believing the Impossible*

God stretched the faith of Abram in many ways. God told Abraham that he would have a son. Moving to an unknown country was a risk, but the promise of having children as an old, childless couple was physically impossible. Even Abram thought God needed help here. Rather than resting in God's promise, Abraham began to create his own plan.

Are we any different from Abraham? God is stretching our faith, for example, when He asks us to watch a family member suffer with cancer or to forgive someone who has terribly wronged us. These become opportunities for us to trust God to cause all things to work together for our eternal good (Rom. 8:28).

Introduction for Youth

Topic: *An Enormous Family*

A number of Christian organizations report that the tendency of individuals in the West toward independence is a threat to the traditional family structure. These agencies report that it is difficult for us to place our lives and our future in the hands of anyone else. Within our control, the outcome might not be an incredible success, but at least it will be predictable and safe. However, our God desires that we instead step into a wonderful world of adventure with Him at the controls.

How can we entrust our existence to God, especially when it seems impossible at times? Nonetheless, the record of Scripture and of our own experiences in following the Lord tell us that He seems to love the word "impossible." He most often does not work through our agenda, and we do not always see Him working in ways we understand. But as He did with Abram, He also asks us to learn to trust His heart. Indeed, this is the first step in becoming a part of His eternal family, along with the rest of Abram's spiritual offspring.

Concepts for Children

Topic: *Expect God to Keep His Promises*

1. God promised to protect Abram (Abraham).
2. God promised to give Abram a son.
3. Abram believed what God promised.
4. God has also made promises to us in the Bible.
5. God is pleased when we accept His promises.

Lesson Commentary

I. ABRAM'S ACCEPTANCE OF GOD'S PLEDGE: GENESIS 15:1-6

A. God's Declaration: vs. 1

After this, the word of the LORD came to Abram in a vision: "Do not be afraid, Abram. I am your shield, your very great reward."

The Lord appeared to Abram in a vision at night. At this time, the patriarch would have been about 85 years old. God told Abram not to be afraid, for the Lord was his "shield" (15:1). The underlying Hebrew noun figuratively refers to God as Abram's protector (see Pss. 7:10; 84:9) and recalls the statement Melchizedek made in Genesis 14:20. There the patriarch learned that the Creator had given him victory over his enemies. Though Abram had rejected the spoils of war offered by the king of Sodom, the most high God would reward him in great abundance (15:1). Indeed, while the patriarch had accumulated material wealth, the Creator was his real source of blessing.

B. Abram's Dilemma: vss. 2-3

But Abram said, "O Sovereign LORD, what can you give me since I remain childless and the one who will inherit my estate is Eliezer of Damascus?" And Abram said, "You have given me no children; so a servant in my household will be my heir."

Abram was respectful when he addressed God as the "sovereign LORD" (Gen. 15:2). In referring to God by this title, the patriarch affirmed that the Creator is the eternal, all-powerful master of the universe. Abram recognized that God's promises depended on the patriarch having descendants, but he was still childless. Also, because he and Sarai were both old, they had no hopes of producing children on their own. In that day, the desire to have children—especially sons—was great. With no clear understanding of immortality, people believed that children provided the opportunity for a kind of earthly immortality. A son could carry on his father's name and take over the family's possessions.

Abram concluded that he would have to leave his estate to a favored servant, Eliezer of Damascus, rather than to a son of his own (vs. 3). Between 1925 and 1941, more than 4,000 clay tablets were discovered among the ruins of Nuzi, near the modern city of Kirkuk in Iraq. These tablets provide fascinating glimpses into everyday life at the time of the patriarchs. Some of the tablets reveal that in Nuzi it was customary for a childless man to adopt someone to carry on his name and inherit his property. This is just what Abram planned to do with Eliezer of Damascus before Isaac was born.

C. God's Promise of Many Descendants: vss. 4-5

Then the word of the LORD came to him: "This man will not be your heir, but a son coming from your own body will be your heir." He took him outside and said, "Look up at the heavens and count the stars—if indeed you can count them." Then he said to him, "So shall your offspring be."

The Lord was sensitive to Abram's concern about being childless. That said, God did not go along with the patriarch's plan to make Eliezer the owner of Abram's property after he died. Instead, the Creator affirmed that a son originating from his "own body" (Gen. 15:4) would inherit his estate. The Lord did not end there, either, in revealing His future plans to Abram. While the patriarch was looking ahead just one generation, God saw the whole future and knew about the multitude of people who would regard Abram as their ancestor.

So in a dramatic move, the Lord led Abram outside his tent and directed him to look upward at the nighttime sky of Palestine. It's helpful to remember that this was an era long before the invention of electric lights. On a clear night, the stars shone brilliantly against the blackness of space. Thousands upon thousands of points of light were visible in the heavens. In fact, there were literally too many to count. As Abram fixed his gaze on myriad stars, he heard the Lord pledge that the elderly patriarch would have as many descendants as the seemingly limitless stars in the sky (vs. 5).

D. Abram's Belief in God's Promise: vs. 6

Abram believed the LORD, and he credited it to him as righteousness.

God's amazing pledge gave Abram security, calmed his nerves, and settled his fears. Whereas before the patriarch was doubtful about having a child, he now fully "believed the LORD" (Gen. 15:6). In this context, the Hebrew verb rendered "believed" means "to consider something to be reliable or dependable." The idea is that Abram regarded the Lord as being fully trustworthy in honoring His promise and bringing it to pass. Because the patriarch completely accepted the divine pledge, God honored his faith. The text says the Lord "credited it to him as righteousness." "Credited" is an accounting term that refers back to Abram's trust in God. He demonstrated by his belief that his loyalty to God was genuine and his commitment was steadfast. In turn, the Lord counted him as righteous.

Paul quotes this verse in Romans 4:3 and Galatians 3:6 to combat the false teaching that salvation is based on merit or good works. The apostle pointed to Abraham (Abram) to demonstrate that God credits people with righteousness and forgives their sins as a result of them believing the promise of the Gospel. Paul illustrated his point by saying that workers' wages are not given to them as a gift, but rather because it is owed to them (Rom. 4:4). If salvation can be attained by works, then it cannot be called the gift of God. Conversely, for the person who does not work but rather places faith in God, that person's faith is credited as righteousness (vs. 5). Abraham is an illustration of the second type of person.

The apostle further illustrated his point from the life of David (vss. 6-8). Paul quoted David's words in Psalm 32:1-2 to show the blessedness of one whose account has been credited with God's righteousness. The latter is appropriated through faith, apart from works. Because of God's grace, sins are covered, and the Lord will never hold a person's wrongdoing against him or her. To drive his point home, Paul raised the question as to whether justification by faith is only for the Jews (the circumcised) or for the Gentiles (the uncircumcised) as well (Rom. 4:9). The apostle, in appealing once more to Abraham, argued that the patriarch was not declared righteous as a result of faith plus circumcision. Also, he was not justified as a consequence of faith plus keeping the Mosaic law. Instead, he was pardoned by faith alone.

In verse 10, Paul raised the important question as to whether Abraham was justified before or after he was circumcised. The apostle quickly answered that "it was not after, but before." The Book of Genesis makes this clear. Hagar, Abraham's wife, gave birth to Ishmael when Abraham was 86 years old (see 16:16). It was sometime after this that God instructed the patriarch to circumcise all his male descendants as a sign of the covenant. This was done when Abraham was 99 years old (see 17:24). It would seem, then, that Abraham's circumcision took place some 13 years after God credited his response of faith as righteousness.

Next, Paul pointed out that Abraham was circumcised as a "sign" (Rom. 4:11) or "seal" that he had already been justified by faith. In other words, the circumcision was a testimony to the patriarch's justifying faith. This ultimately means, then, that Abraham is not just the spiritual ancestor of the Jews, but is, in fact, the forebearer of all who believe, including the Gentiles. Of course, Abraham is also the father of believing Jews (vs. 12). The upshot is that circumcision alone was not enough to render a Jew right with God. Like the Gentiles, the Jew could only be justified by faith and not by observing the Mosaic law.

In further support for his argument, Paul said it was not through the law that Abraham received the promise that "he would be heir of the world" (vs. 13). In point of fact, God's promise to the patriarch—contained in the Abrahamic covenant in Genesis 12:1-3—occurred several centuries before God gave the law through Moses (see Gal. 3:17). Among other things, God promised Abraham that he would have many descendants, and that through his offspring the peoples of the earth would be blessed (see Gen. 12:3). This is probably what Paul was referring to in saying that Abraham "would be heir of the world" (Rom. 4:13). This incredible promise was given several hundred years before the giving of the Mosaic law.

Paul then pointed out that if the Jews could become Abraham's heirs by simply keeping the law, then "faith has no value" (vs. 14; more literally, "faith has been made empty"). In such a situation, "the promise is worthless" (or "the promise has been made invalid"). Expressed differently, to assert that God's blessing goes to the lawkeepers amounts to saying that God's promises to those who have faith (which would include Abraham and David) are meaningless. The fact is, when we try to keep the law, we always end up being under God's wrath (vs. 15). Keeping a list of commandments and ordinances to gain God's favor (and salvation) only produces spiritual arrogance.

The purpose of the Mosaic law was to reveal sin, not to bring about justification.

In arguing for this fact, Paul affirmed that where there is no law, there is no transgression. Put another way, if people don't know right from wrong, then in one sense they cannot be held accountable for their actions. Nonetheless, as Paul pointed out in Romans 1, even those who do not have the written code of Moses have the moral law of God written upon their hearts. So all people intuitively know right from wrong, and therefore all are responsible for their actions and are without excuse before the Creator.

II. GOD'S REASSURANCE TO ABRAM: GENESIS 15:12-18

A. Abram's Sleep: vs. 12

As the sun was setting, Abram fell into a deep sleep, and a thick and dreadful darkness came over him.

God's covenant with Abram had two main provisions: descendants and land. With the matter of the heir settled, the Lord reminded Abram of His promise of the land to which He had called the patriarch (Gen. 15:7). The people as numerous as the stars would need a place to live, and that place was the land of Canaan. Abram asked the "sovereign LORD" (vs. 8) how he could be sure he would receive the land. Probably, we should not take this as a sign of weakened faith on Abram's part. He just wanted some kind of pledge of God's intention.

Graciously, the Lord was willing to give Abram the reassurance he sought. In the present situation, God chose to copy a common practice of that time used to confirm covenants. This observation reminds us that the Lord is always eager for His truths to be presented in ways that people can understand. In Abram's day, covenants were accompanied by confirming and binding oaths. The parties to a covenant would agree to certain punishments if they were to fail in their responsibilities as spelled out by the covenant. These oaths were represented by a symbolic passage through death. By walking between the parts of dead animals, the parties to the covenant symbolically declared, "May I die like these animals, especially if I am untrue to the covenant" (see Jer. 34:18-20).

At God's instruction, Abram gathered animals and split the larger ones in two. He laid them on the ground, forming a corridor between the animal parts. Then Abram waited until the end of the day, which included driving away birds when necessary (Gen. 15:9-11). We can only imagine how tired the elderly patriarch must have felt by this time, especially after spending hours performing tasks requiring heavy physical labor. It's not surprising that when the sun went down, Abram fell into a deep, trancelike sleep. At some point, a terrifying "darkness" (vs. 12) enveloped him, and he was gripped with fear.

B. God's Explanation: vss. 13-16

Then the LORD said to him, "Know for certain that your descendants will be strangers in a country not their own, and they will be enslaved and mistreated four hundred years. But I will punish the nation they serve as slaves, and afterward they will come out with great possessions. You, however, will go to your fathers in peace and be buried at a good old age. In the fourth generation your descendants will come back here, for the sin of the Amorites has not yet reached its full measure."

Since Abram would not live long enough to see how his descendants would possess the land, God explained what would happen. The Lord foretold that the Israelites would become "strangers" (Gen. 15:13) or sojourners in a foreign land, and there they would be oppressed as "slaves" for four centuries (see Exod. 12:40-41). It was then that God planned to end the cruel treatment of His chosen people. He revealed that He would execute judgment on Egypt, free the Israelites from their captivity, and enable them to depart with many "possessions" (Gen. 15:14). The Book of Exodus records the historical fulfillment of these events. Abram, of course, would not experience any of this. The idiomatic expression "go to your fathers" (Gen. 15:15) refers to death. In the patriarch's case, he would pass away in a state of "peace" and be advanced in years by the time of his burial.

The Hebrew noun rendered "generation" (vs. 16) is used here in a broad sense to refer to a long span of life. The immediate context suggests that at that time, one generation was about 100 years. Thus, after four generations, or four centuries, the Lord would liberate His people from Egypt. In God's prediction, His mention of the "sin of the Amorites" gives us some clues as to how His providence works. The Hebrews' conquest of the promised land would have a secondary purpose in punishing the Amorites (standing for all the sinful residents of Canaan). As was noted in lesson 1, archaeologists have shown that the people of Canaan were involved in such evil practices as child sacrifice, idolatry, religious prostitution, and divination. Even so, God was patient with them and would not annihilate them until they were fully deserving of judgment.

C. God's Pledge concerning Canaan: vss. 17-18

When the sun had set and darkness had fallen, a smoking firepot with a blazing torch appeared and passed between the pieces. On that day the LORD made a covenant with Abram and said, "To your descendants I give this land, from the river of Egypt to the great river, the Euphrates."

At the conclusion of God's predictive speech to Abram, the Lord enacted the ceremony for which Abram had prepared. God's holy presence, symbolized by a "smoking firepot" (Gen. 15:17) and a "blazing torch," passed between the animal parts. As a result of this divine action, the covenant was now legally binding. Put differently, God had ratified His intention to fulfill all His promises to Abram. In human agreements, both parties to a covenant usually passed between the dead animals. In this case, however, only the Lord did so, for His promises were unconditional. Since the fulfillment of the promise depended on the Lord alone, Abram was merely a spectator.

Verse 18 literally reads "cut a covenant." This refers back to the slaughtering of the animals mentioned in verse 10. In verse 18, God defined the extent of the land He would give to the patriarch's descendants. It lay between the "river of Egypt" (probably one of the seasonal rivers in the Negev) in the south to the Euphrates River in the north. At that time, this territory was occupied by at least 10 different people groups. According to some scholars, during the reigns of David and Solomon, the Israelites exercised political and economic control over all the land promised to Abram, that is, the territory occupied by the groups of people mentioned in verses 19-21 (see 1 Kings 4:21, 24).

Discussion Questions

1. What made Abram so "afraid" (Gen. 15:1)?
2. How does it encourage you to know that God is your protector?
3. Why did Abram choose his servant, Eliezer, to be his heir?
4. What do you think it means to believe in the Lord?
5. In the covenant ratification ceremony, why did only God pass through the animal parts?

Contemporary Application

When Pam chose to become a teacher, she knew she wanted to touch children's lives, just as her mother, who was also a schoolteacher, had done. What Pam had not counted on was the fact that some children would seem so untouchable. I recall her saying to me, "I had a student whom I'll call Gary who I can only describe as obnoxious and obstinate. He was so much trouble, I thought I was being specially punished when I had to teach him for both sixth and seventh grade."

Pam had little real faith that Gary would ever change. Pam said, "But he surprised me. To my amazement, he changed when he discerned I was truly trying to care for him, that I was trying to like him as a person. That realization made a genuine difference for our relationship and for him as a person. After he graduated, I saw him at a mall, and he called out to me. We chatted for a while, and I was just floored. I would have sworn he would be one of the kids who would walk the other way if he saw me coming."

Many of us live with Garys every day—people we are sure will never change—and we see situations that look hopeless or impossible. We may know that God is powerful enough to change any life, or any situation, but it is something else altogether to expect such changes. This week's lesson offers a memorable glimpse into the joy that comes when God's people learn to move from knowledge to faith. It can be hard to believe that God can do all things and is working even when we cannot see Him operating. Even when we do not always see Him working in ways we understand, He asks us to learn to trust His heart.

The Lord Provides

Scripture

Background Scripture: *Genesis 22:1-14*

Scripture Lesson: *Genesis 22:1-2, 6-14*

Key Verse: "*I know that you fear God, because you have not withheld from me your son, your only son.*" Genesis 22:12.

Scripture Lesson for Children: *Genesis 22:1-2, 6-14*

Key Verse for Children: *Some time later God tested Abraham. He said to him, "Abraham!" "Here I am," he replied.* Genesis 22:1.

Lesson Aim

To encourage trusting God through life's tests.

Lesson Setting

Time: Between 2081–2080 B.C.

Place: Canaan

Lesson Outline

The Lord Provides

   I. God's Command to Abraham: Genesis 22:1-2
   A. *God's Summons: vs. 1*
   B. *Abraham's Response: vs. 2*

   II. Abraham's Unwavering Obedience:
       Genesis 22:6-14
   A. *Bringing the Required Items: vs. 6a*
   B. *Anticipating God's Provision: vss. 6b-8*
   C. *Obeying God Unconditionally: vss. 9-10*
   D. *Affirming Abraham's Commitment: vss. 11-12*
   E. *Substituting a Ram for Isaac: vss. 13-14*

Introduction for Adults

Topic: *Passing the Test*

It seems that a black man named Anthony who was from St. Thomas in the Virgin Islands, somehow came under the influence of Count von Zinzendorf, the saintly German leader of the Moravians in the 18th century. Anthony, it turned out, had been a slave. He told how his fellow slaves wanted to hear the story of the kindly God from the lips of missionaries.

Anthony, however, warned that the missionaries could gain entrance to St. Thomas and the slaves only if they went as slaves. It seemed to everyone that the situation was hopeless. Who would be able to pass such a test of sincerity? Who would have the courage to preach under such terrible conditions?

Amazingly, two Moravian men, Leonard Dober and Tobias Leopold, stepped forward. Dober and Leopold had themselves sold as slaves and sent to the Caribbean, where they suffered and eventually died. Despite this, the loss of them planted a strong Christian church in the area. Like their spiritual ancestor Abraham, these two missionaries were willing to make the ultimate sacrifice in obedience to the will of God.

Introduction for Youth

Topic: *The Ultimate Test*

Ron's sister, Pamela, was sick and needed a kidney transplant. Ron's kidney would be a perfect match. Ron's parents knew that if he went through surgery and donated one of his kidneys, it would save his sister's life.

Physicians carefully explained the procedure. Ron realized that he was being asked to give up something important to himself. Understandably, his parents did all they could to keep him from feeling pressured.

Thankfully, Ron agreed to the procedure without any reservations. He saw the entire process as a test of love for his sister. Likewise, Abraham considered his actions as a test of love for God. Both Ron and Abraham responded accordingly.

Concepts for Children

Topic: *God Takes Care of Abraham*

1. God decided to test Abraham's faith.
2. Abraham's test took place at Mount Moriah.
3. God told Abraham to offer his son as a sacrifice.
4. God provided the sacrifice for Abraham in place of Isaac.
5. God is pleased when we trust and obey Him.

Lesson Commentary

I. GOD'S COMMAND TO ABRAHAM: GENESIS 22:1-2

A. God's Summons: vs. 1

Some time later God tested Abraham. He said to him, "Abraham!" "Here I am," he replied.

In Genesis 20, we see Abraham repeating a sin he had committed earlier (12:10-20). After moving into the Negev, Abraham again identified Sarah as his sister to protect himself. Abimelech, the king of Gerar, took Sarah into his harem. Before long, God warned Abimelech to return Sarah to Abraham. For a second time, Abraham found himself reprimanded by a pagan king for lying. But then Abimelech gave Abraham benefits and cleared Sarah's name.

As promised, Abraham and Sarah did indeed have a son of their own. Chapter 21 reveals that Sarah, at the age of 90, gave birth to a boy, whom her husband named Isaac. Abraham, who was 100 years old, circumcised Isaac in obedience to the Lord's command (vss. 1-5; see 17:9-14). Later, at the feast celebrating Isaac's weaning, Sarah caught Ishmael mocking Isaac. This prompted Sarah to insist that Abraham send away Hagar and Ishmael (21:6-10).

God assured Abraham that He would make Ishmael into a great nation. This was as much as saying that Abraham could send his older son away in good conscience (vss. 11-13). After leaving Abraham's household, Hagar and Ishmael began to suffer from thirst. But then when hope was almost gone, God provided water and told Hagar what He had earlier told Abraham about Ishmael's future (vs. 18). About the same time, the Philistine king, Abimelech, established a treaty with Abraham for peaceful coexistence. The patriarch stayed on at the treaty-making site, Beersheba, in southern Canaan (vss. 22-34).

An examination of chapter 22 reveals that the Lord often tests the faith of His followers. Though He does not tempt us to do evil (see Jas. 1:13), He does allow trials to come into our lives for various reasons, including to prove the authenticity of our faith (see 1 Pet. 1:6-7). In our present text, we discover how God tested the faith of Abraham to see whether he would be obedient. Specifically, the Lord required him to demonstrate confidence in the promises of the covenant. The patriarch's test could hardly have been more severe. It began with God summoning Abraham by name, followed by the patriarch responding as the Lord's ready and attentive servant (Gen. 22:1).

B. Abraham's Response: vs. 2

Then God said, "Take your son, your only son, Isaac, whom you love, and go to the region of Moriah. Sacrifice him there as a burnt offering on one of the mountains I will tell you about."

The Lord began His instructions to Abraham by emphasizing the unique place Isaac occupied in the patriarch's life as his "only son" (Gen. 22:2) by Sarah, the offspring in whom all the divine promises resided. God also affirmed Abraham's deep affection for Isaac. The Lord directed Abraham to take his beloved son with him to the land of Moriah. At this time, the patriarch was living in Beersheba, at the southernmost point of the promised land (see 21:33-34). Genesis 22:2 does not state where the "region of Moriah" is, but the text does say that the patriarch traveled three days to get there (vs. 4). This is about how long it would have taken him to go from Beersheba to the vicinity of what is now Jerusalem, a distance of about 48 miles.

According to 2 Chronicles 3:1, Solomon built the temple on Mount Moriah. Thus, the spot (approximately, at least) where Abraham nearly sacrificed his son became the sacred place where for centuries his descendants would offer animals. Also, nearby was the hallowed spot where the Messiah would become the all-sufficient sacrifice (see Heb. 13:11-14). In short, at the mount of Moriah, the Father spared Abraham's son but not His own (see Isa. 53:4-6).

Even though Abraham loved Isaac, God still called upon the patriarch to present his son as a "burnt offering" (Gen. 22:2) on a soon-to-be disclosed mountain. In later Israelite history, a burnt offering involved the sacrifice of a bull, ram, or male bird (a dove or young pigeon) to the Lord. The animal had to be without blemish. The worshiper first laid his or her hands on the animal, signifying its role as a sacrificial substitute. Next, a priest tossed blood from the animal against the altar. Finally, the priest burned the animal on the altar (see Lev. 1; 6:8-13; 8:18-21; 16:24). The burnt offering was significant for several reasons. It was a voluntary act of worship and atoned for the participant's unintentional sins. The burnt offering also was an expression of total devotion to the Lord.

The biblical text gives no indication that God told Abraham anything more than the initial command he received. Only the reader knows that the Lord meant this act as a test. We can only wonder how objectionable God's directive to Abraham must have felt. The command must have also seemed inconsistent with everything the Lord had promised the patriarch. How could he slay the one through whom, according to God's own word, the promises of the covenant would be fulfilled? Nonetheless, the directive from the Lord was clear. Though Abraham did not know what was ahead for him, he chose to obey God and take Isaac to the region of Moriah to offer the boy as a sacrifice.

II. ABRAHAM'S UNWAVERING OBEDIENCE: GENESIS 22:6-14

A. Bringing the Required Items: vs. 6a

Abraham took the wood for the burnt offering and placed it on his son Isaac, and he himself carried the fire and the knife.

The divine command to sacrifice Isaac is one of the most difficult in Scripture to understand. Some scholars have tried to soften the horror by claiming that this account merely shows how ancient peoples finally moved beyond human sacrifice and learned to placate God by offering up livestock. But the Bible is not an anthropology textbook. The point of this account is how the Lord calls us to radical trust and commitment. For instance, we note that real faith has an element of anguish to it. Abraham certainly would have felt this anguish.

Despite any qualms, the patriarch showed his trust in God by trudging up the mountain with Isaac. It was early in the morning when Abraham got up, saddled his donkey, and cut the wood needed for the burnt offering. In addition to Isaac, the patriarch took two young servants with him on the three-day journey (Gen. 22:3). During this time, Abraham had the opportunity to reconsider his options and change his mind. But he remained committed to the task the Lord had commanded him to perform.

On the third day of the trek, the patriarch caught sight of the place in the distance for the intended sacrifice (vs. 4). He directed his two servants to stay where they were and look after the donkey used for carrying supplies. Abraham explained that in the interim, he and his son would travel farther, spend some time in worship, and return to the servants (vs. 5). Here we see the patriarch displaying confidence in God. Even though Abraham intended on obeying the Lord, the patriarch believed that God could raise his son from the dead (see Heb. 11:17-19).

Abraham carried some coals in a clay pot to ignite a fire and a knife to kill the sacrifice. The patriarch also had his son carry the wood for his own sacrifice (Gen. 22:6). This is remarkably like Jesus, who would carry His own cross on the way to His crucifixion (see John 19:17). We should not think of Isaac as a little boy at the time of this incident. The Hebrew noun translated "boy" (Gen. 22:12) can refer to a man old enough to serve in the military (see 1 Chron. 12:28). Most likely, Isaac was in his late teens or early twenties when his father took him to be sacrificed on Mount Moriah, especially since the son was able to carry the wood by himself up to the appointed place.

B. Anticipating God's Provision: vss. 6b-8

As the two of them went on together, Isaac spoke up and said to his father Abraham, "Father?" "Yes, my son?" Abraham replied. "The fire and wood are here," Isaac said, "but where is the lamb for the burnt offering?" Abraham answered, "God himself will provide the lamb for the burnt offering, my son." And the two of them went on together.

Perhaps at first there was silence as Abraham and his beloved son made their way to the appointed place (Gen. 22:6). But then Isaac broke the silence by commenting on the one item that was missing to complete the intended sacrifice. He asked his father about the "lamb" (vs. 7) that was traditionally used for a "burnt offering." Abraham explained to Isaac that God would provide the lamb. Of course, the patriarch did not know how the Lord would do this, only that somehow He would supply the necessary substitute.

For the moment, Abraham's confident response must have encouraged his son as they made the rest of the journey together (vs. 8). Both of them knew that their trust in God would not be disappointed. Their attention was focused on the Lord's character, especially the truth that He is the great provider, even when His people seem to have no hope. Centuries later, Jesus told a group of His Jewish contemporaries that Abraham rejoiced as he looked forward to the time of the Messiah's coming (John 8:56). Through the patriarch, the Father gave the world an early glimpse into what He would one day do through His Son, who is the "Lamb of God" (1:29, 36).

C. Obeying God Unconditionally: vss. 9-10

When they reached the place God had told him about, Abraham built an altar there and arranged the wood on it. He bound his son Isaac and laid him on the altar, on top of the wood. Then he reached out his hand and took the knife to slay his son.

Abraham knew about no other option but to proceed with the sacrifice of his son. When the two came to the divinely designated spot, the patriarch built a crude altar out of uncut rocks and dirt. Then, after Abraham arranged the wood on the altar, he tied up Isaac, his son, and placed him on top of the wood (Gen. 22:9). Isaac's heart must have skipped a beat or two as he saw his father take the knife in his hand to slaughter his son (vs. 10). Isaac certainly was able to know what was happening. From all appearances, he quietly and willingly went along with the sacrifice. His obedience to his father as he prepared the offering reveals Isaac's confidence in God. Like Isaac's father, the son believed that the Lord's promises would be fulfilled through him, regardless of what happened. Unquestionably, this was Isaac's finest hour.

D. Affirming Abraham's Commitment: vss. 11-12

But the angel of the LORD called out to him from heaven, "Abraham! Abraham!" "Here I am," he replied. "Do not lay a hand on the boy," he said. "Do not do anything to him. Now I know that you fear God, because you have not withheld from me your son, your only son."

The "angel of the LORD" (Gen. 22:11) is distinct from other angels in the Old Testament. In some passages, a difference cannot be made between the angel of the Lord and the Lord Himself (see Gen. 16:7-13; 21:17; 22:11-18; 31:11-13; 48:15-16; Exod. 3:2-10; Judg. 2:1-3; 6:12-14; 13:21-22). The worship of angels is forbidden in Scripture (see Rev. 22:8-9), but the angel of the Lord accepted worship (see Josh. 5:13–6:2). Because of these characteristics, many believe that the appearances of the angel of the Lord were theophanies, that is, manifestations of God in visible form. Since the angel of the Lord seems never to have appeared after the Incarnation, some think this special messenger of God was the preincarnate Messiah.

With no time to spare, the Lord's angel called down from heaven to stop Abraham from slaying his son. The heavenly emissary referred to the patriarch twice by name to signal the urgency of the situation, and Abraham answered as the Lord's humble, willing servant (Gen. 22:11). Abraham had made the decision to go through with the sacrifice in obedience to God. Because the patriarch had passed the divinely appointed test, it was unnecessary for him to actually slaughter Isaac (vs. 12). Abraham's obedience did not take God by surprise, but the test was necessary to mature and develop the patriarch's spiritual character. He had shown that he genuinely feared the Lord. In the Old Testament, to fear God meant to wholeheartedly revere Him and follow Him in absolute obedience (see Gen. 20:11; 42:18; Job 1:1; Isa. 11:2). The Lord's test of Abraham also provided a way for God to show the world how He would make salvation possible through the patriarch's greatest descendant, the Lord Jesus, who gave His life on the cross as a "ransom for many" (Mark 10:45).

E. Substituting a Ram for Isaac: vss. 13-14

Abraham looked up and there in a thicket he saw a ram caught by its horns. He went over and took the ram and sacrificed it as a burnt offering instead of his son. So Abraham called that place The Lord Will Provide. And to this day it is said, "On the mountain of the Lord it will be provided."

After the Lord's angel told Abraham to stop the sacrifice, he saw a ram caught by its horns in a nearby thicket. Consequently, the patriarch offered the ram on the altar in place of Isaac (Gen. 22:13). Before the sacrifice, Abraham promised his son that God would provide an animal for the offering (see vs. 8). And the patriarch was correct. So afterward, he called the place of the sacrifice *Yahweh-Yireh*, meaning "The Lord Will Provide" (vs. 14). This statement foreshadowed what would later come, when the Father provided His Son as a sacrifice for our sins. Just as the ram took the place of Isaac, the Lord Jesus took our place on the cross. And because of that, our sins can be forgiven, and we can be declared righteous by the Father (see 2 Cor. 5:21).

Abraham's obedience demonstrated his confidence in God's covenant promises. The Lord's angel again called to the patriarch from heaven with a resounding confirmation of those promises (vss. 15-16). The emissary declared that numerous descendants would come from the patriarch, that they would one day conquer their enemies, and that through these descendants God's blessing would extend to the entire world (vss. 17-18). Clearly, the Lord was pleased with Abraham's obedience. With his son safe and with the reaffirmation of the covenant ringing in his ears, the patriarch must have been filled with joy as he reunited with his servants and returned to Beersheba (vs. 19).

The Lord may be leading us along paths that seem illogical to us. With our limited perspective, we cannot see God's purpose in what He sends our way any more than Abraham could understand why God would summon him to sacrifice his son. Nevertheless, we can trust the Lord completely, for we know He cares for us. And someday we will be able to see all He has accomplished in our lives. This truth is found in 1 Corinthians 13:12. Paul said that presently believers knew God only partially. Yet the apostle looked forward to a time when the redeemed would know God fully.

Discussion Questions

1. Why do you think God decided to test Abraham?
2. If you were Abraham, how do you think you would have responded to God?
3. What emotions do you think Isaac felt as he and his father journeyed to the designated spot?
4. How does the faith of Abraham shine through in his response to God's command concerning Isaac?
5. Why is it sometimes difficult for believers to trust God through life's trials?

Contemporary Application

God's decision to test Abraham is the underlying reason for an episode in the patriarch's life that otherwise seems illogical and even cruel. Abraham was told to take his only son to be offered on an altar. At first, the patriarch had no idea the Lord was going to stop him. Why would Abraham heed God's directive? And why would the Lord command him to sacrifice Isaac?

God may never ask of us what He asked of Abraham. Even so, as His followers we will endure testing of some kind. The trials we go through in life also may seem illogical and unfair. Like Job, we may be overwhelmed by everything happening at once—for example, a parent dies, a loved one abandons us, and a money crisis occurs, all in a few months.

It is natural to wonder why God allows us to undergo such times of testing. From Deuteronomy 13:3, we learn that He may want to separate us from other things that have taken His place in our lives, such as money, a career, our home, or even our family. Jesus emphasized this truth in Matthew 22:37, when He urged us to love God with every aspect of our being. We also discover from James 1:3-4 that the more hardships we endure, the stronger we may become and the more we may be able to help out others in their times of distress.

Often, the *why* of our testing is less important than how we react to it. Our response should be similar to the obedient manner in which Abraham dealt with his test from God. The patriarch simply trusted that whatever the Lord commanded was the right thing to do, no matter what. Also, Abraham was convinced that God would provide for him, regardless of what occurred.

Both Abraham and Isaac knew that because they trusted God, they would not be disappointed. Trusting the Lord is always the wisest thing we can do, even when we don't understand what is happening to us or why. We can respond to God in this way, for we know that He is the eternal light in the world of darkness that surrounds us.

According to the Promise

Scripture

Background Scripture: *Luke 1:26-56; Galatians 3:6-18*
Scripture Lesson: *Luke 1:46-55*
Key Verse: *Mary said: "My soul glorifies the Lord and my spirit rejoices in God my Savior."* Luke 1:46-47.
Scripture Lesson for Children: *Luke 2:1-16*
Key Verse for Children: *The angel said to them, "Do not be afraid. I bring you good news of great joy that will be for all the people."* Luke 2:10.

Lesson Aim

To emphasize the value of glorifying the Lord and rejoicing in Him.

Lesson Setting

Time: About 6–5 B.C.
Place: The hill country of Judea

Lesson Outline

According to the Promise

    I. The Mercy and Might of the Lord: Luke 1:46-50
        A. *The Response of Joy: vss. 46-47*
        B. *The Reason for Joy: vss. 48-50*
   II. The Faithfulness and Justice of the Lord: Luke 1:51-55
        A. *The Reversal for Fortunes: vss. 51-53*
        B. *The Divine Pledge to Be Merciful: vss. 54-55*

Introduction for Adults

Topic: *Celebrating Promises Fulfilled*

Often when we pray, our main intent is to do nothing else but thank and praise God for honoring His promises to us. But then we find ourselves distracted by a flood of anxious requests for His help. In those moments, it seems virtually impossible to refrain from asking God for things.

Yes, the Lord wants us to bring our requests to Him in prayer. Nevertheless, our petitions should be made within the context of praise (Phil. 4:6). We can thank the Father for His grace, goodness, and mercy, especially in sending His Son. These are the things that Mary praised God for in her prayer (Luke 1:46-55).

The next time you find yourself filled with turmoil, why not take a few moments to worship God? As you praise Him, He will calm your spirit and renew your strength. I can think of no better way to handle the stresses of life!

Introduction for Youth

Topic: *A Timeless Promise*

The Lord's promise to send the Messiah to Israel was fulfilled in the life of Mary. When she visited Elizabeth, she was met with words of praise for being chosen to be the mother of the Lord. In response, Mary proclaimed her own privileged role, then declared how her son Jesus would humble the proud and mighty while bringing mercy to God's people.

None of us can know exactly how Mary felt, but all of us can express a similar attitude toward God for faithfully keeping His promises. Put differently, as followers of Jesus Christ, we can gladly exalt the Father in our hearts and before others because He fulfills what He has pledged to do through His Son.

Concepts for Children

Topic: *The Joy of Jesus' Birth*

1. An angel named Gabriel told Mary that she would give birth to Jesus.
2. Mary visited Elizabeth and told her the good news.
3. Joseph and Mary traveled to Bethlehem to be registered for a census.
4. Mary gave birth to Jesus and placed Him in a manger.
5. Mary praised God for the miracle in her life, and so can we.

Lesson Commentary

I. THE MERCY AND MIGHT OF THE LORD: LUKE 1:46-50

A. The Response of Joy: vss. 46-47

And Mary said: "My soul glorifies the Lord and my spirit rejoices in God my Savior."

For several hundred years, God's voice through the prophets had been silent in Israel. The Roman army had nearly crushed the Jews' hopes that the promised Messiah would come to deliver them. Had God forgotten His people? The Jews enjoyed limited political and religious freedom at this time. Roman administrators had appointed the civil and religious leaders of Judea. When small bands of zealots tried unsuccessfully to fight against foreign occupation, the Roman military quickly and brutally subdued their revolts. The average Jew found few reasons to be optimistic about the future.

Nonetheless, when the fullness of time came, God sent the angel Gabriel to a young woman in Nazareth (Luke 1:26). This small town was 16 miles west of the southern end of the Sea of Galilee. Located near a major trade route, the village was frequently visited by Roman soldiers and Gentile merchants. Mary was betrothed to a man who was descended from King David, the family from which the prophets had said the Messiah would come (vs. 27). For Jewish women at this time, betrothal could occur as early as 12 years old (though Mary was probably older than this), and the betrothal period normally lasted for about a year.

We find little information about Joseph in the Gospels, though we do know that he was a descendant of David, the husband of Mary, and the legal guardian of Jesus. By trade, Joseph was a carpenter (Matt. 13:55). We can deduce from Scripture that Joseph possessed great integrity and firm moral conviction (1:19). Regardless of what God desired of him, Joseph was willing to obey (1:24; 2:14, 21). Because he was a devout Jew, Joseph no doubt made sure Jesus received good spiritual training during His adolescent years in Nazareth (Luke 2:39-40, 51-52). Joseph is last mentioned when Jesus was 12 years old (vss. 42-48). Many scholars think Joseph had died by the time Jesus entered His public ministry (4:14-15).

When Gabriel appeared to Mary, the angel brought her good news. Indeed, the angel greeted Mary with a term that is used only one other place in the New Testament. In Luke 1:28, it is translated as "highly favored." The phrase implies that the Lord had singled Mary out for a special blessing. Paul used the same word in Ephesians 1:6, where believers are told that God loved us in Christ "to the praise of his glorious grace, which he has freely given us." From this we see that to be highly favored conveys more than just being shown grace. It is to have grace lavished upon us.

Mary's understanding of God's grace explains why she was taken aback at Gabriel's greeting. Mary's "why me?" kind of response reflected humility (Luke 1:29, 48), but also surprise. In fact, Mary seemed more startled by the angel's grace-greeting than his appearance. Mary didn't consider herself particularly special, but God did. Indeed, that's the surprise of grace. And the Lord is still surprising people with His grace. The Father has told us in His Word that even though we're sinners and undeserving of His grace, we are nonetheless highly favored in the Son.

Through Mary, God would bestow His grace upon many. Gabriel's salutation, however, was troubling to Mary. Indeed, the presence of the angel was strange and perplexing. Naturally Mary was thrown into turmoil (vs. 29). What could this mean? Why had the angel visited her? It was vital for God to send Gabriel to speak with Mary before she became pregnant because she was a virgin and her pregnancy would cause her distress and shame. In addition, she would have no idea who this child was. Gabriel came to prevent any fears and anxieties that Mary might otherwise have felt. The angel also came so that the young woman could prepare for this great event.

Before Gabriel continued his message, he calmed Mary's fears. He had come to bring her good news, not to alarm her (vs. 30). The angel then told Mary how God was to bless her. She would give birth to a Son and was to call Him "Jesus" (vs. 31). In Jewish culture, a child's name was supposed to indicate the essence of his or her personality. *Jesus* is the Greek form of the Hebrew name *Joshua*, and emphasizes the deliverance of the Lord. Mary's Son would save people from sin and death (Matt. 1:21).

The prophet Isaiah had promised that a virgin would conceive and bear a son (Isa. 7:14). Mary's Son would be that child, this miracle being possible because He would also be the "Son of the Most High" (Luke 1:32). Furthermore, He would fulfill what Isaiah had prophesied about the one who would rule on David's throne (Isa. 9:6-7). God had promised David that his kingdom would be established forever (2 Sam. 7:16). In fact, David's descendants reigned over Judah until the Exile (586 B.C.). The angel's reference to the "throne of his father David" (Luke 1:32) meant that God would now restore the broken line of David's succession. Indeed, Gabriel revealed to Mary that her Son would fulfill that promise, reigning forever (vs. 33).

Mary asked the obvious question. How could she, who had not been physically intimate with any man, become pregnant (vs. 34)? While Mary's question provides Scripture's best verification for the virgin conception of Jesus, Mary's words also show a strong and thinking mind. She was confident enough in her relationship with God to ask appropriate questions. Incidentally, both Mary and Zechariah asked Gabriel how God could do the seemingly impossible. The difference in their queries is that Mary asked how it was possible, while Zechariah (evidently in doubt) asked, "How can I be sure of this?" (vs. 18). Zechariah asked for a sign, which Gabriel granted in the form of Zechariah's muteness.

Gabriel probably anticipated Mary's confusion, for he was prepared to explain God's message to her. The angel said Jesus would need no man to father Him, for the Spirit of God would come upon Mary (vs. 35). In the Old Testament, the

Hebrew counterpart to "overshadow" is the episodes in which the cloud covered the tabernacle when the glory of God descended upon it (for example, Exod. 40:34-35). When the Holy Spirit later came upon Mary, she became the instrument of Jesus' incarnation. Being the "Son of God," Jesus is holy, not because He was dedicated to God, but because He is God.

Although Mary had not asked Gabriel for a sign, he pointed toward evidence that God's power was already at work. He mentioned Mary's relative Elizabeth, who had long been barren but was now pregnant (Luke 1:36). The angel assured Mary that what he said to her would come to pass, for with God nothing is impossible (vs. 37). Human promises sometimes fail, especially when people lack the resources or inclination to keep them. God, however, always fulfills His word. He always comes through. In this regard, Isaiah noted, "Surely the arm of the LORD is not too short to save" (Isa. 59:1).

Mary's response to Gabriel perhaps helps explain why God had chosen her. Many disturbing questions may have been running through her mind: *Will Joseph believe the unimaginable? What will my friends and neighbors think when they learn I am pregnant? Will I be branded the worst of sinners, rather than God's chosen instrument?* Nevertheless, Mary did not argue with the angel. Instead, she humbly submitted to God when He gave her a responsibility (Luke 1:38). Scripture describes faith as "being sure of what we hope for and certain of what we do not see" (Heb. 11:1). Mary had such faith. Though she did not fully understand Gabriel's message, she accepted God's promise. Faith says, "I will believe the 'impossible' as fact because the Lord says so." We put our faith into action when we obey God in this way.

After the angel departed, Mary hurried to visit Elizabeth at her home in the hill country of Judea (Luke 1:39-45). In the song Mary uttered while there (traditionally known as the Magnificat), she rejoiced in her privilege of serving God's purposes. Mary began by exalting or praising the Lord (vs. 46). His greatness was evident in providing salvation for all who put their trust in His Son (vs. 47), the suffering Servant of Isaiah 53. God's glory was also seen in choosing a humble young woman named Mary to give birth to the Christ child.

B. The Reason for Joy: vss. 48-50

"For he has been mindful of the humble state of his servant. From now on all generations will call me blessed, for the Mighty One has done great things for me—holy is his name. His mercy extends to those who fear him, from generation to generation."

Mary most likely belonged to the tribe of Judah, and possibly was herself a descendant of David (Matt. 1:1-16; Luke 1:32). We see much of Jesus' early life through Mary's eyes, as she treasured all sorts of things that happened to Him and pondered in her heart what they might mean (Luke 2:19, 51). This information, unique to Luke, has led some to conclude that Mary was one of the eyewitnesses Luke interviewed when he gathered material for his Gospel (1:2). Mary was also an eyewitness to Jesus' first miracle—the turning of water into wine at the wedding feast in Cana of Galilee (John 2:1-11). On another occasion, Mary and Jesus' brothers wished to see Him while He was teaching the multitudes (Luke 8:19). When Jesus was crucified, Mary stood near the cross. It was then that Jesus gave her over to the care of John (John 19:25-27). After Jesus' resurrection, Mary was in the upper room along with the rest of the disciples as they awaited the coming of the Holy Spirit (Acts 1:14).

In connection with Mary, the Greek noun rendered "servant" (Luke 1:48) comes from a verb that means "to serve as a slave." The underlying idea is to be subject to the will of another. Such a concept would have been objectionable in Greek thought. It was commonly taught that achieving one's potential for excellence was the foremost duty of every person. Such a self-centered mindset is far removed from Mary's attitude. She saw herself as the Lord's humble servant. Rather than loathe the idea, she rejoiced in the fact that God had visited her with His grace. Mary was overjoyed to serve the Lord in such a significant way. Mary's submissive disposition mirrors that of God's Son. He came to serve others, not to be served by them (see Matt. 20:28; Mark 10:45). The Son was so committed to the will of the Father that the Son died a criminal's death on the cross so that the lost might be saved (see Phil. 2:5-8). Here we see that serving is the highway to greatness and the key to a transformed value system.

Despite Mary's status in Jewish society as a lowly servant girl, generations to come would call her "blessed," for God had manifested His grace on her. "Blessed" describes the joy experienced by those whom God favors, a joy shared with and by others. There is an appropriate appreciation for Mary, because what God did through her is totally unique. Nevertheless, some traditions have moved beyond admiring her to worshiping her. For some, Mary is seen as equal with Jesus, and they render a devotion to her that should be reserved only for the Savior. Mary herself would have deflected such veneration. After all, she was "humble" and rejoiced not in her own status but in "God my Savior" (vs. 47).

Mary referred to the Lord as being mighty and holy (vs. 49). He alone is the sovereign Ruler of the universe and absolutely set apart from sin. Yet, despite God's exalted status, He willingly had done and would do great things for Mary (especially through her Son). In particular, the Messiah would make the mercy of the Lord available to all who repent and believe. Mary alluded to this truth when she declared that God showers His mercy from one generation to the next on those who fear Him (vs. 50). This refers to those who show God a reverential respect for His sovereignty.

There are strong literary and thematic parallels between Mary's song and Hannah's ode of praise, which is recorded in 1 Samuel 2:1-10. For instance, Mary, like Hannah, extolled God's greatness. Also, both women are called God's servants (see 1:11), which draws attention to their availability to do the Lord's will. Mary's situation was much different from Hannah's. While Hannah sang for joy after her stigma of barrenness was gone, Mary sang for joy in the face of possible (though undeserved) alienation and shame. Mary chose not to focus on what others might think of her, but on what God thought of her and what she knew of Him.

II. THE FAITHFULNESS AND JUSTICE OF THE LORD: LUKE 1:51-55

A. The Reversal for Fortunes: vss. 51-53

"He has performed mighty deeds with his arm; he has scattered those who are proud in their inmost thoughts. He has brought down rulers from their thrones but has lifted up the humble. He has filled the hungry with good things but has sent the rich away empty."

Mary represents people of faith throughout history who have looked to the Lord as their ultimate source of deliverance. Such hope is not in vain, for God has manifested power with His mighty arm. By way of example, the Lord is known for dispersing the proud because of the haughty imaginations they entertain in their heart (Luke 1:51). Mary was rebuking the sheer arrogance of the proud, who thought that power was their sovereign right. The Lord had toppled such authoritative rulers from their thrones and exalted those of lowly or humble position (vs. 52).

The contrast between the mighty and the lowly dominates the literary landscape of Luke's Gospel. The broader truth is that God cares for those whom the powerful ignore. Verse 53 continues this emphasis by declaring that God has satisfied the hungry with good things. Meanwhile, He has sent the rich away with empty hands. "Good things" refers not merely to material abundance, but to blessings that come from knowing God.

B. The Divine Pledge to Be Merciful: vss. 54-55

"He has helped his servant Israel, remembering to be merciful to Abraham and his descendants forever, even as he said to our fathers."

The Lord's mercy extended even to the nation and people of Israel. They were the recipients of His help and the objects of His unfailing love (Luke 1:54). Mary's song emphasizes that Israel had a special role in serving the Lord and making Him known to the world. This truth is reinforced in verse 55, where Mary reiterated God's promise to Abraham and his descendants (see Gen. 22:16-18). The Lord would remain forever true to His pledge to bless His chosen people. Now, through the covenant with Abraham, God's promises and mercy would extend to all peoples in all generations, especially through faith in the Messiah. Luke 1:56 reveals that Mary remained with Elizabeth for about three months before returning to her hometown of Nazareth.

Discussion Questions

1. What prompted Mary to lift up the Lord in praise?
2. Why is it important for us to affirm that God is our Savior?
3. In what ways had God blessed Mary?
4. How did Mary see the Lord dealing with the strong and the weak?
5. How is it possible for us to praise God in all things?

Contemporary Application

My wife and I were 36 when we learned that we would be parents. After a time of extended waiting to finally have a child of our own, the confirmation that a baby was coming was probably the most wonderful news either of us had ever received. We certainly felt that God had exceedingly blessed us.

This marvelous good news was not the only occasion for celebration. When my wife's dear friend passed away a few years ago, it could have been a time of great sorrow. She was certainly one of the sweetest persons I have known. As a practicing physician, she had brought healing to many lives. Yet, her loving and warm spirit had enriched the lives of far more.

Though this woman died in her early 40s, her family and friends celebrated her farewell into the presence of Christ because she had been so close to Him. We all could rejoice because, as James 1:2 says, we should consider it nothing but joy when we fall into various trials. The reason is that God is making us complete in Him (see vss. 3-4). That is also why we can glorify the Lord and rejoice in Him regardless of the situations we are facing.

God Watches over Joseph

Scripture

Background Scripture: *Genesis 39:1-23*
Scripture Lesson: *Genesis 39:7-21*
Key Verse: *"How then could I do such a wicked thing and
sin against God?"* Genesis 39:9.
Scripture Lesson for Children: *Genesis 39:7-21*
Key Verse for Children: *The* LORD *was with him; he showed
him kindness.* Genesis 39:21.

Lesson Aim

To encourage unwavering commitment to the Lord,
regardless of the consequences.

Lesson Setting

Time: About 1898 B.C.
Place: Egypt

Lesson Outline

God Watches over Joseph

  I. Joseph's Sterling Character: Genesis 39:7-10
     A. *Potiphar's Wife Tempts Joseph: vs. 7*
     B. *Joseph Refuses to Morally Compromise: vss. 8-10*
 II. Joseph's Unjust Imprisonment: Genesis 39:11-21
     A. *The Trap Is Set: vss. 11-12*
     B. *The False Accusation Is Made: vss. 13-15*
     C. *The Blatant Charge Is Repeated: vss. 16-18*
     D. *The Wrongful Imprisonment Is Enforced:
        vss. 19-20a*
     E. *The Lord Shows Kindness to Joseph: vss. 20b-21*

Introduction for Adults

Topic: *A Life of Integrity*

Adults in your class probably consider themselves to be people of integrity. It would be extremely difficult for them not to conform to the laws and regulations of society. They may fudge here and there, such as driving five miles over the speed limit, but they wouldn't flagrantly disregard the laws of the land, such as driving through red lights.

At times, however, your students are faced with situations in which they must obey God or give in to an authority that challenges their commitment to the Lord. When that occurs, they need to understand that they should set aside their desire to be "good" citizens, "good" employees, "good" adult children, or even "good" spouses if they are to be obedient children of God. This is neither easy nor pleasant, but with God's help it can be done. Joseph's life is proof of that.

Introduction for Youth

Topic: *No Means No!*

There are times when saved teens, like Joseph, will feel pressure from peers to do what is wrong. If they say *no* to the temptation, they run the risk of being rejected, shunned, or ostracized. But if they yield to the enticement, they compromise their faith and undermine their witness for the Savior.

Understandably, these dire prospects can easily squelch the enthusiasm youth have for the things of Christ. Praying with the teens in your class is one way to address this issue. Another way is to invite them to share their perspective on the challenges they face in living for Jesus. Finally, you can remind your students of the presence and power of the Spirit to work through them to impact their peers for the Savior.

Concepts for Children

Topic: *A Faithful Young Man*

1. Potiphar's wife tried to get Joseph to do things that were wrong.
2. Joseph was brave in obeying God.
3. Potiphar had Joseph thrown into prison.
4. God was with Joseph while he was in prison.
5. God will give us the courage to do what is right.

Lesson Commentary

I. JOSEPH'S STERLING CHARACTER: GENESIS 39:7-10

A. Potiphar's Wife Tempts Joseph: vs. 7

And after a while his master's wife took notice of Joseph and said, "Come to bed with me!"

Most of the narrative in the last 14 chapters of Genesis is devoted to the life of Joseph. The faith this son of Jacob showed in the midst of distressing circumstances has encouraged believers through the centuries. The first 11 verses of chapter 37 explain the friction that developed between the teenage Joseph and other members of his family. First, we learn that Joseph, at the age of 17, told on his brothers. They had done something they shouldn't have while away from home tending the flocks. Joseph saw the wrongdoing and let Jacob know about it.

Though the biblical text does not tell us so, the brothers undoubtedly had hard feelings toward Joseph because of his reporting on them. Jacob increased the friction between the older brothers and Joseph by showing preference for Joseph. Jacob loved Joseph more because he was born to Jacob in his old age. As a matter of fact, Joseph was his youngest son, next to Benjamin. Jacob may also have preferred Joseph because Joseph was the first son of Jacob's favorite wife, Rachel. Jacob disclosed his favoritism by giving Joseph a special outer garment. As Joseph wore the robe, it must have become a constant irritation to the other brothers. It reminded them that their father loved Joseph best.

Next, we read about two dreams. In the ancient world, dreams were widely believed to predict the future. This belief was right in the case of Joseph's dreams. God sent the dreams to show the superior blessings He would give Joseph. In the first dream, Joseph saw himself and his brothers binding sheaves of grain in the field. This was a normal harvest scene. But suddenly, his brothers' sheaves bowed down to Joseph's sheaf. When Joseph told his brothers about his dream, the brothers correctly interpreted it to mean that one day they would bow down to Joseph. This literally happened when Joseph became a ruler in Egypt. Of course, the brothers did not like the idea of serving their younger brother. Because of the dream, the brothers' hatred of Joseph rose a notch higher.

In Joseph's second dream, he saw the sun, moon, and eleven stars bow down to him. This time Joseph described the dream to his father as well as to his brothers. Now even Joseph's indulgent father was upset with Joseph. Jacob accurately interpreted the dream to mean that he and his wife Leah (Joseph's mother, Rachel, had died by this time), and his sons would all bow down to Joseph. This dream, too, referred to the future when Joseph would be a ruler in Egypt. The biblical text says that Jacob did not forget his son's dreams. But the next event in Joseph's life made their fulfillment seem impossible.

Verses 12-36 recount how Joseph's brothers sold him into slavery in Egypt. Shortly after Joseph's dreams, most of Jacob's sons took his flocks many miles away to the north. A desire to get away from Joseph may have been one reason why they traveled so far away from their home in the Valley of Hebron. But if so, it did no good, for Jacob sent Joseph after them to find out how they were doing. Neither the son nor the father could have known that more than 20 years would pass before they laid eyes on each other again. Joseph caught up with his brothers near Dothan. When they saw Joseph approach, the brothers formed a plan to kill him and blame his death on a wild animal. Uncontrolled jealousy and hatred had brought them to such an intention.

The oldest brother, Reuben, offered an alternative to the plan of immediately killing Joseph. Reuben suggested his siblings put Joseph in a nearby cistern—a stone-lined hole in the ground used to store water. At that moment, the cistern was empty. The brothers adopted the plan. But before they put Joseph in the pit, they took from him the robe that had so inflamed their jealousy. At dinnertime, Judah suggested that the brothers sell Joseph to some Midianite merchants who were passing by their camp. As he pointed out, that way they could avoid the sin fratricide (brother killing) and make some money at the same time. The brothers liked this idea.

Reuben was not present when his brothers sold Joseph. So, when Reuben got back, Joseph was gone. Since it was too late to help Joseph, Reuben went along with the deception. The siblings dipped Joseph's robe in goat's blood and, when they returned home, showed it to their father. They knew full well that Jacob would interpret the bloodied robe to mean that Joseph had been killed by a wild beast. The father, concluding that his favorite son was dead, went into mourning. But of course, Joseph was not dead. He was in Egypt, where the Midianites resold him. Far from home, Joseph found himself the slave of Pharaoh's "captain of the guard" (vs. 36). This title perhaps means that Potiphar, as a high-ranking official in the Egyptian royal court, was in charge of the soldiers who guarded Pharaoh's jail and carried out executions as ordered.

Chapter 39 resumes the narrative concerning Joseph. Once Joseph became the slave of Potiphar, the quality of the young Hebrew's character began to show itself (vs. 1). He did not wallow in self-pity, but energetically carried out the tasks set before him. Verse 2 emphasizes that the Lord was with Joseph, as seen in the success he enjoyed while living in the household of his "Egyptian master." Even though Joseph was separated from everyone and everything familiar to him, still God was with him. Therefore, Joseph's sadness did not turn into despair. He responded positively to the turn of events in his life, and God blessed his work (see Acts 7:9-10).

Potiphar, as an experienced leader, quickly noticed Joseph's abilities (Gen. 39:3). So Potiphar promoted Joseph from common house servant to personal attendant, and then to steward of the entire household (vs. 4). In each position Joseph undertook, he experienced God's blessing (vs. 5). Soon Joseph had Potiphar's complete confidence. Joseph ran everything in the house without any supervision (vs. 6). Joseph's disposition reflects what Paul urged slaves: "Whatever you do, work at it with all your heart, as working for the Lord, not for men" (Col. 3:23). In short, Joseph demonstrated the value of that biblical principle long before Paul was born. Joseph gave himself wholeheartedly to his tasks.

Eventually, though, Joseph's smooth sailing became turbulent. Like his mother, Joseph was well built and good looking (see Gen. 29:17). He was probably in his late teens when he came into the service of Potiphar. As the young Hebrew grew into manhood, his physical attributes caught the eye of Potiphar's wife. And it was not long before she began to make bold advances toward Joseph (39:7). The narrative surrounding the way in which Joseph handled this temptation possibly is one of the reasons for the strong admonitions in Proverbs 5 through 7 about the adulterous woman who tries to seduce young men in a brazen manner.

B. Joseph Refuses to Morally Compromise: vss. 8-10

But he refused. "With me in charge," he told her, "my master does not concern himself with anything in the house; everything he owns he has entrusted to my care. No one is greater in this house than I am. My master has withheld nothing from me except you, because you are his wife. How then could I do such a wicked thing and sin against God?" And though she spoke to Joseph day after day, he refused to go to bed with her or even be with her.

The typical house in ancient Egypt had a front entrance, a chamber used for both living and sleeping, and a storeroom in the back portion of the structure. Evidently, Potiphar's wife lounged on her bed well into the day. She may have strategically located herself in alluring attire to catch the attention of Joseph, openly flirting with him (perhaps out of boredom), and thereby seducing him. Thankfully, despite the efforts of Potiphar's wife, the young Hebrew slave refused to morally compromise (Gen. 39:8).

Joseph cited two reasons for his refusal. First, adultery would be unfair to the man who had trusted him. After all, Joseph noted that no other servant had been given greater authority. Though Joseph was only a slave, he did not want to violate the confidence of his master. Second, since Potiphar had not kept back anything from Joseph except his master's wife, it would be unthinkable for Joseph to act in such an immoral way and thereby "sin against God" (vs. 9; see Ps. 51:4). While the law of Moses had not yet been written, Joseph recognized the wrongness of adultery.

Joseph could easily have rationalized giving in to the temptation. After all, he was far from home. Who would know? Also, God had allowed the young Hebrew to become a slave in Egypt. So why should Joseph honor God? Moreover, Potiphar's wife was in a position to either help or hinder Joseph's career. Conventional thinking might suggest that it was foolish for Joseph to oppose her. None of these rationalizations, though, were sufficient to get Joseph to give in to the woman's seductions (Gen. 39:10). That's because he had a vital personal relationship with

God. Also, it was out of that relationship that Joseph had developed a clear sense of right and wrong. Thus, when temptation sprang upon him, he was ready with reasons why it would be wrong for him to yield to the enticement.

II. JOSEPH'S UNJUST IMPRISONMENT: GENESIS 39:11-21

A. The Trap Is Set: vss. 11-12

One day he went into the house to attend to his duties, and none of the household servants was inside. She caught him by his cloak and said, "Come to bed with me!" But he left his cloak in her hand and ran out of the house.

Despite Joseph's principled stance, it did not deter Potiphar's wife from continuing to pressure the young Hebrew to give in to her advances. Moreover, as they lived in the same home, Joseph could not avoid Potiphar's wife forever. And indeed, one day Joseph found himself alone with her in the house while doing his work. At the time, there were no other household servants present (Gen. 39:11). Potiphar's wife quickly capitalized on the situation. She grabbed Joseph by the cloak and begged him once more to be physically intimate with her. By this time, Joseph had given up trying to reason with Potiphar's wife. Instead of arguing with her, Joseph slipped from her grasp and ran outside, leaving the outer garment in her hands (vs. 12).

B. The False Accusation Is Made: vss. 13-15

When she saw that he had left his cloak in her hand and had run out of the house, she called her household servants. "Look," she said to them, "this Hebrew has been brought to us to make sport of us! He came in here to sleep with me, but I screamed. When he heard me scream for help, he left his cloak beside me and ran out of the house."

The cloak in the hands of Potiphar's wife became the occasion for a deviant plan (Gen. 39:13). Evidently, she was deeply vexed with Joseph. Who was he, a slave, to deny her any pleasure? In retaliation, Potiphar's wife would see to it that Joseph was punished! Specifically, Potiphar's wife concocted a false accusation against the young Hebrew. Since Potiphar was not at home at the time, his wife screamed for help to attract any Egyptian servants within earshot. Perhaps with a tone of indignation, she declared to them that she had screamed because Joseph tried to rape her.

In the wife's accusation, she stressed Joseph's foreign origin and attempted to make the Egyptian slaves also feel humiliated by the Hebrew slave's alleged transgression (vs. 14). We don't know whether the other domestic servants were taken aback by Potiphar's wife nor how they felt about Joseph. But at least now they could serve as witnesses that their mistress had screamed and that when they had come running, she had been holding Joseph's outer garment (vs. 15).

C. The Blatant Charge Is Repeated: vss. 16-18

She kept his cloak beside her until his master came home. Then she told him this story: "That Hebrew slave you brought us came to me to make sport of me. But as soon as I screamed for help, he left his cloak beside me and ran out of the house."

Potiphar's wife had engineered a situation that was guaranteed to succeed. For instance, she had a cadre of sympathetic bystanders who could vouch for her story. Also, she held on to the material evidence—the cloak—until her husband came home (Gen. 39:16). When Potiphar arrived, his wife probably wasted no time to repeat her well-rehearsed testimony. She accused Potiphar of bringing a Hebrew slave into their home, which in turn gave him the opportunity to attempt a shameful act (vs. 17). The wife's statement also shifted the blame from herself to her husband. Indeed, the wife tried to make herself look heroic by claiming that she prevented the alleged attempt at rape from happening when she screamed for help. The implication is that this quick thinking on her part caused the Hebrew slave to panic, drop his outer garment, and flee outside (vs. 18).

D. The Wrongful Imprisonment Is Enforced: vss. 19-20a

When his master heard the story his wife told him, saying, "This is how your slave treated me," he burned with anger. Joseph's master took him and put him in prison, the place where the king's prisoners were confined.

The wife of Potiphar was masterful in twisting the facts to her fullest advantage. For added effect, she even called Joseph "your slave" (Gen. 39:19). The idea is that Potiphar bore full responsibility for the humiliating circumstance that now hung like a dark cloud over the entire Egyptian household. Potiphar's response was predictable. But it's unclear with whom he was more furious, his wife or Joseph. We can only guess how many other times the wife tried to manipulate the circumstances to her advantage, even if it meant casting her husband in the least favorable light. Perhaps he knew his wife well enough to have some doubts about her tale.

In any case, Potiphar decided to commit Joseph to the prison reserved for political prisoners (vs. 20). This possibly was the most comfortable detention center available. This raises the question as to why Potiphar didn't have Joseph executed for his alleged crime, as Potiphar easily could have done since it was a capital offense. One possibility is that he wanted to be lenient toward Joseph because of the Hebrew slave's excellent service in the past.

E. The Lord Shows Kindness to Joseph: vss. 20b-21

But while Joseph was there in the prison, the LORD was with him; he showed him kindness and granted him favor in the eyes of the prison warden.

While Joseph was in a relatively comfortable prison, his experience was by no means easy (Gen. 39:20). The injustice of his treatment must have wounded Joseph as much as it would anyone—and this is in addition to being betrayed by his own brothers. Yet, despite these horrific setbacks, Joseph did not despair. He remained faithful to God because God remained faithful to him. The Hebrew text of verse 21 can be literally rendered "and [the LORD] extended to him loyal love." God's steadfast mercy is evident in giving Joseph favor in the sight of the head jailer of the prison.

Discussion Questions

1. What circumstances led to Joseph being a slave in the household of Potiphar?
2. Why do you think Potiphar's wife would compromise their marriage by pressuring Joseph to lie with her?
3. What does Joseph's response to his enticement to sin say about his character?
4. How would you have felt if you faced the kinds of false charges Potiphar's wife brought against Joseph?
5. With whom do you think Potiphar was more furious, his wife or Joseph? Explain.

Contemporary Application

The issue of maintaining an unwavering commitment to God goes far beyond mere legal matters. Many "laws" are unwritten—cultural expectations, prevailing attitudes in society, pressure from peers, the influence of traditions, and so on. All these weigh heavily upon believers, who must choose between the ways of people and the ways of God. When the ways of people are morally neutral, there's no problem. But when they violate God's principles, a choice is required.

To choose for God in the face of popular opinion requires great courage and conviction. That is why we, like Joseph, need the indwelling power of the Spirit (see Gen. 41:38). And that is why we, like him, need to bathe our circumstances in prayer. We may never be placed in a prison for a crime we never committed, but every day we face other kinds of challenges to our faith. Also, every day we need the same devotion to God that motivated Joseph.

Overcoming challenges to our faith is a two-stage process. It begins with a clear understanding of God's will as revealed in Scripture and exemplified in the Lord Jesus. This understanding clarifies our purpose in this world so that we can recognize our God-given task in any situation. And we experience victory by drawing upon the Holy Spirit's enabling power to fulfill God's purpose for us regardless of the opposition we encounter.

Joseph Finds Favor

Scripture

Background Scripture: *Genesis 41:1-52*
Scripture Lesson: *Genesis 41:37-45, 50-52*
Key Verse: *Pharaoh asked them, "Can we find anyone like this man, one in whom is the spirit of God?"* Genesis 41:38.
Scripture Lesson for Children: *Genesis 41:37-45, 50-52*
Key Verse for Children: *Pharaoh said to Joseph, "I hereby put you in charge of the whole land of Egypt."*
Genesis 41:41.

Lesson Aim

To note that God's wisdom can enable us to help others.

Lesson Setting

Time: 1885 B.C.
Place: Egypt

Lesson Outline

Joseph Finds Favor
  I. Joseph's Rise to Power: Genesis 41:37-40
    A. *Pharaoh's Approval of Joseph's Plan: vs. 37*
    B. *Pharaoh's Selection of Joseph: vss. 38-40*
  II. Joseph's Oversight of Egypt:
    Genesis 41:41-45, 50-52
    A. *Pharaoh's Ratification of Joseph's Appointment:*
      vss. 41-43
    B. *Joseph's New Life as Pharaoh's Vice-Regent:*
      vss. 44-45
    C. *Joseph's New Family: vss. 50-52*

Introduction for Adults

Topic: *Real Success*

Isambard Brunel had a dream of building a great ship to sail from England to Australia. In 1857, he launched the *Great Eastern*. She was 693 feet long, five times the size of any ship afloat! With five gilded and mirrored salons and 800 cabins, the vessel was supposed to be a floating palace. While the predecessor of the modern ocean liner never made much money, she successfully laid the transatlantic cable that ushered in the age of modern instant communication.

Joseph's dreams were greater than Brunel's. Joseph's dreams were of God's power and activity in the adult Hebrew's life and the lives of all those in the world around him. By any measure, his life was characterized by real success. God is also able to unfold similar aspirations in our lives and empower us to be successful in our service to others.

Introduction for Youth

Topic: *From the Prison to the Palace*

Fe Wale, a Presbyterian Filipino pediatrician, directs the Marina Clinic outside of Dumaguete in the southern Philippines. At one point she was captured by rebels, who insisted that she perform the surgery required to remove a bullet from their leader. They refused to accept the fact that as a pediatrician, the last surgery she had done was in medical school years earlier. So with a prayer, some boiling water, and a makeshift operating table, she successfully performed the operation.

Today, Fe Wale's community health workers, wearing identifying T-shirts, are free to work unhampered in the rural areas where many other services have ceased because of the threat of rebel activity. For this saved pediatrician, it is an amazing dream come true. Joseph's rise to power from being a prisoner to the second-in-command in Egypt is even more astounding. God is also able to make our dreams of service for Him come to pass in His time and in His way.

Concepts for Children

Topic: *Faithfulness Is Rewarded*

1. Pharaoh wanted someone to help him solve a big problem.
2. Pharaoh asked Joseph for help because Joseph obeyed God.
3. Pharaoh made Joseph a very powerful person in Egypt.
4. As Joseph helped Pharaoh, Joseph remained faithful to God.
5. God wants us to remain faithful to Him as we help others.

Lesson Commentary

I. JOSEPH'S RISE TO POWER: GENESIS 41:37-40

A. Pharaoh's Approval of Joseph's Plan: vs. 37

The plan seemed good to Pharaoh and to all his officials.

After Joseph had an initial encounter with Pharaoh's cupbearer and baker, the cupbearer forgot about Joseph. Then, two more years passed when Pharaoh experienced his own dreams. In the first one, he found himself standing on the banks of the Nile River, the source of Egypt's prosperity and power. He saw seven ugly, gaunt cows devour seven fat, healthy-looking cows (Gen. 41:1-4). In Pharaoh's second dream, he saw seven heads of shriveled and withered grain swallow up seven heads of plump, well-formed grain (vss. 5-7). The next morning the Egyptian ruler summoned all his priests who were experienced with magic, divination, and soothsaying, but none of them could interpret his dreams (vs. 8).

The incident triggered the memory of Pharaoh's cupbearer, who recalled his own prior experience with Joseph (vss. 9-13). This prompted the ruler to order Joseph's immediate release from prison (see Ps. 105:20). After he had shaved and changed clothes, Joseph found himself standing before the most powerful man in the known world. Pharaoh's request was straightforward. He needed Joseph to interpret his troubling dreams. The young man stated that while he didn't have any innate ability to do this, God would supply the interpretation the ruler desperately desired (Gen. 41:14-16). Having this assurance, Pharaoh recounted his dreams (vss. 17-24).

We can only imagine how clearheaded the Egyptian ruler became as he focused his attention on the lowly, foreign prisoner appearing before him. Joseph explained that both dreams of Pharaoh had the same meaning. The God whom Joseph worshiped and served—despite his years of hardship and isolation—was using him to disclose to Pharaoh what the Lord would soon do (vs. 25). Joseph pointed out that the seven fat cows and the seven plump heads of grain both represented seven years of prosperity (vs. 26). In contrast, the seven gaunt, ugly cows and the seven withered heads of grain represented seven years of famine (vs. 27).

Joseph's reference to the "east wind" merits further comment. In the Middle East, a hot wind off the desert often shrivels and destroys crops in agricultural areas such as Israel and Egypt. In Israel, this wind is called the *sirocco* and regularly blows from the east, off the Arabian deserts, in late spring and early fall, with devastating effects (Jer. 4:11-12; Ezek. 19:10-12; Hos. 13:15). Egypt has a similar scorching wind, called the *khamsin*, that blows in from the deserts and wilts crops in the Nile River valley.

Through his explanation, Joseph clarified the significance of the symbolism in Pharaoh's two dreams. God gave the Hebrew the correct interpretation so that he in turn could make known to the powerful ruler what the Lord was about to do

(Gen. 41:28). In this regard, both dreams had identical messages. There would be seven years of abundance in the kingdom (vs. 29). Then, following the time of plenty, there would be seven years of terrible famine. In fact, it would be so widespread and horrific that all the prosperity would be forgotten and wiped out because of the devastating effects of the famine (vs. 30).

Joseph's announcement of a kingdom-wide famine posed a real threat to Egypt's dominance on the international scene. A brief episode of drought might be endured without much concern. But the disaster Joseph foretold would be so severe and prolonged that it could decimate the powerful nation situated along the Nile River (vs. 31). The Hebrew ex-prisoner noted that Pharaoh's experience of two versions of the same dream was God's way of signaling to the ruler that the matter was divinely decreed and would soon occur (vs. 32).

Because God was sure to act as He had declared through Joseph, the Hebrew urged Pharaoh to take immediate action. In particular, the Egyptian ruler was advised to find someone who was wise and discerning. Such an individual would be aware and informed as well as mature and experienced. This person would also exhibit keen insight and good judgment. Joseph recommended that this even-tempered and morally grounded overseer be placed in charge of a nationwide program (vs. 33). Next, Joseph recommended that Pharaoh appoint officials throughout the land to collect one-fifth of the produce harvested during the seven plentiful years (vs. 34).

The commissioners Joseph advised being appointed would have responsibility for gathering all the excess food and grain during the seven years of abundance to come. In turn, the officials—operating under the authority of Pharaoh—were to stockpile these supplies in the royal storehouses located in various cities throughout the realm (vs. 35). By adopting this strategy, Pharaoh would ensure that there would be enough food to eat when the seven years of famine came. To do otherwise would bring about widespread starvation, resulting in the eventual ruin of the nation. Joseph's proposed course of action was the only way for Egypt to survive the calamity (vs. 36). Not surprisingly, the advice Joseph gave made sense to Pharaoh and all his officials (vs. 37).

B. Pharaoh's Selection of Joseph: vss. 38-40

So Pharaoh asked them, "Can we find anyone like this man, one in whom is the spirit of God?" Then Pharaoh said to Joseph, "Since God has made all this known to you, there is no one so discerning and wise as you. You shall be in charge of my palace, and all my people are to submit to your orders. Only with respect to the throne will I be greater than you."

As the royal court deliberated over who should be appointed to oversee the entire operation, Pharaoh openly wondered whether they could find a better person than Joseph, a wise person in whom resided the spirit of God (Gen. 41:38). The ruler's rhetorical question expected a negative answer. Throughout the ancient Near East, kingship was believed to have been established by the pagan gods of the people. The monarch was viewed as representing and often embodying the authority of the local deity. Therefore, the inhabitants of a region believed a king ruled by divine right. Monarchs were also believed to have direct access to divine wisdom. Pharaoh's remark implied that Joseph displayed unparalleled foresight and prudence, which even exceeded that of the king.

Furthermore, throughout the ancient Near East, there were three distinct classes of wise men: enchanters, astrologers, and diviners. Enchanters were those who practiced conjuring and divination, the art of foretelling the future by signs. Astrologers were probably priests or magi who maintained the traditions of the native religion. Diviners, like enchanters, would interpret signs. In Joseph's day these signs took many forms, including dreams or the casting of lots. Some diviners examined the patterns found in animal organs or the remains in a cup after the liquid was poured out. Joseph distinguished himself from all these pseudo-wise men by receiving direct revelation from God about the future.

Joseph, of course, had spent a number of years in prison, which proved to be the watershed of his life. During that dark period, God humbled and matured him. The Lord also enabled him to acquire and refine his organizational and leadership skills. The former Hebrew prisoner came to see that God had a grander purpose for his hardships. The Lord permitted Joseph to be sold into slavery in Egypt to bring about the rescuing of many lives. This included those of his immediate family, through whom the blessings of the covenant would be transmitted to the world (see 45:5). Thus, despite the harm his siblings intended to cause, God's nobler intent was to bring about widespread good (see 50:20).

Joseph's first meeting with Pharaoh was the starting point for all these things to happen. Egypt's ruler took at face value Joseph's earlier statement that God had revealed to him the meaning of the king's dreams (41:16). Moreover, Pharaoh was convinced that the Hebrew—though a foreigner—was the wisest and most discerning person throughout the entire realm (vs. 39). Thus, it made sense to appoint the 30-year-old to be the national overseer. In order for Joseph to direct the project, he would manage the household of Pharaoh and have charge over all his officials and inhabitants. They were to submit to the Hebrew's commands. Only the Egyptian ruler would rank higher than Joseph and retain supreme authority (vs. 40; see Ps. 105:21; Acts 7:10).

A consistent theme in Proverbs is the comparison between the way of wisdom and the way of foolishness. The way of wisdom leads to a clear conscience, meaningful relationships, and a full life. The path of foolishness leads to frustration, heartache, and eventual ruin. As the collection of wisdom sayings repeatedly reminds us, being prudent is always the superior choice. The benefits of wisdom far outweigh the consequences of foolishness. People like Joseph who follow the way of wisdom tend to succeed. Those who follow the way of foolishness eventually come to ruin.

II. JOSEPH'S OVERSIGHT OF EGYPT: GENESIS 41:41-45, 50-52

A. Pharaoh's Ratification of Joseph's Appointment: vss. 41-43

So Pharaoh said to Joseph, "I hereby put you in charge of the whole land of Egypt." Then Pharaoh took his signet ring from his finger and put it on Joseph's finger. He dressed him in robes of fine linen and put a gold chain around his neck. He had him ride in a chariot as his second-in-command, and men shouted before him, "Make way!" Thus he put him in charge of the whole land of Egypt.

"Egypt" (Gen. 41:41) refers to the country in the northeast corner of Africa. In ancient times, its territory extended from the first waterfall of the Nile River in the south to the Mediterranean Sea in the north (about 650 miles). The only inhabitable areas were the narrow Nile Valley and the broad alluvial Nile delta through which the long river reached the Mediterranean Sea. Egypt was the home of one of the earliest civilizations. Its culture was rich and complex, having developed over a period stretching from about 3000 B.C. to Roman times.

It was over all the "land of Egypt" that Pharaoh placed Joseph. In a sense, he became the nation's grand vizier. It was unusual for Pharaoh to appoint a foreigner for such a vital task as preparing for a famine and to give him so much power in the kingdom. It was especially unusual for the Egyptian ruler to place a relatively young, unknown, and unproven prisoner in an office of such great authority. Only God could have made such an act possible. Joseph had risen from slavery and prison to be the second most powerful person in Egypt, but God's plans for Joseph were just beginning.

To make the appointment official, the Egyptian ruler gave the former Hebrew prisoner the signet ring off his own finger. The ring would be used to mark clay or wax on royal documents and guarantee their authenticity. Moreover, Pharaoh clothed Joseph in fine linen robes, which were typically reserved for Egyptian royalty, and hung a chain made of solid gold around his neck (vs. 42). The clothing and gold chain were appropriate to Joseph's status as the nation's vice-regent. Pharaoh went even further by authorizing Joseph to ride in the chariot next to his own. As the royal entourage passed by a crowd, officials would command onlookers to kneel down and make way for the nation's governor (vs. 43).

B. Joseph's New Life as Pharaoh's Vice-Regent: vss. 44-45

Then Pharaoh said to Joseph, "I am Pharaoh, but without your word no one will lift hand or foot in all Egypt." Pharaoh gave Joseph the name Zaphenath-Paneah and gave him Asenath daughter of Potiphera, priest of On, to be his wife. And Joseph went throughout the land of Egypt.

Pharaoh declared that while he was the supreme ruler of the land, Joseph was his viceroy. This meant that without his permission, no one would be allowed to do anything, including lifting a hand or a foot (Gen. 41:44). In accordance with the custom of the day, Pharaoh gave Joseph the Egyptian name "Zaphenath-Paneah" (vs. 45), the meaning of which remains uncertain. Two prominent suggestions are "god speaks, he lives" and "sustainer of life." Also, during the seven years of abundance, Joseph married Asenath, the daughter of Potiphera. He was a prominent Egyptian priest who served at On (located ten miles northeast of modern-day Cairo), a temple used in the worship of a sun god named Ra. "Asenath" may mean "she belongs to (the goddess) Neith."

C. Joseph's New Family: vss. 50-52

Before the years of famine came, two sons were born to Joseph by Asenath daughter of Potiphera, priest of On. Joseph named his firstborn Manasseh and said, "It is because God has made me forget all my trouble and all my father's household." The second son he named Ephraim and said, "It is because God has made me fruitful in the land of my suffering."

As the second-in-command in Egypt, Joseph shouldered the responsibility of implementing the plan he had outlined to Pharaoh and his court officials. Joseph was 30 years old at this time (Gen. 41:46), which indicates that his rise to power from slavery occurred within a span of 13 years (see 37:2). For the next seven years, the land produced large, abundant harvests (41:47). During this time, Joseph collected all the excess food and stored it in the nation's cities (vs. 48). The grain was so vast in quantity that it was comparable to the sand found on a seashore (vs. 49).

In ancient Egypt, farming followed a regular cycle. First, the Nile River would flood the land in September, October, and November, providing moisture and a layer of rich soil in which to plant crops. If the Nile did not flood because of low rainfall upstream, famine would follow. After the flood, farmers would plant their crops immediately, before the ground dried out. Then they would harvest the crops in March or April.

Some of the harvest would be given to the town temple for the priests. The rest would be stored in granaries for future use, but a portion was collected as annual taxes by government officials, who carefully counted the harvest. Much of the government's grain went to the pharaoh's storehouses. Consequently, the Egyptians would have been used to an official like Joseph collecting grain for Pharaoh. And Scripture says that Joseph used the circumstances of the famine to increase Pharaoh's influence in Egypt (47:23-26).

Admittedly, there are no Egyptian records that can be linked to the specific drought and famine that Joseph described to Pharaoh, or to the storage and distribution plan he devised. However, an inscription has been found in the tomb of an Egyptian official who lived south of Thebes that describes a similar event. The writing in the tomb of Baba, governor of the city of El-Kab, says that the governor stored up corn during a time of plenty, "and when a famine arose, lasting many years, I distributed corn to the city, each year of the famine."

Before the famine came, Asenath bore Joseph two sons, Manasseh and Ephraim (vs. 50). "Manasseh" (vs. 51) possibly means "he who brings about forgetfulness." The term sounds like and possibly is derived from a Hebrew verb that means "to forget." In a statement reflecting Joseph's faith, he reasoned that the birth of Manasseh represented a dramatic change of circumstance. Egypt's newly appointed vice-regent could now put behind him all the hardship he had experienced, especially in connection with his father's family. Most likely, "Ephraim" (vs. 52) means "to bear fruit" and is derived from a verb that means "twice fruitful" or "double fruitfulness." The name reminded Joseph that in a land where he had endured so much suffering, God had made him fruitful.

Discussion Questions

1. How was it possible for Joseph to go from being imprisoned to the second-in-command in Egypt?
2. If you were Joseph, how would you have felt at suddenly being elevated to such a high position of power?
3. What was Joseph's plan for coping with the coming disaster?
4. What are some ways in which God works through believers today to bring about good?
5. How is Joseph's unwavering faith in God evident in the names Joseph gave to his children?

Contemporary Application

The account of Joseph shows us how God gives us wisdom and how we can use that wisdom to help others. Even though he was only 30 when he went before Pharaoh, Joseph was already wise to God's ways, since he had learned to trust God in hard places. We are wise when we trust God through crises. We can then use that godly wisdom to help others—for instance, as we share with a struggling friend what God has done for us.

Opportunities to help others come when we least expect them. Joseph was brought quickly from the prison to the court of Pharaoh. That is why we must walk close to the Lord every day, so we will be ready when He calls us to serve. We must be prepared to alter direction if God suddenly changes our circumstances.

Moreover, we never know how far reaching the effects of sharing our godly wisdom will be. Joseph interpreted Pharaoh's dreams correctly and saved Egypt. Later, he saved his own family from starvation. Similarly, people will seek our help in times of need if they have seen God in us.

Pharaoh recognized that God spoke through Joseph. People should notice our humility, acts of kindness, and wise advice as God works through us—but He receives the glory for what we do for Him. Joseph gave God the credit for the correct interpretation of Pharaoh's dreams. Likewise, when God gives us wisdom to help others, all the glory belongs to Him.

God Preserves a Remnant

Scripture

Background Scripture: *Genesis 42:1-38; 45:1-28*
Scripture Lesson: *Genesis 45:3-15*
Key Verse: *"So then, it was not you who sent me here, but God."* Genesis 45:8.
Scripture Lesson for Children: *Genesis 45:1-9*
Key Verse for Children: *"God sent me ahead of you to preserve for you a remnant on earth and to save your lives by a great deliverance."* Genesis 45:7.

Lesson Aim

To recognize that God's purposes exceed our plans.

Lesson Setting

Time: 1876 B.C.
Place: Egypt

Lesson Outline

God Preserves a Remnant
  I. Joseph's Disclosure: Genesis 45:3-7
     A. *Joseph's Declaration: vs. 3*
     B. *Joseph's Realization: vss. 4-5*
     C. *Joseph's Explanation: vss. 6-7*
  II. Joseph's Instructions: Genesis 45:8-15
     A. *God's Sovereign Working: vs. 8*
     B. *Joseph's Exhortation: vs. 9*
     C. *Joseph's Promises: vss. 10-11*
     D. *Joseph's Assurance: vss. 12-13*
     E. *Joseph's Brotherly Affection: vss. 14-15*

Introduction for Adults

Topic: *Sharing Blessings*

Jim Elliot, Nate Saint, Pete Flemming, Ed McCulley, and Roger Youderian were martyred in 1956, shortly after they arrived in the jungles of Ecuador to bring the Gospel to the Auca Indians. It was a witness that could not be ignored. They were a testimony that properly placed faith, when eager to share the blessings of the Gospel, is more precious than life itself.

Five years after she watched those martyrdoms, a woman named Dawa became the first Auca Christian. Other conversions followed. Then, 36 years later, the Aucas (properly called the Huaoranis) received their first complete New Testament.

Some wonder if Elliot and his associates could have planned their missionary outreach better and thus worked longer for the Lord. Yet God allows some candles to burn fast and brilliantly, while others (like Joseph) burn long and steadily. Both are a part of His plan of bringing the blessings of His grace to others.

Introduction for Youth

Topic: *Preserving the Family Line*

The sign on the high-school football team's locker room door read: "Everyone is welcome to play football! To play you must: 1. Give 110%! 2. Be at practice everyday! 3. Have a positive attitude! 4. Listen to your coach!" While the sign said *welcome*, there were conditions. Joseph welcomed his brothers unconditionally. Expressed differently, there were no "Gotchas!" to his offer of reconciliation.

Moreover, despite circumstances that looked less than favorable at first, God accomplished His purposes in Joseph's life. And God's plans for Joseph went beyond his brothers' intentions to include the preservation of the family line of Jacob. Sometimes when our plans are frustrated, we feel that God is indifferent or has forgotten us. But we can trust that God loves us and that He has the ability to bring His best out of the worst circumstances.

Concepts for Children

Topic: *A Surprise Reunion*

1. Joseph's brothers were surprised to see him again.
2. Joseph forgave his brothers and wanted them near him.
3. Joseph knew that even in the hard times, God was with him.
4. Joseph knew that God was using him to help his family out of trouble.
5. God also wants to work through us to do important things for Him.

Lesson Commentary

I. JOSEPH'S DISCLOSURE: GENESIS 45:3-7

A. Joseph's Declaration: vs. 3

Joseph said to his brothers, "I am Joseph! Is my father still living?" But his brothers were not able to answer him, because they were terrified at his presence.

Genesis 41:53-57 leaves the impression that life was busy and absorbing for Joseph, both personally and professionally. It became even more so as the seven years of drought and hunger began, for Pharaoh directed his starving people to go to Joseph for the food they needed to survive. The famine extended even to Canaan and impacted its inhabitants. Moreover, chapters 42–44 reveal that as the situation worsened throughout the Fertile Crescent, Jacob was forced to send his remaining sons (except for Joseph's full brother, Benjamin) to Egypt to buy grain for the family. Such a transaction required them to deal directly with Joseph. After recognizing his brothers and remembering the dream of his youth, the powerful overseer of the land began an elaborate test to see what kind of adults his brothers had become over the years.

Joseph started the test by accusing his siblings of being spies and imprisoning them for three days. Joseph then held Simeon as hostage and allowed the other brothers to return to Jacob with food for the family. Joseph also ordered that the money they had brought to buy food be hidden in their sacks of grain. He informed them that to buy more grain and save Simeon, they would have to return before him with Benjamin (42:1-20). Jacob thought he had already lost one of his sons born to Rachel—Joseph. Now the patriarch thought he was in danger of losing his other son born to Rachel—Benjamin—who was probably then in his 20s or early 30s. However, to save the family from starvation, a reluctant Jacob allowed Benjamin to return with his other sons to Egypt. The reformed brothers immediately attempted to return the money that had mysteriously appeared in their grain sacks on the last trip. They also purchased more grain for the family. Then, with Simeon returned to them, they all began their journey back to Canaan (42:21–44:3).

The siblings hadn't traveled far before they discovered another phase of Joseph's test. He had again hidden their money in the grain sacks and had hidden his silver cup in Benjamin's grain sack. Joseph's servant accused Benjamin of the crime and offered to let the other brothers go free while he took Benjamin to become Joseph's slave. Instead of saving themselves, the brothers risked their lives by returning to Egypt to plead for Benjamin's freedom. Judah functioned as the spokesperson for the group (44:4-32). After offering a summary and explanation of recent events, Judah concluded by pleading with Joseph to be kept in Egypt as a slave in place of Benjamin. The young man, in turn, would be permitted to return with his other brothers to their home in Canaan (vs. 33). Judah explained that the alternative would involve him returning to his aged father without Benjamin, and Judah could not bear to witness the devastation Jacob would feel (vs. 34).

Judah's speech proved that he was not the same person who years earlier had come up with the idea of selling Joseph to Midianite traders. It had taken a long time, but the Lord had worked changes in Judah's heart. As he was telling about Jacob's sorrow and was offering himself as a substitute for Benjamin, Joseph must have listened with rising emotion. He had wanted to find out if the selfish, vengeful brothers he had known in his youth had changed. By means of an elaborate test, Joseph verified that his siblings had not only matured, but also become God-fearing adults. Finally, the overseer could hide his feelings no more. Not for a minute longer could he stand in front of his brothers and pretend to have a merely official interest in them.

Joseph's brothers must have been stunned when they heard him command his attendants to leave the room (45:1). Probably all along Joseph had been talking to his siblings through an interpreter to disguise the fact that he could understand their Hebrew speech. The tender reunion that was about to occur would be a family matter, and presumably Joseph didn't want any outsiders around to distract him and his brothers. Moses described Joseph's emotional release as so powerful that his weeping could even be heard by the servants who had departed from the area. Somehow the household of Pharaoh also learned about the incident, perhaps by means of an official report (vs. 2). The sons of Jacob were shocked to hear the second-most powerful person in Egypt declare, "I am Joseph!" (Gen. 45:3). For more than 20 years, his siblings thought of Joseph as enslaved or dead. Since meeting the nation's viceroy, they never for a moment suspected that the person dressed in Egyptian finery and speaking the Egyptian language was their long-lost brother. But there he stood, saying in Hebrew that he was their sibling (see Acts 7:13).

Joseph followed up his self-revelation by asking about the father he had not seen for over two decades. Beyond question, this was the concern closest to the heart of the overseer. Thus, he was eager to have more news about his father. Until this point, Joseph would have aroused suspicion by showing too much interest in Jacob. Joseph's brothers made no reply to his question, for they were still in shock over finding themselves in the presence of their sibling. Evidently, they had not mentioned the name of the brother who—as the cover-up story went—had been killed by an animal (see Gen. 42:13; 44:28). Thus perhaps Joseph's using his own name convinced them of his true identity. Now they were confused and terrified and undoubtedly wondered if he would eliminate them for what they had done to him.

The biblical text portrays Joseph as an emotional, sensitive man. The moment when he revealed his identity to his brothers is not the first time in the narrative that he cried. He did so briefly but secretly when he had Simeon taken from his brothers and held prisoner (42:24). Then he showed even more emotion when he first saw his brother Benjamin. So his brothers would not see him cry, he left them and wept by himself for a while in his private room (43:30). Later, he would weep "for a long time" (46:29) when he saw and embraced his father, Jacob, after the passage of more than 20 years.

B. Joseph's Realization: vss. 4-5

Then Joseph said to his brothers, "Come close to me." When they had done so, he said, "I am your brother Joseph, the one you sold into Egypt! And now, do not be distressed and do not be angry with yourselves for selling me here, because it was to save lives that God sent me ahead of you."

Thinking that perhaps the brothers did not believe Joseph was who he said he was, the vice-regent called them to him so that they could take a closer look at his face (Gen. 45:4). Then he repeated his claim to be Joseph, the sibling whom they long ago had sold into slavery. Only Joseph himself could have known the secret that they had mistreated him so shamefully. Of course, Joseph's brothers were dumbfounded by his disclosure. The person they had terribly wronged was now in a position of absolute power over them. He could imprison, enslave, or execute his siblings with just a word. The overseer's emotional outburst only added to their fear of his vengeance. However, like his brothers, he was a different person than the 17-year-old who was thrown into a cistern.

During their time of reunion, Joseph reassured his petrified brothers that he was not interested in revenge. He was able and willing to forgive his siblings because he had learned to look at his trials from a godly perspective. Instead of Joseph concentrating on his brothers' evil intentions, he focused on God's supreme plan of blessing him with success and saving people from destruction. Thus Joseph urged his siblings not to be angry with themselves for their past misdeeds. Ultimately, God had been working in the circumstances that had brought Joseph to Egypt. Though the brothers' actions in the past were despicable, God had used their decisions to place Joseph in a position of authority so that he could rescue Egypt and his own family (vs. 5; see 50:20).

The truth of God's oversight over all that occurred lay at the heart of the reconciliation between Joseph and his brothers. None of them could reverse the wickedness the siblings were guilty of committing against Joseph. But the realization that God can bring good out of evil paved the way for the severed relationship to be restored and rehabilitated. That which was humanly impossible to achieve the Lord sovereignly brought about in His own time and in His own way.

C. Joseph's Explanation: vss. 6-7

"For two years now there has been famine in the land, and for the next five years there will not be plowing and reaping. But God sent me ahead of you to preserve for you a remnant on earth and to save your lives by a great deliverance."

Joseph explained that the two years of famine that had already passed would extend to seven. (This means that he was now 39 years old.) During this time, the drought would be so severe that neither plowing nor harvesting would occur (Gen.

45:6). This would be just as true for the family of Jacob as for the entire nation of Egypt. Without immediate assistance and long-term help, the Israelite clan would not likely survive. Over the years, Joseph had plenty of time to reflect on the strange turn of events his life had taken. As a person of faith, he could discern God's purposes in what had happened to him. God would use Joseph to preserve a "remnant" (vs. 7) of His people. Joseph's words reminded his brothers of the great peril facing their family and implied that they would be rescued only because God had something special in store for the Israelite clan.

II. JOSEPH'S INSTRUCTIONS: GENESIS 45:8-15

A. God's Sovereign Working: vs. 8

"So then, it was not you who sent me here, but God. He made me father to Pharaoh, lord of his entire household and ruler of all Egypt."

The main point of Joseph's explanation is that ultimately God—not Jacob's sons—was responsible for sending the former Hebrew slave and prisoner to Egypt. Joseph said that the Lord had made him a "father to Pharaoh" (Gen. 45:8). Joseph was speaking figuratively of someone giving others advice, as parents would to their children. In the case of Pharaoh, he relied on Joseph's foresight and prudence. In the years since the Egyptian ruler had appointed him as second-in-command, the Hebrew had proved his trustworthiness and dependability. Both the royal household and the entire land of Egypt were in good hands.

"Pharaoh" was the official title of the rulers of Egypt. The name itself derived from an Egyptian word meaning "great house." Before the name came to be applied to the person of the ruler himself, it was used to refer to the royal palace and the Egyptian court. By the time of Joseph, it was commonly used to refer to the ruler. The name pharaoh was a title and, as such, was not the personal name of the Egyptian rulers.

B. Joseph's Exhortation: vs. 9

"Now hurry back to my father and say to him, 'This is what your son Joseph says: God has made me lord of all Egypt. Come down to me; don't delay.'"

Since the first time Joseph's brothers had appeared before him, the overseer had worked out a plan for the family. He would settle them in Egypt. Joseph knew that the Israelite clan had to act quickly to survive the famine, which had several more years to go. Thus, he directed his brothers to exhort their father not to delay in relocating the entire family. As reassurance that this was the divinely ordained course of action, Joseph noted that God had made him "lord of all Egypt" (Gen. 45:9). We can only imagine the impression left on Joseph's brothers as they possibly heard attendants command everyone within earshot to kneel down in the presence of the nation's overseer (see 41:43).

C. Joseph's Promises: vss. 10-11

"'You shall live in the region of Goshen and be near me—you, your children and grandchildren, your flocks and herds, and all you have. I will provide for you there, because five years of famine are still to come. Otherwise you and your household and all who belong to you will become destitute.'"

Joseph's plan was to settle the entire Israelite clan—family members, their livestock, and all their possessions—in the land of Goshen (Gen. 45:10). This region was located in the northeastern section of the Nile River delta. Though the area is not large (about 900 square miles), it was considered some of the best territory in Egypt. With irrigation, it was an excellent site for grazing and for growing certain crops. The Hebrew people were still living in the region at the time of the Exodus, four centuries later. Joseph, as the second-in-command in Egypt, promised to provide the Israelite clan what it needed and would watch over it, especially in the five years of famine that remained. Left on their own in Canaan, Jacob's family would either die from starvation or scatter from the plight of its destitution. Joseph wanted to ensure that the entire group remain together and safe in Egypt (vs. 11).

When Jacob's family moved to Egypt, it had to cross barriers greater than the rocky Sinai Peninsula to make this new land its home. Not only were Egypt and Canaan on different continents, but also they contrasted sharply in terms of agricultural practices and societal traditions. For instance, Egypt was rich in crops, livestock, and precious metals, but Canaan's primary enterprise was shepherding, which the Egyptians despised (see 46:34). At that time, Egypt was an intellectual and cultural center of the ancient world, while Canaan was mostly an intellectual and cultural backwater. Most Egyptians were brown skinned, with stiff brown hair. Most Canaanites had olive-colored complexions and straight dark brown or black hair. Without Joseph's power in the royal court, it is unimaginable that the Israelite clan of nomadic shepherds would have received such a gracious welcome from Pharaoh in the sophisticated, cosmopolitan nation over which he ruled (see 47:1-12).

D. Joseph's Assurance: vss. 12-13

"You can see for yourselves, and so can my brother Benjamin, that it is really I who am speaking to you. Tell my father about all the honor accorded me in Egypt and about everything you have seen. And bring my father down here quickly."

Joseph wanted there to be no doubt among his siblings that he truly was their long lost brother. Here we find Joseph dispensing with an interpreter and speaking directly to his brothers (Gen. 45:12; see 42:23). The viceroy urged his brothers to tell their father how much Joseph was honored in Egypt and the collaborating details of what they saw. Joseph reasoned that their personal testimony would convince Jacob to relocate his entire family from Canaan to Egypt (45:13).

E. Joseph's Brotherly Affection: vss. 14-15

Then he threw his arms around his brother Benjamin and wept, and Benjamin embraced him, weeping. And he kissed all his brothers and wept over them. Afterward his brothers talked with him.

With the important explanations over, Joseph embraced and wept with his brothers, beginning with the youngest (Gen. 45:14). Benjamin was Joseph's only full brother and the only one innocent in regard to the overseer. Earlier, when Joseph was pretending to be an Egyptian, he must have wanted more than anything to embrace Benjamin and the others. The high-ranking official did not have to restrain himself anymore. This mutual display of emotion and the conversation that followed completed the family reunion (vs. 15). Whatever bitterness Joseph may have felt toward his brothers was all gone now. They had nothing to fear from him, for he had forgiven them.

Discussion Questions

1. Why were Joseph's brothers terrified in his presence?
2. What reason did Joseph give for being in Egypt?
3. What plan did Joseph have for the Israelite clan?
4. Have you known a time in your life when you realized God worked something good out of a difficult circumstance?
5. Have you ever had to struggle over whether to forgive abuse from other family members?

Contemporary Application

When leaders Mark and Jana set out with their youth group for Pennsylvania from Michigan, they knew the church's bus was not in the best shape. Still, they had not expected to stop dead in bumper-to-bumper traffic on an Ohio interstate exit ramp—on a Sunday morning. There was little the group could do but push the stalled bus onto the shoulder, raise the hood, and pray for help.

Soon a woman on her way to church stopped to find out how she could help. "Well," Mark said, "we need a mechanic." "There's a mechanic in our church," the woman said. "Let's see what I can do." Once at church, the woman interrupted the service to tell the congregation about the group's plight and ask for assistance. She returned to the broken-down bus with a few other churchgoers. "I can repair the bus," one man said. Another pulled Mark aside and said, "I would like to put your group up for the night at our church while you wait for the repair. I would also like to buy your dinner."

That breakdown taught the group important lessons about God's faithfulness. It could have been a time of grumbling and frustration. Instead, they were all reminded that God's purposes exceed our plans, especially as He works to accomplish His will in our lives. We must simply remember whose children we are—and enjoy the ride.

Passing on Abraham's Promise

Scripture

Background Scripture: *Genesis 50:1-26*
Scripture Lesson: *Genesis 50:15-26*
Key Verse: "*You intended to harm me, but God intended it for good to accomplish what is now being done, the saving of many lives.*" Genesis 50:20.
Scripture Lesson for Children: *Genesis 50:15-26*
Key Verse for Children: "*You intended to harm me, but God intended it for good.*" Genesis 50:20.

Lesson Aim

To explore reasons why believers must forgive.

Lesson Setting

Time: *1859–1805* B.C.
Place: *Egypt*

Lesson Outline

Passing on Abraham's Promise
  I. Joseph Reassures His Brothers: Genesis 50:15-21
      A. *The Brothers' Fear: vs. 15*
      B. *The Brothers' Request: vss. 16-17*
      C. *The Consoling Words of Joseph: vss. 18-21*
  II. Joseph Dies and Is Buried: Genesis 50:22-26
      A. *The Long Life of Joseph: vss. 22-23*
      B. *The Request Made by Joseph: vss. 24-25*
      C. *The Ending of Joseph's Life: vs. 26*

Introduction for Adults

Topic: *The Power of Forgiveness*

A woman dropped out of her Bible class on Wednesday evenings to attend a course on assertiveness training. To her surprise, she discovered that the course's emphasis was on standing up for one's rights and contriving to get redress for any slights. "I thought the course would help me get over my shyness," she later related. "But they tried to get me to leave behind what they called my religious hang-ups, like being a forgiving person."

This woman learned how radical God's demands are on members of His faith community. This woman also found that God's way runs counter to the world's way. The latter truth is clearly evident in the life of Joseph. Instead of seeking to get even with his brothers, who had harmed him greatly, Joseph chose to forgive them—freely and unconditionally. As followers of the Lord Jesus, we are also called to be as forgiving in our relationships with others.

Introduction for Youth

Topic: *I'm Not a Hater!*

Until 2011, the entertainment industry knew that when a celebrity was in trouble, she or he could turn to Oprah Winfrey. After a spot on her show, a few confessions, and some tears to wash away iniquities, she or he was as good as new.

Is this all that constitutes repentance? Is this true forgiveness? No, true forgiveness starts with sincere repentance for the wrong and a resolution not to repeat the action. True repentance means a new direction. It is given to the individual by other believers and by the Lord Jesus, not a celebrity like Oprah Winfrey.

The episode involving Joseph and his brothers is a case in point. The older siblings genuinely repented of their past transgressions against Joseph. And he responded by refusing to bear a grudge against them. Instead, he forgave them for what they had done. This week's lesson encourages us to strive to be the same way.

Concepts for Children

Topic: *Victory from Hardship*

1. When Jacob died, Joseph's brothers became afraid.
2. Joseph's brothers wondered whether he might want to get even with them.
3. When the brothers visited Joseph, he spoke kindly to them.
4. Joseph's brothers learned that he had forgiven them.
5. God wants us to forgive those who do mean things to us.

Lesson Commentary

I. JOSEPH REASSURES HIS BROTHERS: GENESIS 50:15-21

A. The Brothers' Fear: vs. 15

When Joseph's brothers saw that their father was dead, they said, "What if Joseph holds a grudge against us and pays us back for all the wrongs we did to him?"

After Joseph made himself known to his brothers (Gen. 45:1-15), he provided them with carts in which they would bring their families back to Egypt. Joseph also sent a whole caravan of food and gifts for his father. Not only would these items please Jacob, but also they would serve as proof that Joseph still loved and honored his father (vss. 16-24). Jacob must have spent the weeks that his sons were away from home worrying about them, especially Benjamin. And the patriarch must have been overjoyed when all 11 appeared at his door safe and sound. Even more astounding, though, was his realization that Joseph was alive and the grand vizier of Egypt. Jacob vowed to go to Joseph before the patriarch's death (vss. 25-28).

Chapters 46 and 47 reveal that Jacob fulfilled his vow. He left Canaan with all his family members, servants, livestock, and possessions. Joseph traveled from his home and met Jacob in the land of Goshen. Then, after the reunion, Joseph escorted his father's caravan to Pharaoh and presented his father and brothers to Egypt's ruler. In keeping with Pharaoh's recommendation, Joseph provided land and food for the Hebrew immigrants. Joseph himself, though, continued in his government position, saving lives while at the same time enriching Pharaoh. Meanwhile, Jacob's family remained in Egypt even after the famine ended, probably because it was prospering. But Jacob knew his family's true home was in Canaan. So, as the patriarch neared his death, he made Joseph promise to bury him in Canaan with his father and grandfather.

Jacob's blessing of Ephraim and Manasseh, along with the patriarch's adoption of Joseph's two sons, is recounted in chapter 48. This is followed in 49:1-28 with the record of Jacob's blessing of his natural sons. The patriarch's words prophetically anticipate the characteristics of the tribes that would come from the men. Jacob disclosed that the tribes of Judah and Joseph (that is, Manasseh and Ephraim) had the greatest future. After Jacob finished the address to his sons, he repeated his request that he be buried in the cave of Machpelah along with his ancestors and his wife Leah. Then Jacob died at the age of 147 (in 1859 B.C.; vss. 29-33).

Joseph led the way in displaying grief over the death of his father. This included Joseph placing himself across Jacob's body and embracing him (50:1). Once Joseph's initial display of grief was over, he gave orders for the physicians under his management to embalm Jacob's body (vs. 2). Apparently, the patriarch was made into a mummy. This was the usual treatment in Egypt for the body of an important person who had died. Ordinarily, professional embalmers, not physicians, were called in to mummify a body. Joseph may have wanted physicians to embalm his father so as to avoid the religious ceremonies that typically went along with the procedure. According to records dating from a period shortly after Joseph's time, the embalming process usually took 70 days. Jacob's embalming, taking place earlier and perhaps in a simpler form, was completed in only 40 days. But the mourning went on for another 30 days (vs. 3). Since a pharaoh was mourned for 72 days (only two days more than Jacob), the patriarch's mourning period shows the great honor he was accorded.

At the end of the 70-day mourning period, Joseph sought permission from Pharaoh's royal court to leave the country to bury Jacob. For some reason, Joseph did not make this request to Pharaoh in person (vs. 4). In Joseph's request, he played on the Egyptian monarch's respect for the dead. Joseph mentioned the oath he had given to his father to bury Jacob in the land of Canaan (vs. 5). Pharaoh was quite willing to let Joseph go for such a purpose (vs. 6). In Egypt, funeral processions were major spectacles. Jacob's entourage was no exception. His body was accompanied by Joseph, his brothers, and other members of their family. Also, out of respect for Joseph, many senior Egyptian courtiers accompanied the body (vss. 7-8). To protect such an important crowd, mounted soldiers went along (vs. 9).

The destination of the funeral procession was the cave of Machpelah, not far from Mamre. Apparently, those in the procession did not take the shortest route to the burial site. Instead, they went around the Salt Sea and came at their destination from the north. They may have wanted to avoid problems with the Philistines in the area lying between Egypt and Mamre. The entourage stopped for a week at the threshing floor of Atad (vs. 10). We don't know where the spot was, except that it was near the Jordan River. But here, at this point of entering the promised land, the group observed another mourning period. For this reason, the local residents named the place Abel Mizraim, which means "mourning of the Egyptians" (vs. 11). Eventually, the body arrived at its final resting place: the cave of Machpelah (vss. 12-13). Probably, here there were additional ceremonies. Then, everyone in the entourage returned to Egypt (vs. 14).

Sometime after Jacob's death, his 10 oldest sons began feeling vulnerable. After all, their father was no longer around to protect them from their powerful brother. The Hebrew verb rendered "holds a grudge" (vs. 15) literally means "to hate" or "to retain animosity against." Joseph's siblings feared he might now want to seek revenge for their selling him into slavery many years earlier. Accounting terminology is used to refer to Joseph seeking to be repaid in full for the harm (literally "evil") his brothers did to him.

B. The Brothers' Request: vss. 16-17

So they sent word to Joseph, saying, "Your father left these instructions before he died: 'This is what you are to say to Joseph: I ask you to forgive your brothers the sins and the wrongs they committed in treating you so badly.' Now please forgive the sins of the servants of the God of your father." When their message came to him, Joseph wept.

After talking over their situation, the brothers settled on a plan. They wanted to get things straightened out between themselves and Joseph once and for all. The plan involved the brothers sending a message to Joseph claiming that Jacob left instructions for Joseph to forgive his brothers (Gen. 50:16). In that day, the requests of a dying clan leader were given much weight. The posthumous statement attributed to Jacob labeled his sons' crimes against Joseph as "sins" (vs. 17) and "wrongs." "Sins" refers to offenses and rebellious deeds, whereas "wrongs" denotes wicked, injurious actions. Together, these terms emphasize the extent of the cruelty Joseph's brothers inflicted on him. The brothers humbly referred to themselves as "servants of the God" of Jacob and begged Joseph to pardon their trespasses and absolve their guilt.

Some scholars think the brothers made up the instructions they said were from Jacob. These specialists reason that if Jacob had wanted to give instructions of this sort to Joseph, he could have done so at the deathbed interview. Regardless of whether parts of the message were a fabrication, Joseph readily accepted his brothers' request to be forgiven and wept when he heard the message. It had been at least 17 years since Joseph had assured his brothers that he bore no grudge. As far as we know, in all the intervening years, Joseph had done nothing to harm them. And, in fact, he had helped his brothers in many ways. This was enough to make a grown person cry.

C. The Consoling Words of Joseph: vss. 18-21

His brothers then came and threw themselves down before him. "We are your slaves," they said. But Joseph said to them, "Don't be afraid. Am I in the place of God? You intended to harm me, but God intended it for good to accomplish what is now being done, the saving of many lives. So then, don't be afraid. I will provide for you and your children." And he reassured them and spoke kindly to them.

The brothers followed their message in person. In Joseph's presence, they prostrated themselves and referred to themselves his "slaves" (Gen. 50:18). By the brothers putting themselves at the mercy of Egypt's viceroy, they were right back where they had been all those years before (see 44:14, 16). Then, just as Joseph had done years before, he dealt tenderly with his brothers. He encouraged them not to be fearful. He would not judge them, for that was up to God (50:19; see Rom. 12:19).

Next, Joseph gave his brothers the same explanation for his slavery that he stated before (see Gen. 45:5). On the one hand, the brothers meant to "harm" (50:20; literally, "do evil against") Joseph. On the other hand, God brought a good outcome out of the brothers' wickedness, namely, the preservation of "many lives" in Egypt and Canaan, especially those of Jacob's clan. And now Joseph vowed to continue providing for his brothers and their families, just as the grand vizier had done while Jacob was alive. Then, Joseph consoled his brothers with reassuring words that touched their hearts (vs. 21).

II. JOSEPH DIES AND IS BURIED: GENESIS 50:22-26

A. The Long Life of Joseph: vss. 22-23

Joseph stayed in Egypt, along with all his father's family. He lived a hundred and ten years and saw the third generation of Ephraim's children. Also the children of Makir son of Manasseh were placed at birth on Joseph's knees.

The final verses of Genesis are reserved for a description of Joseph's end. He finished out his life in Egypt amid his larger family (Gen. 50:22). At one time, Jacob had said Joseph would become a "fruitful vine" (49:22), and Joseph began to see that prediction come true. He even lived long enough to see the descendants of Ephraim to the "third generation" (50:23). If placing children on one's knees was a sign of adoption (see 48:12), then Joseph evidently adopted some of his great-grandchildren, including giving them special inheritance rights. (Makir was an important clan in the tribe of Manasseh; see Judg. 5:14).

B. The Request Made by Joseph: vss. 24-25

Then Joseph said to his brothers, "I am about to die. But God will surely come to your aid and take you up out of this land to the land he promised on oath to Abraham, Isaac and Jacob." And Joseph made the sons of Israel swear an oath and said, "God will surely come to your aid, and then you must carry my bones up from this place."

As the time of Joseph's death approached, he called his brothers together. Of course, some of them may have died by this time. The Hebrew noun rendered "brothers" (Gen. 50:24) can refer to other relatives. Perhaps, if some of Joseph's brothers had passed away, they were represented by their sons, Joseph's nephews. Even though Joseph had found power and wealth in Egypt, his heart was in the land God had promised to the patriarchs—Abraham, Isaac, and Jacob. Consequently, Joseph wanted to be buried in Canaan, as his ancestors had been. But the viceroy did not ask his brothers to bury him there right after his death, as in the case of Jacob. Instead, Joseph made his brothers vow to carry his bones with them when they returned to the promised land.

Scripture reveals that Joseph's wishes were respected. At the time of the Exodus, Moses made sure the Hebrews took with them the bones of Joseph (see Exod. 13:19). Eventually, Joseph was buried in the tract of land Jacob had purchased near Shechem (see Josh. 24:32). At the time Joseph made his request to be buried in Canaan, he assured his next of kin that God would come to help them, particularly in leading them back to the promised land (Gen. 50:25). Possibly, the Hebrews were already beginning to experience the oppression that would become full-scale slavery by the time of Moses. As Exodus discloses, it was this oppression that prevented God's people from immediately burying the bones of Joseph in Canaan. Nonetheless, Joseph had perfect confidence in the deliverance promised by God.

C. The Ending of Joseph's Life: vs. 26

So Joseph died at the age of a hundred and ten. And after they embalmed him, he was placed in a coffin in Egypt.

Genesis 50:26 states that Joseph died when he was 110 (in 1805 B.C.), which was regarded by the Egyptians as an ideal age at which to pass away. Many references to that effect have been found in ancient Egyptian writings. Joseph's death at 110 must have confirmed to the Egyptians that God's blessing had indeed been on Joseph's life. Next, Joseph was embalmed and placed in a coffin, where his body would await transport to the land of promise. According to ancient Egyptian belief, the dead lived on in another world and continued to need their bodies. Thus, the Egyptians developed advanced embalming techniques. First, embalmers would remove most internal organs. Then, they would place the body in natron (that is, sodium carbonate) to dry out the tissues. Finally, they would wrap the body in linen bandages and place it in a coffin. Well-preserved mummies have been found dating back to the time of Joseph and even earlier.

From start to finish, Genesis is a book of history, and its historical account concerning such luminaries as Jacob and Joseph is trustworthy because it was inspired by God. That said, we should not expect Genesis to provide a complete or systematic history of time from its origin until the Hebrews' Egyptian sojourn. The author's concern was not history for history's sake. Instead, he used true historical figures and events to teach truths about God and humankind. For instance, consider the fact that Genesis, which opened with the beginnings of life on earth, ended with a dead man in a coffin. In Romans 6:23, Paul declared that the wages of sin is death. Even so, the believers' hope for eternal life can be found in the faith of the patriarchs. Each patriarch, including Joseph, died in full confidence of God's grace (see Heb. 11:22). The Lord's redemptive program began with the family of Abraham, Isaac, and Jacob. But His plan all along was to bless all peoples throughout the earth. And He is doing this as people everywhere put their temporal lives and eternal future in the hands of the Savior, the Lord Jesus.

This far-reaching perspective concerning the patriarchs is explored at length in Hebrews 11. The phrase "by faith" begins the author's comments concerning Abraham, Isaac, Jacob, and Joseph (see vss. 17, 20-22). We learn that the last of these three blessed their sons in a way that caused them to look to the future for the fulfillment of God's promises (see Gen. 27:27-29, 38-40; 48:15-16; 50:24-25). Each of these patriarchs maintained his faith in God and His promises, even at the time of his death and even though the fulfillment of those promises must have seemed uncertain. Earlier, the author stressed that it is impossible to please God without faith (Heb. 11:6). In fact, anyone who approaches God must first believe that He exists. Furthermore, the person who approaches God must also believe that He greatly rewards "those who earnestly seek him."

Like the world of the patriarchs, our world, too, often tries to convince us that since we can neither see nor touch God, He does not exist. Therefore, the implication is that we cannot be confident that He provides salvation. At those times, we need to allow Scripture to remind us that there are realities vital to temporal life—and to eternal life—that we cannot see or touch. Our faith provides assurance of God's love for us. It also enables us to rest upon His provision of salvation (vs. 1).

Discussion Questions

1. Was there any basis for Joseph's brothers becoming afraid after their father died?

2. If you were Joseph, how would you have felt after hearing Jacob's final instructions?

3. Why do you think Joseph's brothers felt it was necessary for them to prostrate themselves in front of their brother?

4. In what way is the faith of Joseph evident in the statement he made in Genesis 50:20?

5. What are some ways you can console those who have apologized to you for their offenses against you?

Contemporary Application

The 17th-century English poet and clergyman George Herbert once wrote, "He that cannot forgive others, breaks the bridge over which he himself must pass if he would ever reach heaven; for every one has need to be forgiven." When we stand in judgment against others, no matter how just our cause seemingly is to us, in effect we are discounting the great mercy Jesus has shown to us. How can we say that another person's offense against us is even comparable to our offense against God?

Yet it takes divine empowerment to truly forgive people for some of the worst wrongs done to us. Therefore, we always need to seek God's help in rising above our weakness of character, our anger and self-pity, and our desire to hate and find some way to pay back evil for evil. We need the Lord's help to let go of those feelings of rage and resentment, and instead pay back evil with good, while trusting God's ability to carry out justice.

The American humorist and writer Mark Twain said, "Forgiveness is the fragrance the violet sheds on the heel that has crushed it." When people observe how we have been unjustly treated and how forgiveness radiates from our presence, they will sense Jesus' fragrance coming from us. Indeed, as Paul stated, "We are to God the aroma of Christ among those who are being saved and those who are perishing" (2 Cor. 2:15). When we forgive as Jesus has taught us, we become a special people—a blessing to God and others, as well as to ourselves.

Out of Egypt

Scripture

Background Scripture: *Exodus 1:8-14, 15:1-27*
Scripture Lesson: *Exodus 15:1-3, 19, 22-26*
Key Verse: *When Pharaoh's horses, chariots and horsemen went into the sea, the* LORD *brought the waters of the sea back over them, but the Israelites walked through the sea on dry ground.* Exodus 15:19.
Scripture Lesson for Children: *Exodus 15:1-3, 19, 22-26*
Key Verse for Children: *The Israelites walked through the sea on dry ground.* Exodus 15:19.

Lesson Aim

To recognize that God has the power to deliver those trapped by circumstances.

Lesson Setting

Time: *1446* B.C.
Place: *Red Sea*

Lesson Outline

Out of Egypt

    I. The Lord's Defeat of the Enemy:
        Exodus 15:1-3, 19
        A. *Triumph from the Lord: vs. 1*
        B. *Deliverance from the Lord: vss. 2-3*
        C. *Protection from the Lord: vs. 19*
   II. The Bitter Waters of Marah: Exodus 15:22-26
        A. *The Lack of Fresh Water: vss. 22-23*
        B. *The Provision of Fresh Water: vss. 24-25a*
        C. *The Lord's Decree: vss. 25b-26*

Introduction for Adults

Topic: *Following a Trusted Leader*

Detours often result in disasters. An American traveler driving through Germany missed a detour sign because he couldn't read German. Soon he was hopelessly bogged down in a small town where the streets had been torn up.

Perhaps that's the way it must have seemed to the Israelites. Their detour out of Egypt might have looked like a looming disaster, for the enemy was quickly overtaking them. However, in the case of the Israelites, the supposed detour was really God's leading. Through it He would protect them. All they had to do was trust Him.

Many times when we face unexpected turns in our lives, we might wonder whether God is in control. We have the maps to our lives pretty much figured out, and then God says, "Take a different road. Go south." The Red Sea crossing indicates that it is best for us to follow God's lead. He makes no mistakes and will watch over us every step of way. Even when it looks as if we are trapped, He reminds us to trust Him and to go forward.

Introduction for Youth

Topic: *Free!*

What's it like to be a slave? We cannot imagine the experience, because we enjoy unparalleled freedom. However, depression, fear, and despair come at us from different directions today through broken homes, broken promises, sickness, emotional and physical abuse, violence in our neighborhoods and schools, substance abuse, and suicide.

But the account of Israel's Red Sea crossing is one of God's protection of His people. The narrative also gives us many reasons for hope in the midst of despair. Teenagers readily admit their need for courage and hope. They need courage to be faithful to the Savior. Also, they need hope to handle the myriad severe crises they confront.

The biblical account reminds us that the Father is with us today in the person of His Son. Jesus said He would never leave or forsake His people. When we feel trapped between the metaphorical Egyptians and the Red Sea, we need to pray and cry out to Him for protection.

Concepts for Children

Topic: *Rescued from the Enemy*

1. God saved His people from their enemies.
2. God's people sang a song of praise to Him.
3. God's people said that He would protect them.
4. God's people learned that He wants them to obey Him.
5. God will always be with us and help us do what is right.

Lesson Commentary

I. THE LORD'S DEFEAT OF THE ENEMY: EXODUS 15:1-3, 19

A. Triumph from the Lord: vs. 1

Then Moses and the Israelites sang this song to the LORD: "I will sing to the LORD, for he is highly exalted. The horse and its rider he has hurled into the sea."

The backdrop to Exodus 15 is the Israelites' crossing of the Red Sea. Chapters 6 through 11 detail the judgment of plagues on Egypt. Then, in chapter 12, the focus shifts to the Lord's institution of Passover (vss. 1-20), followed by His striking of Egypt's firstborn (vss. 21-30). The Israelites' departure from Egypt is recounted in verses 31-42. Especially pertinent is the fact that God's chosen people had spent 430 years in Egypt when the Lord led them out. The actual Red Sea crossing is discussed in 13:17–14:31.

When the Israelites left their first encampment at Succoth, they apparently traveled southeastward to the edge of the desert of Etham, where they set up their second encampment (13:20). During the Israelites' journey, God led them in a visible and reassuring way. He provided a pillar of cloud to lead them during daytime travel, and a pillar of fire for nighttime travel (vs. 21). Also, because the pillar of cloud or of fire always remained in front of the Israelites, they were assured that they were being guided by God's own presense (vs. 22).

After the Israelites had been encamped at Etham for perhaps a few weeks, the Lord gave Moses an instruction that must have seemed strange at the time (14:1). God told Moses to lead the Israelites back toward Egypt (vs. 2). To encamp near Pi Hahiroth would place the Israelites within striking distance from the city of Rameses, the headquarters of Pharaoh and his military. God explained to Moses why He wanted the people to make this change in direction. The Lord said such rerouting would lead Pharaoh to believe the Israelites didn't know where they were going. From Pharaoh's perspective, the Israelites would seem to have come to a dead end. The sea would block them at the front and the desert at all other sides (vs. 3).

Because God continued to harden Pharaoh's heart, the Egyptian ruler would begin his pursuit of the Israelites in the desert. This was according to the sovereign plan of the Lord, who would prove to Pharaoh, the Egyptians, and the Israelites that He is the one true God. So, according to His command, the Israelites moved north and set up their third encampment near Baal Zephon (vs. 4). God had set the stage for the Israelites to be trapped by the Egyptians on one side and the sea on the other. All was going exactly according to God's redemptive plan.

Amazingly, even the deaths of the Egyptians' firstborn were not enough to make up the minds of Pharaoh and his officials. When Pharaoh learned that the Israelites had fled Egypt, he and his officials decided they should not have let the Israelites go. Pharaoh remembered that the Israelites had been an incredibly valuable workforce.

The loss of the Israelites' slave labor would be devastating to Egypt's economy (vs. 5). Consequently, Pharaoh prepared his army and stormed into the desert after the Israelites. The Egyptian forces caught up with their former slaves at the Israelite encampment opposite Baal Zephon (vss. 6-9).

When the Israelites saw that an army was after them, they became panic stricken. First, they cried out to the Lord, probably complaining that He had not protected them (vs. 10). Then they accused Moses of deceiving them by leading them into the desert to die (vs. 11). The Israelites' retort about wishing they had remained in Egypt suggests they had forgotten the despair of the situation from which they had been delivered (vs. 12). Thankfully, Moses did not react with a quick temper or agitation. Instead, he responded with patient instruction. Moses directed the people not to be afraid and to trust the Lord to rescue them from their Egyptian foes (vs. 14).

God wanted His people to move on, not complain (vs. 15). Of course, in front of Moses and the Israelites stood a body of water, and behind them were the charging Egyptians. So the Lord told Moses to part the waters by raising his staff and stretching his hand out over the banks of the sea (vs. 16). God promised to do the rest. The Lord told Moses that the Israelites would cross the sea on dry land and that the Egyptians would follow. But the Egyptians would not catch up with the Israelites, for God said He would destroy Pharaoh once and for all (vs. 17). The Lord added that He would gain glory through this mighty act (vs. 18).

Apparently, the Egyptians and the Israelites were in close proximity when the angel of God moved from the front to the rear of the Israelites (vs. 19). The angel, who had been a guide, now became a guardian. The pillar of cloud, which had guided the Israelites by day, also moved from the front to the rear of their formation that night. In turn, this obscured the oncoming Egyptians' view of the Israelites. Throughout the night, neither the Egyptians nor the Israelites came near the other (vs. 20). As Moses stretched out his hand (indicating to the people that what was about to happen was not a natural phenomenon), the Lord split the sea with a strong east wind (vs. 21). Through the night the wind blew, banking up great walls of water and drying the ground that had been the bottom of the sea (vs. 22).

Next, the Israelites began their movement across, and the Egyptians followed (vs. 23). Then, about 2 a.m. to dawn, the wheels of Pharaoh's chariots twisted off, perhaps because they were sinking into the soft ground. When the entire Egyptian army became incapacitated, they realized that the Lord had intervened on behalf of His people, which prompted the Egyptians to attempt an escape (vss. 24-25). By this time, the Israelites were safe on the other side of the Red Sea (vs. 29). The Lord again had Moses stretch his hand over the banks of the sea (vs. 26). Moses did as God had instructed, causing walls of water to crash down on the Egyptians (vs. 27).

Despite the enemies' efforts to make it back to shore, not a single soldier or chariot survived the devastating rush of water (vs. 28). The Israelites could see the bodies of the Egyptian soldiers washing up on the shore (vs. 30). The aftermath of the great miracle God had worked reinforced the Israelites' trust in the Lord and in Moses, God's faithful servant (vs. 31). Now that Moses and the Israelites were completely free from the oppression of the Egyptians, God's people began to sing to Him a song of praise and thanksgiving. They did so as a collective person—"I will sing" (15:1), noting that the Lord had exalted Himself through His glorious victory over the Egyptians. This observation is evident in the fact that God successfully threw the horses and riders of the enemy into the Red Sea.

B. Deliverance from the Lord: vss. 2-3

"The LORD is my strength and my song; he has become my salvation. He is my God, and I will praise him, my father's God, and I will exalt him. The LORD is a warrior; the LORD is his name."

Exodus 15:2 reinforces the praise offered in verse 1 for God's mighty work at the Red Sea (see Ps. 118:14; Isa. 12:2). He deserved honor for saving the Israelites from death or recapture by their foes. Both Old and New Testaments point out that believers should offer praise to God for His perfections, for His mighty works, and for His gracious benefits. While praising the Lord is viewed as a mark of His people (see Eph. 1:13-14; Phil. 1:11; 1 Pet. 2:9), one of the marks of unbelievers is their refusal to offer praise and thankfulness to God (see Rom. 1:21; Rev. 16:9). Unlike them, the Lord's followers affirm Him to be their strong defender and the one who gives them victory. The appropriate response is for every generation of believers to praise God and extol Him for His greatness (Exod. 15:2).

Verse 3 pictures the Lord as a mighty "warrior." The idea is that no one better understands how to fight and defeat the enemy in battle. This truth is demonstrated by God's strength and power overthrowing the Egyptians. He is depicted as commanding the hosts of heaven and earth from His throne room. There is an underlying assurance that despite the age-old battle between good and evil, the righteous remnant is preserved from all threats from the enemy. The Israelites respectfully gave God the credit for defeating the forces of the Egyptians. The chosen people also proclaimed that "the LORD is his name" (see 3:4-15). It's possible this statement was a final taunt to Pharaoh, who had earlier asked, "Who is the LORD, that I should obey him and let Israel go?" (5:2).

C. Protection from the Lord: vs. 19

When Pharaoh's horses, chariots and horsemen went into the sea, the LORD brought the waters of the sea back over them, but the Israelites walked through the sea on dry ground.

The song next turns to some of the details of God's victory in the Israelites' behalf. The people sang about Pharaoh and his army being inundated by the waters of the sea and drowning (Exod. 15:4). The Lord, by His awesome power, broke the enemy in pieces (vs. 5). Also, by the abundance of His majesty, the Lord overthrew those who rose up against Him (vs. 6). His anger blazed out against His foes, consuming them like straw (vs. 7). The Israelites compared the east wind that divided the Red Sea to the blast of God's nostrils (vs. 8). And after mentioning the Egyptians' arrogance (vs. 9), the Israelites recounted how the waters collapsing on the enemy was due to the blowing of God's breath (vs. 10).

At a pivotal point in the song, the chosen people declared that the Lord was incomparable among the false gods worshiped by unbelievers. None of these powerless, lifeless idols could match the Lord's holy majesty, awesome splendor, and mighty acts (vs. 11). After all, God had caused the Egyptians to be gulped down into the earth, figuratively speaking (vs. 12). The situation was very different for the Israelites. By His steadfast love, God led His people, whom He had "redeemed" (vs. 13). Moreover, by His strength the Lord guided the Israelites to their sacred home. Most likely, "holy dwelling" is a metaphorical reference to the promised land, though it might also refer to the future house of worship that would someday be constructed.

God's deliverance of His people would cause other nations to fear Israel (vss. 14-16). The order in which these nations are listed—Philistia, Edom, Moab, and Canaan—roughly previews the route the Israelites would follow in their travels toward their sacred home. While the Israelites praised God for His power, they realized that they were a people who had been purchased or acquired by God. Therefore, they had every reason to believe that the Lord would establish them in their new land. He would succeed in planting them on His holy mountain, the special place reserved for His own dwelling (vs. 17). The song concludes with a final burst of praise for God. The Israelites rejoiced in the fact that the Lord's reign will last forever (vs. 18). Verse 19 recaps the supernatural event that occurred at the Red Sea. A vast number of Egyptian horses, chariots, and drivers went into the sea, only to be drowned by its surging waters. Meanwhile, the Israelites walked on dry land through the middle of the sea.

Verse 20 describes how Miriam, Moses' sister, launched into her own song of praise. At this time, Miriam must have been in her 90s, since she was a young girl at the time of Moses' birth (and Moses was now in his 80s; see 2:4, 7-8). As Miriam played her hand-drum (or tambourine) and sang, other women began following her, playing hand-drums themselves and dancing to her song. It was very common in ancient times for women to dance on occasions of military victory. Miriam is the first woman in the Bible to be called a prophetess. Numbers 12:2 records that she made the claim to have spoken God's word, just as Moses and Aaron had. Also, Micah 6:4 reports that the Lord delivered Israel from the Egyptians by the hand of Moses, Aaron, and Miriam. Clearly, Miriam played an important role in the events that transpired during the Exodus. Like the song of Moses, Miriam's ode recounted God's deliverance of the Israelites (Exod. 15:21).

II. THE BITTER WATERS OF MARAH: EXODUS 15:22-26

A. The Lack of Fresh Water: vss. 22-23

Then Moses led Israel from the Red Sea and they went into the Desert of Shur. For three days they traveled in the desert without finding water. When they came to Marah, they could not drink its water because it was bitter. (That is why the place is called Marah.)

After Moses led the Israelites away from the shores of the Red Sea, the lawgiver shepherded them southeast into the Desert of Shur (located in the northwestern portion of the Sinai Peninsula; see Num. 33:8). The chosen people continued traveling south for three more days in the desert, all the while finding no water (Exod. 15:22). When the Israelites arrived at Marah, they found they were not able to drink its water because of it being "bitter" (vs. 23) in taste. Evidently, the water was salty and brackish, which explains the place being called Marah, which means "bitter."

B. The Provision of Fresh Water: vss. 24-25a

So the people grumbled against Moses, saying, "What are we to drink?" Then Moses cried out to the LORD, and the LORD showed him a piece of wood. He threw it into the water, and the water became sweet.

The Hebrew verb rendered "grumbled" (Exod. 15:24) refers to more than just incidental complaining. Behind the Israelites' murmuring was rebellion, in which they questioned the Lord's motives and abilities (see Exod. 16:2; 17:3; Num. 14:2; 16:11, 41). Since the people could not directly voice their dissatisfaction to God, they targeted Moses with the question of what they were going to drink. Undoubtedly, Moses was tired of the Israelites' frequent whining. This time, in response to their murmuring, the lawgiver prayed earnestly to the Lord for help. God, in turn, answered Moses' plea by instructing him to toss a piece of wood (possibly a branch from a nearby tree) into the water. When Moses did so, the water became "sweet" (Exod. 15:25), that is, safe to drink.

C. The Lord's Decree: vss. 25b-26

There the LORD made a decree and a law for them, and there he tested them. He said, "If you listen carefully to the voice of the LORD your God and do what is right in his eyes, if you pay attention to his commands and keep all his decrees, I will not bring on you any of the diseases I brought on the Egyptians, for I am the LORD, who heals you."

While the Israelites were encamped at Marah, God issued a binding ordinance for them. It was a statute that would test them at that moment as well as into the future (Exod. 15:25). The reason the Lord did is that the Israelites had just demonstrated their true nature. Specifically, instead of trusting God to provide for their needs, they had manifested their lack of belief by grumbling. The decree the Lord gave was straightforward. He wanted His people to "listen carefully" (vs. 26) to His commands and keep them. The point of the ordinance was that the Israelites were to learn to rely completely on God. They were to heed His directives, do what He considered to be right, and abide by all His "commands" and "decrees." As they did so, the Lord promised to protect them from the various diseases He had inflicted on the Egyptians. He, the Israelites' divine Healer, would provide for their needs. In turn, they were to trust Him at every step of the way along the path of their earthly sojourn.

Discussion Questions

1. What feelings come to mind for you as you read the song of Moses?
2. Why is it important for believers to look to God for strength in times of difficulty?
3. Do you think the Israelites had a real reason to murmur against Moses? Explain.
4. What are some ways God might currently be testing your faith in Him?
5. In what sense do you believe God is the divine Healer?

Contemporary Application

Imagine an escape artist performing before a packed auditorium. Handcuffs secure his wrists behind his back. A padlocked chain encircles his ankles. A blindfold covers his eyes. Volunteers from the audience then lift him into a coffin-sized box and nail down the heavy lid. The artist's assistant stands to one side of the stage, where a giant stopwatch is on display. She sets the hands ticking. The artist has 10 minutes to escape or else he will run out of air.

Now imagine the artist inside the box. The key he had hidden in his mouth has fallen out of his reach. He can hear the audience counting down the time he has left. He knows that unless he gets help soon, he will die. The time ticks down to almost nothing. Finally, the artist cries out for help, and the assistant orders the box torn open. In a moment, the dazed artist is freed by the volunteers, and the audience responds with grateful applause.

The main message of the Bible is that we cannot help ourselves, not one bit. Much as we would like to have the key to our own salvation, so we could effect our own rescue, we need to admit to ourselves that we have lost the key and cannot be our deliverers. Just as only God could rescue the Israelites from their Egyptian taskmasters, so too only the Lord has the power to deliver us from sin and give us eternal life.

Perhaps at times we have faced something like the Red Sea and thought that we had finally gone beyond the point where the Lord could be of any help. But we have the historically reliable testimony of Scripture, of those we know, and even of our own experience to tell us that God is bigger than whatever we are facing. He is never late, and His plan is always good, though we may not see it from our current perspective.

Justified by Faith

Scripture

Background Scripture: *Galatians 1:1–2:21*
Scripture Lesson: *Galatians 2:15-21*
Key Verse: *"I have been crucified with Christ and I no longer live, but Christ lives in me. The life I live in the body, I live by faith in the Son of God, who loved me and gave himself for me."* Galatians 2:20.
Scripture Lesson for Children: *Galatians 2:15-21*
Key Verse for Children: *"The life I live in the body, I live by faith in the Son of God, who loved me and gave himself for me."* Galatians 2:20.

Lesson Aim

To emphasize the importance of relating to the Savior on the basis of faith alone.

Lesson Setting

Time: Either A.D. *48–49 (the South Galatian theory) or* A.D. *53–57 (the North Galatian theory)*
Place: Either the churches in a geographic area called Galatia that was located in central Asia Minor (now Turkey; the North Galatian theory) or the churches in the southern part of the Roman province of Galatia (the South Galatian theory)

Lesson Outline

Justified by Faith
   I.   Faith-Righteousness, Not Works-Righteousness: Galatians 2:15-18
        A. *Being Justified by Faith: vss. 15-16*
        B. *Affirming That All Are Sinners: vss. 17-18*
   II. New Life in the Son: Galatians 2:19-21
        A. *Dying to the Law: vs. 19*
        B. *Living by Faith: vss. 20-21*

Introduction for Adults

Topic: *Seeking Something to Believe In*

Paul declared that the good news about Christ did not embarrass him, for the Gospel represented the power of God at work in saving everyone who believes (Rom. 1:16). Sadly, we find many people in our culture who reject the importance of getting right with God by believing the truth of the Gospel.

According to the polls, a lot of people claim to be "religious." Nevertheless, many in the West take little account of God. Perhaps there is little fear of facing a holy God because the idea of sin has virtually been abolished.

The Gospel, which Paul proclaimed, won't make the evening news on television. It won't even make newspaper headlines. It's thus the responsibility of believers to carry the Good News far and wide so that all may hear it and have the opportunity to be saved. Perhaps the Father in His grace might use your proclamation of the Gospel to prompt some who hear it to get right with Him by trusting in His Son.

Introduction for Youth

Topic: *Got Faith?*

A man bought two batteries, took them home, and inserted them into his tape recorder. Surprisingly, nothing happened. He then returned the batteries to the store and received two new ones. However, he eventually discovered that his problem was not with the batteries but rather with the way he had inserted them.

The same sort of thing happens when we carve out our own plans for pleasing God. We trick ourselves into thinking that, regardless of what we do, God is pleased most of the time. This reasoning reflects the mindset of a college student who said that God would accept him because he did what was right 99 percent of the time. This is flawed thinking, for as James 2:10 says, the person who keeps all of the laws except one is as guilty as the person who has broken all of God's laws.

Who, then, has the power to obey God? Apart from Christ, no one has this ability. But the good news is that through faith in Him we not only are declared righteous but also receive power to obey God. With Jesus at our side, we can live in a way that genuinely pleases God.

Concepts for Children

Topic: *I Believe*

1. God showed His love for us by sending us His Son, Jesus.
2. God wants us to believe in Jesus for salvation.
3. God wants us to tell other people about Jesus.
4. Jesus wants us to live for Him.
5. Jesus wants us to love one another.

Lesson Commentary

I. FAITH-RIGHTEOUSNESS, NOT WORKS-RIGHTEOUSNESS: GALATIANS 2:15-18

A. Being Justified by Faith: vss. 15-16

"We who are Jews by birth and not 'Gentile sinners' know that a man is not justified by observing the law, but by faith in Jesus Christ. So we, too, have put our faith in Christ Jesus that we may be justified by faith in Christ and not by observing the law, because by observing the law no one will be justified."

The location of the churches addressed in Galatians is a matter of debate that centers on two prominent theories. The North Galatian theory holds that Paul wrote the epistle for believers living in the old, ethnic area called Galatia in north-central Asia Minor. Though the Book of Acts does not mention Paul's journey there, supporters of this view believe that he visited the area on his second missionary journey and wrote the Letter to the Galatians shortly afterward, about A.D. 53–57. The South Galatian theory suggests that Paul wrote Galatians to churches in the southern area of the Roman province of Galatia, in the cities of Antioch, Iconium, Lystra, and Derbe. We know that Paul founded churches there on his first missionary journey (Acts 13–14). Proponents of this view disagree whether Paul wrote Galatians before the Jerusalem Council (mentioned in Acts 15:1-29) or afterward. If the apostle wrote Galatians after the Council, it is surprising that he did not mention the event, as it dealt with the same issues that are covered in the epistle.

Regardless of which view is preferred, it is clear that during Paul's absence from the Galatians, some Jews who professed being Christians had come among them and had begun calling into question the apostle's authority and spreading false doctrine. Today these false teachers are called Judaizers. The legalists apparently taught that faith in Christ is not adequate for acceptance by God. Obedience to the Mosaic law, or at least to parts of it, is also necessary. Consequently, they were trying to enforce the law on the Gentile believers in Galatia.

The Judaizers' teaching drew a fierce reaction from Paul. In the apostle's mind, to make the law mandatory for salvation is, in effect, to nullify the Gospel. Salvation is by grace through faith in the Son alone, apart from the works of the law. Believers are not bound by the law but are free in the Messiah. Paul could not immediately go to Galatia to straighten out the churches in person. So he wrote to them, defending his teachings and his status as an apostle (Gal. 1–2), explaining Christian freedom from the law (3–4), and encouraging the Galatians to live out their freedom in Christ (Gal. 5–6).

After Paul's strong condemnation of the false teachers at the beginning of this letter, he went on to make a case for his ministry and message (1:10–2:10). He revealed that before his conversion, he had been a zealous supporter of Judaism and its ancient traditions. But through Paul's conversion, the Lord gave him a new message, the true Gospel. God confirmed this message through revelation and the positive recognition of the other apostles, including James, Peter, and John. Beginning in 2:11, Paul related a circumstance involving hypocritical behavior on the part of Peter. Since Peter was acting improperly, Paul wasted no time in censuring Peter in a personal and possibly public confrontation. Peter's inappropriate behavior concerned his refusal to fellowship with Gentile believers in the church at Syrian Antioch because they did not keep all the Jewish rules. For instance, before eating church meals and the Lord's Supper, they did not wash ritually as the law required. According to Jewish tradition, such omissions meant Jews should not associate with them. Nevertheless, the Jewish Christians in Antioch overlooked the infractions committed by their Gentile associates. Indeed, the two groups ate together, and in other ways lived in harmony.

At some point, Peter came to Syrian Antioch, presumably to contribute temporarily to the church work going on there. Initially, Peter participated fully with the Gentile Christians, as did the other Jewish Christians, since he had learned not to call anyone unclean (see Acts 10:28). But all that changed after some legalists from Jerusalem arrived in Syrian Antioch (Gal. 2:12). Not much is known about these men or why James sent them to Antioch. They may have carried a message to Peter from James that changed Peter's mind. At any rate, somehow the pro-circumcision group caused Peter to begin drawing back from the Gentile Christians. Once Peter set the example, other Jewish Christians in Syrian Antioch began drawing back from Gentiles too. Even more disappointing to Paul was the hypocritical behavior of Barnabas, who had been Paul's partner in evangelizing the Gentiles. Barnabas allowed himself to be led astray by the Judaizers (vs. 13).

The Jewish observance of circumcision (the act of removing the foreskin in males) has its roots in God's command to Abraham (see Gen. 17:9-27). The Lord told the patriarch to be circumcised and to circumcise all the males of his household. This practice was to be repeated on all of Abraham's male descendants as well as others in the covenant community. The performance of this rite represented an oath confirming the covenant. Circumcision meant, "If I am untrue to the covenant, may I be cut off like my foreskin." Over time, some legalistic Jews began to see circumcision not as a sign of a relationship with God, but as the means to a relationship with Him. This overvaluation of circumcision started to negatively influence the early church. Paul's view was that while Jews were free to decide whether to circumcise themselves and their male offspring, one should not try to force Gentile believers to be circumcised.

Jesus' atoning sacrifice had broken down the wall of hostility that once divided Jews and Gentiles (see Eph. 2:14-18). Now Paul was horrified to see that wall being rebuilt in the church at Syrian Antioch. To prevent further damage being done to the Body of Christ, Paul took quick and decisive action. Since Peter had started the defection by his public actions, Paul decided to rebuke him publicly. Undoubtedly, Paul thought that by doing so, he could change the minds of others, too. The first part of Paul's strategy was to point out to Peter the inconsistency of his actions (Gal. 2:14). Paul noted that before the Judaizers arrived, Peter, a Jew, had lived like a Gentile (by ignoring Jewish laws and customs). So why was he now demanding that Gentiles live like Jews (by following those laws and customs)? To say one thing and do another is the essence of hypocrisy.

Peter was not alone in his pretense. The other Jewish believers in the church at Syrian Antioch, except Paul, also stood condemned in this matter. Accordingly, Paul broadened his speech to address all those who were "Jews by birth" (Gal. 2:15) and not sinners from among the Gentiles. The latter is how Jews in that day commonly referred to non-Jews. For centuries, Jewish legalists believed they could make themselves acceptable to God by obeying the Mosaic law, but they were mistaken. No one can perfectly obey the law, so no one can be justified by keeping the law. In fact, that was never the law's purpose. Paul's fellow Jewish believers had learned that sinners can be justified only through faith in the Messiah (vs. 16). In short, it was not just Gentiles who needed the Savior; Jews needed Him too.

B. Affirming That All Are Sinners: vss. 17-18

"If, while we seek to be justified in Christ, it becomes evident that we ourselves are sinners, does that mean that Christ promotes sin? Absolutely not! If I rebuild what I destroyed, I prove that I am a lawbreaker."

In Paul's day, the Greek verb translated "justified" (Gal. 2:17) signified a court setting with a judge declaring an individual "not guilty." The idea of justification comes from a judge pronouncing someone to be righteous or innocent of a crime. The word had a technical forensic application of a onetime rendering of a positive judicial verdict. Paul used the term to refer to God's declaration that the believing sinner is righteous because of the atoning work of the Messiah on the cross. This perspective is evident in Romans 1:17, where Paul talked about a "righteousness from God . . . that is by faith." The noun translated "righteousness" comes from a root word that means "straightness" and refers to that which is in accordance with established moral norms. In a legal sense, righteousness means to be vindicated or treated as just.

From a biblical perspective, God's character is the definition and source of righteousness. As a result, the righteousness of human beings is defined in terms of God's holiness. Because the Lord solely provides righteousness, it cannot be produced or obtained by human efforts. God makes His righteousness available to all people without distinction. Just as there is no discrimination with Him in universally condemning all people as sinners, so God does not show partiality by offering righteousness to one particular ethnic group. The Lord freely gives it to all people—regardless of their race or gender—when they trust in the Messiah.

Against this backdrop, we find that God's law serves several purposes. First, it is like a mirror that reflects the perfect righteousness of the Lord and a person's own sinfulness and shortcomings. While the law does not cause people to sin, it frames their actions as sin by revealing God's evaluation of what they have done (see Rom. 7:7). Second, the law not only shows people their sin, but also steers them away from it and toward the Savior (see Gal. 3:19-24). The law is like a map. While it does not mark out the road to God, it does show a person the landscape of a God-pleasing life once he or she is traveling on the road. Third, the law may restrain evil. Admittedly, the law cannot change the wicked bent of the human heart. Nevertheless, the law can somewhat inhibit anarchy by its threats of judgment, especially when those threats are reinforced by civil codes that administer punishment for confirmed transgressions (see Deut. 13:6-11; 19:16-21; Rom. 13:3-4).

Paul's teaching that we are justified by faith, and not by works, led some critics to charge that he was encouraging Jews to become sinners (namely, breakers of the law). For example, when Paul encouraged Jewish believers to have fellowship with Gentile believers, he was said to be going against Jewish laws. Paul was concerned, because at first glance one might conclude that his teaching promoted sin (Gal. 2:17). The critics also claimed that Paul's teaching not only degraded the value of the law, but also disgraced the Messiah. "Absolutely not!" was Paul's response. Jesus did not further any Jewish believer's sinning just because the new convert abandoned law keeping as the way to salvation. In fact, for Christians to revert to the Jewish law is really to break the law (vs. 18). Paul may have been thinking of Peter's attempt to rebuild the wall of hostility between Jew and Gentile that had been torn down by the Gospel. Peter's efforts reinstated the condemnation of the law. Paul argued that the lawbreaker was not the one who looked to the Messiah in faith for justification. Instead, it was the one who looked to the law for justification.

II. NEW LIFE IN THE SON: GALATIANS 2:19-21

A. Dying to the Law: vs. 19

"For through the law I died to the law so that I might live for God."

Paul declared that he had stopped living for the Mosaic law, for the law had put him to death. Through the law, he realized how spiritually dead he was and how much he needed the Redeemer. When Paul trusted in the Messiah for salvation, the apostle was identified with Jesus' death, burial, and resurrection. Through spiritual union with the Son, Paul died to the law so that he could live for God (Gal. 2:19). Paul expanded on these important theological truths in Romans 6:3-8. He noted that all believers who are baptized into Christ were also baptized into His death. Believers are also raised as Jesus was raised from the dead in order to live a new life. Through the identification of believers with the Messiah, their old sinful selves were crucified with Him so that sin might lose its power in their lives. The upshot is that believers are no longer slaves to sin because they have been freed from its once irresistible power.

In Paul's day, Roman slaves were often devalued as individuals, and stripped of ordinary rights and privileges. Frequently, slaves would carry the name of the master (some were even branded with the name of the master) and left with no identity of their own. However, when a slave master died, his power and influence died as well. Thus, a slave would be set free from the owner's control once that master died. Paul said that believers who are baptized into Christ experience something similar in the spiritual realm. Just as Jesus died on the cross, the sin nature of believers was crucified as well. Also, just as Jesus rose from the dead, likewise His followers live a new life through their identification with Him. And just as a branch is grafted into a tree, so too believers grow together with Christ. Moreover, just as a grafted branch receives its life from the life flow of the branch, in a corresponding way Jesus' followers receive life from Him.

B. Living by Faith: vss. 20-21

"I have been crucified with Christ and I no longer live, but Christ lives in me. The life I live in the body, I live by faith in the Son of God, who loved me and gave himself for me. I do not set aside the grace of God, for if righteousness could be gained through the law, Christ died for nothing!"

God established the Mosaic law to show people their need for a fuller relationship with Him—a relationship made available through faith in the Messiah. Popular opinion sees faith as irrational. It's supposedly believing something even when your mind tells you not to. In contrast, the biblical concept of faith includes both reason and experience. Such faith, however, is not limited to what we can see. It makes unseen spiritual realities perceivable, not by willing them into existence, but by a conviction that what God has said about them is true (see Heb. 11:1). Biblical faith is rooted in the knowledge of God (see vs. 6). Those who possess this faith believe that God exists and that He rewards those who truly want to know Him.

Faith is so foundational to the Christian life that one cannot be in a relationship with the Lord Jesus apart from it. In a sense, we who have trusted in the Messiah for salvation have been nailed to the cross with Him and have also spiritually died there with Him. Furthermore, we have been united with Him in His resurrection. Now that we have been saved, Jesus lives within us, and we look to Him for direction in life (Gal. 2:20). The point of justification is not only to save us, but also to make it possible that we can live our lives for God. Because of our union with the Son, we share in His resurrection power. This does not mean that our old sin nature is completely eradicated. But it does mean that through faith, we can limit its power and experience victory over it. Rather than lead to increased sinfulness, our union with the Redeemer gives us the power to live a holy life.

Paul was insisting that a person who trusted in the Messiah was changed. To think about going back to the former way of life was absurd to one who had become a new creation. Though the possibility of sinning remained, the Son gave the believer the power to resist the temptation to sin, something the Mosaic law could never do. Apparently, the Judaizers claimed that Paul nullified God's grace in giving Israel the law when the apostle taught that Gentiles did not have to obey all the law. Far from it, said Paul. He did not set aside the grace of God. Instead, the apostle established God's grace by teaching that justification and right behavior are possible through the Messiah rather than through the law (vs. 21). Besides that, if righteousness before God could be obtained by human effort, then Jesus would not have died upon the cross. Moreover, if the law could bring about salvation, then the Redeemer died for no purpose. Any believer who relies on human effort for salvation essentially undermines his or her own faith.

Discussion Questions

1. In Paul's day, what sorts of tensions existed between Jews and Gentiles?
2. Why isn't it possible to be justified by observing God's law?
3. What difference has believing in the Lord Jesus made in your life?
4. Why would it be wrong to declare that the doctrine of justification by faith promotes sin?
5. How would you define the true Gospel to your unsaved peers?

Contemporary Application

Paul's Letter to the Galatians emphasizes the centrality of the Messiah in the apostle's thought and life. In this way Paul becomes a good role model for us. Do we trust in anything other than the Son to make ourselves pleasing to God? At every point of our decision making, do we ask ourselves what the Savior would have us do?

In answering these questions, we come to see that it is not enough to disregard false teachers. We should also listen to godly ones. These are believers who reject the notion of being saved by good works and affirm the truth of being declared righteous through faith in Christ. In addition to remaining true to the Gospel, they teach Jesus' followers how to remain faithful to God, how to be more like the Messiah, and how to serve Him. Good teachers will help believers comprehend these things about the Lord. That's why, in today's supermarket of religious ideas, Christians should beware. They should accept only what conforms to the Gospel of the Son.

Moreover, it is our duty to proclaim to others that eternal life is not moored to a system of legalistic rules. Rather, it is anchored to the Messiah. We also have a responsibility to tell unbelievers that the Father gives salvation to those who believe in His Son. As we depend on the Lord Jesus, He will give us the strength we need to make Him known to the lost.

Freed from Law

Scripture

Background Scripture: *Galatians 3:1-14*

Scripture Lesson: *Galatians 3:1-14*

Key Verse: *[Christ] redeemed us in order that the blessing given to Abraham might come to the Gentiles through Christ Jesus, so that by faith we might receive the promise of the Spirit.* Galatians 3:14.

Scripture Lesson for Children: *Galatians 3:1-14*

Key Verse for Children: *The law is not based on faith; on the contrary, "The man who does these things will live by them."* Galatians 3:12.

Lesson Aim

To be reminded of the Father's spiritual blessings to all who trust in His Son for salvation.

Lesson Setting

Time: Either A.D. *48–49 (the South Galatian theory) or* A.D. *53–57 (the North Galatian theory)*

Place: Either the churches in a geographic area called Galatia that was located in central Asia Minor (now Turkey; the North Galatian theory) or the churches in the southern part of the Roman province of Galatia (the South Galatian theory)

Lesson Outline

Freed from Law

I. Faith in the Crucified Messiah: Galatians 3:1-5
   A. *Believing the Message about the Messiah: vss. 1-2*
   B. *Experiencing the Presence and Power of God: vss. 3-5*

II. Abraham—A Case in Point: Galatians 3:6-9
   A. *Abraham's Spiritual Children: vss. 6-7*
   B. *Being Blessed Along with Abraham: vss. 8-9*

III. Redeemed from the Curse of the Law: Galatians 3:10-14
   A. *The Way of Faith: vss. 10-12*
   B. *The Messiah's Saving Work: vss. 13-14*

Introduction for Adults

Topic: *The Place of Ultimate Trust*

Hundreds of millions of dollars are given away every year to winners of state lotteries. To claim your prize, you have to produce a ticket showing the winning numbers. On some occasions, officials wait for days for someone to show up with a rightful claim to the money. Many weeks no one claims the prize, because no one matches the numbers, and the jackpot is rolled over.

From the madness surrounding multimillion-dollar prizes, one would think the lottery is the biggest thing anyone could ever win in his or her life. Meanwhile, what is really the biggest jackpot of all often goes unclaimed. It's a prize that brings lasting satisfaction and eternal life—nothing a lottery prize could ever do for us.

People fail to realize what the Father has done for them in His Son (see Gal. 3:8-9, 13-14). And so they fail to claim the spiritual wealth that comes through faith in Him. The multitude of God's blessings in Christ are waiting to be claimed, and we do not need a lottery ticket to win. The question is, what prevents us from coming to the one who is the place of ultimate trust?

Introduction for Youth

Topic: *Free at Last!*

Grandpa tried to help his 8-year-old grandson put together a new toy. "I know how to do this," the boy said, rejecting his grandfather's assistance. Perhaps initially we might think such an attitude represents childish pride. But then it's sobering to realize that this way of thinking is evident in many adolescents.

"I don't need your help" means we feel self-sufficient. When we have such an attitude, it's humiliating to admit that we need help. Perhaps this is the greatest stumbling block that keeps many younger and older people—like the legalists of Paul's day—from coming to faith in Christ (see Gal. 3:1-5). After all, who wants to admit he or she is enslaved to sin? And who wants to say that only God can free him or her from sin's bondage?

The Gospel cuts to the heart of the issue—our stubborn pride and willful independence from God. Until we understand and admit out spiritual need, we will not be prepared to come to the Lord on His terms. It's only when we accept our inability that we will be ready to receive the Father's gift of salvation through faith in His Son.

Concepts for Children

Topic: *I Am Free*

1. Jesus died on the cross to free us from our sins.
2. When we believe in Jesus, God forgives our sins.
3. When we believe in Jesus, God gives us His Spirit.
4. Abraham is a person who put his faith in the Lord.
5. The Holy Spirit helps us to do what God wants.

Lesson Commentary

I. FAITH IN THE CRUCIFIED MESSIAH: GALATIANS 3:1-5

A. Believing the Message about the Messiah: vss. 1-2

You foolish Galatians! Who has bewitched you? Before your very eyes Jesus Christ was clearly portrayed as crucified. I would like to learn just one thing from you: Did you receive the Spirit by observing the law, or by believing what you heard?

At this point in his letter, Paul began a more systematic argument against the position of the Judaizers. Carefully, line upon line, the apostle presented reasons and proofs concerning why the believers in the church at Galatia should not depend upon the Mosaic law to earn God's favor (Gal. 3–4). To set the stage for his argument, Paul asked his readers a series of pointed questions (3:1-5). The apostle prefaced his queries with the unusual address "foolish Galatians" (vs. 1). Paul did not mean they were half-witted. Rather, he accused them of not using their God-given intelligence to the best advantage. They should have known better than to believe the Judaizers. Also, by calling his readers "Galatians," rather than "brothers" as before (see 1:11), the apostle adopted a more formal tone suiting his message.

Paul's first question was one he did not actually expect his readers to answer: "Who has bewitched you?" He and they both knew he was talking about the Judaizers. The Greek verb rendered "bewitched" refers to the casting of a spell and figuratively points to the act of deception. In a manner of speaking, some of Paul's readers had been duped by the visitors among them. Immediately after the first question, the apostle reminded the Galatians that they had heard him preach the truth about Jesus' crucifixion. In fact, Paul had described the Savior's atoning sacrifice at Calvary and its significance so plainly that it was as though the Galatians had seen the event with their own eyes. Here is another reason the Galatians should have known better than to be taken in by the Judaizers' doctrine, since that teaching in effect made the Son's death unnecessary (see 2:21).

The Greek verb translated "clearly portrayed" (3:1) literally referred to the posting of a notice or placard in a public place. In New Testament times the word was often used to describe a father's proclaiming that he would not be responsible for the debts of a wayward son. Paul used the same expression to convey the opposite message. On the Father's behalf, the apostle had vividly set forth the image of the Son crucified. In this case, the message of the public notice was not that the Father refused responsibility for the sin debt of humanity, which the Son had taken on Himself. Rather, because of the death of His Son, the Father had canceled the sin debt for all who believe.

Once Paul brought the image of Jesus' death and its significance to the minds of the Galatians, the apostle next asked them the central question: How did they receive the Spirit of God? The Judaizers would have argued that Paul's readers had to obey the law of Moses before receiving the Spirit. The apostle, however, said the Galatians received the Spirit after hearing about the Messiah and trusting in Him for salvation (vs. 2). As was the case for the recipients of Paul's letter, all the spiritual blessings we receive from the Father are based on our faith in His Son.

B. Experiencing the Presence and Power of God: vss. 3-5

Are you so foolish? After beginning with the Spirit, are you now trying to attain your goal by human effort? Have you suffered so much for nothing—if it really was for nothing? Does God give you his Spirit and work miracles among you because you observe the law, or because you believe what you heard?

In Galatians 3:3, Paul maintained that his readers began their Christian life in the Son by the Spirit. Therefore, it would have been foolish for them to continue in that life by their own power. Indeed, they were powerless to complete in their own strength what God's Spirit had started in them. The "human effort" Paul mentioned is a reference to observing the Mosaic law. Verse 4 suggests that the apostle's readers had "suffered" for their faith. Admittedly, we don't have any record of the believers at Galatia being persecuted, even though of course it is possible that they were mistreated before Paul wrote his letter to them. In referring to the suffering experienced by his readers, the apostle maintained that if they now abandoned the Gospel, their adversity would be in vain.

Finally, Paul repeated his central question (see vss. 2, 5). The wording of the question in verse 5 is slightly different from in verse 2, notably in the addition of the word "miracles." This may refer to gifts and works of the Spirit that the Galatians enjoyed since their salvation. The apostle asserted that God had given the believers at Galatia His Spirit and worked miracles in their lives because they had trusted in the Messiah, not because they had obeyed the Mosaic law. While we may be inclined to join Paul in his feeling of indignation at the Galatians' betrayal of all God had done for them, we should first take a look at ourselves. Do we ever forget all we have been through as Christians—both the good and the bad experiences—when a particularly appealing temptation appears? If we keep in touch with the Spirit and use our God-given intelligence, we may be able to avoid mistakes that would sidetrack us in our spiritual journey.

II. ABRAHAM—A CASE IN POINT: GALATIANS 3:6-9

A. Abraham's Spiritual Children: vss. 6-7

Consider Abraham: "He believed God, and it was credited to him as righteousness." Understand, then, that those who believe are children of Abraham.

After calling on the Galatians to remember their own experiences with the Savior, Paul proceeded to strengthen his argument for the superiority of grace over the law by appealing to Scripture. The apostle's first scriptural teachings were grouped around the figure of Abraham (Gal. 3:6-9). As we learned in earlier lessons this quarter, Abraham was one of a family of idol worshipers in the Mesopotamian city of Ur around 2091 B.C., when the living God called him to move to Canaan. At the age of 75, Abraham obeyed. He and the members of his clan never had a permanent home in Canaan, but rather ranged across it as nomads, and even lived for periods in neighboring areas. Yet God blessed them, and Abraham became wealthy. God repeatedly promised Abraham that he would have a son and that his descendants would possess the land of Canaan. Finally, when Abraham was 100 years old, his son Isaac was born. The patriarch of Israel died at the age of 175 (see Gen. 11:26–25:11).

Evidently, Paul's opponents had taught the Christians at Galatia that male Gentile believers needed to be circumcised, as Abraham had been, to truly become the patriarch's spiritual children and participate in God's blessings upon Abraham. So Paul had to set the record straight. In discussing Abraham, the apostle may have used the same Bible passages the Judaizers had used, only interpreting them differently. One example would be Genesis 15:6 (Gal. 3:6). One night, God promised Abraham that He would give him descendants as numberless as the stars. Long before the Mosaic law existed, the patriarch believed God's promise that he would have a son and, through the son, many descendants. God accepted Abraham's faith and declared that the patriarch was in a right relationship with Him because of it.

Paul was saying that we can become justified before God in the same way as Abraham, namely, through faith. Of course, Abraham's faith was in a promise, since he lived before the advent of the Lord Jesus. Yet the patriarch's faith in the divine promise, like saving faith in the Messiah, involved believing God. All who trust in the Father through the Son are declared righteous. For this reason, all who have saving faith are the spiritual children of Abraham (vs. 7). Even Gentiles, who are neither physically descended from Abraham nor necessarily circumcised, can become children of Abraham through faith in the Messiah.

This view contrasts sharply with the perspective of the Judaizers, who maintained that Abraham had so much righteousness (in terms of good works) that he had a surplus of merit. Allegedly, this merit was available to the patriarch's descendants. Many first-century Jews also believed Abraham was a perfect example of a person who is justified by performing good works. In Romans 4:2, Paul fully agreed that the patriarch was a righteous individual and that, as such, he had something to boast about before people, "but not before God." As was noted in lesson 2, Paul substantiated his point in verse 3 by quoting from Genesis 15:6 (just as the apostle had done in Gal. 3:6). In short, Abraham's life was a perfect illustration that righteousness before God is by faith, not by works.

B. Being Blessed Along with Abraham: vss. 8-9

The Scripture foresaw that God would justify the Gentiles by faith, and announced the gospel in advance to Abraham: "All nations will be blessed through you." So those who have faith are blessed along with Abraham, the man of faith.

The inclusion of Gentiles in Abraham's spiritual family was part of God's plan from the beginning. Paul personified the Scripture, saying that it "foresaw" (Gal. 3:8) God's justification of Gentiles and "announced" the Gospel to Abraham. This means that God, represented by His Word, preached the Gospel of grace for Gentiles even as early as Abraham's day. This occurred when God declared to the patriarch, "All nations will be blessed through you" (see Gen. 12:3; 18:18; 22:18).

The Lord Jesus is a descendant of Abraham. Through the Son, the Father's grace is available to people of all nations. Expressed differently, through the Son, the blessings the Father promised to Abraham are distributed worldwide in the form of salvation and life in the Spirit. Just as the patriarch believed God's promise and was blessed, so too all who believe the truth of the Gospel are blessed (Gal. 3:9). Many people mistakenly view the Old Testament as having little more than historical value for Christians. Yet we should be thrilled to realize that many promises of the Old Testament are applicable to believers of all time. Indeed, we are spiritual children of Abraham!

II. REDEEMED FROM THE CURSE OF THE LAW: GALATIANS 3:10-14

A. The Way of Faith: vss. 10-12

All who rely on observing the law are under a curse, for it is written: "Cursed is everyone who does not continue to do everything written in the Book of the Law." Clearly no one is justified before God by the law, because, "The righteous will live by faith." The law is not based on faith; on the contrary, "The man who does these things will live by them."

The Judaizers argued from the Hebrew Scriptures that one had to meticulously obey the Mosaic law to be justified in the eyes of God. To counter this falsehood, Paul may have turned to many of the same passages used by his opponents, though the apostle understood them in a completely different way. The gist of Paul's response is found in Galatians 3:10-13. Here he made four points, backing up each one with a scriptural quotation. Then, in verse 14, the apostle made a concluding observation.

Paul's first point is that all who rely on doing the works of the Mosaic law to be justified are "under a curse" (vs. 10). By this, the apostle meant that God regards them as being guilty and condemned. The explanation Paul gave for this claim is found in Deuteronomy 27:26. The original purpose of this verse was to encourage obedience to the law. But taken at face value, the verse shows that people are mistaken to trust in the law for salvation. After all, no one can ever perfectly keep the law without the Father's grace through His Son. The legalists had failed to acknowledge that the law of Moses contains such stringent requirements that no one can keep them perfectly.

Paul's second point is that the law justifies no one (Gal. 3:11). In support of this truth, the apostle quoted Habakkuk 2:4. In its original context, this verse explains that righteous people live by faith, unlike wicked people, who live by selfishness.

Paul built on this thought by declaring that those who trust God, rather than their own efforts (such as observing the law), are counted righteous. For the third of Paul's four points, he said that law and faith are mutually exclusive as a means of producing righteousness (Gal. 3:12). As Leviticus 18:5 shows, law keeping is a matter of doing rather than of believing. Faith, on the other hand, is a matter of believing. Here we discover that the law is not based on faith, for it promises life only to those who perfectly heed its commands. As believers, we realize that our obedience will always be imperfect. The implication is that apart from the Father's grace in the Son, we are eternally lost.

B. The Messiah's Saving Work: vss. 13-14

Christ redeemed us from the curse of the law by becoming a curse for us, for it is written: "Cursed is everyone who is hung on a tree." He redeemed us in order that the blessing given to Abraham might come to the Gentiles through Christ Jesus, so that by faith we might receive the promise of the Spirit.

The first of Paul's four points said that all who rely on doing the works of the Mosaic law are "under a curse" (Gal. 3:10). In the last of the apostle's four points, he told how people are "redeemed" (vs. 13), or ransomed, from the curse pronounced by the law. When the Messiah hung on the cross, He took upon Himself the guilt and condemnation connected with our transgressions. The apostle substantiated his point by citing Deuteronomy 21:23. This verse says that a person who was executed on a tree was under a curse and thus had to be buried the same day. In ancient societies, the body of an executed criminal was sometimes hung on a tree as an added insult or a public warning. Old Testament law prohibited this practice and encouraged same-day burials because an executed person was accursed (see vss. 22-23). By extension, it could be said that Jesus was cursed (and bore our curse) because He hung on a wooden cross to die. Jesus went through this to free us from the curse of the law.

In a concluding observation, Paul took the subject of redemption from the law's curse and linked it with what he had said earlier about blessings through Abraham (see Gal. 3:6-9), and even earlier about receiving the Spirit (see vss. 2, 5). Specifically, the reason Jesus paid the ransom for us was so that the blessing God promised to Abraham would become available to all believers, regardless of whether they were Gentiles or Jews. The Father receives all the praise for ensuring that His Son did not experience the shame of the crucifixion in vain. It was the Father's will that His Son become our atoning sacrifice in order that people from all nations might be blessed through Him. It was also so that the Father could give believing sinners His promised Holy Spirit (vs. 14). We should never cease to be grateful for the suffering Jesus endured for our sake on the cross. He didn't have to experience it to redeem Himself. Instead, He willingly rescued us because He loves us.

Discussion Questions

1. Why was legalism attractive to the believers at Galatia? Why is it attractive to people today?
2. What evidences might we, as Christians, be able to cite that the Father has given us His Spirit?
3. Why do we need the righteousness the Father offers us when we trust in His Son?
4. What lessons about faith can we learn from Abraham?
5. Why was it necessary for the Son to die on the cross to fulfill the Father's promise to Abraham?

Contemporary Application

For many, finding joy in life is the object of a never-ending search. Some people seek happiness in alcohol and drugs. Others look for fulfillment in illicit relationships. Still others try to obtain satisfaction in the supercharged world of fame and popularity.

Paul taught that the Lord Jesus is the only source of fulfillment, satisfaction, and joy. The apostle also declared that the Son is the one we must turn to in faith if we are to be made right with the Father. We can neither be forgiven nor receive the Spirit by doing good works. We must set aside our self-made righteousness and receive by faith the one who is pure righteousness and truth—the Lord Jesus.

Faith in the crucified and risen Savior is also the basis for the believers' hope. We cannot build our eternal future on what we own, how many good things we have done, or even our family heritage. Only trusting in the Messiah will ensure that we have salvation and eternal life with God.

Abraham is an excellent example of faith. In answering God's call to move to an unknown land, the patriarch represents the kind of faith that we should have, especially when the Lord seems to be calling us elsewhere to serve Him. If we are facing such a move, we can trust God to plant us where He desires. We know that the Lord will provide for us and use us as His witnesses.

Heirs to the Promise

Scripture

Background Scripture: *Galatians 3:15-29; 4:1–5:1*
Scripture Lesson: *Galatians 3:15-18; 4:1-7*
Key Verse: *So you are no longer a slave, but a son; and since you are a son, God has made you also an heir.* Galatians 4:7.
Scripture Lesson for Children: *Galatians 3:15-18, 21-29*
Key Verse for Children: *You are all sons of God through faith in Christ Jesus.* Galatians 3:26.

Lesson Aim

To understand that believers are heirs of the Father's salvation promises through faith in His Son.

Lesson Setting

Time: Either A.D. *48–49 (the South Galatian theory) or* A.D. *53–57 (the North Galatian theory)*
Place: Either the churches in a geographic area called Galatia that was located in central Asia Minor (now Turkey; the North Galatian theory) or the churches in the southern part of the Roman province of Galatia (the South Galatian theory)

Lesson Outline

Heirs to the Promise
  I. The Law and the Promise: Galatians 3:15-18
    A. *An Example from Daily Life: vss. 15-16*
    B. *God's Unchangeable Promise: vss. 17-18*
  II. The Status of Slaves and Minors: Galatians 4:1-7
    A. *Under the Care of Guardians: vss. 1-3*
    B. *Adoption with Full Rights: vss. 4-7*

Introduction for Adults

Topic: *Understanding Values*

Perhaps some of the students in your class have lived with failure this week. Sunday morning may find them hurting because they can never seem to satisfy a demanding sibling, spouse, friend, or supervisor. Constant criticism may be eroding their sense of worth.

Be sure to share with your students the good news that the Father has given us the free gift of eternal life through faith in His Son. We do not have to measure up to some rule or standard before God will accept us. Because Jesus died on the cross and rose from the dead, all who trust in Him can enjoy the abundant love and fellowship of God.

Introduction for Youth

Topic: *The Benefits of Adoption*

In our achievement-oriented society, a person is often valued only for what he or she does. Grades become the measure of a student's worth. Job performance determines promotion or the termination of employment. In sports, one bad season can mean the end of a coach's career. Society has little tolerance for failure.

This worldly way of thinking is unhealthy and undesirable inside the church. God does not accept us because we have achieved certain spiritual goals. In fact, it is impossible to please Him on our own. When we relate to Him on the basis of grace and faith, we are adopted as His adult sons and daughters, and we go from being slaves to heirs.

Concepts for Children

Topic: *I Am Growing*

1. God made a promise to Abraham.
2. When we believe in Jesus, we will receive the promise given to Abraham.
3. When we believe in Jesus, we become part of God's family.
4. God wants us to serve Him out of love, not fear.
5. God wants us to tell others—even if they are different from us—about Jesus and His love for them.

Lesson Commentary

I. THE LAW AND THE PROMISE: GALATIANS 3:15-18

A. An Example from Daily Life: vss. 15-16

Brothers, let me take an example from everyday life. Just as no one can set aside or add to a human covenant that has been duly established, so it is in this case. The promises were spoken to Abraham and to his seed. The Scripture does not say "and to seeds," meaning many people, but "and to your seed," meaning one person, who is Christ.

In Galatians 3:15, Paul softened his tone by calling his readers "brothers." Then, the apostle returned to Abraham as a key to understanding the Gospel. Paul noted that it was long after Abraham's time when God introduced the covenant He made with Moses and instituted the law. In doing so, God did not cancel or even change the covenant He previously made with Abraham. The covenant with the patriarch—namely, the divine pledge that all the families on earth would be blessed through him (see Gen. 12:3)—was a lasting promise. In our day, once a contract has been signed, it cannot be changed (that is, unless both sides agree to alter it). The same situation was true of formal agreements ratified between people in Paul's day.

Based on the Greek noun translated "covenant" (Gal. 3:15), it seems that the legal instrument the apostle had in mind was a will. Even so, the binding nature of the compact was the same for any legal agreement of the day, including covenants. Paul referred to the way human covenants cannot be changed to illustrate that God's covenant with Abraham remained unaltered, even after the establishment of the Mosaic covenant and law. Evidently, the Judaizers in Galatia had taught that since the law of Moses had been introduced, the blessings of Abraham could be received only by those who meticulously kept the legal code. Paul countered that God's covenant with Abraham took the form of a promise to him and his "seed" (vs. 16; see Gen. 12:7; 13:15; 17:7; 24:7), which is a figurative reference to the patriarch's offspring. Depending on the context and usage, both the Hebrew and the Greek words for "seed" can be either plural or singular. From Paul's perspective, the word clearly referred to one person, namely, the Messiah, who was Abraham's greatest descendant (Gal. 3:16). Thus, in the Lord Jesus—and only in Him—does God bless all nations.

B. God's Unchangeable Promise: vss. 17-18

What I mean is this: The law, introduced 430 years later, does not set aside the covenant previously established by God and thus do away with the promise. For if the inheritance depends on the law, then it no longer depends on a promise; but God in his grace gave it to Abraham through a promise.

Paul's argument is that the law God gave to Moses, even though it came 430 years after the covenant God ratified with Abraham, did not invalidate the earlier "promise" (Gal. 3:17). The Mosaic and Abrahamic covenants merely existed side by side. Perhaps the apostle's reference to 430 years was based upon Exodus 12:40-41, verses that refer to the period of the Hebrews' sojourn in Egypt. The actual period between the beginning of the Abrahamic covenant and the beginning of the Mosaic covenant was somewhat longer. Be that as it may, Paul maintained that despite the addition of the Mosaic law, the inheritance or blessing of Abraham's descendants continued to be based on God's "promise" (Gal. 3:18).

Paul next asked and answered two questions that might naturally have arisen in his readers' minds because of his previous comments. The first question asked why the Mosaic law was given. The apostle explained that it was added as a temporary provision by which the Father prepared people for the Messiah's advent. To be more specific, God established the law alongside the promise to reveal to people their "transgressions" (vs. 19). Put another way, the law represented God's perfect moral standard and how much people violated it (see Rom. 5:20). Accordingly, when the Son came as the fulfillment of the Father's promise, the chosen people should have been ready and willing to seek the forgiveness of their sins by trusting in the Messiah.

Unlike God's promise to Abraham, which was permanent, the Mosaic law was temporary and intended as a means of getting people ready for the advent of the Redeemer. Even though the law came from God, it was administered through angels by an intermediary. The latter refers to Moses, who was God's representative to His people. Most likely, the tradition that the law was handed down by angels (see Acts 7:38, 53; Heb. 2:2) was based on Deuteronomy 33:2 and Psalm 68:17. Normally, binding agreements that require an intermediary are those in which both parties are active. The covenant of Moses fits this description, for while God gave the law, His people were responsible to obey it. God's covenant with Abraham was entirely different, for it had only one active party, namely, the Lord. Because He is the one and only God (Gal. 3:20; see Deut. 6:4), He has the right and authority to act alone when He chooses to do so. In the case of Abraham, God unilaterally gave His promise to the patriarch and unconditionally pledged He would fulfill it.

In Galatians 3:21, Paul posed his second question. Do the distinctions between the Mosaic law and the Abrahamic covenant mean there is a conflict between these two? The short answer is not at all. The longer explanation is that the law and the divine promises are not opposed to one another, for they merely worked on different levels. The law had been practiced with varying degrees of success over a period of several centuries, yet it was unable to impart new life to its adherents. Only God in His grace can spiritually regenerate the lost. Thus, Paul concluded that a right standing before God was not based on the law. Moreover, Scripture revealed that the entire created order, including all people, is imprisoned under the power of sin (vs. 22). Expressed differently, the law not only brought about a knowledge of sin, but also placed all humanity under its curse (see Deut. 27:26).

The preceding arrangement remained in effect until the advent of the Messiah, who fulfilled God's promise to Abraham. During Jesus' earthly ministry, He faithfully carried out God's will. In this regard, the Cross is the supreme demonstration of the Son's unswerving devotion to the Father. Those who trust in the Messiah for salvation receive God's promise of freedom (Gal. 3:23). In the Roman world, wealthy families often had a servant who supervised the conduct of the family's sons. Paul compared the Mosaic law to this servant. In a manner of speaking, the law held us in its protective custody. The law was also like a guard who kept us locked up as prisoners until the time when we would believe in the Redeemer (vs. 23). Paul had already noted that all are prisoners of sin (vs. 22). There's a sense in which being a prisoner of the law is not much different, except that the law reveals sin in us and provokes it to action (see Rom. 7:5, 7-11).

The Greek noun rendered "put in charge" (Gal. 3:24) refers to a guardian or guide for younger children. In Bible times, a tutor was a slave who trained and instructed his master's children. For instance, the tutor might be responsible for pointing out and punishing improper behavior. In a figurative sense, the Mosaic law operated as a tutor by revealing sin and condemning it. The law continued in this function until the Messiah's advent. Now that the Father has established faith in Him as the way to be declared righteous, we no longer need the law as our custodian (vs. 25). Just as a child's guardian is no longer needed when the child grows up and becomes an adult, so the law was superseded by the coming of the Savior.

Jewish Christians could have been said to have grown up (in terms of their relationship to the Mosaic law) and reached spiritual adulthood (in terms of their relationship to the Messiah). Admittedly, the Gentile believers in Galatia had not been raised according to the law. Nonetheless, they had also become spiritual adults when they trusted in the Messiah for salvation. The reality of this truth is the reason why Paul called the Galatians "sons of God" (vs. 26). The Greek noun translated "sons" refers to those who have reached adulthood. The apostle's point is that the Father's spiritual children reach adulthood, not by keeping the law, but by trusting in His Son.

Paul described salvation not only as becoming adults in God's spiritual family, but also as being "baptized into Christ" (vs. 27) and "clothed . . . with Christ." The apostle's use of the Greek verb translated "baptized" reminded his readers of their baptismal ceremonies. Paul was referring to their close identification with and participation in the Messiah's death and resurrection (see Rom. 6:3-5). Furthermore, the Galatian believers spiritually wore the Savior like they physically wore clothing. Put another way, they took on His righteousness by faith. The advent of the Redeemer made it possible for people to become children of God. Also, through faith, they are baptized into and clothed with the Messiah.

Jesus' coming broke down worldly divisions, such as those based on distinctions of race, social status, and gender (vs. 28). This means that such distinctions have no bearing on who can become a follower of the Savior. It also means that all people in society should be seen as persons of worth. The three social distinctions Paul mentioned were significant ones in his day. Prejudice existed between Jews and non-Jews over religious, political, and cultural issues. Hundreds of thousands of people in the Roman Empire were enslaved by others. Women had limited legal rights and were often looked down upon by men. Thankfully, through the valid influence of Christian principles, many of these social divisions have been abolished. This truth is reinforced by Paul's statement in verse 29 that all who have trusted in Christ are Abraham's spiritual descendants and heirs.

II. The Status of Slaves and Minors: Galatians 4:1-7

A. Under the Care of Guardians: vss. 1-3

What I am saying is that as long as the heir is a child, he is no different from a slave, although he owns the whole estate. He is subject to guardians and trustees until the time set by his father. So also, when we were children, we were in slavery under the basic principles of the world.

In order for Paul to drive home his point concerning the status of the believer in Christ, the apostle used one more illustration based on the customs of his day. The apostle established a hypothetical situation in which a father apparently had died, leaving behind a young son, a minor, as the heir of his father's estate. The property and assets actually belonged to the child, but he could not control it until he reached the age specified by the father in the trust (Gal. 4:1). The child was subject to "guardians and trustees" (vs. 2), or tutors and managers, who were in complete control of the child.

As far as having freedom to act and decide on his own, the child was no different from a slave. Paul took the child's "slavery" (so to speak) as symbolic of our spiritual slavery before coming to faith in the Messiah. We were enslaved to the "basic principles of the world" (vs. 3). Much debate has centered on what Paul meant here. To list just three suggestions made by Bible scholars, the apostle may have been referring to the law, to angels and demons, or to the superstitions of pagan religions. Regardless of which option is preferred, Paul was drawing attention to the enslaved status of a person before receiving the Gospel of grace concerning the Savior.

B. Adoption with Full Rights: vss. 4-7

But when the time had fully come, God sent his Son, born of a woman, born under law, to redeem those under law, that we might receive the full rights of sons. Because you are sons, God sent the Spirit of his Son into our hearts, the Spirit who calls out, "Abba, Father." So you are no longer a slave, but a son; and since you are a son, God has made you also an heir.

It was onto the dark and dreary scene of slavery that Paul shone the glorious light of freedom in the Son. With great care, the apostle gave his statement about Jesus' advent (Gal. 4:4). In the Father's exercise of His will, He chose the moment for His Son's birth. It was the climax toward which the divine plan had been moving throughout the ages. All that happened in the coming of the Redeemer, in His earthly ministry, and in His death was under the most precise scrutiny of the Father.

Paul affirmed Jesus' virgin birth ("born of a woman," not of man) and His obedience to the law ("born under law"). In the fullest sense of the word, God became sinless man in the person of the Lord Jesus so that He might identify with us. In the Messiah's death on the cross, He accomplished His purpose in providing redemption for all those "under law" (vs. 5). He shared the curse of the law with all of us (see 3:13) and became the permanent sacrifice for our sins (see 2 Cor. 5:21). The Greek verb translated "redeem" (Gal. 4:5) literally refers to a ransom or payment and points to Jesus bringing us out of our slavery.

Paul brought his earlier illustration to a climax by describing those who have received the Messiah as having received their full inheritance. This is more than just a legal maneuver in which repenting sinners are adopted into God's family as children. When we receive "the Spirit of his Son" (vs. 6), we actually share the spiritual life of God in our daily experience. This new relationship revolutionizes our prayer lives. We approach the Father, not as slaves who are apologetic and fearful. Rather, we who have experienced this new freedom in the Lord Jesus come as children of the King. "Abba, Father" is an address of love and intimacy reserved for children who are fully aware of their standing with their father (see Rom. 8:15).

Slavery was widespread in the Roman Empire of Paul's day. Most slaves got that way by being born to slaves. Others lost their freedom when they became prisoners of war or were kidnapped by pirates and sold to slave traders. Some people even sold themselves into slavery. Slaves were generally treated well. Most were well fed and well clothed. They had the right to have families, control their own money, and defend themselves in court. Many were educated at their owner's expense, and some held posts of importance.

Because of their security, slaves were often better off than poor free people, many of whom lived in the streets. Most owners set their slaves free after a few years. The reason for such an action might be to show gratitude, to save money, or to make the slaves available for military service. Frequently, masters established their freedmen in business, and then became partners in the business. Slavery in the Roman world of the first century A.D. was not as bad as it could have been, but it was still slavery. Paul used slavery repeatedly as a symbol of a negative condition.

Galatians 4:7 sums up Paul's argument. The believers at Galatia were no longer slaves to the basic principles of the world, but now were God's spiritual children and heirs of the covenant promises. The same is true of all believers. We are entitled to all the benefits and privileges of being full-fledged members of God's family. Because the Father loves us as His children, He will graciously give us all good things in connection with His Son (see Rom. 8:32).

Discussion Questions

1. In what sense was the covenant that God made with Abraham a lasting promise?

2. Why does God's establishment of the Mosaic law not invalidate the Abrahamic covenant?

3. Before the advent of the Messiah, how did the Mosaic law function as a tutor or manager for God's people?

4. In what ways are we, as believers in Christ, like adult heirs in an ancient Roman household?

5. Why is it better for us to count on our heavenly inheritance than any earthly one?

Contemporary Application

In the movie *Rain Man*, a young adult named Charlie Babbit is summoned home when he hears that his wealthy father has died. When the lawyer reads the father's will, Charlie discovers that his father has left him only two items from the large estate: a vintage car and some prize-winning rosebushes. The will reflected the father's own disappointment in his son, who remained estranged from him over several years. Charlie had not lived up to the father's expectations. As a result, Charlie's father had withheld his son's inheritance.

What a contrasting picture this is to the inheritance God has promised His spiritual children. Our heavenly Father does not promise our inheritance based on our performance, that is, on our ability to keep the Mosaic law. Instead, His promise to us is solely based on our faith in His Son. Also, no secret document hides the details of our eternal inheritance. The Bible is clear as to what believers will inherit. The benefits include all the promises contained in God's new covenant: salvation; the Holy Spirit; eternal life; perfect love, joy, and peace; no more pain and tears; a dwelling place in the presence of God; a new, immortal body; the authority to rule and reign with the Messiah; all the wealth of God's kingdom—indeed, the list could go on and on!

The Father won't ever take His promises away from us, no matter how much we may struggle in life, no matter how we may feel we may have failed, and no matter how insignificant our existence may seem to us. Our confidence that our inheritance won't be taken away lies in the fact that it has been secured for us by the Father's perfect Son, the Lord Jesus. We can become heirs in God's spiritual family because of the Messiah's finished work on the cross. Also, we receive our eternal inheritance by grace through faith in the Savior.

Fruits of Redemption

Scripture

Background Scripture: *Galatians 5:2–6:18*
Scripture Lesson: *Galatians 5:22–6:10*
Key Verse: *The fruit of the Spirit is love, joy, peace, patience,
kindness, goodness, faithfulness, gentleness and self-control.
Against such things there is no law.* Galatians 5:22-23.
Scripture Lesson for Children: *Galatians 5:22–6:10*
Key Verse for Children: *As we have opportunity, let us do
good to all people, especially to those who belong to the family
of believers.* Galatians 6:10.

Lesson Aim

To recognize the importance of relying on the Spirit to
be productive, godly Christians.

Lesson Setting

Time: Either A.D. *48–49 (the South Galatian theory) or* A.D.
53–57 (the North Galatian theory)
*Place: Either the churches in a geographic area called Galatia
that was located in central Asia Minor (now Turkey; the
North Galatian theory) or the churches in the southern part of
the Roman province of Galatia (the South Galatian theory)*

Lesson Outline

Fruits of Redemption
  I. The Fruit of the Spirit: Galatians 5:22-26
      A. *The Fruit Delineated: vss. 22-23*
      B. *The Sinful Nature Rejected: vss. 24-26*
  II. The Spirit-Led Life: Galatians 6:1-10
      A. *Sharing Each Other's Troubles: vss. 1-6*
      B. *Reaping What One Sows: vss. 7-10*

Introduction for Adults

Topic: *Bearing One Another's Burden*

Regardless of what one thinks of the recovery movement so popular today, it has had a tremendous impact upon our society. Obviously, it has struck a nerve. People are looking for inner healing. They want to recover emotionally.

Where can people go to share their burdens with others in a nonthreatening environment? Should they always have to turn to secular psychologists for the answers to their problems? As we will learn in this week's lesson, God wants us to reach out to others with the love of Christ. When our lives are controlled by the Spirit and manifesting His fruit, we can bring healing to those who are full of emotional pain.

Introduction for Youth

Topic: *Fruit Does a Body Good*

The young man was desperate to discover God's will. In fact, the teen felt so confused that he looked for a sign from heaven. He concluded that if he received a letter with a certain stamp on it, he would be sure of God's will. This sort of thinking has more superstition to it than faith.

God confronts us with choices so that we can learn to trust Him for the answers. The basic principle is that we live by faith, not by sight. Choosing to live that way means we are open to learning from our mistakes, from our foolishness, and from our violations of God's will.

We are not alone in this difficult but important venture. The Father sent the Spirit to be our helper. We can be confident that when we develop a keen sense of the Spirit's leading, He will guide us in the path of truth and virtue, and enable us to bear abundant spiritual fruit. He will also uphold us in the most difficult circumstances of life. Of this we can be certain.

Concepts for Children

Topic: *I Am Helpful*

1. The Spirit helps us to obey God.
2. The Spirit helps us love others around us.
3. The Spirit gives us joy and peace in our lives.
4. The Spirit helps us to be kind and patient with others.
5. With the Spirit's help, we can control how we act.

Lesson Commentary

I. THE FRUIT OF THE SPIRIT: GALATIANS 5:22-26

A. The Fruit Delineated: vss. 22-23

But the fruit of the Spirit is love, joy, peace, patience, kindness, goodness, faithfulness, gentleness and self-control. Against such things there is no law.

We learn in Galatians 5:15 that Paul's readers were (in a manner of speaking) guilty of "biting and devouring each other" like wild beasts. We don't know the exact causes of this intense strife in the Galatian churches, but the discord was serious enough for the apostle to warn his readers that they might consume each other. It's not easy to go from fighting one another to loving one another, but that is possible if we live by the Spirit (vs. 16). The Spirit makes it possible for us to resist our wayward impulses. When we give into them, it leads us to cause strife and commit sins. We may want to do good, but if we obey the dictates of our sinful human nature, we will not do good (vs. 17). We can do good only if we live by the Spirit. The reason is that our sinful nature and the Spirit are in opposition to each other, and each have opposite goals. When we are led by the Spirit, we do not do the evil prompted by our sinful nature, and neither are we under the Mosaic law (vs. 18).

Presumably, the Judaizers had told Paul's readers that if they did not obey the law, the only other option was for them to obey their own sinful nature. But the apostle said there is a third option, namely, we can obey the Spirit. Up until this point in his letter, Paul had talked generally about how wrong it is to indulge one's sinful nature and how right it is to live by the Spirit. Now, the apostle got specific about what he meant by these two diametrically opposed options. He also described the negative consequences of indulging the sinful nature and the positive benefits of living by the Spirit. For instance, when the wayward impulses of one's fallen human nature are gratified, the results are "obvious" (vs. 19). This probably means that it is plain to see that these acts are wrong, even without the aid of the Old Testament law. Also, it is evident that these acts spring from the sinful nature.

Paul listed 15 sinful acts to represent all the ways people do evil (vss. 19-21). The representative nature of the catalog is made clear by his addition of "and the like" at the end (vs. 21). Many sinful acts did not make the apostle's list, but that makes them no less sinful. Paul may not have intended to list the 15 sinful acts in any particular order. Nonetheless, they seem to fall into four categories. The list includes three vices of sensuality (sexual immorality, impurity, debauchery), two vices associated with heathen religions (idolatry, witchcraft), eight vices of interpersonal conflict (hatred, discord, jealousy, fits of rage, selfish ambition, dissensions, factions, envy), and two vices related to the misuse of alcohol (drunkenness, orgies).

The acts of the sinful nature that Paul listed are highly varied, but they all are alike in arousing God's wrath. So the apostle warned his readers about the consequences of these sins. As Paul had told the Galatians earlier when he was with them, those who practiced such things would not "inherit the kingdom of God" (vs. 21). This does not mean that every believer who commits a sin is prevented from inheriting God's kingdom. Rather the apostle's statement indicates that people who continually commit these acts of the sinful nature thereby demonstrate that they are not following the Lord Jesus and have no place in His eternal kingdom. Nevertheless, believers can learn from Paul's warning how seriously God views human sin.

To balance the list of acts of the sinful nature, the apostle presented a list of godly virtues produced by those who yield their lives to the Spirit. This list, too, is representative rather than exhaustive. The items mentioned are some of the effects appearing in the lives of those in whom the Spirit of God dwells. Paul used a singular word for "fruit" (vs. 22). He could have said "fruits," but he did not. He may have wanted to suggest that the aspects of the fruit of the Spirit develop and grow together like a bunch of grapes. They are not separate pieces of fruit existing independently of each other. All the elements of the fruit of the Spirit should be found in all believers. Love is at the top of the apostle's list of spiritual fruit because all the other virtues develop from it. Love is the opposite of the selfishness of the flesh. Joy and peace follow. Paul then listed patience, gentleness, goodness, faithfulness, meekness, and self-control. The apostle noted that the Mosaic law contained a curse against those who failed to keep it. But that curse does not apply to those who are bearing the fruit of the Spirit, because they are thereby fulfilling what the law intended (vs. 23).

In stepping back from Paul's two different lists, we see that while the "acts of the sinful nature" (vs. 19) are many, the "fruit of the Spirit" (vs. 22) is a singular, internal attitude that comes from the Spirit controlling our lives. For this reason, each part of the "fruit" is worth looking at in more detail. "Love" is seeking the well-being of others despite who they are. "Joy" means having happiness despite our circumstances. "Peace" is the harmony in our relationship with God that brings tranquility to our minds. "Patience" means putting up with others when severely tried. "Kindness" is our acting toward others in a way similar to how God treats us. "Goodness" involves behaving in a generous way toward others. "Faithfulness" means showing that others can always rely on us, while "gentleness" (vs. 23) is proving that we have the power to control ourselves in adverse situations. Finally, "self-control" means demonstrating the Spirit's presence with victory over fleshly desires.

B. The Sinful Nature Rejected: vss. 24-26

Those who belong to Christ Jesus have crucified the sinful nature with its passions and desires. Since we live by the Spirit, let us keep in step with the Spirit. Let us not become conceited, provoking and envying each other.

Unbelievers are not able to bear the fruit of the Spirit because they do not have the Spirit. Though they may have respectable qualities, they are still ruled by their flesh and act in keeping with that nature by seeking to satisfy their passions and desires. Believers, however, can bear the fruit of the Spirit. They receive the Spirit when they trust in the Messiah. At the moment of salvation, their sinful nature (in one sense) is crucified, or put to death (Gal. 5:24). This is because Jesus earned the right to break sin's grip of control over believers when He hung on the cross, and He sets them free from sin when they believe in Him. In another sense, of course, the Christian life is a daily process of believers putting their sinful nature to death. We cooperate with God by letting go of our past sinful ways and taking up a holy way of living.

Though believers already have the Spirit living in them, they are not automatically under His control. They need to consciously yield to Him as He leads and empowers them. Because the Spirit is the source of every believer's life, they should also allow Him to direct its course (vs. 25). Paul gave a few specific examples of what he did not mean by keeping in step with the Spirit: being conceited, provoking others to anger, and envying others (vs. 26). Most likely, these were particular problems among the Galatian believers. They are also some specific kinds of unspirituality that we should avoid.

Admittedly, at times our sinful nature can seem overpowering to us. Nonetheless, by faith we recognize our victory over it through faith in Christ and the necessity of our constantly being renewed through our walk in the Spirit. Because of what the Lord Jesus did on the cross, we can, by faith, appropriate His victory into our lives and live in obedience to Him through the Spirit. Such a humble attitude keeps us from becoming inflated with pride, a vice that can destroy Christian fellowship, as was happening in the Galatian churches. The latter truth notwithstanding, we have assurance in the Son of victory over the flesh in the heat of the spiritual battle. Moreover, the change that the Savior brings to our lives as believers shows itself in the fruit of the Spirit.

II. THE SPIRIT-LED LIFE: GALATIANS 6:1-10

A. Sharing Each Other's Troubles: vss. 1-6

Brothers, if someone is caught in a sin, you who are spiritual should restore him gently. But watch yourself, or you also may be tempted. Carry each other's burdens, and in this way you will fulfill the law of Christ. If anyone thinks he is something when he is nothing, he deceives himself. Each one should test his own actions. Then he can take pride in himself, without comparing himself to somebody else, for each one should carry his own load. Anyone who receives instruction in the word must share all good things with his instructor.

In Galatians 6, we find a number of specific instructions about Christian living, combined with warnings and encouragements. Most likely, Paul chose these instructions because they related to specific problems in the church at Galatia. The instructions do not spell out all that is expected of those who live by the Spirit. But they do provide some representative examples that can serve as models for us as we make our own decisions. The apostle began by dealing with situations in which believers are "caught in a sin" (vs. 1). The idea behind this phrase is not that others have found out someone's sinning, but rather that the sinner has allowed himself or herself to be trapped or enticed by sin. Once the person's sinning has become public knowledge, Paul said those who were spiritual should help restore the transgressor. The idea is that other Christians should support and guide the struggling believer as he or she recovers from the sinning.

Restoration of church members who have sinned can mean different things depending on factors in the situation. Here are some possible steps in restoration: (1) The restorers help those sinning recognize the gravity of their sin, come to a point of true repentance, and confess their sins privately and (if necessary) publicly. (2) The restorers help those who sinned accept God's forgiveness once the ones who sinned have genuinely repented. (3) The restorers help the repentant sinners plan strategies to deal with the effects of their sin and to change their behavior. (4) The restorers help the reformed sinners move back into full participation in church life and service.

This process of restoration requires sensitivity on the part of the restorers. Its purpose is to draw sinners toward spiritual healing, not to make them feel bad. Therefore, restoration must be done gently, not harshly or vindictively. Unless restoration is performed carefully, those who sinned can rebel and fall into worse sin. This process can also harbor dangers for the restorers. By putting them in a position of moral authority, it may tempt them to feel superior. That's why Paul warned restorers to watch themselves lest they become proud, thus falling into sin themselves. We all have cause for humility.

Next, Paul broadened the area of Christians' concern for each other to include those who suffer all kinds of "burdens" (vs. 2). This translates a Greek noun that originally referred to heavy weights. The apostle used it to refer to misfortunes that fall on us and threaten to crush us. He said believers must help one another bear these burdens of misfortune until the weight has lightened. The burdens the apostle referred to may include grief, illness, and persecution—in fact, anything that may hurt or hinder believers. The tense of the verb translated "carry" indicates that we are to keep on shouldering each other's burdens as long as our help is needed. In this way, we fulfill "the law of Christ" (namely, His teachings). This includes loving not only our neighbor but also our enemy, with God's love being the model.

If there was a problem in the Galatian churches with believers not helping one another, it was probably due to the arrogance of those who considered themselves to be free of such burdens. That would explain why Paul warned against prideful self-deception (vs. 3). The apostle also supplied a defense against arrogance—self-testing (vs. 4). The idea is to measure ourselves against God's will as revealed in Scripture. From this we can gain a proper perspective on our failings as well as take satisfaction in what we have achieved by His grace. Paul also urged us to carry our own "load" (vs. 5), which translates a Greek noun that originally referred to a traveler's pack. According to apostle, the "pack" all believers carry is our responsibility before God for our own actions. No one can carry another's load of responsibility. Thus, if we are wise, we will be realistic about where we stand with the Lord.

Verse 6 seems to have no direct relation to the verses that come before or after it. Evidently, Paul slipped in this counsel because Christian teachers in Galatia were not getting the appreciation they deserved. The phrase "share all good things" bears close inspection. First, the word "share" indicates that Paul wanted his readers to support their teachers because they wanted to, not because they had to. Elsewhere, the apostle taught that supporting ministers is a duty (1 Cor. 9:7-18). But here he was concerned with attitude. It should be one of willingness, even cheerfulness (see 2 Cor. 9:7). Second, we should note that the phrase "all good things" (Gal. 6:6) is general enough to include both material support, such as a salary and gifts, as well as immaterial support, such as prayer and respect. Wouldn't it be wonderful if Paul's counsel in this verse were no longer needed? But it is still needed. Many faithful pastors and other church leaders today are forced to do their work with too little pay and too little cooperation from those whom they serve.

B. Reaping What One Sows: vss. 7-10

Do not be deceived: God cannot be mocked. A man reaps what he sows. The one who sows to please his sinful nature, from that nature will reap destruction; the one who sows to please the Spirit, from the Spirit will reap eternal life. Let us not become weary in doing good, for at the proper time we will reap a harvest if we do not give up. Therefore, as we have opportunity, let us do good to all people, especially to those who belong to the family of believers.

Serving others requires unselfishness and dependence on God's Spirit. But those who do not do the hard work of Christian living had better not kid themselves that God will spiritually bless them (Gal. 6:7). People who perform the acts of the sinful nature rather than bear the fruit of the Spirit will not be eternally rewarded, for God will not be mocked. Unlike people, He cannot be fooled, and His justice is perfect. Furthermore, there is a simple relationship between how people live and how God judges and rewards them (vs. 8). By way of example, a farmer who sows barley cannot expect to harvest wheat. Similarly, those who obey the callings of the flesh (and thereby give evidence of their unregenerate state) cannot expect to receive eternal life from God. Instead, they will earn eternal destruction. Happily, though, the opposite of this truth is that if we live by the Spirit, we will enjoy eternal life.

Paul feared that his readers, who had started well in their faith, were losing enthusiasm for Christian living. The Judaizers' false teachings and the Galatians' own unethical living had weakened their spiritual vitality. Thus, the apostle portrayed the heavenly reward awaiting the faithful—namely, an intimate relationship with God—as an incentive to renew their efforts at doing good (vs. 9). This incentive is one we sometimes need too. The longer our Christian lives stretch on, the more likely we are to suffer fatigue and to hear the voice of discouragement whispering in our ears. Paul himself must often have thought, *I can't go on!* and *What's the use?* But he persevered to the end, and, with God's help, we can persevere as long as necessary too. In this regard, the Christian life is not a sprint but a marathon. God provides strategic opportunities for us to do good to others (vs. 10). We should try to discern these opportunities and eagerly act on them. Helping unbelievers is an excellent way to witness without words to God's goodness. But if anything, we should be more eager to help other Christians, since we are all part of God's family.

Discussion Questions

1. Why does Paul speak of the *fruit* of the Spirit, rather than the *fruits* of the Spirit?
2. Why did Paul place such a strong emphasis on crucifying the passions and desires of the flesh?
3. Why is it important to refrain from comparing ourselves to others, especially in the things of Christ?
4. Why is it vital for us to financially support those in the ministry?
5. Have you ever felt weary of doing good? What encouraged you to continue doing good?

Contemporary Application

Sin versus the Holy Spirit seems like a battle that will never end. Once we think we have licked sin, it pops up somewhere and we fall prey to it. Sounds rather discouraging, doesn't it? But in this battle we never fight alone. With the Holy Spirit living in us, and with the encouragement and prayers of fellow Christians, we can win the battle.

Perhaps we are most vulnerable when we think we don't need other people. And possibly that's why Paul envisaged a fellowship of believers together fighting the battle against sin, rather than fighting against each other. He talked about our being individually responsible, but he also called us to be responsible for one another.

Our individualistic society militates against our receiving help, prayer, counsel, and admonitions from one another. But as we keep in step with the Spirit, we will also be much more inclined to depend on our fellow believers and strengthen them in their faith. They in turn will minister to us, and together we will glorify God through the spiritual victories that He brings about in our lives.

Wisdom's Part in Creation

Scripture
Background Scripture: *Proverbs 8*
Scripture Lesson: *Proverbs 8:22-36*
Key Verse: *Listen to my instruction and be wise; do not ignore it.* Proverbs 8:33.
Scripture Lesson for Children: *Proverbs 8:22-35*
Key Verse for Children: *The LORD brought me forth as the first of his works, before his deeds of old.* Proverbs 8:22.

Lesson Aim
To more fully appreciate the value of godly wisdom.

Lesson Setting
Time: Sometime during the reign of Solomon (about 970–930 B.C.)
Place: Jerusalem

Lesson Outline
Wisdom's Part in Creation

  I. Affirming Wisdom's Role in Creation: Proverbs 8:22-31
    A. *Wisdom's Creation: vss. 22-23*
    B. *Wisdom's Antiquity: vss. 24-26*
    C. *Wisdom's Presence at the Beginning: vss. 27-29*
    D. *Wisdom's Involvement at the Beginning: vss. 30-31*
 II. Hearing Wisdom's Call: Proverbs 8:32-36
    A. *Heeding Wisdom: vss. 32-33*
    B. *Remaining Attentive to Wisdom: vs. 34*
    C. *Experiencing Life through Wisdom: vss. 35-36*

Introduction for Adults

Topic: *Wise Up!*

In Bible times there was a custom of double invitations. When a great feast or a celebration was planned, the host would send out invitations to all those he wanted to attend. This was so those invited would know to plan for the appointed time.

When the moment came for the actual feast or celebration, the host would send out a servant to go back to all those who had been invited. The servant would tell them that the time had come and they were now to attend the wonderful event. In fact, failure to come would be considered a serious offense.

Perhaps your students should consider this week's lesson as an opportunity to accept Lady Wisdom's invitation to partake of her delightful offerings. They will discover that nothing can compare with the treasures of understanding to be found in the wisdom of God.

Introduction for Youth

Topic: *Got Wisdom?*

Think about all of the advertising slogans that appeal to our self-interests and self-gratification. Not all of them are evil, of course, but they help shape the values and choices that determine the outcomes of our lives.

For teenagers, the power of advertising and peer pressure make it exceedingly difficult to follow God's wisdom. It takes tremendous courage to stand out from the crowd and say that the world's appeals amount to foolishness.

In this week's lesson, we find a powerful model for Christian young people to follow. God's wisdom is personified as a woman speaking out in public for righteousness and morality. There is a time to stand up and be counted, not in some obnoxious way, but with love and patience. God's wisdom must be heard and followed if we are to be saved from the consequences of wrong choices that violate God's standards of holiness.

Concepts for Children

Topic: *Learn from Wisdom*

1. Each day brings us many opportunities to obey God.
2. We hurt ourselves and others when we make wrong choices.
3. God loves to give us His wisdom and guidance for our lives.
4. Knowing God's commands is more important than anything else.
5. God promises to guard and protect those who listen to Him.

Lesson Commentary

I. AFFIRMING WISDOM'S ROLE IN CREATION: PROVERBS 8:22-31

A. Wisdom's Creation: vss. 22-23

"The LORD brought me forth as the first of his works, before his deeds of old; I was appointed from eternity, from the beginning, before the world began."

The sages of the ancient nations often personified wisdom as Solomon did in Proverbs 8. The king, by embodying the concepts of understanding and discernment, made wisdom more than a system of information and principles. Also, by referring to wisdom as a female person, Solomon transformed wisdom from an "it" into a "she." Thus, as a living being, Lady Wisdom became a proper noun and was able to interact with the world around her. In point of fact, it is in this chapter that Lady Wisdom gave the reader a concise autobiographical sketch.

This female figure spoke with divine authority (1:20-33) and played a role in Creation (chap. 8). The meaning of this exalted female figure in a strongly male-centered society has been the topic of much debate, for female imagery begins (chaps. 1–9) and ends (chap. 31) the book. Most likely, Solomon meant Lady Wisdom to be an extension of God's characteristics. Similarly, her direct opposites— Woman Folly, Woman Stranger, and the adulteress—represent every form of evil opposed by God. In all likelihood, Lady Wisdom was modeled after the real roles of teacher, counselor, and household planner that Israelite women played in their homes and societies.

As a "person," Lady Wisdom was able to rebuke the foolish, commend the prudent, and display a wide range of emotions. In a manner of speaking, she stood by God at the creation of the universe and resisted her personified nemesis, Woman Folly. Moreover, as a living being, Lady Wisdom was able to go to those who needed her and reach them with a timely message of righteousness and prudence. She did not stand idly by and wait for them to seek her out. Also, she had no problem calling attention to herself (8:1).

Solomon portrayed Lady Wisdom as a fiery, determined preacher who represented everything that was good about God. Lady Wisdom could be found at every intersection and on every hilltop (vs. 2). She was present at the gates of every small town and large city where the leadership met to hold court (vs. 3). Anywhere society might gather, she was present to proclaim the truth and seek justice. No one was beyond the hearing of her voice. Lady Wisdom was no respecter of persons. She showed no partiality toward any race or social class. Indeed, she raised her voice to all of humanity (vs. 4).

Lady Wisdom's objective was to train and correct the immature, the inexperienced, and the naïve. These foolish ones were not necessarily people with evil intentions. Instead, they are often young people who blindly follow selfish and immoral leadership. Many times they would not consider the natural consequences of their actions. Lady Wisdom came to these simpletons and offered to teach them knowledge and improved judgment. She gave them the opportunity to change their foolish ways before they were beyond her reach (vs. 5).

In Lady Wisdom's personified sketch, she described some of her more important qualities and abilities. For instance, she was an excellent counselor who offered sound judgment and understanding. Moreover, she was endowed with great power (vs. 14). By means of it, she set up and maintained the governments of the world. Monarchs and nobles owed their authority to her—even though some refused to acknowledge it (vss. 15-16). Those who valued Lady Wisdom would be blessed by her in return. Also, those who sought her out would find her (vs. 17). They would be rewarded by her with great riches and honor (vs. 18). Even so, the wealth and accolades would be of little value when compared to the intimacy they would enjoy with Lady Wisdom (vss. 19-21).

Lady Wisdom continued this portion of her personal sketch by flashing back to some of her earliest memories. At the dawn of time, before God brought the rest of creation into existence, He formed Lady Wisdom. God established her long ago—in fact, before He made the heavens and the earth (vs. 22; see Gen. 1:1). Moreover, it was in eternity past, before the world existed, that God appointed Lady Wisdom for her exalted role (Prov. 8:23). This made her foundational to all God would do. Solomon placed these declarations in Lady Wisdom's mouth so she could claim the rights and responsibilities of the firstborn. As such, she possessed influence over other aspects of Creation. Also, as the firstborn, Lady Wisdom served as the family representative between God and those who followed her. Therefore, the prudent did not act without first consulting Lady Wisdom.

B. Wisdom's Antiquity: vss. 24-26

"When there were no oceans, I was given birth, when there were no springs abounding with water; before the mountains were settled in place, before the hills, I was given birth, before he made the earth or its fields or any of the dust of the world."

In Proverbs 8:24 and 25, the phrase "I was given birth" appears. The latter, which recalls the Creation account recorded in Genesis 1, points to the antiquity of Lady Wisdom and emphasizes the importance of her firstborn status. Lady Wisdom was with God long before there were any deep oceans or springs overflowing with fresh water. Even before God set in place earth's mountains and hills, Lady Wisdom was present. She even preceded the formation of the planet, along with its continents, fields, and first handfuls of soil (Prov. 8:26).

Because of the references to Lady Wisdom being the firstborn of creation and the artisan at God's side during the Creation, some Bible scholars think that chapter 8 is a description of the Messiah prior to the Incarnation. They hold to this opinion even though wisdom is personified here as a woman. In church history, the heretical movement called Arianism picked up on this idea and attempted to use passages such as verses 22-31 to prove that the Lord Jesus was a created being. They claimed that Jesus could not be coeternal with the Father and the Spirit if in fact Jesus did not eternally exist, as described in this passage of Scripture.

It is an erroneous assumption, though, to equate the Lord Jesus with Lady Wisdom. The Messiah is a living person, whereas Lady Wisdom is a metaphorical personification. Moreover, John 1:1 reveals that the Son eternally preexisted with the Father and the Spirit before the creation of the universe and everything in it. Also, in 8:58, Jesus declared to the religious leaders that before Abraham was born, the Son already existed from eternity past. Even Colossians 1:15 refutes the heretical teaching that Jesus of Nazareth is a created being. Paul described the Son as the "firstborn over all creation." The latter does not mean that Jesus was the first entity that the Father brought into existence, but rather that the Son holds preeminence over all creation (even wisdom). Put another way, He exercises full authority over the entire universe as its sovereign Lord (see Matt. 28:18; Rev. 19:16).

C. Wisdom's Presence at the Beginning: vss. 27-29

"I was there when he set the heavens in place, when he marked out the horizon on the face of the deep, when he established the clouds above and fixed securely the fountains of the deep, when he gave the sea its boundary so the waters would not overstep his command, and when he marked out the foundations of the earth."

Once again, wisdom's antiquity is underscored by her presence with God at the dawn of Creation. When the Lord established the heavens, wisdom was already there (Prov. 8:27). She was also present during a host of other creation activity, including the following: when God marked out the horizon on the world's oceans; when He set the clouds above and established the earth's deep foundations (vs. 28); when God established boundaries for the sea so that the waters would not spread beyond their confines; and when He laid foundations to support the planet (vs. 29).

D. Wisdom's Involvement at the Beginning: vss. 30-31

"Then I was the craftsman at his side. I was filled with delight day after day, rejoicing always in his presence, rejoicing in his whole world and delighting in mankind."

Lady Wisdom was more than an idle spectator while God created the heavens and the earth. She was an active participant. Solomon described wisdom as the Lord's master "craftsman" or skilled architect (Prov. 8:30). The Hebrew term rendered "craftsman" is the same word used to describe Bezalel, who designed and organized the building of the tabernacle (see Exod. 31:1-3). Just as Bezalel used his exceptional abilities as he worked under the leadership of Moses, so Lady Wisdom used her extraordinary talents as she assisted God in His Creation.

Lady Wisdom did not recall her work for God as being a tedious process. Instead,

Lady Wisdom remembered every moment of her work as a joyful experience both for her and the Lord (Prov. 8:30). The reason for this joy was not merely pride in wisdom's accomplishments. Her happiness was the natural result of the Lord taking delight in her. The joy Lady Wisdom felt being in God's presence carried over to the entire world her hands had helped to create. Indeed, Lady Wisdom's love for God's creation, especially humankind, was boundless (vs. 31). When we ask God for wisdom, we are requesting something that has been around since the foundation of the world. We can trust God's wisdom because of its vast experience and depth of insight. Certainly there is nothing we can face that God's wisdom has not seen countless times in the lives of others.

II. HEARING WISDOM'S CALL: PROVERBS 8:32-36

A. Heeding Wisdom: vss. 32-33

"Now then, my sons, listen to me; blessed are those who keep my ways. Listen to my instruction and be wise; do not ignore it."

Lady Wisdom closed her discourse by inviting the people of God to listen and learn from the message she preached at every intersection and gathering place. Those who heeded the instruction and guidance offered by Lady Wisdom were truly "blessed" (Prov. 8:32). She wanted everyone to know that it was not too late to respond to her call. Her persistence in attempting to reach the foolish was a strong sign of her love for those who were created in the image of God. Lady Wisdom's perseverance is an example of God's tenacious attempts to reach people today. If the discerning responded, they would experience Lady Wisdom's blessings. But if they ignored her, they would become increasingly steeped in their foolishness (vs. 33).

Students of Proverbs have noted that many of the maximums in the book were originally addressed to young men as wisdom from fathers to sons (1:8; 2:1; 3:1; 4:1; 8:32). This reflects the nature of ancient Israelite culture, in which sons were expected to inherit positions of leadership within the family and nation. It would be incorrect to assume, however, that because Proverbs has a masculine tone, women are excluded from either the giving or receiving of the book's teaching. For instance, Solomon repeatedly urged youth to pay attention to the instruction of their mothers (1:8; 6:20; 10:1; 30:17). Similarly, the principles and warnings of the book apply just as much to young women as they do to young men. This is especially true in our culture, where both genders dabble in many of the same vices.

Another feature of Proverbs is the instruction given by both parents and grandparents. A valid inference from this is that God desires both parents to be involved in the tutoring and mentoring of the younger members of the family. In ancient Israelite culture, fathers typically took the lead as sources of guidance and direction, and mothers offered governing principles based on God's Word (1:8; 4:1; 6:20). In addition, 4:3-4 suggests that grandparents have an important role to play in the instruction of children, since Solomon is passing on to his children the wisdom given to him by his father, David. It's in this way that a family is to train children in the right way (22:6).

B. Remaining Attentive to Wisdom: vs. 34

"Blessed is the man who listens to me, watching daily at my doors, waiting at my doorway."

Because Lady Wisdom was not willing to give up, she again invited the prudent to follow her and reminded them of the benefits that would come if they obeyed. As in Lady Wisdom's previous invitations, she used a Hebrew verb that is rendered "listen." This term carried with it the idea of hearing with a desire to obey and a readiness to act. Lady Wisdom's invitation to the discerning to meet her at her home is a stark contrast to the offer of the adulteress. Unlike the promiscuous woman, who sought her victims in the darkness, Lady Wisdom searched for the upright in the light of the day (vs. 34; compare 7:9-10).

C. Experiencing Life through Wisdom: vss. 35-36

"For whoever finds me finds life and receives favor from the LORD. But whoever fails to find me harms himself; all who hate me love death."

Another contrast between the adulteress and Lady Wisdom is seen in the consequences the prudent would receive for their visit. The promiscuous woman would curse the foolish with death. Lady Wisdom would bless the righteous with favors from the Lord and a full and abundant life. The discerning who sought Lady Wisdom would be blessed with wealth, honor, and a purposeful existence (Prov. 8:35). Lady Wisdom closed this passage with a warning about ignoring her. Those who chose not to follow her were in reality just hurting themselves. She would not actively punish those who refused to follow her. She simply would not be there to protect them from the natural consequences of their own folly (vs. 36).

Why do some people deafen their ears to the call of Lady Wisdom? Perhaps her path is perceived as too rugged or steep. The path of folly, however, seems to offer a smooth ride. Sometimes, taking the path of Lady Wisdom can seem painful, but in the end it is always worth it. Here we are reminded of the two ways of life Jesus graphically depicted in Matthew 7:13-14. One way He called the narrow gate and road, and the other He called the wide gate and road. The restricted passage leads to life, while the unrestricted passage leads to destruction. In ancient times, city gates were massive wooden doors in a town wall through which traffic passed. Such gates were often reinforced with bronze or iron to provide greater security. They were opened during the day to allow the citizens to come and go, but they were closed at night as a safety measure. And in the event of an attack, the gates were shut and barred to keep out the enemy.

Perhaps while looking at the crowds gathered before Him (vs. 28), Jesus noted that the narrow gate—the one that led to eternal life—was rather small and the road connected with it was constricted. Because of this few people ever found themselves traveling down this path. In other words, a smaller number of people turned to the Savior in faith for eternal life. Jesus stated that the broad gate—the one that led to destruction—was quite wide and the road connected with it was spacious. It had ample room for the droves of people making their way along its easy, gliding path. The point is that a larger number of people reject the Savior and thus experience eternal separation from Him. Throughout life people are faced with making decisions concerning whom they will marry, where they will live and work, and what they will buy. More important than any other decision they make is the one concerning eternal life. Will they choose the path of life or the path of ruin? While it might be more popular to choose destruction, picking deliverance through faith in the Son is far wiser.

Discussion Questions

1. In what ways does Lady Wisdom make her presence known to us?
2. Why do people often fail to take notice of God's wisdom?
3. What do we learn about the character of God by the declarations made about Lady Wisdom in Proverbs 8:22-36?
4. Why do you think the Lord accorded Lady Wisdom such a prominent role in the world's creation?
5. What attitude do you think Lady Wisdom had toward the creation of humankind?

Contemporary Application

Scan your daily newspaper to see how many stories substantiate the truth of Proverbs 8. How many of the reported conflicts occurred because someone, or a group of people, chose foolishness instead of wisdom? "Those who fail to find me," we can hear Lady Wisdom declaring, "harm themselves." In some cases, the harm comes to others as well. Despite this, many people refuse to listen to God. Tragically, some individuals listen only after they have been hurt.

In contrast, Lady Wisdom proclaims, "Whoever finds me finds life." The deepest satisfaction comes from knowing God's Word and obeying His injunctions recorded in it. Our obligation as responsible, prudent Christians is to offer life and to warn of destruction. We must be faithful watchers on the wall, crying out with wisdom for people to be careful and to choose God's path of uprightness over the wicked, destructive ways of the world.

Moreover, this week's lesson speaks of the choices we face as we move along the path of life. Lady Wisdom, in Proverbs 8, speaks to us, telling us that her ways lead to life. Other ways bring only destruction. When we ask God for discernment, we are requesting something that has been around since the foundation of the world. We can trust God's wisdom because of its vast experience and depth of insight. Certainly there is nothing we can face that God's wisdom hasn't seen thousands of times in the lives of others.

The Word Became Flesh

Scripture

Background Scripture: *John 1:1-14*

Scripture Lesson: *John 1:1-14*

Key Verse: *The Word became flesh and made his dwelling among us. We have seen his glory, the glory of the One and Only, who came from the Father, full of grace and truth.* John 1:14.

Scripture Lesson for Children: *John 1:1-14*

Key Verse for Children: *The Word became flesh and made his dwelling among us.* John 1:14.

Lesson Aim

To explore the significance of Jesus being fully divine and fully human.

Lesson Setting

Time: A.D. 26

Place: Judea

Lesson Outline

The Word Became Flesh

I. The Divinity of the Son: John 1:1-8
 A. *The Son's Eternal Preexistence: vss. 1-2*
 B. *The Son's Role in Creating the World: vs. 3*
 C. *The Son as Light and Life: vss. 4-5*
 D. *The Witness of John the Baptizer: vss. 6-8*

II. The Humanity of the Son: John 1:9-14
 A. *Those Who Rejected the Son: vss. 9-11*
 B. *Those Who Received the Son: vss. 12-13*
 C. *The Incarnation of the Son: vs. 14*

Introduction for Adults

Topic: *From the Beginning*

Ed and Laura decided to host a Bible study on the Gospel of John to their unbelieving friends. During the first session, a man objected to the statement that before the dawn of time, Jesus already existed. This person could not reconcile this point with his understanding that Jesus was born on Christmas.

Because Ed and Laura had grown up in Christian homes, it never occurred to them that anyone would take issue with the truth of the Incarnation. The man's agitation gave the couple an opportunity to explain the fact that Jesus is not just someone whose birth we celebrate on Christmas. As this week's lesson reminds us, He is the divine, incarnate Word, the eternal God breaking into history in human form to change the world forever.

Introduction for Youth

Topic: *Always Been There*

For months they had corresponded, one writing at a polished desk in a cramped Chicago-area apartment, the other at a worn kitchen table in a large Wisconsin farmhouse. Finally, the two decided to meet: the farm "boy" in his 40s and the city "gal" at 39. In the early 1960s, through the mail, they had fallen in love. But only face-to-face communication would bring the marriage proposal.

Young people need the abstract made tangible. In coming to earth, the eternal Son of God entered space and time to make the Father's love visible. Human eyes could see it, ears could hear it, and hands could touch it. The apostle John left no doubt about that (see John 1:1; 1 John 1:1). Jesus is God, but He is also a human being. And His desire is to communicate with those He created, including the young people in your class.

Concepts for Children

Topic: *In the Beginning*

1. Jesus is the Word of God.
2. Jesus was with the Father and the Spirit when the world began.
3. Jesus brings life and light into the world.
4. John told people about Jesus.
5. Jesus also wants us to tell other people about Him.

Lesson Commentary

I. THE DIVINITY OF THE SON: JOHN 1:1-8

A. The Son's Eternal Preexistence: vss. 1-2

In the beginning was the Word, and the Word was with God, and the Word was God. He was with God in the beginning.

The heretics of John's day lauded the spiritual aspect of existence but scoffed at the physical realm. Both Genesis 1:1 and John 1:1 serve as a corrective to such a distorted view of reality. For instance, the creation activity recorded in Genesis 1 was first of all physical in nature. Yet there was a spiritual element to it that reflected the immaterial aspect of existence (see Heb. 11:3). In fact, Genesis 1:31 notes that God considered everything He had made to be "very good." Comparably, the account in John 1 is first of all spiritual in nature. Nonetheless, the recreation of the physical realm is equally in view (cf. Isa. 65:17; 66:22; 2 Pet. 3:13; Rev. 21:1). Like the introductory material in Genesis, the introductory material in John anticipates the end of the age when the eternal kingdom is established. This is made possible by the redemption secured by the Son at Calvary, though it will not be fully consummated until His second advent (cf. Rom. 8:18-23; Heb. 9:26-28).

John 1:1, by declaring that the "Word was with God," indicates that the Son and the Father (along with the Spirit) enjoyed an intimate, personal relationship. Moreover, when the apostle said "the Word was God," John meant the fullness of the Godhead resided in the Son and the Father (as well as the Spirit). In other words, John noted in the strongest possible terms that the Word was God (see John 5:18; Rom. 9:5; Phil. 2:6; Col. 2:9; Heb. 1:3; 2 Pet. 1:1). The abiding truth of the Christian faith is that the three members of the Godhead, though distinct personalities, share the same divine nature (see John 8:58; 10:30; 17:11). These truths are reiterated in John 1:2. Before the creation of the world, the Word already existed. Because the Son is uncreated, He is not dependent on anyone or anything. Instead, everyone and everything depends on Him for their existence.

B. The Son's Role in Creating the World: vs. 3

Through him all things were made; without him nothing was made that has been made.

John 1:3 again points us back to the Creation account of Genesis 1. The apostle portrayed the divine Word as the master builder who commanded everything into existence (see Col. 1:16; Heb. 1:2). According to John 1:3, not one thing that has come into being did so apart from the Son. In brief, physical and spiritual reality as we know it would not exist apart from the Messiah.

C. The Son as Light and Life: vss. 4-5

In him was life, and that life was the light of men. The light shines in the darkness, but the darkness has not understood it.

Contrary to the prevailing Greek thought of the day, the Word was not an impersonal, rational force that remained detached from life within the universe. Instead, the Son, as the Creator of the world, is the giver and source of life (John 1:4; see 5:26; 10:28; 14:6). In 1:4, the apostle had both physical and eternal life in mind. Later, in 17:3, Jesus declared that eternal life is much more than unending existence. It is being in an intimate, personal relationship with the Father, the only true God, and His Son, Jesus the Messiah, whom He sent to earth.

Psalm 36:9 states that God is the origin and provider of life. Furthermore, He is the repository of all knowledge and insight, which is symbolized by "light." The apostle possibly had this verse in mind when he proclaimed that the Word, who is life itself, likewise is the "light" (John 1:4) of all people (see 2 Cor. 4:6). In Scripture, light represents what is good, true, and just, while darkness symbolizes what is evil, counterfeit, and immoral. Iniquity and injustice are linked to darkness, whereas holiness and purity are associated with light. An ongoing emphasis in the fourth Gospel is that Jesus' disciples live in the light, while Satan's followers abide in the darkness.

It would be incorrect to conclude from John 1:4 that all the lost will come to the saving light of the Messiah. After all, 3:19 states that the unsaved "loved darkness instead of light" (see vs. 20). Rather, the emphasis in the fourth Gospel is on the Son being "the light of the world" (8:12), that is, the glorious presence of God, who extends the promise of eternal life to all who are willing to receive it (see 1:12). The Messiah is the one who "shines in the darkness" (vs. 5). Indeed, the Son's radiant presence never ceases to pierce through the darkness. The idea is that the Messiah's mission included overcoming what is characterized by error and falsehood. Both before and after Jesus' incarnation, His light continued to shine so that the lost might move from unbelief (darkness) to belief (see 12:46). Even death itself could not snuff out the light of the Word, for He conquered death through His bodily resurrection (see 20:1-9).

There are various ways of rendering the last part of 1:5. The Greek verb rendered "understood" means "to seize" or "to grasp." When applied metaphorically to the darkness spoken of in this verse, the emphasis seems to be on its inability to understand, master, and extinguish the light of the Son. This truth is verified by the fact that unsaved people, who are immersed in the value system of fallen human society, fail to grasp the light of Christ, for their minds are darkened by Satan (see 2 Cor. 4:4; 1 John 5:19). As expected, they are not only hostile to the Messiah, but also to His followers (see John 15:18–16:4). Indeed, one of the major emphases of the fourth Gospel is the ongoing struggle between the forces of belief and unbelief.

D. The Witness of John the Baptizer: vss. 6-8

There came a man who was sent from God; his name was John. He came as a witness to testify concerning that light, so that through him all men might believe. He himself was not the light; he came only as a witness to the light.

As the Synoptic Gospels reveal (see Matt. 3:1-12; Mark 1:2-8; Luke 3:1-20), the Father commissioned John as a prophet to prepare the hearts of the people of his day for the coming of the Son (see Jer. 7:25). The fourth Gospel complements these accounts by focusing on the nature of the Baptizer's witness as it related to the life-giving, light-bearing Word. False teachers, in denying the true identity of the Son, had failed to appreciate the central role that the Son served in the Father's plan of redemption. That is why the introductory portion to the fourth Gospel stresses both the full divinity and humanity of the Messiah, and the testimony of the Baptizer is central to this emphasis.

Like the prophets in the Old Testament era, God commissioned and dispatched John to declare the truth about the Messiah (1:6). Because of the Baptizer's powerful preaching, some had mistakenly identified him as the Redeemer. Though John himself was not the light (vs. 8), he bore witness to the light so that as many as possible might put their trust in the Son and thereby receive eternal life (vs. 7). In accordance with Deuteronomy 17:6 and 19:15, John was one of several witnesses who confirmed the truth regarding the Savior.

By way of example, in John 5:31-47, the Son identified four different but interconnected testimonies that validated the truthfulness of His messianic claims: John the Baptizer, the Son's own works of power (or miracles), God the Father, and Scripture (in particular, Moses; see 8:17-18). While the other sources of testimony may have ranked higher in importance than John's (cf. 5:36), his was nonetheless significant (see Matt. 11:11). Indeed, due to the witness the Baptizer gave, Jesus referred to him as a "lamp that burned and gave light" (John 5:35). During the time the Baptizer's testimony shone brightly, others benefited from it and rejoiced in it, thus confirming his appointment by God.

II. THE HUMANITY OF THE SON: JOHN 1:9-14

A. Those Who Rejected the Son: vss. 9-11

The true light that gives light to every man was coming into the world. He was in the world, and though the world was made through him, the world did not recognize him. He came to that which was his own, but his own did not receive him.

The problem with counterfeit teachers in John's day meant believers were being deceived by imposters who claimed they were spokespersons for God (see 1 John 4:1-6). The witness of the Baptizer verified that the Word, in sharp contrast to the dubious claims of others, is the "true light" (John 1:9). The emphasis here is on the Son being the real, genuine, and authentic Word of God who has come "into the world." Elsewhere in the fourth Gospel, the Messiah is spoken of as coming into the world (see 6:14; 9:39; 11:27; 16:28). In fact, in 12:46, Jesus directly referred to Himself as a light that has come into the world so that all those who believed in Him would not remain in darkness. Through His incarnation, the Son brings the light of divine truth to a sin-darkened world and in so doing discloses the spiritual need that all people have for salvation. All who encounter the light can either choose to receive or renounce it (see 3:19-21). Only those who believe in Him are enlightened in the truest sense of the word.

Against the backdrop of false teachers who denied the truth of the divine Word's full and real humanity, John declared that the Messiah genuinely came to earth for a period of time. He is the same one spoken of earlier in 1:3 as bringing the universe into existence. Even humanity, with its vaunted culture and achievements, owed its existence to the Word. Amazingly, the inhabitants of the planet failed to recognize Him as the Messiah (vs. 10). This is especially true of the rulers of this sin-cursed era. Had they known who Jesus truly was, they would not have "crucified the Lord of glory" (1 Cor. 2:8).

Even when the Son conducted His earthly ministry among His own people in their homeland, they failed to receive Him as the Messiah (John 1:11). In verse 10, the emphasis is on unsaved humanity as a whole failing to recognize the Word. But in verse 11, the censure is stronger and narrower in focus. His own nation, including the religious elite of His day, refused to accept and welcome Him as their Savior and Lord (see John 12:37-41; Acts 7:51-53). None of this caught the Father off guard, for He sovereignly planned that His Son should be rejected and crucified by the ruling powers as well as raised from the dead (see Acts 2:23-24; 4:27-28).

B. Those Who Received the Son: vss. 12-13

Yet to all who received him, to those who believed in his name, he gave the right to become children of God—children born not of natural descent, nor of human decision or a husband's will, but born of God.

While many spurned the Word, not all did. The latter group are those who put their faith in Jesus' "name" (John 1:12). Moreover, those who became His disciples, acknowledged Jesus' integrity, affirmed His messianic claims, and received or accepted Him as the Redeemer. This equates to believing that Jesus is the eternal and fully divine Word (see 20:31). Undoubtedly, the apostle was familiar with heretical ideas that said belief was nothing more than an intellectual assent. In contrast, John stressed that trusting in the Son denoted far more than this. It was staking one's eternal future on Him.

The saving mission of the Word included making God known to humankind. In this case, those who put their faith in the Messiah received the right, or legal entitlement, to become God's children (1:12). Belief in the Son makes the recipient's freedom, capacity, and capability to undergo this change of status a reality. This is a situation in which believing sinners are adopted into God's family and receive all the corresponding rights and privileges that go along with it (see Rom. 8:14-17; Gal. 4:4-6). Additionally, the Father delivers them from the power of darkness and transfers them to the kingdom of His beloved Son (Col. 1:13).

The false teachers John was combating maintained heretical notions about how one became united with God. To refute counterfeit declarations that it was a human-centered, self-initiated process, the apostle declared that those who become God's children are not spiritually reborn in this way (see Jesus' comments in 3:3, 5, 7-8). Specifically, regeneration is not a matter of "natural descent" (1:13) from human parents; nor is it the outworking of fleshly human desires, regardless of whether such are characterized by virtue or vice; nor does it result from any human volition whatsoever.

There is no insinuation here that the flesh in its unfallen state is inherently wicked. Rather, the point is that the new birth is the result of God's gracious action. He sovereignly brings it about (see 2 Cor. 5:17; Gal. 6:15; Titus 3:5) when people put their faith in the Son (see Eph. 1:13; 2:8-9). The re-creation of the fallen human nature signifies a new start for believing sinners. They are transformed in their volition, emotions, and actions (see Rom. 12:1-2). Despite the assertions of heretics, this inner renewal is not the result of people, apart from the Spirit, willing themselves to change by acquiring knowledge. The new birth is entirely the work of the triune God and becomes a reality when people receive the Son for salvation.

C. The Incarnation of the Son: vs. 14

The Word became flesh and made his dwelling among us. We have seen his glory, the glory of the One and Only, who came from the Father, full of grace and truth.

John 1:14 spotlights the incarnation of the divine Word, who "became flesh" so that the lost might be saved (see Matt. 1:21; Luke 2:11). Expressed differently, the second person of the Trinity left the grandeur of heaven to take upon Himself a full and genuine human nature, including a human body, without surrendering any of His divine attributes (see Phil. 2:6-8). The result was the perfect union between His divine and human natures in one person (see Col. 1:19; 2:9; Heb. 1:3). The Greek verb rendered "made his dwelling" is more literally rendered "tabernacled." This recalls the Israelite shrine in the wilderness in which the glory of the Lord was manifested (see Exod. 25:8; 40:34-35; 1 Kings 8:10-11). Jesus of Nazareth, by taking up temporary residence among the people of His day, voluntarily chose to live within the limitations of natural human experience.

Throughout Jesus' earthly ministry, His followers carefully observed Him in all sorts of situations. John, as part of the Twelve, could personally attest to the "glory" (John 1:14) of the one who came from heaven (see Matt. 17:1-13; Mark 9:2-13; Luke 9:28-36). The idea behind the Greek term rendered "glory" (John 1:14) includes the notions of splendor and grandeur. But perhaps even more than this, "glory" implies the presence of worth, significance, and honor. When applied to the Son (see Phil. 2:9-11; Heb. 1:3)—who is the embodiment of truth, wisdom, goodness, mercy, and grace (to name a few virtues)—it means He fully deserves to be worshiped as the Creator and Ruler of the universe (see John 20:28). The glorious life and ministry of the Son (witnessed by John and others) included the miracles Jesus performed (see John 2:11; 11:4) as well as His death, resurrection, and ascension (see 7:39; 12:23, 28; 13:31-32; 17:1, 4-5).

The Greek term rendered "One and Only" (1:14) denotes something that is distinctively unique, special, or one of a kind. The idea is that Jesus is the one and only Son of the Father (see John 3:16, 18; 1 John 4:9). The superlative nature of the Word is highlighted by the apostle's declaration that He is full of "grace" (1:14) and "truth." In the Old Testament, the equivalent notions would be God's enduring love and faithfulness (see Gen. 24:27; Ps. 26:3), which were the basis for His covenant mercy to His people through Moses and others (see Exod. 33:18-19; 34:6-7; Ps. 25:10; Jonah 4:2). From a New Testament perspective, the Lord's grace, or unmerited favor, is the reason believers are saved (see Eph. 2:8). This redemption in turn is made possible through the atoning sacrifice of the Messiah, who through His incarnation has made the Father known to humankind (vs. 18).

Discussion Questions

1. How was it possible for the Word, who eternally existed, to become a human being in time and space?
2. What role did John the Baptizer serve with respect to the Messiah?
3. What does it mean to you to receive Jesus and how does this come about?
4. What sort of glory did John the apostle and others see in Jesus?
5. In what ways has Jesus made the Father known to you as a believer?

Contemporary Application

The Bible's diagnosis of the human condition is that we are sinful and separated from God. Yet the Lord longs to live in loving relationship with us. How, then, can sinful people and a holy God be reconciled? God's answer is Jesus Christ— the one who came as God in human form.

In His full humanness, Jesus faced and triumphed over temptation, never giving in to it. Because of this, He was eligible to give His life for the sinful. His pure sacrifice satisfied God's requirements for dealing justly with sin. Moreover, since Jesus is fully God, when He had successfully met every obstacle to His mission, He exercised His authority over sin and death, setting believers free from the ultimate destruction of these powers.

In our human experience, we cannot relate to Jesus' complete sinlessness. But we can relate to the weaknesses, vulnerability, temptation, pain, loneliness, and loss He suffered while He walked in our shoes (see Heb. 4:15). What a comfort it is to know that Jesus understands what we are going through as we struggle!

In light of these truths about Jesus, verse 16 encourages us to approach God's throne of grace with the assurance of receiving the mercy and help we need in our time of need. Jesus is the one-of-a-kind Savior who makes our relationship with God not only a possibility through His power, but also a meaningful and relevant reality through His compassion.

The Wedding at Cana

Scripture

Background Scripture: *John 2:1-12*
Scripture Lesson: *John 2:1-12*
Key Verse: *This, the first of his miraculous signs, Jesus performed at Cana in Galilee. He thus revealed his glory, and his disciples put their faith in him.* John 2:11.
Scripture Lesson for Children: *John 2:1-12*
Key Verse for Children: *[Jesus] . . . revealed his glory, and his disciples put their faith in him.* John 2:11.

Lesson Aim

To recognize that Jesus is concerned with our ordinary problems.

Lesson Setting

Time: A.D. 26
Place: Cana and Capernaum

Lesson Outline

The Wedding at Cana
  I. The Social Dilemma: John 2:1-5
      A. *Jesus at the Wedding: vss. 1-2*
      B. *Mary's Request: vss. 3-4*
      C. *Mary's Faith: vs. 5*
  II. The Display of Jesus' Glory: John 2:6-12
      A. *The Savior's Command: vss. 6-8*
      B. *The Master's Discovery: vss. 9-10*
      C. *The Disciples' Faith: vs. 11*
      D. *The Journey to Capernaum: vs. 12*

Introduction for Adults

Topic: *The Good Stuff*

The biblical account of the wedding ceremony at Cana in Galilee (see John 2:1-12) reminds us that social embarrassments come in all sizes, shapes, and colors. But rarely do they open doors for discussions about spiritual issues. This is because it's hard for people to make the connection between everyday life and God's will.

Nevertheless, seeing is believing when people observe how Christians handle not just social embarrassments but also the deeper issues of life. For instance, many people take notice when they see a person of faith finding the strength to endure trials, hardships, and sufferings.

Consider how extraordinary it is to witness Christians refusing to take revenge when others have wronged them (see Prov. 20:22). It's also exceptional when a believer uses a gentle response to defuse a potentially explosive situation (see 15:1). Jesus' followers may not be able to turn ordinary water into fine wine (in a manner of speaking, the "good stuff"), but they can lead people to faith in the Son by the way they follow His commands in ordinary situations.

Introduction for Youth

Topic: *He's Got the Power!*

What does it take to believe in Jesus? Miracles? Visions? Facts? Testimonies of others? Generations raised on believing only hard data find it difficult to accept the reliability of other kinds of facts. In response, believers over the centuries have noted that Christianity appeals to the facts of history, which are clearly recognizable and available to everyone. This observation applies to the miracle of Jesus turning water into wine (the subject of this week's lesson).

Believing in Jesus is not a blind leap of faith into the dark void of ignorance. Rather, it is an intelligent decision that is informed by eyewitness accounts (see 1 Cor. 15:1-8). Jesus' original followers wrote about what He did so that we might trust in our all-powerful Savior for eternal life (see John 20:30-31). As the Son said to Thomas in verse 29, "blessed are those who have not seen and yet have believed."

Concepts for Children

Topic: *Good Things Come When Needed*

1. Jesus, His followers, and His mother went to a wedding at Cana in Galilee.
2. When Jesus' mother noted that the wine was gone, Jesus told the servants to fill six stone jars with water.
3. Those at the wedding soon discovered that Jesus had turned the water into wine.
4. Jesus used this miracle to show His glory.
5. Jesus has the power to meet our every need.

Lesson Commentary

I. THE SOCIAL DILEMMA: JOHN 2:1-5

A. Jesus at the Wedding: vss. 1-2

On the third day a wedding took place at Cana in Galilee. Jesus' mother was there, and Jesus and his disciples had also been invited to the wedding.

Our lesson for this week deals with Jesus turning water into wine. In the preceding chapter of John's Gospel, we learn that the Son is the living Word, that He eternally existed with the Father and the Spirit before time began, and that He came to earth as a human being so that the lost might be saved (1:1-18). As John the Baptizer declared, Jesus is the Lamb of God "who takes away the sin of the world" (vs. 29). It's no wonder, then, that so many people would be willing to become His followers (vss. 35-51).

One of John's goals was to convince people to trust in Jesus as the Messiah, the Son of God, and consequently find eternal life in Him (20:30-31). The apostle's inclusion of seven signs (see 2:11), or attesting miracles, in the first 12 chapters of the fourth Gospel help to accomplish that overarching purpose. The wondrous deeds persuasively demonstrate the messianic identity, power, and authority of the Lord Jesus. Just as in the period of Moses, the great lawgiver and leader of Israel, God intervened in human history, so now with the coming of the Word (1:1-2, 14, 18), God involves Himself in a new way to bring about eternal redemption for those who believe (see Deut. 11:3; 29:2).

Jesus' first recorded miracle took place at a wedding feast, which His disciples and His mother also attended (John 2:1-2). The marriage celebration was a symbolic reminder that the age of the Messiah had dawned and inaugurated the blessings of the future Kingdom (see Gen. 49:11; Isa. 25:6; Jer. 31:5; Hos. 2:22; Joel 3:18; Amos 9:13). The backdrop of this wedding feast was an array of purification rites described in the Old Testament, all of which found their ultimate fulfillment in the Son. The time reference in John 2:1 suggests the Messiah arrived the third day after He and His followers left the Jordan River area, where the Baptizer had been headquartered. The presence of Mary at the celebration indicates that the bride or groom (or both) was a close friend of the family, rather than just an acquaintance of Jesus and His disciples. It is unclear why no mention is made of Joseph. He may have been deceased by this time.

The changing of water into wine (fermented grape juice) occurred at Cana in Galilee. This village is only mentioned two other times in the fourth Gospel—4:46 and 21:2. The latter reference identifies Cana as the home of Nathanael, who had just been chosen to follow Jesus (1:47). Since Cana was a small town, more than likely Nathanael would have also known the newly married couple. The exact location of this village remains unknown. Two suggested sites are near Nazareth, where Jesus grew up with His family. One is a group of ruins called Khirbet Kana, about nine miles north of Nazareth. However, some think that the present village of Kafr Kanna, about four miles northeast of Nazareth, is the actual location, with its abundant springs and fig trees. Some of the Crusaders identified this location as Cana, and it fits well with the descriptions of medieval travelers, who describe a church in this location supposedly containing at least one of the original water jars from the wedding.

B. Mary's Request: vss. 3-4

When the wine was gone, Jesus' mother said to him, "They have no more wine." "Dear woman, why do you involve me?" Jesus replied. "My time has not yet come."

In Jesus' day, wedding festivals could last up to a week. On such occasions, banquets would be prepared to accommodate many guests. The attendees would spend their time celebrating the new life to be enjoyed by the married couple. Archaeological evidence indicates that entire villages would be invited to a wedding celebration. Also, to refuse such an invitation was considered an insult. The wedding meal itself consisted of bread dipped in wine. Typically, the guests would call for innumerable toasts. After that, more visiting, eating, and drinking would occur (though this was rarely an occasion for drunkenness).

Wine diluted with water was the accepted beverage of the times, and people were accustomed to it. Because of a lack of water purification processes, this mixture was safer to drink than water alone. Careful planning was needed to accommodate all who came. This was imperative, for the strong, unwritten rules of hospitality implied that it was humiliating to be caught in short supply of some necessary item. Even the poorest Jewish parents would scrimp and save enough money to provide plenty of food and wine for their children's wedding. Yet, for some unknown reason, the bridegroom failed to supply enough of the latter for the duration of the festivities (John 2:3). Perhaps more guests came than he had anticipated, or perhaps they stayed longer than he had planned.

Few details are given of what happened next. Evidently, someone reported the predicament to Mary, who then went to her son. Perhaps Jesus was seated at a table with His disciples and enjoying the festivities. One possibility is that Mary quietly sat down next to Jesus and discretely told Him the wine had run out. It is clear from Jesus' response that Mary's statement implied more than a simple observation of fact. Implicit in her words was a request for Jesus to do something about the situation so that the bridegroom could avoid being socially embarrassed. According to verse 11, Jesus had not yet performed any miracles. Thus at this point in the account we can only speculate as to what Mary had observed in Jesus that would give her the idea He could somehow resolve the problem.

It is unlikely that Mary expected Jesus to send the people home, for that was not His prerogative. Also, Mary probably did not want Him to send His disciples into town to buy more wine, for they surely lacked the funds to do so. It is possible Mary had seen Jesus on other occasions do kind and helpful things for hurting people. Perhaps in the privacy of neighborhood life, Jesus was known as an extraordinary and caring person. Regardless of what Mary may have been thinking, Jesus gave her a startling and provocative answer. He did not say either yes or no. Instead, He asked Mary why she had come to Him for help. Without waiting for her reply, Jesus' words indicate that He was no longer under His mother's authority. While Jesus continued to honor Mary, His actions were governed by the mission His Father in heaven had given Him (see 8:28-29). In brief, the goal of the Son was to die on the cross in order to atone for the sins of the world (see 1:29).

Jesus was neither cruel nor harsh in His remarks to His mother. "Dear woman" (2:4) was a common term of address that implied no disrespect (see Matt. 15:28; Luke 13:12; John 4:21; 8:10; 19:26; 20:15). Such observations notwithstanding, in offering this response, Jesus wanted Mary to think of Him not so much as the child whom she had parented, but rather as the Redeemer of Israel. Jesus used a social situation to point to a spiritual reality. In fact, the contrast between the wedding crisis and His mission could not have been more vivid. The Savior's query, "why do you involve me?" (John 2:4), spotlights Mary's desire that Jesus do something to help a family avoid social embarrassment. Also, the follow-up statement, "My time has not yet come," stressed that Jesus' atoning sacrifice at Calvary, resurrection from the dead, and return to the Father in glory was a more eternally relevant issue (see 12:23, 27; 13:1; 17:1).

C. Mary's Faith: vs. 5

His mother said to the servants, "Do whatever he tells you."

From what transpired, it is clear that Jesus had not offended Mary. In fact, she seemed to instinctively know that Jesus would intervene in a constructive manner. At this point, Mary returned to the servants and possibly told the head steward to do whatever Jesus directed (John 2:5). Although Mary did not know what Jesus might have in mind, she nevertheless trusted Him to initiate what was prudent. Here we see that despite the awkwardness of the situation, the Lord Jesus conducted Himself impeccably in the social affairs of His community. Though His redemptive mission was lofty, He was not above mingling with people on all levels, so that they might be drawn to Him in saving faith (vs. 11). Jesus' response to Mary shows that the Savior knew and controlled His eternal future (10:17-18). Mary, in turn, submitted to Jesus' decision about how to handle the situation.

II. *THE DISPLAY OF JESUS' GLORY: JOHN 2:6-12*

A. The Savior's Command: vss. 6-8

Nearby stood six stone water jars, the kind used by the Jews for ceremonial washing, each holding from twenty to thirty gallons. Jesus said to the servants, "Fill the jars with water"; so they filled them to the brim. Then he told them, "Now draw some out and take it to the master of the banquet." They did so.

The Messiah apparently wasted no time in taking action. Perhaps after getting up from where He had been sitting, He went to the nearby spot where there were six empty stone jars (John 2:6). Then no doubt after praying silently to His heavenly Father, Jesus told the servants to fill the jars with water (vs. 7). Mary's faith was honored when Jesus did His first miracle at this humble peasant wedding. Jesus performed the miracle in such a way as to not draw attention to Himself or the shortage of wine at the feast.

The six stone vessels at the wedding feast normally kept the family's water supply fresh and cool. The jars of varying size each could hold about 20 to 30 gallons of water (all total, roughly between 120 and 180 gallons of liquid), which the Jews used to wash their hands and vessels according to the Mosaic law's requirements. Apparently, because of the number of wedding guests, the water in the six jars had been used up, so they needed to be refilled. The servants might have been puzzled by Jesus' unusual sounding command. Why take ordinary water to the master of ceremonies (vs. 8)? Despite whatever doubts the servants may have had, they did not complain. Instead, they did exactly what Jesus said.

B. The Master's Discovery: vss. 9-10

And the master of the banquet tasted the water that had been turned into wine. He did not realize where it had come from, though the servants who had drawn the water knew. Then he called the bridegroom aside and said, "Everyone brings out the choice wine first and then the cheaper wine after the guests have had too much to drink; but you have saved the best till now."

After the servants filled the jars to the top with water, they then dipped some out and took it to the person in charge of the festivities (usually a servant or friend of the bridegroom). When this individual tasted the water now turned into wine, he was so pleasantly surprised that he commended the bridegroom for his good taste (John 2:9). The master of ceremonies noted that it was customary for the host (such as the bridegroom) to serve the best wine first and then later to bring out the less expensive wines. But the bridegroom was congratulated for the brilliant stroke of keeping the best wine until last (vs. 10).

C. The Disciples' Faith: vs. 11

This, the first of his miraculous signs, Jesus performed at Cana in Galilee. He thus revealed his glory, and his disciples put their faith in him.

Jesus' first sign at Cana in Galilee was experienced not so much as a miracle, but rather as a wonderful discovery (John 2:11). Only the Messiah and the servants initially knew what had happened. Jesus evidently took no unusual action, such as touching the stone jars or commanding the water to turn into wine. Most likely, a simple prayer brought about the attesting sign. Jesus did not call for a pause in the festivities, and He did not summon everyone's attention. He also did not tell those present to gather around and see how He had changed water into wine. Rather,

Jesus performed His miracle in a quiet and humble manner. John 1:3 reveals that the Word is the Creator of all things. In fact, acts of creation and transformation are part of His nature (see 2 Cor. 5:17).

Jesus' turning water into wine should be understood in terms of what the Old Testament said about the coming Redeemer. In the messianic age, the Lord would host a great feast complete with the best food and overflowing wine, symbolizing great joy (see Isa. 25:6; Joel 2:19, 24; 3:18; Amos 9:13-15). In fact, one non-biblical description of the messianic age describes it as a time of great fertility, with grapes so large that just one would produce about 120 gallons of wine. Wine, however, could also symbolize suffering, since its color suggested blood, and drinking its dregs was a sign of punishment (see Pss. 60:3; 75:8; Jer. 25:15-16). Jesus symbolically linked wine with His blood at the Last Supper, which He celebrated when His hour had indeed come (see John 2:4; 13:1; 18:11).

We do not know how Jesus changed the water into wine at Cana in Galilee, only that He did it instantaneously and without fanfare. But we do know that Jesus used this miracle to validate His claim to be the Messiah (a truth that would later lead to His crucifixion). All the miracles of Jesus were signs that He performed to demonstrate His power so that people would trust in Him. It is true that Jesus healed and helped people in dire situations, and they were blessed in this way by His miracles. Yet, in the end, Jesus' foremost goal was to relieve the deepest spiritual needs of people. The Messiah's changing the water into wine unveiled His glory (that is, His divine nature, presence, and power; see Exod. 24:15-18; 34:29-35; 40:34-38), and the disciples believed in Him as the Anointed One (John 2:11). His glory was seen in two aspects at Cana—His love for the neighborhood people and His control over the elements of nature.

From the beginning verses of his Gospel, John—a devoted follower of Jesus and an eyewitness of His miracles—emphasized as one of his major themes the Savior's mastery over all creation. John's chief means of doing so was to describe in detail seven signs that Jesus performed. Jesus' turning water into wine revealed Him as the source of life (2:1-12). The healing of the royal official's son showed Jesus to be master over distance (4:46-54). The healing of the invalid at the pool of Bethesda revealed Jesus as the master over time (5:1-17). The feeding of over 5,000 showed Jesus to be the Bread of life (6:1-14). Jesus' walking on water and stilling the storm revealed Him as master over nature (6:16-21). The healing of the man blind from birth showed Jesus to be the Light of the world (9:1-41). And the raising of Lazarus from the dead revealed that Jesus has power over death (11:17-45).

D. The Journey to Capernaum: vs. 12

After this he went down to Capernaum with his mother and brothers and his disciples. There they stayed for a few days.

After Jesus attended the wedding in Cana, He traveled some 20 miles northeast to Capernaum (John 2:12), where He stayed for a few days with His mother, brothers (see Matt. 1:24-25; 12:46; Mark 3:21; 6:3; Luke 8:19), and disciples (see John 1:35-51). Capernaum, the home of some of Jesus' followers, served as the Lord's headquarters during a large portion of His public ministry (see Matt. 4:13; Mark 1:21; 2:1). It was a fishing village built on the northwest shore of the Sea of Galilee. Capernaum hosted a Roman garrison that maintained peace in the region. Major highways crisscrossed at Capernaum, making it militarily strategic. Because of its fishing and trading industries, the city was a melting pot of Greek, Roman, and Jewish cultures.

Discussion Questions

1. Why do you think Mary approached Jesus, who had not yet performed any miracles, about the wedding host's running out of wine?
2. Why did Jesus' turning the water into wine give rise to the disciples' belief?
3. In what way did Jesus' performance of this miracle reveal His glory?
4. How has Jesus turned some ordinary aspect of your life into something extraordinary?
5. Do you find it hard to keep trusting in Jesus when you find yourself in a situation that you don't understand? How do you maintain your faith during those times?

Contemporary Application

Jesus brought good news to a broken world. He announced that God's kingdom was at hand, and that all people should repent and believe in the Gospel (Mark 1:15). Jesus did so not from the isolation of a religious commune, but rather from the everyday world inhabited by ordinary people.

For instance, a neighborhood wedding provided the ideal setting for Jesus to show His love and power (John 2:1-12). Suddenly He was no longer just a carpenter from Nazareth (see Mark 6:3). Rather, He was the Messiah of Israel, the one who inspired faith and obedience.

People today also need to see Jesus in this way. He is much more than a famous painting or statuesque religious figure. When we trust in Him, He remains ever present to help us through our ordeals. And regardless of the nature of our problems, He is there to watch over and strengthen us.

Clearly, then, our Savior is not confined to the sanctuary. Instead, He is present in every place of life. He wants us to find salvation and peace through faith in Him. And He calls us, as His followers, to declare the message of His love and care to the lost so that He can fill their empty lives with joy and purpose. What a wonderful gift we have to share with others!

God's Word Saves

Scripture

Background Scripture: *John 3:11-21; Numbers 21:4-8*
Scripture Lesson: *John 3:11-21*
Key Verse: *"God so loved the world that he gave his one and only Son, that whoever believes in him shall not perish but have eternal life."* John 3:16.
Scripture Lesson for Children: *John 3:11-21*
Key Verse for Children: *"God so loved the world that he gave his one and only Son, that whoever believes in him shall not perish but have eternal life."* John 3:16.

Lesson Aim

To appreciate the importance of trusting in the Son for eternal life.

Lesson Setting

Time: A.D. 27
Place: Jerusalem

Lesson Outline

God's Word Saves

  I. The Importance of Faith in the Son: John 3:11-15
      A. *An Inability to Believe: vss. 11-12*
      B. *Jesus' Redemptive Mission: vss. 13-15*
  II. The Two Ways of Responding to the Son: John 3:16-21
      A. *The Father's Gift of His Son: vs. 16*
      B. *The Son's Goal of Saving the Lost: vs. 17*
      C. *The Contrast between Faith and Unbelief: vs. 18*
      D. *The Contrast between Light and Darkness: vss. 19-21*

Introduction for Adults

Topic: *A New Life*

As the guests headed out that Friday night in July 1981 to dance at a new hotel in Kansas City, Missouri, no one expected that 100 people wouldn't return. The hotel had been beautifully and carefully constructed. The architects and builders knew of no flaw in the suspended bridges that hung one, two, and three stories above the main floor. But as people danced on them, the bridges started to sway and then collapsed, plunging many to their deaths.

Tragic construction flaws can go unnoticed. More generally, uncertainties in life get ignored. Nicodemus, for instance, thought he had constructed a good foundation for his spiritual life based on following the Mosaic law. But Jesus saw the tragic flaw in this way of thinking. Nicodemus wasn't building a foundation on and overcoming his uncertainties through the Spirit. May we not make the same mistake with our eternal future. Instead, may we find new life through faith in the Messiah.

Introduction for Youth

Topic: *Saved!*

Seeing—and understanding—God's kingdom in its full glory cannot be done by casual observers, offhand inquirers, or those who have no commitment to God's Word. Those who maintain otherwise do not have God's Spirit and remain unsaved.

As Jesus told Nicodemus, we cannot see the kingdom of God unless we are born again. Only then do our eyes adjust to God's way of seeing things. Through faith in His Son, we are saved. As a result, we receive the Holy Spirit and a new vision on life, both temporal and eternal in nature.

Concepts for Children

Topic: *Love Leads to Action*

1. Nicodemus, an important Jewish leader, wanted to know God better.
2. Jesus said that knowing the Father better started by trusting in His Son for salvation.
3. Only God's Spirit can give one new life and make one a child of God.
4. God's Spirit is in complete control when it comes to imparting eternal life.
5. Jesus wants us to believe in Him so that we can become members of God's family.

Lesson Commentary

I. THE IMPORTANCE OF FAITH IN THE SON: JOHN 3:11-15

A. An Inability to Believe: vss. 11-12

"I tell you the truth, we speak of what we know, and we testify to what we have seen, but still you people do not accept our testimony. I have spoken to you of earthly things and you do not believe; how then will you believe if I speak of heavenly things?"

John 3:1 introduces us to Nicodemus, who was both a Pharisee and a member of the "Jewish ruling council," or Sanhedrin. Verse 10 adds that Nicodemus was "Israel's teacher." This reference has led some to think that he had a special position as the premier instructor to the nation. The more likely option is that Jesus affirmed the status of Nicodemus as a highly esteemed rabbi among his religious peers. In a later episode, Nicodemus defended Jesus before the Sanhedrin (see 7:51). The faith of Nicodemus eventually progressed to the point where he openly assisted in the burial of the Messiah (see 19:39-42).

Nicodemus might have been one of the religious leaders who saw Jesus clearing the temple area and performing various signs during the Passover festival (see 2:13-23). Evidently, Jesus' miracles had impressed the esteemed Pharisee (3:2). In brief, Nicodemus had seen the signs as the Lord's seal of approval on Jesus. Perhaps Nicodemus also felt that with all his self-righteousness, something was still missing. Or possibly Nicodemus was questioning Jesus on behalf of some members of the Sanhedrin. The night visit may mean that Nicodemus did not want to be seen publicly talking with Jesus. Or it may mean that Nicodemus wanted a long conversation, which would be more possible at the end of the day. In any case, the Light of the world was about to illumine this seeker of truth with good news of the new birth and the new order He was about to inaugurate.

Nicodemus addressed Jesus with high respect by calling Him "Rabbi" and acknowledging that God had sent Him to teach the Jewish people. But at this point, Nicodemus did not realize he was in the presence of the one who is the Son of God. In fact, the Pharisee regarded his conversation with Jesus as one peer discussing doctrine with another. Undoubtedly, to the surprise of Nicodemus, Jesus did not respond to his flattering remark, but spoke directly to the subject at the heart of the ruler's greatest need—eternal salvation. Jesus' statement immediately undercut what Nicodemus had believed and taught as a Pharisee, namely, that if one wanted to be right with God, he or she must strive to perfectly obey the Mosaic law. With profound insight, Jesus told Nicodemus that, in order to see God's kingdom, a person must be "born again" (vs. 3).

The Greek word rendered "again" can also mean "from above" (see 3:31; 19:11) and probably both meanings are intended here. Scripture teaches that in a divine act of grace, the Holy Spirit entirely revitalizes the fallen human nature of believing sinners (see Rom. 12:1-2; Eph. 4:22-24; Col. 3:9-10; Titus 3:5-7; 1 Pet. 1:3). In this decisive moment, God miraculously raises them from spiritual death to new life. The desires, goals, and actions of the regenerate are so radically changed that they want to live for God and serve others (see 2 Cor. 5:17). To see God's kingdom (as a result of the new birth) means to experience fully the redemptive blessings associated with the rule of the Lord in one's life, both in the present and throughout eternity. Even such a respected religious leader as Nicodemus needed to be spiritually reborn. And only God's power, not human effort, could transform the Pharisee's sinful heart (as well as that of all people; see John 1:13).

Nicodemus interpreted Jesus' statement in an overly literal way. Specifically, the religious leader thought the Savior was talking about an adult reentering the womb of his or her mother and going through the process of physical birth a second time (3:4). Perhaps Nicodemus had been attempting to earn God's favor for years and had failed. To strive to do even more would seem like an act of futility. The response of Nicodemus to Jesus can be viewed in at least two ways: either Nicodemus did not understand Jesus, or Nicodemus did not like where the conversation was headed and chose to be ignorant of Jesus' true meaning. In either case, Nicodemus was searching for more information from the Messiah.

Jesus noted that the rebirth was spiritual, not physical, and could only be accomplished by the Holy Spirit (vs. 5). There are three noteworthy views concerning the meaning of the phrase rendered "of water and the Spirit." Some think Jesus was referring to the theological meaning behind baptism. Since Jesus' ministry came shortly after that of John the Baptizer, John's baptism of repentance was on everyone's minds. Put another way, Nicodemus needed to repent and be born of the Spirit to see God's kingdom. Others maintain the reference is to water (the fluid in the amniotic sac) associated with the birth of a child. Thus, Jesus was referring to both physical and spiritual births. Still others note that Nicodemus, as a scholar, should have known those Old Testament passages where "water" (as cleansing) and "spirit" (or "wind") are both mentioned (see Isa. 32:15; 44:3-5; Ezek. 18:31; 36:25-27; 37:9-10; Titus 3:5). These symbolize new life from above and anticipate the coming age in which the Messiah brings redemptive blessing to God's people.

Jesus' main point was that entrance into the divine kingdom could not be obtained by keeping the law or by belonging to the right race or people. The Messiah explained that what is born of physical heritage is physical (namely, weak and mortal in nature). In contrast, what is born of the Spirit is spiritual (namely, eternal and immortal in nature; John 3:6). Jesus urged Nicodemus not to be amazed that the new birth was a necessity for anyone to enter God's kingdom (vs. 7). Perhaps the two were standing on the flat roof of a house and talking when a gust of wind arose. Accordingly, the Messiah took the opportunity to compare the work of the Spirit to the wind (vs. 8). In fact, in both Hebrew and Greek the same word can mean either "spirit" or "wind." One cannot see the wind or understand its origin, but its effects can be seen. In the same way, people cannot see the Spirit at work within someone's heart, but people can watch the dramatic changes in that individual's life. Just as people cannot control the wind, so the Spirit does as He pleases in regenerating believing sinners.

Nicodemus admitted that he did not understand Jesus' words (vs. 9). The religious leader's reply should probably be taken as a plea for help, not as a questioning of Jesus' response. Nicodemus wanted to know how he could experience this seemingly mysterious and enigmatic new birth. Jesus, in turn, was surprised that Nicodemus did not understand the concept of the new birth (vs. 10). As a prominent teacher, he should have been familiar with Old Testament prophetic passages that speak of a new life and a new heart (see Jer. 31:33). The Son noted that He, along with the Father and the Spirit, spoke about what they knew. And these truths were affirmed by the witness of the Old Testament prophets, John the Baptizer, and the first disciples of Jesus concerning what the Son said and did. Regrettably, though, many of the Pharisee's contemporaries did not accept the truth about Jesus (John 3:11). If they did not believe what Jesus said about things that happen on earth (particularly, spiritual regeneration), they would have much more difficulty in believing what He said about things that happen in heaven (vs. 12).

B. Jesus' Redemptive Mission: vss. 13-15

"No one has ever gone into heaven except the one who came from heaven—the Son of Man. Just as Moses lifted up the snake in the desert, so the Son of Man must be lifted up, that everyone who believes in him may have eternal life."

Thankfully for Nicodemus, he was talking with someone who could speak with authority regarding eternal matters. While the Jews possessed God's revelation in the Mosaic law (see Rom. 9:4), no one but the Son of man had ever gone into heaven or come back to describe it (see John 1:51; 3:31; 6:41-42). Also, because Jesus is the divine, incarnate Word, He alone can unveil heaven's true nature to humanity (3:13; see 1:18). He revealed to Nicodemus truths that cannot be discovered by experience or logic, including how the new birth is possible. Jesus referred to a historical event recorded in the Pentateuch involving the Israelites. As they were about to go around Edom in their path to the promised land, the people grumbled against God and Moses. The people also complained about the "miserable food" (Num. 21:5) they had to eat in the wilderness.

In response, God sent "venomous snakes" (vs. 6) into the Israelite camp until the people cried out in repentance. The number and variety of snakes in Israel, Sinai, and Egypt are numerous, but only a small percentage are potentially lethal. One of the most poisonous species in the Middle East is the cobra. Another deadly species is the viper. The adder, which is mentioned in Jeremiah 8:17, was possibly the desert viper. The snakes that attacked the Israelites in the desert (Num. 21:6) were probably carpet vipers. Vipers can strike without provocation and their bite can kill within a few days. The Bible almost always portrays the snake as a symbol of evil, so the analogy that Jesus makes in John 3:14 is unusual.

Next, the Lord instructed Moses to make a bronze replica of a poisonous snake, attach it to a pole, and lift it up so everyone could see it. Those who were bitten could look at the object and live (Num. 21:8). The Son equated His coming death on the cross to Moses lifting up the snake in the wilderness. The word translated "lifted up" (John 3:14) can mean both lift up (as on a cross) and exalt (as to heaven; see 8:28; 12:32, 34). This information serves as a reminder that the Messiah's death became the stepping-stone to His exaltation. Furthermore, through the Son's death on the cross, believing sinners become citizens of the divine, heavenly kingdom. They realize their condition as being similar to that of the ancient Israelites. Regardless of the age in which people live, they are guilty of disobedience, under God's judgment, and unable to rescue themselves. Their only hope is to accept the provision of salvation the Father makes in the Son. In particular, when they look to the Cross in faith, they are saved, just as looking at the bronze snake brought relief to the Israelites (3:14-15).

II. THE TWO WAYS OF RESPONDING TO THE SON: JOHN 3:16-21

A. The Father's Gift of His Son: vs. 16

"For God so loved the world that he gave his one and only Son, that whoever believes in him shall not perish but have eternal life."

It is quite probable that Jesus was still speaking until the end of John 3:15, for only He used the phrase "Son of Man" in the four Gospels. It is also possible that the apostle's reflection starts with verse 16, since Jesus' death is spoken of in the past tense after verse 15. Regardless of whether John was recording Jesus' words to Nicodemus in verses 16-21 or adding to this dialogue what Jesus had taught His disciples, these verses reveal the truth about the nature and extent of God's love for the lost. The Father, being motivated by His infinite love for humanity, sent His "one and only Son" to die for the sins of the world. God summons all people on earth to put their faith in the Messiah—not only assenting to what He said as true, but also entrusting their lives to Him. Those who believe in the Redeemer will not suffer eternal separation from God, but will enjoy a reconciled, deeply satisfying relationship with the Son and His heavenly Father.

B. The Son's Goal of Saving the Lost: vs. 17

"For God did not send his Son into the world to condemn the world, but to save the world through him."

The Greek noun rendered "world" (John 1:17) is an important term in the fourth Gospel. In its most basic usage, the noun refers to an ornament, such as in 1 Peter 3:3, where it is used to mean the "adornment," namely, the ornamentation of jewelry and clothing. The term can also be used of the universe with its orderly ornamentation of stars and planets. Eventually, the noun came to refer to the earth, since (from the human perspective) that is the most important part of the universe, and also people, since they are the most significant inhabitants of the planet.

In the fourth Gospel, "world" most often refers to the majority of people and their temporal pursuits. John's "world" is hostile to the Savior and to His followers because of their association with Him (see 7:7; 15:18-19). Amazingly, despite the world's hatred of God, He still loves it and gave His Son so that its people might receive eternal life (see 3:16). Verse 17 explains that the Father's ultimate purpose in sending His Son into the world was not to condemn humankind for its guilt and eternally punish the lost. Rather, it was to provide the way of salvation for them.

C. The Contrast between Faith and Unbelief: vs. 18

"Whoever believes in him is not condemned, but whoever does not believe stands condemned already because he has not believed in the name of God's one and only Son."

The salvation of the lost through the Son has been the Father's supreme desire since Adam and Eve sinned in the garden of Eden. Those who refuse God's provision will perish. The fact that salvation is for all who believe implies judgment for those who reject the Messiah. While John emphasized that the Redeemer came to offer eternal life, the apostle could not ignore the destiny of those who spurned the "one and only Son" (John 3:18; see 1 Pet. 2:8; 1 John 5:10-12). He alone is God's provision for salvation (see Heb. 6:4-8).

D. The Contrast between Light and Darkness: vss. 19-21

"This is the verdict: Light has come into the world, but men loved darkness instead of light because their deeds were evil. Everyone who does evil hates the light, and will not come into the light for fear that his deeds will be exposed. But whoever lives by the truth comes into the light, so that it may be seen plainly that what he has done has been done through God."

The declaration "this is the verdict" (John 3:19) leaves readers with the impression that throughout Jesus' ministry, He was on trial, a situation that mirrors the courtroom language of the Old Testament (see Isa. 43–48). In the fourth Gospel, the evidence for Jesus is presented at length. As was noted in lesson 2, in accordance with Deuteronomy 17:6 and 19:15, several witnesses are also presented in the fourth Gospel, and each confirmed the truth regarding Jesus as "the Christ, the Son of God" (20:31). The heavenly court of divine justice forms the backdrop of the Father's condemnation of those who reject the Son. The fact is that God sent the one who is Light into the world (see 1:2-5, 9). Tragically, though, morally depraved people love the darkness of Satan and sin (3:19).

Because the lives of the unsaved are characterized by disobedience (see Eph. 2:2) and steeped in wickedness (see Rom. 1:32), they dread the possibility of coming in faith to the Light. Also, because they realize He will expose their sins, they hate Him and His followers all the more (John 3:20; see 15:18-25). In contrast are those who practice the truth revealed by the Lord Jesus. They demonstrate by their lives of piety and integrity that they readily come to the Light. They do not fear any kind of exposure—not because they are free from sin, but because they want to be cleansed by God's grace. When others see that God enables them to be people of rectitude and virtue, He is glorified (3:21).

Discussion Questions

1. What sort of heavenly truths did Jesus declare to the people of His day?
2. What is necessary for people to receive eternal life?
3. Why would the Father give His beloved Son to the world?
4. What can you do to convince as many of your peers as possible to trust in the Messiah?
5. Why do you think the unsaved love the darkness of sin more than the light of the Son?

Contemporary Application

Not all doubts are objectionable. Doubts about faith can either lead us closer to the truth or gradually sink us into disbelief. Sometimes people have doubts, but they refuse to ask questions to resolve them. In this case there is a false sense of comfort in using doubts as an excuse not to hold oneself accountable to the truth. In addition, allowing doubts to go unresolved often results in a loss of conviction and belief. Thankfully, Nicodemus wrestled with his doubts.

A more contemporary example would be Mark, who was in his final year of high school. He was having the time of his life, or so it seemed. But at the end of the year, a gentle sophomore girl named Charlene, whom Mark respected and admired, wrote the following in his yearbook:

"Mark, I have enjoyed our friendship, and I will miss having you around next year. There is one thing I want to tell you before you go out into the big world. I know you are searching for happiness, but you will never find true happiness until you find Jesus. He is the only One who can give you the peace you are looking for."

When Mark read this entry, Charlene's words were like a razor cutting right through the superficial externals of his life to the heart of his need for something real and lasting. That night Mark called Charlene and asked what she had meant by "finding Jesus." Charlene then described her own relationship with Christ and invited Mark to her youth group. Mark came that week. And after asking the youth leader many questions, he received the Father's grace and forgiveness through the Son.

Mark was reborn that night into a new way of experiencing life. He was spiritually delivered into God's kingdom through faith. And if you were to ask Mark, he would tell you that that event has made all the difference in his life. Since then, two decades have passed. Mark has graduated from a Christian college, served as a youth pastor, and worked with mentally-handicapped adults. And his relationship with Jesus continues to grow, giving his life meaning and purpose.

Jesus Testifies to the Truth

DEVOTIONAL READING

John 8:28-38

DAILY BIBLE READINGS

Monday March 26
  Psalm 43 Led by Truth and Light

Tuesday March 27
  Psalm 86:8-13 Walking in God's Truth

Wednesday March 28
  John 18:1-11 Arrest of Jesus

Thursday March 29
  John 18:12-18 Denial of Jesus

Friday March 30
  John 18:19-24 Questioning of Jesus

Saturday March 31
  John 8:31-38 What Is Truth?

Sunday April 1
  John 18:28-37 "Are You the King?"

Scripture

Background Scripture: *John 18–19*

Scripture Lesson: *John 18:28-37*

Key Verse: *"You are a king, then!" said Pilate. Jesus answered, "You are right in saying I am a king. In fact, for this reason I was born, and for this I came into the world, to testify to the truth. Everyone on the side of truth listens to me."* John 18:37.

Scripture Lesson for Children: *John 18:28-37*

Key Verse for Children: *[Jesus said,] "I came into the world, to testify to the truth."* John 18:37.

Lesson Aim

To take a stand for the truth about the Son, regardless of the consequences.

Lesson Setting

Time: A.D. *30*

Place: Jerusalem

Lesson Outline

Jesus Testifies to the Truth

  I. Pilate Questioning the Religious Leaders: John 18:28-32
      A. *Handing Jesus Over to Caiaphas: vs. 28*
      B. *Exploring the Charges against Jesus: vss. 29-30*
      C. *Fulfilling Jesus' Prediction that He Would Be Crucified: vss. 31-32*
  II. Pilate Questioning the Son: John 18:33-37
      A. *The Query about Jesus' Kingship: vss. 33-34*
      B. *The Nature of Jesus' Kingdom: vss. 35-36*
      C. *The Reason for Jesus' Advent: vs. 37*

Introduction for Adults

Topic: *No Foolin'!*

When President Eisenhower's advisors counseled him to lie about the American U-2 spy plane that had been shot down over the Soviet Union, he refused. He wanted no part in trying to fool the American people, regardless of how serious the consequences might be for U.S.–Soviet relations.

When Jesus stood for truth before Pilate, the consequences were dreadful. Pilate emerged as a weakling. Those national leaders and the Jerusalem mob emerged as haters of the truth. Jesus died (and rose again) for His stand, but because He refused to deny His claims to be God's Son, He goes down in history as the one who changed the world.

Truth has a power that cannot be suppressed. Many individuals since Pilate have tried, but they have all failed. Jesus Christ has prevailed. The Bible has prevailed. And God's truth still draws people to faith in the Son.

Introduction for Youth

Topic: *Keeping It Real*

How did the poor chicken, which provides us food in abundance, ever become the symbol of cowardice? Anyone who has ever faced the reality of a determined rooster will tell you something about its fierceness. Regardless of how it all started, we know how people tend to call others "chicken." That label has induced all kinds of reckless—and often tragic—behavior.

It would be easy to say that the Roman ruler, Pilate, chickened out when he caved in to the mob and agreed to execute Jesus. But before we say that we would never do such a thing, we need to ask ourselves how tall we stand when someone demands our Christian credentials. If we are real with ourselves, do we sense that we would chicken out when others ridicule us or challenge our faith, or do we run for cover?

What makes the difference? It's ultimately the courage and faith that Jesus gives to us in our moment of need. Facing hostile interrogators is never easy, but we gain strength each time we make our public profession of faith in Christ.

Concepts for Children

Topic: *Action Requires Courage*

1. When a Roman ruler named Pilate tried to release Jesus, the religious leaders refused to let it happen.
2. When Pilate asked Jesus who He was, Jesus said He was a King.
3. Pilate told the Jewish leaders he could find nothing wrong with Jesus.
4. Despite Pilate's efforts, he decided to give in to the people's demands to have Jesus put to death.
5. God wants us to have the courage to believe in Jesus, not turn away from Him in unbelief.

Lesson Commentary

I. PILATE QUESTIONING THE RELIGIOUS LEADERS: JOHN 18:28-32

A. Handing Jesus Over to Caiaphas: vs. 28

Then the Jews led Jesus from Caiaphas to the palace of the Roman governor. By now it was early morning, and to avoid ceremonial uncleanness the Jews did not enter the palace; they wanted to be able to eat the Passover.

Jesus' arrest took place while He and His followers were in a privately owned "olive grove" (John 18:1) located slightly east of Jerusalem on the lower slopes of the Mount of Olives. Because the Savior regularly spent time with the Twelve in the olive grove, Judas knew he could find Jesus and His followers there (vs. 2). The chief priests and Pharisees had given Judas a detachment of Roman soldiers and temple guards to accompany the betrayer to Jesus (vs. 3). At this point, Jesus stepped forward and identified Himself to the authorities (vss. 4-7).

Jesus' expert use of satire is seen in Luke 22:52-53. He noted that a small army had come to arrest Him, as though He were a kind of dangerous revolutionary. Jesus incisively pointed out how ludicrous that looked by saying He had been accessible to the authorities every day while teaching in the Jerusalem temple. Yet no one had made a move to arrest Him. The Savior knew the authorities came after Him in the dead of night because they wanted the darkness to conceal their deed. Also, symbolically it was appropriate for such an evil action to be undertaken in the darkness. At that point, all the disciples deserted Jesus and fled (see Matt. 26:56; Mark 14:50).

Nothing now stood in the way of Jesus' arrest. So the squad of Roman soldiers, their commanding officer, and the temple guards seized Jesus and tied Him up (John 18:12). The latter action was possibly standard procedure in that day. We can only imagine the emotional shock this turn of events must have caused for Jesus' disciples. The contingent first escorted Jesus to Annas, the father-in-law of Caiaphas, who was the high priest at that time (vs. 13). The latter was the same individual who previously had advised the Jewish leaders that it was to their advantage for "one man [to die] for the people" (vs. 14). This is a reference to John 11:49-50. The idea is that it was politically expedient for an innocent person to be executed for the sake of preventing an entire nation from perishing. While Annas and Caiaphas interrogated Jesus, Peter stood outside. There Peter denied Jesus three times. Once the rooster crowed, Peter realized that he had denied the Lord just as Jesus had foretold (John 18:15-18, 25-27).

After Caiaphas and members of the Sanhedrin claimed Jesus was guilty of blasphemy, they took Him to Pilate. In A.D. 26, Pontius Pilate replaced Valerius Gratus as governor of Judea. Pilate is mentioned not only in the Gospel accounts, but also by the Jewish writers Josephus (A.D. 37–100) and Philo (20 B.C.–A.D. 50), and by the Roman historian Tacitus (A.D. 56–117). In addition, the name "Pilate" appears on coins, and in an inscription found at Caesarea Martima. As a governor, Pilate was responsible for the administration of the province of Judea, including judicial matters. Josephus states that Pilate had the power to execute. He was also responsible for collecting taxes and tribute, disbursing funds to the provinces, and sending revenues to Rome. Despite these duties, the office of governor of Judea was not the most prestigious in the empire.

A number of incidents occurred during Pilate's rule (A.D. 26–36) that resulted in skirmishes between the governor and the Jews. Pilate got off to a bad start when he introduced into Jerusalem images in honor of the reigning emperor, Tiberius. These articles, which were religiously offensive to the Jews, aroused such a protest that Pilate transported the items to Caesarea. In another incident, Pilate constructed an aqueduct with the use of Jewish funds, giving rise to rebellion that was put down with bloodshed. Josephus, however, reported that the Jews were upset, not over the money involved, but over what was done with the water. Scholars have concluded that the unrest was due to the lack of concern by Pilate for the water's ritual purity as it came into Jerusalem.

Tensions sometimes erupted into riots. Mark 15:7 reports the insurrection that apparently was well known in Jesus' time, though now is unknown. Luke 13:1 describes an encounter with Galileans "whose blood Pilate had mixed with their sacrifices." Josephus and Philo also reported events that may be connected to these Gospel references. Jesus' opponents made the most of these tensions between a Roman governor and his Jewish constituency by accusing Jesus of rebelling against the emperor (John 19:12). In fact, Jesus was accused of claiming to be a Jewish king (18:33-34).

Although the Jewish rulers wanted Jesus crucified, they did not have the authority to carry it out themselves. Pilate and his Roman troops were in Jerusalem in case the celebration of the Passover Feast erupted into a revolt. The Jews brought Jesus to Pilate with the intention of persuading the Roman governor to pronounce the death sentence on Him. It was in the early hours of the morning when the Sanhedrin had the accused taken to Pilate (vs. 28). The Jewish leaders could do so at this early hour because Roman officials typically began their working day at first light. This timing also suited the Sanhedrin's plans to have Jesus executed as soon as possible. Since the religious leaders believed that entering a Gentile residence ceremonially defiled them for seven days, and since they wanted to participate in the Passover Feast, they refused to enter Pilate's palace.

B. Exploring the Charges against Jesus: vss. 29-30

So Pilate came out to them and asked, "What charges are you bringing against this man?" "If he were not a criminal," they replied, "we would not have handed him over to you."

Because the religious leaders refused to enter the governor's residence, Pilate had to come out to them to determine the crime they had charged against Jesus (John

18:29). It is remarkable that a powerful Roman governor such as Pilate felt obliged to leave his palace and question his Jewish subjects about their complaint. When he did so, the officials responded disrespectfully by noting that they would not have gone to all this trouble of bringing Jesus to Pilate if Jesus were not a criminal (vs. 30). They evaded Pilate's question since they lacked any evidence that Jesus had broken a specific Roman law. Throughout the entire ordeal that unfolded before Jesus, He faced His enemies' hostility with God-inspired boldness and courage because He had prayed. The Son had given Himself to the will of the Father. And now Jesus surrendered to the tide that would sweep Him directly to the cross. He had no hesitation to offer Himself freely as a sacrifice for the sins of humankind (see Mark 10:45; John 1:29).

C. Fulfilling Jesus' Prediction that He Would Be Crucified: vss. 31-32

Pilate said, "Take him yourselves and judge him by your own law." "But we have no right to execute anyone," the Jews objected. This happened so that the words Jesus had spoken indicating the kind of death he was going to die would be fulfilled.

Initially, Pilate urged the Jewish leaders to take Jesus away and judge Him by their own laws. However, they refused to comply. Instead, Jesus' antagonists reminded the governor that only Roman officials were permitted to execute someone sentenced to die for a capital offense (such as treason; John 18:31). John the apostle (and writer of the fourth Gospel) noted that this turn of events was divinely foreordained. God allowed these things to happen so that Jesus' prediction about the way in which He would die (namely, by crucifixion) would be fulfilled (vs. 32; see 12:32-33; 18:32). In other words, God was in control of everything that happened to Jesus. The Lord foreordained even the Savior's arrest, trial, abuse, and crucifixion.

II. PILATE QUESTIONING THE SON: JOHN 18:33-37

A. The Query about Jesus' Kingship: vss. 33-34

Pilate then went back inside the palace, summoned Jesus and asked him, "Are you the king of the Jews?" "Is that your own idea," Jesus asked, "or did others talk to you about me?"

The Greek word rendered "palace" (John 18:33) was also called the Praetorium. The latter term originally referred to the praetor, or tent, of a commander in a military camp. Later the word was applied to the official residence of Roman governors in various cities of the provinces where they ruled. There are two possible locations for the Praetorium in Jerusalem. The first is the Fortress (or Tower) of Antonia, which was located northwest of the temple area (on the prominent elevation alongside the southern slope of Mount Bezetha). The second spot is the palace of Herod near the Jaffa Gate at the westernmost part of the old city of Jerusalem.

Previously, the religious leaders had convicted Jesus because He claimed to be divine (10:33; 19:7). In the eyes of the authorities that was blasphemy. But this was a religious offense, not a civil crime. While a Roman official might question the sanity of a person who claimed to be God, he would not likely put a person to death for such a cause. Consequently, the Jewish officials changed their indictment from blasphemy to sedition. They accused Jesus of claiming to be the king of the Jews. They made it sound as though Jesus had set Himself up in opposition to Caesar, which would be a treasonable offense.

Pilate, of course, was no fool. He could easily see through the religious leaders' pretense of loyalty to the emperor. The governor also knew they were jealous of Jesus because He was a threat to their power. Yet Pilate had to look into the case (see Mark 15:10). As the governor began to do so, Jesus must have seemed like an unusual prisoner to Pilate. After all, he would have been accustomed to defendants shouting their innocence. But Jesus acted differently. It was as though He intended to die and would do nothing to interfere with His destiny. For instance, when Pilate asked whether Jesus was "the king of the Jews" (John 18:33), the accused countered with a question. He asked whether the governor was inquiring about Jesus' identity on his own initiative or was interrogating Jesus on behalf of what Caiaphas and the Sanhedrin had said (vs. 34).

B. The Nature of Jesus' Kingdom: vss. 35-36

"Am I a Jew?" Pilate replied. "It was your people and your chief priests who handed you over to me. What is it you have done?" Jesus said, "My kingdom is not of this world. If it were, my servants would fight to prevent my arrest by the Jews. But now my kingdom is from another place."

Pilate's response to Jesus spotlights the frustration the governor felt at Jesus' vague answer (John 18:35). In interrogating Jesus, Pilate was trying to uncover the facts. The governor wanted to know whether the charge of sedition was true and (thus) whether Jesus was guilty of treason. As verses 33-35 indicate, Pilate had some doubt about the veracity of the accusations and didn't immediately abandon his efforts in the midst of Jesus' vague response.

The governor's question "Am I a Jew?" suggests that he scoffed at the notion that he could have any personal interest in the controversy between Jesus and the religious leaders. Pilate made it clear that he certainly was not a Jew. In fact, it was Jesus' own people who demanded that the governor investigate the matter. Pilate was only concerned about whether Jesus had committed a crime against Roman law. Thus, when the governor asked Jesus what He had done (vs. 35), Jesus took the opportunity to acknowledge that He was a king. But the Savior explained that He was not a ruler over an earthly kingdom. If He were, His followers would have taken up arms and fought His arresters. That they did not all attack showed that His kingdom was of another realm (vs. 36).

In Jesus' day, the concept of "kingdom" was rooted in the Old Testament. The term most often referred to the reign or royal authority of a king. Jewish people prayed daily for the coming of God's reign. When they prayed for His kingdom, they did not doubt that God presently reigned over His creation. Yet they longed for the day when God would rule unchallenged and all peoples would acknowledge Him. Most Jews, therefore, associated this kingdom with the coming of a Jewish ruler who would lead his people to victory over their enemies (see John 6:15; Acts 1:6).

In contrast, the Romans guarded the title of "king." Anyone who, without the emperor's permission, claimed to be even a client king was committing the offense of high treason. Thus, Jewish leaders—like the high priest Caiaphas and the Jerusalem aristocracy—who helped keep peace for the Romans, wanted to stop any would-be kings who might stir up trouble with Rome (John 11:47-50). Oddly enough, Pilate had a different understanding than the Jewish leaders of Jesus' reference to the kingdom. Pilate, as a Roman, knew reports of Cynic philosophers who wandered around claiming to be kings while possessing nothing. Such philosophers lacked respect for rulers, yet were without political ambition for themselves. As thinkers, they spoke about truth and about reigning, but to a Roman pragmatist they were relatively harmless. This seems to be the case with Jesus.

C. The Reason for Jesus' Advent: vs. 37

"You are a king, then!" said Pilate. Jesus answered, "You are right in saying I am a king. In fact, for this reason I was born, and for this I came into the world, to testify to the truth. Everyone on the side of truth listens to me."

Pilate exclaimed that Jesus had finally admitted to being a king. The underlying idea in John 18:37 is that if the governor wanted to call Jesus a king, then Jesus would not dispute Pilate's statement. Jesus, however, focused on His purpose for coming into the world instead of debating His title. Jesus' purpose was to bear witness to the truth. He then added that all who sought the truth would listen to Him who is "the way and the truth and the life" (14:6). Implicit in Jesus' statement was a question that asked whether Pilate was willing to listen concerning the truth. The governor shrugged off Jesus' statement by cynically retorting, "What is truth?" (18:38).

Without waiting for an answer, Pilate returned to the crowd outside and stated that he had found nothing that would indicate that Jesus was dangerous to the state. Since the governor was a shrewd politician, he suggested that Jesus be released according to their custom in which the Romans freed one Jewish prisoner during each Passover Feast. This way Pilate could avoid offending those Jewish officials who wanted Jesus convicted of a crime and yet not execute a man he believed to be innocent of any wrongdoing. Nevertheless, the governor could not resist a scornful jab by referring to Jesus as their "king" (vs. 39). The crowd, however, shouted for the release of Barabbas and not Jesus (vs. 40). Since Barabbas had taken part in the local rebellion against the Romans, the crowd probably viewed him as a national hero. Mark and Luke called him a murderer (see Mark 15:7; Luke 23:19).

Discussion Questions

1. Why did the religious leaders scheme to have Jesus arrested?
2. How do you think Pilate felt about the charges the religious authorities brought against Jesus?
3. How would you describe Pilate's standards for decision-making?
4. What did you do in a situation where you struggled to act fairly and objectively on what you knew to be true?
5. How can fear affect the decisions that we make?

Contemporary Application

Although North American believers in the twenty-first century do not suffer flogging and crucifixion as a result of their commitment to God, they should not be surprised if others occasionally treat them badly for any number of reasons. For instance, they might be excluded from a social event because they are labeled as being too "religious," or a peer might spread false rumors about them because of their devotion to Christ.

Because of sin, mistreatment is inevitable in this world. Thus believers should expect it. Those who are not for Christ are against Him. Thus, as believers live for the Lord, unbelievers will oppose them. Even fellow believers will occasionally let Christians down and do something that hurts them.

This does not mean that believers should intentionally try to irritate others and invite mistreatment. But they should also not be devastated when it happens. In fact, when Christians truly seek to follow God's call for their lives, some unbelievers will disapprove of it. If adults who are Christian never encounter any opposition to their faith, it may be an indication that they are not as overt in their walk with Christ as they ought to be.

Whatever mistreatment the members of your class might experience, Jesus is the supreme example for them to follow. When He was cursed, He blessed His detractors; when He was persecuted, He patiently endured the mistreatment; and when He was slandered, He humbly entrusted His circumstances to the Father.

If believers are ostracized by their peers for being perceived as excessively "spiritual," their first reaction might be outrage. However, a more Christlike response is for them to refrain from losing their temper. By demonstrating patience, adults who are Christian might have an opportunity to share their faith with their unsaved acquaintances.

The Living Word

Scripture

Background Scripture: *John 20:1-23*
Scripture Lesson: *John 20:1-10, 19-20*
Key Verse: *The disciples were overjoyed when they saw the Lord.* John 20:20.
Scripture Lesson for Children: *John 20:1-10, 19-20*
Key Verse for Children: *The disciples were overjoyed when they saw the Lord.* John 20:20.

Lesson Aim

To affirm the truth that Jesus rose from the dead.

Lesson Setting

Time: A.D. *30*
Place: Jerusalem

Lesson Outline

The Living Word

I. The Empty Tomb: John 20:1-10
    A. *Mary's Report: vss. 1-2*
    B. *Peter and John's Immediate Response: vss. 3-4*
    C. *Peter and John's Initial Investigation: vss. 5-8*
    D. *Peter and John's Lack of Understanding: vss. 9-10*

II. The Savior's Appearance to His Disciples: John 20:19-20
    A. *The Savior's Reassuring Statement: vs. 19*
    B. *The Disciples' Joy: vs. 20*

Introduction for Adults

Topic: *Dawn of a New Day*

One of the common testimonies of people whose heart ailments have been treated with bypass surgery is that they have found new life. Instead of feeling weak, tired, and short of breath, they now have energy to do things they could not do before. It is as if a new day of opportunity has dawned for them.

Jesus' resurrection does the same sort of thing for us in the spiritual realm. At one time we were "dead in . . . transgressions and sins" (Eph. 2:1). But when we trusted in Jesus for salvation, we passed from death to life (vs. 5). This is possible because we have been identified with Jesus' death, burial, and resurrection (see Rom. 6:1-4).

If we think of our old, sinful life as dead and buried, we have a powerful motive to resist sin. We now have the option of consciously choosing to treat the temptations and desires of the old nature as if they were dead. Such is possible because of the wonderful new life we have in Jesus.

Introduction for Youth

Topic: *The Word Lives On!*

Our heads nod as we hear the expression "Familiarity breeds contempt." But through overuse its meaning has become dulled. In *God Came Near*, Max Lucado sharpens that meaning for us.

"[Familiarity] won't steal your salvation; he'll just make you forget what it was like to be lost. You'll grow accustomed to prayer and thereby not pray. Worship will become commonplace and study optional. With the passing of time he'll infiltrate your heart with boredom and cover the cross with dust so you'll be 'safely' out of reach of change."

Yes, the risen and living Word invites doubters to view His nail-pierced hands and touch His wounded side so that their questions will be answered and their faith in Him solidified. But He also invites spiritually anesthetized believers to fully appreciate their Savior's sacrifice and thereby rekindle their faith.

Concepts for Children

Topic: *Rejoicing in New Life*

1. We learn in the Bible that Jesus died on the cross for us.
2. The Bible also teaches that Jesus rose from the dead.
3. Various people saw Jesus after He rose from the dead.
4. Mary Magdalene was one of those who saw the risen Lord.
5. Jesus wants us to share the truth of His resurrection with others.

Lesson Commentary

I. THE EMPTY TOMB: JOHN 20:1-10

A. Mary's Report: vss. 1-2

Early on the first day of the week, while it was still dark, Mary Magdalene went to the tomb and saw that the stone had been removed from the entrance. So she came running to Simon Peter and the other disciple, the one Jesus loved, and said, "They have taken the Lord out of the tomb, and we don't know where they have put him!"

The Savior's crucifixion is the historical prelude to His resurrection from the dead. After the crowd outside the Praetorium insisted on Barabbas's release, Pilate ordered his soldiers to flog Jesus. They pressed a crown of thorns on Jesus' head and wrapped a purple robe around Him. Then they mocked Him and smacked Him in the face (John 19:1-3). Perhaps Pilate thought this harsh treatment of Jesus would elicit the crowd's sympathy for Him. No such compassion was demonstrated, however. After telling the people once more that he found Jesus innocent of any charge, and after parading Him before them in ridiculous attire, Pilate presented Jesus to them (vss. 4-5).

Pilate soon became disgusted with the heartless attitude of the Jewish officials. He told them to crucify Jesus themselves. Yet they argued that their law required that He be executed since He professed to be God's Son (vss. 6-7). The governor withdrew and asked Jesus to reveal His origin. Jesus' silence infuriated Pilate, who reminded this peasant that as governor he possessed the authority to free Him or sentence Him to die on the cross (vss. 8-10). Pilate's comment, however, failed to impress Jesus. He told the governor that any authority he had over his prisoner was granted by God. While Pilate had the power to sentence Jesus to death, Caiaphas had delivered Him to the Roman governor. Therefore, Caiaphas was guilty of a worse sin (vs. 11).

When Pilate sought some way of letting Jesus go, the Jewish rulers warned him loudly that such an act would be treason to Caesar (vs. 12). Faced with this implied threat, Pilate ordered Jesus to stand before His accusers while the governor sat on the judgment seat (vs. 13). It was Friday morning of the Passover week when Pilate pointed to Jesus and contemptuously said to the crowd that He was their King (vs. 14). The people had turned into a mob thirsty for blood. They repeatedly yelled for Jesus to be crucified. Pilate asked them whether they really wanted him to do this. Ironically, the chief priests who had condemned Jesus for blasphemy proclaimed Caesar to be their only monarch. Thus, having exhausted all attempts to free Jesus, Pilate finally yielded to their demands and commanded his soldiers to take Jesus away to be crucified (vss. 15-16).

The details of Jesus' crucifixion are recorded in 19:17-27, His death is discussed in verses 28-37, and His burial is the focal point of verses 38-42. Joseph of Arimathea, a wealthy and prominent member of the Sanhedrin (see Matt. 27:57;

Mark 15:43), was instrumental in arranging for the Messiah's burial. Though Joseph had kept his faith in Jesus a secret because he was afraid of his colleagues, he had not consented to the council's decision to condemn Jesus (see Luke 23:50-51). Now that Jesus had been executed, Joseph openly expressed his devotion to the Savior by boldly seeking Pilate's permission to allow him to bury Jesus in Joseph's own tomb (John 19:38; see Matt. 27:60).

After Pilate gave his consent, Joseph and Nicodemus took the body of Jesus away. Nicodemus was another member of the Jewish ruling council and the Pharisee who had come to Jesus at night to inquire about the kingdom of God (see John 3:1-15). The two retrieved Jesus from the cross and prepared His body for burial. Nicodemus had brought about 75 pounds of myrrh and aloes, and together they dabbed strips of linen with the spices and wrapped Jesus' body with the cloths in keeping with the proper burial customs of the Jews (19:39-40). Joseph and Nicodemus took Jesus' body to a new tomb that was empty of any other corpses. John also mentioned that the tomb was in a garden, which is another indication that Jesus was not buried in a public cemetery. The tomb was apparently close to the execution site. This was fortunate since sundown, which was fast approaching, would mark the beginning of the Passover Sabbath (vss. 41-42).

Mary Magdalene was one of the women who stood near the cross upon which Jesus was executed (vs. 25). And early Sunday morning, while it was still dark, Mary was the first disciple to come to the tomb where Jesus' body had been placed (20:1). Mark informs us that Mary came to Jesus' tomb after the Sabbath to pour spices over His body, a cultural expression of love for the dead person (Mark 16:1). Such devotion on Mary's part was not unusual. After all, Jesus had exorcised seven demons from her (Luke 8:2). As an early follower of Jesus, Mary proved to be an energetic and caring woman. She not only traveled with Jesus, but also contributed to the needs of the group.

When Mary came to the tomb, she saw that "the stone had been removed from the entrance" (John 20:1). She and the other women with her wondered how they would be able to move the massive stone away from the entrance. Their concern vanished when they discovered that the rock had already been removed. Though it was still early, they were able to see that Jesus' tomb was empty. Mary dashed to Peter and the "other disciple" (vs. 2), who most likely was John. Mary frantically told them that people had transferred Jesus' body to a place she and the other women did not know. Mary probably thought that Jesus' enemies had stolen His body and had not considered the possibility that God had raised Him from the dead.

B. Peter and John's Immediate Response: vss. 3-4

So Peter and the other disciple started for the tomb. Both were running, but the other disciple outran Peter and reached the tomb first.

Understandably, Peter and John were alarmed by Mary's news. This prompted the two disciples to run to Jesus' tomb to see for themselves whether the body was missing (John 20:3). It turns out that John outran his peer and thus arrived first at the empty sepulcher (vs. 4).

For centuries skeptics have considered the Gospel writers' resurrection accounts as myth or legend. In this regard, it is significant that after Jesus' resurrection He first appeared to Mary Magdalene and then assigned to her the responsibility of informing His disciples of His return to the Father. In ancient Judaism the witness of women mattered very little judicially and socially. Thus no ancient Jewish author would have made up such a story with a woman being the first witness to this important event. Further undermining Mary's testimony was her being from Magdala, a city Jewish rabbis condemned for its wickedness. And she had a history of demon possession (see Luke 8:2). Thus even if she seemed cured, her testimony would have been questioned.

Consequently, John's account fortifies the historical fact of Jesus' resurrection. Why didn't the Savior first appear to Peter or John? Jesus' logic isn't the same as that of the prevailing culture. And the testimony of His death and resurrection is still being entrusted centuries later to unlikely candidates who, like Mary, will follow through faithfully. The major truth to be proclaimed at Easter is that Jesus Christ, our Savior, has risen from the dead. Knowing this makes all the difference in the world. It spells the difference between despair and joy, and between turmoil and peace.

C. Peter and John's Initial Investigation: vss. 5-8

He bent over and looked in at the strips of linen lying there but did not go in. Then Simon Peter, who was behind him, arrived and went into the tomb. He saw the strips of linen lying there, as well as the burial cloth that had been around Jesus' head. The cloth was folded up by itself, separate from the linen. Finally the other disciple, who had reached the tomb first, also went inside. He saw and believed.

In ancient times, the entrance to private burial chambers was often less than three feet high. Thus an adult would have to bend down to look inside. John did this and saw the strips of linen that had been used to cover Jesus' body. But John decided not to go into the tomb (John 20:5). When Peter arrived, he immediately entered the sepulcher (vs. 6). The apostle saw both the strips of linen and the face cloth that had been placed around Jesus' head. The cloth was rolled up in a spot by itself (vs. 7). These details indicate that thieves had not stolen Jesus' body, for it is unlikely that anyone who had come to remove the corpse would have bothered to unwrap it before removing it. Shortly thereafter, when John went inside the tomb, he saw the evidence and "believed" (vs. 8).

D. Peter and John's Lack of Understanding: vss. 9-10

(They still did not understand from Scripture that Jesus had to rise from the dead.) Then the disciples went back to their homes.

The full extent of what John believed is not explicitly stated in the biblical text. Did he believe that Jesus had risen from the dead, or did John now believe Mary, who had told Peter and John that the tomb was empty? The answer is not clear. What is clear is that neither Peter nor John had a full understanding at this time of Scripture's teaching about Jesus' resurrection (John 20:9). Once Peter and John were done checking out the scene, they returned to their lodgings in Jerusalem (vs. 10).

II. THE SAVIOR'S APPEARANCE TO HIS DISCIPLES: JOHN 20:19-20

A. The Savior's Reassuring Statement: vs. 19

On the evening of that first day of the week, when the disciples were together, with the doors locked for fear of the Jews, Jesus came and stood among them and said, "Peace be with you!"

Mary evidently had returned to the tomb with Peter and John. At this point Mary had not yet figured out that Jesus had risen from the dead. Mary still thought bandits had stolen Jesus' body, and this possibility so traumatized Mary that she "stood outside the tomb crying" (John 20:11). At some point Mary decided to look in the tomb, and when she did, she saw two white-robed angels sitting at the head and foot of the place where the body of Jesus had been lying (vs. 12). Even while Mary was reexamining the tomb, she had continued to weep. This prompted the angels to ask her, "Woman, why are you crying?" (vs. 13). Mary explained that she was grieved over the fact that Jesus' body had somehow been stolen. The fact that Mary couldn't attend to Jesus' body and give Him a decent burial could have added to Mary's distress. She still did not realize that her Lord had risen from the dead.

At that moment Mary sensed the presence of another person. She turned and saw a man standing outside the tomb with her, but she did not realize the man was Jesus (vs. 14). Either there was something different about the risen Lord that prevented not only Mary but also other of His friends from immediately recognizing Him (see Luke 24:13-31; John 21:4), or they were supernaturally prevented from recognizing Him until the time was right. Mary thought that He was the gardener (John 20:15). Jesus first addressed Mary as "Woman," just as the angels had done. Like the angels, Jesus asked Mary why she was weeping, but also inquired as to whom she was seeking. Previously, she had thought that Jesus' enemies might have stolen His body, but now Mary hoped that this man, whom she assumed was responsible for the upkeep of this private cemetery, might have moved the body. She did not answer Jesus' questions, but implored Him to reveal the whereabouts of the Savior's body if He had carried it away. Mary promised to return the body to the tomb herself.

Once Jesus had described Himself as the Good Shepherd. He said that when He calls His sheep by their name, they will know His voice (see 10:3). Something like this must have occurred here with Mary, for she recognized the Lord when she heard Him say her name. Her immediate reaction was to turn toward Jesus again, but this time to exclaim, "Rabboni!" (20:16). Mary had spoken in Aramaic, which was the language the people of Palestine commonly spoke in Jesus' day. John explained to his readers that "Rabboni" meant "Teacher."

According to Matthew 28:9, when Mary Magdalene and another Mary encountered the risen Lord, they fell to the ground, clasped His feet, and worshiped Him. John's account provides us with further insight into this incident by revealing Jesus' instruction to Mary not to cling to Him (John 20:17). It wasn't that Jesus forbade Mary to touch Him at all. Rather, the phrase "Do not hold on to me" conveys the idea of "don't clutch tenaciously to me." Mary wanted to never let go of the Lord she thought she had lost, but He had an ascension for Himself and an assignment for her. Mary was to return to the disciples with the great news of Jesus' victory over death.

Although Jesus had not yet ascended into heaven, He wanted to assure His disciples that shortly He would be returning to His heavenly Father. The Son spoke of His Father and His God as their Father and God. Now that Jesus' redemptive work was fully accomplished, the reconciliation between God and His spiritual children was complete. Appropriately, Mary obeyed Jesus by rushing to the disciples. Mary told them that she had actually seen the risen Lord. Mary also related the message Jesus had entrusted to her. Mary's abrupt ascent from the depths of grief to the heights of joy probably astonished the rest of the disciples (vs. 18).

After Jesus first appeared to Mary of Magdalene, other people encountered Him on that extraordinary Sunday. Luke 24:13-35 records Jesus' meeting and discussions with Cleopas and his companion on the road to and at Emmaus, as well as mentions Jesus' earlier appearance to Peter. John, however, skipped these incidents and went to the evening's events of which he was an eyewitness. Many of Jesus' disciples, which included most of the apostles, had secretly convened to discuss the strange yet marvelous reports that their Lord had risen from the dead. Nevertheless, since they still feared the religious officials, they bolted the doors (John 20:19).

As the disciples talked, Jesus suddenly stood among them. John did not explain how Jesus could have entered the house when the doors were locked. Clearly, Jesus' glorified body had powers and capabilities it did not reveal before His death and resurrection from the dead. Jesus greeted His friends by exclaiming, "Peace be with you!" Although this phrase was a common Hebrew greeting, Jesus probably said it to allay their fears at His sudden and unexpected appearance.

B. The Disciples' Joy: vs. 20

After he said this, he showed them his hands and side. The disciples were overjoyed when they saw the Lord.

Luke 24:37-38 reveals that Jesus' followers initially thought He was a ghost. John 20:20 indicates that to convince the disciples that their Savior's body had substance,

He showed His pierced hands and side. Luke 24:39 adds that Jesus invited His followers to touch Him and verify for themselves that He was not a ghost. Once the disciples were convinced of Jesus' identity and presence, they were overcome with joy (John 20:20). Like Mary, they too traveled from the depths of despair to the pinnacle of happiness in a matter of seconds!

Discussion Questions

1. Why do you think Mary felt compelled to return to Jesus' tomb early Sunday morning?
2. If you were Peter and John, how would you have felt upon hearing Mary's statement that Jesus' body had been stolen?
3. Why do you think John initially hesitated to go inside the tomb?
4. What evidence at the tomb did Peter and John find for Jesus' resurrection from the dead?
5. In what ways has Jesus brought peace to your life as a believer?

Contemporary Application

We may tend to minimize the despair and darkness of those who saw the death of Jesus because we know that He rose from the dead. But the first-century disciples did not know the rest of the account when Jesus was crucified. At times our position is similar to theirs. This side of heaven we see only death and despair, when in reality God has rescued us from both and is preparing a place for us with Him (see John 14:1-2).

Jesus' victory over death is the foundation for our faith and the source of our hope. Paul stressed that we can stand on these unshakable facts: Jesus died for our sins and was resurrected on the third day (1 Cor. 15:3-4). Also, if that victory over death had not happened, our faith would be in vain and those who die would be truly lost (vss. 17-18). Thankfully, Christ rose from the dead, and His resurrection is just the first, for all believers will follow in His path (vs. 20).

Through the Son's resurrection, the Father has rewritten the presumed ending of our life accounts. Death is just the beginning of a new chapter in our walk with Him. The resurrection hope should shine in our moments of darkness, reminding us that the tomb was empty. Moreover, we can join all believers in giving thanks to the Father for the victory we have through His Son (vs. 57).

Cleansing the Temple

Scripture

Background Scripture: *John 2:13-22*
Scripture Lesson: *John 2:13-22*
Key Verse: *To those who sold doves [Jesus] said, "Get these
out of here! How dare you turn my Father's house into a market!"* John 2:16.
Scripture Lesson for Children: *John 2:13-22*
Key Verse for Children: *To those who sold doves [Jesus]
said, "Get these out of here! How dare you turn my Father's
house into a market!"* John 2:16.

Lesson Aim

To recognize that Jesus demands respect and worship.

Lesson Setting

Time: A.D. *27*
Place: Jerusalem

Lesson Outline

Cleansing the Temple
  I. Jesus' Decisive Action: John 2:13-17
    A. *Traveling to Jerusalem: vs. 13*
    B. *Buying and Selling in the Temple Courts: vs. 14*
    C. *Clearing the Temple Courts: vss. 15-17*
  II. Jesus' Prophetic Response: John 2:18-22
    A. *The Demand for a Sign: vs. 18*
    B. *The Veiled Reference to Jesus' Resurrection:
       vss. 19-22*

Introduction for Adults

Topic: *Restoration and Re-creation*

An old saying warns us, "If you find the perfect church, don't join it, because you'll wreck it." Because of our sinful natures, this is always a possibility. On the other hand, God calls His purified people to worship in a purified way. There's no room for ungodliness in Christ's Body.

There have always been periods throughout history where the people of God needed their relationship with Him restored. This was certainly true in Jesus' day. When He saw the wretched conditions around the temple, He decided to risk the fury of the religious authorities. Yes, this was a time to challenge worship that had been corrupted by commercialism. Pure worship was a worthwhile goal that required drastic action.

How easy it is to slip over the line and make worship into a business. This danger lurks everywhere. Therefore, we need constant reminders to purify our hearts and our worship.

Introduction for Youth

Topic: *Cleaning Up and Setting It Right!*

The young army private took his customary place on his lower bunk in the barracks. As he climbed beneath his sheets, he looked up and spotted some pieces of palm leaves stuck between the springs and mattress of the upper bunk.

The private's curiosity was piqued, and he learned that the soldier occupying that bunk had brought the palms back from chapel. This was the first time the private had encountered anyone who took his or her Christian faith so seriously. The realization spurred the private to clean up his spiritual act (so to speak) and get right with God.

There are many ways we can prepare to witness to our faith. We can use outward symbols, like wearing a cross or putting a bumper sticker on our car. We can also prepare inwardly by developing better habits of prayer, Bible study, worship, and Christian fellowship.

When our character shows that we love Jesus, other people will notice that we are different. How we live should be consistent with the faith we profess. When we walk our talk (as the saying goes), God will give us many opportunities to tell others about Jesus.

Concepts for Children

Topic: *Jesus Brings Order*

1. Jesus went to Jerusalem during a time called Passover.
2. Jesus went into the courts of the temple.
3. Jesus saw people buying and selling in the courts.
4. Jesus put a stop to what He saw.
5. Jesus showed by His actions that He wants us to put Him first in our lives.

Lesson Commentary

I. JESUS' DECISIVE ACTION: JOHN 2:13-17

A. Traveling to Jerusalem: vs. 13

When it was almost time for the Jewish Passover, Jesus went up to Jerusalem.

When it was nearly time for the celebration of the Jewish Passover in the winter of A.D. 27, Jesus traveled about 80 miles south from Capernaum to Jerusalem. Passover was one of several yearly sacred festivals the people of God observed. These special days had different purposes and varying kinds of observances, but they all were meant to deepen the people's devotion to the Lord and give them occasions for joy and celebration.

Passover was the first festival on the calendar and possibly signified the most important holy feast to the Israelites. During this sacred event, they would commemorate the final plague in Egypt, when the angel of death passed over the firstborn of the Israelites, while killing the firstborn of the Egyptians (see Exod. 12:1-30). Passover was to begin on the evening of the fourteenth day of the first month (Lev. 23:5). The Israelites would kill a lamb and on that evening eat a special meal. It was designed to remind them of the meal their ancestors ate on the first Passover night, before leaving Egypt (see Num. 9:1-14; 28:16; Deut. 16:1-7; Matt. 26:17; Mark 14:12-26; John 2:13; 11:55; 1 Cor. 5:7; Heb. 11:28).

The fourth Gospel records at least three separate Passover celebrations that occurred during the time of Jesus' earthly ministry: the first in 2:13 and 23; the second in 6:4; and the third in 11:55, 12:1, 13:1, 18:28, 39, and 19:14. Some think that the Jewish festival mentioned in 5:1 was Passover, though Pentecost and Tabernacles are two other strong possibilities. Depending on the separate number of Passover celebrations appearing in John's Gospel, Jesus' ministry could have lasted as long as three and a half years. This statement is based on the premise that the Passovers appear in strict chronological order. Another option is that the material in the fourth Gospel is arranged topically. In turn, this would leave open the possibility that the account of Jesus clearing the temple courts actually occurred later in His public ministry.

The Synoptic Gospels record a similar episode occurring in the week preceding Jesus' crucifixion, specifically after His triumphal entry into Jerusalem (see Matt. 21:12-17; Mark 11:12-18; Luke 19:45-46). Those favoring the view that the episodes in the fourth Gospel are topically arranged consider the two temple-clearing incidents as being one and the same. In contrast, those who regard the material in John's Gospel as being sequenced chronologically argue for two separate episodes. This view is supported by the writer's emphasis throughout his narrative on mentioning specific times, places, facts, and details. Also, the content and wording of the fourth Gospel and the Synoptic Gospels about the temple-clearing incident are markedly different. Regardless of which view is preferred, Jesus' statement in John

2:19 most likely forms the basis for the accusations voiced by false witnesses at the Redeemer's trial before the Sanhedrin (see Matt. 26:61; Mark 14:58) and for the spectators' taunting remarks at His crucifixion (see Matt. 27:40; Mark 15:29).

B. Buying and Selling in the Temple Courts: vs. 14

In the temple courts he found men selling cattle, sheep and doves, and others sitting at tables exchanging money.

The temple area Jesus entered with His disciples was a complex of courts, porticoes, and buildings on a large raised platform. The court of the Gentiles, where the money changers and merchants were set up, was the outermost section of the temple complex. It was paved with marble and formed a square three-quarters of a mile in circumference. Several porticoes or meeting places located there were often used by Jesus for teaching. According to Jewish tradition, this was also the place where the Levites (who assisted the priests) ate and slept. This outer court was the only spot in the temple where the Gentiles were allowed. It was separated from the inner courts by a stone railing a few feet high. Warnings were posted along the barrier in Greek and Latin, telling Gentiles they would be put to death if they entered any of the other inner courts.

The importance of the temple for the Jewish people cannot be overstated. To begin, the shrine had an indispensable theological function to serve. It was the place where the Lord manifested His holy presence in Judea. It was also the spot where sacrifices were made in response to God's gracious choice of Israel as His people. In the sanctuary, God's people could spend time in prayer. Moreover, its design, furniture, and customs were object lessons that prepared the people for the Messiah.

Additionally, the temple had important political and economic roles to play in Jewish society. It was the institution that held together the entire covenant community—the past as well as the present and the future. The shrine gave political identity to the people. Access to its courts identified who was properly a citizen and who was excluded. From an economic perspective, rooms in the temple functioned as a treasury—in effect, the society's bank. Because of the sanctuary's demands for tithes and offerings, a large portion of the Jewish economy passed through the temple personnel and storehouses. In brief, without the shrine, God's people had little opportunity to pull together as a coherent society to face the challenges of the future.

On the day Jesus arrived, the temple courts were filled with activity and noise as merchants and bankers did business with worshipers. Every day, and especially during the Passover celebration, pilgrims who had traveled from near and distant locations offered many types of sacrifices (John 2:13). Vendors close to the temple sold ceremonially pure animals to the worshipers for this purpose. Money changers converted foreign coins into the proper currency so that visitors could buy the animals they needed and also pay the required half-shekel temple tax (see Exod. 30:13-16). Tragically, the presence of all this commercial activity prevented Gentile converts to Judaism from being able to worship and pray in the only approved spot of the temple area (John 2:14).

C. Clearing the Temple Courts: vss. 15-17

So he made a whip out of cords, and drove all from the temple area, both sheep and cattle; he scattered the coins of the money changers and overturned their tables. To those who sold doves he said, "Get these out of here! How dare you turn my Father's house into a market!" His disciples remembered that it is written: "Zeal for your house will consume me."

The Messiah, being filled with indignation at the enormity of the injustice, took bold and decisive action. To symbolize God's authority and judgment, Jesus made a whip out of cords of rope and began to flail it in the air, perhaps in a wide, circular motion. He chased people out of the temple area, and opened the pens housing their sheep and cattle to let these animals escape. He also turned over the tables of the money changers and scattered their coins on the ground (John 2:15).

Next, Jesus went to the merchants selling doves and ordered them to remove the birds from the area. Perhaps He opened some of the cages in which the doves were kept so they could more easily fly away. He ordered that the rest be removed and that the house of His Father no longer be turned into a marketplace of merchants (vs. 16). This is possibly an allusion to Zechariah 14:21, in which the Hebrew term rendered "Canaanite" could also be translated "merchant" or "trader." The idea is that in the day the Lord established His messianic kingdom, He would remove all those involved in commercial activity from His temple. Jesus' cleansing of the temple did not mean that no true worship of God was occurring there. For example, there are Gospel accounts of devout people such as Zechariah, Simeon, and Anna humbly worshiping God in the temple (see Luke 1:8-10; 2:25-38).

From Jesus' earliest years, He was aware of His special relationship with His heavenly Father, including God's desire that the temple in Jerusalem be a sacred place for worship and prayer (see 2:49). This attitude is reflected in Jesus' efforts at the start of His earthly ministry to clear the temple area of all profane activity. This set in motion a long chain of events that led to His atoning sacrifice on the cross. After the Messiah's resurrection from the dead, His disciples remembered the prophecy recorded in Psalm 69:9, which foretold that Jesus' fervent devotion for the Lord's house burned in Him like a fire. As the second half of this verse prophesies, the Redeemer's love for the things of God would raise the ire of His enemies (see Rom. 15:3). The antagonists did not realize that the insults they hurled at the Father, fell on the Son.

As the divine, incarnate Word, Jesus is the Lord and the messenger of the covenant about whom Malachi 3:1-4 said would come to spiritually purify and morally refine God's people. This is in keeping with the Old Testament teaching that God maintained a burning zeal and passion for the covenant community and would deal with all rivals firmly. As John 2:17 indicates, anyone who was spiritually unfaithful to the Lord Jesus would experience His hand of discipline (see Prov. 3:11-12; Heb. 12:5-6). Similarly, James 4:5 states that God intensely longs for the spirit He has caused to dwell in us. The idea is that when God's people become unfaithful in their commitment, He zealously desires to have them return to Him in faithfulness and love. For that reason, when they opt for friendship with the world, it provokes God to anger. Indeed, He will not permit them to have divided loyalties between Himself and the world.

II. JESUS' PROPHETIC RESPONSE: JOHN 2:18-22

A. The Demand for a Sign: vs. 18

Then the Jews demanded of him, "What miraculous sign can you show us to prove your authority to do all this?"

At some point, the temple authorities were alerted to the unfolding events and rushed to the scene to investigate. When they saw what Jesus had done, they demanded an explanation for His actions (John 2:18). They considered Jesus to be a counterfeit rabbi who operated without being properly ordained. They were also convinced that whatever claim Jesus made to exercise divine authority was illegitimate. In short, they regarded Him to be a false prophet. For these reasons, the religious leaders demanded proof of Jesus' legal right to disrupt the commercial activities occurring in the temple area.

The Greek noun rendered "sign" most likely refers to some sort of miracle that would certify Jesus' status as the Son of God. In Paul's writings, the apostle noted that as a precondition to accepting the Gospel, educated Jews demanded miraculous signs (see Matt. 12:38; 16:1, 4; Mark 8:11-12; John 2:18; 6:30), while learned Greeks insisted on worldly erudition (1 Cor. 1:22). But what was an intolerable offense to the Jews and utter nonsense to the Gentiles—the Messiah's atoning sacrifice at Calvary (see Deut. 21:23; Gal. 3:13)—was the only way for people to come to a saving knowledge of God (1 Cor. 1:23). The phrase "Christ crucified" was a startling contradiction in terms. To the religious elite, a reference to the Messiah was closely associated with power and triumph, while remarks about the cross were synonymous with weakness and defeat. In contrast, for those summoned by the Father to redemption—both Jews and Greeks—the Son was the epitome of God's power and wisdom (vs. 24; see Rom. 1:4, 16; Col. 2:3).

B. The Veiled Reference to Jesus' Resurrection: vss. 19-22

Jesus answered them, "Destroy this temple, and I will raise it again in three days." The Jews replied, "It has taken forty-six years to build this temple, and you are going to raise it in three days?" But the temple he had spoken of was his body. After he was raised from the dead, his disciples recalled what he had said. Then they believed the Scripture and the words that Jesus had spoken.

In response to the religious authorities, Jesus declared that when they tore down "this temple" (John 2:19), He would rebuild it once more "in three days." Ironically, Jesus' resurrection is the only authentication of His divine nature that He promised to give the authorities (see Rom. 1:3). They failed to understand His claim that if they tore down the temple of His body, He would reestablish its viability within three days (John 2:20-21). The religious leaders thought the Messiah was referring to the temple of Herod the Great, which the king began to renovate and reconstruct around 19 or 20 B.C. The shrine was not completed until A.D. 64, during the reign of Herod Agrippa. A 46-year timeline implies a date of around A.D. 27 for the Passover mentioned in verse 13.

On other occasions (recorded in the Synoptic Gospels), Pharisees and teachers of the law demanded to see Jesus perform a sign to authenticate His divine authority. In response, He declared that the only certifying mark they would receive was that of Jonah. The prophet was facing certain death during the three-day period in which he lay entombed in the belly of a huge sea creature (see Jonah 1:17). The Lord restored Jonah to life by setting him free from his predicament.

This incident foreshadowed Jesus spending a comparable amount of time buried in the depths of the earth. Jesus' own resurrection from the dead would be the supreme validation of His messianic power and authority and serve as a sign that He was superseding the old temple order (see Matt. 12:38-41; 16:1-4; Luke 11:16, 29-32). After Jesus' body was raised from the dead, the Holy Spirit enabled the disciples to remember what the Redeemer had said, including the meaning and significance of His teachings (John 2:22; see 14:26). What the Son had prophesied, fulfilled what the Father had promised in the Old Testament. Jesus' disciples believed the Scriptures and the sayings Jesus had spoken about them.

In the fourth Gospel, there is theological significance to the clearing of the temple courts as one of Jesus' first public acts. From the start of the Savior's earthly ministry, the judgment of God rested on the established civil and religious authorities. Jesus' bold action at the Jerusalem shrine is an end-time event that signals the nearness of the day of the Lord.

The temple-cleansing episode also points to the truth that God is purifying His spiritual children (see 1 Pet. 4:17) and establishing them as a new temple in which the Spirit dwells (see 1 Cor. 3:16-17; 6:19; Eph. 2:19-22; 1 Pet. 2:5). The latter was the reason why the old order, represented by the shrine built by Herod the Great, would give way to the new order, represented by the temple of Jesus' body. With the advent of the Messiah as the final expression of God's Word (see John 1:1, 14, 18), all the divine blessings anticipated under the old covenant were brought to fruition, including being cleansed from sin, experiencing the delight of salvation, and enjoying unbroken fellowship with the Lord (see Isa. 25:6-9; 56:7; Jer. 31:31-34; Rev. 21:22).

Discussion Questions

1. Why do you think Jesus felt it was important to go to Jerusalem during the time for the Jewish Passover festival?
2. If you were with Jesus when He entered the temple courts, how would you have responded to all the buying and selling taking place?
3. What reason did Jesus give for His actions in the temple courts?
4. What theological aspects of the temple cleansing did Jesus' disciples later recognize in the event?
5. Why did Jesus think it was important so early in His ministry to talk about His crucifixion and resurrection?

Contemporary Application

Jesus' cleansing of the Jerusalem temple is a historical event recorded in all four Gospels. That said, the episode also symbolizes what He wants to do in our lives today. Does He receive from us the undivided attention He deserves? What things in our lives might be blocking our worship of Him? What does the Savior need to clean out (so to speak) to make our lives a "house of prayer" (Matt. 21:13)?

As we reflect on these questions, we come to see that we cannot develop a personal relationship with Jesus without an investment of our time. Frantically busy as many of us are, we often find it difficult to find time to spend with the Savior. Yet intimacy with Jesus demands that we determine to set aside a regular time each day to develop a personal relationship with Him. This is a necessary prelude to worshiping Him.

While the Father has determined that developing our intimacy with the Son is mainly a private and personal enterprise, the Father desires that our worship of the Son often be a public matter. This includes times of corporate worship on Sunday, but it also involves openly praising Jesus throughout the week. Doing so is part of what He intended when He directed His followers to be His witnesses. At the minimum, His disciples are to bring Him and His deeds to the public's attention.

Since Jesus has died for our sins and changed our lives, we should say so to others. If we have found Him to be the one who hears our prayers, let us report it. Let us recount joyfully every good and perfect deed that Jesus has done. To an age that has lost its way, despairs of finding truth, and seeks to discover a life worth living, let us praise Jesus for what He has done for us. In addition, we benefit when we praise God for His Son. For in doing so, we are reminded of how wonderfully blessed we are to have Jesus' love and friendship.

Woman of Samaria

Scripture

Background Scripture: *John 4:1-42*
Scripture Lesson: *John 4:7-15, 23-26, 28-30*
Key Verse: [Jesus said,] *"The water I give him will become
in him a spring of water welling up to eternal life."*
John 4:14.
Scripture Lesson for Children: *John 4:7-15, 23-26, 28-30*
Key Verse for Children: [Jesus said,] *"The water I give
him will become in him a spring of water welling up to eternal
life."* John 4:14.

Lesson Aim

To realize that only Jesus can satisfy our deepest needs
and longings.

Lesson Setting

Time: A.D. 27
Place: Samaria

Lesson Outline

Woman of Samaria

  I. The Samaritan Woman's Conversation with Jesus:
     John 4:7-15, 23-26

    A. The Savior's Request: vss. 7-9

    *B. The Savior's Comment about Living Water:
      vss. 10-12*

    *C. The Savior's Explanation of What He Meant:
      vss. 13-15*

  II. The Belief of Many Samaritans in Jesus:
     John 4:28-30

    A. The Woman's Invitation to Her Peers: vss. 28-29

    B. The Response of the Samaritans: vs. 30

Introduction for Adults

Topic: *Turning Life Around*

A person doesn't have to spend much time around a school yard to realize that children can be cruel. Even on the first day of school, it doesn't take more than a few minutes for names like "fatty," "four-eyes," and a range of other, harsher labels to echo across the playground.

Sadly, the name-calling doesn't end with graduation. We adults simply find more civilized and socially acceptable reasons for being prejudiced toward others. While eyeglasses may not keep us out of the "right" groups, our weight, social status, IQ, income, career choices, and religious beliefs might. As long as there are differences between people, they will find reasons to turn their backs on or take a disliking to one another.

In this week's lesson, it is clear that Jesus understood the needs, both spoken and unspoken, of a Samaritan woman at a well. It was obvious she had been ostracized by those around her. But Jesus looked beyond that fact to her deeper, spiritual needs and offered her a way to turn her life around: an eternal relationship with God. He was the starting point for her to overcome prejudice. The same is no less true of us today.

Introduction for Youth

Topic: *The Thirst Quencher*

In Jesus' day, the Jews had no dealings with the Samaritans due to the great hostilities between the two groups. Beyond that, a Jewish man did not engage a woman in public conversation. Jesus violated these well-established customs when He began talking with the woman at the well about how she could quench her spiritual thirst.

In today's world, teens may find that people in the household of faith are different from the people they encounter at school or even in their neighborhoods. Like Jesus, they should be willing to accept those from backgrounds other than their own and to do so with genuineness and humility. Like the woman at the well, Jesus wants to use saved adolescents to reach out to their friends and peers and thereby satisfy their spiritual thirst for eternal life.

Concepts for Children

Topic: *Jesus Restores Life*

1. A Samaritan woman came to get water from Jacob's well.
2. Jesus, a Jew, asked the woman to give Him a drink of water.
3. The woman was shocked by the request, because Samaritans and Jews usually did not have social contact with one another.
4. Jesus showed by His example that faith and fellowship in God are not limited by our differences as people.
5. God wants us to reach out to others with His message of grace and hope.

Lesson Commentary

I. THE SAMARITAN WOMAN'S CONVERSATION WITH JESUS: JOHN 4:7-15, 23-26

A. The Savior's Request: vss. 7-9

When a Samaritan woman came to draw water, Jesus said to her, "Will you give me a drink?" (His disciples had gone into the town to buy food.) The Samaritan woman said to him, "You are a Jew and I am a Samaritan woman. How can you ask me for a drink?" (For Jews do not associate with Samaritans.)

The fourth Gospel leaves as indefinite the time interval between the visit of Nicodemus to Jesus and the testimony of John the Baptizer concerning the Savior (John 3:22-36). In turn, the chronological relation between these sections and Jesus' conversation with a Samaritan woman (4:1-42) is not specified. Most likely, the latter occurred sometime during the winter of A.D. 27. Even at this early stage in Jesus' ministry, He encountered opposition from the Pharisees and scribes. They began to envy His growing popularity. They also resented His challenges to their traditions and hated His exposure of their hypocrisy. Undoubtedly, the religious leaders wondered whether Jesus had political aspirations and worried about how His increasing influence would affect their control over the people. The Pharisees and scribes allowed their petty concerns to blind them to the truth that Jesus is the fulfillment of the Mosaic law.

Perhaps sympathizers within the Sanhedrin (for example, someone such as Nicodemus) kept Jesus informed of the disapproval of the Jewish leadership over His activities. For instance, the Pharisees were alarmed by the many disciples He won and baptized, particularly that they exceeded the number of followers John had gained (vs. 1). Verse 2 is the author's parenthetical clarification that it was Jesus' disciples, not the Savior Himself, who actually baptized others in His name. Elsewhere it is revealed that He gave the Twelve authority to cast out evil spirits and heal every kind of disease and sickness (see Matt. 10:1; Mark 3:14-15). John had already provoked the Pharisees, and Jesus probably did not want to clash with the religious establishment of Jerusalem at this time. Thus, He decided to return to Galilee by the shortest route, which was through the province of Samaria, a journey that took about three days (John 4:3-4; see 7:1).

One of the historic landmarks in Palestine was Jacob's well at the foot of Mount Gerizim (located southwest of Mount Ebal). Centuries earlier, after the Israelites entered the promised land, they gathered in front of Mount Gerizim and Mount Ebal to hear Joshua read the blessings and curses recorded in the Mosaic law (Deut. 27:12-13; Josh. 8:33-35). This incident was one reason why the Samaritans insisted that God had to be worshiped on Mount Gerizim rather than in Jerusalem (see John 4:20). Despite this difference of opinion between the Jews and the Samaritans, there were similarities between their faiths. For instance, both practiced circumcision as a religious rite and both looked for the Messiah.

Also, like the Jews, the Samaritans believed in a final judgment with the Messiah handing out rewards and punishments. Moreover, by Jesus' day they had forsaken all idolatry, as had the Jews.

It was around noon when Jesus came to Jacob's well. Most likely, it was a shaft that burrowed deeply (perhaps more than 100 feet) into solid limestone rock. A low stone wall possibly encircled the spring-fed well (see vss. 11-12) and formed a ledge upon which a weary and exhausted traveler such as Jesus could sit (vs. 6). In that culture, it was the job of women to draw water from wells by using jugs or animal skins attached to ropes. Because the heat was probably most intense at this time of the day, women normally drew water at sunset (see Gen. 24:11). Thus, it was unusual for the Samaritan woman to come at midday. Perhaps she had an urgent need for the water. But since there were other wells nearer to Sychar (less than a mile away to the northeast), she probably came to this well at that moment in order to avoid the other women of the community. The woman at the well might have been shunned by the other women because of her apparently tainted character.

By that point in the exchange, the Savior's disciples had gone into the village to buy food (John 4:8). This left Jesus alone at the well when He asked the Samaritan woman for a drink (vs. 7). Respected Jewish teachers of that day rarely, if ever, volunteered to speak with a woman in public. Also, no Jewish man would ever make himself ceremonially unclean by drinking from a Samaritan's cup. Given this cultural context, it is understandable why the woman at the well was astonished by Jesus' request. She even noted the centuries-old wall of enmity between the two groups of people (vs. 9). Incidentally, to be called a Samaritan was the worst form of insult (see 8:48). In fact, some religious leaders would not even say the name "Samaritan" (see Luke 10:37).

B. The Savior's Comment about Living Water: vss. 10-12

Jesus answered her, "If you knew the gift of God and who it is that asks you for a drink, you would have asked him and he would have given you living water." "Sir," the woman said, "you have nothing to draw with and the well is deep. Where can you get this living water? Are you greater than our father Jacob, who gave us the well and drank from it himself, as did also his sons and his flocks and herds?"

Rather than get drawn into a longstanding racial conflict, Jesus redirected the woman's attention to her deepest spiritual need. By referring to Himself as "living water" (John 4:10), Jesus wanted the woman to recognize Him as God's gracious provision of salvation to the lost (see John 3:16; Gal. 2:20; Eph. 5:25). The Messiah implied that because He is the Son of God, He could give the woman water much greater than that from the well. In the original, the phrase rendered "living water" (John 4:10) typically referred to fresh, pure water that flowed in rivers, streams, and springs. In the Old Testament, the Lord referred to Himself as "the spring of living water" (Jer. 2:13). He also described the heavenly blessings He offered as "living water" (Zech. 14:8). These metaphors would have resonated with those living in the hot, arid climate of Israel. The community of faith would depend on the Lord to nourish and refresh them spiritually for all eternity (see Ps. 36:9; Isa. 12:3; 44:3; 49:10; 55:1; Jer. 17:13).

The woman responded to Jesus' peculiar statement with two questions. First, she asked how He planned to get this drinkable water, especially since He was without the means to obtain it from the well (John 4:11). Second, the woman attempted to provoke Jesus by asking whether He was greater than Jacob. The well he left for the Samaritans to enjoy had provided water for the famed patriarch, his family, and their livestock. The woman became skeptical at the possibility that Jesus was superior to Jacob (vs. 12; see 8:53). The woman may have been comparing Jesus' apparent unimportance with the Samaritans' importance as descendants of Jacob and Joseph. This would imply that the woman did not need what the Messiah offered.

In point of fact, Jesus was infinitely greater than Jacob and all other esteemed individuals in the Old Testament. By way of example, the prophet Isaiah had promised that a virgin would conceive and bear a son (Isa. 7:14). Mary's Son would be that child, the absolutely great Messiah of Israel. This miracle was possible because He would also be the "Son of the Most High" (Luke 1:32). Furthermore, He would fulfill what Isaiah had prophesied about the one who would rule on David's throne (Isa. 9:6-7). God had promised David that his kingdom would be established forever (2 Sam. 7:16). As it happened, David's descendants reigned over Judah until the Exile (586 B.C.). The angel's reference to the "throne of his father David" (Luke 1:32) meant that God would now restore the broken line of David's succession. Indeed, Gabriel revealed to Mary that her Son would fulfill that promise, most of all as He ruled forever in majestic splendor (vs. 33).

C. The Savior's Explanation of What He Meant: vss. 13-15

Jesus answered, "Everyone who drinks this water will be thirsty again, but whoever drinks the water I give him will never thirst. Indeed, the water I give him will become in him a spring of water welling up to eternal life." The woman said to him, "Sir, give me this water so that I won't get thirsty and have to keep coming here to draw water."

Jesus adroitly sidestepped the Samaritan woman's provocation by noting that even water from Jacob's well quenched thirst for only a short time (John 4:13). But the eternal life Jesus offered would abundantly satisfy the spiritual thirst of people forever (see 10:10). God's gift of salvation was comparable to a fountain of water that vigorously welled up in believers in an inner, unending, and overflowing supply (4:14). The idea of a perpetual torrent of water intrigued the woman, who pictured it as something that would replace her daily trips carrying a heavy pot to and from the well. She took Jesus literally and focused on personal convenience rather than anything spiritual (vs. 15).

The Redeemer, however, had a different agenda, one that involved getting the woman to see her need for eternal life. To achieve this goal, Jesus focused on the woman's sin, which stood in the way of her accepting what He offered. Jesus began by telling the woman to go and get her husband (vs. 16). In turn, she stated that she was not married. The Messiah affirmed the truthfulness of the woman's statement, adding that she had been divorced five times and was now living immorally (vss. 17-18). Suddenly it dawned on the woman that Jesus was not an ordinary person. Indeed, to have such remarkable discernment, He must be a prophet (vs. 19; namely, a divinely inspired person with supernatural knowledge and insight). Perhaps in an attempt to deflect the conversation away from her sinful lifestyle, the woman brought up the controversy between Samaritans and Jews regarding the proper place to worship (vs. 20). To her it was a suitable religious question for a prophet to give his authoritative assessment.

The Jews recognized that God had instructed Solomon to build a temple in Jerusalem. They could go there to offer sacrifices and to worship Him. Meanwhile, the Samaritans argued that worship of God should be performed at Mount Gerizim, where they claimed many blessed events occurred. The Samaritans taught that Abraham proved his faithfulness and obedience to God when the patriarch offered his son, Isaac, on Mount Gerizim. The Samaritans also taught that Abraham and Melchizedek met on this mountain. More importantly, the Samaritans believed the Lord commanded Moses to build an altar on Mount Gerizim for God's people to worship Him. Since the Samaritans regarded only the Pentateuch (Genesis through Deuteronomy) as sacred, they naturally dismissed the Jewish belief that the center of worship should be at the temple in Jerusalem. In contrast, the Jews claimed that the Samaritans distorted the Scriptures. This controversy over the proper place to worship God only added to the enmity between the Jews and Samaritans.

Jesus used the mention of the debate to strike at the heart of the woman's problem. She was concerned with an external aspect of worship, that is, the right place to revere God. Jesus made her focus on the internal aspect of worship, namely, revering God with a cleansed heart. Here we see that the woman's frame of reference needed to be adjusted. Jesus began to do this by bluntly stating that in the coming day of fulfillment, it would not matter where people worshiped—be it Mount Gerizim or Mount Zion (vs. 21). After all, the Messiah surpassed in importance all earthly shrines and sanctuaries, even the temple in Jerusalem.

Next, Jesus addressed the issue the woman had raised. The Samaritans acknowledged the true God, but they worshiped Him in ignorance. Since they considered only the Pentateuch as sacred, they ignored the prophets. The Jews worshiped God as He revealed Himself in the entire Hebrew Bible. The Messiah clearly sided with the Jews on this issue by identifying Himself with them through the emphatic use of the Greek word rendered "we" (vs. 22). God had chosen the Jews to be the vehicle through which He would reveal His plan of redemption.

The time was soon coming, however, when a Jew, a Samaritan, or any other person could freely worship the Lord—as long as that person did so in spirit and truth (vs. 23). Indeed, the opportunity had been inaugurated with the Messiah's advent (which included His death, resurrection, and ascension). To worship in spirit is to do so from the heart, not merely to go through the motions of worship. The latter is frequently characterized by an obsession with being at the right place and performing approved rituals. To worship in truth is to revere the Father as He has disclosed Himself in the Son (see 1:18), not as would-be worshipers have created God in their own minds. Indeed, He actively seeks people who worship Him with sincerity and dedication. Jesus, in declaring God to be "spirit" (4:24), meant He is immaterial in His existence.

Upon hearing the truths Jesus spoke, the Samaritan woman started to wonder whether He was more than just a prophet (vs. 25). The woman thus voiced the hope of both Samaritans and Jews, namely, that the Messiah would come. In Bible times, it was commonly believed that whenever the Anointed One came, He would explain all the enigmas of life. At this point, Jesus directly told the Samaritan woman that He was the Messiah (vs. 26). Evidently, the political overtones associated with Jewish misconceptions of the Messiah did not prevail in Samaria, thus making it relatively safe for Jesus to identify Himself unambiguously in this way.

II. THE BELIEF OF MANY SAMARITANS IN JESUS: JOHN 4:28-30

A. The Woman's Invitation to Her Peers: vss. 28-29

Then, leaving her water jar, the woman went back to the town and said to the people, "Come, see a man who told me everything I ever did. Could this be the Christ?"

Just as Jesus was finishing His conversation with the woman, His disciples returned with some food. Because of cultural prejudice against women, His disciples were astonished to discover Him talking to the Samaritan woman in public. Yet they had been with Him long enough to know not to question their Master, who by His actions was teaching them to break down the walls of prejudice (John 4:27).

Meanwhile, the woman abandoned her jug of water at the well and hurried back to the village. Her excited response shows the profound impression Jesus had made on her (vs. 28). In the woman's effort to tell others in the village about the newcomer, she completely forgot about her initial reason for going to the well (vs. 29). (Undoubtedly, she planned to return to it.) Meeting Jesus also helped the woman forget the shame she may have carried for years. She seemed thrilled that Jesus was able to tell her everything she ever did (a slight overstatement) and still talk with and accept her. The woman did not say to the villagers, "I have found the Messiah," but asked humbly, "Could this be the Christ?"

B. The Response of the Samaritans: vs. 30

They came out of the town and made their way toward him.

The woman's indirect approach aroused the interest of the Samaritans without overtly stating any conclusion. Because of the woman's reputation, it is doubtful her neighbors would have accepted her assessments. But by simply relating what had happened, the woman generated considerable interest. While John 4:30 does not indicate how many came, it gives the impression that a large number of residents from Sychar responded to the woman's invitation.

Discussion Questions

1. Why was the Samaritan woman surprised when Jesus asked her for a drink?
2. What was the gift of God to which Jesus referred?
3. Why did the woman raise the issue of proper worship?
4. What about Jesus' identity do you learn from His conversation with the Samaritan woman?
5. Why do we turn to things besides Jesus to fulfill our needs?

Contemporary Application

Human beings are extraordinary creatures. We are shaped and molded in the image of God. Also, the human mind is able to create, discover, and explore the depths of the universe. The psalmist rightly declared that we are "fearfully and wonderfully made" (Ps. 139:14).

Despite all our vast knowledge and skills, human beings are still unable to conquer and solve many of life's basic problems. We still struggle with loneliness and depression. And in a land of seemingly unlimited resources, many people feel destitute and alienated, with little or no sense of purpose in life.

Echoing the prophet's words, we are frail and like grass that withers and fades with the passing of time (Isa. 40:6-8). Out of our innermost self, we often cry for something or someone to give us peace and comfort. Before we can experience God's help and consolation, we must first recognize our own human frailty.

The void that exists in the lives of each of us can be filled only by the Lord Jesus. When we invite the living Messiah to come into our hearts, He supplies the freeing power from the bondage of evil and sin's oppression. Jesus also helps us deal with loneliness, depression, and insecurity we might feel at times. He comforts us through His presence and the promises of His Word. Jesus also consoles us through the indwelling Holy Spirit and the loving support of Christian friends.

As we allow Jesus to meet our deepest needs, we should respond by exploring new ways in which we can minister to people in need. Often we concentrate so much on what we cannot do that we fail to consider what we can do. The important point is that we begin thinking about how we can match the gifts God has given us with the needs around us. Helping does not often require great wealth or a huge investment of time. God is able to use whatever we have in ways that are humanly impossible.

Healing the Blind Man

Scripture

Background Scripture: *John 9*

Scripture Lesson: *John 9:1-17*

Key Verse: *Some of the Pharisees said, "This man is not from God, for he does not keep the Sabbath." But others asked, "How can a sinner do such miraculous signs?" So they were divided.* John 9:16.

Scripture Lesson for Children: *John 9:1-17*

Key Verse for Children: *"Go," [Jesus] told him, "wash in the Pool of Siloam" (this word means Sent). So the man went and washed, and came home seeing.* John 9:7.

Lesson Aim

To more fully appreciate that Jesus is the Light of the world.

Lesson Setting

Time: A.D. 29
Place: Jerusalem

Lesson Outline

Healing the Blind Man

I.   The Healing of the Blind Man: John 9:1-12
     A. *The Disciples' Question: vss. 1-2*
     B. *The Savior's Response: vss. 3-5*
     C. *The Savior's Directive to the Blind Man: vss. 6-7*
     D. *The Astonishment of the Neighbors: vss. 8-9*
     E. *The Healed Man's Explanation: vss. 10-12*
II. The Interrogation of the Healed Man: John 9:13-17
     A. *The Man's Recounting of the Miracle: vss. 13-15*
     B. *The Debate among the Religious Leaders: vss. 16-17*

Introduction for Adults

Topic: *What Comes First?*

Operation Overlord was the name given to the Allied invasion of western Europe. The event began on June 6, 1944, with the largest invasion fleet in history conducting an amphibious landing on the northern coast of France. This became the starting point for a massive Allied thrust eastward through France and on into the heart of Nazi Germany.

As a result of Operation Overlord, the darkness of oppression gave way to the light of freedom. On an even grander scale, when people turn to Christ for salvation, the light of His glory shines in their hearts to overcome the darkness of sin. And once the redeemed have encountered the risen Lord, they no longer want to wallow in the mire of transgression. Instead, they make sure that He comes first in their lives.

Introduction for Youth

Topic: *Rules You Don't Keep*

Photosynthesis is the process by which plants use the energy from sunlight to produce sugar. Without adequate light, plants eventually die. They may shed leaves, especially older ones. Flowering plants may fail to produce buds. And variegated plants may revert to solid green.

For saved teens the light of Christ is just as important for their eternal vitality. It is the risen Lord who sustains them, not their dogged efforts to heed a long list of rules. He alone guides them in the path of uprightness and steers them away from the way of the wicked. Apart from Him your students will go astray and spiritually wither, but in vital union with Him, they will grow and thrive.

Concepts for Children

Topic: *Jesus Heals*

1. Jesus healed a blind beggar so that the people could see God's goodness.
2. Some people did not believe that Jesus healed the blind man.
3. When we know that Jesus has helped us, we want to worship Him.
4. Jesus wants us to follow in the light of salvation and truth that He offers us.
5. The light of Jesus helps us to avoid evil in our pathway.

Lesson Commentary

I. THE HEALING OF THE BLIND MAN: JOHN 9:1-12

A. The Disciples' Question: vss. 1-2

As he went along, he saw a man blind from birth. His disciples asked him, "Rabbi, who sinned, this man or his parents, that he was born blind?"

The sixth sign featured in the fourth Gospel reveals Jesus as the Light of the world (John 8:12; 9:5). The miracle demonstrated His infinite superiority to all the Old Testament prophets, for none of them ever cured blindness (9:30-33). Giving sight to the blind was a messianic activity foretold in the Old Testament (see Exod. 4:11; Ps. 146:8; Isa. 29:18; 35:5; 42:7), and it validated Jesus' claim to be the Son of God (John 20:30-31). This healing also illustrated the way Jesus opens spiritual eyes to God's truth. Most likely, the Son performed the miracle while in Jerusalem in the fall of A.D. 29, not long after the festival of Tabernacles had ended.

Perhaps as Jesus and His disciples exited out of an open gate of the Jerusalem temple (see Acts 3:1-7), they encountered a beggar who had been born blind (John 9:1). In that day, begging was the only means of support for those with a severe physical disability like congenital blindness. It is not hard to imagine him sitting on a straw mat and holding up a saucer into which sympathetic passersby could drop their coins. Most likely, Peter, as the spokesperson for the Twelve, asked Jesus whether the man's blindness was a result of his own sins or those of his parents (John 9:2; see Exod. 20:5; 34:7; Ps. 109:13-15; Isa. 65:6-7). In the first century A.D., it was widely believed that sin caused all suffering, especially such a serious condition as blindness. Some of the rabbis of the period speculated that one could sin in the womb before birth, thereby causing one to be born blind. Others suggested that possibly one could sin in a preexistent state and thereby cause an affliction at birth.

B. The Savior's Response: vss. 3-5

"Neither this man nor his parents sinned," said Jesus, "but this happened so that the work of God might be displayed in his life. As long as it is day, we must do the work of him who sent me. Night is coming, when no one can work. While I am in the world, I am the light of the world."

Perhaps because the Twelve had been exposed to countless disabled beggars, their compassion for the blind man seemed to be minimal. For them he had been reduced to a theological riddle. They assumed this man's suffering was the result of someone's offense against God, but they did not understand how. While sin may be the cause of some affliction, as clearly indicated in Scripture (see John 5:14; 1 Cor. 11:27-30), it is not always the case necessarily (see Ezek. 18; 2 Cor. 12:7). Jesus reflected this view in His clear and direct response to the disciples' question. The Messiah stated that the man's blindness was not due to his sin or his parents'

sins. Rather, he had been born blind so that the Lord's power, as seen in the working of a miracle, could be displayed in the man (John 9:3). Expressed differently,
though the Father had not inflicted this man with blindness, the Son promised to
eliminate this beggar's disability to demonstrate God's compassion and glory (see
John 11:4, 40; 1 Pet. 4:12-19).

Jesus declared that as long as it was daytime, it was necessary for He and His disciples to perform the deeds of His Father, who sent the Son to earth as His
emissary. Once nighttime arrived, no further work could be done (John 9:4). In
this verse, daytime metaphorically referred to the bodily presence of the
Redeemer, while nighttime denoted the passing of His earthly ministry as a result
of His crucifixion. The divinely ordained tasks included giving sight to the blind
and revealing God's truth to the lost.

Jesus was the Light that unveiled God's plan of redemption to a dying world.
Correspondingly, it was not enough to be theologically correct about the cause of
the man's blindness. More importantly, something had to be done about it. Next,
Jesus reassured His disciples that while He was still on earth, He was the "light of
the world" (vs. 5). He did not mean that He somehow ceased being the light once
He ascended to heaven. Rather, the Savior meant the light of His presence shone
brightly among people when He was on earth doing His Father's will. The Son
would prove His claim by giving the blind man the ability to see.

C. The Savior's Directive to the Blind Man: vss. 6-7

Having said this, he spit on the ground, made some mud with the saliva, and put it on the man's eyes.
"Go," he told him, "wash in the Pool of Siloam" (this word means Sent). So the man went and washed,
and came home seeing.

The fourth Gospel provides no indication that Jesus was asked to heal the man.
Evidently, while the Twelve stood by and watched, Jesus took the initiative to spit
on the ground, make mud with the saliva, and smooth the mud over the blind
man's eyes (9:6). In that day, many people believed that saliva possessed the power
to cure physical ailments. The ancient world thought that the saliva of someone of
particular importance was especially effective in the treatment of blindness.

While Jesus could have cured the man without such a hands-on procedure, per-
haps this outcast needed the Savior's reassuring, personal touch. Jesus also used
His spit on two other recorded occasions, namely, to give hearing to a deaf man
(Mark 7:33) and sight to another blind man (8:23). Just as God had originally
made human beings out of the dust of the ground (see Gen. 2:7), so too the
Messiah used clay to create a seeing pair of eyes for the blind man (see Job 10:9;
Isa. 45:9; Jer. 18:6). Because it was a Sabbath, the religious leaders considered this
activity as a form of work that violated their traditions (see John 9:14).

The Redeemer told the beggar to go and wash in the Pool of Siloam, in which
the latter term means "sent" (vs. 7). Just as the Father had sent the Son into the

world (see 4:34; 5:23, 37; 7:28; 8:16, 18, 26, 29, 42; 10:36; 12:44; 14:24), so now the Son was sending the blind beggar to the pool, which was probably a substantial distance from the temple. This would have called for a degree of faith from the man (see 2 Kings 5:10-14). Hezekiah originally built the reservoir southeast of Jerusalem. An underground tunnel carved out by the king's workers carried water to the pool from the Gihon Spring in the Kidron Valley. During times of siege, having clear access to water was imperative (2 Kings 20:20; 2 Chron. 32:30). In Jesus' day, during the festival of Tabernacles, worshipers would draw water from the pool and pour it out at the base of the altar in the Jerusalem temple.

D. The Astonishment of the Neighbors: vss. 8-9

His neighbors and those who had formerly seen him begging asked, "Isn't this the same man who used to sit and beg?" Some claimed that he was. Others said, "No, he only looks like him." But he himself insisted, "I am the man."

Just as Jesus directed, the blind man picked up his belongings, including a walking stick, and gradually made his way to the pool. Perhaps after finding an open spot, he knelt down by the edge of the pool, set his walking stick to one side, cupped some water in his hands, and began rubbing it in his eyes. A growing sense of excitement must have filled the man as he began to see. For the first time in his life, his once useless eyes were now able to gaze upon an array of images, colors, and movements. His neighbors and others who knew him as a blind beggar could not miss the joy he expressed over the miracle that had occurred in his life (John 9:8). Some thought the man was the former blind beggar, while others who did not recognize him thought the completely healed man was someone else. In the midst of the debate, the man kept insisting that he was the same person (vs. 9).

E. The Healed Man's Explanation: vss. 10-12

"How then were your eyes opened?" they demanded. He replied, "The man they call Jesus made some mud and put it on my eyes. He told me to go to Siloam and wash. So I went and washed, and then I could see." "Where is this man?" they asked him. "I don't know," he said.

When the neighbors and acquaintances of the former blind beggar asked how the miracle occurred (John 9:10), he testified to them in a simple and straightforward manner what Jesus had done (vs. 11). Then, when asked where Jesus might be, the man said he did not know (vs. 12). Evidently, the onlookers wanted to speak to Jesus themselves (as did the neighbors of the Samaritan woman at the well; see 4:28-30). As the narrative in John 9 develops, there is a corresponding increase in the cured man's understanding of Jesus' identity and commitment to Him as the Messiah. The former beggar first referred to Jesus as a "man" (vs. 11), then as a "prophet" (vs. 17), and finally as an emissary from God (vs. 33). The healed man also doubted whether Jesus ever sinned (vs. 25). Though the one-time beggar was eventually banned from the synagogue by the religious leaders (vs. 34), that did not deter him from putting his faith in Jesus as the Son of Man and worshiping Him as Lord (vss. 35-38).

II. THE INTERROGATION OF THE HEALED MAN: JOHN 9:13-17

A. The Man's Recounting of the Miracle: vss. 13-15

They brought to the Pharisees the man who had been blind. Now the day on which Jesus had made the mud and opened the man's eyes was a Sabbath. Therefore the Pharisees also asked him how he had received his sight. "He put mud on my eyes," the man replied, "and I washed, and now I see."

Perhaps the healed man bore witness to Jesus in the precincts of the temple. If so, this caught the attention of the religious authorities, who directed the temple police to bring the former beggar to them for questioning (John 9:13). Undoubtedly, the man felt some anxiety as he was escorted into a large chamber and made to stand before his interrogators. Most of them were likely seated behind a long table with various important documents spread out in front of them. One person would have recorded what occurred at this makeshift tribunal, including any decisions involving the healed man and Jesus, his benefactor.

The previous series of incidents in the temple involving the preacher from Nazareth were fresh in the minds of the Pharisees. Thus, they were keen to investigate this new development, which had taken place on the Sabbath (vs. 14). When the authorities questioned the man about the circumstances surrounding his healing, he gave an even shorter account than he had to his neighbors. He just reported the facts (vs. 15).

B. The Debate among the Religious Leaders: vss. 16-17

Some of the Pharisees said, "This man is not from God, for he does not keep the Sabbath." But others asked, "How can a sinner do such miraculous signs?" So they were divided. Finally they turned again to the blind man, "What have you to say about him? It was your eyes he opened." The man replied, "He is a prophet."

The healed man's response confirmed in the minds of some of the Pharisees that despite Jesus' claims, He was not from God. After all, Jesus dared to break their Sabbath traditions (for example, by kneading together spittle and dirt to make a clay-like paste), which they considered as sacred and binding as the Mosaic law. The implication is that Jesus was an enemy of the Jewish nation. Others, however, wondered how someone whom they concluded was a sinner could perform such an amazing miracle. Despite the disagreement among the inquisitors, those antagonistic toward Jesus seemed to be in the majority (John 9:16).

Next, when the panel asked the former beggar for his opinion about the miracle-working Nazarene, the man called Jesus a prophet (vs. 17; see 2 Kings 2:19-22; 4:18-44; 5:1-14). One can only imagine the commotion such a statement created among the Pharisees. Despite the evidence, the tribunal refused to believe that Jesus was the Messiah. They rejected the fact that the Father had sent the Son and empowered Him. But the authorities were perplexed as to how to invalidate the miracle and brand Jesus as a fraud. The religious leaders acted as if they were standing in judgment over the former beggar and the Galilean who had healed him. But ironically the panel's rejection of the Son of God meant they were the ones who stood condemned as sinners before the Father (see John 3:36; 5:22-23; 9:39).

The tribunal continued their investigation by summoning the man's parents for questioning (9:18). Perhaps in the interim, the healed man was escorted out of the chamber. Once the temple guards brought in the parents, the religious leaders asked them how their son, despite being born blind, was now able to see (vs. 19). The couple gave a non-committal response. They affirmed that the man being questioned was their son and that he had been born blind (vs. 20). But the parents declined to speculate how he had overcome his disability. Undoubtedly with a tone of respect, the couple asked the inquisitors to question their son, who was mature enough to give legal testimony for himself (vs. 21). The couple responded in this way because they feared being banned for life from attending the synagogue. Since the latter was the heart of their religious and social existence, to be excommunicated meant being cut off from their cultural identity as Jews. The parents had heard this was the penalty for acknowledging Jesus as the Messiah (vss. 22-23).

Most likely, the authorities had the temple guards escort the couple out of the chamber before bringing their son back in for further questioning. Once the healed man was standing before the panel, he was formally placed under oath and directed to promise before God that he would speak the truth (see Josh. 7:19). For the Pharisees this meant declaring the itinerant preacher to be a sinner, for He violated their ban against doing any kind of work on the Sabbath (John 9:24). The former beggar refused to speculate as to whether Jesus was a sinner. All the man could say, undoubtedly with a deep measure of gratitude, is that whereas before he was congenitally blind, he could now see, and this was due to the miraculous intervention of Jesus (vs. 25). Because the tribunal was convinced that the Nazarene was a fraud, they struggled to make sense of the healed man's testimony. When they asked him what Jesus had done (vs. 26), the man became exasperated. Instead of rehearsing the facts again, the former beggar asked with biting sarcasm whether they also wanted to become disciples of Jesus (vs. 27).

Perhaps by this point it dawned on the healed man that even the risk of being expelled from the synagogue would not stop him from becoming a follower of Jesus. Of course, such a notion infuriated the religious leaders. The panel heaped insults on him by declaring that while he had chosen to follow a charlatan, they were loyal disciples of Moses (vs. 28). The authorities were convinced that God had spoken to Moses and that the preacher from Galilee was a fraud (vs. 29). Despite the truth Jesus had declared in the synagogue, the miracles He had performed, and the testimony others had given on His behalf, the religious hierarchy still refused to acknowledge Him as the Son of God. Their efforts, however, to intimidate the healed man backfired. Rather than incriminate Jesus of wrongdoing, the man noted that the tribunal's doubt concerning Jesus was remarkable. After all, the Nazarene had given sight to someone who once was congenitally blind (vs. 30).

Discussion Questions

1   Why did the disciples think the blind man's condition was due to sin?
2.   What did Jesus mean when He claimed to be the Light of the world?
3.   How did the beggar's peers respond to the fact that he was no longer blind?
4.   What explanation did the beggar give when asked how his eyes were opened?
5.   Why is it important to share with others that Jesus is the Light of the world?

Contemporary Application

Karen sat next to her sister Lisa and listened to her sister's shallow breathing. Karen had no idea how long she would be able to communicate with her. Lisa was dying of cancer. So Karen began to pray: "Lord, my sister is dying. Ever since I became a Christian, I have told her about You, Lord, but she just ignored me or changed the subject. Lord, I don't want my sister to go to hell. Could You please help me to tell her clearly once again about Jesus? Would You please take the blinders off of her mind and her heart so she can understand that she needs You? Please, Lord, help me."

As Karen prayed, she held her Bible with one hand and touched her sister's hand with the other. Karen began to read John 9:5, explaining that Jesus is the Light of the world. When Karen finished, she asked her sister if she wanted to pray with her about making a decision for Christ. Lisa shook her head no. Presentations like this one go on each day all over the world. The claims of Jesus as the source of spiritual truth and hope are clearly stated and unbelievers are asked to respond. Some accept the Lord Jesus and others reject Him.

No magic formula or miracle prayer can force a person to receive the Son. Even some of those who saw Jesus' miracles (such as the healing of a man born blind) and heard the voice of God "would not believe in him" (12:37). Even many of the religious leaders failed to believe in Jesus because He did not come in the form they had expected. The populace was hoping for a powerful, wealthy, warrior king. Instead, Jesus came as the humble Son of man, ready to give His life.

Still today, people do not accept the Messiah because He does not come to them in the way they expect Him to. He preaches servanthood instead of power, and sacrifice rather than glory. These truths can be hard to accept. But we know that Jesus' claims about Himself being the Light of the world (see 8:12) demand a response from every person. Also, we need to be open to doing everything we can to lead others to Him. It's true that not everyone will accept the Savior. Nevertheless, as believers we must not keep our faith to ourselves due to fears of what might happen to us. Instead, we need to keep praying and taking advantage of opportunities to share the claims of the Lord Jesus.

The Bread of Life

DEVOTIONAL READING

Psalm 107:1-9

DAILY BIBLE READINGS

Monday April 30
John 6:1-15 Feeding the Hungry

Tuesday May 1
John 6:16-21 Walking on Water

Wednesday May 2
John 6:36-40 Giving Eternal Life

Thursday May 3
John 6:41-51 Offering Living Bread

Friday May 4
John 6:60-65 The Life-giving Spirit

Saturday May 5
John 6:66-71 To Whom Can We Go?

Sunday May 6
John 6:22-35 The True Bread of Heaven

Scripture

Background Scripture: *John 6*
Scripture Lesson: *John 6:22-35*
Key Verse: *Jesus declared, "I am the bread of life. He who comes to me will never go hungry, and he who believes in me will never be thirsty."* John 6:35.
Scripture Lesson for Children: *John 6:22-35*
Key Verse for Children: *Jesus declared, "I am the bread of life. He who comes to me will never go hungry."* John 6:35.

Lesson Aim

To investigate the meaning of Jesus being the Bread of life.

Lesson Setting

Time: A.D. *29*
Place: Sea of Galilee, Capernaum

Lesson Outline

The Bread of Life

  I. The Aftermath of Jesus Walking on the Water: John 6:22-24
     A. *The Realization of the Crowd: vss. 22-23*
     B. *The Search for Jesus: vs. 24*
  II. The Son as the True Bread from Heaven: John 6:25-35
     A. *The Father's Approval of the Son: vss. 25-27*
     B. *The Necessity of Belief in the Son: vss. 28-29*
     C. *The Father's Provision of the Son: vss. 30-33*
     D. *The Son Declares Himself to Be the Bread of Life: vss. 34-35*

Introduction for Adults

Topic: *Nourishment for Life*

Jim Collins and Jerry Porras are the authors of *Built to Last: Successful Habits of Visionary Companies.* This book compares what they have identified as "visionary" companies with selected organizations in the same industry. The former had a number of common characteristics. For instance, almost all had some type of core ideology that guided the company in times of upheaval and served as a constant benchmark.

Where can adults find lasting results for their life endeavors? Where can they go for unending spiritual satisfaction? The answer is Jesus Christ. When He is the center of their life, it has genuine meaning and lasting purpose. Encourage your students to turn to Him to meet their deepest eternal longings for fulfillment.

Introduction for Youth

Topic: *Better than Bread!*

Recently, the humble bread loaf has made a comeback. In fact, for specialty bakeries and bread-only retail stores business couldn't be better. It's not hard to understand bread's incredible popularity. Even teens find the smell alluring and the taste appealing.

Bread, as some used to say, is the staff of life. Indeed, for many in the West it is impossible to imagine life without this source of food. What bread accomplishes for the human body, Jesus brings about for the human soul. As the teens will learn in this week's lesson, the Messiah is the only true source of eternal nourishment for those who put their trust in Him.

Concepts for Children

Topic: *Jesus Is the Living Bread*

1. The crowd searched for Jesus because they wanted Him to give them more food to eat.
2. God the Father and Jesus the Son work together to fill the needs of all who believe in Jesus.
3. All who believe in Jesus will live with Him forever.
4. Jesus wants us to believe in Him so that He can bless us.
5. We can find rest in Jesus, even as we serve people in need.

Lesson Commentary

I. THE AFTERMATH OF JESUS WALKING ON THE WATER: JOHN 6:22-24

A. The Realization of the Crowd: vss. 22-23

The next day the crowd that had stayed on the opposite shore of the lake realized that only one boat had been there, and that Jesus had not entered it with his disciples, but that they had gone away alone. Then some boats from Tiberias landed near the place where the people had eaten the bread after the Lord had given thanks.

The context of John 6 is the Savior's feeding of over 5,000 people. It also represents a major turning point in the thematic development of the fourth Gospel. Up until this time in the narrative, Jesus' ministry was primarily in Jerusalem, but now it shifts to Galilee. This change of venue brings the Son's identity as the Messiah into sharper relief. For instance, the signs He did recalled the miraculous ways in which God intervened on behalf of His people in the Book of Exodus, specifically the first Passover event, the departure from Egypt, and the provision of manna in the desert. Jesus is shown to be the fulfillment of the law's types and prophecies, the one whom the Father has sent into the world to do His will. Perhaps more than before, the distinction between and consequences of belief versus unbelief are differentiated. People in the category of unbelief become increasingly intense in their rejection of and hostility toward the Messiah.

Apart from the Resurrection, Jesus' feeding of over 5,000 people is the only miracle that is recorded in all four Gospels. It shows the Redeemer to be the Bread of life. The fact that John retold an incident that was probably already well-known is an indication of the impact this miracle had on people. The "some time after this" (John 6:1) reference is indefinite, though verse 4 says it was near the time when the Passover was about to be celebrated in Jerusalem. A probable date for the episode is the spring of A.D. 29, which was just one year before the crucifixion of the Anointed One.

The author provided no explanation concerning the Messiah's journey north from Jerusalem to Galilee. According to Matthew 14:13, Jesus retreated from the crowds to a remote place after hearing about the execution of John the Baptizer. The solitary spot was likely in the area of Bethsaida (see Luke 9:10), a town located on the northeast shore of the Sea of Galilee. John 6:1 notes that Jesus withdrew by crossing over to the far side of the lake. But by the time the fourth Gospel was written, the lake was called "the Sea of Tiberias," named after the Roman emperor who reigned during Jesus' earthly ministry.

After the miraculous feeding of the large crowd (vss. 2-11), Jesus told His disciples to gather the fragments that were left on the ground so that none of the food would go to waste (vs. 12). This instruction would not have seemed unusual to His disciples since it was customary for servants to pick up and eat the leftovers after a Jewish feast. It was also in keeping with the Jewish belief that bread is a gift from

God and must not be left lying around. Most likely, the disciples did not use small wicker baskets, but rather larger ones normally used for carrying sizable quantities of food and other supplies. The disciples filled their 12 baskets with the remaining pieces of bread (vs. 13).

The feeding of the multitude was clearly a miracle from the hand of the Messiah, yet He did not perform it in isolation. He let the Twelve have a part in working the miracle, such as by setting out the food for the people. And even before Jesus began to perform the miracle, He challenged His followers to come up with their own plan for feeding the crowd. In this way the deed became a collaborative effort from beginning to end. Imagine the disciples' feeling of excitement in cooperating with the Redeemer in feeding the multitude. That thrill, that sense of involvement, was necessary to their training. Jesus had not called them to stand aside and watch Him work. Neither was He sending them to work without His help. The disciples were partners with the Lord Jesus in His ministry of redemption.

The miraculous supply of food prompted many to wonder if Jesus was the prophet that Moses referred to in Deuteronomy 18:15 and 18 (John 6:14). Whether this prophet was to be a forerunner of the Messiah or the Messiah Himself is unclear, though the Pharisees questioned John the Baptizer as if the Prophet and the Messiah were separate people (see 1:20-21). In any case, the crowd saw significant signs in Jesus' ministry that He was someone worthy of being the Prophet whom Moses described. For instance, Jesus miraculously fed the people a kind of Passover (6:4) that filled 12 baskets with leftovers—symbolically, one for each of the 12 tribes. Further, Jesus' miracles hinted at what the people were expecting when the Messiah would come, namely, that abundant wine would flow and enough food to feed all Israel would fall like manna from the heavens (see Amos 9:13). In their desperation, the people wanted to force Jesus to be their king. But the kind of ruler they wanted, a brigand who would overthrow Israel's oppressors, was not in God's plan (see John 18:36-37; Acts 1:6; Rom. 14:7).

The Messiah came to offer forgiveness from sin and an enduring relationship with God (see Jer. 31:31-34). Thus, the Son retreated into the hills to spend the night in prayer with His Father (Matt. 14:23; Mark 6:46; John 6:15). Just prior to this, Jesus dismissed the crowds. He also directed His disciples to get into a boat without Him, cross over to the west side of the lake, and head to Capernaum (Matt. 14:22; Mark 6:45; John 6:16-17). As the Twelve made their way, a gale-force wind sent huge waves crashing against the sides of the boat (Matt. 14:24; John 6:18). At times on the Sea of Galilee, the sudden appearance of violent storm episodes occurred. Evidently, the disciples spent most of the night fighting the elements as they tried to cross. Despite their efforts, they only went about three miles, which placed them near the middle of the lake (Mark 6:47; John 6:19).

In the hours immediately preceding dawn, Jesus saw the trouble His disciples were in and came to them by walking on the lake (Matt. 14:25; Mark 6:48; see Job 9:8). Not even the wind, waves, and gravity could stop the one who is the Lord of all creation (see Job 38:8-11; Pss. 29:3-4, 10-11; 65:5-7; 77:19; 89:9; 107:23-32; Isa. 43:2, 16). When Jesus' form appeared mysteriously out of the darkness like a ghost, the disciples' minds must have turned to the old Jewish superstition that a spirit seen at night brings disaster. In this case, they mistook Jesus for a ghost (Matt. 14:26; Mark 6:49-50). It seems that whenever the Savior was absent, the Twelve fell into distress through lack of faith. Jesus quickly calmed their fears. Undoubtedly, the familiar sound of His voice identifying Himself reassured His disciples that they would not be harmed (Matt. 14:27; John 6:20).

After Jesus entered the boat, the turbulent wind died down (Matt. 14:32; Mark 6:51). The Twelve were completely dumbfounded over what had taken place, including the episode in which Jesus rescued Peter as he attempted to walk on the water (Matt. 14:28-31). On impulse, the disciples worshiped the Messiah, exclaiming Him to be the Son of God (vs. 33). Then perhaps in what seemed like a moment of time, the boat and all its passengers immediately reached the shore of the lake (John 6:21). The next day, the crowds who had stayed on the east side of the lake realized that there had been only one boat there. They saw that the Twelve set off in the vessel and that Jesus had not gone with them (vs. 22). Several boats from Tiberias landed near the spot where Jesus had miraculously fed thousands of people (vs. 23). (Between A.D. 18 and 22, Herod Antipas founded the city and named it after the Roman emperor, Tiberius Caesar.)

B. The Search for Jesus: vs. 24

Once the crowd realized that neither Jesus nor his disciples were there, they got into the boats and went to Capernaum in search of Jesus.

Eventually, the crowd saw that Jesus and His disciples had left. And so some of the people embarked in the boats. They used these vessels to travel across the lake. Once they reached the opposite side, they began looking for the Savior at Capernaum (John 6:24).

II. THE SON AS THE TRUE BREAD FROM HEAVEN: JOHN 6:25-35

A. The Father's Approval of the Son: vss. 25-27

When they found him on the other side of the lake, they asked him, "Rabbi, when did you get here?" Jesus answered, "I tell you the truth, you are looking for me, not because you saw miraculous signs but because you ate the loaves and had your fill. Do not work for food that spoils, but for food that endures to eternal life, which the Son of Man will give you. On him God the Father has placed his seal of approval."

Once the people found Jesus, they asked when He had arrived (John 6:25). In addition to those who had witnessed the multiplication of bread and fish, others from Capernaum also likely showed up. After they heard what Jesus had done the previous day, they probably wanted to see Him perform the same kind of miracle for them (see the demand of the crowd recorded in vs. 30). Though Capernaum was

Jesus' headquarters during His Galilean ministry, and though Peter and some of the other disciples had their families there, the residents of the city rejected the one who is the Son of God. Their unbelief prompted Jesus to foretell Capernaum's destruction (Matt. 11:23-24; Luke 10:15).

Jesus, who knew the hearts of all people (see John 2:24), sidestepped the issue of when He arrived on the other side of the lake. Instead, He dealt directly with the people's motives for seeking Him. Since the Redeemer had provided them with a miraculous meal, they wanted more (6:26). They were so focused on satisfying their physical needs that they did not even consider the spiritual implications of this sign. Jesus admonished them not to put a priority on obtaining material desires, which had no lasting value, but to seek eternally lasting spiritual nourishment. Jesus was speaking metaphorically of everlasting life, which He, as the Son of Man, gave to believers. He had the right to do so because God the Father had placed His seal, or mark, of approval on the Son's ministry and messianic claims (vs. 27). In ancient times, a seal, or signet, was a small engraved object that was created to produce an image in soft clay or wax. The presence of a seal on a document, container, or storage compartment guaranteed that the contents were authentic and carried the endorsement of the monarch or emperor.

B. The Necessity of Belief in the Son: vss. 28-29

Then they asked him, "What must we do to do the works God requires?" Jesus answered, "The work of God is this: to believe in the one he has sent."

The crowds misunderstood Jesus when He talked about working for the food that endures forever. They thought He meant rules and regulations they had to keep in order to earn God's favor. Thus, they wanted to know exactly what God demanded of them (John 6:28). In response, Jesus explained that the "work" (vs. 29) of God was simply to trust in His emissary, the one who is the embodiment of the Mosaic law. Faith in Him would lead to eternal life (see Eph. 2:8-9; Titus 3:5).

C. The Father's Provision of the Son: vss. 30-33

So they asked him, "What miraculous sign then will you give that we may see it and believe you? What will you do? Our forefathers ate the manna in the desert; as it is written: 'He gave them bread from heaven to eat.'" Jesus said to them, "I tell you the truth, it is not Moses who has given you the bread from heaven, but it is my Father who gives you the true bread from heaven. For the bread of God is he who comes down from heaven and gives life to the world."

Rather than entrust their eternal future to Jesus, the throng demanded to know what miracle He would perform to convince them to make such a commitment (John 6:30). Unless He could prove to them that He was greater than Moses, the famed lawgiver and leader of Israel, the crowd refused to accept Jesus' claim to be the promised Redeemer (vs. 31). This is because popular opinion among some Jews of the day was that when the Messiah came, His arrival would be accompanied by a miracle that exceeded the feat God performed in the desert on behalf of Moses.

For 40 years, God rained down heavenly food, in the form of manna, for an entire nation (see Exod. 16:4, 15; Neh. 9:15; Pss. 78:24-25; 105:40). By comparison, Jesus' one-time provision of inexpensive barley bread to a multitude of people seemed junior-grade. But in point of fact, the eternal Word performed other miraculous signs that exceeded anything ever done by Moses. This included giving sight to a man born blind (see John 9:1-7, 30-32) and restoring Lazarus to life (11:1-44). Jesus solemnly assured the crowd that it was actually God, not Moses, who gave their ancestors manna to eat (see Deut. 8:3). The latter, while the Father's genuine and gracious provision, was not meant to be an end in itself. Rather, the manna foreshadowed the ideal and eternally satisfying life now made available in the Messiah. In the fullest and most perfect way, He is the "true bread from heaven" (John 6:32). The Son came to earth to make new life available to the world (vs. 33).

D. The Son Declares Himself to Be the Bread of Life: vss. 34-35

"Sir," they said, "from now on give us this bread." Then Jesus declared, "I am the bread of life. He who comes to me will never go hungry, and he who believes in me will never be thirsty."

Despite the clarity of the Savior's explanation, the crowds misunderstood Him to be referring to literal, physical loaves of bread. They even asked Jesus to give them this source of nourishment from then on (John 6:34; see 3:4; 4:15). Jesus' response in 6:35 is the first of the seven "I am" declarations in the fourth Gospel that point to the Son's divine nature. With Exodus 3:13-15 as the contextual backdrop, the Lord Jesus revealed Himself to be the ever-present, ever-living God of Israel (see John 1:1-2; 8:58; Heb. 13:8; Rev. 1:4, 8; 4:8; 11:17; 16:5). By declaring Himself to be the "bread of life" (John 6:35), the Son revealed that only in Him can a person find the sustenance necessary to nourish one's soul. Specifically, Jesus' statement was an invitation for the crowd to place their faith in Him. All who did would never be spiritually hungry or thirsty again.

The various "I am" declarations in the fourth Gospel are accompanied by discourses. These help to contrast Jesus with the legalistic religious practices of His day, especially obsolete rituals. For example, Jesus being the Bread of life implies that He satisfies the longings of people in a way that no other person or group could ever do. His being the Good Shepherd (see John 10:11) indicates that other spiritual shepherds were untrustworthy and self-serving. Together, the "I am" declarations in the fourth Gospel make a profound theological claim for Jesus. As the fulfillment of the Mosaic law, He does not just represent the Father, but also manifests His presence in the world (1:18). Also, because Jesus is the radiance of God's glory and the exact representation of His being (Heb. 1:3), the Son can work, speak, and act as the Father's counterpart. People should direct their spiritual longing and need to Jesus because He is the eternal Word (John 1:1, 14).

Discussion Questions

1. How did the people react when Jesus miraculously fed them?
2. How did Jesus feel about the crowd's reaction to His miracle?
3. What does Jesus' claim of being the Bread of life really mean to you?
4. What are some of the futile and inadequate ways people use to nourish their souls?
5. What do you spiritually feed on each day?

Contemporary Application

In the West, bread was once something that was served with every meal. But as people have become more weight conscious, bread is often labeled as one of the villains that contribute to an unwanted wider waistline. Even though bread is still considered part of an essential food group, bread consumption is often discouraged. In Jesus' time, however, it wasn't that way. A typical Jewish family in His day woke up each morning to the smell of freshly baked bread. It was present at each meal and a dominant food item both physically and symbolically throughout Israel. A day without bread was like an entire 24-hour period without sunshine.

Thus, when Jesus told the people twice "I am the bread of life" (John 6:35, 48), He wanted them to understand that He meant, "I am an essential part of your daily life." They (and we) should not try to live a day without Jesus being an integral aspect of it. The Savior also wanted the people to realize that He was the food for their eternal existence. As He told Satan in Matthew 4:4, people do not "live on bread alone, but on every word that comes from the mouth of God." Jesus is both the divine Word (John 1:1) and the Bread of life. As the life-giving bread, He is not just imparting eternal salvation. He Himself is the gift. Thus, whoever understands that truth and receives Him by faith will not be spiritually hungry anymore.

Even if bread is no longer an essential food item in our society as it was in the time of Jesus, it still represents everything we need physically to survive. Jesus, of course, can meet those needs (see Matt. 6:31-33). But more importantly, He wants to fulfill our eternal needs. After all, we require spiritual food for our souls more than we need our daily slice of bread.

The Good Shepherd

Scripture

Background Scripture: *John 10:1-18*
Scripture Lesson: *John 10:7-18*
Key Verse: *When he has brought out all his own, he goes on ahead of them, and his sheep follow him because they know his voice.* John 10:4.
Scripture Lesson for Children: *John 10:7-18*
Key Verse for Children: *[Jesus said,] "I am the good shepherd; I know my sheep and my sheep know me."* John 10:14.

Lesson Aim

To recognize the Lord Jesus as our Shepherd and Guide.

Lesson Setting

Time: A.D. 29
Place: Jerusalem

Lesson Outline

The Good Shepherd

I. Finding Eternal Life in the Son: John 10:7-10
    A. *Jesus as the Gate of the Sheep: vs. 7*
    B. *Jesus as the Source of Salvation: vss. 8-10*
II. Experiencing the Son's Unfailing Love: John 10:11-18
    A. *Jesus as the Good Shepherd: vs. 11*
    B. *Self-Serving Leaders: vss. 12-13*
    C. *Jesus' Sacrificial Commitment: vss. 14-15*
    D. *Jesus' Other Sheep: vs. 16*
    E. *Jesus' Supreme Authority: vss. 17-18*

Introduction for Adults

Topic: *Following Good Leaders*

The young man faced a critical decision. He had been active in his church as a teenager and college student. Then he was offered an attractive position at a large company after he graduated from school. But he wondered whether he should first consider Christian ministry. He feared the risks involved and the negative opinion of others.

But then the young man heard a sermon on the meaning of discipleship that changed his thinking. He decided to follow Jesus into full-time ministry, not because the business world was wrong or evil, but because he believed the Lord's will for him lay in a different area. (Many other believers, of course, have honored God by serving Him in the business world.)

Later on, after more than 50 years of devoted service to Christ, the minister thought about God's faithfulness to him. He recognized that discipleship means trusting the Good Shepherd to take care of us, no matter what.

Introduction for Youth

Topic: *Leaders You Don't Follow*

On July 11, 2004, a two-car accident occurred in Wilmington, Delaware. One of the cars had rolled over, and the driver—an adult male—was trapped inside. Units from the Wilmington Fire Department were dispatched to the scene and worked alongside paramedics to remove and stabilize the driver. Due to the quick action of these professionals, they were able to treat the driver within 15 minutes.

Firefighters and paramedics such as these work hard every day to ensure the safety of the public. Their concern for the well-being of others reminds us of our Lord's protection of us from evil, especially leaders who are unscrupulous. As our Good Shepherd, Jesus ensures that nothing in all creation will separate us from the love of our heavenly Father (see Rom. 8:38-39).

Concepts for Children

Topic: *The Good Shepherd*

1. Jesus said He was like a good shepherd.
2. Jesus meant that He leads and protects His followers.
3. Jesus also noted that He gave His life for us on the cross.
4. Jesus knows and loves each of us.
5. We can depend on Jesus to watch over us at all times.

Lesson Commentary

I. FINDING ETERNAL LIFE IN THE SON: JOHN 10:7-10

A. Jesus as the Gate of the Sheep: vs. 7

Therefore Jesus said again, "I tell you the truth, I am the gate for the sheep."

The events recorded in John 10–12 took place in the last six months of Jesus' life. It was not long after the Jewish festival of Tabernacles (around October, A.D. 29) that Jesus declared Himself to be the Good Shepherd. Then two months later, during the festival of Dedication (around December, A.D. 29), the Son claimed to be God. Perhaps not long after that (during the winter of A.D. 29), Jesus validated His claim to be the resurrection and the life by raising His deceased friend, Lazarus, from the dead. Finally, it was six days before the Passover was about to start (in the spring of A.D. 30) that the Messiah made His triumphal entry into Jerusalem. These various episodes, in their unique ways, help establish that Jesus, especially in the temple of His body, is the reality to which the rites and rituals connected with the shrine in Jerusalem pointed.

It seems that Jesus' continued to address the same Pharisees who had questioned Him about the issue of spiritual blindness (see 9:40-41). The shabby way in which the religious leaders had treated a former blind beggar (whom Jesus had healed) called into question their ability to shepherd God's people (see vss. 28-29, 34). Sometime during Ezekiel's ministry (593–571 B.C.), the prophet censured the religious leaders of his day for the deplorable way in which they cared for the covenant community. Ezekiel declared that in the kingdom age, the sovereign Lord would shepherd His flock in a manner characterized by kindness, sensitivity, and compassion. Indeed, at that time, a ruler like David would ensure that peace, equity, and righteousness prevailed (Ezek. 34:1-31; see Ps. 80:1; Isa. 40:10-11; 56:9-12; Zech. 10:2; 11:5, 8). Scripture discloses that Jesus is the end-time Shepherd who one day restores the prosperity of the Lord's sheep (see Heb. 13:20; 1 Pet. 5:4; Rev. 7:17). In truth, Jesus is the messianic King who brings to pass all that God's spokespersons foretold in the Old Testament (see Pss. 2:6-12; 89:4, 20, 29; Isa. 9:6-7; 11:1; Jer. 23:5-6; 30:9; Hos. 3:5; Amos 9:1-15; Mic. 5:2; Luke 1:31-33).

The Pharisees who conversed with Jesus in Jerusalem in October, A.D. 29, should have readily understood the implications of His identifying Himself as a shepherd, since they would have been familiar with sheep husbandry. They grasped the importance of herding sheep into pens and protecting them from hostile forces. They appreciated the seriousness with which shepherds assumed their role as guardians over their sheep. Thus, when Jesus told His listeners to pay careful attention to His analogy of Himself as a shepherd, He wanted them to understand how He could be a shepherd to them. He wanted them to listen to His voice as the Word of God and follow His leading. Also, Jesus wanted them to know to what length He would go in caring for them and how much they could mean to Him as His sheep.

Sadly, the majority of the religious leaders of the day refused to follow the one who is the culmination of all that was prophesied in the Mosaic law (see Rom. 10:4). Consequently, they remained in spiritual blindness and condemned because of their sin. Their intent was to serve their own interests and to use their positions of leadership to exploit the masses. People became objects to promote the self-serving agendas of the religious leaders. Jesus, fully realizing this, solemnly declared in John 10:1 that not every spiritual leader who claimed to be honest and upright truly was. The Messiah used the analogy of the shepherd and his or her flock to convey His remarks. In that day, there were different kinds of sheepfolds. Evidently, Jesus was referring to a courtyard in front of a house. Such a compound was surrounded by a stone wall, which was often covered with briers for protection. There was usually only one entrance or door to the enclosure. This prevented the sheep from wandering out and also kept predators from entering in.

The Son warned His listeners against thieves and robbers who were not concerned for the welfare of the sheep, but for their own self-interest. These bandits would try to sneak into the fold through some way other than through the proper entrance, that is, the gate. Who were these thieves and robbers to whom Jesus was referring? Since the Messiah had recently told some experts in the law that they remained guilty of sin, His listeners undoubtedly included these leaders among the thieves. Certainly, the Pharisees had set themselves up as the shepherds of God's people, and many of them attempted to lead the people astray by turning them against Jesus. In 9:39-41, Jesus contrasted the Pharisees with the former blind beggar. Now the Son contrasted them with Himself.

Unlike thieves and robbers, the shepherd entered through the gate (10:2). Only the shepherds who guarded the sheep had the right to enter the fold through this entrance. The gatekeeper knew this, and that is why he would open the entryway for the shepherds. Much speculation has been written about who the gatekeeper in this allegory represents. For instance, some believe the individual symbolizes leaders in the church who make sure that no one but the Messiah is guiding their congregations. In fact, however, there may be no specific identity necessarily intended. In any case, the sheep recognize the voice of their shepherd, who calls them by their names (vs. 3).

Since a pen often enclosed several herds of sheep, each shepherd had a unique name for calling his or her sheep from among the other animals. The shepherd would not only bring them out of the pen, but also go ahead of them (vs. 4). A good shepherd in Palestine never drove his or her sheep from behind, but trained the animals to follow by listening to the shepherd's voice. On the other hand, if a stranger tried to call the sheep, they would panic at the sound of his or her voice (vs. 5). Jesus' listeners should have understood His parable, but most of them did not. If they were truly His sheep, they would have recognized His voice and followed Him. Their spiritual deafness prevented them from comprehending what He was trying to teach them (vs. 6).

Jesus resumed His discourse with another allegorical statement: "I am the gate for the sheep" (vs. 7). This is the third of the Son's "I am" statements recorded in the fourth Gospel. Some sheep pens did not have a gate, and the shepherd would serve as the door by lying across the opening. This not only kept the sheep inside the fold, but also kept out potential intruders. In addition, a good shepherd inspected his or her sheep at the gate and tended to their needs and wounds. The Son of God was declaring that He constantly looked out for His sheep, checked for injuries, and was ready to heal them.

B. Jesus as the Source of Salvation: vss. 8-10

"All who ever came before me were thieves and robbers, but the sheep did not listen to them. I am the gate; whoever enters through me will be saved. He will come in and go out, and find pasture. The thief comes only to steal and kill and destroy; I have come that they may have life, and have it to the full."

In Jesus' day, the raising and breeding of domestic sheep was a major part of the local economy. Indeed, wealth was often defined in terms of how large a flock one owned. Local residents used sheep to provide meat, wool, and milk. They made arrowheads, needles, scrapers, and lances from the bones of these animals. They also made curtains, leather, and clothing from sheep hides. Even the horns of sheep were valuable for use as musical instruments and containers for olive oil. City dwellers often kept a small number of animals that they grazed outside the city walls and brought home with them at night or left under guard in protected sheep-folds. In contrast, the flocks of tent dwellers were cared for by family members or by shepherds hired for the job.

The necessities of the task meant that shepherds often lived apart from cities and villages. Alone or with a small group of other shepherds, they were people of the outdoors who were responsible for caring for themselves as well as their flocks. Some, such as the part-time hirelings, could be irresponsible in times of threat or danger. The positive biblical pictures of a shepherd focus on those who care for the welfare of their animals. In addition to finding adequate shelter for the sheep, the best shepherds also had to lead them to good pasturelands and ample supplies of water. Knowing that their flocks were easy prey, shepherds spent part of their time warding off attacks from savage animals. If necessary, shepherds were willing to risk their own lives to ensure the safety of the flock. Perhaps these caretakers are the reason why, throughout the ancient world, the concept of "shepherd" was a recognized image or title for a nation's leader.

In Jesus' analogy of the shepherd and the sheep, He emphasized that as the one gate to the fold, He is the person who determines who can enter into God's kingdom. There is no other way into the Father's fold except through faith in the Son (John 10:9). Other people who claimed to represent the Father had preceded the Son, but they were thieves and robbers (vs. 8). They had distorted the truth and, consciously or unconsciously, tried to take God's people from His fold. Jesus was not talking about the Hebrew prophets of the Old Testament era, but about the aberrant religious hierarchy of His day. Furthermore, thieves have only one goal on their minds—to get what they want regardless of the destruction it causes. With Jesus at the gate, however, not only is the flock protected, but the needs of the sheep are also met (vs. 10). Expressed differently, only in the Messiah is the abundant, deeply satisfying life made available.

II. EXPERIENCING THE SON'S UNFAILING LOVE: JOHN 10:11-18

A. Jesus as the Good Shepherd: vs. 11

"I am the good shepherd. The good shepherd lays down his life for the sheep."

In John 10:11, Jesus declared, "I am the good shepherd." This is the fourth of His "I am" statements recorded in the fourth Gospel. When the Son said He was "the good shepherd," He portrayed Himself as the ancient Hebrews viewed God (see Gen. 48:15; 49:24; Pss. 23:1; 28:9; 78:52; Jer. 23:1-3; Ezek. 34:12, 15). The Messiah was not only identifying Himself as God, but also distinguishing a particular characteristic of Himself as God. As the nobleminded and trustworthy Shepherd, Jesus promised to sacrifice Himself for His sheep.

Jesus' statements are like an extended parable that reveal the loving and gracious heart of God. In Bible times, Jewish teachers often told stories called parables to illustrate whatever moral principle they were trying to communicate. These parables might have one central point or include several points of comparison. Sometimes spokespersons for God would tell a parable or a riddle that hearers would understand only if they had the key to the interpretation. Thus, with some parables the details had symbolic significance. This teaching device was a way of encouraging the faithful to consider deeply the spokesperson's words and to separate out the uncommitted. The stories conveyed truth to attentive hearers who were eager to understand. At the same time, the figurative language veiled truth from persons who did not want to believe it, such as the religious elite of Jesus' day (see Matt. 13:10-17; Mark 4:10-12; Luke 8:9-10).

B. Self-Serving Leaders: vss. 12-13

"The hired hand is not the shepherd who owns the sheep. So when he sees the wolf coming, he abandons the sheep and runs away. Then the wolf attacks the flock and scatters it. The man runs away because he is a hired hand and cares nothing for the sheep."

In contrast to the Lord Jesus, hired hands would not risk their lives for the sheep. They fulfilled their duties of caring for the flock, not out of concern for them, but for their own self-interest—that is, the wages they were paid. If a wolf threatened to assault the sheep, the hirelings would not endanger themselves, but would instead abandon the flock and flee for safety (John 10:12). Consequently, the wolf would be able to attack and disperse the sheep (vs. 12). Jesus' disapproval of the hired hand's response contrasts with other views of the day. For example, the Mishnah (a major work of rabbinic Judaism) taught that the hired shepherd was required to defend the sheep if only one wolf attacked. If more than one wolf struck, however, the hireling would not be blamed for abandoning the sheep.

C. Jesus' Sacrificial Commitment: vss. 14-15

"I am the good shepherd; I know my sheep and my sheep know me—just as the Father knows me and I know the Father—and I lay down my life for the sheep."

Once more, Jesus said He is "the good shepherd" (John 10:14). The knowledge that Jesus has of His sheep and they of Him goes beyond mere recognition. They have an intimate familiarity with each other in the same way the heavenly Father and His Son know each other (vs. 15). In fact, the love and concern Jesus has for each one of His sheep is so great that He willingly laid down His life for all of them.

D. Jesus' Other Sheep: vs. 16

"I have other sheep that are not of this sheep pen. I must bring them also. They too will listen to my voice, and there shall be one flock and one shepherd."

Jesus made it clear that His sacrificial act would include not only Jewish believers but Gentile believers as well. His current followers composed His present flock, but later Gentiles would also hear His summons to salvation and become His disciples. When this occurred, there would not be two flocks under one shepherd—that is, a Jewish-Christian church and a Gentile-Christian church—but one united flock shepherded by the Messiah (John 10:16; see John 3:16-17; 11:52; 17:20-23; 1 Cor. 12:13; Gal. 3:28; Eph. 2:11-22; 3:6; 1 Pet. 2:4-5, 9-10).

E. Jesus' Supreme Authority: vss. 17-18

"The reason my Father loves me is that I lay down my life—only to take it up again. No one takes it from me, but I lay it down of my own accord. I have authority to lay it down and authority to take it up again. This command I received from my Father."

Since perfect harmony exists between what the Father wills and what the Son does, it is only natural that the Father should love His Son. But Jesus' willingness to sacrifice His life in obedience to God's plan did not cause the Father to love Him, for that love has existed from the beginning. Moreover, God's love was an expression of His approval of His Son's laying down His life—only to raise Him up from the dead. Jesus wanted it understood, however, that His death would not be forced upon Him. He would lay down His life voluntarily (John 10:18). Indeed, the Son of God had the authority—that is, the power and the right—not only to sacrifice His life but also to take it back again in resurrection. The Father Himself gave this authority to the Son (vs. 18; see John 13:1; 15:13; Acts 2:23-24; 4:27-28).

Discussion Questions

1. What sterling character qualities associated with good shepherds did Jesus spotlight for consideration?
2. Why did Jesus use the parable of the good shepherd and his flock?
3. How can Jesus be both the door (or gate) for the sheep as well as their shepherd?
4. Why would Jesus, as our Good Shepherd, sacrifice Himself for us?
5. How is the love of the Father for us demonstrated in the sacrifice of His Son on the cross?

Contemporary Application

Imagine a sheep named Eunice who had a shepherd whom she knew to be good and kind, always taking excellent care of her. There were times, however, when Eunice would begin to doubt the shepherd's abilities and his intentions for her.

For instance, Eunice hated it when the shepherd led her up long, steep slopes. She would get so tired and leg weary. Of course, the shepherd made frequent stops so Eunice could rest, and he would come to speak softly to her and check her for injury. Nonetheless, the walk was tough, and it almost always peeved Eunice that the shepherd would require her to make such a journey at all. There were even times she became so irritated that she would refuse to get up from her resting spot. Eunice had to admit, though, that there was always something worthwhile at the end of these long treks—a green pasture, a pool of clear water, or a safe place for a peaceful night's rest.

A host of dangers regularly threatened the flock. Wolves and lions lurked, razor-sharp briers could cut or tear skin, and even the sheep's own unwise decisions could bring disaster to themselves or to the whole flock. Eunice knew that she need not be terrified by any of these things, for the shepherd was well able to defend his sheep from predators and bind up their wounds.

Sometimes, however, Eunice got careless. Months of peace and safety would lull her into holding the false notion that just having the shepherd nearby was enough to keep harm away. One time she nearly walked into a rushing river. The shepherd rescued her with the crook of his staff. From that day on, each time Eunice spied the shepherd's rod and staff, a wave of comfort would roll over her.

This week's lesson reminds us just how much we have to be grateful for when the Lord Jesus is the one tending our lives. As we feel our gratitude toward the Savior for His care, we should not hold back or shy away from expressing our thankfulness to Him. He loves to hear our praise and know that we enjoy and appreciate His provision for our lives.

The Resurrection and the Life

Scripture

Background Scripture: *John 11:1-27*

Scripture Lesson: *John 11:17-27*

Key Verse: *Jesus said to [Martha], "I am the resurrection and the life. He who believes in me will live, even though he dies."* John 11:25.

Scripture Lesson for Children: *John 11:17-19, 32-44*

Key Verse for Children: *Jesus said to [Martha], "I am the resurrection and the life. He who believes in me will live, even though he dies."* John 11:25.

Lesson Aim

To consider the implications of Jesus' claim to be the resurrection and the life.

Lesson Setting

Time: A.D. 29

Place: Bethany

Lesson Outline

The Resurrection and the Life

   I. Dealing with the Tragedy of Death: John 11:17-19
      A. *The News of the Death of Lazarus: vs. 17*
      B. *The Comforting Presence of Friends: vss. 18-19*
  II. Accepting the Truth of Jesus' Claims: John 11:20-27
      A. *Martha's Confidence in Jesus: vss. 20-22*
      B. *Martha's Belief in the Resurrection: vss. 23-24*
      C. *Jesus' Declaration Concerning Himself: vss. 25-26*
      D. *Martha's Affirmation of Faith: vs. 27*

Introduction for Adults

Topic: *Life That Does Not End*

Why does time seem to drag on when we're waiting for something important like a surgeon's report? Waiting often tests our faith in and commitment to God.

Consider Mary and Martha. Their patience was tested through days of waiting for Jesus. When He finally came, it looked as if it was too late, for their brother Lazarus had already died and was buried. Then the bereaved sisters told Jesus that had He come earlier, He could have prevented the tragedy from happening.

Like Mary and Martha, how many times have we said "If only" to God? "If only" is the antithesis of trust and obedience. If we live with regrets or harbor resentment against God, we cannot enjoy spiritual wellness and unending new life He offers.

Scripture tells us that God acts on our behalf according to His will, love, and wisdom (Rom. 8:28). Thus, it never pays to second-guess God's timing. This means Jesus never arrives too late to help us. We can rest assured that He will do what is best for us in His perfect will.

Introduction for Youth

Topic: *Life That Doesn't End*

The restoring of Lazarus to life was the most powerful miracle of Jesus recorded in the Gospel of John. This close friend of the Savior had truly died. And Jesus, out of His great love for Lazarus, brought him back from the grave.

Perhaps the greatest miracle, however, is being born again. After all, before coming to faith in Christ, we were spiritually dead and condemned because of our sins. We obeyed Satan rather than God, and followed the passions of our evil nature rather than the desires of the Spirit (Eph. 2:1-3).

But because the Father is rich in mercy and loves us greatly, He gave us new life through faith in His Son. We have been identified with Jesus' death, burial, and resurrection. In fact, God sees us as being seated with Jesus in the heavenly realms (vss. 4-6). Now that is what it means to be alive again!

Concepts for Children

Topic: *He Lives Again*

1. Lazarus, a close friend of Jesus, had died, and his friends were sad.
2. The sisters of Lazarus—Mary and Martha—wondered why it took so long for Jesus to come to them.
3. When Jesus finally came, He brought Lazarus back to life.
4. From this miracle we see that Jesus has power over death.
5. When we trust in Jesus, He forgives our sins and gives us new life.

Lesson Commentary

I. DEALING WITH THE TRAGEDY OF DEATH: JOHN 11:17-19

A. The News of the Death of Lazarus: vs. 17

On his arrival, Jesus found that Lazarus had already been in the tomb for four days.

John 11 narrates the episode involving the death of Lazarus and Jesus' restoration of him to life. Verse 1 states that Lazarus lived in Bethany with his sisters, Mary and Martha. The village was located on the east side of the Mount of Olives, along the road leading toward Jericho. Somehow Lazarus became ill, and his condition worsened to the point that Mary and Martha turned to Jesus for help (vs. 3). The sisters undoubtedly had seen Him perform many miracles. They were convinced of Jesus' ability to help Lazarus. The message to the Savior most likely took about a day to reach Him. He, in turn, remained in Bethany two more days (vs. 6), and it probably took about a day for Jesus and His disciples to reach Bethany. It may be that Lazarus died before the messenger reached Jesus. If so, this explains how Lazarus could have been in the grave for four days (vs. 17).

Most likely, Jesus sensed His disciples' concern for Lazarus and for this reason gave them an explanation that both reassured and puzzled them. First, the Messiah sought to allay the fears of the Twelve by noting that the illness would not "end in death" (vs. 4). Jesus did not mean that Lazarus would not physically die, but that the end of his condition would be life, not death. Second, Jesus explained that both He and the Father would be glorified in the situation. Third, Jesus did not rush off to Bethany in a panic. Instead, He stayed where He was for two more days (vs. 6). One reason for this delay is that the Son operated according to the Father's timetable, not the timetables of people. A second reason is that the delay would ensure Lazarus had been dead long enough to prevent others from either misinterpreting the miracle as a fraud or as merely a resuscitation.

Jesus must have surprised His disciples by announcing that He was setting out for Bethany, which was in the province of Judea (vs. 7). The choice was theirs as to whether they would accompany Him despite the peril that awaited. When the Twelve voiced concern for Jesus' safety, He responded with an adage probably common at the time, but that had added meaning coming from Him (vs. 8). During the winter season, there were typically 12 hours of daylight. With this in mind, the Redeemer spoke of walking in the light and in the darkness. People who walk in the light do not stumble, because they can see, but people who walk in the darkness stumble because they cannot see. This is not only true with regard to physical conditions, but also true with regard to a person's spiritual journey. As long as the Son operated in the Father's will, no harm would come to Jesus. Similarly, only those who walk with the Messiah, the light of the world, can see and avoid stumbling (vss. 9-10).

Next, Jesus explained that Lazarus had "fallen asleep" (vs. 11), which was a euphemistic reference to death (see Gen. 47:30; Matt. 27:52; Mark 5:39; Acts 7:60; 1 Cor. 15:51; 1 Thess. 4:13). Jesus also stated that He was going to Bethany so that He could wake up Lazarus. The disciples took Jesus to mean that Lazarus was literally sleeping, and so they were confused (John 11:13). In their minds, if Lazarus were sleeping, that meant he would also get better on his own (vs. 12). Realizing His disciples' confusion, Jesus stated plainly that Lazarus had died (vs. 14). The Son of God again demonstrated His supernatural power to know things beyond normal human ability. Then He explained that this incident would give His followers another opportunity to believe in Him (vs. 15).

If Jesus had been with Lazarus during the final moments of his life and healed him of his sickness, the opportunity for an even greater miracle would have been lost. Jesus intended to use the death of Lazarus as an occasion to demonstrate His power over death to the disciples and others. This was not a trivial desire on the part of the Savior. He knew that His closest followers needed their faith in Him clarified, matured, and strengthened.

Consider, for example, the dialogue between Martha and Jesus, which is recorded in verses 17-27. Despite Jesus' statement that Lazarus would rise again, Martha failed to grasp what He was saying. Instead, she affirmed a more general theological truth about the resurrection of the righteous. Even when Jesus plainly declared Himself to be "the resurrection and the life" (vs. 25), Martha still could not quite understand what this meant for Lazarus. Though Martha affirmed Jesus' messiahship (vs. 27), she remained unaware of the fact that Jesus would restore Lazarus to life. Furthermore, Martha's sister, Mary, and their friends remained just as oblivious to the truth of what Jesus said He would do for Lazarus (vss. 28-37).

Verse 16 records the statement made by Thomas, who was also called Didymus. Both names literally mean the "twin" (see Matt. 10:3; Mark 3:18; Luke 6:15; Acts 1:13). It is not known whom this disciple's twin sibling might have been (whether a brother or sister). Thomas was also known as the doubter because he initially refused to accept the testimony of the other disciples concerning the risen Lord (see John 20:24-29). In the episode involving Lazarus, Thomas challenged his peers to go with Jesus back to Judea, where death seemed imminent for all of them (vs. 16). This is the first time John mentioned Thomas. His comment shows his leadership and courage, even though he struggled with doubts.

After Jesus and His group arrived in Bethany, they learned that four days earlier the body of Lazarus had been placed in a tomb (vs. 17). Since a dead body decayed quickly in the hot local climate, the family of Lazarus would have had his body anointed, wrapped, and laid in the family tomb soon after he had expired. The four days is significant in that Jesus would not have reached His friend while he was still alive, even if the Savior had left Perea immediately after hearing about the illness of Lazarus. The delay was to assure, in the minds of the people, that the raising of Lazarus from the dead was truly a miracle.

B. The Comforting Presence of Friends: vss. 18-19

Bethany was less than two miles from Jerusalem, and many Jews had come to Martha and Mary to comfort them in the loss of their brother.

Since Jerusalem was no more than a few miles from Bethany (John 11:18), a number of Jews from the city paid their respects to Martha and Mary during their time of grief (vs. 19). Evidently, this family had a commanding influence or was popular among the local people. The proximity between Bethany and Jerusalem indicates that news of the miracle would have circulated quickly throughout the holy city.

II. ACCEPTING THE TRUTH OF JESUS' CLAIMS: JOHN 11:20-27

A. Martha's Confidence in Jesus: vss. 20-22

When Martha heard that Jesus was coming, she went out to meet him, but Mary stayed at home. "Lord," Martha said to Jesus, "if you had been here, my brother would not have died. But I know that even now God will give you whatever you ask."

When the sisters of Lazarus heard that Jesus was approaching their village, Martha went out to greet Him, while Mary remained in the house (John 11:20). On the surface, Martha's first words to Jesus appear to be a veiled rebuke (vs. 21). After all, she previously scolded Jesus for her sister's apparent idleness (see Luke 10:40). Martha, however, probably knew that Jesus could not come in time to heal her brother of his illness. Thus Martha's comment was more likely an expression of regret that Jesus could not be present, a feeling the sisters probably spoke about quite often during the previous four days.

Martha's next remark might be interpreted as a sign of a remarkable faith in Jesus' power to raise people from the dead (John 11:22). Later, however, Martha was the one who complained when Jesus ordered the stone to be removed from the entrance to the tomb of Lazarus (see vs. 39). It is possible that Martha was merely noting that she still had faith in Jesus, for Martha was certain that God granted Jesus whatever request He asked (vs. 22).

B. Martha's Belief in the Resurrection: vss. 23-24

Jesus said to her, "Your brother will rise again." Martha answered, "I know he will rise again in the resurrection at the last day."

The Savior declared to Martha that her brother would rise from the dead (John 11:23). In turn, Martha showed that she had not thought about Jesus' bringing Lazarus back to life at that time. Instead, Martha voiced the view of the Pharisees that God would resurrect the just at the last day (vs. 24; see Isa. 26:19; Dan. 12:2; Matt. 22:23; Acts 23:7-8). Jesus' statement may have been said to Martha and her sister many times by others to comfort them, and now it may have sounded hollow to her.

C. Jesus' Declaration Concerning Himself: vss. 25-26

Jesus said to her, "I am the resurrection and the life. He who believes in me will live, even though he dies; and whoever lives and believes in me will never die. Do you believe this?"

Jesus' response to Martha is incredible. He could have said that He would resurrect Lazarus. Instead, Jesus asserted, "I am the resurrection and the life" (John 11:25). His declaration is the fifth of seven "I am" statements that highlight His divinity and messiahship. Jesus, in fact, is the life of the age to come, and all who put their trust in Him will experience the resurrected life (vs. 26).

When Jesus asked Martha whether she believed what He was saying, He was actually asking her whether she believed in Him. The Messiah wanted her (and all other people) to begin experiencing right now the joys of eternal life. The raising of Lazarus was intended to foster such faith in the Son of God. And the apostle's inclusion of this miracle in the fourth Gospel was designed to encourage people down through the ages to put their trust in Jesus as the Messiah (see 20:30-31).

D. Martha's Affirmation of Faith: vs. 27

"Yes, Lord," she told him, "I believe that you are the Christ, the Son of God, who was to come into the world."

Regardless of Martha's fretful nature, she had amazing faith in Jesus. Martha not only replied positively but was also clear about what she believed—that Jesus is the Messiah, God's only divine Son. Furthermore, Martha affirmed that Jesus left heaven and entered the world by becoming a human being (John 11:27). Few, if any, could have affirmed the Son any better than Martha. Her confession of faith parallels that voiced by Peter (see Matt. 16:16). Then Martha left Jesus outside her village and went back home and told Mary that the Teacher wanted to see her (John 11:28). Naturally, Mary took Jesus' request as a command and hurried to the place where Martha had conversed with Him.

Mary was in such a rush to comply that her Jewish comforters took notice and followed her. They assumed that she was going to continue her mourning at her brother's tomb and thought they would join in her grieving (vss. 29-31). Although Mary's words are almost identical to her sister's first words to Jesus, her actions departed dramatically from Martha's. Mary fell at the feet of the Lord Jesus in homage to Him and wept as she spoke (vs. 32). Mary, too, believed Jesus had the power to heal her brother of his illness, but now it was apparently too late.

The Messiah eventually arrived at the tomb where the body of Lazarus had been placed. Verse 33 says that at the sight of the wailing, Jesus was "deeply moved in spirit and troubled." On one level, the phrase suggests Jesus was touched with sympathy at the sight and perhaps indignant at the sorrow caused by death that sin has brought to the human condition. On another level, though, the Savior seemed agitated by the unbelief of His closest followers. The Messiah had plainly stated that He would restore Lazarus to life. Nonetheless, Martha and Mary, instead of rejoicing over what the Son was about to do, remained filled with despair over their brother's death. This attitude of unbelief and doubt is reflected in the statement made by some of the onlookers (recorded in vs. 37).

So that Jesus could demonstrate His divine power at Lazarus's tomb, He asked where the burial site was located (vs. 34). As the sisters directed Jesus to the grave, He showed His grief by crying (vs. 35). The Greek word used to describe His tears suggests a quiet mourning, not the loud wailing of the other mourners. In response to Jesus' tears, some of the bystanders noted how much He loved His friend (vs. 36), while others wondered why He had not healed Lazarus of his sickness. After all, Jesus was able to restore sight to a blind man several months earlier (vs. 37; see 9:1-7). None of the onlookers, however, were anticipating the awesome display of glory that was about to take place in their presence. God's glory often shines brightest when circumstances seem like they could not be more dark.

One can only imagine the emotions the Son felt as He approached the tomb of Lazarus, a cave with a stone rolled across its entrance (11:38). In Jesus' day, people used caves carved in the limestone rock of a hillside as tombs. These graves were large enough for people to walk inside, and a tomb could hold several corpses. Martha did not understand why Jesus would want the stone removed from the tomb's entrance. She noted that after four days the smell from the decomposing corpse of Lazarus would be terrible (vs. 39). The Messiah, ever patient in the midst of such confusion, stated once again that if Martha had faith, she would witness the glory of God (for example, in Jesus' restoring Lazarus to life; vs. 40).

Unlike the Egyptians, the Jews neither tightly wrapped the body of the deceased nor embalmed it. Instead, they loosely wrapped the body in linen cloth and added spices between the layers and folds. The aromatic spices helped to counteract (but not completely eliminate) the objectionable odors resulting from the decomposition of the corpse. One can only imagine the bewilderment and skepticism among the onlookers. Though Jesus' command to remove the stone from the tomb of Lazarus seemed to go against common sense, it was done anyway (vs. 41).

The prayer voiced by the Son, which is recorded in verses 41 and 42, is not so much a petition as it is an expression of thanksgiving to the Father. The Anointed One knew in advance that the Father would grant His request, and so the Redeemer gave thanks for this. Jesus declared in the hearing of the onlookers that the Father always answered His requests. Jesus stated this openly, not for His own benefit, but rather for the sake of the bystanders. It was His desire that in seeing the miracle, they would believe His claim to be the Messiah. In restoring Lazarus to life, Jesus would prove that He is the master of death. Ironically, though, this miracle would set in motion a series of events that would lead directly to His arrest and eventual execution. Yet even in the Son's crucifixion, both He and the Father would be glorified (see 17:1, 5).

When Jesus had finished praying, He simply and directly commanded Lazarus to exit from the tomb (11:43). In one sense, this served as a preview of the power of the Son that will be fully displayed in the final resurrection when all who have died will hear His voice and live (see 5:25, 28-29). Lazarus, who had been unquestionably dead, came out of the tomb. His hands and feet were still wrapped with strips of burial cloth, and a separate cloth covered his face. Next, Jesus told the people to unwrap the burial clothes and headcloth from Lazarus and let him go (11:44). By doing this, they would know that Lazarus was truly alive and that his appearance was not merely a magic trick.

Discussion Questions

1. Upon Jesus' arrival at Bethany, what did the people report to Him?
2. How did others reach out to the bereaved in their time of loss?
3. What was Martha's initial response to Jesus upon seeing Him? How do you think you would have responded?
4. How did Martha convey a clear and strong faith in Jesus?
5. In what sense is Jesus "the resurrection and the life" (John 11:25) to you?

Contemporary Application

The raising of Lazarus called forth faith from Mary and Martha, and from many of the Jews who witnessed the miracle. Tragically, however, it angered the religious leaders and convinced them that Jesus had to be executed. When people consider Jesus today, some are so impressed that they give themselves fully to Him in faith. Others, however, do not take Him and His miracles seriously. They do not believe that He is the one and only source of eternal life.

One of the great values of trusting in Jesus is finding Him to be a real person who invites us to cast all our cares upon Him. We know that He identifies with our sorrows. When we suffer the loss of a loved one we know that Jesus understands how we feel.

Christians have a sure hope in the face of sickness and death, and people need to hear about our faith and hope. One of the best ways is to invite them to study the life of Jesus. He prayed that people would believe in Him because He restored Lazarus to life. When we invite people to consider the miracles that Jesus performed, we give them an opportunity to believe and be saved.

Like Mary and Martha, we can become sad and distraught when events don't turn out the way we'd hoped. But God works in mysterious ways. From the human point of view, all appeared to be lost when Lazarus died. But then Jesus reversed the situation by restoring Lazarus to life. This episode would only be eclipsed by Jesus' resurrection from the dead.

The Messiah's resurrection is a promise of our own resurrection and our own victory over sin, suffering, and death. Though our ultimate victory will be realized when we one day join the Lord Jesus in heaven, we can also be victors here on earth. It's possible because the focus of our faith is on Jesus and we are remaining faithful to God's will.

The Way, Truth, and Life

Scripture

Background Scripture: *John 14:1-14*

Scripture Lesson: *John 14:1-14*

Key Verse: *Jesus answered, "I am the way and the truth and the life. No one comes to the Father except through me."* John 14:6.

Scripture Lesson for Children: *John 14:1-14*

Key Verse for Children: *Jesus answered, "I am the way and the truth and the life. No one comes to the Father except through me."* John 14:6.

Lesson Aim

To emphasize that Jesus is the only way to the Father.

Lesson Setting

Time: A.D. 30
Place: Jerusalem

Lesson Outline

The Way, Truth, and Life

  I. The Way to the Father: John 14:1-7
      A. *The Exhortation to Trust in Jesus: vs. 1*
      B. *The Promise of Spending Eternity with Jesus: vss. 2-4*
      C. *The Reminder about Jesus Being the Only Way: vss. 5-7*
  II. The Father and the Son: John 14:8-14
      A. *Seeing the Father through the Son: vss. 8-9*
      B. *Unity between the Father and the Son: vss. 10-11*
      C. *Greater Works through Faith in the Son: vss. 12-14*

Introduction for Adults

Topic: *Finding Direction for Life*

For people who are blind or visually impaired, daily tasks that others don't even think about can be a real challenge. That's why at its inception, the concept of a guide dog was revolutionary. The seeing-eye dog has helped to enhance the independence, dignity, and self-confidence of people who are blind by enabling them to travel safely and independently.

In the spiritual realm, we are all born blind. Left on our own, we would stumble about in the darkness of sin. Thankfully, the Father has sent His Son to be our spiritual guide. Only He can lead us in paths of righteousness and help us avoid the pitfalls of sin.

Introduction for Youth

Topic: *No Other Way!*

A Global Positioning System (GPS) uses satellites to help people navigate through unfamiliar territory. The GPS is extremely accurate in letting users know their precise location and the direction in which they should head to reach their destination. The system remains effective even in the worst weather conditions.

Just as military and civilian users rely on the GPS to help them get from one locale to the next, so too Jesus is the believers' spiritual "compass" pointing them to God. In addition, the Son is the only pathway to the Father. Moreover, divine truth and eternal life can only be found in the Savior. Indeed, He alone is the hope of teens.

Concepts for Children

Topic: *Jesus Gives True Life*

1. Jesus encouraged His followers not to worry but to put their faith in Him.
2. Jesus was returning to heaven to prepare a dwelling place for His followers.
3. Jesus is the way to the Father as well as the source of truth and life.
4. Jesus makes the Father known to believers.
5. When we belong to Jesus, He will do great things through us.

Lesson Commentary

I. THE WAY TO THE FATHER: JOHN 14:1-7

A. The Exhortation to Trust in Jesus: vs. 1

"Do not let your hearts be troubled. Trust in God; trust also in me."

The Last Supper is the next event spotlighted in John's Gospel. During this final meal, Jesus demonstrated what it truly means to be a servant. Even though He was the Son of God, He humbled Himself by washing the feet of His disciples. The act was so deferential that at first Peter refused to allow the Lord to wash his feet. Jesus told Peter and the others that unless this was done, He could not accept them as one of His own. After washing their feet, Jesus explained that He had set an example for them. In particular, it was symbolic of how they were to serve one another (13:1-17).

At Jesus' last supper with His closest disciples, the Lord spoke at length about the purpose of His earthly ministry and their responsibilities as His chosen apostles. Jesus also warned that one of their number would betray Him and said that He was about to depart from them. In particular, Jesus noted Peter's denials, which probably further disturbed the disciples. Although they had proclaimed their faithfulness to Him, Jesus knew that they would falter during His darkest hour. They would need some comforting words to look back on. In difficult circumstances, it is often helpful to look to the words of Jesus as a source of encouragement.

The Savior began by urging His disciples to calm their troubled hearts. The way to do this was to put their trust in the Father as well as in the Son. John's use of the Greek verb rendered "trust" (John 14:1) can be interpreted in many ways. It would not be surprising if the apostle intended multiple meanings to enrich Jesus' exhortation. Here are possible renderings of John verse 1b: two commands—"Believe in God, believe also in me"; two statements—"You believe in God, you also believe in me"; a statement followed by a command—"You believe in God, believe also in me"; a command followed by a statement—"Believe in God, you also believe in me"; a question followed by a command—"Do you believe in God? Believe also in me"; and a statement followed by a question—"You believe in God. Do you also believe in me?"

In any case, it is remarkable that Jesus focused on comforting His followers rather than dealing with His own needs. The treachery of Judas and the fickleness of the rest of the disciples did not prevent the Savior from remaining a calming presence among them. He proved once again to be the ultimate source of peace.

B. The Promise of Spending Eternity with Jesus: vss. 2-4

"In my Father's house are many rooms; if it were not so, I would have told you. I am going there to prepare a place for you. And if I go and prepare a place for you, I will come back and take you to be with me that you also may be where I am. You know the way to the place where I am going."

Jesus spoke about heaven, perhaps to further ease the minds of His followers. He referred to heaven as a large house, belonging to His Father and having plenty of room. Though Jesus was leaving the disciples, He was going there to prepare a place for them. Jesus told the disciples that if this were not so, He would not have made this promise to them (John 14:2). The pledge, however, was true. And so the disciples could count on Jesus one day returning to bring them back with Him to heaven (vs. 3). This promise of being reunited with the Savior would be fulfilled no matter what happened to Him or to them. Throughout Jesus' public ministry He had been teaching these disciples what it meant to be His followers. Now He told them that they should know the way to where He was going. As they followed that way, they would end up there with Him (vs. 4). No matter how rough the path, believers can always look forward to their final destination, knowing Jesus is there waiting for them.

C. The Reminder about Jesus Being the Only Way: vss. 5-7

Thomas said to him, "Lord, we don't know where you are going, so how can we know the way?" Jesus answered, "I am the way and the truth and the life. No one comes to the Father except through me. If you really knew me, you would know my Father as well. From now on, you do know him and have seen him."

Thomas openly expressed his confusion. He was probably speaking for the other disciples as well. They did not know where Jesus was going, and they did not know the way (John 14:5). After all, how could they? Had not Jesus already said that where He was going, they could not come (see 13:33)? They understandably were dumbfounded. Jesus' reply to Thomas is the most profound "I am" declaration in the fourth Gospel. Jesus not only identified who He was, but made it clear that He is the only possible path to God (14:6). When Thomas asked Jesus the way, Jesus did not hand him a road map and give him directions. Jesus told all of them that He Himself is the way to God. In a few hours some of His followers would see Jesus hanging on a cross and would wonder how this could be true. After His resurrection, they would understand that as the one who died for their sins, He is the only link between God and repentant sinners.

Today, when many nonbelievers are told that Jesus is the only way to God, they are deeply offended. Accusations of bigotry, narrow-mindedness, and arrogance toward those who believe this abound. Nevertheless, there simply is no other path to God. Despite all the lies that were charged against Jesus during His public career and since, Jesus' words, deeds, and character have shown Him to be the embodiment of truth. Nothing He ever taught has proved unreliable. In Him we see the truth of God in action. And what better proof of knowing that Jesus is the life than His spectacular resurrection. Indeed, only Jesus has the power over life and death. Previously, Jesus' disciples had not fully known Him. They had seen glimpses of His true identity and had a partial understanding of who He was—but they had not fully experienced Him. If they had, they would have known that they were seeing what God the Father is like by seeing the Son. In the coming days, however, they would know Jesus and thus they would know God (vs. 7).

II. THE FATHER AND THE SON: JOHN 14:8-14

A. Seeing the Father through the Son: vss. 8-9

Philip said, "Lord, show us the Father and that will be enough for us." Jesus answered: "Don't you know me, Philip, even after I have been among you such a long time? Anyone who has seen me has seen the Father. How can you say, 'Show us the Father'?"

Centuries before the time of the Redeemer, Moses made one of the boldest requests ever petitioned before God: "Now show me your glory" (Exod. 33:18). The word "glory," when used of God, refers to the radiant display of His person, that is, His glorious revelation of Himself to humanity. This definition is borne out by the many ways the word is used in Scripture. For example, brilliant light consistently accompanied the divine manifestation (see Matt. 17:2; 1 Tim. 6:16; Rev. 1:16).

Since no human being can see God in His full glory and live, what Moses requested was more than the Lord would grant—for Moses' own good. Nevertheless, God did agree to place Moses in a crevice and then cause His glory to pass by (Exod. 33:19-23). What actually occurred during Moses' encounter with the glory of God? As a human being, Moses could not stare directly into the glory of God Himself. To do so would be fatal. So God protected Moses from accidentally viewing His glory by placing His hand over Moses' face until His glory had passed by.

It was only after God's glory had passed by that He removed His protecting hand. At that moment Moses caught a glimpse of God's back. But what does this mean? Did Moses actually see the back of God? From other passages we know that God is spirit (John 4:24) and, as such, is invisible (Col. 1:15). Also, the Hebrew word translated "back" (Exod. 33:23) carries connotations of "aftereffects." So what Moses saw was probably a manifestation of God and His glory. And yet Moses did not see God's glory directly. But once it had gone past him, God allowed him to view the results—the afterglow—that His glorious presence had produced.

This incident was a vivid reminder to the Jews of Jesus' day that it was impossible to see God directly and survive. The Messiah's disciples probably shared the same apprehension about seeing God. Thus, when Philip asked Jesus to show the Father to them, Philip was likely making a request to see God in the same way Moses had. If Jesus could do that for them, they would be satisfied and it would end any doubts they had (John 14:8).

Jesus was disappointed that Philip still did not understand His statement about knowing and seeing God (see vs. 7). The disciples had spent nearly three years with the Son. There was no need for Philip or any of them to ask Him to show them the Father. If they truly knew the Lord Jesus, they would have known that to see Him was to see the Father's divine nature (vs. 9). Later New Testament writers made similar affirmations. For instance Paul stated that the incarnate Son was "in very nature God" (Phil. 2:6) as well as the "image of the invisible God" (Col. 1:15). Moreover, in the Messiah "all the fullness of the Deity lives in bodily form" (2:9). And according to Hebrews 1:3, "the Son is radiance of God's glory and the exact representation of his being."

B. Unity between the Father and the Son: vss. 10-11

"Don't you believe that I am in the Father, and that the Father is in me? The words I say to you are not just my own. Rather, it is the Father, living in me, who is doing his work. Believe me when I say that I am in the Father and the Father is in me; or at least believe on the evidence of the miracles themselves."

Jesus continued to describe His unity with God the Father (and the Spirit) by asking His disciples whether they believed He was in the Father and the Father was in Him. Jesus was forcing His disciples to consider what would have been outrageous to the Jewish mind—that a person could be one in essence with Yahweh (the Lord)—while expecting them to believe it. In fact, Jesus' words and works were a revelation of the triune Godhead, for the Father gave the Son the words He spoke and performed through Jesus the works He did (John 14:10). There are at least three reasons why Jesus had to be fully divine. First, only someone who is the infinite God could bear the full penalty of all the sins of all who would believe in Him. Second, no mere human or creature could ever save people. Only God Himself could (see Jonah 2:9). Third, only someone who was truly and fully God could be the one mediator between God and human beings (1 Tim. 2:5), both to bring us back to God and to reveal God most fully to us (John 14:9).

Once more Jesus exhorted His disciples to believe that He is in the Father and the Father is in Him. After living with Jesus and experiencing the life He lived, they should have taken Him at His word. But even if they could not at this point, they could at least base their belief on the miraculous signs they had witnessed (vs. 11). The Messiah was presenting faith based on miracles as second best. The best foundation of faith is Jesus' proven character, especially when a wished-for miracle does not appear.

Jesus performed many miracles during His earthly ministry, some of which are not recorded in the four Gospels. His miracles were extraordinary expressions of God's power. When the Son performed a miracle, the Father directly altered, superseded, or counteracted some established pattern in the natural order. The miracles of Jesus served several purposes. First, they confirmed His claim to be the Messiah. Second, they validated the Son's assertion that He was sent by the Father and represented Him. Third, they substantiated the credibility of the truths Jesus' declared to the people of Israel. Fourth, they encouraged the doubtful to put their trust in the Son. Fifth, they demonstrated that the one who is love was willing to reach out to people with compassion and grace.

C. Greater Works through Faith in the Son: vss. 12-14

"I tell you the truth, anyone who has faith in me will do what I have been doing. He will do even greater things than these, because I am going to the Father. And I will do whatever you ask in my name, so that the Son may bring glory to the Father. You may ask me for anything in my name, and I will do it."

Jesus told the disciples that those who believed in Him would do even greater things than what He had been doing (John 14:12). Jesus certainly was not saying that they would possess greater powers than Him, nor that they would perform greater miracles. Evidently, Jesus was talking about the mighty works of conversion. Whereas Jesus' ministry was primarily confined to Galilee and Judea, they would take the Gospel to distant lands. Yet they could do none of this unless the Son first returned to the Father.

Without a doubt, the Savior knew His followers could not serve Him effectively in their own power. They would need supernatural assistance. In particular, they would need the gift promised by the Father—the Holy Spirit. When the Spirit came, the disciples would be filled with courage and the ability to witness about Jesus. Their testimony would not be confined to Jerusalem. They would take the message to the surrounding regions of Judea and Samaria, and even to the ends of the earth (Acts 1:8). They could do this knowing that the Father had given the Son all authority in heaven and earth (Matt. 28:18).

These truths notwithstanding, the essential nature of prayer in doing God's work effectively must not be forgotten. When we make our request known to God through Jesus' name, Jesus Himself will do it (John 14:13). Of course, Jesus was not providing a magical formula to be used as though one were bidding a genie to grant a wish. Nor did it mean that Jesus would always fulfill the request in the way His followers desired. Instead, Jesus was referring to requests whose primary purpose is to glorify God, and thus are in line with God's will.

Here we see that answered prayer brings honor to the Trinity. The Spirit intercedes on our behalf (Rom. 8:26), and the Son represents us as our advocate before the Father (1 John 2:1). The Father in turn works through our petitions and circumstances to bring about His will. In this regard, we know that God is able to do exceedingly more than what we could ever ask or think (Eph. 3:20). The Messiah's statements do not limit the power of prayer. Instead, they require the petitioner to make his or her request consistent with the character of the Son and in accordance with the will of the Father (John 14:14). Once we focus our requests on fulfilling the will of God, we will desire nothing less. Since we pray in Jesus' name, He promised that He will do it. Thus, Jesus will be the one who is glorifying His heavenly Father. The two not only are one, but they also bring glory to each other.

The Messiah stated that those who genuinely loved Him also kept His commands (vs. 15). As an encouragement to those who would love and obey Him, the Son promised that His disciples would have the indwelling of the Holy Spirit. The third person of the Trinity would come and make His home in believers so that their love could be clearly defined and their obedience could be carefully directed. The Son, referring to the Spirit as "another Counselor" (vs. 16), indicated that the latter is the same kind of advocate, intercessor, and comforter as the Messiah Himself was to the disciples. Expressed differently, the Spirit comes to the believers' aid to help them meet every challenge to their faith. As the Spirit of truth, He reveals the truth about God, shows what is true, and leads believers into all truth (vs. 17). In these ways, the Spirit remains ever present to help believers understand, accept, and apply what the Son commanded.

Discussion Questions

1. Why would trusting in the Lord Jesus have calmed the troubled hearts of the disciples?
2. In what sense was Jesus going to prepare a place for His disciples?
3. In what sense is Jesus the way?
4. How is it possible for us to find truth and life in Jesus?
5. How does the Godhead work together to answer our prayers?

Contemporary Application

David and Christine had never traveled overseas before. Now they were actually making plans for 10 days in western Europe, with stops in France, Belgium, Switzerland, and Germany.

David was earnestly listening to some French language tapes, trying to memorize key phrases in French (such as "Help! We're lost!"), when the doorbell rang. It was a special-delivery letter from his uncle Gabe, a missionary stationed just outside Paris. "Instead of just stopping by on your way through," Gabe wrote, "why don't you and Chrisine stay with us? We can give you the grand tour, help with the language—you don't speak French or German, do you?—and make sure nobody takes advantage of you."

David smiled in relief as he turned off the French language tape and went to share the news with his wife. Suddenly he knew the whole trip was going to be better than they had thought. With Gabe and his family as their companions, they were certain to have a great time. And even though David thought he might still try out some of his French, Gabe would be there to make sure he didn't get snails when he wanted steak.

As this week's lesson points out, Jesus knew how beneficial it can be to have a traveling companion, someone to help us make sense of what we are experiencing, empower us to try new things, comfort us when things do not work out, and lead us on the most productive path. As the way, the truth, and the life (John 14:6), Jesus is our lifelong companion and guide. Indeed, apart from Him, we cannot do God's will (see 15:5).

Rules for Just Living

Scripture
Background Scripture: *Exodus 22:1–23:9*
Scripture Lesson: *Exodus 23:1-9*
Key Verse: *"Do not follow the crowd in doing wrong. When you give testimony in a lawsuit, do not pervert justice by siding with the crowd."* Exodus 23:2.
Scripture Lesson for Children: *Exodus 23:1-9*
Key Verse for Children: *Blessed are they who maintain justice, who constantly do what is right.* Psalm 106:3.

Lesson Aim
To recognize the importance of cultivating a life of justice, mercy, and integrity.

Lesson Setting
Time: 1446 B.C.
Place: Mount Sinai

Lesson Outline
Rules for Just Living
   I. Living in a Virtuous Manner: Exodus 23:1-3
      A. Being an Honest Person: vs. 1
      B. Being a Person of Integrity: vss. 2-3
  II. Living in an Upright Manner: Exodus 23:4-9
      A. Being Kind to Others: vss. 4-5
      B. Being an Advocate for Justice: vss. 6-7
      C. Refusing to Accept a Bribe: vs. 8
      D. Refusing to Oppress Others: vs. 9

Introduction for Adults

Topic: *Justice for All*

"Envy is wanting what another person has and feeling badly that I don't have it. Envy is disliking God's goodness to someone else and dismissing God's goodness to me. Envy is desire plus resentment. Envy is anti-community," asserts John Ortberg in *Love Beyond Reason: Moving God's Love from Your Head to Your Heart.*

An envious heart is incapable of showing justice, mercy, and humility. It is too preoccupied. Have you witnessed the results of envy? Envy frequently makes its way into criminal acts. But on a private level, envy is damaging too. Its seed of discontentment quickly grows into the weed of resentment. This weed can choke relationships—even among Christians.

So how does a believer eradicate this weed? Extermination begins with developing a right attitude toward God and the blessings He, in His wisdom, bestows.

Introduction for Youth

Topic: *Don't Twist Justice*

The father regularly taught his son to do what is right. One day, while they worked together with some other men, the language became exceedingly profane. When the lad joined in the talk, his father reminded him that such language was inappropriate.

God expected the Israelites to live up to His high moral standards. This included promoting, not twisting, justice. Instead, once the chosen people were settled in the promised land, they began to wallow in the ways of their corrupt neighbors, allowed immorality and injustice to prevail, and hypocritically worshiped the Lord.

It's perilously easy for us who are Christians to go through the motions of worship, prayer, and other religious activities. We forget that God wants us to grow in our love for Him, to mature in our spiritual wisdom and understanding, and to become more like Jesus in our thoughts and actions. Exodus 23:1-9 helps us to see how important it is to cultivate a life of justice, mercy, and integrity.

Concepts for Children

Topic: *Doing What's Fair!*

1. God wants us to treat each other fairly.
2. God wants us to be kind to those who dislike us.
3. God wants us to help people from other countries who live among us.
4. God does not want us to join with others in hurting anyone.
5. God is pleased when we do the right thing, even when no one is watching.

Lesson Commentary

I. LIVING IN A VIRTUOUS MANNER: EXODUS 23:1-3

A. Being an Honest Person: vs. 1

"Do not spread false reports. Do not help a wicked man by being a malicious witness."

God called Moses to lead the Israelites out of Egypt to the promised land. Though Moses was raised for 40 years in Pharaoh's court, he nonetheless did not ignore the plight of God's people. He killed an Egyptian who was beating a Hebrew slave, then fled into the wilderness of Midian (Exod. 2:11-15; Acts 7:23-29). Another 40 years passed, during which time Moses married and tended sheep (Exod. 2:16-22). Egypt probably became a distant memory. Yet at the right moment, God shared with 80-year-old Moses the plan He had in place all along. It was a plan that revealed God's love and concern for Moses and all of the Israelites. Moses was to be God's instrument in leading His people out of captivity and into the promised land. God had not forgotten the Israelites, nor had He forgotten the promises He made to their forebears (Exod. 3:7-22; Acts 7:30-34).

The account of the Israelites' escape from Egypt is recorded in Exodus 5:1–14:31 (see Acts 7:36). So that Pharaoh would let the Israelites leave, God brought 10 plagues on Egypt. The waters of the Nile River turned to blood. Then frogs, lice, and flies descended on the land. A pestilence infected Egypt's cattle. Then came hail, locusts, and darkness. Even so, Pharaoh's heart was hardened, and he would not let the Israelites leave Egypt. In the last plague, which led to the death of all the firstborn of Egypt, the Israelites' firstborn were "passed over," and God instituted the celebration of the Passover (Exod. 12:1-30). Finally, Pharaoh let the Israelites' depart, but then he changed his mind and pursued them until he trapped them between his army and the uncrossable waters of the Red Sea. It was at this point that God parted the sea for the Israelites, then closed it again to drown the Egyptian army. The bodies of the adversaries that washed up on shore reminded the Israelites' of God's protection for them.

Exodus 15:22–19:2 detail the Israelites' journey from the Red Sea crossing to Mount Sinai. The Israelites reached God's mountain in the third month of their journey out of Egypt (19:1). Moses then climbed Mount Sinai to speak with God (chap. 20). While Moses was still atop Mount Sinai, he received from God more laws to guide the Israelites' behavior (21:1). One of the first sets of these laws dealt with the Israelites' relationship with their slaves (vss. 2-11). Slavery was a way of life among the ancient peoples. In fact, slavery was practiced by almost every culture that kept historical records: the Egyptians, Sumerians, Babylonians, Assyrians, Phoenicians, Syrians, Moabites, Ammonites, Edomites, Greeks, and Romans. Among most ancient peoples, slaves were considered strictly as property and were granted no personal rights. This was not the case, however, among the Israelites. Though slaves were considered property, they had certain rights defined under the Mosaic law. In some cases, the slave was treated as a member of the family.

This emphasis on equity and justice is found in various laws concerning personal injuries (vss. 12-36) and property (22:1-15). These are followed by an assortment of laws centered on the general issue of social responsibility (vss. 16-31). Some of the brief commands in this section reiterate directives God had given to His people earlier, while others are new directives. Undergirding all these commands was God's compassion for the unfortunate. From the beginning of His relationship with the Israelites, God maintained a special concern for those who were less fortunate than others. In keeping with His compassion, He commanded that the corners of fields were not to be reaped, so that food would be left for the needy (Lev. 19:9-10). He also promised a special blessing to those who reflect His compassion for the poor (Prov. 19:17), and judgment against those who oppress the poverty-stricken. Additionally, God made provision for destitute sojourners who were not a part of the nation of Israel. For instance, gleanings from the harvest were to be left for them (Deut. 24:19-21).

Above all, the Lord wanted His people to be holy. He also wanted a people devoted to His purposes. One way the Israelites could demonstrate their holiness was to avoid eating the meat of an animal that had been attacked and killed by wild beasts (Exod. 22:31). Another way they could practice holiness was by living in a virtuous manner. The starting point was their decision to be honest in their dealings with one another. Behind this commitment was the realization that the Lord is a God of justice. Indeed, His desire for justice among His people can be seen in the laws He prescribed for them. For example, the ordinances recorded in 23:1-9 were intended to demonstrate the spirit in which impartial justice was to be administered by the Israelites.

To help secure justice, God commanded that His people not spread baseless reports about each other (vs. 1). This included an injunction against circulating malicious gossip and unfounded rumors (see Exod. 20:16; Lev. 19:16; Deut. 5:20; 19:16-21; Ps. 27:12; Prov. 19:5). Also included was a ban against joining hands with evil and unscrupulous persons. No one in the covenant community was to assist a guilty person in a scheme to bring down an innocent party by offering a corrupt testimony. Likewise, God did not want the Israelites helping to bring about a mistaken judgment or to contribute to the cause of evil. This concern was especially important in Israel. Many crimes had stiff punishments, including death. And since a case could be decided on the testimony of two or three witnesses, it was important to make sure that false witness not be offered in court, thereby resulting in someone's wrongful punishment (see Num. 35:30; Deut. 17:6; 19:15).

B. Being a Person of Integrity: vss. 2-3

"Do not follow the crowd in doing wrong. When you give testimony in a lawsuit, do not pervert justice by siding with the crowd, and do not show favoritism to a poor man in his lawsuit."

Another way the Israelites were instructed to maintain impartial justice was by being people of integrity. For example, they were not to join a group that was determined to act wickedly (Exod. 23:2). God called His people to individual responsibility in doing what is right according to His Word, not according to what other people are doing. Furthermore, being part of a crowd would not exempt anyone of guilt. Also, following a throng of agitators could get a person into great trouble. Jesus aptly warned that "wide is the gate and broad is the road that leads to destruction, and many enter through it" (Matt. 7:13).

Exodus 23:2 echoes verse 1 by warning against offering testimony in a lawsuit that agrees with the majority opinion but perverts justice by bringing about a corrupt decision (see Lev. 19:15, 33; Deut. 1:17; 16:19; 24:17; 27:19; 1 Sam. 8:3). Exodus 23:3 adds that God's people were prohibited from showing partiality in a legal proceeding to someone just because of that person's poverty. Giving preferential treatment to the poor because of their destitution was just as wrong as condemning the rich because of their wealth. In every situation, God wanted the Israelites to seek out the truth and be impartial in their judgment. The critical issue is whether the accused party—either rich or poor—was guilty or innocent.

II. LIVING IN AN UPRIGHT MANNER: EXODUS 23:4-9

A. Being Kind to Others: vss. 4-5

"If you come across your enemy's ox or donkey wandering off, be sure to take it back to him. If you see the donkey of someone who hates you fallen down under its load, do not leave it there; be sure you help him with it."

Living in an upright manner complemented living in a virtuous manner. A starting point in this regard was making the effort to be kind to others. For instance, in order for the Israelites to be God's representatives to the rest of the world, it was important that they would exhibit justice and compassion—even to their enemies and to those who hated them. (The present context refers to another member of the covenant community.)

Thus, God commanded that His people help those in need, and He gave them two examples. In the first one, an Israelite encountered the "ox or donkey" (Exod. 23:4) of their foe wandering away. In an agriculturally based society, it was common for some animals to be grazing, while other beasts were used to carry heavy burdens. Also, there were times when someone would come upon a stray (see 1 Sam. 9:3, 20). The kind gesture was to return the animal to its owner. In the second example, an Israelite came upon the "donkey" (Exod. 23:5) belonging to an antagonist. The pack animal had either stumbled or collapsed under the heavy load that it was carrying, and now it lay helpless. The quickest way to correct the problem was for two people to stand on each side of the animal and simultaneously lift its load. The compassionate response would not be to ignore the enemy, but to stop and offer help (see Deut. 22:1-4; Prov. 25:21).

Ultimately, God knew that acts of compassion could help transform enemies into friends. Moreover, these commands show that God has always wanted His people to be considerate and helpful toward those who revile them. As a matter of fact, Jesus later instructed His followers, "Love your enemies and pray for those who persecute you" (Matt. 5:44). Admittedly, this instruction is not easily followed by any of us, but it is the high calling of those who are disciples of the Messiah. Jesus Himself gave us an example of caring for our enemies when He prayed for those who nailed Him to the cross (Luke 23:34).

B. Being an Advocate for Justice: vss. 6-7

"Do not deny justice to your poor people in their lawsuits. Have nothing to do with a false charge and do not put an innocent or honest person to death, for I will not acquit the guilty."

Living in an upright manner included being an advocate for justice. So, while the impoverished were not to be given special privileges in the legal system, neither were they to be denied justice (Exod. 23:6). The context here is litigation being brought before a judge and the prohibition is against the legal process being subverted. The general point is that truth was to be sought in every case regardless of the social status of those involved. Accordingly, the righteous were to keep their distance from those falsely accusing someone of committing a crime. Likewise, the upright were banned from bringing capital punishment on those who were "innocent or honest" (vs. 7). As before, God was warning against giving spurious testimony and against wrongful punishment. He realized that false witnesses could corrupt the nation's entire system of justice.

An example of denying justice to the poor would be the episode involving Naboth's vineyard (1 Kings 21). We know relatively little about him except that he was from Jezreel in the northern kingdom of Israel. Perhaps during a time of relative peace during the reign of Ahab (874–873 B.C.), the king was able to spend time at his winter palace in Jezreel and pursue the leisurely activity of gardening. When Ahab stated that he wanted Naboth's vineyard, the owner refused to trade or sell the property. Then Ahab's wife, Jezebel, used the king's authority to arrange for the elders and nobles who lived in Jezreel to try, convict, and execute Naboth on the false charge of cursing God and the king. Jezebel's ruthless actions were consistent with the way pagan monarchs of the ancient Near East ruled.

When the news of Naboth's death was reported to the queen, she in turn went to her husband and told him to take possession of the vineyard. Jezebel explained that Naboth was no longer alive. Amazingly, it isn't even recorded that Ahab asked what caused the death of the Jezreelite. The king simply got up and took possession of the property. Ahab evidently was thrilled to learn that Naboth was dead. And without Naboth to object, Ahab was fully prepared to disregard God's standards and seize the property that did not really below to him. However legal the king's actions might have seemed by ancient Near Eastern customs, they represented clear violations of God's law. Ahab could see that Naboth had been the victim of terrible crimes.

The Lord would not overlook the injustice that had been committed, and He would not let Ahab close his eyes to it. So God sent Elijah the Tishbite to condemn the king for his crime. The Lord told Elijah that Ahab had gone to take possession of Naboth's vineyard and that the prophet would find the king there. Elijah was to confront the guilty monarch with the truth. Even though Ahab had not personally murdered Naboth, God held the king responsible for this wicked injustice. Ahab's sin was one of deliberate and willful ignorance, of permitting someone to commit evil on his behalf and for his benefit without his asking any questions or seeking to stop it. Through Elijah, God made it clear that Ahab would pay a heavy penalty for acting unjustly. The Old Testament's death penalty for murder would apply even to the king. Specifically, dogs would lick up Ahab's blood in the same place they licked up the blood of Naboth.

C. Refusing to Accept a Bribe: vs. 8

"Do not accept a bribe, for a bribe blinds those who see and twists the words of the righteous."

A "bribe" (Exod. 23:8) is a gift of money or possessions to persuade someone to act illegally or dishonestly. This included paying off judges or demanding a fee just to hear a case. Bribery was a common problem in the ancient Near East. In fact, it was so severe that some societies prescribed the death penalty for a person caught offering or taking a bribe. God's law, however, did not stipulate a specific penalty for this offense, but did consider it an unlawful act. The Lord declared that bribes can cause judges to act greedily rather than justly. Likewise, bribes have the effect of thwarting a just person's testimony, thus allowing a guilty person to go free. Moreover, accepting a bribe makes impartial justice an impossibility (see Deut. 10:17; 16:19; 27:25; Ps. 26:10; Prov. 6:35; 15:27; 17:8; Isa. 1:23; 5:23; Mic. 3:11; 7:3).

D. Refusing to Oppress Others: vs. 9

"Do not oppress an alien; you yourselves know how it feels to be aliens, because you were aliens in Egypt."

The Hebrew verb rendered "oppress" (Exod. 23:9) literally means "to crush" and refers to actions that are abusive and overbearing. In this case, the object of such maltreatment were foreigners, with the likely context being an inequitable judgment rendered in a legal court. The reason the Israelites were to treat resident aliens fairly and objectively is that God's people had a long history as foreigners in Egypt for 430 years (see Exod. 22:21; Lev. 19:33-34). The Lord was calling for a sense of interracial justice among His people. They knew, perhaps better than any of the pagans living around them, that aliens usually had no family nearby to protect them if they were attacked. God said foreigners deserved protection. Throughout Scripture, the Lord is portrayed as showing compassion for the world's marginalized people. In fact, widows, orphans, the poor, and foreigners were often objects of God's special concern.

Discussion Questions

1. What are some examples that come to mind for you of malicious gossip?
2. How can believers resist the temptation to follow a crowd in doing what is evil?
3. Why is it wrong to show favoritism either to the rich or the poor?
4. What are some ways you can think of to help those who do not like you?
5. How might your church reach out to foreigners in your community with the good news of Christ?

Contemporary Application

The injustices referred to in Exodus 23:1-9 have a strangely modern ring to them. For example, it parallels that of the wealthy people in our recent global financial crisis. These individuals unjustly gained billions of dollars while impoverishing masses of ordinary people. It seems that some who are rich share a timeless selfishness that puts one's own happiness above all other considerations.

Do we not all experience the temptation to covet possessions and to seek personal satisfaction? If so, can we be sure that any of us are free from unjust attitudes and actions? Notice how the focus of our own satisfaction unfailingly leads us into unjust actions. First, it crowds God out of our thinking. While being consumed by our own desires, we cannot simultaneously love the Lord with all our heart. Nor will we be really interested in what God wants from us. We will neither meditate on His law nor apply His commands to our conduct.

Second, a primary concern with our own pleasure prevents us from truly loving our neighbors. Instead of being compassionate to them and doing good to people, we will use others as a means to satisfy our own desires. Third, selfishness leads us to abuse the power and influence that we do have and to proceed toward our goals by any means possible. We become unwilling to accept the responsibilities that come with privilege. Instead, we call on all our resources to get where we want to go, no matter who gets hurt.

Since promoting justice involves obeying God's commands for dealing rightly and fairly with others, it cannot grow in a soil of selfishness. Ultimately, injustice grows from carelessness about others and not being interested in whether they are treated equitably. Furthermore, injustice is so happy over getting what it wants that it has no time to mourn over anyone who is hurt. That's because when we care too much for ourselves, we don't really care about anyone else.

Living as God's Just People

Scripture

Background Scripture: *Leviticus 19:9-18, 33-37*
Scripture Lesson: *Leviticus 19:9-18, 33-37*
Key Verse: *"The alien living with you must be treated as one of your native-born. Love him as yourself, for you were aliens in Egypt. I am the LORD your God."* Leviticus 19:34.
Scripture Lesson for Children: *Leviticus 19:9-18, 33-37*
Key Verse for Children: *"Love your neighbor as yourself."* Leviticus 19:18.

Lesson Aim

To make our love for God and others the highest priority in our lives.

Lesson Setting

Time: 1446 B.C.
Place: Mount Sinai

Lesson Outline

Living as God's Just People
  I. How to Treat Our Neighbors: Leviticus 19:9-18
    A. *Showing Concern for Our Disadvantaged Neighbors:
       vss. 9-10*
    B. *Being Principled in Our Dealings with Our
       Neighbors: vss. 11-13*
    C. *Treating Our Neighbors Humanely: vs. 14*
    D. *Dealing with Our Neighbors Equitably: vss. 15-16*
    E. *Being Forthright and Kindhearted with Our
       Neighbors: vss. 17-18*
  II. How to Treat Foreigners: Leviticus 19:33-37
    A. *Being Charitable to Foreigners: vss. 33-34*
    B. *Being Honest in Our Transactions with Foreigners:
       vss. 35-36*
    C. *Remaining Obedient to God: vs. 37*

Introduction for Adults

Topic: *Acting with Compassion*

The biblical command that we love one another is likely to be greeted with a big yawn. We've heard that before. What else is new? We must confront spiritual inertia on this point. We can name a few people who seem to act with compassion, but in too many cases we live in isolation chambers.

If this diagnosis seems too negative, perhaps we could take an anonymous survey of people in our Sunday school classes and churches. We could find out (1) if people feel they receive love from fellow Christians, and (2) how they demonstrate love for one another. Whatever the outcome, we have to seek the Holy Spirit's conviction to stir up obedience to our Christian duty to love those around us.

Introduction for Youth

Topic: *Justice by Caring*

We like to sing, "They'll know we are Christians by our love," which is straight from the teaching of Scripture. But how much harder it is to practice the words and make it the basis for real social justice. Any group of Christian adolescents is bound to include some who are not especially lovable. In fact, they may turn us off by their quirky behavior.

Yet we cannot dodge the hard commands of Leviticus 19:18 and 34. To love unconditionally is our inescapable imperative and the source of one of God's greatest blessings. Failure to do so negates our Christian profession. Perhaps we need to confess our bad attitudes and listless behavior. Out of our weakness we must ask the Lord to make us more loving toward others, including those who may turn us off.

Concepts for Children

Topic: *Just Do It!*

1. God wants us to share with people in need.
2. God wants us to be kind and fair to others around us.
3. God wants us to accept others, even though they might be different than us.
4. We can show love to others because God has loved us.
5. When we show the love of Jesus to others, God watches over us and takes care of us.

Lesson Commentary

I. HOW TO TREAT OUR NEIGHBORS: LEVITICUS 19:9-18

A. Showing Concern for Our Disadvantaged Neighbors: vss. 9-10

"When you reap the harvest of your land, do not reap to the very edges of your field or gather the gleanings of your harvest. Do not go over your vineyard a second time or pick up the grapes that have fallen. Leave them for the poor and the alien. I am the LORD your God."

The first seven chapters of Leviticus provide instructions about the five main types of sacrifices to be offered at the altar. Making sacrifices reminded the Israelites—who were meant to be holy people dedicated to God—that sin has consequences and must be dealt with. Chapters 8–10 deal with the ordination of priests. Chapters 11–16 relate the laws concerning what is clean and unclean. And chapters 17–27 deal with the mandates for holy living.

There are three different types of law recorded in Leviticus. Moral laws specified the type of personal and community behavior that always is the duty of God's people. Civil laws took the principles expressed in the moral law and applied them to Israel's national situation. And ceremonial laws detailed rituals and customs associated with the nation's sacrificial system. Furthermore, the laws, purposes, and character of God are intriguingly portrayed in Leviticus.

Many practices of the people surrounding the Israelites were an abomination to God. In the material that makes up chapters 18–20, Moses transmitted rules to keep the Israelites a holy people, that is, distinctly different from those around them. These laws condemned such offenses as sexual immorality, social injustice, and idolatry. The emphasis on maintaining personal holiness is clear in 19:2.

There the Lord, through Moses, declared to the Israelites that the holiness of God was the basis for them also being holy. Expressed another way, the chosen people were to be pure in their attitudes and upright in their actions because the Lord was morally spotless in His character. Likewise, the Israelites were to be truthful in their words and benevolent in their deeds, for this mirrored the holy nature of God. Such a virtuous way of life was demonstrated by the Israelites treating their parents with respect and observing the Sabbath (vs. 3). Also, they showed their unwavering commitment to the Lord by refusing to venerate idols (vs. 4).

Verses 5-8 deal with the proper way for the Israelites to eat the fellowship offering. The purpose of the latter was to express the people's desire to enjoy harmony, not only between God and themselves, but also among themselves. This offering included a communal meal consisting of the meat of either a lamb or a goat. The sacrifice had to be eaten the day it was offered or no later than the following day. Whatever was left over on the third day had to be burned with fire. It could not be eaten then, for the offering was considered desecrated and so ritually unacceptable to God. Those who ate this contaminated food would be guilty of profaning what was supposed to be set apart as sacred to the Lord. In turn, the transgressors would bear the punishment for their iniquity, namely, being cut off from the faith community.

Verses 9 and 10 shift the focus to those times in the agricultural season when the Israelites harvested their crops. The Lord, through Moses, commanded the chosen people not to cut all the grain from the corners of their fields. Additionally, they were prohibited from picking up what the harvesters dropped. The reference here is to gleaning. This was the process of going back over a field, orchard, or vineyard after the main harvest to gather every last bit of produce. The law prohibited landowners from gleaning their lands. Instead, the poor and the foreigner were given the privilege of gathering whatever the harvesters had missed. By instituting a law related to gleaning, God showed His concern for the impoverished and the alien (see Deut. 23:4-5; 24:19-22).

To emphasize the statute, God punctuated it with the declaration, "I am the LORD your God" (Lev. 19:10). This was a reminder of who stood behind the commandment. It was also an announcement of who owned the land. Ultimately, the land belonged to the Lord. Also, God provided the land for people to grow their food, and gave them strength for plowing, sowing, cultivating, irrigating, and harvesting. Thus, what grew on the land actually belonged to the Lord. He graciously gave it to His people to provide for their needs. But this gift was given with the provision that the poor be allowed to eke out a living by picking up the leftovers. If the people followed God's ways, there would be food for everyone (see 26:4-5).

B. Being Principled in Our Dealings with Our Neighbors: vss. 11-13

"Do not steal. Do not lie. Do not deceive one another. Do not swear falsely by my name and so profane the name of your God. I am the LORD. Do not defraud your neighbor or rob him. Do not hold back the wages of a hired man overnight."

The list of injunctions in Leviticus 19:11-13 restate several of the divine rules appearing in the Ten Commandments (see Exod. 20:1-17; Deut. 5:5-21). The prohibition against stealing is closely related to the commandment not to covet (see Exod. 20:17; Deut. 5:21). Also, the rest of the Mosaic law contains directives against stealing people (Exod. 21:16) as well as property (22:1-4). The biblical prohibition against theft is one that should affect our lives today. For instance, how honestly do we file our tax return? Do we ever take home supplies provided only for office use? Do we ever loaf on the job? All such activities—amounting to forms of stealing—are encompassed in Leviticus 19:11.

The injunctions against lying and deceiving others mirrors the commandment forbidding giving false testimony against one's neighbor (see Exod. 20:16; Deut. 5:20). We are also reminded of Exodus 23:1, which we studied last week, and its ban on spreading false reports and helping the guilty by being a malicious witness against the innocent. Leviticus 19:12 forbids God's chosen people from using His name to swear a falsehood. Otherwise, the transgressors would be guilty of putting shame on God's name, who declared Himself to be the eternal, sovereign Lord. Similarly, Exodus 20:7 and Deuteronomy 5:11 forbid the Israelites from misusing the name of the Lord, especially for insincere or frivolous purposes. Using God's name in an oath when there was no intention of keeping it was one way to infringe on this commandment. More generally, the Israelites were never to use the Lord's name for evil purposes.

Leviticus 19:13 prohibits being cruel to one's neighbor by either cheating or robbing them. Moreover, the Israelites were to promptly pay their hired workers. Deuteronomy 24:14-15 clarifies that day laborers tended to be lowly and impoverished, and they could either be Israelites or foreigners living within Israel. In that culture, it was common practice for hired workers to be paid at the end of the day so that they could use their earnings to buy food for themselves and their families (see Matt. 20:8). Thus, withholding wages overnight until the following morning was potentially harmful to those trying to earn an honest living. Furthermore, the disadvantaged laborer could cry out to the Lord for help. In that case, God would declare the dishonest employer to be guilty of violating His law.

C. Treating Our Neighbors Humanely: vs. 14

"Do not curse the deaf or put a stumbling block in front of the blind, but fear your God. I am the LORD."

In ancient Israel, the disadvantaged included the deaf and the blind. Unlike today, though, people with these disabilities were severely hampered from earning a living and often had to resort to begging (see John 9:1, 8). Leviticus 19:14 forbid the Israelites from treating the marginalized in a degrading manner. This prohibition included reviling them and taking advantage of their impaired circumstance. To those within the covenant community who might be tempted to prey on the weak among them, this verse admonished that they were to fear God, their Lord.

Proverbs 1:7 states that the reverent fear of God is the starting point of all Hebrew wisdom. On the one hand, the idea is not an irrational feeling of dread and impending doom. On the other hand, fearing the Lord is more than courteous regard. It is an attitude of obedience and worship that comes from a deep awareness of God's sovereignty and power. The Lord is to be revered in awe and obeyed unconditionally. Additional incentive is found in 3:34, which reveals that the proud cannot receive God's overflowing grace. In contrast, He shows favor to the humble and oppressed (see Jas. 4:6; 1 Pet. 5:5).

D. Dealing with Our Neighbors Equitably: vss. 15-16

"Do not pervert justice; do not show partiality to the poor or favoritism to the great, but judge your neighbor fairly. Do not go about spreading slander among your people. Do not do anything that endangers your neighbor's life. I am the LORD."

Last week's lesson contained injunctions against perverting justice, either by siding with the rich or showing partiality to the destitute, especially in a matter involving a lawsuit (see Exod. 23:2-3). A similar directive appears in Leviticus 19:15 in which the Israelites were prohibited from dealing unjustly in rendering any decision. Examples of the latter included being favorably predisposed to the impoverished or being inclined to honor the rich and powerful. In contrast to these perversions of justice, the members of the covenant community were enjoined to judge their fellow citizens fairly.

Moreover, the Israelites were to be kind and considerate in how they treated one another. This could not happen, though, when one person spread malicious gossip and rumors about their neighbors (see Exod. 23:7). If others took these slanderous remarks at face value, it could lead to the victimization of the one being falsely accused, particularly in a court of law. Because God was the Lord and Judge of every Israelite, His chosen people were not to do anything that might unnecessarily jeopardize the life of their peers (Lev. 19:16).

E. Being Forthright and Kindhearted with Our Neighbors: vss. 17-18

"Do not hate your brother in your heart. Rebuke your neighbor frankly so you will not share in his guilt. Do not seek revenge or bear a grudge against one of your people, but love your neighbor as yourself. I am the LORD."

The general injunction against hating one's "brother" (Lev. 19:17) could be expanded to include all people. This certainly is the case in 1 John 4:7, where the apostle urged believers to show love for one another. Love is not a natural trait or a learned behavior, for its origin is from God. Thus all who practice Christian love show that they have been born of God and that they have an intimate relationship with Him. John's point is that love is the natural expression of a Spirit-filled life. The ability to truly love grows out of fellowship with God. For John, the new birth, fellowship with God, and the practice of Christian love are all intimately woven together to form the core of genuine Christian character. Moreover, believers should love one another because God is the source of love and because He is in fact the essence of love (vs. 8).

There are times when believers must confront one another, and do so by speaking the truth in a spirit of love (see Eph. 4:15). This idea is behind the latter half of Leviticus 19:17, where the Israelites were directed to be candid in reproving their fellow citizens when they sinned. Otherwise, those who either ignored or minimized the transgression could be accused of approving or aiding the guilty party in their trespass. There would be times, of course, when God's people were the victims of crime. In those instances, it would be wrong for them to seek vengeance or harbor resentment against a fellow Israelite. The more godly response for the Lord's chosen people was to depend on God to right all wrongs (see Deut. 32:35; Rom. 12:19) and to have the same love for their neighbor that they had for themselves (Lev. 19:18; see Matt. 5:43-44; 19:19; Luke 10:27; Rom. 13:9; Gal. 5:14).

Centuries later, when an expert in the Mosaic law asked Jesus which of the commandments was the greatest one, He named two (see Matt. 22:34-40; Mark 12:28-31). The first was the importance of loving God with every aspect of one's being (see Deut. 6:5). The second equally vital commandment was for believers to love their neighbors as themselves (see Lev. 19:18). The idea is that we need to work out our love for God in daily life. A supreme love for God will always find expression in unselfish love for others. The importance of doing the latter is seen in Jesus' statement recorded in Matthew 22:40, namely, that the entire Old Testament depends on loving God and others. Expressed differently, the Mosaic legal code is illumined and deepened by the presence of Christlike love (see Matt. 5:17; 7:12; Rom. 8:4; 13:8-10). Furthermore, just as the Savior loved us and gave His life for us, we also should reach out to others in a caring manner (see 1 John 4:9-12).

II. HOW TO TREAT FOREIGNERS: LEVITICUS 19:33-37

A. Being Charitable to Foreigners: vss. 33-34

"When an alien lives with you in your land, do not mistreat him. The alien living with you must be treated as one of your native-born. Love him as yourself, for you were aliens in Egypt. I am the LORD your God."

A life of submission to God is not just seen in loving one's neighbor. It also includes being compassionate to foreigners (see Exod. 23:9). This truth forms the context for Leviticus 19:33, in which the Israelites were told not to oppress immigrants living among them. The injunction goes beyond being polite but detached in one's treatment of resident aliens. It included treating foreigners as if they were native citizens in the land of Israel. More specifically, God's chosen people were to show the same kindness and consideration to immigrants as they personally would want to be shown. After all, the Israelites were once despised aliens in Egypt, that is, before the Lord, their God, set them free from their bondage (vs. 34).

B. Being Honest in Our Transactions with Foreigners: vss. 35-36

"Do not use dishonest standards when measuring length, weight or quantity. Use honest scales and honest weights, an honest ephah and an honest hin. I am the LORD your God, who brought you out of Egypt."

Like societies today, the Israelites had business dealings among themselves and with neighboring peoples. The Lord, who had redeemed the Israelites out of Egypt, was characterized by faithfulness and truth (see Deut. 32:4; Ps. 31:5; Isa. 65:16). Likewise, His chosen people were to be known for their honesty and integrity in all their commercial transactions. This included not trying to cheat when measuring "length, weight or quantity" (Lev. 19:35). Also included was the use of correct scales and weights, along with accurate containers for measuring dry goods or liquids (vs. 36; see Prov. 11:1; 16:11; 20:10, 23). In Moses's day, an "ephah" (Lev. 19:36) measured about four gallons or one third of a bushel, while a "hin" was equal to about a quart.

C. Remaining Obedient to God: vs. 37

"Keep all my decrees and all my laws and follow them. I am the LORD."

Leviticus 19:37 served as a general reminder to the Israelites of their obligation to the Lord. Their nation was founded on a variety of "decrees" and numerous "laws." Both individually and collectively, these statues and regulations were to be followed. As noted earlier, the central focus of the Israelites' obedience was their love for God and other people. Indeed, a commitment to the Lord was seen in how His people treated others around them, whether native-born citizens or resident aliens in their midst.

Discussion Questions

1. Why were the Israelites not to be greedy when they harvested their grain?
2. What negative impact do you think lying and deception have on interpersonal relationships?
3. Why is it important for believers to do whatever they can to empower the disadvantaged to be successful?
4. How might you befriend an immigrant living in your community?
5. What are some ways you can be an example of honesty to your peers?

Contemporary Application

There is a lawyer's instinct in all of us that seeks careful definitions of our Christian duties. This suggests we suffer from a cold creedalism that can strangle tangible expressions of love. However, God's command to love all people transcends legal niceties (Lev. 19:18, 34). We cannot separate our duties to others from our duties to God. Saying the right words, praying the right prayers, and singing the right hymns cannot make up for a lack of love (1 Cor. 13:1-3).

We have to confess our coldness and our preoccupation with ourselves. And we have to admit how hard it is to find the time and the resources to show Christlike love to hurting people. Together, we must encourage one another to make our churches places where love springs into action. Otherwise, we may look outwardly holy, but be inwardly full of hypocrisy.

This week's lesson reminds us of the importance to give love for God and others the highest priority in our lives. We are more likely to help others if we remember the last time someone helped us. If we maintain a safe distance from those in need, we can avoid feelings for them. But Scripture tells us we don't have an excuse good enough to stay at arm's length from them (so to speak). We should stop and extend mercy to anyone we have the opportunity and resources to help (Lev. 19:9-10).

Celebrate Jubilee

Scripture

Background Scripture: *Leviticus 25:8-55*
Scripture Lesson: *Leviticus 25:8-12, 25, 35-36, 39-40,
47-48, 55*
Key Verse: *"Consecrate the fiftieth year and proclaim liberty
throughout the land to all its inhabitants. It shall be a jubilee
for you."* Leviticus 25:10.
Scripture Lesson for Children: *Leviticus 25:8-22*
Key Verse for Children: *"Consecrate the fiftieth year and
proclaim liberty throughout the land."* Leviticus 25:10.

Lesson Aim

To stress that only God provides true security and freedom from worry.

Lesson Setting

Time: 1446 B.C.
Place: Mount Sinai

Lesson Outline

Celebrate Jubilee

  I. The Year of Jubilee: Leviticus 25:8-12
    A. *Counting Off Seven Sabbath Years: vs. 8*
    B. *Consecrating the Fiftieth Year: vss. 9-12*
 II. The Redemption of Property: Leviticus 25:25,
    35-36, 39-40, 47-48, 55
    A. *Buying Back Property: vs. 25*
    B. *Helping Impoverished Neighbors: vss. 35-36*
    C. *Treating Fellow Citizens Humanely: vss. 39-40*
    D. *Retaining the Right of Redemption: vss. 47-48*
    E. *Living as Servants of the Lord: vs. 55*

Introduction for Adults

Topic: *Making a Fresh Start*

W. P. Keller states that "there is an unfortunate tendency among some Christians to withdraw from society. There lurks the inclination to retreat into sheltered secluded situations." This resistance to involve ourselves in ministry can grow out of an attitude of apathy or futility.

It should come as no surprise, then, that saved adults typically feel that what they do or can do to serve the Lord is unimportant. Supposedly, since they aren't leaders or doing something that radically improves the impoverished culture in which they live, their ministry or possible ministry isn't important. They may wonder, "What difference does my ministry make to the disadvantaged?"

Making a fresh start—as represented in the Jubilee year observed by the Israelites—is the perfect remedy for such a defeatist attitude. According to Bill Bennett, in our effort to impact our culture and society, what really matters is "what we do in our daily lives—not the big statements that we broadcast to the world at large, but the small messages we send through our families and our neighborhoods and our communities."

Introduction for Youth

Topic: *Justice That Frees*

Imagine you purchase a ticket to fly from the closest international airport in your area to London, England. After checking in your luggage and boarding the plane, you find your assigned seat and get comfortable for the long flight.

Soon after taking off, however, you notice that the plane does not seem to be heading in any specific direction. Puzzled by it, you ask a flight attendant if anything is wrong. She responds, "Oh, don't worry. The pilot decided to scrap the planned itinerary. We're just flying around the area for a while before landing. Relax and enjoy the ride."

Most teens would protest over the pilot's decision as being unfair. Just as they would want the plane to be flying to a specific destination, so God wants their lives to be filled with such direction and purpose that justice is promoted. From this week's Scripture passage we will learn that God wants saved adolescents to pursue their ministries with equity and fairness and in this way promote lasting freedom for themselves and others around them.

Concepts for Children

Topic: *Let Freedom Ring!*

1. It is good for believers to take time to rest and praise God.
2. We please God when we thank Him for providing for us.
3. Giving to others in need honors God and brings His blessing.
4. God wants us to be good neighbors to everyone around us.
5. When our faith is in God, we have true freedom from worry.

Lesson Commentary

I. THE YEAR OF JUBILEE: LEVITICUS 25:8-12

A. Counting Off Seven Sabbath Years: vs. 8

"Count off seven sabbaths of years—seven times seven years—so that the seven sabbaths of years amount to a period of forty-nine years."

In Leviticus 25:8, God directed His people to count off seven Sabbath years, or seven sets of seven years, for a total of 49 years. According to verse 1, the Lord made known His will to "Moses on Mount Sinai." What follows in the next seven verses are details regarding the Sabbath year. Then in verses 8-55, God provided regulations concerning the Jubilee year. Throughout the chapter we find the Lord, as the royal sovereign over the promised land, issuing decrees that were intended to prevent the land and its tenants from being exploited (see vs. 23).

In terms of the Sabbath year, we see an analogy being played out. Specifically, just as God's people needed a time of rest, the promised land also needed to remain fallow for a season. The people were instructed to plow the fields and harvest the crops for six years, but during the seventh year they were to let the land lie idle (Exod. 23:10-11). The Lord promised that the harvest of the sixth year would be sufficient to sustain them until they took in another harvest (Lev. 25:20-22). God said the crops that grew unattended in the seventh year were to be left for poor people as well as for wild animals (Exod. 23:11).

The Lord's initial establishment of the Sabbath forms the backdrop for the commands involving the Sabbath year and the year of Jubilee. In verse 12, God reminded the Israelites to observe a day of rest. He said that adherence to this law would enable animals and human laborers to be "refreshed." The latter renders a Hebrew verb that literally means "to breathe" or "to take breath." The idea is that God's Sabbath would be like a "breath of fresh air" (in a manner of speaking).

B. Consecrating the Fiftieth Year: vss. 9-12

"Then have the trumpet sounded everywhere on the tenth day of the seventh month; on the Day of Atonement sound the trumpet throughout your land. Consecrate the fiftieth year and proclaim liberty throughout the land to all its inhabitants. It shall be a jubilee for you; each one of you is to return to his family property and each to his own clan. The fiftieth year shall be a jubilee for you; do not sow and do not reap what grows of itself or harvest the untended vines. For it is a jubilee and is to be holy for you; eat only what is taken directly from the fields."

In the fiftieth year, the Israelites were to blow a trumpet throughout the entire promised land. "Trumpet" (Lev. 25:9) renders a Hebrew noun that refers to the curved horn of a ram. The blast took place on the "Day of Atonement," which was the tenth day of the seventh month (namely, Tishri, which occurred in September–October). Hebrew religion was highly concerned with ceremonial cleanness and uncleanness. When people became unclean, they could become clean again by following the proper ritual. But since there were so many laws about cleanness, it was inevitable that some people would become unclean without knowing it and consequently would pollute the sanctuary. So once a year on the Day of Atonement (celebrated today as Yom Kippur), the high priest performed a special ritual to restore the tabernacle to cleanness (16:16, 19). This was the only ritual important enough for the high priest to risk his life by entering the most holy place, where God's presence dwelt (vs. 2).

The Israelites, by heeding the observances detailed in verses 3-10, would set the fiftieth year apart as holy. It would also be a time to announce "liberty" (25:10) to all the inhabitants of the promised land. The original can also be translated "freedom" and points to being released from one's outstanding obligations. It was to be a year of "jubilee." Some think the underlying Hebrew noun literally means "ram" and can also denote the horn of a ram. If so, the thematic association with verse 9 is reinforced. The jubilee would become an opportunity for all property that had been sold to be restored to the original owner or the descendants. Likewise, it would be a time when any who had been sold as slaves would be emancipated and returned to their clans (vs. 10).

During this sacred season, the Israelites were not allowed to plant their fields. Likewise, they were banned from harvesting the grain that grew by itself and gathering the grapes from their "untended vines" (vs. 11). The reason for this wide-ranging prohibition is given in verse 12. The fiftieth year was to be a time of "jubilee" in which the Israelites, by their actions, treated the season as "holy" or sacred. Nonetheless, the people were only permitted to eat what was taken "directly from the fields." Expressed differently, they were only allowed to consume what the fields would have otherwise produced on their own, apart from any cultivation.

II. THE REDEMPTION OF PROPERTY: LEVITICUS 25:25, 35-36, 39-40, 47-48, 55

A. Buying Back Property: vs. 25

"If one of your countrymen becomes poor and sells some of his property, his nearest relative is to come and redeem what his countryman has sold."

Throughout Israel's tenure in the promised land, the Lord remained its rightful owner. He considered the people to be tenants to whom He gifted a parcel of land. Through the enactment of the "Year of Jubilee" (Lev. 25:13), God undercut any tendency on the part of the wicked rich to exploit the poor. It was His will that in the fiftieth year, all property that had been sold was to be returned to its original owner or that person's ancestors. The observance of this injunction had the added benefit of helping to keep the family structure intact.

God was not banning the buying and selling of property between Israelite neighbors. Instead, He was preventing one party from taking unfair "advantage" (vs. 14) of another party in the commercial transaction. The price was to be set according to the "number of years" (vs. 15) remaining until the next jubilee. Similarly, property was to be sold based on the number of years that were left before the occurrence of the upcoming jubilee. This meant that any lease on a property was to last no more than 50 years (see 27:18, 23). Accordingly, when there were a considerable number of years remaining, the price of the property could be set higher. In contrast, if the number of years left were fewer, the lease price was to be set lower. After all, what was really being sold were the actual number of harvests the land could produce until the next Jubilee year (25:16).

The bottom line in all transactions was to treat one's neighbor fairly. After all, the Israelites were the chosen people of the Lord, their God. One way they showed their "fear" (vs. 17) for Him was by not cheating or exploiting their neighbor. Moreover, the Lord commanded His people to obey Him. This included following His "decrees" (vs. 18). This renders a Hebrew noun that can also be translated "statutes" or "ordinances." Likewise, the Israelites were to obey God's "laws." This renders a noun that can also be translated "regulations" or "edicts." By heeding the Lord's injunctions, the people would ensure their safe dwelling in Canaan. Also, the land would produce an abundance of crops. The Israelites not only would eat their fill but live securely in the land (vs. 19).

Deuteronomy 11:13-15 provides a helpful, clarifying perspective. Moses declared to a new generation of Israelites that they were to love the Lord, their God, and serve Him with their entire heart. Their commitment to doing so would be demonstrated by paying close attention to His commandments. Their faithful obedience would result in God sending rain on the land when it was needed (particularly, in the autumn and spring), resulting in an abundance of grain, wine, and olive oil. The Lord would also bless His people with lush pasturelands for their livestock, and the Israelites themselves would have all the food they could ever want to eat.

Perhaps it seemed counterintuitive to the Israelites to observe the Sabbath year and Jubilee year. Leviticus 25:20 considers the possibility of the people wondering what food there would be to "eat in the seventh year," especially when all forms of planting and harvesting of crops was forbidden for such an extended period of time. God reassured His potentially anxious people that He would send His "blessing" (vs. 21) on the land in the sixth year. In fact, the harvest would be large enough to satisfy the nutritional needs of the inhabitants for "three years."

This was necessary, for in the eighth year when the Israelites began again to plant their fields, they would be eating what they harvested in the sixth year. Due to the Lord's blessing, His people would have enough to eat until they harvested their crops in the "ninth year" (vs. 22). Ultimately, God was the sovereign owner and Lord of Canaan. Consequently, He had the right to remove the Israelites from the promised land, especially if they failed to heed His injunction against permanently selling any portion of the land. In reality, they resided in Canaan as foreigners and strangers. It was as if the Lord were leasing the land to "tenants" (vs. 23), not deeding private property to residents who had inalienable rights to the same.

Deuteronomy 6:10-12 reveals that Canaan was the Lord's good and generous gift to the Israelites. Moses realized that it would be easy for even a new generation of God's chosen people to forget Him when times were good. Therefore, the lawgiver told the Israelites to always remember all that the Lord had done for them, so that they would love Him with all their heart, soul, and strength. In fulfillment of the promise God had made to Abraham, Isaac, and Jacob—the Israelites' ancestors—God provided a way for them to come to the brink of inheriting the promised land. Moses informed the people that the land they would possess would have large, splendid cities, houses full of good things, wells, vineyards, and olive trees. All these things they would enjoy not because they had earned them, but because the land and all that was in it would be a gift from God.

Before the people began to enjoy the land and their freedom in it, Moses warned them not to forget that God had delivered them from slavery and brought them to the land of promise. The lawgiver's statement emphasized what the Lord had done and would do for them and not what they had done or could do for themselves. The power that would make them into a prosperous nation would be from the Lord and not from themselves. Therefore, they were never to forget what He had done for them, especially if they wanted to continue to enjoy His blessings. Moses, by reminding the Israelites about their terrible experiences in Egypt, was, in effect, warning them that tragedy could again befall them if they did not remember the Lord and His gifts to them.

Leviticus 25:24 reiterates how important it was for the Israelites to observe the Sabbath year and the Jubilee year. It did not matter which portion of Canaan held "as a possession" was being sold from one party to another. With every purchase, the provision had to be made for the original owner (or the descendants) to redeem what was sold. Verse 25 conveys a similar mindset. If any Israelite within the covenant community became impoverished (for example, due to crop failure, illness, and so on), and sold some of their property, the nearest relative had the moral obligation to buy back what had been sold.

B. Helping Impoverished Neighbors: vss. 35-36

"If one of your countrymen becomes poor and is unable to support himself among you, help him as you would an alien or a temporary resident, so he can continue to live among you. Do not take interest of any kind from him, but fear your God, so that your countryman may continue to live among you."

The "Year of Jubilee" (Lev. 25:13) was intended to be more than a time for the land to lie idle. Every fiftieth year, it signified a period of liberation and restoration. It was an opportunity for a new beginning for the promised land and its inhabitants (especially the poor). Outstanding loans were to be cleared, and land that had been sold was to be returned to the original owners. The Lord was so serious about

His people observing the Sabbath year and the Jubilee year that noncompliance would result in the Israelites being exiled from the promised land (see Lev. 26:34-35; 2 Chron. 36:21). In fact, those who later returned from Babylonian captivity renewed their commitment to observe these sacred institutions (see Neh. 10:31).

The generosity of spirit reflected in the Jubilee year is seen in the Lord's command for His chosen people to help their impoverished neighbors. Specifically, if any of the Israelites' fellow citizens became destitute and unable to make a living, nearby family, neighbors, and friends were to provide financial support. The help given was to mirror what the Israelites would offer to a foreign resident and enable the destitute Israelite to remain in the promised land (Lev. 25:35). Furthermore, God's chosen people were not to gouge any impoverished Israelites by charging them interest in either money or goods. Ultimately, it was a reverential fear of God that compelled wealthier individuals to assist their destitute fellow citizens so that they could remain in the covenant community (vs. 36). This is the same Lord who rescued His chosen people from Egypt and gave them Canaan as their inheritance (vs. 38).

C. Treating Fellow Citizens Humanely: vss. 39-40

"If one of your countrymen becomes poor among you and sells himself to you, do not make him work as a slave. He is to be treated as a hired worker or a temporary resident among you; he is to work for you until the Year of Jubilee."

Leviticus 25:39 discusses a situation in which destitute Israelites sold themselves to one of their fellow citizens in order to pay off outstanding debts. God prohibited His chosen people from forcing impoverished Israelites to work as slaves and be treated as mere property. Instead, the indigent were to live within the faith community as hired workers or resident foreigners. That said, once the Jubilee year arrived, any remaining balance owed by the poverty-stricken was to be forgiven (vs. 40). At that time, those who were destitute, along with their children, would be able to return to their clans and ancestral property (vs. 41).

D. Retaining the Right of Redemption: vss. 47-48

"If an alien or a temporary resident among you becomes rich and one of your countrymen becomes poor and sells himself to the alien living among you or to a member of the alien's clan, he retains the right of redemption after he has sold himself. One of his relatives may redeem him."

Leviticus 25:47 raises the issue of Israelites becoming indebted to prosperous resident foreigners. This is a situation in which the destitute become indentured servants to the immigrant or to a member of the immigrant's family. The Mosaic law declared that those who were impoverished still kept their right of redemption. So, even if they could not redeem themselves, a close relative could buy them back (vs. 48). Of course, if Israelites who were indentured servants obtained the means to pay off the remainder of their debt to a resident foreigner, they were allowed to do so (vs. 49).

E. Living as Servants of the Lord: vs. 55

"For the Israelites belong to me as servants. They are my servants, whom I brought out of Egypt. I am the LORD your God."

Leviticus 25:55 states an important fact, namely, that the Israelites were God's chosen people and members of His covenant community. As such, all of them were His "servants," whom He took out of the land of Egypt. This truth did not just apply to the generation of Israelites who left Egypt, but also to their descendants. All of them were to worship and serve the Lord and God of their ancestors.

Discussion Questions

1. Why did God require His people to count off seven Sabbath years?
2. What was the Day of Atonement?
3. In what sense was the fiftieth year a Jubilee year?
4. Why does God's Word stress to us the importance of not exploiting one another?
5. How inclined would you be to forgive the debt owed to you by a fellow Christian? Explain.

Contemporary Application

Every day we choose to serve either God or the world system. And how we decide is based on whether we see God as our only source of true security and freedom from worry. In turn, our "little" choices quickly harden, like cement, into habits. Every self-centered decision gives Satan a little more control. However, each time we choose God's will, we make a deposit in our heavenly bank account.

In the financial world, investors use money to make more money. In a manner of speaking, the Spirit is like a broker who is continually reinvesting God's resources in His children's lives. The Father first invested in us when He sent His Son to buy us back from Satan's kingdom. Now the resulting "dividends" include the fruit of the Spirit (Gal. 5:22-23).

Leviticus 25:55 reminds us that everything we have belongs to God. Since we are the Lord's stewards, we are obligated to use our possessions, time, and energy as investments for our Master. Every act of faithful stewardship adds to our spiritual treasure. Where, then, is our heart focused? Are we using our resources to invest in God's kingdom? The answers to these questions indicate that the contents of our character matter more to God than the size of our stock portfolio.

The Heart of the Law

Scripture

Background Scripture: *Deuteronomy 10:1-22; 16:18-20*
Scripture Lesson: *Deuteronomy 10:12-22; 16:18-20*
Key Verse: *What does the LORD your God ask of you but to fear the LORD your God, to walk in all his ways, to love him, to serve the LORD your God with all your heart and with all your soul, and to observe the LORD's commands?* Deuteronomy 10:12-13.
Scripture Lesson for Children: *Deuteronomy 10:12-22*
Key Verse for Children: *What does the LORD your God ask of you?* Deuteronomy 10:12.

Lesson Aim

To emphasize that God's people need His value system.

Lesson Setting

Time: 1406 B.C.
Place: Plains of Moab

Lesson Outline

The Heart of the Law
  I. Living for the Lord: Deuteronomy 10:12-22
    A. *Obeying the Lord: vss. 12-13*
    B. *Being Chosen by the Lord: vss. 14-15*
    C. *Being Committed to the Lord: vss. 16-17*
    D. *Being Compassionate to Others: vss. 18-19*
    E. *Serving the Lord: vss. 20-22*
  II. Establishing Equity in the Land: Deuteronomy 16:18-20
    A. *Appointing Judges: vs. 18*
    B. *Promoting Justice: vss. 19-20*

Introduction for Adults

Topic: *Loving as We Are Loved*

Everyone who has gone through military basic training knows what the drill sergeant's idea of "perfection" means. One speck of dust anywhere in the barracks can bring down the wrath of the inspectors. In civilian industry this attitude used to be called "zero defects."

When we consider our lives, we know that we have not reached such a high standard, especially in terms of morality. But that is not an excuse to slack off and settle for second best. Whether it's our character, our maturity, or our compassion for others, we should make every effort to grow in these and other areas.

Because we are joined to the Lord by faith, we have the resources we need to be upright in thought and virtuous in conduct. Moreover, God's love for us empowers us to show unconditional love to others. Indeed, with the Lord's help and the encouragement of His people, we can aim for the noble goal of being holy in our lives.

Introduction for Youth

Topic: *The Heart of the Matter*

A new generation of Israelites was poised to enter and conquer the promised land. In their possible exhilaration over this prospect, the Israelites might not have anticipated all the moral and social dangers that would soon confront them. Therefore, God called to them to renew the covenant, or agreement, He had originally made with the previous generation. By virtue of the fact that they were about to inherit Canaan, the Israelites belonged to the Lord and would be expected to live accordingly.

Rarely do saved teens think the stakes are so high. Rarely do they put their commitment to the Savior in terms of a solemn agreement. Rarely do they even recall the covenant they made when they trusted in the Son and joined His church. Rarely do they even hear those vows, except when new members are welcomed into the fellowship. During the class session, emphasize to your students that their unwavering commitment to the Lord is seen by them loving Him with all their heart and soul (see Deut. 10:12).

Concepts for Children

Topic: *What God Requires*

1. Moses reminded the people of the covenant God made with them.
2. Moses called the people to obey the commandments God set down.
3. The people were not to forget that God alone had delivered them from slavery in Egypt.
4. The people were to be faithful to God.
5. Our love for God encourages us to love others around us.

Lesson Commentary

I. LIVING FOR THE LORD: DEUTERONOMY 10:12-22

A. Obeying the Lord: vss. 12-13

And now, O Israel, what does the LORD your God ask of you but to fear the LORD your God, to walk in all his ways, to love him, to serve the LORD your God with all your heart and with all your soul, and to observe the LORD's commands and decrees that I am giving you today for your own good?

Moses began the Book of Deuteronomy with an account of Israel's journey from the Sinai peninsula to Kadesh Barnea, where the Israelites rebelled against God, first by refusing to enter the promised land and then by engaging the Canaanites in battle without the Lord's consent (chap. 1). Because of the Israelites' sin, they had to wander in the desert for about 38 years, until all but the faithful had perished (2:1-23). Moses then described Israel's victories over the Amorites, whose kingdoms east of the Jordan were granted to the Reubenites, Gadites, and Manassites (2:24–3:20). Moses also explained why the Lord forbade him to cross the Jordan, and how He chose Joshua to lead Israel into the promised land (vss. 21-29). Moses again warned Israel to obey God's laws and not to commit idolatry, explaining that the Lord is the only true God (4:1-40). After commenting on the cities of refuge, Moses introduced the Ten Commandments (vss. 41-49).

Next, Moses reminded the Israelites that God had made a covenant with them, and they in return had to obey the Lord. Then, as Moses restated the Ten Commandments God had given to him at Horeb, the Israelite leader reminded the people about the laws telling them how to honor God (5:1-15). These were followed by the divine injunctions dealing with community life (vss. 16-21). After that, Moses told how the people had responded to the Ten Commandments by promising to obey them. In turn, God was pleased with their response, but He also desired that their obedience and faithfulness would remain constant. Furthermore, Moses reminded the people that if they continued to honor God with their obedience, they could expect long and prosperous lives in Canaan (vss. 22-33).

In chapter 6, Moses declared that the Lord was one God (in distinction from the many gods of the religions flourishing in Canaan). The Israelites were only to worship and serve the Lord. Moses also told the Israelites that to remain a faithful community down through the years, each generation would have to impress upon its children the importance of knowing God's commands and obeying them (vss. 1-9). Moses wanted the people to recognize that while they were to love the Lord, they were not to take Him for granted. The Israelite leader urged them to maintain their reverence for God's power and to be careful not to provoke His anger. Moses reminded the people that as long as they did what was right and good in God's sight, their inheritance of the land would remain secure (vss. 10-19).

Moses wanted the Israelites to anticipate how they would answer when their children asked about the meaning of the Lord's commands. Moses told the people to recount for their children God's delivering them from Egyptian slavery and to remind their children that obeying God would result in long lives and prosperity in the promised land (vss. 20-25). As Moses continued to address the Israelites on the plains of Moab, he shifted his focus from God's laws that were to regulate their lives in the promised land to the attitudes they were to have as they seized and dwelt in that land. Since the inhabitants of Canaan were hostile toward the Lord, Moses instructed the Israelites either to destroy them or drive them out so that they would not be a snare to God's people (chap. 7). Because Moses would not accompany them into Canaan and thus would not be able to instruct them again in person, he repeated his admonition never to forget the Lord (chap. 8).

Moses said that God was opening the land for Israelites, not because of their righteousness, but because of the wickedness of the Canaanites (9:1-6). Moses reminded the Israelites of their own unworthiness, such as when they worshiped the golden calf (vss. 7-29). Next, after recounting God's giving of the Ten Commandments and the resuming of their journey toward the promised land (10:1-11), Moses once more urged the people to live for the Lord. He addressed them collectively as "Israel" (vs. 12) and rhetorically asked what the Lord, their God, expected from them. In actuality, it was quite straightforward. They were directed to love their Creator and Redeemer with their all their "heart" and "soul," that is, with complete fervor and emotional commitment. Moreover, the Israelites were to keep the Lord's commandments and heed His statutes, for doing so would ensure their well-being in the promised land (vs. 13).

B. Being Chosen by the Lord: vss. 14-15

To the LORD your God belong the heavens, even the highest heavens, the earth and everything in it. Yet the LORD set his affection on your forefathers and loved them, and he chose you, their descendants, above all the nations, as it is today.

Unlike the local tribal deities venerated by the Canaanites, the God of the Israelites was the Ruler of all creation. This included the "highest heavens" (Deut. 10:14), earth itself, and every single thing the planet contained. Furthermore, among all the peoples of the earth, the Israelites enjoyed a distinctive status as those whom God said would bear His name. Centuries earlier, He showed His loving favor to the patriarchs (that is, Abraham, Isaac, and Jacob). They, along with their descendants, enjoyed the Lord's "affection" (vs. 15) and experienced His loving care. Moreover, God in His grace picked the Israelites, out of all earth's inhabitants, to be His chosen people. This truth was validated by the fact that a new generation of Israelites stood ready to take control of the promised land.

C. Being Committed to the Lord: vss. 16-17

Circumcise your hearts, therefore, and do not be stiff-necked any longer. For the LORD your God is God of gods and Lord of lords, the great God, mighty and awesome, who shows no partiality and accepts no bribes.

Centuries earlier, when Abraham was 99 years old, the Lord told the patriarch to be circumcised and to circumcise all the males of his household. This practice was to be repeated on all Abraham's male descendants as well as others in the covenant community (Gen. 17:10-14). Circumcision was not unknown at that time. In fact, anthropologists tell us that tribes in America, Africa, and Australia practiced circumcision from earliest times. In Abraham's day, some Egyptians and perhaps others in the Near East practiced circumcision. But for Abraham's household, circumcision was new and symbolized the covenant. For the patriarch, the practice represented an oath affirming the covenant. Circumcision meant, "May I be cut off like my foreskin if I am untrue to the covenant." The cutting of circumcision reflected the literal meaning of the phrase "to make a covenant," which is "to cut a covenant."

This historical information forms the backdrop to the Lord's statement to a new generation of Israelites to "circumcise" (Deut. 10:16) their "hearts." In a metaphorical sense, they were to cut away the thick calluses from their innermost being and thereby become receptive and responsive to the Lord. Ultimately, it was the grace of God that enabled His chosen people to be successful in cleansing their hearts (see Deut. 30:6; Jer. 4:4; 9:26). Furthermore, the Lord directed the Israelites to cease being "stiff-necked" (Deut. 10:16). This idiom was based on the familiar scene of a draft animal refusing to submit to the yoke or rein of its owner. Despite the owner's efforts, the animal would not bend its neck to pull a load. Tragically, the Israelites had a prior history of stubbornly rejecting what God commanded (see Exod. 32:9; 33:3, 5; 34:9; Deut. 9:13).

In Deuteronomy 10:17, Moses declared that the Redeemer of His people was the supreme God and Lord of the universe. Unlike the powerless and lifeless idols worshiped by the Canaanites, Israel's God was strong in power and to be greatly feared. Moreover, He was unbiased and could not be bought off with money. From these truths the Israelites were to recognize that God demanded exclusive loyalty from them. They could have no other gods before Him. They were to confess and believe in His total sovereignty as the one true God. Because He had given Himself to His people, He was to be their ultimate focus. He would not accept anything else's vying for their worship and adoration.

Early peoples of Mesopotamia worshiped hills, trees, streams, and large stones, all of which were thought to contain some form of deity. This type of idolatry is represented in the Old Testament by the Asherah pole (Judg. 6:25-32). Egyptians worshiped the sun, the life-giving Nile River, and many animals, such as the scarab beetle, cow, and crocodile. The religion of the Canaanites was particularly vile with its sexual immorality and child sacrifice. When the Israelites conquered Canaan, God commanded His people to utterly destroy Canaanite idols (Exod. 23:24; 34:13; Num. 33:52; Deut. 7:5). Tragically, the Israelites often fell prey to idolatrous practices and thus invited God's judgment on the nation.

D. Being Compassionate to Others: vss. 18-19

He defends the cause of the fatherless and the widow, and loves the alien, giving him food and cloth-
ing. And you are to love those who are aliens, for you yourselves were aliens in Egypt.

The Lord of Israel was not a remote, uninvolved deity. Instead, He was compassionate and gracious in His dealings. He not only refused to show favoritism, but also made sure that the marginalized (such as orphans and widows) were treated fairly. What's more, He took loving care of resident foreigners by seeing that they got "food and clothing" (Deut. 10:18). One way God brought the latter about was through the kindheartedness of His chosen people. He wanted them to treat immigrants with the same loving care as He did, especially since the Israelites once were despised foreigners in the land of Egypt (vs. 19; see Exod. 23:9).

In Jesus' day, the religious leaders taught others to love their neighbors and hate their enemies (Matt. 5:43; see Lev. 19:18). The idea of hating one's enemy, however, was an extra-biblical injunction maintained by the authorities. It was based on a narrow understanding that a neighbor included only one's fellow Jew. Jesus, however, called His followers to love, bless, and pray for their enemy as well as their neighbor. Such compassion would demonstrate that Christ's followers were true children of their heavenly Father (Matt. 5:44-45). Jesus was stressing that goodwill must not allow itself to be limited by ill will. In fact, those who were genuine children of the Father demonstrated their parentage by their moral resemblance to Him who is love. Here we see that the standard believers were to adopt was that of God Himself. As His children, they were to reflect His image in all they did.

E. Serving the Lord: vss. 20-22

Fear the LORD your God and serve him. Hold fast to him and take your oaths in his name. He is your
praise; he is your God, who performed for you those great and awesome wonders you saw with your own
eyes. Your forefathers who went down into Egypt were seventy in all, and now the LORD your God has
made you as numerous as the stars in the sky.

Moses told the Israelites that they were to live in reverential fear of the Lord, serve Him as their true God, and remain unwavering in their loyalty to Him. Also, their oaths were only to be made in His name and backed up by His authority (Deut. 10:20). Furthermore, the chosen people were to make the Lord the sole object of their praise. After all, it was the God of Israel who did tremendous—even staggering—miracles when He freed them from slavery in Egypt (vs. 21). So great was His power that even the hearts of the Canaanites melted in fear at the thought of His awesome presence going before the advancing Israelite army (see Josh. 2:9-11).

It's true that when the ancestors of the Israelites first entered Egypt, they numbered only 70 (see Gen. 46:27; Exod. 1:5). Centuries later, the situation was far different, for the sovereign Lord had made His chosen people seem almost as "numerous as the stars in the sky" (Deut. 10:22; see Gen. 15:5-6). In Old Testament times, there was no pollution or bright lights from nearby cities to deter a person's view of the sky. Thus, while the Israelites did not have the benefit of a powerful telescope, they no doubt could grasp something of the vastness of space. Even today, scientists speak of stars as being trillions of miles away from us and describe the universe in terms that at times can seem hard to comprehend. Many of us can recall times when we gazed up into the sky on a clear night and saw countless stars extending from one end of the horizon to the other. If this was the case for God's people, we can only infer how puny they must have felt against the immense expanse of the heavens above which God had set His glory (see Ps. 8:1-4).

II. ESTABLISHING EQUITY IN THE LAND: DEUTERONOMY 16:18-20

A. Appointing Judges: vs. 18

Appoint judges and officials for each of your tribes in every town the LORD your God is giving you, and they shall judge the people fairly.

Both individually and collectively, the Israelites were to live for the Lord. One way to ensure that this remained true throughout the covenant community was by establishing equity in the land. The starting point would be the appointment of honest judicial leaders. They, along with subordinate civil magistrates, were to be fair in the decisions they made in the villages God was giving the twelve tribes of Israel. The Hebrew noun rendered "town" (Deut. 16:18) is literally "gates." It points to the customary practice of the day in which the local elders gathered at the entrance of a city to render important decisions (see Ruth 4:1, 11; Job 29:7; Lam. 5:14).

B. Promoting Justice: vss. 19-20

Do not pervert justice or show partiality. Do not accept a bribe, for a bribe blinds the eyes of the wise and twists the words of the righteous. Follow justice and justice alone, so that you may live and possess the land the LORD your God is giving you.

Because the God of Israel was unbiased (see Deut. 10:17), the leaders of His people were to be people of integrity. In the process of them making judicial decisions, whether large or small, they were prohibited from twisting the law, playing favorites, and taking bribes. Instead of being wise and upright, leaders who allowed themselves to be bought off became inept, self-serving, and corrupt (16:19). For that reason, Moses urged the present and future leaders of Israel to pursue unadulterated "justice" (vs. 20). In point of fact, it was the only way for the chosen people to really live and possess the land the sovereign Lord was giving to them as an inheritance.

Discussion Questions

1. Why does the Lord want us to serve Him with all our heart and soul?
2. How are believers benefited by heeding God's commands?
3. In what ways has the Lord enabled you to spiritually flourish?

4. What are some ways God might use you to defend the cause of the disadvantaged?

5. Why is it important for believers to promote the presence of justice in government?

Contemporary Application

Tom flies his own airplane. He stressed that it is important for him to follow the regulations of the Federal Aviation Administration. He also believes that Christians must heed what the Lord has commanded in Scripture.

"I have become aware of how much the air traffic control system is like God's presence with us. I do a good deal of my Synod travel flying my own plane. So it is not surprising that I am thinking about flight safety! Whenever I make a flight, I have to prepare carefully. My preparation begins by checking my currency logs. Next, I prepare and file a flight plan of where I would like to go. Then I get a detailed weather briefing and do a careful preflight inspection of the plane. Sometimes this preparation to fly can take as much time as the flight itself!

"The air traffic control system itself is awesome. My aircraft is tracked all the way to my destination by a gigantic computer with the help of radar. A host of highly trained air traffic controllers direct my flight, warn me of other traffic, vector me around thunderstorms, alert me if I deviate from my assigned heading or altitude, and provide me with a sector of safe airspace. I am in constant radio contact with these controllers, and sometimes I talk with as many as twenty or thirty of them during the course of a trip. It is reassuring to have someone there to help me when I need it!

"All of my flight and the activity of the air traffic controllers are precisely and extensively codified by the Federal Aviation Administration. Rather than resent these regulations, I have come to value them. Each regulation has been carefully researched, tested, and evaluated for its primary purpose: to provide aircraft with a safe and reliable flying environment. I know that these regulations are also strictly enforced, and that if I fail to follow them, I am not only endangering my own safety and that of others, but I can be punished for the violation."

Similarly, when we heed God's Word, we are ensuring our own spiritual safety and survival.

Samuel Administers Justice

Scripture

Background Scripture: *1 Samuel 7:3-17*
Scripture Lesson: *1 Samuel 7:3-11, 15-17*
Key Verse: *"Commit yourselves to the LORD and serve him only, and he will deliver you."* 1 Samuel 7:3.
Scripture Lesson for Children: *1 Samuel 7:3-11, 15-17*
Key Verse for Children: *"Commit yourselves to the LORD and serve him only, and he will deliver you."* 1 Samuel 7:3.

Lesson Aim

To learn that God's people should remain committed to serving Him only.

Lesson Setting

Time: About 1050 B.C.
Place: Mizpah and its environs

Lesson Outline

Samuel Administers Justice

I. Dealing with Idolatry: 1 Samuel 7:3-6
  A. *Getting Rid of Idols: vss. 3-4*
  B. *Getting Right with the Lord: vss. 5-6*
II. Defeating the Enemy: 1 Samuel 7:7-11, 15-17
  A. *The Threat of a Philistine Attack: vs. 7*
  B. *The Intercession of Samuel: vss. 8-9*
  C. *The Rout of the Philistines: vss. 10-11*
  D. *The Judgeship of Samuel: vss. 15-17*

Introduction for Adults

Topic: *Rescued!*

After losing her four-year-old son, Sheila felt overwhelmed with grief. For months it seemed as if she just crawled through her days. She especially struggled to forgive the person who had run over her child. She found herself filled with bitterness over not understanding why God allowed this tragedy to happen.

Sheila discovered that prayer was the way God rescued her from her resentment and helped her overcome her depression. By regularly communing with the Lord, Sheila was able to move beyond her grief and put herself in the loving hands of the Almighty. The adults in your class also need to know that when they spend time in prayer with God, He will hear and respond. As with Samuel and the Israelites, though, it is often in ways far more profound and meaningful than the students could ever imagine.

Introduction for Youth

Topic: *Security through Justice*

In "Process Spirituality: Being versus Doing," Kenneth Boa notes that praying to God should be a daily practice. It starts early in life when we seek to "form the habit of holy leisure." We purposely seek out "quiet places and times" to be "alone with the Lord." Our goal is to "restore our passion and intimacy with Christ." The resulting "restoration and renewal," especially after "periods of intense activity," enables us to remain energized in "our outward service" for God.

The teens in your class can benefit from knowing these scriptural truths. Be sure to emphasize that Samuel must have valued his times of quiet solitude with the Lord. And undoubtedly, communing with Him in prayer was a key factor in Samuel remaining effective in establishing security and justice throughout Israel. The same thing can be said for your students, especially as they pray about their activities and endeavors.

Concepts for Children

Topic: *Samuel: A Just Judge*

1. The Israelites depended on a strong leader, Samuel, to speak on their behalf with God.
2. Samuel was fair in the way he led the Israelites.
3. Samuel wisely chose prayer as a means to help the Israelites.
4. Samuel was an example of the power of prayer.
5. When we pray to God, we know that He will hear and respond to our requests.

Lesson Commentary

I. DEALING WITH IDOLATRY: 1 SAMUEL 7:3-6

A. Getting Rid of Idols: vss. 3-4

And Samuel said to the whole house of Israel, "If you are returning to the LORD with all your hearts, then rid yourselves of the foreign gods and the Ashtoreths and commit yourselves to the LORD and serve him only, and he will deliver you out of the hand of the Philistines." So the Israelites put away their Baals and Ashtoreths, and served the LORD only.

At the beginning of 1 Samuel, the Israelites were at a religious low point. The priesthood was corrupt, the judges tended to be dishonest, and the people showed open disdain for God and His Word. In addition, Israel was a loosely organized, weak federation of tribal states. The abusive rule of judges and the infighting among the tribes caused the people to long for a monarchy such as they saw in the surrounding nations. First Samuel reveals that though the handsome and tall Saul appeared to be well suited for leading a nation, his reign ended in tragedy because he violated the Mosaic law. David contrasted sharply with Saul. Though David was from an undistinguished rural family, he had a remarkable faith in God. Also, though he made mistakes, he always turned back to God for mercy.

In preparation for the nation's move into the new era, Samuel was called to repair the moral fabric and restore the spiritual vitality of a people who had drifted far from God. Samuel finished the work of the judges and launched the monarchy, not by human strength and intuition, but by the power of God through prayer. Along with establishing the monarchy, Samuel aided in launching an order of the prophets so as to bring God's Word to His people (see 19:20). From Samuel's time onward, the prophets promoted the spiritual life of Israel and were the channels through whom God made His will known to both king and commoner.

Chapters 4–7 in 1 Samuel are called "The Ark Narratives" by many Bible scholars. This material focuses on events extending from the removal of the ark of the covenant from Shiloh to its arrival at Kiriath Jearim. First Samuel 4 begins with Israel preparing to meet the Philistines in battle. One of several groups of "Sea Peoples," the Philistines were a great military power and Israel's principal enemy during the time of Samuel, Saul, and David. The Philistines, the only non-Semitic inhabitants of Canaan, came from Caphtor, usually identified with Crete and other Aegean islands (see Deut. 2:23; Jer. 47:4; Amos 9:7). They arrived in Canaan in several waves of migration, one during the patriarchal period (about 2000 B.C.) and another sometime around 1200 B.C. The new immigrants settled on the southern coastal plain of Israel, a region later known as Philistia. The Philistine government was a federation of five lords, each of whom controlled one of five principal cities—Ashdod, Ashkelon, Ekron, Gaza, and Gath. The Philistines used a variety of advanced technologies for their time, and were experts in metalwork, especially iron (see 1 Sam. 13:19-20).

When Samuel was about 13 years old, the Israelites engaged the Philistines in battle at Aphek, a strategic city bordering Philistine territory on the north. The battlefield was most likely the Plain of Sharon. There the Philistines could have made the best use of one of their most effective weapons, the chariot (see 1 Sam. 13:5; 2 Sam. 1:6). Overwhelmed by the Philistines' superior military might, Israel lost 4,000 men (1 Sam. 4:1-2). When it became evident that the battle would go to the Philistines, the elders of Israel called for the ark of the covenant to be brought from Shiloh to the battlefield. They mistakenly believed that the ark was a type of good-luck charm that would turn the tide of battle in Israel's favor (vss. 3-4). The elders in Samuel's day failed to understand that the mere presence of the ark was no guarantee that God would deliver Israel. Indeed, the Philistines fought on to victory, slaughtering 30,000 Israelites in the process and capturing the ark (vss. 9-11).

After the Philistines captured the ark, they took it to Ashdod, where God destroyed their image of Dagon. God caused tumors and plagues of rats to follow the ark wherever it went. After seven months, the Philistine diviners advised the people to return the ark—along with a guilt offering of golden likenesses of the tumors and rats—to appease the God of Israel. The Israelites eventually brought the ark to Kiriath Jearim, located about 10 miles west of Jerusalem. The ark could not be returned to Shiloh because that city had been completely destroyed by the Philistines (around 1050 B.C.; see 5:1–7:1). Twenty years passed with the ark at Kiriath Jearim, and the people of Israel longed for renewed fellowship with the Lord (7:2). The ark was kept in this city from shortly after the battle of Aphek, around 1104 B.C., until David moved it to Jerusalem in 1003 B.C., the first year of his reign over the united kingdom of Judah and Israel (see 2 Sam. 5:5; 6:1-11). The ark had been at Kiriath Jearim 20 years when the events of 1 Samuel 7 took place.

Samuel, at about the age of 33, addressed the nation in his first recorded act of public worship. Years earlier as a boy, Samuel was summoned to serve as prophet, priest, and judge of Israel. While the ministry of priests was a constant in Israel's history, the work of the prophets was tailored to particular periods of crisis. The prophets were God's representatives, proclaiming His message under specific circumstances. While Abraham (Gen. 20:7) and Moses (Deut. 18:15-19) are both called prophets, as a group, prophets first appear in the biblical period during the time of Samuel. Samuel is usually referred to as the last of the significant judges and the first of the prophets. Deuteronomy 18 makes it clear that a true prophet is always called by God (vss. 15, 18), speaks for God, derives authority from God (vs. 19), and cannot fail in the fulfillment of his or her predictions (vs. 22). Nevertheless, Israel was plagued by false prophets. Like weeds they popped up in Israel declaring counterfeit messages of peace and prosperity.

Samuel played a unique and pivotal role in Jewish history. As the last of Israel's significant judges and the first of the prophets during its monarchy, Samuel both served as chief administrator for the Hebrews and selected their first kings.

Because of his unwavering service to the Lord, he was the ideal person of faith for such a profound calling. It was in this role that Samuel challenged the people of Israel to demonstrate their renewed desire to fellowship with the Lord by getting rid of all their foreign gods. If they would, then God would deliver them from the oppressive hands of the Philistines (1 Sam. 7:3). Israel complied and abandoned worship of the Baals and Ashtoreths and the rituals associated with the worship of these pagan deities (vs. 4).

Baal appears to be a general term used to describe the male gods of Canaan. The meaning of the word suggests that each individual Baal was an "owner," or lord, of a particular locality. Because these regional Baals were thought to control fertility in agriculture, the Canaanites made it a priority to secure their favor. Often the Baals were portrayed as weather gods, since the timing and amount of rain were crucial to crop growth and abundance. Ashtoreth was the consort of Baal and was regarded as a goddess of fertility as well as of war. She was worshiped as Ishtar in Babylon and was the forerunner of Aphrodite, the Greek goddess of love and beauty.

At times in Scripture the names of the deities refer to the objects associated with their worship. For instance, when verse 4 notes that the Israelites removed the Baals and images of Ashtoreth, the text most likely refers to the destruction of stone and wood representations of these idols from town or household shrines. This cleansing may have been effective for a while, since Scripture does not mention idol worship among the Israelites during the times of Saul and David. The Canaanite worship of Baal and Ashtoreth included animal sacrifice, using some of the same creatures that Israel sacrificed to the Lord. The worship of Baal also involved male and female temple prostitution, fertility rites using wine and oil, and in some cases human sacrifice (see 1 Kings 14:23-24; Jer. 19:4-5). The degrading nature of these pagan customs shows why God wanted the Canaanites destroyed so that His people would not be influenced by such evil.

B. Getting Right with the Lord: vss. 5-6

Then Samuel said, "Assemble all Israel at Mizpah and I will intercede with the LORD for you." When they had assembled at Mizpah, they drew water and poured it out before the LORD. On that day they fasted and there they confessed, "We have sinned against the LORD." And Samuel was leader of Israel at Mizpah.

After the people disposed of their idols, physically and emotionally, Samuel told them to congregate at Mizpah (1 Sam. 7:5), a city of Benjamin in the region of Geba and Ramah (1 Kings 15:22). Despite numerous references, Mizpah's location remains disputed. At Mizpah, Saul was first presented to the Israelites as their king (1 Sam. 10:17), and the city was also one of the places that Samuel visited on his yearly circuit as Israel's judge (7:16-17).

At Mizpah, it was Samuel's intention to intercede with the Lord on behalf of the

Israelites (vs. 5). There Samuel led the people in a ceremony in which water was poured out before the Lord (vs. 6). This is the only passage in Scripture where the pouring of water is said to be a sign of repentance. Moreover, the people fasted throughout the day and openly confessed that they had sinned against the Lord. The text then adds (almost as an afterthought) that Samuel led (literally "judged") the Israelites at Mizpah. Samuel had appeared on the scene during a time of pervasive, cyclical decline in Israel. Yet, despite the sorry state of affairs, Samuel wasn't afraid to issue the call for spiritual revival in Israel. Under his leadership in the offices of prophet, priest, and judge, stability came to the beleaguered nation.

II. DEFEATING THE ENEMY: 1 SAMUEL 7:7-11, 15-17

A. The Threat of a Philistine Attack: vs. 7

When the Philistines heard that Israel had assembled at Mizpah, the rulers of the Philistines came up to attack them. And when the Israelites heard of it, they were afraid because of the Philistines.

The news that the Israelites had gathered at Mizpah prompted the Philistine rulers into action (1 Sam. 7:7). Perhaps fearing the threat of an insurrection among the Israelites, their overlords mustered their troops in order to attack God's people. In turn, the Israelites became terrified at the prospect of being mauled by Philistines. These warlike people were Israel's major enemy from Samson's day until the time of David. Since their main cities were located in a land corridor often used by invading armies, the Philistines were eventually overrun and disappeared from the annals of history. Their one legacy was the application of their name to the land of Canaan. The region between the Mediterranean Sea and the Jordan River became known as Palestine, or "the land of the Philistines."

B. The Intercession of Samuel: vss. 8-9

They said to Samuel, "Do not stop crying out to the LORD our God for us, that he may rescue us from the hand of the Philistines." Then Samuel took a suckling lamb and offered it up as a whole burnt offering to the LORD. He cried out to the LORD on Israel's behalf, and the LORD answered him.

Because the Israelites felt overwhelmed by the Philistine threat, they implored Samuel to continue making supplication to the Lord on their behalf. Their desire was that God would deliver them from their oppressors (1 Sam. 7:8). This request was agreeable to Samuel. Thus, he sacrificed a nursing lamb to the Lord as well as offered fervent prayer on behalf of the people. The Lord in turn "answered him" (vs. 9). How God responded to Samuel prior to the battle is not known. We can only assume that the prophet clearly recognized God's voice.

C. The Rout of the Philistines: vss. 10-11

While Samuel was sacrificing the burnt offering, the Philistines drew near to engage Israel in battle. But that day the LORD thundered with loud thunder against the Philistines and threw them into such a panic that they were routed before the Israelites. The men of Israel rushed out of Mizpah and pursued the Philistines, slaughtering them along the way to a point below Beth Car.

The burnt offering Samuel made to the Lord was a voluntary act of worship as well as an expression of devotion, commitment, and total surrender to God. In this case, the intent behind Samuel's actions represented the collective desire of the Israelites. Expressed differently, they wanted to make a complete break with their sin (especially their idolatry and immorality) and devote themselves once again in trust and obedience to God. We can be sure that He was pleased with such a response.

The Philistines prepared to attack while Samuel was in the process of offering sacrifices for the nation. As the enemy approached, however, God terrorized the Philistines in a thunderous display of divine power (1 Sam. 7:10). The concussion of noise could have been literal thunder or simply the voice of God. Buoyed by divine support, the Israelites engaged their foes. This led to the Philistines taking flight from the pursuing Israelites in panic and disarray. God's people immediately left Mizpah and chased the Philistines all the way to the hillside below Beth Car. The exact location of the town, whose name means "house of sheep," remains unknown. The Israelites slaughtered every enemy soldier they caught (vs. 11). So complete was the victory that the Philistines did not invade Israel again in Samuel's lifetime.

D. The Judgeship of Samuel: vss. 15-17

Samuel continued as judge over Israel all the days of his life. From year to year he went on a circuit from Bethel to Gilgal to Mizpah, judging Israel in all those places. But he always went back to Ramah, where his home was, and there he also judged Israel. And he built an altar there to the LORD.

After defeating the Philistines, Samuel expressed the people's gratitude to God by erecting a stone monument between Mizpah and Shen. The latter name literally means "the tooth," which could refer to a prominent mountain or hill shaped like a tooth. In any case, the location of Shen is unknown. Samuel called the monument "Ebenezer," which means "stone of help" (1 Sam. 7:12). God's assistance was so great that Israel got back all the land the Philistines had taken, broke the power of the Philistines over other neighboring peoples, and established peace with the Amorites (vss. 13-14). The name "Amorites" is a general designation for the original inhabitants of Canaan (see Josh. 10:5).

Throughout his life, Samuel served Israel as a circuit judge (1 Sam. 7:15). This included him making the rounds from Bethel to Gilgal to Mizpah to his hometown of Ramah (vs. 16-17). This route was roughly 50 miles in circumference. As a judge, Samuel's function was primarily threefold—civil (1 Sam. 7:16; see Exod. 18:16), military (see 1 Sam. 12:11), and religious (see 7:6, 17). In his priestly capacity, Samuel erected an altar to the Lord in Ramah because the tabernacle in Shiloh had been destroyed. In whatever capacity Samuel served, worship was always his first priority (vs. 17).

Discussion Questions

1. Why did Samuel direct the Israelites to abandon their idols?
2. In what way did Samuel intercede for the Israelites?
3. What sin did the Israelites admit they were guilty of doing?
4. What resources do believers have to overcome sin in their lives?
5. Why is it important for believers to be committed to serving only the Lord?

Contemporary Application

"What we believe about God," said the well-known Christian writer A. W. Tozer, "is the most important thing about us." How true are his words! Our beliefs invariably affect our character, our thoughts, and our eternal futures. As Samuel emphasized to the people of Israel during his many years of service, what we believe and trust should be reflected in what we do. If we believe in God, we will prove it through specific actions. Saying we serve only Him when other things control our life is hypocrisy.

It is not hard to find idols in our own society that demand our time and devotion to them. If we were to take one day of our life and analyze how we spend our time, we might be shocked by where our own "idols" may be lurking. The appropriate response is to clean them out, as the Israelites did, so that God's spiritual blessings may follow. Perhaps some of us have never claimed to trust in God and serve Him. If we trust in ourselves, it ultimately will lead only to selfishness and despair. Augustine, the fifth-century church leader, said it well: "Beware of despairing about yourself: you are commanded to put your trust in God, not in yourself."

How can we make God the exclusive focus of our trust and devotion? The answer is found in Scripture. There is a clear call to personal commitment that runs through the Old Testament and into the New Testament. We do not need to attend a graduate school of religion or spend years trying to uncover the alleged "hidden" secrets of the Bible. We need to attend carefully to the message of God's Word and apply its truths.

Samuel is only one of many people who have heeded the teaching of Scripture and given their lives to the Lord in wholehearted service. In the New Testament, people from all walks of life responded to the gospel exhortation to believe in Jesus for eternal life, and they did. Likewise, we need to put our trust in the risen Lord and follow His example of total submission to His Father's will.

Embodying God's Justice

Scripture

Background Scripture: *2 Samuel 22:1–23:7;
1 Chronicles 18:14*

Scripture Lesson: *2 Samuel 23:1-7; 1 Chronicles 18:14*

Key Verse: *David reigned over all Israel, doing what was just
and right for all his people.* 1 Chronicles 18:14.

Scripture Lesson for Children: *2 Samuel 23:1-7;
1 Chronicles 18:14*

Key Verse for Children: *David [did] what was just and
right for all his people.* 1 Chronicles 18:14.

Lesson Aim

To recognize that God blesses those who faithfully
serve Him.

Lesson Setting

Time: About 970 B.C.

Place: Jerusalem

Lesson Outline

Embodying God's Justice

   I. The Lord's Approval: 2 Samuel 23:1-4

      A. The Beloved Psalmist of Israel: vs. 1

      B. The Spirit Speaking through David: vs. 2

      C. The Blessing of Governing Fairly: vss. 3-4

  II. The Lord's Deliverance: 2 Samuel 23:5-7

      A. The Lord's Everlasting Covenant: vs. 5

      B. The Demise of the Godless: vss. 6-7

 III. The Just Rule of David: 1 Chronicles 18:14

Introduction for Adults

Topic: *True to the End*

Promises are the great stuff of life. We make promises when we get married. Our children extract promises from us. And we obtain promises from our employers. God's promise to David of an "everlasting covenant" (2 Sam. 23:5) was so astonishing that we find it difficult to fathom. God pledged to give him a great name, a homeland for the Israelites, and an enduring dynasty (see 7:8-13).

Perhaps these promises sound too much like the pledges that politicians make during their election campaigns. After all, promises are only as good as the one who makes them. (Nothing is worse than a broken pledge!) In David's case, he believed what God promised to him, and this was the basis for David remaining true to God to the end of the king's life.

We likewise are refreshed, encouraged, and inspired by God's promises to us. We live in hope because we believe in the total reliability and trustworthiness of God. He cannot lie (Titus 1:2). Therefore, as the old hymn puts it, we are "standing on the promises of God."

Introduction for Youth

Topic: *Significance through Justice*

We love to ask children, "What do you want to be when you grow up?" Later on, when they finish high school, we may ask, "What are your career goals?" That's when youth begin to wrestle with their dreams. Sometimes it takes years for them to figure out what they want to do with their life.

Since we build our lives on God's will, it's good to remind ourselves what the Lord told David: "I took you from the pasture and from following the flock to be ruler over my people Israel" (2 Sam. 7:8). No high school or college guidance counselor could ever have foretold that career for David. And who could have guessed that his enduring legacy would be that of justice and righteousness (see 2 Sam. 23:3; 1 Chron. 18:14)?

While it's wise to get all the counseling we can, in the end we must trust God to help us make something out of our lives. We can be sure that God's desire for our success as Christians far outweighs our own. Obedience to Him right now will lead to greater opportunities to serve Him in the future.

Concepts for Children

Topic: *David: A Just King*

1. David was the king of Israel for 40 years.
2. David wanted to do what was right as the nation's king.
3. David tried to be fair and kind to everyone.
4. God was pleased with the way David ruled the chosen people.
5. God is always present to help us remain faithful to Him.

Lesson Commentary

I. THE LORD'S APPROVAL: 2 SAMUEL 23:1-4

A. The Beloved Psalmist of Israel: vs. 1

These are the last words of David: "The oracle of David son of Jesse, the oracle of the man exalted by the Most High, the man anointed by the God of Jacob, Israel's singer of songs."

Even though King David was a man of deep faith, his human failings and often ruthless drive to get what he wanted resulted in great distress for himself and his family. Toward the end of David's reign, his kingdom was struck with a three-year famine because of Saul's slaughter of the Gibeonites. David turned over seven of Saul's descendants to the Gibeonites for execution to avenge their loss. Second Samuel 21 ends by cataloging four different battles in which Israel prevailed over the Philistines. Chapter 22 records David's song of praise to the Lord for delivering him from all his enemies, including Saul. David declared that the Lord was his source of strength. God had come to his rescue and given him complete victory over his foes. David concluded by extolling the God of his salvation.

In 23:1-7, we find the "last words of David" (vs. 1). They are reminiscent of the king's ode of joy recorded in chapter 22. Like many of David's psalms, the hymn appearing in 23:1-7 affirms God's faithfulness in keeping His promises. These concluding thoughts are not literally the final statements David ever made. They are more like a concluding, solemn declaration of a leader of Israel whose heart remained faithful to God to the end of his life. Since David used the Hebrew noun rendered "oracle" (vs. 1), this might also be his last inspired utterance. When a true prophet of the Lord spoke an oracle, he declared the very words of God.

David described himself as one of Jesse's sons. An examination of 1 Samuel 16:10-11 indicates that Jesse had eight sons, with David being the youngest. First Chronicles 2:13-15 gives the names of David's brothers, and lists David as the seventh son. Apparently one of David's brothers was excluded from the genealogy in 1 Chronicles, perhaps because he had no offspring. In any case, 1 Samuel 16:12 states that David had a striking presence about him. He is described as glowing with health, and being both bright-eyed and good-looking. The Hebrew adjective translated "ruddy" probably referred to David's reddish hair and complexion, which was enhanced by spending much of his time out in the sun. These features were singled out in a land where dark hair and complexion were the norm.

Second Samuel 23:1 notes that as Israel's king, David was "exalted by the Most High." The latter phrase points to God as the sovereign Lord and creator of the entire universe. In His mercy, He gave David great success in defeating all his enemies (see 7:1). Before this ever happened, though, the "God of Jacob" (23:1) had Samuel anoint David as the next king of Israel (see 1 Sam. 16:12-13). Though at that time David was handsome in appearance, Samuel did not choose him because of his good looks. David was a person after God's own heart, which is the most important quality a leader can have (see 13:14; 16:7). After the anointing, the Holy Spirit came upon David with power, enabling him for the task of leadership. In the Old Testament, the indwelling of the Holy Spirit was often temporary and individual, while in the church age it became extensive and long-lasting. Now, the Holy Spirit indwells all believers as they are incorporated into the body of Christ (see Rom. 8:9), not just certain individuals empowered for some special service to God (see Judg. 3:10; 6:34; 13:25; 14:6; 1 Sam. 10:10; 16:13).

The last part of 2 Samuel 23:1 is literally rendered "the pleasant psalmist of Israel." In a manner of speaking, David was the nation's most beloved and popular lyricist. As Israel's premier psalmist, David was an accomplished musician. Seventy-three psalms are ascribed to him, and he was also instrumental in appointing other singers and musicians to lead in Israel's worship (see 1 Chron. 15:16). David was often the most heroic person in the many hymns he authored. Some have called David's description of himself in 2 Samuel 23:1 as pompous. However, in two of the three descriptions, the king gave God credit for his high positions. David was simply recounting the places to which the Lord had exalted him. David had been elevated to the office of king from a lowly position in an obscure family. Moreover, Jesse's son had been chosen by God to serve as the nation's monarch. He did not strive for or place himself in that position.

B. The Spirit Speaking through David: vs. 2

"The Spirit of the LORD spoke through me; his word was on my tongue."

David's words were far more than poetry set to music. The psalms were written under the inspiration of the Holy Spirit (2 Sam. 23:2). While David used his own thoughts, vocabulary, and style in composing the psalms, the Holy Spirit oversaw the process to make sure that David penned only the words God wanted written. Along with the rest of Scripture, the songs authored by David give practical solutions for living according to God's plan (2 Tim. 3:16). From these passages we can be taught, rebuked, corrected, and thoroughly trained in righteous living. In fact, it is the Bible—with words that have been breathed by God Himself—that equips us to do good (vs. 17). Good works that stem from genuine faith have great value and bear much fruit for God's kingdom.

C. The Blessing of Governing Fairly: vss. 3-4

"The God of Israel spoke, the Rock of Israel said to me: 'When one rules over men in righteousness, when he rules in the fear of God, he is like the light of morning at sunrise on a cloudless morning, like the brightness after rain that brings the grass from the earth.'"

The "God of Israel" (2 Sam. 23:3), who was the source of David's prophetic gift, was also "the Rock of Israel." Hannah, the mother of the prophet Samuel, used a similar title to describe God in her prayer of thanksgiving after Samuel's birth (see 1 Sam. 2:2). The Hebrew noun translated "Rock" can refer to a single large boulder or an entire mountain range. During David's time of exile in the wilderness, he learned how important the mountains and their resources could be. A large boulder provided shade from the desert sun, while serving as a defensive barrier against David's enemies. The mountain ranges also provided many hiding places, like the cave of Adullam, which David used as a headquarters (see 2 Sam. 23:13). In short, the Rock of Israel was a reliable source of refuge and protection for David (see Deut. 32:4, 15, 18, 30-31; 2 Sam. 22:47).

Next, David recorded God's description of the ideal king (2 Sam. 23:3; see Isa. 9:7; 11:1-5; Jer. 23:5-6; 33:15-16; Zech. 9:9). To govern in "righteousness" (2 Sam. 23:3) was to rule in an equitable and virtuous manner. It also meant to lead the nation in the "fear of God." Loving the Lord and relating to Him in reverential fear are so closely linked that in some passages they are virtually synonymous (see Deut. 10:12). As noted in lesson 2, the biblical concept of fearing God does not mean we should be terrified to enter into His presence. To fear God is to approach Him with a sense of worship and awe, recognizing that He alone is worthy to be praised. The ideal king of Israel was to maintain this view of the Lord and inspire it in others. As Christians, we don't have to be leaders to set this kind of example. It should come naturally to us.

David used two word pictures to describe this kind of ruler (2 Sam. 23:4). The one who leads in the fear of God is like the light of dawn on a cloudless morning or the return of the sun after a refreshing rain. "The brightness after rain" could refer to light that occurs during a thunderstorm, which is an allusion to lightning. It causes tender grass to carpet the earth, and it glistens under the refreshing rain (see Ps. 72:1-7). In Revelation 22:16, the Lord Jesus referred to Himself as the Messiah who came from the house and lineage of David. Moreover, Jesus is the "bright Morning Star" who ensures that a new day of salvation will dawn for believers.

II. The Lord's Deliverance: 2 Samuel 23:5-7

A. The Lord's Everlasting Covenant: vs. 5

"Is not my house right with God? Has he not made with me an everlasting covenant, arranged and secured in every part? Will he not bring to fruition my salvation and grant me my every desire?"

Throughout David's tenure as Israel's king, he strove to be a godly and upright monarch. He declared that his "house" (2 Sam. 23:5), that is, his family and dynasty, had been established by God. As before, David was not boasting here, but spoke under the inspiration of the Holy Spirit. This was God's statement of fact about David, not the king's opinion about himself. Ultimately, of course, David's standing before the Lord was a matter of grace. Indeed, David's house was right with God because the Creator had entered into a covenant with David, which the Redeemer had initiated. In turn, He would always deliver David and bring all his desire to fruition.

The latter truths are more fully recounted in 7:8-16. Nathan the prophet related that the Lord in His grace had taken David from being a shepherd boy and made him the king of Israel (vs. 8). God had not only enabled David to subdue his enemies but also made his name famous. In addition, the Lord used David to enable the Israelites to dwell in peace in Canaan. This had never been true since the time of the judges (vss. 9-11). Verses 11-13 record the establishment of God's covenant with David, which amplifies and confirms the promises of His covenant with Abraham (see Gen. 12:1-3). Although the word "covenant" is not specifically stated in 2 Samuel 7, it is used elsewhere to describe this occasion (see 2 Sam. 23:5; Ps. 89:28, 34). Clearly, the issues of 2 Samuel 7 are of immense theological importance. They concern not only the first coming of the Messiah, but also the Savior's eternal rule on the throne of David.

The Hebrew noun rendered "house" (vs. 11) lies at the heart of this passage. David saw his own house (or palace) and desired to build a house (or temple) for the Lord. God declared, however, that He would build a house (or dynasty) for David. Moreover, the king's son would build a house (or temple) for the Lord. In His covenant with David, God promised that the king's descendants would become a dynasty and always rule over Israel. Individual kings were subject to severe punishment (Ps. 89:30-32), but the Lord would never permanently reject the line of David from the throne (vss. 33-37). The New Testament reveals that God's promises to David are fulfilled in the Lord Jesus. He keeps the conditions of the covenant perfectly (Heb. 4:15), serves as the Mediator of the covenant (9:15), and promises to return as the conquering King (Matt. 24:29-31).

David did not have to worry whether his kingdom would endure after his death, for the Lord would make the royal throne of his son secure for all time (2 Sam. 7:13). God also pledged to establish an intimate Father-son relationship with David's descendants. When a Davidic king did wrong, the Lord would punish him just as parents discipline their rebellious children (vs. 14). God's punishment of David's successors would culminate in the loss of land and temple (see 1 Kings 9:6-9). Yet the Lord would never withdraw His love from His covenant people. Furthermore, the Davidic kings did not have to fear that God would remove His loyal love from them as He had with Saul (2 Sam. 7:15; see 1 Sam. 15:28). God's promise to establish forever the dynasty, kingdom, and throne of David would not fail (2 Sam. 7:16), being one day fully realized in the Messiah (see Jer. 33:14-26; Mic. 5:2-5). Because the Lord Jesus has entered into a covenant with those who believe, Christians can also say that we are right with God. Like David's salvation, our deliverance will be brought to fruition when the Messiah returns to permanently establish His kingdom in its ultimate phase.

God used Nathan on a number of other occasions to reveal His will to David. For instance, the Lord later sent Nathan to rebuke David for his multiple sins of coveting, theft, adultery, and murder in his affair with Bathsheba (2 Sam. 12:1-15; Ps. 51). Also, when Solomon was born, God sent word through Nathan to name the child Jedidiah (2 Sam. 12:25). Furthermore, Nathan was involved in advising David on how to arrange the musical service for sanctuary worship (2 Chron. 29:25). And when Adonijah tried to claim the throne of David, Nathan undermined his efforts (1 Kings 1:11-27). The prophet was even part of the delegation that proclaimed Solomon king (vss. 28-45). Nathan later wrote a history in which he described the reigns of David and Solomon (1 Chron. 29:29-30; 2 Chron. 9:29).

B. The Demise of the Godless: vss. 6-7

"But evil men are all to be cast aside like thorns, which are not gathered with the hand. Whoever touch-es thorns uses a tool of iron or the shaft of a spear; they are burned up where they lie."

The destiny of the wicked is radically different from that of the righteous. The Hebrew noun rendered "evil" (2 Sam. 23:6) is literally "Belial" and refers to people who are reprobate and wretched in their character. David compared these godless individuals to "thorns," which is a metaphor of rejection. To gather them with one's hands risked injury. Instead, they were to be handled with an iron instrument or the wooden shaft of a spear. In David's time, soldiers would use both of these items to combat their foes in times of war (vs. 7). Thorns were considered worthless and had to be burned before the farmer could cultivate the land. Unrepentant, wicked rulers would be treated with similar roughness by God. Sadly, most of David's successors would fall into this category.

III. THE JUST RULE OF DAVID: 1 CHRONICLES 18:14

David reigned over all Israel, doing what was just and right for all his people.

First Chronicles opens with nine chapters of genealogies that stretch from Adam to the time of the return from Babylonian captivity. Then the narrative picks up with the death of Saul, and the rest of 1 Chronicles parallels the contents of 2 Samuel. Second Chronicles covers the same time frame as both books of Kings. Chronicles deals only with the kings who reigned from Jerusalem. The northern kings of Israel are mentioned in passing and only when they have significant contact with the southern kingdom.

Concerning David, when he died, he was honored with burial in the old fortress part of Jerusalem, which he had captured for his capital and which bore his name (1 Kings 2:10; see 2 Sam. 5:6-10). The last 33 years of David's reign had been spent in Jerusalem as the king of all the tribes (1 Chron. 18:14). This was after the 7 years in Hebron when only the tribe of Judah acknowledged him as their king (1 Kings 2:11; see 2 Sam. 5:5). Throughout David's entire reign (1010–970 B.C.), he sought to administer justice and righteous to the chosen people (1 Chron. 18:14). Admittedly, he was far from perfect. Be that as it may, David endeavored to be fair and evenhanded in serving the Israelites before God.

Discussion Questions

1. In what sense were David's utterances inspired?
2. What was the basis for the Lord anointing David to be the ruler of Israel?
3. Why was it important for the Spirit to speak through David as Israel's king?
4. In what ways has the Lord proven to be a source of refuge and protection for you?
5. How might the Lord use you to encourage the ungodly to repent and be saved?

Contemporary Application

Kim has volunteered at the homeless shelter in her city for several years. As a result, she has made friends with people she never would have known. She has befriended wayward teens doing community service there, as well as warm, caring retirees who have added a fresh perspective to her life.

One woman, in her 70s, has become a particular encouragement to Kim. Kim has also learned more about the social services in her community and has even taken advantage of the free mental health clinic for herself. Best of all, Kim has been able to watch God work in the lives of disadvantaged people and has become more grateful for the small but adequate apartment in which she lives.

A seeker of God such as Kim has the greatest likelihood of experiencing the spiritual blessings of God. When we let the Lord's concerns rank equal in importance with our own (as David did), our character changes, and we're more apt to experience God's blessings. It's not that service earns blessings or erases problems. Even David faced significant challenges in his life, but he did see the greater purposes of God for which he worked—the building of the nation of Israel—become fruitful.

We also must be careful not to dictate to God just what our spiritual blessings should be. Instead, our goal is to serve the Lord and let Him decide on how, when, and where He will shower His favor on us. Perhaps we will be blessed by seeing someone we have been teaching really grasp what God is about, or by seeing someone advance whom we helped get a job, or by seeing a positive report from a missions agency we have supported for years.

Jesus assures us that His love will always be with us. This remains true, even when some of our noble dreams crumble. Such circumstances remind us to live by faith, not by sight. In fact, the entire Christian life is based on eternal truths, which we cannot see. That is the essence of our faith (Heb. 11:1). Like David, we did nothing to deserve God's blessings, whether past, present, or future. So our foremost response is to praise and thank the Father for giving us eternal life with Him through faith in His Son, Jesus Christ.

Wisdom and Justice

Scripture

Background Scripture: *1 Kings 3; 2 Chronicles 9:8*
Scripture Lesson: *1 Kings 3:16-28; 2 Chronicles 9:8*
Key Verse: *When all Israel heard the verdict the king had
given, they held the king in awe, because they saw that he had
wisdom from God to administer justice.* 1 Kings 3:28.
Scripture Lesson for Children: *1 Kings 3:16-28*
Key Verse for Children: *Israel . . . held the king in awe,
because they saw that [Solomon] had wisdom from God to
administer justice.* 1 Kings 3:28.

Lesson Aim

To discover that a discerning heart is better than power
or riches.

Lesson Setting

Time: 970–930 B.C.
Place: Jerusalem

Lesson Outline

Wisdom and Justice

I. The Claims Made by Two Prostitutes:
1 Kings 3:16-22a
  A. *The Two Prostitutes in the Presence of Solomon:
     vs. 16*
  B. *The First Prostitute's Statement: vss. 17-21*
  C. *The Second Prostitute's Statement: vs. 22a*
II. The Decision Made by Solomon: 1 Kings 3:22b-28
  A. *The King's Summary of Each Prostitute's Statement:
     vss. 22b-23*
  B. *The King's Initial Decree: vss. 24-25*
  C. *The Prostitutes' Differing Responses: vs. 26*
  D. *The King's Wise Ruling: vss. 27-28*
III. The Perspective of the Queen of Sheba:
2 Chronicles 9:8

Introduction for Adults

Topic: *Wisdom and Justice*

Solomon was faced with what seemed like an impossible dilemma to resolve. And it was only his God-given wisdom that enabled the king to make an equitable decision.

Most of us at one time or another have thrown up our hands in despair and shouted, "It's impossible!" That's a normal human response. Perhaps it's a situation at work in which our boss has demanded more from us than is physically possible for us to accomplish. Or maybe we're expected to do a job for which we lack the training and experience. Another scenario may involve our impatience in dealing with personal problems that appear unending.

For Christians today, the gift and ability to discern is important for managing the development of their personal lives and professional careers. But believers should not expect this gift to appear "full-grown" within the moment they begin to receive it from God. Instead, wisdom will come to them in seed form and will continue to mature throughout their entire lifetime. What's important is that discernment gets planted within, and that the students continually water it by obedience and devotion to the Lord.

Introduction for Youth

Topic: *Wisdom through Justice*

Most of your students would affirm the desire to have God's wisdom in their lives. They will be more inclined to do so as a result of learning about an incident in which Solomon had to settle a dispute between two prostitutes.

James 1:5 tells us how it is possible to become more prudent in the decisions we make. We learn that if we lack wisdom, namely the discernment to do what is proper, we should ask God for it. He in turn will help us know what He wants us to do.

This is one of the "promise Scriptures" many newly saved teens memorize and many mature believers rely on. It reminds us that we are not left to our own understanding. The Lord makes His wisdom available for the asking. If time permits, consider spending a few moments with the adolescents in prayer, in which they are given the opportunity to petition God for discernment to make sensible choices.

Concepts for Children

Topic: *Solomon: A Wise Judge*

1. God gave Solomon wisdom.
2. Solomon used his wisdom to make good decisions.
3. The people of Israel were amazed at Solomon's wisdom.
4. God wants to give us wisdom, too.
5. We should use our wisdom to help others make good decisions.

Lesson Commentary

I. THE CLAIMS MADE BY TWO PROSTITUTES: 1 KINGS 3:16-22A

A. The Two Prostitutes in the Presence of Solomon: vs. 16

Now two prostitutes came to the king and stood before him.

First Kings 1 tells how Solomon thwarted Adonijah's early attempt to usurp the throne against David's wishes and became ruler of the mighty nation his father had built. David, upon hearing about Solomon's success, called his favorite son to hear his deathbed directives. David's primary instruction to Solomon was to show his loyalty to the Lord by following His commandments. If Solomon did, David assured his son that the Lord would make him prosper. Though unspoken, David implied that if Solomon and his descendants did not follow the Lord's commandments, they would fail instead of prosper (2:1-4).

By the end of his fourth year as king of Israel, Solomon had severely dealt with any internal threats to his throne. He had also begun dealing with any external threats to his kingdom by making a marriage alliance with the pharaoh of Egypt. Solomon housed his wife somewhere in the old part of Jerusalem until he could build her a palace (3:1). Moreover, at this time the Israelites offered sacrifices at the high places. Despite prohibitions against using once-pagan sites to venerate the Lord, the practice was quite common in Israel before Solomon built the temple (vs. 2). To show his gratitude to God for the stability his kingdom now enjoyed, Solomon traveled to the high place near Gibeon and sacrificed a thousand burnt offerings there to the Lord (vss. 3-4). Though the biblical writer clearly explained that performing an offering on such high places went against God's commandments, He seemed to make allowances for it, since the temple had not yet been built (vs. 2). Also, while the location used to make the offerings was once used for pagan sacrifices, Solomon's intention was to thank and glorify the one true God.

God rewarded Solomon's obedience by speaking with him through a dream. The Lord offered to give the young monarch anything he requested (vs. 5). In response, Solomon noted that God had been exceedingly loyal to His servant David, who walked before the Lord in faithfulness, uprightness, and sincerity. God had demonstrated His steadfast love to David by allowing his son, Solomon, to sit as his successor on his throne (vs. 6). The new monarch was well aware that it was the sovereign Lord, the God of the patriarchs, who enabled Solomon to consolidate his power and serve in the place of his father, David. Solomon also acknowledged that he was a relatively young man and somewhat inexperienced when it came to running an entire nation (vs. 7). The typical wish of Solomon's contemporaries would have included a long life, great riches, or the destruction of enemies. Instead of asking for these, Solomon requested a discerning heart so he could properly govern his kingdom. In making this remarkable request, the young monarch—who was probably about 20-24 years old—admitted that properly ruling the 12 tribes of Israel called for more experience and knowledge than he could claim. Perhaps Solomon's first four years in power had taught him how complicated running a kingdom could be (vss. 8-9).

Solomon's humble request pleased the Lord (vs. 10). In particular, God took note of Solomon's desire for the ability to make wise judicial decisions, rather than be given health, wealth, or even vengeance on his foes (vs. 11). The Lord in turn promised Solomon the wisest and most discerning heart of all time (vs. 12). The Lord also gave Solomon what he had not requested, namely, riches and honor (vs. 13). The result is that David's successor was the greatest monarch of his generation. All Solomon had to do to insure receiving these blessings was to wholly follow the Lord (vs. 14). When Solomon awakened from his sleep, he realized the Lord had spoken to him in a dream (vs. 15). Solomon hurried back to Jerusalem, where "the ark of the Lord's covenant" was and made additional offerings there. These probably were the fellowship offerings of Leviticus 7:11-17 that celebrated the gratitude of the offerer for God's activity in his life. All of the officials of Solomon's court joined him in a feast thanking God for investing the young king with great wisdom and discernment. The feast would have consisted of the animals offered in the fellowship offerings.

Verses 16-28 recount an incident in which Solomon displayed uncanny wisdom. The episode involved a dispute between two prostitutes who claimed the same baby. In turn, they wanted the young monarch to settle the controversy. The time of the incident must have been early in Solomon's reign, for it helped establish his reputation for wisdom (see vs. 28). Evidently, there were occasions when Solomon held open court so that ordinary citizens could bring their complaints to him.

B. The First Prostitute's Statement: vss. 17-21

One of them said, "My lord, this woman and I live in the same house. I had a baby while she was there with me. The third day after my child was born, this woman also had a baby. We were alone; there was no one in the house but the two of us. During the night this woman's son died because she lay on him. So she got up in the middle of the night and took my son from my side while I your servant was asleep. She put him by her breast and put her dead son by my breast. The next morning, I got up to nurse my son— and he was dead! But when I looked at him closely in the morning light, I saw that it wasn't the son I had borne."

Prostitution seems to have been practiced, even though it was unlawful in Israel. Since mostly men traveled, the connection between brothels and public inns was so strong that the Hebrew word for "prostitute" could also mean "innkeeper." The two prostitutes who appeared before Solomon may have lost their customers as their pregnancies advanced. The first prostitute to speak noted that she and the other prostitute shared a house and that she gave birth to her son while both women were living there (1 Kings 3:17). Three days later, the other prostitute gave birth to her son. According to the first prostitute, they and their newborns were the only ones in the house at that time (vs. 18).

It's not hard to imagine the mutual joy both mothers shared at the births of their babies. But then tragedy struck when, according to the first prostitute, the other one accidentally rolled on top of her newborn and suffocated him (vs. 19). Evidently, this death occurred early in the evening, and there were no witnesses to the baby boy's death. This enabled the bereaved mother to devise a heinous plan. Later that night, she got up, took the other mother's baby boy from her side without waking her up, and replaced him with her infant's corpse (vs. 20). When the first prostitute got up the next morning to nurse her baby boy, she was shocked to discover that he was dead. Even more appalling was the fact that when the mother carefully examined the newborn, she realized he wasn't her baby (vs. 21).

C. The Second Prostitute's Statement: vs. 22a

The other woman said, "No! The living one is my son; the dead one is yours."

We can only wonder how conflicted the second prostitute might have felt as Solomon listened to the first version of the tragic account. The bereaved mother had been desperate when she switched the corpse for the other baby. Now she was sufficiently brazen to declare that her son was alive and that the other prostitute's son was dead (1 Kings 3:22). It must have taken a lot of emotional energy for the second prostitute to keep up her pretense.

II. The Decision Made by Solomon: 1 Kings 3:22b-28

A. The King's Summary of Each Prostitute's Statement: vss. 22b-23

But the first one insisted, "No! The dead one is yours; the living one is mine." And so they argued before the king. The king said, "This one says, 'My son is alive and your son is dead,' while that one says, 'No! Your son is dead and mine is alive.'"

The first prostitute must have been horrified when she heard the other prostitute shamelessly lie in the king's presence. But this did not stop the real mother of the baby boy from insisting that he belonged to her and that the other woman's son was dead. For several minutes the two prostitutes argued, with one woman and then the other countering each other's claims (1 Kings 3:22). It was not difficult for Solomon to restate the seemingly irresolvable dispute the mothers had over whose son remained alive (vs. 23). The hard part was in exercising discernment in making a wise ruling. Somehow, the king needed to distinguish between a mother's regard for her son and a selfish woman's desire not to lose having a child. The young monarch needed wisdom to devise a means of eliciting revealing responses from the women.

B. The King's Initial Decree: vss. 24-25

Then the king said, "Bring me a sword." So they brought a sword for the king. He then gave an order: "Cut the living child in two and give half to one and half to the other."

Obviously, Solomon did not have all day to listen to the two prostitutes haggle about who was the actual birth mother for the surviving baby boy. The king also did not have the resources to conduct a forensic analysis of the home where the other infant died. Moreover, Solomon knew nothing about genetic testing to identify which of the two women was telling the truth. Instead, the young monarch directed his court officials to bring him a sword, which they did (1 Kings 3:24). Perhaps the two prostitutes were stunned to hear Solomon order his attendants to use the weapon to slice the baby boy in two, with one half of its corpse being given to one mother and the second half going to the other mother (vs. 25). In this instance, the king was not being cruel. Instead, he astutely chose to order the child's execution to see how each woman would respond.

C. The Prostitutes' Differing Responses: vs. 26

The woman whose son was alive was filled with compassion for her son and said to the king, "Please, my lord, give her the living baby! Don't kill him!" But the other said, "Neither I nor you shall have him. Cut him in two!"

One can ask whether Solomon's scheme revealed the actual biological mother or the woman who was more fit to mother him regardless of their biological relationship. The writer of 1 Kings had no doubt that Solomon used his God-given wisdom and discernment to determine the biological mother. When she heard the young monarch's decree, she could not bear the thought of seeing her baby boy sliced in two and die instantly. The first prostitute's motherly instincts were so strong that she pleaded with the young monarch to spare her infant son by giving him to the bereaved woman. The latter, in contrast, felt no emotion toward the newborn and insisted that he be divided in two. The second prostitute concluded that neither she nor the real mother would have the child (3:26).

D. The King's Wise Ruling: vss. 27-28

Then the king gave his ruling: "Give the living baby to the first woman. Do not kill him; she is his mother." When all Israel heard the verdict the king had given, they held the king in awe, because they saw that he had wisdom from God to administer justice.

The king's savvy plan worked. He was able to use the birth mother's strong yearning for her infant to determine that she had told the truth all along. In turn, Solomon ordered that the first prostitute be given parental custody of the baby boy. After all, since the real mother had been found, it wasn't necessary to execute the newborn (1 Kings 3:27). It did not take long for the news about the young monarch's decision to spread throughout "all Israel" (vs. 28). The covenant community stood in awe of Solomon, for they realized that he truly had God-given "wisdom" to make prudent judicial decisions. It's interesting that this brief account is one of the best-known incidents in the Old Testament. Almost everyone knows that Solomon showed his unusual discernment by proposing to cut a baby in two to reveal that the protective woman was the true mother. This incident still reveals that God did something unusual for the young monarch so that he could administer justice among God's chosen people.

III. THE PERSPECTIVE OF THE QUEEN OF SHEBA: 2 CHRONICLES 9:8

"Praise be to the LORD your God, who has delighted in you and placed you on his throne as king to rule for the LORD your God. Because of the love of your God for Israel and his desire to uphold them forever, he has made you king over them, to maintain justice and righteousness."

Solomon's reputation for wisdom became renowned in the ancient world. For instance, the queen of Sheba traveled from southwest Arabia to Jerusalem to see whether the Israelite king's reputation was warranted (2 Chron. 9:1). Sheba was a kingdom occupying part of modern Yemen and controlling territory in eastern Ethiopia across the Bab el Mandeb, the narrow straits between the Red Sea and the Gulf of Aden. Its capital, Marib, has been excavated by archaeologists. Sheba flourished as the receiver of merchandise from India and Africa that it shipped by camel caravan to Damascus and Gaza. Spices, especially Arabian balm, were Sheba's specialty. The queen of Sheba brought Solomon a camel-caravan load of gold, spices, and precious stones. The spices—associated with perfumes and ointments rather than food—were the most impressive and valued part of her gift (vs. 9).

The queen's personal mission was posing "hard questions" (vs. 1) to Solomon. The queen probably pressed the most puzzling philosophical and religious issues of the day on Solomon to compare his answers with those she had heard from the sages of her court. No vexing issue the queen of Sheba asked Solomon stumped him (vs. 2). Not only did he answer every difficult question, but the quality of his answers surpassed anything the queen had ever heard. They rang true at the deepest spiritual levels. The queen was overwhelmed by the cumulative effect of Solomon's personal wisdom, the splendor of his capital city, the opulence of his court, and the majesty of his worship of God (vss. 3-4).

The queen of Sheba—partly as diplomatic courtesy, but largely as honest confession—confirmed that the dramatic stories she had heard about Solomon were true (vs. 5). The queen had been unable to believe them without personally checking their veracity. After doing so she concluded that words could not convey half of the impact of witnessing the king's wisdom (vs. 6). The queen praised Solomon's officials, who benefited every day from working in the presence and atmosphere created by his wisdom (vs. 7). The queen praised the Lord (whom she identified as Solomon's God) and credited Him for Solomon's unusual abilities and magnificent realm (vs. 8). The dignitary attributed the justice and righteousness of Solomon's government to the Lord's love for His people Israel and His lasting commitment to them.

The queen of Sheba gave Solomon 120 talents of gold, the same amount Hiram king of Tyre had given him in exchange for the 20 towns of Cabul (vs. 9; see 1 Kings

9:11, 14). Perhaps Solomon used this gold to repay Hiram when he was dissatisfied with the towns (see 1 Kings 9:13; 2 Chron. 8:2). The spices in the gift from Sheba stood out because Solomon's shipping venture with Hiram had already netted him great quantities of gold, precious stones, and rare woods. The rare woods went into special applications in the temple and palace and into musical instruments (1 Kings 10:11-12; 2 Chron. 9:10-11). In addition to sharing his wisdom with her, King Solomon lavished gifts on the queen of Sheba in keeping with his stature as a wealthy and powerful monarch (1 Kings 10:13). The Chronicler indicated that the value of Solomon's gifts exceeded those of the queen (see 2 Chron. 9:12).

Discussion Questions

1. What emotions do you think each of the mothers felt as they stood in Solomon's presence?
2. What are the details of the account the first prostitute gave to the king?
3. Why would the mother of the dead baby try to switch infants with the other mother?
4. How do you feel about Solomon's initial decision to give one half of the child's corpse to each mother?
5. What sort of counsel might the Lord want you to share with other believers?

Contemporary Application

Solomon's reign got off to a good start. He received great advice from his father. He had sense enough to accept his inadequacies. And he knew he needed wisdom from the Lord, especially to succeed as king of Israel. This became clear in the episode involving the dispute between two prostitutes.

When we face awesome responsibilities for which we feel unqualified, we can either avoid them or seek God's help. We may not ever have to ask Him how to be a wise ruler of a whole nation, but we still need wisdom to lead our families, churches, and communities.

Oftentimes what we think we need to live differs from what God thinks. Society says we should have lots of money, power, and popularity. But God's Word says our foremost concern should be His kingdom (Matt. 6:33). We can put the Father and His work first, for He has promised to supply all our needs from His glorious riches, which have been given to us in His Son (Phil. 4:19).

Therefore, our main focus should be on spiritually maturing as believers. This involves growing wiser, becoming more patient, demonstrating unconditional love to others, and obeying God in whatever we do (1 Cor. 13:4-7). It means manifesting the fruit of the Spirit, rather than the acts of the sinful nature (Gal. 5:19-23). Setting our sights on riches will only leave us dissatisfied, for even if we get the material possessions we crave, we will still want something more. But if we seek wisdom from God, He will provide it in abundance (Jas. 1:5).

Acting on a Widow's Behalf

Scripture

Background Scripture: *2 Kings 4:1-37; 8:1-6*

Scripture Lesson: *2 Kings 8:1-6*

Key Verse: *The king . . . assigned an official to her case and said to him, "Give back everything that belonged to her, including all the income from her land from the day she left the country until now."* 2 Kings 8:6.

Scripture Lesson for Children: *2 Kings 8:1-6*

Key Verse for Children: *The king . . . said to [an official], "Give back everything that belonged to her, including all the income from her land from the day she left the country until now."* 2 Kings 8:6.

Lesson Aim

To note that God's plan for us may not match our expectations.

Lesson Setting

Time: Between 852–841 B.C.

Place: Israel and Philistia

Lesson Outline

Acting on a Widow's Behalf

  I. The Seven-Year Famine: 2 Kings 8:1-2
    A. *The Directive to Leave Israel: vs. 1*
    B. *The Decision to Relocate to Philistia: vs. 2*
  II. The Restoration of Property: 2 Kings 8:3-6
    A. *The Shunammite's Appeal: vss. 3-5*
    B. *The King's Decision: vs. 6*

Introduction for Adults

Topic: *Restorative Justice*

Who cares for the poor without any preconditions? The ministry of Elisha in the life of the Shunammite woman indicates that God does. And Christians should, too, for it's one way the Lord brings about restorative justice.

During Jesus' earthly ministry, He stood against oppression, and the poor and helpless flocked to Him. Knowing that our Lord cares for the poor does not relieve us of our duty to give time, wisdom, and money to help them. Rather, we who belong to Christ by faith are to be His instruments of goodness and grace to the disadvantaged in society.

We admit that there are risks in being so generous. People who offer help to the poor have sometimes suffered for their efforts. We might worry about channeling our material resources in the wrong direction. We may also be concerned that our benevolent programs are not well managed. While these shortcomings do exist, they should not prevent us from reaching out to people in need. If we wait until all conditions are perfect, we will never find the right time to do anything.

Introduction for Youth

Topic: *Restoration through Justice*

When Elisha ministered to the Shunammite woman and her family, the prophet did so unconditionally. And justice prevailed when Israel's king restored the Shunammite's house and land to her, all due to the sterling reputation Elisha had as God's spokesperson.

There are a number of reasons why Christians should care for others, especially the poor, without expecting anything in return. But perhaps our biggest obstacle in doing so is our consuming self-interest. The world tells us to put ourselves first, to look out for number one.

We know, though, that God hates such pride. When we care for others, we strip ourselves of the desire to be first. We affirm the teaching of Jesus that "it is more blessed to give than to receive" (Acts 20:35). That's a spiritual principle that saved teens dare not ignore, especially if they want to enjoy the eternal delight of God.

Concepts for Children

Topic: *Justice Restored*

1. Elisha was a person who told others about God.
2. God used Elisha to help out a Shunammite woman and her family.
3. Israel's king greatly respected Elisha.
4. Israel's king did what was right by giving back to the Shunammite woman her house and land.
5. God spiritually blesses us for our acts of kindness to others.

Lesson Commentary

I. THE SEVEN-YEAR FAMINE: 2 KINGS 8:1-2

A. The Directive to Leave Israel: vs. 1

Now Elisha had said to the woman whose son he had restored to life, "Go away with your family and stay for a while wherever you can, because the LORD has decreed a famine in the land that will last seven years."

Elisha (848–797 B.C.), whose name means "God is salvation," was the son of Shaphat from Abel Meholah, a town located on the western side of the Jordan River. Elisha was also a statesman and prophet who succeeded Elijah (875–848 B.C.) in being God's official spokesperson (1 Kings 19:16-21). Before Elijah was taken up to heaven, he gave Elisha a double share of his prophetic spirit (2 Kings 2:9-15). The implication is that God blessed Elisha's ministry as Elijah's replacement. Elisha's 51-year ministry in the northern kingdom of Israel encompassed the reigns of Joram, Jehu, Jehoahaz, and Joash. Elisha declared the divine message, lead a prophetic order, advised kings, and anointed monarchs.

Second Kings 8:1 mentions an incident in which God used Elisha to bring a mother's son back to life. The woman was a wealthy resident of Shumen (4:8), a town located about three miles north of Jezreel and near Mount Gilboa. Sometime later, Elisha urged the woman to move her family temporarily to another place. The prophet explained that the Lord had decreed a seven-year famine on Israel to censure the people for disobedience and bring them to repentance (see Joel 2:12-14; Zeph. 3:5-7). The details of Elisha's previous encounter with the Shunammite woman and her son are recorded in 2 Kings 4:8-37. There we learn that as part of Elisha's ministerial duties, he traveled a circuit in which he visited groups of prophets who were under his spiritual care and direction. On one occasion, while Elisha was in Shunem, he met the previously mentioned woman. In turn, she invited the prophet to her home for a meal (vs. 8). After that, whenever Elisha was passing through the town, he would eat with the woman and her husband. Most likely, the man was a prominent leader.

Perhaps it only took a few encounters with Elisha for the Shunammite woman to realize that he was a "holy man of God" (vs. 9). This verse is a reminder that contemplating the holiness of God does not have to be a theological abstraction. When Scripture says that He is holy, it implies He is distinct from and transcends His creation. His holiness also indicates that His character and action are morally pure. Expressed differently, there is no taint of wicked intentions, motives, or desires in whatever He declares, thinks, or does. Accordingly, He is the source of all goodness, wholesomeness, and truth.

Elisha, as a holy person, devoted himself in service to God. While all who belong to the community of faith are called to serve the Lord and their fellow human beings, prophets such as Elisha were consecrated to God's work in a very special way. In 2 Timothy 2:4-6, Paul used the analogies of soldiers, athletes, and farmers to illustrate the single-minded dedication that typified the Lord's servants. Like a solider, ministers of God sought to please Him in everything they did. Also, like an athlete, those devoted to a high and holy calling operated according to the rules of Scripture. Moreover, like a hardworking farmer, agents of truth can anticipate being eternally rewarded for their commitment to the Lord.

Evidently, the Spirit of God was prompting the Shunammite woman to assist Elisha in his proclamation of the divine message. For the woman, this meant going out of her way to show hospitality to the prophet. The woman recommended to her husband that they build a small, fully walled room on the flat roof of their house, which Elisha could easily access by means of an outside staircase. Roofs in that era were used something like suburban decks are used today. Within the small room the woman wanted to place a minimum of basic furniture items, specifically, a bed, a table, a chair, and an oil lamp. Whenever Elisha visited the couple in Shunem, he could lodge in the room (2 Kings 4:10).

From all appearances, the husband agreed to his wife's idea, for verse 11 indicates that the upstairs private room became Elisha's place to stay whenever he passed through Shunem. Undoubtedly, the prophet came to appreciate the convenience of having a private room for himself as he traveled a regular circuit. Perhaps as he rested on the bed his hosts had graciously provided, he wondered what he could do for them. This prompted him to direct his personal servant, Gehazi, to tell the Shunammite woman the prophet wanted to speak to her (vs. 12). The questionable character of Gehazi is seen in the account involving Naaman, the army commander of the king of Aram (or Syria). After Elisha cured Naaman of leprosy, the prophet refused any reward from the Aramean. This decision, however, did not sit well with Gehazi. So he ran after the military official to claim some items for himself. Because of Gehazi's duplicity and greed, Elisha cursed him with the same skin disease from which Naaman had been cured (see 5:20-27).

Elisha spoke to the Shunammite woman through Gehazi. The Hebrew of 4:13 literally says, "you have turned trembling to us with all this trembling." The idea behind this expression is that his wife had gone to a lot of trouble to provide for Elisha's needs. Elisha felt so moved by the woman's generosity that he asked what he could do for her. For instance, the prophet offered to put in a good word for the couple to the king or to the commander of his army. Perhaps Elisha was implying that by speaking on the couple's behalf to these officials, he could convince them to do something beneficial for the couple, such as lower their taxes. The woman's kindness, however, was not mercenary in character. Her hospitality reflected her genuine respect for the prophet as a spokesperson for God. This attitude is seen in the woman's response to Elisha. The Shunammite literally said, "Among my people I am living." By this she meant she abided securely and had all her needs amply met within the community of her extended family and clan. Thus, it was unnecessary for her to look to powerful leaders in government for additional favors.

Elisha was determined to find some way to express his appreciation in a tangible manner to the Shunammite woman. When the prophet asked what he could do for her, Gehazi noted that the woman was childless. Also, there was little prospect that she could bear a son now that her husband was old (vs. 14). In the culture of that day, it meant there would be no male heir to the family estate. Likewise, the family name would not continue after the death of the husband. Once the younger wife became a widow, her own future well-being was placed at risk. In the ancient Near East, the death of a woman's husband could leave her in an abandoned and helpless state. Widowhood was also viewed with reproach by many in Israelite society. Thus, a widow without legal protection was often vulnerable to neglect or exploitation. Sadly, it was far too common for greedy and unscrupulous agents to defraud a destitute widow of whatever property she owned.

When Elisha learned that his generous host was childless, he found a way to personally minister to her. So the prophet directed Gehazi to summon the Shunammite woman. As she stood in the doorway to the upstairs room (vs. 15), she was unprepared for what happened next. Elisha promised that next year at that time, the once barren wife would be holding her own newborn son in her arms. The Shunammite was taken aback by what she heard. While respectfully addressing Elisha as her "lord" (vs. 16), the woman asked this "man of God" not to mislead her, his "servant." The strong response from the Shunammite signaled how deeply she longed to be a mother and how anguished she felt at not being able to conceive.

Elisha had not made an idle promise to his host. Verse 17 reveals that the Shunammite woman did conceive, and at the specified time the following year, she gave birth to a son. This took place in fulfillment of what the prophet had foretold. His gracious host must have felt elated by this hard-to-envision turn of events. We can imagine extended family members and neighbors joining the couple as they celebrated the goodness of the Lord in giving them a son. The child's birth confirmed that Elisha truly was a "holy man of God" (vs. 9).

B. The Decision to Relocate to Philistia: vs. 2

The woman proceeded to do as the man of God said. She and her family went away and stayed in the land of the Philistines seven years.

Over the course of the Shunammite woman's previous encounters with Elisha, she had learned to trust his judgment and value his wise counsel. The Shunammite would need to do so again, especially in light of what the prophet revealed concerning the divine decree of a prolonged famine. The Shunammite decided to sojourn for the seven-year period in Philistia (2 Kings 8:2). As was noted in lesson 5, the territory belonged to the Philistines. It was located between Joppa and Gaza on the coastal plain of southwest Palestine (see Pss. 60:8; 108:9).

II. THE RESTORATION OF PROPERTY: 2 KINGS 8:3-6

A. The Shunammite's Appeal: vss. 3-5

At the end of the seven years she came back from the land of the Philistines and went to the king to be,
for her house and land. The king was talking to Gehazi, the servant of the man of God, and had said
"Tell me about all the great things Elisha has done." Just as Gehazi was telling the king how Elish
had restored the dead to life, the woman whose son Elisha had brought back to life came to beg the kin,
for her house and land. Gehazi said, "This is the woman, my lord the king, and this is her son whon
Elisha restored to life."

In the culture of that day, once a family left its home and land to resettle elsewhere
it was likely that another clan in the community would take control of the proper
ty. This is what happened to the Shunammite woman. After sojourning in Philisti
for seven years, she relocated her family to Israel. (By then, she possibly was a
widow; see 2 Kings 4:14.) Next, she sought audience with Joram to ask him to give
her back her house and field (8:3). At that moment, the king was talking with
Gehazi, who was Elisha's servant. Specifically, Joram wanted Gehazi to give an
account of all the wonderful deeds God's prophet had performed (vs. 4). Clearly
the monarch held Elisha in great esteem. The elder statesman enjoyed a sterling
reputation as the Lord's holy spokesperson.

According to verse 5, Gehazi was recounting the incident in which Elisha brough
the dead back to life. Just then, the Shunammite woman arrived with her teenag
son to ask Joram for her house and field. Gehazi was filled with excitement at th
sight of the Shunammite. Elisha's servant stated that the adolescent was the perso
whom the prophet had brought back to life. Years earlier, a severe headache preced
ed the boy's unexpected death in the lap of his mother (4:18-20). In turn, she ha
her son's body placed on the bed in the guest room used by Elisha (vs. 21). Nex
the Shunammite mounted a donkey and quickly went to see Elisha at Mount Carme
(vss. 22-25). After the prophet learned about the child's death, Elisha traveled bac
with the Shunammite woman to her home (vss. 26-31).

Once the prophet reached the house, he saw the boy's body on the guest bed (v
32). At this point, Elisha went into the room by himself and shut the door, so tha
he could earnestly pray to the Lord in private (vs. 33). Then the prophet place
himself on the lifeless corpse, and as Elisha did so, the child's skin began to gro
warm (vs. 34). Next, the prophet got up and while praying, paced back and fort
several times in the room. After that, he once again stretched himself upon the bo
and this time he sneezed seven times before finally opening his eyes (vs. 35). Elish
directed Gehazi to summon the Shunammite woman, and when she arrived, th
prophet invited her to embrace her son (vs. 36). The mother, now filled with jo
and gratitude, took the child in her arms and left (vs. 37).

Throughout Israel's history, many so-called prophets claimed to speak for Goc
The Lord foresaw the problem and provided two guidelines for discerning fals

from true prophets. First, if a prophet foretold something and it failed to take place, it was proof positive that this person was no spokesperson for an all-knowing God (Deut. 18:21-22; Jer. 28:15-17). Second, if a prophet's message led people away from God and His commandments (Deut. 13:1-3; Jer. 23:13-32; Mic. 3:5-7), then the message was false, and the messenger was a lying prophet. In the case of the Shunammite woman's son being restored to life by Elisha, this was a miracle that confirmed him as a genuine spokesperson for the Lord.

Believers accept the truth that God works miracles in their lives. Miracles may be defined as any extraordinary display of divine, or supernatural, power in the external, visible world. Scripture teaches that miracles are brought about by the immediate intervention and direct will of God (Exod. 7:3; John 3:2). Miracles involve the alteration, superseding, or counteracting of some established order of creation. For example, God might temporarily suspend a gravitational law with reference to water (Exod. 14), or He might halt the movement of heavenly bodies (Josh. 10:12-13). The Lord uses signs and wonders to confirm the message His spokesperson is declaring and to make Himself known to people (Deut. 4:34-35; John 10:38). In fact, those with the gift of miracles use this special ability to substantiate the Gospel message and establish the validity of Scripture (1 Cor. 12:10, 28; Heb. 2:4).

B. The King's Decision: vs. 6

The king asked the woman about it, and she told him. Then he assigned an official to her case and said to him, "Give back everything that belonged to her, including all the income from her land from the day she left the country until now."

Joram did not hesitate to confirm the truthfulness of the account Gehazi had told him. The king asked the Shunammite woman to recall the miracle of how Elisha restored her dead child to life. Without question, the mother was eager to do so, and the presence of her son helped to corroborate what the Shunammite had said. Joram was genuinely impressed by what he heard, so much so that he granted the woman's initial request. The king ordered his attendants to restore to her everything that she owned, which would have been the house and surrounding fields. Moreover, Joram directed that she was to receive the income from the crops her field produced during her seven-year sojourn in Philistia (2 Kings 8:6).

This joyous turn of events reminds us that we need to set aside our preconceived notion of God's plan for our lives and be open to the unexpected. We also need to set aside any limited notions we have of the type of circumstances and people God must work through and allow His limitless creativity to set us free. Admittedly, time and circumstances can operate to erode our trust in God. Nonetheless, as V. Raymond Edmond, the former Chancellor of Wheaton College, once said, "Never doubt in the darkness what God has shown you in the light." Today, in the light of God's Word, we see the truth that the Lord is concerned for us in our struggles and seeks to minister to us where we are.

Discussion Questions

1. What set of circumstances led to Elisha restoring the Shunammite woman's son to life?
2. Why do you think the Lord decreed that a seven-year famine would overtake Israel?
3. If you were the Shunammite woman, would you have abandoned your home and field as she did?
4. How much courage do you think it took for the Shunammite to bring her petition before the king?
5. How do we demonstrate our faith in God when we reach out to others in need, especially when we are experiencing times of great want?

Contemporary Application

From the account of the Shunammite we see that God works in mysterious ways. Most likely, the woman did not anticipate that a seven-year famine would overtake Israel. Also, at first she did not know that Elisha would urge her to leave Israel to sojourn elsewhere. Then there's the challenge the Shunammite faced when she returned to Israel. She had to petition the king for her house and land.

From this week's lesson we come to understand that God, in the unfathomable ways in which He works in our lives, challenges us to go beyond our expectations. His plan may not match what we anticipate will happen. We may have thought we would live in a different place, make more money, or not have so many obstacles when we followed His will. When our plans are not God's plan, we must make a choice. Will we surrender to self-pity over unrealized expectations or accept the unexpected opportunities God has made available to us? For instance, will we follow Peter's example and reach out to people whom we have ignored but whom God wants us to accept, and do things for Him we never thought we could do (see Acts 10:9-35)?

Although God's plan might lead us into uncomfortable or unexpected situations, we can always rely on His wisdom and love. We can also rely on the Lord's ability to guide us—often from unexpected sources—when we are willing to listen. The Shunammite went beyond her initial incredulity to accept the advice given by Elisha concerning the option to temporarily leave Israel. And when God used the king of Israel to bring about the restoration of the Shunammite's house and land, it must have brought her great joy. The Lord works in each of our lives in very different and unexpected ways. Regardless of how He chooses to make His will known and what He brings to pass, we can look forward to Him using us. Our job is to step out in faith and embrace His wonderful plan for our lives.

Making Judicial Reforms

Scripture

Background Scripture: *2 Chronicles 18:28–19:11*
Scripture Lesson: *2 Chronicles 19:4-11*
Key Verse: *[Jehoshaphat] told [the judges], "Consider carefully what you do, because you are not judging for man but for the LORD, who is with you whenever you give a verdict."*
2 Chronicles 19:6.
Scripture Lesson for Children: *2 Chronicles 19:4-11*
Key Verse for Children: *[Jehoshaphat] gave them these orders: "You must serve faithfully and wholeheartedly in the fear of the LORD."* 2 Chronicles 19:9.

Lesson Aim

To discern that renewing our relationship with God requires specific, sometimes costly steps.

Lesson Setting

Time: Between 872–848 B.C.
Place: Judah

Lesson Outline

Making Judicial Reforms
  I. Appointing Judges: 2 Chronicles 19:4-7
    A. *Turning People Back to the Lord: vs. 4*
    B. *Admonishing Leaders to Judge Carefully: vss. 5-7*
  II. Appointing Priests: 2 Chronicles 19:8-11
    A. *Choosing Priests to Administer the Law: vs. 8*
    B. *Admonishing Priests to Serve Faithfully: vss. 9-10*
    C. *Establishing the Religious and Civil Hierarchy: vs. 11*

Introduction for Adults

Topic: *Return to Justice*

The adage is true. *What we don't know can hurt us.* This is especially so in matters involving justice. It even applies to our spiritual renewal. The eleventh edition of *Merriam-Webster's Collegiate Dictionary* says that renewal involves restoring something to freshness or vigor. The process is so thorough that what had become deteriorated is now new.

How can adults experience spiritual renewal, especially in their relationship with God? A consideration of the religious reforms enacted by Jehoshaphat indicates that it requires specific, costly steps. This is particularly the case in terms of the energy spent, the time invested, and the personal sacrifices made. Often both individual and group activities will help foster spiritual renewal and encourage one to make difficult choices and tough decisions.

Most Christians who have sought to renew their relationship with God would agree that the change, though in their best interests, was not easy. They also would concur that the benefits they obtained were worth the effort.

Introduction for Youth

Topic: *Fairness through Justice*

God used Jehoshaphat to turn the hearts of the people back to the Lord. In turn, there was a renewed effort to promote fairness through justice throughout Judah.

A young college student decided to quit school. He knew his father wanted him to take over the family business, but he didn't like that idea. So he hopped into his car and headed west. On the way he grew despondent and didn't know where to turn. Then he remembered that his mother had placed a Bible in the trunk of his car. The young man took the Bible into his motel room and began to read it. Soon God impressed upon him his need to repent and receive Christ as his Savior. The young man decided to return home, finish college, and earn a seminary degree. He is now a Christian educator!

This former student read God's instruction manual, and it brought spiritual renewal to his life. He found direction and purpose by committing himself to Christ. God offers the same hope to us. Thus, if we read and heed His Word, we have the assurance of being inwardly transformed.

Concepts for Children

Topic: *Be Fair with Everyone*

1. Jehoshaphat was 35 years old when he became the king of Judah.
2. Jehoshaphat did things that were pleasing to God.
3. The king chose leaders to make decisions that were fair.
4. God used Jehoshaphat to turn the hearts of the people back to the Lord.
5. God also wants us to always love and serve Him.

Lesson Commentary

I. APPOINTING JUDGES: 2 CHRONICLES 19:4-7

A. Turning People Back to the Lord: vs. 4

Jehoshaphat lived in Jerusalem, and he went out again among the people from Beersheba to the hill country of Ephraim and turned them back to the LORD, the God of their fathers.

The books of Chronicles cover the same time span as the books of Samuel and Kings, but Chronicles is much more than a collection of leftovers. The books of Kings showed the Israelites how to evaluate their kings by God's standards, while the books of Chronicles showed how vital the house of David and the temple were for the future of God's people. First Chronicles opens with nine chapters of genealogies that stretch from Adam to the time of the return from Babylonian captivity. Then the narrative picks up with the death of Saul, and the rest of 1 Chronicles parallels the contents of 2 Samuel. Second Chronicles covers the same time frame as both books of Kings, but Chronicles limits its focus to the monarchs who reigned from Jerusalem. While the northern kings of Israel are mentioned in passing, it is only when they have significant contact with the southern kingdom.

With respect to purpose, 1 and 2 Chronicles were written to provide encouragement for the Jewish exiles freshly back from Babylon. These books taught the importance of the right worship of God through careful but wholehearted observance of temple rituals. Chronicles champions the descendants of David as the rightful protectors of the priests, Levites, and temple. All the genealogies and lists of officials helped the returned exiles reorganize their national and spiritual lives. Today, Chronicles helps Christian readers remember how connected we are to those who came before and who worked hard to leave a godly legacy. These books highlight the efforts of a few devout leaders to advance the kingdom of God within Judah. We should look back to those heroes the Lord has placed in our family and church heritage. Finally, Chronicles was written to a community of faith that had survived the Babylonian captivity, which was the worst disaster in Israel's history since enslavement in Egypt. These books, which at first glance seem no more than dusty accounts of temple musicians and minor government bureaucrats, are words of hope for people on the edge of despair.

Jehoshaphat, whose name means "the Lord has judged," was one of Judah's godly kings. He reigned from 872–848 B.C., and possibly was a coregent with his father, Asa, from 872–869 B.C. Jehoshaphat was 35 years old when he became the king of Judah, and he reigned for 25 years in Jerusalem (1 Kings 22:42; 2 Chron. 20:31). In a manner of speaking, Jehoshaphat followed in his father's footsteps by being careful to do what the Lord approved (1 Kings 22:43; 2 Chron. 20:32). For instance, early in Jehoshaphat's reign, he attempted to eliminate from Judah the hilltop shrines people used to worship pagan deities, along with the sacred wooden poles they used to venerate the Canaanite goddess, Asherah (2 Chron. 17:6).

Despite Jehoshaphat's efforts, though, he was unsuccessful in completely putting an end to these idolatrous practices in Judah (1 Kings 22:43; 2 Chron. 20:33). He was more successful in removing from the land the male shrine prostitutes who managed to survive the purge undertaken during the reign of Asa (1 Kings 15:12; 22:46).

During Jehoshaphat's reign, Judah enjoyed peace with Israel (22:44). Perhaps this was due in part to the fact that early in his time in office, he fortified Judah to resist any attack coming from Israel (2 Chron. 17:1). For instance, Jehoshaphat stationed troops in all Judah's fortified cities and deployed additional garrisons wherever they were needed (vs. 2). Moreover, because he sought to be as godly as his ancestor, David, Jehoshaphat experienced the Lord's favor (vs. 3). Indeed, Jehoshaphat was single-minded in his devotion to God (vs. 6). Judah's king refused to seek guidance from Baal. (As noted in lesson 5, Baal was the fertility and nature god of the Canaanites.) Instead, Jehoshaphat turned to the Lord for help and obeyed His decrees (vs. 4). The Lord made Judah secure, and Jehoshaphat received great tribute and esteem from his subjects (vs. 5).

Judah's monarch understood the central role of the Mosaic law in Judah. For that reason, in the third year of Jehoshaphat's reign, he dispatched his civil and religious officials to teach God's Word in the cities of Judah (vss. 7-9). Also, the Lord made all the neighboring countries afraid to go to war with Judah (vs. 10). Former adversaries such as the Philistines brought Jehoshaphat tribute, while the Arabs brought him large flocks of rams and goats (vs. 11). These developments helped Jehoshaphat to increase in power (vs. 12). To enhance his military might, the king built fortifications and storage cities throughout Judah. In turn, he placed military supplies in these facilities. All of this was used to support an elite corp of seasoned warriors, who were strategically placed throughout the land (vss. 13-19).

Jehoshaphat's reign was marred by his political and military alliance with wicked King Ahab of Israel (18:1). During one infamous episode, both Ahab and Jehoshaphat joined forces at Ramoth Gilead to battle the king of Aram (or Syria). In this conflict, Jehoshaphat survived, while Ahab perished (vss. 28-34). After Jehoshaphat returned safe and sound to Jerusalem (19:1), a prophet named Jehu confronted the king about his involvement with Ahab. The Lord declared His displeasure with Jehoshaphat for his involvement with Israel's wicked ruler (vs. 2). Be that as it may, God affirmed the commendable deeds Jehoshaphat had accomplished during his reign. This included his efforts to follow the Lord's will and purge Judah of its Asherah poles (vs. 3). More generally, Jehoshaphat's tenure as Judah's king was characterized by religious reform. Even though his palace was in Jerusalem, he traveled throughout the nation—from the southern-most city of Beersheba to the northern-most towns in the hill country of Ephraim. As the king traversed the nation, he encouraged his subjects to follow the Lord, the God of their ancestors (vs. 4).

B. Admonishing Leaders to Judge Carefully: vss. 5-7

He appointed judges in the land, in each of the fortified cities of Judah. He told them, "Consider carefully what you do, because you are not judging for man but for the LORD, who is with you whenever you give a verdict. Now let the fear of the LORD be upon you. Judge carefully, for with the LORD our God there is no injustice or partiality or bribery."

As part of Jehoshaphat's religious reform efforts, he established a judicial system. This included the selection and appointment of judges to serve throughout Judah, as well as in each of its fortified towns (2 Chron. 19:5). The Mosaic law decreed that these magistrates were to be fair and objective in the decisions they rendered. They were prohibited from perverting justice, showing favoritism, and taking bribes. Instead, they were to let the rule of law prevail and righteousness be their guide (Deut. 16:18-20). In every circumstance, the magistrates were to think carefully before pronouncing a judgment. After all, they were not just rendering decisions on behalf of human beings, but more importantly to please the Lord. He promised to be with them in every case for which they rendered a just verdict (2 Chron. 19:6).

Throughout the process, the magistrates were to revere the Lord and weigh their decisions in a thoughtful and discerning manner according to the teachings of His Word. They were to remember that God, who is the supreme Judge, would not tolerate any form of corruption in the judicial process (vs. 7). God may have used Jehoshaphat's commitment to Scripture to strengthen the devotion of His people to His Word. Undoubtedly, this desire to follow the Hebrew sacred writings helped keep the hope of the nation alive during its long years of exile in Babylon. The truths of God's Word would also give the people encouragement and fortitude during the difficult time of restoration to the land that followed.

Leaders, judges, and officials served different roles, but each of these groups was made up of Israel's elders. The elders were considered qualified for leadership by reason of age and experience. The Israelites had maintained and recognized elders even during the years they spent in Egyptian bondage. At the time of Moses, there were a fixed number of them, namely, 70. Their primary duty was the spiritual oversight of the people. Leaders had administrative duties over the various clans and often were given oversight of military operations. As the name implies, judges usually performed judicial duties by resolving disputes among the people. Officials had clerical duties and were responsible for recording the events of a community's history. These elders, leaders, judges, and officials represented their individual tribes as well as all the people of Israel at national assemblies.

II. APPOINTING PRIESTS: 2 CHRONICLES 19:8-11

A. Choosing Priests to Administer the Law: vs. 8

In Jerusalem also, Jehoshaphat appointed some of the Levites, priests and heads of Israelite families to administer the law of the LORD and to settle disputes. And they lived in Jerusalem.

Jehoshaphat's religious reform efforts included creating a judicial role for the Aaronic priests, Levites, and Israelite family leaders who lived in Jerusalem. Evidently, the religious officials decided on matters that had to do with the Mosaic law, while the prominent heads of Israelite clans mediated disputes involving civil affairs (2 Chron. 19:8). By organizing and centralizing the process in this way, Jehoshaphat helped to ensure the entire system ran in a consistent and equitable fashion.

B. Admonishing Priests to Serve Faithfully: vss. 9-10

He gave them these orders: "You must serve faithfully and wholeheartedly in the fear of the LORD. In every case that comes before you from your fellow countrymen who live in the cities—whether bloodshed or other concerns of the law, commands, decrees or ordinances—you are to warn them not to sin against the LORD; otherwise his wrath will come on you and your brothers. Do this, and you will not sin."

When it came to the operation of the judicial process, Jehoshaphat left nothing to chance. He instructed the priests, Levites, and prominent family leaders to fulfill their duties in reverence for the Lord. Their hearts were to be characterized by honesty, integrity, and pure motives (2 Chron. 19:9). The magistrates would be required to hear a variety of cases involving their fellow citizens who lived in the outlying towns. Some issues would seem weighty, such as murder. In contrast, other issues would appear to be far less consequential, such as disputes involving the interpretation of the Mosaic law (which contained numerous directives, rules, and regulations). Regardless of the nature of the case, the religious and civil officials were to urge God's people not to violate His decrees. If the magistrates failed to forewarn their fellow citizens, God would hold these officials and their colleagues responsible for the resulting moral failure of the nation. In turn, His wrath would fall upon Judah's magistrates. The way for them to avoid incurring any guilt was by conscientiously heeding Jehoshaphat's orders (vs. 10).

C. Establishing the Religious and Civil Hierarchy: vs. 11

"Amariah the chief priest will be over you in any matter concerning the LORD, and Zebadiah son of Ishmael, the leader of the tribe of Judah, will be over you in any matter concerning the king, and the Levites will serve as officials before you. Act with courage, and may the LORD be with those who do well."

Jehoshaphat went further in delineating religious and civil judicial responsibilities. Specifically, in all disputes involving the Mosaic law, the magistrates were to report to Amariah, the chief priest (who is mentioned only here). Furthermore, all civil issues (that is, those pertaining to the king) were to be brought to Zebadiah. He was the son of Ishmael—the most prominent leader in the tribe of Judah. Though Amariah and Zechariah would not be micromanaging the judicial process, they were to have the final say in the settling of all disputes within their respective domains of responsibility. Furthermore, no one person would be expected to shoulder all the work that arose within the judicial system. That is why Jehoshaphat decreed that the Levites were available to keep order in the courts and ensure that justice was served.

Perhaps before a large gathering before his royal court, the king encouraged his officials to be bold and diligent in the execution of their responsibilities. After all, the Lord pledged to be with those who strove to do their best in making sure that righteousness prevailed throughout the realm (2 Chron. 19:11). In a convocation such as this there would be tremendous pressure to conform. No one could see into the hearts of others. No one could tell who was sincere and who was hypocritical. Promises would be easy to make in the heat of the moment but hard to keep when the lure of idolatry beckoned. Nevertheless, Jehoshaphat did all he could to bring God's laws into the conscious awareness of the magistrates. The Mosaic law was the basis of the king remaining wholehearted in his commitment to follow the Lord. For the bulk of Jehoshaphat's reign in Judah, the people did not turn away from the God of their ancestors.

This commitment to the Lord is found later in Jehoshaphat's reign when a coalition of Moabites, Ammonites, and Meunites attacked Judah from the direction of Edom (20:1-2). Understandably, the king was afraid. So he declared a nationwide fast and decided to seek the Lord's help (vs. 3). Jehoshaphat and a large number of the nation's religious and civil leaders assembled in front of the new courtyard of the Jerusalem temple (vss. 4-5). The shrine was the place where God had pledged to show His presence among His people. Thus it was a fitting spot for the king and his subjects to meet. Verses 6-12 record the prayer that Jehoshaphat spoke in the presence of his subjects. The nation's monarch affirmed that the Lord of heaven ruled over all the nations of the world. He was so powerful and mighty that no one could oppose Him. He was the one who freed His people from Egypt and enabled them to successfully drive out the inhabitants of Canaan. Moreover, during any national calamity—whether a war, an epidemic, or a famine—they knew they could pray to the Lord and He would rescue them. So Judah's king asked God to help His chosen people as they faced the onslaught of a huge invading army.

Assembled with Jehoshaphat and the nation's leaders were their wives, infants, and other children (vs. 13). Just then, the Lord's Spirit came upon a Levite named Jahaziel, who was present in the crowd (vs. 14). He declared that Jehoshaphat and his subjects would not have to fight their adversaries, for the Lord would give His people the victory. The people of Judah could march out against the enemy, for the nation knew that God would be with them (vss. 15-17). In response to this prophecy, Jehoshaphat bowed to the ground and worshiped the Lord. Likewise, all those in attendance did the same (vs. 18). Then the members of the Levite clans of Kohath and Korah stood up and shouted praises to God (vs. 19). Verses 20-30 recount how the Lord defeated Judah's foes, enabled His people to gather a large amount of plunder, and instill fear among the surrounding nations. In summary, for the remainder of Jehoshaphat's reign, the Lord gave him security on every side.

Discussion Questions

1. What motivated Jehoshaphat to turn the hearts of his fellow citizens back to the Lord?
2. Why did Jehoshaphat appoint judges throughout Judah?
3. Why were the judges to serve the Lord faithfully and wholeheartedly?
4. Why are we sometimes reluctant to renew our relationship with God?
5. What are some specific ways we can express our zeal for the Lord?

Contemporary Application

When we first become Christians, our relationship with God feels strong. We are eager to do whatever He asks, and we desire to conform our lives to His will. Over time, however, our devotion may wane. We start worrying about our problems and become distracted by the pressures of life. Before long, we realize that we are not as close to the Lord as we wanted to be. If our relationship with God has weakened to a certain extent, it will take some time for us to renew it.

The reforms that Jehoshaphat undertook suggest that renewing our relationship with the Lord requires specific, sometimes costly steps. It is good for us to be aware of this truth before we begin the process of drawing closer to Him. Otherwise, we might become so discouraged or demoralized that we will quickly give up when the situation becomes tough.

As we seek to renew our relationship with the Lord, we should first examine our inner spiritual lives. For example, do we think about things that are pure and wholesome, or do we tend to dwell on matters that are immoral or offensive? How eager are we to pray to God, study His Word, and give Him praise? If we are honest with ourselves, we will probably discover at least one area of our inner lives that needs to be changed.

We should next examine the external aspects of our spiritual lives. For instance, which is more important to us—fellowshiping with God's people or doing questionable things with our unsaved acquaintances? What is our attitude toward worshiping with other believers? How enthusiastic are we to share the good news of Christ with our unsaved family members and friends? Do we go out of our way to encourage other believers who are struggling in their faith?

Self-evaluation will be painful at times. As part of the renewal process, the Lord will bring to mind areas of our lives He wants to change. It might be the way we think, the words we use, or the activities we do. Regardless of how God brings about change in our lives, His ultimate goal will be to draw us closer to Him.

Praise for God's Justice

Scripture

Background Scripture: *Psalm 146:1-10; Exodus 21–23; Isaiah 58*

Scripture Lesson: *Psalm 146:1-10*

Key Verse: *Blessed is he whose help is the God of Jacob. . . . He upholds the cause of the oppressed and gives food to the hungry.* Psalm 146:5, 7.

Scripture Lesson for Children: *Psalm 146:1-10*

Key Verse for Children: *Blessed is he whose help is the God of Jacob. . . . He upholds the cause of the oppressed and gives food to the hungry.* Psalm 146:5, 7.

Lesson Aim

To remember that God is worthy of praise because of His greatness, goodness, and glory.

Lesson Setting

Time: Between 538–400 B.C.

Place: Jerusalem

Lesson Outline

Praise for God's Justice

   I. Refusing to Trust in People: Psalm 146:1-4
      A. *A Declaration of Praise: vs. 1*
      B. *A Call for a Life of Praise: vs. 2*
      C. *A Warning against Misplaced Trust: vss. 3-4*
  II. Depending Exclusively on God: Psalm 146:5-10
      A. *God, the Source of Help and Hope: vs. 5*
      B. *God, the Creator: vs. 6*
      C. *God, the Faithful One: vss. 7-9*
      D. *God, the Eternal King: vs. 10*

Introduction for Adults

Topic: *Executing Justice*

"There isn't any justice" is the common refrain of people who think they have been cheated by the "system." No doubt such complaints seem reasonable in some cases, being caused by what we call a miscarriage of justice. However, we must be careful not to jump to premature conclusions, for often we do not know all the facts.

When considering the issue of justice, our own integrity is important to safeguard. For instance, we should avoid all appearances of unseemly behavior, even when others have wronged us. We should also avoid wallowing in bitterness, for an angry, resentful heart brings no pleasure to God, and it can destroy our spiritual vitality. The Lord is honored and pleased when we leave the issue of justice in His hands (see Ps. 146:6-9).

Introduction for Youth

Topic: *Justice through Human Experience*

The teenager complained to his father about the family rules. The father explained that he was trying as best he could to establish Christian values within the home. His desire was not to make his son miserable, but rather to please God. The father explained, "I am answerable to God for how I run my family. One day I will stand before the Lord, and He will evaluate how I exercised my responsibilities as your father."

That was a new thought for the teenager. He knew he lived under his father's authority, but he had not considered that his father was accountable to an even higher authority. God is the Judge, not just of teenagers, but also of their parents and everyone else (for example, pastors and teachers).

These observations remind us that God wants us to help one another do the best we can to carry out His will for our lives. After all, He is our source of help and hope (see Ps. 146:5). Our "Maker" (vs. 6) is pleased when we strive to be fair and honest in all our relationships, rather than taking advantage of one another or showing favoritism of any kind.

Concepts for Children

Topic: *A God of Justice*

1. The psalmist praised God for making heaven and earth.
2. There are wicked people who try to disobey God, but He will not let them succeed in their plans.
3. God comes to the aid of those who need help and gives them reasons to be joyful.
4. God cares about how we treat others, especially people in need.
5. God wants us to be kind and fair to other people.

Lesson Commentary

I. REFUSING TO TRUST IN PEOPLE: PSALM 146:1-4

A. A Declaration of Praise: vs. 1

Praise the LORD. Praise the LORD, O my soul.

The Psalms are songs and prayers written over hundreds of years by many poets. Probably groups of these psalms were collected at different times. By the third century B.C., the book had received its final form, presumably through the efforts of temple musicians. The best-known author of psalms was David. In fact, more sacred songs are attributed to him than to any other author. Furthermore, biblical historians recorded that David was "Israel's singer of songs" (2 Sam. 23:1) and that he organized the sanctuary's music program (1 Chron. 15:3-28). In addition to David, several people are claimed as authors by the psalm titles. They are Moses, Solomon, Asaph (a Levite choir director), the Sons of Korah (a group of Levite musicians), Heman the Ezrahite (the founder of the Sons of Korah), and Ethan the Ezrahite (probably also called Jeduthun). Of the several authors, only David is represented in each of the book's major divisions.

Neither the composer nor the occasion of Psalm 146 are known. Most likely, this sacred ode was written by a member of the postexilic community living in Jerusalem (between 538–400 B.C.). The psalm is a hymn of descriptive praise due to its emphasis on the person and character of God. The predominant theme is that people should put their hope and trust in the Lord, not in any human entity. After all, people have no control of their individual destinies, and cannot guarantee the well-being of others. Moreover, people and their institutions prove to be unreliable. In contrast, the psalmist declared God to be the all-powerful Creator and the sovereign King of the universe (vss. 6, 10). Also, He is compassionate toward the marginalized of society (vss. 7-9). The covenant community is reminded that the Lord is utterly trustworthy in supplying all human needs, and His love is always available to the disadvantaged.

For these reasons, the psalmist began his hymn with the declaration, "praise the LORD" (vs. 1). The Hebrew for this phrase is *Hallelu Yah*, from which we get our English term *hallelujah*. The underlying thought behind the word—to give exuberant praise to God—is based on the Hebrew verb *hâlal*, which means "to be boastful" or "to praise." *Hâlal* was only one of several terms the Hebrews used to speak about praise. Experts tell us they had seven distinct words to express subtle nuances of adoration to God. The Hebrews joined the word *Yah*, which is a shortened form of *Yahweh* (the covenant name of the Lord) to the verb *hâlal*. The combined phrase basically meant "Praise the LORD!" Some form of the Hebrew phrase *hâlal Yah* appears 33 times in the Psalms alone. Also, every time it appears in the Old Testament, it is translated. For example, Psalm 113:1 renders it, "Praise the LORD." In the New Testament, however, the word *hallelujah* occurs only four times, all in the first six verses of Revelation 19. This explains why many have called this Scripture passage the New Testament *Hallelujah Chorus.*

The composer of Psalm 146:1 stated that he would give praise to God with his "soul." The soul has been traditionally understood as the immaterial essence or life-giving principle of human beings. Be that as it may, in Hebrew thought, the body and soul are combined in one person. Expressed differently, everyone is viewed as an indivisible whole. This implies that a person is not just a soul or spirit who temporarily dwells in an earthly body that will be discarded at death. Instead, in the Old Testament, the soul or spirit denoted the entire person or individual as a living being. Scripture reveals that even after the death of one's physical body, the soul continues to exist (see Matt. 10:28; Jas. 5:20; Rev. 6:9; 20:4). This condition is ended when the dead are resurrected at the end of the age (see 1 Cor. 15:35-55).

B. A Call for a Life of Praise: vs. 2

I will praise the LORD all my life; I will sing praise to my God as long as I live.

The Psalms arose from a long tradition of Hebrew poetry. We can observe this because most books of the Old Testament, beginning with Genesis, contain at least some fragments of poetry. Hebrew poetry is flexible in form and rhythm. Nonetheless, most Hebrew poetry exhibits a distinguishing characteristic called parallelism. This term simply means that two (or sometimes three) lines of poetry are, in one way or another, parallel in meaning. A case in point would be Psalm 146:2. In the first line, the composer stated his basic intention of praising the Lord throughout his life. Then, in the second line, the poet advanced the thought by declaring that he would sing praises to God as long as he existed. In a manner of speaking, the hymnist would make melody even with his dying breath to the Creator-King.

C. A Warning against Misplaced Trust: vss. 3-4

Do not put your trust in princes, in mortal men, who cannot save. When their spirit departs, they return to the ground; on that very day their plans come to nothing.

The poet was familiar with the tendency for people to place their confidence in individuals who wielded power and influence, such as nobles, princes, and monarchs. The truth, though, is that these leaders are mere mortals who have no special abilities to deliver anyone from their plight (Ps. 146:3). One day they, too, die, and it is then that their life's breath departs. Meanwhile, their corpse returns to the earth. In a moment, all their cherished projects and dreams perish with them (vs. 4).

Ecclesiastes 3 conveys similar thoughts. Solomon noted that despite the efforts of individuals to exceed the parameters of their existence, they remain as mortal as any other creature on the planet (vs. 18). Also, like animals, people both breathe and are destined to die. Every creature is made from the same minerals and chemicals of the ground, and in death that is where all of them return (vs. 20; see Gen.

3:19; Pss. 49:12, 20; 103:14). No living entity can escape this destiny. In light of this sobering truth, people of faith choose to revere the Lord and obey Him (see Eccles. 12:13-14).

The preceding observations do not categorically rule out the likelihood of immortality for people. Indeed, other passages of Scripture reveal a distinction between the respective fates of humans and animals. While people have an after-life that is dealt with by God, all other earthly creatures cease to exist when they physically expire. In the Old Testament, there is an emerging awareness of the truth that there is life after death for people (see Pss. 16:9-11; 49:15; 73:23-26; Isa. 26:19; Dan. 12:2). With the advent of the Messiah, the truth of the resurrection has been fully and clearly revealed in the Gospel (see John 5:24-29; 2 Tim. 1:10).

II. DEPENDING EXCLUSIVELY ON GOD: PSALM 146:5-10

A. God, the Source of Help and Hope: vs. 5

Blessed is he whose help is the God of Jacob, whose hope is in the LORD his God.

In contrast to the sorrow that results from trusting in mere mortals for salvation, is the eternal joy of turning to the "God of Jacob" (Ps. 146:5) for help. Those who put their hope in the covenant-keeping Lord of Israel are truly "blessed." The latter renders a Hebrew noun that is the functional equivalent of the Greek adjective translated "blessed" in the Beatitudes (see Matt. 5:3-12). Both the Hebrew and Greek terms denote the abiding presence of joy in those who are the recipients of God's favor. Psalm writers often used the Hebrew noun to "congratulate" (in a manner of speaking) someone who had learned to trust God, whose sin was forgiven, or who knew how to care for the poor. When God's people used the Hebrew noun, they expressed a kind of "holy envy." They were not saying that a person would be blessed. They were celebrating a person who had learned to live God's kind of life.

B. God, the Creator: vs. 6

The Maker of heaven and earth, the sea, and everything in them—the LORD, who remains faithful forever.

Genesis 1:1 reveals that everything in the universe owes its existence to God. This truth is reiterated in Psalm 146:6. Here we find the composer referring to Israel's God as the one who made "heaven and earth," as well as the oceans of the world and all the creatures who inhabit the seas. He is eternally "faithful" to keep every promise He has ever made. This truth is a source of assurance for believers, who have made the Lord the foundation of their faith and the basis for their hope. Psalm 104 likewise refers to the Lord as the Creator and one true God. He also is to be both trusted, worshiped, and praised. As the poet sang about the glory of the Lord's creation, he exclaimed at "how many are [God's] works" (vs. 24). Whether it be the lights in the sky, the heavens and the waters, the land and vegetation, the sun, moon, and stars, the fish and birds, or the animals, people, and food to sustain them, the Lord in His wisdom made them all. This sentiment reflects the mindset of the covenant community in ancient times. They looked at the world with reverence because it reflected the glory of its Creator.

Furthermore, Psalm 104 produces a magnificent poetic and musical commentary on the creation. Even the structure of the psalm draws praise in that it is modeled quite closely on the day-by-day creation events recorded in Genesis. Indeed, as the psalmist described in grandiose detail the daily acts of creation, he seemed to preach in glowing terms that what God created on each day is reason enough to praise Him. It is clear that the psalmist used the various stages of creation as his starting points for praise. But as he developed each creation-day theme, there is a constant anticipation for more, especially for the later days of the creation. For instance, in verses 25-26, the writer focused on the immense seas with their many forms of aquatic life. The rich variety of the world's oceans stood as a testimony to the enormity of God's wisdom. That said, the Lord's wisdom is especially evident in humans. People have abilities and aptitudes that far exceed those of other creatures. To illustrate, humankind has made abundant use of the world's seas. This includes the fact that people and nations have built all kinds of sailing vessels to travel over the oceans.

Psalm 8 is another example of this God-centered way of thinking. David extolled the Creator for His enormous skill, care, and precision in giving shape to the world and populating it with plant and animal life. The one who made the heavens, moon, and stars (vs. 3) also crowned humankind with glory and honor (vs. 5). The Lord gave men and women dominion over His wonderful works. He graciously put them in charge of His expansive and marvelous creation (vs. 6), which includes tame and wild animals (vs. 7), birds, and sea creatures (vs. 8). These truths remind us how important it is for us to consider God's power and wisdom in His created universe. The earth is built on the Lord's foundations, and He guarantees its permanence. Though one day the present heavens and the earth will be destroyed (2 Pet. 3:10), God will create new heavens and a new earth that will last forever (Isa. 65:17; Rev. 21:1). The same power that upholds the world also provides a firm foundation for believers. Such a great God is worthy of devotion and praise from His people (Ps. 8:9).

C. God, the Faithful One: vss. 7-9

He upholds the cause of the oppressed and gives food to the hungry. The LORD sets prisoners free, the LORD gives sight to the blind, the LORD lifts up those who are bowed down, the LORD loves the righteous. The LORD watches over the alien and sustains the fatherless and the widow, but he frustrates the ways of the wicked.

The sovereign Creator is the one who defends the cause of the marginalized in society. Specifically, He vindicates those who have been crushed by the wicked, He feeds the hungry, and He releases the imprisoned (Ps. 146:7). Likewise, Israel's just God enables the blind to see, He lifts the burdens of those who are bent down from their heavy loads, and He is unfailing in His love for the upright (vs. 8). Furthermore, the King of the universe protects the foreigner and sustains the orphan and the widow. In contrast, the Lord overturns the plans of the wicked. For instance, God makes evildoers reap the harmful aftermath of their actions (vs. 9).

Psalm 82 focuses in-depth on God's judgment of the wicked. In this drama, God is pictured as presiding over a "great assembly" (vs. 1), namely, the royal court of heaven. In this somber setting, the Lord pronounces judgment against the "gods." Most likely, this is a sarcastic reference to the world's evil human leaders (such as judges and kings). In ancient times, it was common for the nation's rulers to be honored as divine beings, or to take upon themselves the title of a pagan deity. Some think these leaders issued their decrees in the names of certain false gods in order to claim more authority for themselves. The point of verse 1 is that ultimately all authorities are accountable to the Lord. He measures the integrity of those to whom He has delegated power according to their treatment of the poor, the orphaned, the afflicted, and the needy. Sadly, as verse 2 makes clear, many of the rulers of the nations surrounding Israel were guilty of handing down unjust decisions. They showered special favors on the wicked, rather than punishing them for their crimes.

God accused the rulers of the nations of the earth with a variety of social injustices. For instance, they had failed to "defend the cause" (vs. 3), or give fair judgment, to the disadvantaged in society, such as the destitute and the oppressed, as well as widows and orphans. God appointed earthly leaders to rescue the "weak and needy" (vs. 4) from the grasp of evil people. Tragically, the opposite happened. These verses summarize the teaching of the Mosaic law and indicate God's basic desire that the defenseless would find a haven of justice in the law courts of the nation in which they lived. Instead of judging fairly, the rulers misjudged, and instead of coming to the aid of the disadvantaged, the leaders exploited them. By showing favoritism to the wicked (vs. 2), the wicked kings and judges trampled the cause of the righteous.

D. God, the Eternal King: vs. 10

The LORD reigns forever, your God, O Zion, for all generations. Praise the LORD.

Psalm 146:10 closes out the hymn with a declaration of the truth of the Lord's eternal reign. Here, "Zion" is figuratively used to refer to Jerusalem (the city of David). Throughout all generations, God remains the sovereign King over the eternal city and its inhabitants. For this reason, the chosen people are enjoined to give Him unending praise.

Discussion Questions

1. Why is it shortsighted for believers to put their trust in other human beings?
2. What would life be like if the Maker of heaven and earth withdrew His sustaining hand?
3. What end awaits the unjust rulers of the world?
4. What groups do you consider to be truly powerless today? How might you speak up for these people?
5. What are we saying to God when we neglect to praise Him for His eternal reign?

Contemporary Application

This week's lesson seeks to draw us to praise God for that which goes beyond our human explanation. We come to see that He is worthy of praise because of His greatness, goodness, and glory. We learn that He is both Lord and King, whose greatness is beyond discovery.

When we are astounded by the wonder of God's creation, we are more likely to praise Him than when we attempt to explain the world rationally. For example, to realize that a single tongue of a solar flare is more than 40 times the diameter of the earth causes amazement. And even rapidly counting nonstop, it would take us thousands of years to number the stars in just one galaxy. Amazingly, the universe contains untold numbers of galaxies.

When we praise our great and awesome God, we honor Him for the way He graciously takes care of us. We also have an opportunity to express our gratitude to Him for His marvelous deeds and wonderful goodness. Recalling the Lord's compassion on our lives helps us to realize that we are His mortal, dependent creatures who exist to serve and worship Him.

Oppositely, when we neglect to praise God for His goodness and grace, we indicate that we do not appreciate what the Lord has done. We take for granted His abundant provision of food, clothing, and shelter. We trivialize the value of His sovereign care of the world. In our arrogance, we communicate to God that we do not need or want Him and that we can survive and prosper by ourselves.

We know, however, that such an approach to life is to be shunned. Instead, we are called to visibly give thanks to God for His unfailing love and kindness. When we do, we bear witness to the unsaved that every person needs God for present life and future hope. Our words of praise and gratitude to the Lord might even encourage the unsaved to consider the truths of Christ and turn to Him in faith for new life and eternal joy.

A Righteous Lord

Scripture

Background Scripture: *Isaiah 9:1-7*
Scripture Lesson: *Isaiah 9:2-7*
Key Verse: *For to us a child is born, to us a son is given, and the government will be on his shoulders. And he will be called Wonderful Counselor, Mighty God, Everlasting Father, Prince of Peace.* Isaiah 9:6.
Scripture Lesson for Children: *Isaiah 9:2-7*
Key Verse for Children: *For to us a child is born, to us a son is given.* Isaiah 9:6.

Lesson Aim

To rejoice because the promised Messiah has come.

Lesson Setting

Time: 740–700 B.C.
Place: Judah

Lesson Outline

A Righteous Lord
  I. God's Light: Isaiah 9:2-3
      A. *The Coming Dawn: vs. 2*
      B. *The Coming Joy: vs. 3*
  II. God's Judgment: Isaiah 9:4-5
      A. *The Oppressor's Yoke: vs. 4*
      B. *The Warrior's Garments: vs. 5*
  III. Messiah's Reign: Isaiah 9:6-7
      A. *The Messiah's Names: vs. 6*
      B. *The Messiah's Justice: vs. 7*

Introduction for Adults

Topic: *Hope in Spite of Darkness*

Gary Smalley cites four things that many individuals perceive as the basis for their hope but that are ultimately undependable. People can bring us hope. Unfortunately, though, we can't control them. Places can bring us hope. But the fact is, we get bored with them. Possessions can offer us hope. Yet we never seem to get enough. A position of prominence can bring us hope. Sadly, though, we never seem to be able to climb high enough.

Ultimately, for believers, the Savior is their source of hope, even in the midst of dark periods in their lives. His saving presence brings spiritual light (Isa. 9:2), and His just rule is the reason Christians anticipate a bright eternal future (vss. 6-7). In turn, this encourages them to convey new hope to people around them.

Introduction for Youth

Topic: *Justice Fulfilled*

Not all the presents we receive really make a difference. Some of the stuff we get on special occasions (such as graduations, birthdays, holidays, and so on) is easily disposable, and some of it we don't even want. Sometimes when we are asked what we want to get, we feel hard-pressed to think about what we really need.

What a wonderful opportunity, then, for special occasions to be a time when we can give presents that will change people's lives! For example, we can give the gift of forgiveness in which we pledge to get over past hurts and grudges. We can also give the gift of reconciliation to our friends, and the gift of peace and healing for people suffering emotionally and physically.

Most of all, by proclaiming the Gospel, we can share the gift of peace through faith in the Savior, the true Prince of Peace (Isa. 9:6). And why shouldn't we do this, for He came to make people whole by filling their lives with justice. What He has to offer really counts—both now and in eternity.

Concepts for Children

Topic: *A Mighty Ruler*

1. Isaiah promised that the Savior was bringing hope to God's people.
2. Isaiah promised that the Savior was bringing joy to God's people.
3. Isaiah promised that the Savior was bringing freedom to God's people.
4. Isaiah promised that the Savior was bringing peace to God's people.
5. We should thank God for the special gift of the Savior.

Lesson Commentary

I. GOD'S LIGHT: ISAIAH 9:2-3

A. The Coming Dawn: vs. 2

The people walking in darkness have seen a great light; on those living in the land of the shadow of death a light has dawned.

God's people had rebelled against Him by embracing idolatry and witchcraft. Their spiritists and mediums, however, had brought them "no light" (Isa. 8:20). There was trouble, anguish, and dark despair (vs. 22). Indeed, the "distress" and "gloom" of verse 22 are carried over into 9:1. In Isaiah's prophecy, chapter 9 stands at a pivotal turning point. King Ahaz had stubbornly refused to seek God's help and protection. Instead, he latched onto the Assyrians. However, in God's plan Assyria would become His "razor" (7:20) of judgment. Isaiah predicted terrible times ahead. People would starve and curse God (8:21). Distress, darkness, and gloom would overcome them (vs. 22). Isaiah envisioned this blanket of darkness descending upon the land of Zebulun and Naphtali.

Zebulun was the tenth son of Jacob; his mother was Leah. The tribe of Zebulun controlled a large area of land in Galilee that was mostly uninhabited. There were no great cities in this region. The southern border was the Kishon River, which gave this tribe considerable power over the trade routes. They shared Mount Tabor with the tribe of Issachar. Naphtali was the sixth son of Jacob; his mother was Bilhah. The land of Nahtali was a large strip west of the Sea of Galilee and the upper Jordan. This territory was among the most fertile in the region, and it included 19 fortified cities. The famous Canaanite city of Hazor was located within these borders. The Israelites did not conquer this city until late in the period of the judges. Consequently, the Canaanite religious rituals and beliefs tainted Israel and specifically Naphtali.

God did not intend for His people to experience anguish and gloom forever. In fact, He promised to one day honor them and make their land great. He would fulfill His word by bringing a great light of deliverance and hope to His people (9:1).We learn from verse 2 how God would directly address the needs of His people. He would replace their dark and gloomy existence with "great light." Additionally, the Lord would bring renewal (which is implied by the light dawning or shining) on all who live in the land. The result will be a complete reversal of the people's deplorable condition.

In this verse, as in other parts of Scripture, darkness and light are used in symbolic ways. For instance, darkness is used to represent human ignorance of God's will, especially as such ignorance is manifested in sin. In contrast, light has been associated with the presence, truth, and redemptive activity of God. The origin of light rests with God, and He is the very essence of light. This indicates that He is the ultimate source of all knowing and understanding. Conversely, darkness rests with Satan, and he is the very essence of darkness. This implies that he is the ultimate source of all ignorance, superstition, and oppression.

Notice that the prophecy in verse 2 uses a tense that indicates past action: "The people walking in darkness *have seen* a great light; . . . a light *has* dawned" (emphasis added). It reads as if what is described has already taken place. This is a common feature of Hebrew prophecy, indicating absolute certainty that a declaration will come to pass. (The prophecies of verses 3 to 7 also use a past tense.) A diamond always sparkles more brightly when set against a dark velvet backdrop. Even so, the "light" announced in 9:2 blazes more brilliantly against the backdrop of 8:18-22. The prophecies of chapters 9–12 may have applied in a limited degree to King Hezekiah or to another king of Judah. But they apply in the fullest sense to Jesus, the Messiah. He would bring a great light of deliverance and hope to His people. The Messiah would offer salvation to both Jews and Gentiles (42:6; 49:6). As we know from biblical history, the people of Israel had to wait over 700 years before Jesus, "the light of the world" (John 8:12), shone in splendor upon them.

B. The Coming Joy: vs. 3

You have enlarged the nation and increased their joy; they rejoice before you as people rejoice at the harvest, as men rejoice when dividing the plunder.

There were two major factors that produced immense anguish in the hearts of the Israelites living during the time of Isaiah. First, the people rebelled against God, leaving many feeling spiritually empty and confused. Second, God disciplined His people for their sinful ways. He allowed the king of Assyria to attack and destroy much of Israel. It would be hard for us to imagine the turmoil God's people experienced as a result of these devastating invasions. This week's lesson shows us that because of their unhappiness, they needed God's promise of the coming Messiah to give them joy. When Isaiah first made this prophecy known, he sought to give the Israelites good news in which they could rejoice. Even today, all God's people can likewise rejoice because their Savior and Lord has come.

The advent of the Messiah would have concrete results. For example, instead of decreasing the nation by judgment so that only a remnant was left, the Messiah's coming would bless the nation so that it would enlarge (Isa. 9:3). The future Assyrian oppression of Israel would leave its citizens feeling humiliated and diminished as a people. But Isaiah's prophecy pointed to a future day when the peace and prosperity of God would prevail. Isaiah's exuberance about the Messiah's coming joy led the prophet to compare the event to the satisfaction farmers have at harvesttime or the delight soldiers experience when dividing the plunder of a conquered foe. This joy of God's people is in marked contrast to the gloom mentioned in verse 1. Isaiah likely was overwhelmed by the broad vision of the future—with all its various judgments and blessings—that he was permitted to glimpse. He may have been moved to awe-filled silence, reverence, and worship. God's deliverance should also inspire praise and worship in us. Likewise, such should spring from enlarged hearts that are focused on God.

II. GOD'S JUDGMENT: ISAIAH 9:4-5

A. The Oppressor's Yoke: vs. 4

For as in the day of Midian's defeat, you have shattered the yoke that burdens them, the bar across their shoulders, the rod of their oppressor.

One reason for the great joy mentioned in Isaiah 9:3 is that the Messiah would lift the people's burdens from their shoulders (vs. 4). They bore a heavy yoke. (This was a wooden frame that was placed on the necks of animals to hold them together while they worked.) The people also carried a massive bar across their shoulders and were beaten with a rod by the enemy. Isaiah thought about the time when the Israelites were delivered from Midianite oppression.

Genesis 25:2 and 4 say that the Midianites were descendants of Abraham and Keturah. Tragically, the Midianites usually were foes rather than friends of the Hebrew people. (The land of Midian was located principally in northwest Arabia, though the Midianites roamed throughout portions of northern Sinai, the Negev, and the southern Transjordan region.) Despite the fact that the Midianites once had a powerful army, God used Gideon and 300 Israelite soldiers to overwhelm their foe (Judg. 7:19-23). Similarly, the Messiah would release His people from their burden by shattering the power of their oppressors. This prophecy had a more immediate fulfillment in Jerusalem's miraculous deliverance from an Assyrian siege in 701 B.C. (Isa. 37:36-37).

B. The Warrior's Garments: vs. 5

Every warrior's boot used in battle and every garment rolled in blood will be destined for burning, will be fuel for the fire.

In ancient times, nations such as Assyria often used bloodstained uniforms from past battles as a deliberate scare tactic to frighten enemies in an upcoming battle. Perhaps Isaiah had this background information in mind when he declared that in the day of peace, uniforms would never again be bloodstained by war. Likewise, battle gear would no longer be issued. Moreover, the prophet declared that the boots of the enemy that had marched across God's promised land and desecrated it with their violence and wickedness would be thrown into the fire. Also, every uniform of the oppressor stained with the blood of slain Israelites would be incinerated (Isa. 9:5). The idea is that the clothing of war would be rendered obsolete at the Messiah's coming. There would be no more need for such clothing, since Jesus' reign would be characterized by perfect peace. From this information, we see that the Lord's triumph over the enemy would be complete, and His redemption of His people would be absolute.

II. MESSIAH'S REIGN: ISAIAH 9:6-7

A. The Messiah's Names: vs. 6

For to us a child is born, to us a son is given, and the government will be on his shoulders. And he will be called Wonderful Counselor, Mighty God, Everlasting Father, Prince of Peace.

Isaiah gave many reasons for joy and celebration—the oppressor's yoke would be broken, battle gear would be destroyed, and God would redeem His people. Isaiah's prophecy took an abrupt turn with the announcement of the birth of someone who would one day be the King of kings. Isaiah envisioned this birth as having been already accomplished: "A child is born . . . a son is given" (Isa. 9:6). Expressed differently, God's promises would be fulfilled no matter how far-fetched they might seem. The prophecy pointed to the Lord Jesus' incarnation. He was born in the normal human way as a baby in Bethlehem.

Matthew 1:20 reveals that centuries later, an angel of the Lord appeared in a dream to a man named Joseph. God's heavenly messenger disclosed that the child in the womb of Mary, Joseph's future wife, had been conceived by the Holy Spirit. Just as God's Spirit was instrumental as the agent of the natural Creation (Gen. 1:2), even so the Spirit of God was the divine agent in the conception of Jesus' human nature (Luke 1:35). Creation before the Fall was pronounced "very good" (Gen. 1:31), and likewise Jesus' human nature was preserved from any taint of inherited sin. The angel also announced that Joseph was to name Mary's child "Jesus" (Matt. 1:21). *Jesus* is the Greek form of *Joshua*, which means "the Lord saves" or "the Lord is our salvation." As Joshua—Moses' successor—had led the Israelites into the promised land, so Jesus—God's Son—would lead many into God's salvation.

Isaiah 9:6 declares that Israel's Redeemer would carry the government "on his shoulders." This may be a reference to the royal robe worn by ancient kings. Such robes hung on the shoulders and represented authority to rule. Down through the years, Israel had suffered through the reigns of many wicked, apostate kings. The coming Messiah, however, would rule uprightly for the good of God's people. The Savior would be God's just and faithful King. These truths are evident in the four names or descriptions Isaiah gave the Messiah. As the "Wonderful Counselor," He brings the words of life to His people. Humanity undoubtedly would be less besieged by psychological problems if it seriously acknowledged Christ as a wonderful counselor. The Messiah also is the "Mighty God." The image in this verse is that of a valiant and stout fighter who is without equal. The emphasis is on the Messiah's ability to defend the cause of His people and protect their interests. With Him on their side, no foe would overcome them or threaten their existence.

Furthermore, the Lord Jesus is the "Everlasting Father." The word "Father" refers to the Messiah's role as an ideal king. His rule is eternal and filled with compassion. When He reigns on the throne of David, the Messiah will provide for and watch over His people. Not one of their temporal and eternal needs will be overlooked or neglected by Him. Additionally, the Messiah is the "Prince of Peace." This indicates more than the absence of war. The Messiah will bring peace in the fullest sense of the word—peace between God and people as well as between person and person. Also, during the reign of the Lord Jesus, spiritual healing and wholeness will prevail throughout society. When we look at these majestic, descriptive titles, we conclude that no human emperor has ever come close to living up to them. Many rulers and kingdoms have come and gone, but none of them has achieved what Isaiah prophesied. The fulfillment will only come when Jesus returns.

B. The Messiah's Justice: vs. 7

Of the increase of his government and peace there will be no end. He will reign on David's throne and over his kingdom, establishing and upholding it with justice and righteousness from that time on and forever. The zeal of the LORD Almighty will accomplish this.

The child mentioned in Isaiah 9:6 "will reign on David's throne" (vs. 7). This is an important prophecy in light of the New Testament's numerous references to David, many of which actually pertain to his greatest descendant, Jesus Christ. God promised David a kingdom that would have no end (1 Chron. 17:10-14). This could not have referred to the kingdom of David's son, Solomon, and his other short-term successors, for the Israelite kingdom divided (1 Kings 12:19). Also, both resulting kingdoms eventually came to an end (2 Kings 17:18; 2 Chron. 36:17-21). Nevertheless, the line of David continued and eventually culminated in the birth of Jesus (Matt. 1:1). Luke 1:32 says, "the Lord God will give him the throne of his father David." In fact, the Messiah will "reign over the house of Jacob forever; his kingdom will never end" (vs. 33). Thus, we see that in Jesus the divine promise to David was and is fulfilled.

We learn from Isaiah 9:7 that the reign of the Messiah will be characterized by peace. His government will be ever expanding and never ending. Fairness and justice will be the hallmarks of His rule, and His passionate commitment for His people will guarantee that all the divine promises to them will be fulfilled. This verse mentions "the zeal of the LORD Almighty." This phrase depicts God as a jealous lover who refuses to desert His people. His zeal is filled with devotion and single-minded allegiance, and this is the reason why His promise to the Israelites concerning the Davidic kingdom would be fulfilled (37:32; 42:13).

Jesus came over six centuries after Isaiah's prophecy, and He came as a suffering Servant who would bring more than an earthly blessing. He came to bring all people—not only the Jews—an abundant spiritual life that would continue throughout eternity in heaven. Thus, God's Son would be the light that would pierce through and shine on a dark and sinful world. Jesus Christ would be the Lord's answer to a world filled with pride and arrogance. The coming of the Messiah would not establish a new political order, but rather fulfill the promise of an ideal King.

Discussion Questions

1. What great light would the people walking in darkness see?
2. What symbols of rejoicing are found in Isaiah 9:3 and 5?
3. How has Jesus been the Mighty God to you?
4. How has Jesus been the Everlasting Father to you?
5. In what ways is the authority of Christ continuing to grow today?

Contemporary Application

"Rejoice greatly," sings one line of Handel's *Messiah*. Why rejoice? Because "light has come into the world" (John 3:19). People who walk in darkness can see a great light (Isa. 9:2).

In Charles Dickens's *Great Expectations*, an eccentric old woman named Miss Havisham has spent most of her time in a dark room—since the day of her scheduled wedding when her fiancé jilted her. At the end of the book, a young man named Pip throws open the curtains that have kept the room shrouded in darkness for years. As light rushes in, all is exposed.

Light flooded into our world when Christ came (John 1:5, 9). By His presence, He dispelled the darkness of superstition and ignorance. Through His ministry of teaching and healing, He shone the light of God's truth and purity for the whole world to see.

In his book *The Gift of Worship*, C. Welton Gaddy tells the story of when, at the beginning of the Christmas holidays one year, the renowned scholar and lecturer, Paul Tillich, went downtown in New York City to worship with a small congregation in a storefront church. The pastor was one of Tillich's students. Tillich listened with dismay as the young preacher related the Christmas story to a beleaguered group of uneducated people using the language of the lecture hall. After the service ended, the brilliant teacher, with tears in his eyes, approached his student. Tillich said, "Son, just tell them that God became a man in Jesus of Nazareth."

Do we have any reason for rejoicing because Jesus has come and will one day return to reign? Indeed, we do! We no longer blindly stumble in darkness. Instead, the Savior has made us aware of God's love for and goodness toward us. We are also assured that, in the day when Jesus returns to reign, He will bring peace, righteousness, and unparalleled blessing to all who have trusted in Him. Because of these wonderful truths, we can rejoice!

A Righteous Branch

DEVOTIONAL READING
Psalm 33:1-5

DAILY BIBLE READINGS

Monday August 13
  1 Timothy 6:11-16 Pursue Righteousness

Tuesday August 14
  1 John 2:28–3:3 God's Children Now

Wednesday August 15
  Proverbs 11:27-31 The Righteous Will Flourish

Thursday August 16
  Isaiah 60:17-22 All Shall Be Righteous

Friday August 17
  Psalm 33:1-5 The Lord Loves Righteousness and Justice

Saturday August 18
  Psalm 116:5-19 The Gracious and Righteous Lord

Sunday August 19
  Jeremiah 23:1-6; 33:14-18 The Lord Is Our Righteousness

Scripture

Background Scripture: *Jeremiah 23:1-6; 33:14-18*
Scripture Lesson: *Jeremiah 23:1-6; 33:14-18*
Key Verse: *"The days are coming," declares the LORD, "when I will raise up to David a righteous Branch, a King who will reign wisely and do what is just and right in the land."* Jeremiah 23:5.
Scripture Lesson for Children: *Jeremiah 23:1-6; 33:14-18*
Key Verse for Children: *"In those days and at that time I will make a righteous Branch sprout from David's line; he will do what is just and right in the land."* Jeremiah 33:15.

Lesson Aim

To recognize that a self-focused life is not God's plan.

Lesson Setting

Time: 626–585 B.C.
Place: Jerusalem

Lesson Outline

A Righteous Branch

  I. The Promise of New Leaders: Jeremiah 23:1-6
     A. *Rogue Shepherds: vss. 1-2*
     B. *A Restored Flock: vss. 3-4*
     C. *A Righteous Branch: vss. 5-6*
  II. The Reaffirmation of the Covenant: Jeremiah 33:14-18
     A. *Fulfilling the Divine Promise: vs. 14*
     B. *Providing Salvation and Safety: vss. 15-16*
     C. *Pledging an Unending Reign: vss. 17-18*

Introduction for Adults

Topic: *The Just Leader*

Justice is much more than meting punishment to criminals. In God's view of things, justice requires that we use what we have to help meet the needs of others. Justice also demands that we do not exploit other people to get what we want. Justice moreover demands that we set aside our materialistic ambitions so that we can address suffering and hardships.

Injustice, then, is more than the absence of justice. It is also the failure to do the right things when we can. Judah's rogue leaders were guilty of this. They could have helped God's people but they didn't, choosing instead to gratify their own selfish desires (see Jer. 23:1-2). The disrepute connected with their deeds shouts to us a powerful message about how easy it is not only to fail the Lord, but also to ignore His warnings.

Introduction for Youth

Topic: *Embrace the Righteous Shepherd*

Retailers face huge obstacles trying to keep up with the fast-changing tastes of teenagers. One year's fashions are next year's disappointments. The teen market in the West is driven by the impulse to have everything new right away. How hard it is for adolescents to resist this consuming urge. If they are aware of what is happening, they struggle not to be swept along with the idea that we obtain happiness with a brilliant array of designer clothes, fast muscle cars, and so on.

Judah's rogue leaders tried to buy security and happiness by abusing their power and authority, but they utterly failed in their attempts (see Jer. 23:1-2). We cannot afford to follow their self-centered example. If we put our trust in Jesus, our Righteous Shepherd (see 23:5-6; 33:15), we are guaranteed eternal joy and peace with Him in heaven. What more could we possibly want?

Concepts for Children

Topic: *A Just Leader*

1. God compares His children to sheep.
2. Those who lead God's children are like shepherds.
3. God wants those who lead His children to be kind and fair.
4. God wants His children to respect those who lead them.
5. Jesus is the best example of what it means to lead others faithfully.

Lesson Commentary

I. THE PROMISE OF NEW LEADERS: JEREMIAH 23:1-6

A. Rogue Shepherds: vss. 1-2

"Woe to the shepherds who are destroying and scattering the sheep of my pasture!" declares the LORD. Therefore this is what the LORD, the God of Israel, says to the shepherds who tend my people: "Because you have scattered my flock and driven them away and have not bestowed care on them, I will bestow punishment on you for the evil you have done," declares the LORD.

The chronological setting of Jeremiah's prophecies in chapters 1–20 is not crystal clear. In chapters 21–45, however, the prophecies tend to link themselves to their historical context. Jeremiah 21 leaps ahead to 588 B.C. during the reign of King Zedekiah. Nebuchadnezzar's Babylonian army had prepared to lay siege to Jerusalem. It's likely that Jeremiah delivered this prophecy at about the time of the events described in chapters 37 and 38. He advised the populace to surrender to the Babylonians and instructed the nobility of Judah to adopt justice as their operating principle of government. Nothing else could protect them from Babylon.

Chapter 22 probably jumps back to the time of King Jehoiakim. Its theme is similar, however, to the previous chapter's call for righteousness and justice. Jeremiah looked back on the four kings preceding Zedekiah. Josiah, who sought to reform the faith and morals of the nation, was held up as the standard. Josiah's son Shallum (who ruled briefly as Jehoahaz) was deported by the Egyptians. Jehoiakim, another son of Josiah, was installed in Shallum's place. Jehoiakim was addicted to luxury and was indifferent to the poverty of the people. His son Jehoiachin reaped the consequences of his father's unrighteousness when Nebuchadnezzar dragged him to Babylon.

As the unrighteous leaders of Judah steered the nation toward certain destruction at the hand of the Babylonians, Jeremiah continued his call for righteous leaders. To describe leadership, the prophet borrowed an image from the agricultural community that was often used by other biblical writers—the shepherd (see, for example, Ps. 78:70-72). The shepherds Jeremiah condemned seem to have been the kings of Judah (see Jer. 21–22), false prophets (see 23:9-10), and priests (vs. 11). Shepherds were supposed to protect the flock, but Judah's shepherds destroyed it (see vs. 1). Instead of keeping the flock together, Judah's shepherds scattered them. The Lord promised to punish the evil shepherds of Judah.

Verse 2 continues the divine oracle against the leaders who ruled over Judah's inhabitants. These self-serving officials failed in their solemn responsibility of caring for God's chosen people, and the tragic outcome was that they would be dispersed and driven into exile. The Lord solemnly affirmed that He would punish the nation's officials for what they had done. This verse uses a Hebrew verb that means to "attend to" or "inspect." Because the leaders of Judah had not attended to their sheep by caring for them, the Lord would attend to the leaders by judging them. Later prophets of Israel continued to develop the metaphor of righteous and unrighteous shepherds (see Ezek. 34; Zech. 10:2; 11:15-17). Even today, we often regard church leaders as shepherds (1 Pet. 5:1-4). And tragically, there are church leaders whose false teaching scatters and destroys the sheep. These ministers drive people away from the church by preaching insipid messages or by serving up misleading exhortations to social service. As a result, the flock wanders off looking in vain for what will satisfy their souls.

B. A Restored Flock: vss. 3-4

"I myself will gather the remnant of my flock out of all the countries where I have driven them and will bring them back to their pasture, where they will be fruitful and increase in number. I will place shepherds over them who will tend them, and they will no longer be afraid or terrified, nor will any be missing," declares the LORD.

The biblical concept of a righteous "remnant" (Jer. 23:3) that survives a devastating judgment or terrible calamity is based on God's faithfulness in keeping the Mosaic covenant (see Deut. 4:27-31). Centuries earlier, as a new generation of Israelites were poised to enter the promised land from the plains of Moab, Moses joined with the priests to remind the Israelites that they were the people of God (Deut. 27:9-10). Moses also described how blessings would come to those Israelites who fully obeyed the Lord, and how curses would befall those who disobeyed His commands and decrees (chap. 28).

Then, Moses implored the Israelites to obey God's laws. But the Israelite leader must have realized that at some future point among the coming generations of Hebrews, the people might turn away from God and disregard His decrees and statutes. And when it happened, God would allow foreign powers (such as the Assyrians and Babylonians) to conquer the Israelites, take them from the promised land, and disperse them around the known world. Sometime after that had taken place, the Israelites would come to their senses and realize that their dispersion had occurred because of their disobedience. At that time, Moses said, the people of Israel would recall the words and the laws of the Lord (30:1).

Moses foresaw the return of a righteous remnant to the Lord and how they would then obey Him with all their heart and soul (vs. 2). Just as the Israelites had cried out to the Lord in the midst of Egyptian bondage, they would again cry out to the Lord in the midst of their dispersion in Babylon. Also, just as the Lord had heard their cries from Egypt, He would also hear their cries while dispersed throughout the Fertile Crescent. Most importantly, Moses knew God would forgive the Hebrews and would again make a way for them to return to their homeland from wherever in the ancient Near East they had been scattered. Moses stressed that repentance would reverse the Israelites' deplorable circumstance. When God saw the people's repentant hearts, He would pour out His compassion on the righteous remnant (vs. 3). Throughout Moses' final address to God's people, he invariably reminded them of the Lord's compassion. No matter how grievous the sin, God would always forgive a repentant people—or person. Moreover, while emphasizing God's greatness as well as His compassion, Moses said that no matter how far away the Israelites' enemies might take the Hebrew descendants from their land, God would reach out and bring them back home (vs. 4). Moses also promised that when the Israelites' descendants would return to their homeland, the Lord would make them more prosperous and numerous than they had been before (vs. 5).

Jeremiah 23:3 builds on the preceding promises with the statement of God's pledge to a future generation of His chosen people. One day He would regather those of the "remnant of [his] flock" from all the countries where He had driven them. In 25:10-11, Jeremiah used stark poetic pictures to predict the disappearance of peaceful, civilized life from Judah and the surrounding nations. Their land would be replaced with a wasteland, and they would enter 70 years of servitude to Babylon (see 29:10). The writer of Chronicles saw these 70 years as a sabbath rest for the land. This was time that had accumulated during 490 years when the people had neglected to allow the land to rest every seventh year, according to the law (2 Chron. 36:21; compare Lev. 25:1-7). Even though God would use the Babylonians as His divine tool of judgment, they would themselves have to be judged one day (Jer. 25:12-14). Nebuchadnezzar and Babylon were guilty of great cruelty and arrogance. The land of Babylon faced permanent desolation because of the guilt of its conquering armies. Jeremiah's prophecy of judgment on Babylon was fulfilled when the Medes and Persians conquered the nation (Dan. 5:30-31).

Though the prophecy recorded in Jeremiah 23:3 included the Babylonian captivity, God's declaration went beyond it to the regathering of Jewish exiles from there during the time of Zerubbabel and Ezra. Furthermore, Jeremiah hinted at yet another time—the second advent of the Messiah—that would see a worldwide scattering and returning of God's people (see Matt. 24:31; Mark 13:27). Previously, Jeremiah 3:14-18 had offered a glimpse of the messianic age, but did not focus on the Messiah Himself. In 23:3, the Lord promised to gather His flock from all the countries where He had exiled them in punishment. Once back in their home pasture, His sheep would then thrive and multiply (see Gen. 1:28). Furthermore, the Lord promised to give caring shepherds to His regathered flock. These leaders would be individuals of integrity and committed to justice. They would provide for the restored remnant so they could be free of fear and harm. These leaders would also feed the sheep with divine truth so they could repose in the joy and peace of their Lord. God pledged that not one member of His flock would turn up lost or missing (Jer. 23:4).

C. A Righteous Branch: vss. 5-6

"The days are coming," declares the LORD, "when I will raise up to David a righteous Branch, a King who will reign wisely and do what is just and right in the land. In his days Judah will be saved and Israel will live in safety. This is the name by which he will be called: The LORD Our Righteousness."

The Lord revealed through Jeremiah that future peace would come when God raised up David's "righteous Branch" (Jer. 23:5). This is the King and Messiah from David's family tree (see Isa. 4:2; 53:2; Zech. 3:8; 6:12; Matt. 19:28). A similar promise is found in Isaiah 11:1, which harks back to the desolation of Judah predicted in 6:9-13. The prophet pictured the royal family of God's chosen people as a chopped-down tree. Unlike the Assyrians, who were cut down never to rise again, the stump of David's father, Jesse, contained the promise of new life. He would continue the dynasty of David in fulfillment of the promise recorded in 2 Samuel 7:16. This Ruler would be the opposite of the ungodly leaders who lived in Jeremiah's day. The reign of David's righteous Branch would be characterized by wisdom and understanding. Moreover, God the Son would establish justice and righteousness in the promised land (Jer. 23:5; see 2 Sam. 8:15; 23:3; Ps. 72:1-2; Isa. 52:13).

Jeremiah 23:6 points to a future day when under the rule of the Messiah, Judah and Israel would be reunited (see Jer. 3:18; 30:3; 31:27, 31; Ezek. 37:15-28; Hos. 1:11). Also, the chosen people would enjoy safety, live securely, and be eternally redeemed. After all, the Messiah would shield them from the physical and spiritual attacks of their enemies. In the kingdom age, the Messiah would go by the name, "The LORD Our Righteousness" (Jer. 23:6). Put another way, God the Son would be the source of justice and vindication for the chosen people. This is the same name the Messiah would impart to a new Jerusalem (see 33:16). In fact, He would become the embodiment of "righteousness, holiness and redemption" (1 Cor. 1:30) for all who put their faith in Him.

To show the splendor of the renewed Jerusalem, the Lord declared through Jeremiah that coming events would alter the Israelites' view of history. In Jeremiah's day, the watershed event of Israel and Judah's history was considered to be the exodus from Egypt. It was the greatest known example of God's power, so much so that the Israelites would affirm their oaths by referring to the Exodus (Jer. 23:7). But the future would change the people's figure of speech. No longer would they guarantee their words by the certain memory of their ancestors' departure from Egypt. Instead, they would refer to an even greater epoch-making event, namely, the return and restoration of the chosen people from worldwide dispersion to the promised land (vs. 8; see 16:14-15). Ultimately, Jeremiah was writing about the regathering of Israel in the future day of the Lord.

II. THE REAFFIRMATION OF THE COVENANT: JEREMIAH 33:14-18

A. Fulfilling the Divine Promise: vs. 14

"'The days are coming,' declares the LORD, 'when I will fulfill the gracious promise I made to the house of Israel and to the house of Judah.'"

Jeremiah wrote chapters 32 and 33 during Nebuchadnezzar's 18-month siege of Jerusalem (587–586 B.C.). The authorities imprisoned the prophet on false charges of trying to desert to the Babylonians. Eventually, they transferred him from a dungeon to confinement in the courtyard of the guard house in the palace of the king (see 33:1). Zedekiah complained to the prophet about his forecasts of doom for Jerusalem and everyone in it, implying that Jeremiah's actions left the king no choice but to confine him. Jeremiah's cousin visited him during his confinement and offered to sell him family property in Anathoth. The Lord instructed Jeremiah to buy the field as an object lesson that the people of Judah had a future in the land, despite their upcoming defeat by the Babylonians. Even during the siege, Jeremiah confessed confidence in the Lord. God again spoke about the necessity of judging, and He renewed His promise of future blessing. For instance, in verse 14, the Lord declared through Jeremiah that a future day was coming in which God would fulfill His blessed pledge to the chosen people. The reference to both the houses of Israel and Judah indicated that despite their worldwide dispersion, all the tribes would be reunited in the land of their ancestors.

B. Providing Salvation and Safety: vss. 15-16

"In those days and at that time I will make a righteous Branch sprout from David's line; he will do what is just and right in the land. In those days Judah will be saved and Jerusalem will live in safety. This is the name by which it will be called: The LORD Our Righteousness.'"

Jeremiah 33:15 reiterates the promise of a "righteous Branch" in 23:5. The Lord pledged to bring to the throne of David an upright and virtuous descendant. The reference is to the Messiah, whose rule over the chosen people in the future kingdom age would be characterized by justice and righteous. Never before had the chosen people even experienced such an honest and fair monarch. At that time, the land of Judah would enjoy safety and Jerusalem would live in security. Undoubtedly, the physical circumstance would reflect an inward spiritual truth, namely, the regenerate status of all the chosen people. At that time, calling Jerusalem "The LORD Our Righteousness" (33:16) would emphasize the truth that God had provided justice for the upright remnant. Once again, the Lord would dwell among His people, vindicate them, delight in them, and cherish them (see Isa. 62:2-4; Jer. 3:17; Ezek. 48:35; Zech. 8:3).

C. Pledging an Unending Reign: vss. 17-18

"For this is what the LORD says: 'David will never fail to have a man to sit on the throne of the house of Israel, nor will the priests, who are Levites, ever fail to have a man to stand before me continually to offer burnt offerings, to burn grain offerings and to present sacrifices.'"

The Lord pledged through Jeremiah that in the kingdom age, David would never lack a successor to rule over all the people of Israel (Jer. 33:17). Likewise, there would always be Levitical priests on hand to offer up "burnt offerings" (vs. 18), sacrifice "grain offerings," and offer other types of "sacrifices" (see Num. 25:13) in the Jerusalem temple. Even though God's hand of judgment would fall on the land and people of Israel, He covenant promises to them would come to pass.

Their fulfillment was as assured as His commitment to sustain the day-and-night cycle of creation (Jer. 33:20-21). Indeed, the Lord pledged to make David's descendants and the Levitical priests as innumerable as the stars in the sky and the grains of sand on a seashore (vs. 22).

Discussion Questions

1. Why were Judah's leaders so derelict in performing their responsibilities?
2. What led to the scattering of the chosen people from the promised land?
3. How would the blessing of God be evident once His people were reestablished in Judah?
4. What are some ways you have seen God fulfill His promises to you in His Word?
5. In what tangible ways can believers reflect the character of the Savior by promoting justice and righteousness?

Contemporary Application

Greatness, according to Jeremiah, wasn't about outward signs of wealth and power. The ignominy of Judah's rogue shepherds made this truth abundantly clear. Even today, having a gigantic home, a spacious corner office, the latest model car, or designer clothes is not God's goal for us. Rather, it's to be fair and just in all dealings.

Nonetheless, selfishness seems to dominate the human heart. For instance, we may spend a lot of time trying to get a "good deal," even though it means not paying folks what their work is worth. We may argue for tax breaks that favor our own income group, with no regard to how they affect others in lower income groups. Or we may simply not pay much attention to our neighbors' needs. We may be oblivious to the hurts and pains of the people who live next door to us, or the other people whom we see every day.

The needs are great, both where we live and around the world. Consider, for example, that 35,000 children under the age of five die every day in developing countries from diseases that are largely preventable. With the basics of clean water, clean power, and vaccinations, this number would shrink considerably. What would it mean for us as the body of Christ to be kind, fair, and compassionate in a needy world such as ours?

The bottom line is that each of our actions needs to be regarded with the following question in mind: Is this the kind, helpful thing the righteous remnant would do, or the greedy, self-focused sort of thing Judah's rogue shepherds would do? Our world will be a better place, and our own lives will be better, the more we take care of others as much as ourselves.

God with Us

Scripture

Background Scripture: *Ezekiel 34*
Scripture Lesson: *Ezekiel 34:23-31*
Key Verse: *"I will place over them one shepherd, my servant
David, and he will tend them; he will tend them and be their
shepherd."* Ezekiel 34:23.
Scripture Lesson for Children: *Ezekiel 34:23-31*
Key Verse for Children: *"Then they will know that I, the
LORD their God, am with them and that they, the house of
Israel, are my people, declares the Sovereign LORD."*
Ezekiel 34:30.

Lesson Aim

To learn that our holy God restores us by His grace.

Lesson Setting

Time: 592 B.C.
Place: Jerusalem, Babylon

Lesson Outline

God with Us
   I. The Lord as Israel's Shepherd and Prince:
       Ezekiel 34:23-24
       A. *The Promise of a Davidic Shepherd: vs. 23*
       B. *The Promise of a Davidic Prince: vs. 24*
   II. The Lord's Covenant of Peace with Israel:
       Ezekiel 34:25-31
       A. *The Lord's Pledge: vs. 25*
       B. *The Blessings of the Covenant: vss. 26-27a*
       C. *The Safety and Security of the Covenant: vss. 27b-28*
       D. *The Provisions of the Covenant: vs. 29*
       E. *The Reassurance of the Lord: vss. 30-31*

Introduction for Adults

Topic: *Meeting Our Deepest Need*

"Any god I use to support my latest cause, or who fits comfortably within my understanding or experience, will be a god no larger than I and thus not able to save me from my sin or inspire my worship or empower my service. Any god who fits the contours of me will never really transcend me, never really be God."

Those words of Donald W. McCullough, from *The Trivialization of God*, emphasize the need for us to remember that God is greater than we can ever conceive Him to be. A lowercase "god" cannot be the same as our uppercase "God."

These observations are important to remember when we think about God's ability to meet our deepest needs. As Ezekiel stressed to the exiles in Babylon, only the Lord is able to restore our lives when we sit overwhelmed in the midst of its ruins (see Ezek. 34:25-29). His infinite and incomprehensible grace provides the building material to reclaim run-down lives. And He alone is powerful enough to do the job (see vss. 30-31).

Introduction for Youth

Topic: *God's Covenant*

Sometimes to break the ice (so to speak) in a new group we ask people questions like, "If you had one wish, what would it be?" or, "Who would you like to be?" The answers help us to get to know one another better.

Imagine your reaction if someone said, "I'd like to have a new heart and a new spirit within me." Wow! That would really be a discussion starter. For most of us, though, such an idea would be too uncomfortable to talk about with others.

We find it hard to verbalize our deepest needs. We also find it difficult to talk to God about our innermost desires. Why can't we be more honest with Him? We know we need to spiritually mature, so why can't we ask God to help us grow more Christlike? The situation doesn't have to remain this way. After all, God promises through His "covenant of peace" (Ezek. 34:25) to change our hearts, if we will let Him.

Concepts for Children

Topic: *A Caring Presence*

1. Ezekiel was someone who spoke for God.
2. Ezekiel told the people that God cared for them and wanted to restore them.
3. Those who follow God experience His favor.
4. The example of a shepherd and sheep provides a picture of God's care for His people.
5. God has promised to deliver, provide for, and be present with us.

Lesson Commentary

I. THE LORD AS ISRAEL'S SHEPHERD AND PRINCE: EZEKIEL 34:23-24

A. The Promise of a Davidic Shepherd: vs. 23

"I will place over them one shepherd, my servant David, and he will tend them; he will tend them and be their shepherd."

Ezekiel, whose name means "God strengthens," was the son of Buzi, a priest of the family of Zadok (Ezek. 1:3). What is known about Ezekiel's life comes from the information he gives in his book. Also, his prophecies contain dates more specific than almost any others in the Old Testament. This makes it possible to correlate Ezekiel's declarations with Babylonian records and date many of the prophet's oracles (for example, see 1:1-3; 8:1; 20:1; 24:1; 26:1; 29:1, 17; 30:20; 31:1; 32:1, 17; 33:21; 40:1). In 597 B.C., when Ezekiel was about 25 years old, the Babylonians took him into exile with Jehoiachin and about 10,000 other Jews (see 2 Kings 24:10-17). When Ezekiel was 30 years old and living in the Jewish colony of Tel Aviv on the Kebar River (near the ancient city of Nippur), he heard God's call to be His prophet (Ezek. 1:2-3; 3:15; about 593 B.C.). Apparently, Ezekiel was a person of some stature among the leaders of his people, for the prophet's home became a central meeting place (see 3:24; 8:1; 14:1; 20:1). Ezekiel was married. But 10 years into the exile, his wife died suddenly, perhaps due to a plague (see 24:15-18). Evidently, the couple was childless.

Throughout Ezekiel's ministry, which continued until 571 B.C. (see 29:17), he tried to help his fellow exiles deal with the fact that they were far from their homeland. He taught them that the Lord was close at hand to sustain them during their time of displacement. Ezekiel's oracles, like those of Jeremiah, fall into three major categories: declarations against Israel, especially before the fall of Jerusalem in 586 B.C.; pronouncements against the nations, such as Egypt and Tyre; and words of consolation for Israel's future, including visions of a restored nation and a new temple (chaps. 33–47). Like Jeremiah, Ezekiel is known for his symbolic acts to convey God's message, such as shaving his head and burning some of his hairs to show God's destruction of Jerusalem (chap. 5). The context of this week's lesson is the aftermath of the fall of Jerusalem. Based on 2 Kings 25:8, this occurred on August 14, 586 B.C. Five months later, on January 8, 585 B.C., someone who had escaped from the city of David arrived in Babylon and told Ezekiel about Jerusalem's demise (Ezek. 33:21).

A pivotal reason for the foreboding event was the despicable manner in which the rulers of Israel had led God's people. The civil and religious authorities were like greedy, self-serving shepherds who tended to their own needs but failed to care for the Lord's flock (34:1-2). God had appointed the rulers of Israel to feed and lead everyone in the nation, including the poor and oppressed. But instead of relieving the plight of the disadvantaged, the wicked rich exploited and abused parents, foreigners, widows, and orphans (see 22:7). Metaphorically speaking, the elitists took advantage of God's less-fortunate sheep by eating their "curds" (34:3), clothing themselves "with the wool," and butchering their "choice animals." Meanwhile, the Lord's flock remained neglected and unprotected (vs. 4). Consequently, God's sheep wandered in every direction and fell victim to the attacks of predators (vs. 5). In all this, none of Israel's contemptuous rulers bothered to look for the lost sheep and guide them back to safety (vss. 6-8).

The sovereign Lord held the wicked and wayward rulers of His people accountable for their criminal behavior (vss. 9-10). God pledged to rescue His abused sheep from the clutches of their marauders, particularly by removing the latter from their positions of power. Moreover, the Lord promised to look for His scattered sheep, bring them back to their homeland, and feed them (vss. 11-13). Within Israel the restored flock would graze in lush pastures and lie down in peace (vss. 14-15). While God planned to bandage the injured and strengthen the weak, He would judge the wicked rich for their iniquities (vs. 16). Because the powerful elitists had grown fat and strong at the expense of their fellow sheep, the Lord declared He would separate the haves from the have-nots. He knew which ones consumed the greenest grass and trampled what remained after they had filled their stomachs. While the rulers were privileged to drink clean water, they made sure the disadvantaged only had muddy water to drink. In short, the poor and oppressed had nothing fit to consume (vss. 17-19).

Israel's all-powerful God would no longer permit His flock to be abused in this way. He committed Himself to personally judge between the sheep that had grown fat and the rest that had become scrawny (vs. 20). In a manner of speaking, the wicked rich had pushed with their side and shoulder at their disadvantaged peers. Also, the elitists had thrust their "horns" (vs. 21) at all the weak sheep until the latter were scattered far from the flock. The time had come for the Lord to rescue His forlorn sheep and not allow them to be "plundered" (vs. 22) anymore. Indeed, He planned to judge every member of His flock by separating the good from the bad.

God declared His intent to set over His people one spiritual shepherd from the family of His servant, King David (vs. 23). This ruler like David would feed and lead the chosen people in a way they had never experienced before. In the years leading up to the first century A.D., no descendant from the royal line of David fulfilled what Ezekiel described. From a New Testament perspective, this promise looks forward to the eternal kingdom of the Messiah. The reign of God's Servant—the Lord Jesus—will be characterized by righteousness, peace, and prosperity. In fact, His rule will surpass anything seen or experienced during the glory years of David and Solomon's reign (see Ps. 89:4, 20, 29; Isa. 9:6-7; Jer. 23:5-6; Luke 1:31-33).

B. The Promise of a Davidic Prince: vs. 24

"I the LORD will be their God, and my servant David will be prince among them. I the LORD have spoken."

The Lord pledged that in the messianic kingdom, He would be the God of His chosen people (Ezek. 34:24). Likewise, His "servant David" (Jesus) would reign as "prince" among the redeemed (see 37:24-25; 44:3; 45:7, 16-17, 22; 46:2-18; 48:21-22). This idyllic Prince stands in sharp contrast to the corrupt princes who ruled over the Israelites (see 7:27; 12:10, 12; 19:1; 21:25; 22:6, 25). In 34:24, the Savior is called "David" because He would embody the royal ideal described in the Old Testament (see Isa. 11:1; Jer. 30:9; Hos. 3:5; Amos 9:11-15; Mic. 5:2). This King would be the opposite of the ungodly rulers of Ezekiel's day. As we learned in last week's lesson, David's righteous Branch would "reign wisely and do what is just and right in the land" (Jer. 23:5). His name would be known as "The LORD Our Righteousness" (vs. 6), a name He would impart by association to a new Jerusalem (see 33:16).

II. THE LORD'S COVENANT OF PEACE WITH ISRAEL: EZEKIEL 34:25-31

A. The Lord's Pledge: vs. 25

"I will make a covenant of peace with them and rid the land of wild beasts so that they may live in the desert and sleep in the forests in safety."

The Hebrew noun rendered "covenant" (Ezek. 34:25) can also mean "pledge" or "agreement." The covenant the Lord made with Israel at Mount Sinai followed a common form throughout the ancient Near East for agreements made between high kings and peoples who swore allegiance to them. A formal covenant contained: (1) a preamble identifying the king; (2) a historical prologue about the king's past relations with the people; (3) a catalog of the demands placed on the people and the obligations of the king; (4) a covenant ratification ceremony detailing blessings for obedience and curses for disobedience; and (5) a list of witnesses and directions for carrying out the covenant. The covenant, as it appears in Deuteronomy, parallels this form: preamble (1:1-4), historical prologue (1:5–4:43), demands of the covenant (4:44–26:19), blessings and curses (27:1–28:29), and witnesses to testify to the covenant (4:26; 31:26).

All the covenants God establishes with His people have "peace" (Ezek. 34:25) as their goal. The Hebrew noun is *shalom*, a term that denotes safety, tranquility, and prosperity. Ezekiel specifically had in mind the new covenant of Jeremiah 31:31-34 (see Ezek. 37:26), which the Lord Jesus inaugurates in peace (see John 14:27; Phil. 4:7). Through His atoning sacrifice on the cross, the Messiah makes it possible for believing sinners to be at peace with God (see Rom. 5:1; 8:1). Indeed, the Son's redemptive work at Calvary is the basis for God's people being reconciled to Him (Rom. 5:9-11; 2 Cor. 5:18-20). Jesus, as the Good Shepherd of God's sheep, said that He came to bring new life in all its abundance and fullness to His followers (John 10:10). He enables them to live "in safety" (Ezek. 34:25) and experience freedom from fear. In the messianic kingdom, none of life's dangers would threaten the ability of the redeemed to enjoy God's richest blessings. The Lord promised to chase away the wild animals from the desert and the forest, enabling His people to inhabit these one-time places of danger in safety (see Ps. 104:20-21; Jer. 5:6). The imagery is none other than that of paradise restored.

B. The Blessings of the Covenant: vss. 26-27a

"I will bless them and the places surrounding my hill. I will send down showers in season; there will be showers of blessing. The trees of the field will yield their fruit and the ground will yield its crops."

The future day of renewal is set against a backdrop of agricultural bounty. With respect to the Hebrew noun rendered "bless" (Ezek. 34:26), it denotes the abundant provision of life that God graciously gives to His people (see Gen. 12:1-3). The Lord promised not only to bless the covenant community, but also the regions around His holy hill (namely, Jerusalem and its environs). God pledged to make the autumn and spring showers come down in due season (see Jer. 5:24). He also declared that the orchards would bear fruit and the fields would yield bumper crops (Ezek. 34:27). In a region known for its dry seasons and periods of drought, the inhabitants would regard the consistent and plenteous supply of rain as a source of blessing. It would remind God's people of the sorts of divine graces mentioned in the Mosaic covenant (see Lev. 26:4-6).

C. The Safety and Security of the Covenant: vss. 27b-28

"The people will be secure in their land. They will know that I am the LORD, when I break the bars of their yoke and rescue them from the hands of those who enslaved them. They will no longer be plundered by the nations, nor will wild animals devour them. They will live in safety, and no one will make them afraid."

Throughout the Israelites' existence, they endured the oppression of such regional powers as Egypt, Assyria, and Babylon. In the future messianic kingdom, God pledged that His people would dwell securely in the promised land (Ezek. 34:27). The Lord figuratively referred to the bondage of His people as "bars of . . . yoke." In ancient times, the yoke typically was a wooden harness used to connect a pair of animals (such as oxen) to an agricultural tool such as a plow. Placing the yoke over the necks of two animals enabled them to work more efficiently and effectively. The metaphorical yoke enslaving the Israelites would be broken and the figurative chains shackling them would be destroyed. In that day when they were rescued from their captors, they would know that their God is the Lord. The pagan nations would no longer plunder God's people, and not even wild beasts would kill and eat them (vs. 28), so great would be the Lord's protection of the remnant. He would ensure that they lived securely in the promised land, with no one to terrify them. In short, they would have nothing and no one to fear.

D. The Provisions of the Covenant: vs. 29

"I will provide for them a land renowned for its crops, and they will no longer be victims of famine in the land or bear the scorn of the nations."

Nehemiah 9:36-37 sheds light on the difficult conditions under which God's people had to exist, first during the time of the Babylonians and then the Persians. Their livelihood disappeared to pay the crippling taxes that their pagan overlords imposed on the covenant community. However, the Lord promised that in the latter days all this would change. Then He would give them fertile fields, ones that produced enormous amounts of crops. As a result, the remnant would never again go hungry in the promised land. Also, God would put an end to foreign nations sneering in contempt at the redeemed (Ezek. 34:29).

E. The Reassurance of the Lord: vss. 30-31

"Then they will know that I, the LORD their God, am with them and that they, the house of Israel, are my people, declares the Sovereign LORD. You my sheep, the sheep of my pasture, are people, and I am your God, declares the Sovereign LORD."

In the Book of Ezekiel, the prophet noted that Israel's God wanted His people to know that He is the Lord (see 6:7; 7:4, 9; 11:10, 12; 12:20; 34:30). In fact, Yahweh used times of judgment and restoration to convince the remnant that He is sovereign over all creation. He also wanted them to know that He abided with them, just as He had abided with Abraham and his descendants (see Gen. 15:7; Exod. 6:7). The omnipotent Lord reassured the exiles that all those who belonged to the "house of Israel" (Ezek. 34:30) were His people and He was their God. He returned to the shepherding metaphor to remind the remnant that they were the sheep of His pasture, the flock that He fed and led (vs. 31).

On two occasions recorded in the Gospels, Jesus was moved to compare the multitudes who flocked to Him in words reminiscent of these verses. Early in Jesus' teaching ministry, He looked out over the crowd and "had compassion on them, because they were harassed and helpless, like sheep without a shepherd" (Matt. 9:36). Also, before Jesus fed over five thousand, He consented to teach the multitude because "he had compassion on them, because they were like sheep without a shepherd" (Mark 6:34). Later Jesus compared His concern for His people with that of other teachers. "I am the good shepherd. The good shepherd lays down his life for the sheep. The hired hand . . . abandons the sheep and runs away" (John 10:11-12). Jesus offered Himself as the Good Shepherd who fulfilled the Old Testament prophecies.

The Bible does not tell us all we'd like to know about the nature of life in the messianic kingdom. We know that in God's presence we will experience joy, blessing, and comfort. As seen in Genesis 3:22-24, God expelled Adam and Eve from Eden so they would not eat fruit from the tree of life. God did not want them to live forever in their sinful state. But in Revelation 7:17, the Lord Jesus leads the redeemed to the waters of life. The imagery is that of a shepherd guiding his sheep to a freshwater spring in the desert. Salvation from the death that sin brought into the world will be complete. In heaven the righteous will enjoy unending life.

Discussion Questions

1. How does the future shepherd like David stand in contrast with those who ruled God's people in the past?
2. What sorts of things will this future shepherd do for us, the redeemed?
3. What was the nature of the covenant of peace that God said He would make with His people?
4. What blessings associated with this new covenant have you already experienced?
5. How would the remnant come to know that Israel's God is the Lord?

Contemporary Application

Restoration follows cleansing. That principle works when we take a bath, when we confess our sins, and when we forgive each other and give up our grudges. How pleasant it is to put on clean clothes; how much more delightful it is to be restored to God and one another.

Before we apply soap to our bodies, we have to be convinced that we need a shower. The spiritual counterpart of this is that we must admit that we really have offended God and other people by our behaviors. That's the hard part. Many people are unconvinced that they need to be spiritually renewed. They refuse to admit the consequences of their sins. They fail to see the necessity of the cleansing that Jesus offers them.

Ezekiel exposed sin for what it is—a disgrace to God. The prophet also declared that God offers forgiveness and complete restoration to those who come to Him in humility and faith. After all, the Lord is our only hope for the future.

In their fallen state people are a little like spiritual zombies. By every natural indication they appear to be alive. For example, they are able to think, breathe, and communicate just as any self-aware person would. From God's perspective, however, there is no spiritual life. They do not enjoy intimate fellowship, and they are completely oblivious to His presence.

A radical change takes place when sinners trust in Christ. They experience new life. This means the Spirit graciously replaces their fallen human nature with a new one. Their relationship with God is restored, their rebelliousness and unbelief are supplanted by obedience and dependence, and their hatred is exchanged for unconditional love.

The world might scoff at the idea of receiving new life in Christ. Believers know from God's Word, however, that this is a reality. Remember, lasting inner renewal cannot be purchased. The lost must put their faith in Christ in order to experience the new birth.